Voices From the Dust

A Book of Mormon Commentary

Volume Two

Mosiah thru Alma

Philip M. Hudson

"Thou shalt speak out of the ground and thy speech shall be low out of the dust, and thy voice shall be as one that hath a familiar spirit and shall whisper out of the dust". (2 Nephi 26:16).

"I will proceed to do a marvellous work among this people, even a
marvellous work and a wonder: for the wisdom of their wise men shall perish,
and the understanding of their prudent men shall be hid."
(Isaiah 29:14).

Copyright 2023 by Philip M. Hudson.
Published 2023.
Printed in the United States of America.
All rights reserved.

No portion of this book may be reproduced,
stored in a retrieval system, or transmitted
in any form or by any means, mechanical,
electronic, photocopy, recording, scanning,
or other, except for brief quotations in
critical reviews or articles, without
the prior written permission
of the author.

ISBN 978-1-957077-51-2

Illustrations - Google Images.
This book may be ordered from
online bookstores.

Publishing Services
by BookCrafters, Parker, Colorado.
www.bookcrafters.net

Joseph Smith "has translated the book, even that part which I have commanded him, and as your Lord and your God liveth, it is true." (D&C 17:6).

"And I saw another angel fly in the midst of heaven, having the everlasting gospel to preach unto them that dwell on the earth, and to every nation, and kindred, and tongue, and people."
(Revelation 14:6).

We must
drag our broken
and bleeding bodies
to the Church, because it
is there that we will receive
the transfusions of a spiritual
element. It is a heavenly dialysis
center where worldly contaminants
might be removed from our systems,
because, honestly, we are not capable of
accomplishing the task on our own. The
necessary resources are only to be found
within the Atonement of Christ, that is a
doctrine which is unambiguously taught
by every prophet in The Book of Mormon.

Nephi taught: "And if ye shall believe in Christ ye will believe in these words, for they are the words of Christ, and he hath given them unto me; and they teach all men that they should do good. And if they are not the words of Christ, judge ye - for Christ will show unto you, with power and great glory, that they are his words, at the last day; and you and I shall stand face to face before his bar; and ye shall know that I have been commanded of him to write these things."
(2 Nephi 33:10-11).

"Take thee one stick, and write upon it, for Judah, and for the children of Israel his companions: then take another stick, and write upon it, For Joseph, the stick of Ephraim, and for all the house of Israel his companions. And join them one to another into one stick; and they shall become one in thine hand." (Ezekiel 37:16-17).

Our greater
understanding
of the Plan of God
that is revealed in The
Book of Mormon blesses
our lives in many ways. Its
power creates the opportunity
for dynamic change, as wisdom
flows along established channels.
Moreover, personal accountability,
responsibility, and commitment to
obedience expand. The humble need
to serve strengthens connections of
brotherhood and sisterhood while it
generates interdependency within
a community of true believers in
which any cultural differences
are effectively expunged. We
are no longer strangers or
foreigners. We've become
fellowcitizens with the
Saints, within the
household of
God.

When we
open up The Book
of Mormon for the first
time, there will be revealed
a strait and narrow path that
stretches away to a soft glow of
light on the eastern horizon.
At that very moment, our
real journey to Christ
will only have just
begun.

Table of Contents

"Scripture consists not in what we read, but in what we understand."
(St. Hilary).

Acknowledgements

Acknowledgements..1

Preface

Preface...3

Introduction

Introduction..5

The Book of Mosiah
130 B.C - 91 B.C.

Chapter 1..15
Chapter 2..21
Chapter 3..27
Chapter 4..33
Chapter 5..37
Chapter 6..41
Chapter 7..43
Chapter 8..45
Chapter 9..49
Chapter 10..51
Chapter 11..53
Chapter 12..55
Chapter 13..57
Chapter 14..59
Chapter 15..61
Chapter 16..69
Chapter 17..77
Chapter 18..81

Chapter 19..........89
Chapter 20..........93
Chapter 21..........95
Chapter 22..........101
Chapter 23..........103
Chapter 24..........107
Chapter 25..........111
Chapter 26..........115
Chapter 27..........121
Chapter 28..........127
Chapter 29..........133

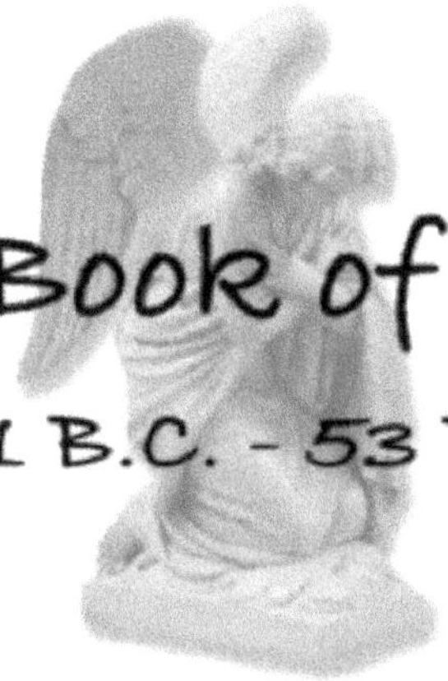

The Book of Alma
91 B.C. – 53 B.C.

Chapter 1..........145
Chapter 2..........151
Chapter 3..........155
Chapter 4..........157
Chapter 5..........167
Chapter 6..........181
Chapter 7..........183
Chapter 8..........189
Chapter 9..........193
Chapter 10..........197
Chapter 11..........201
Chapter 12..........205
Chapter 13..........213
Chapter 14..........219
Chapter 15..........223
Chapter 16..........227
Chapter 17..........231
Chapter 18..........239
Chapter 19..........243
Chapter 20..........247

Chapter 21......251
Chapter 22......255
Chapter 23......259
Chapter 24......261
Chapter 25......265
Chapter 26......267
Chapter 27......271
Chapter 28......275
Chapter 29......277
Chapter 30......281
Chapter 31......291
Chapter 32......299
Chapter 33......307
Chapter 34......311
Chapter 35......315
Chapter 36......319
Chapter 37......321
Chapter 38......329
Chapter 39......331
Chapter 40......335
Chapter 41......339
Chapter 42......343
Chapter 43......355
Chapter 44......359
Chapter 45......361
Chapter 46......365
Chapter 47......369
Chapter 48......371
Chapter 49......377
Chapter 50......379
Chapter 51......383
Chapter 52......387
Chapter 53......391
Chapter 54......395
Chapter 55......397
Chapter 56......399
Chapter 57......403
Chapter 58......405
Chapter 59......407
Chapter 60......409
Chapter 61......413
Chapter 62......417
Chapter 63......421

Observations

Observations...473

Author's Note

Author's Note..465

Addendum
A Sampling of Scriptures
(Mosiah - Alma)

Addendum..473

Commentary and Compendium Index

Commentary and Compendium Index..553

Acknowledgements

The creation of my Commentary would have been impossible without stability and support on the home front. In the early years of its genesis, my children Tara, Joanna, Christopher, Patrick, Elizabeth, Kathryn, and Andrew tolerated the late hours when their sleep must have been interrupted many times by the incessant tapping on my keyboard. Later, when I was preoccupied with endless revisions, their insight and suggestions helped to define and refine the work. I will always remember the conversations we had concerning the lessons we learned from the scriptures. Often, listening to their perspective propelled me in new directions that expanded my appreciation of themes that I would have otherwise only narrowly or superficially addressed. Their example always gave me courage and the inspiration to make the study of The Book of Mormon relevant to our family's circumstances.

Throughout the process, my wife Jan has stood by my side and put up with my fixation on this project in countless ways. Without her constant support, my efforts would have fallen far short of my envisioned goal. She became the rudder of my ship, guiding me past unseen rocks and reefs. She has been my helm, holding steady when winds of adversity blew, and has been my telltale, who always alerted me to threatening squalls. She has been my keel, who helped me to move against the current and the wind, and my mainsheet, who held firm with just enough pressure to prevent me from capsizing when I was dangerously heeled over. She has been my safety-line, providing security when my footing was unsure and the foaming sea was streaming across my deck. She has been my compass, showing me the way, especially when the course was unclear, my chart, warning me of hidden dangers, and my barometer, cautioning me to take heed of impending storms. She has always been my lookout, standing as my faithful sentinel whenever I became distracted by trivial concerns. It was she who held the line that trailed in my wake, offering the promise of safety whenever I slipped and fell overboard. She has been and ever will be the wind that fills my sails. Jan and I may be partners in this great adventure, but she is my better half.

In The Book
of Mormon, we are
exposed to a constant
flow of insight, intuition,
inspiration, and revelation
that basically streams forth in
a downpour of divine direction.
it blesses us was we walk along
illuminate pathways, and we
exercise our faculties of mind
and spirit. The book leads us
to the community of Christ,
so that, together, we may
collectively experience
the guidance of the
Holy Ghost.

Preface

I have always wanted to write a Commentary on The Book of Mormon. In 1981, when the New English Language Edition of the Standard Works was published, I began to comprehensively organize my card files and correlate them with the marginal notations that I had made over the years in my copies of the scriptures. These references became the foundation of my written impressions in this Commentary.

Collating my source material was daunting, especially before the age of word processing began in earnest, with the introduction of personal computers in the early 1980s.

I have attributed quotations to original authors whenever possible, as well as when I have editorialized the thoughts expressed by others. In many cases, however, the language in my Commentary will naturally reflect the teachings of leaders in The Church of Jesus Christ of Latter-day Saints. Of course, I alone am responsible for the content of these volumes. I hope my interpretation of the teachings of The Book of Mormon will cultivate your interest to dig deeper into the themes woven into its tapestry. My only goal is to help you to expand your insights into the foundation truths, core doctrines, and eternal principles that are the celestial guideposts embedded within its verses.

Hugh Nibley observed: "Men fool themselves, when they think for a moment that they can read scripture without ever adding something to the text or omitting something from it". Therein lies the power inherent in its study. We glean insight and understanding every time we investigate the word of God. I have learned to love the scriptures, and I often think of St. Hilary, who wrote: "Scripture consists not in what we read, but in what we understand". In my Commentary, I have consistently tried to anchor to the scriptures the ideas swirling around in my head.

Utilization of a Commentary does not replace personal scripture study. The spiritual awakening that accompanies prayerful efforts to understand the mysteries of God through the study of His word cannot be achieved through another person's interpretation. Perhaps, though, my own perspectives on the eternal themes expressed within The Book of Mormon will be helpful to you as you read and seek your own guidance. It is my hope that you will use this Commentary only to assist you in your own personal journey to Christ.

Our challenge is to enlist the aid of the Holy Ghost as we process the world around us. Many years ago, Dallin Oaks said: "Latter-day Saints know that learned or authoritative commentaries can help us with scriptural interpretation, but we maintain that they must be used with caution. Commentaries are not a substitute for the scriptures any more than a good cookbook is a substitute for food. When I refer to "commentaries", I mean everything that interprets scripture, from the comprehensive book-length commentary to the brief interpretation embodied in a lesson or an article, such as this one".

"One trouble with commentaries", he continued, "is that their authors sometimes focus on only one meaning to the exclusion of others. As a result, commentaries, if not used with great care, may illuminate the author's chosen and correct meaning but close our eyes and restrict our horizons to other possible meanings. Sometimes, those other less obvious meanings can be the ones most valuable and useful to us as we seek to obtain answers to our own questions. This is why the teaching of the Holy Ghost is a better guide to scriptural interpretation than is even the best commentary".

I could not agree more heartily with these wise words of counsel from President Oaks. As a matter of fact, every time I proofed a chapter (and I did this many times) I found myself scribbling additional notes in the margins and thinking to myself, "Why didn't I see that before?". That is precisely what I hope will be the experience of everyone who takes the time to read my Commentary. I trust the process will motivate you to search the scriptures more carefully and to be instructed by the Spirit, as you do so, that you might be led in directions that will prove to be personally illuminating.

I would expect that my older grandchildren who read this Commentary will be impacted in ways that are different from my adult children or my contemporaries. I hope that my observations will touch you differently each time you read them. When I am long-gone, perhaps the considerable thought that went into its production will generate a palpable bond that will span the years separating us. Maybe, the gulf that then divides us will not be as great, and our shared energies will pave the way to an eventual joyous reunion.

Know that I have been exhilarated when I have found wisdom and great treasures of knowledge, even hidden treasures, in the scriptures. These doctrinal themes have become pearls that I might have overlooked had I taken only a cursory glance. I hope that I am planting seeds so that you might harvest greater understanding, as well.

I had the opportunity to visit the Holy Land many years ago. We stopped, too briefly, at Qumran. The Dead Sea Covenantors lived there, and in the ruins of their library, I was able to pause and reflect upon their Eleventh Hymn that had been recovered from parchments hidden within caves high above their community. The translation reads, in part: "Behold, for mine own part I have reached the intervision, and through the spirit thou hast placed within me, come to know Thee, my God". In similar fashion, Moses wrote: "But now, mine own eyes have beheld God; but not my natural, but my spiritual eyes, for my natural eyes could not have beheld; for I should have withered and died in his presence; but his glory was upon me; and I beheld his face". (Moses 1:11)

I am continually reminded of Nephi's counsel to press forward with complete dedication and steadfastness, or confidence and a firm determination in Christ, having a perfect brightness of hope, or perfect faith, and charity, or a love of God and of all men. If we do this, he promised, feasting upon the word of Christ, or receiving strength and nourishment from the scriptures, and endure to the end in righteousness, we shall have eternal life, that is the greatest gift God can bestow upon His children. (See 2 Nephi 31:20). It is with love that I extend to you the invitation to enjoy my Commentary.

Introduction

Cicero wrote: "The first law for the historian is that he shall never dare utter an untruth. The second is that he shall suppress nothing that is true. Moreover, there shall be no suspicion of partiality or of malice in his writing". The accounts in The Book of Mormon abridged by the prophet-historian Mormon were true to the mandate given by Cicero. Although, as Washington Irving brooded: "It is the rule that history fades into fable; fact becomes clouded with doubt and controversy; the inscription moulders, and columns, arches, and pyramids are but heaps of sand, and their epitaphs, nothing but characters written in the dust", yet The Book of Mormon stands as a shining example of the divine model.

The Book of Mormon "is the witness that testifies to the passing of time. It illuminates reality, vitalizes memory, provides guidance in daily life, and brings us tidings of antiquity". It is the "evidence of time, the light of truth, the life of memory, the directress of life, committed to immortality". (Cicero, "De Oratore", ii, 36). In its pages, "the centuries roll back to the ancient age of gold". (Horace, "Odes", IV, ii, 39).

Those who read The Book of Mormon undertake an incredible journey through thousands of years of history as the pages of a profound text unfold before the panorama of great civilizations. Within its pages lies the intrigue of ancient Asia, as warlords battle for supremacy, the tension in Jerusalem mounts as rival empires of the Near East struggle for power, and the faithful prepare for a journey to a land of promise beyond the horizon of their vision.

The Book of Mormon may be devoured as if it were literally the bread of life, and those who read it feast upon the word of God and feel exhilaration as prophets counsel us from the dust. We seek, and yearn, and strive, and wrestle for our blessing, realizing that "unto some it is given by the Holy Ghost to know that Jesus Christ is the Son of God, and that he was crucified for the sins of the world", while "to others it is given … the word of knowledge". (D&C 46:13 & 18).

The Book of Mormon makes the bold claim that its pages contain "the fulness of the Gospel". (D&C 42:12). Even members of The Church of Jesus Christ of Latter-day Saints sometimes misinterpret this to mean that there will be found within its pages detailed instructions regarding every doctrinal principle that governs our lives in the last days, and that the Nephite Saints participated in every ordinance of the Gospel as we know it. But it is we, and not they, who live in the Dispensation of The Fulness of Times, when the knowledge of the ages is being revealed. The Book of Mormon Saints only received "the fulness of the Gospel", in the sense that they were given instruction for their own needs, and sufficient for their own salvation.

The Title Page of The Book of Mormon is an overview of its history, and was written by the Prophet Mormon who inserted it into the last leaf of the collection of plates. (See H.C., 1:71). It was translated by Joseph Smith and moved by him to the beginning of the book. It forthrightly explains that the book was written for doubters, "to the convincing of the Jew and Gentile" that Jesus is The Christ. But it also makes the astounding acknowledgement that it might contain mistakes. This admission, however, refer to faults other than theology. Joseph Smith assured the Saints that "The Book of Mormon (is) the most correct of any book on earth, and the keystone of our religion, and a man (will) get nearer to God by abiding by its precepts, than by any other book". (H.C., 4:461).

Most evidence suggests that he and Oliver Cowdery "began their work of translation" in April 1829, beginning with The Book of Mosiah, and that during the month of May they translated to the end of The Book of Moroni. They then translated the Title Page, and finally The Small Plates of Nephi and The Words of Mormon before the end of June. The text of the Title Page was used as the book's description on the copyright form filed on June 11, 1829. (See "Encyclopedia of Mormonism", V. 1, Book of Mormon Translation by Joseph Smith, John Welch).

The translation was unlike that of any other text, inasmuch as it was accomplished "through the mercy (and) power of God". (D&C 1:29). This is as specific an explanation as is found regarding just how Joseph created an evenly flowing and coherent narrative spanning a thousand years of history, that stands revealed today without the benefit of subsequent editorial revision. During his lifetime, he tended to let the record speak for itself. With an understanding of the revelatory process, we are drawn to the book itself rather than to the specific means of translation, and without distraction we focus on the challenge left by Moroni: "And when ye shall receive these things, I would exhort you that ye would ask God, the eternal Father, in the name of Christ, if these things are not true; and if ye shall ask with a sincere heart, with real intent, having faith in Christ, he will manifest the truth of it unto you, by the power of the Holy Ghost". (Moroni 10:4, see verse 5).

Jesus Christ Himself testified of the book's historical and doctrinal accuracy. Joseph Smith "translated the book, even that part which I have commanded him, and as your Lord and your God liveth, it is true". (D&C 17:6, see D&C 19:26). For emphasis, the Savior used an ancient Hebrew oath in His witness. "Because he could swear by no greater, he sware by himself". (Hebrews 6:13).

Sometimes, those who are learning about the Restoration of the Gospel ask why the Church does not still possess the plates from which the Nephite history was translated. But as Hugh Nibley pointed out: "The presence of the plates would only prove that there are plates, and no more. It would not prove that Nephites wrote them, or that an angel brought them, or that they had been translated by the gift and power of God. A far more impressive claim is put forth when the whole work is given to the world as a divinely inspired translation". (Hugh Nibley, "An Approach to The Book of Mormon", p. 17-18).

Thus, The Book of Mormon stands on its own merits, in sharp contrast to the confusion surrounding most biblical scholarship. For example, "there are so many Greek New Testament manuscripts (over 5,000) that effective management and citation in a critical text amount to highly selective and careful genealogical classification into families, so that over 150,000 alternative readings can be grouped and profiled in a useful way. Also, the American Bible Society has counted over 24,000 differences among only six separate pre-1830 editions of the 1611 King James Version of the Bible". (FARMS Report).

No wonder that, in the Sacred Grove, Joseph Smith learned of the sects of Christendom that "they were all wrong" and that "all their creeds were an abomination". (J.S.H. 1:19). Organizations or teachings that do not lead us clearly and unambiguously toward salvation and exaltation in the Celestial Kingdom are abominable in the sight of God because they thwart the stated purpose of The Plan of Salvation, which is to guide us unerringly and bring to pass our immortality and eternal life. (See Moses 1:39). It was such confusion, in Joseph Smith's mind, that led to his Theophany and introduced the world to the Dispensation of The Fulness of Times.

Today, there is remarkable harmony within the Church regarding the dogma embedded within The Book of Mormon. Every day throughout the world, millions of Latter-day Saints open their translations of this scripture and are exposed to the same identical doctrinal themes. Contrast this unity of the faith with the thousands of denominations that interpret, with significant differences and sometimes-heated discussions, hundreds of variants of single biblical verses of scripture. It is far better that the Church proclaims that The Book of Mormon has been translated by the gift and power of God through the Prophet Joseph Smith. This leaves little room for conflicting doctrinal interpretation either within or outside the Church.

So important is The Book of Mormon, that right after its publication on March 26, 1830, the faithful met in Fayette, New York, and officially organized The Church of Jesus Christ of Latter-day Saints on April 6, 1830. Fully ten years earlier, Joseph Smith had communed with The Father and The Son in the Sacred Grove. Three years after that theophany, he received several documented visits from the Angel Moroni. Between 1823 and 1830, he became personally acquainted with all of the important characters in The Book of Mormon and enjoyed additional visits from Moroni. Still, the Church could not be organized until the Nephite scriptures that had been miraculously handed down to us were ready for publication.

Joseph Smith is listed in that first edition as the books' "author and proprietor". Thus, enemies of the Church have claimed that he wrote it, but the truth is simply that in accordance with the copyright laws of the State of New York at the time, someone had to be listed as author and proprietor of a text, and Joseph Smith was the logical choice.

In the past, paragraph two in the Introduction invited misunderstanding, because Lamanites were identified therein as the "principal" ancestors of the American Indians. (This introduction was written by Bruce R. McConkie in 1981, and was not part of the original translation of the text). Archaeological, anthropological, and genetic research suggests that the civilizations whose histories are recorded in The Book of Mormon lived in rather narrowly defined geographical areas in Meso-America. Certainly, there are many Native Americans today whose lineage may be traced to peoples other than Nephites and Lamanites who co-inhabited the Americas two thousand years ago. In any event, the 2007 change of one word in the Introduction, eliminating the word "principal" from the phrase "the principal ancestors of the American Indians..." and rendering it "among the ancestors of the American Indians..." invites a clearer understanding of the intent of the Introduction that was originally written by McConkie.

In their written testimony found at the beginning of the text, three witnesses accorded honor to the "Father, and to the Son, and to the Holy Ghost, which is one God". Better than other Christians, Latter-day Saints understand the nature of the Godhead. They recognize the individuality of each member of the Holy Trinity, while acknowledging the spiritual rapport between the Father, Son, and Holy Ghost, and between Them and true believers who enjoy a Holy Communion as they have become "one" in a spiritual sense.

Eight additional witnesses saw and handled the plates and described them as "having the appearance of gold". (See J.S.H. 1:34). We really do not know how many of the plates were actually made of gold. The 24 Gold Plates of Ether are the only ones that are identified in the text of The Book of Mormon as having been made of gold. (See Mosiah 8:9). We do know, however, that they were heavy. These witnesses "hefted" the bound plates that are estimated to have weighed in the neighborhood of 36 kilograms. The plates from which Joseph translated The Book of Mormon may have been thin sheets of gold, (see "Testimony of Joseph Smith", J.S.H., 1:34) but the text itself suggests that, in general, the Nephite prophets engraved their records on a variety of metals.

The Three Witnesses to The Book of Mormon wrote only that they had "seen the plates which contain this record" without reference to the specific composition of the metal, although they went into great detail to describe the engravings themselves and their purpose to benefit humanity. Various record-keepers referred to "plates of ore". (See

1 Nephi 19:1, Mosiah 21:27, and Mormon 8:5). When the prophets referred to a specific material, it was generally to "brass". (See 1 Nephi 3:3, 3:12, 3:24, 4:16, 4:24, 4:28, 5:10, 5:14, 5:18-19, 13:23, 19:21-22, 22:1, 22:30, 2 Nephi 4:2, 4:5, 5:12, Omni 1:14, Mosiah 1:3, 1:16, 10:16, 28:11, 28:20, Alma 37:3, 3 Nephi 1:2 & 10:17). "Plates of gold" are mentioned only in Mosiah 8:9 and 28:11, where they specifically refer to the 24 Gold Plates of Ether. Mormon, who had access to all the records and who abridged many of them, never referred to plates of gold.

His son Moroni twice referred to the plates, but only in reference to hiding them in the earth. (See Ether 15:11 & Mormon 8:4). Likewise, "Ammaron, being constrained by the Holy Ghost, did hide up the records which were sacred, yea, even all the sacred records which had been handed down from generation to generation, which were sacred". (4 Nephi 1:48-49). It may simply be that the custodians of the record were more focused on the message than on the material.

Because gold itself was much more plentiful in the Lands of The Book of Mormon, it many have not mattered to them of what material the plates were crafted. Jacob reported that his people, who still had an "Old World" mindset, had "begun to search for gold, and for silver, and for all manner of precious ores". Note that Jacob qualified as "precious" the ore his people sought. "In the which," or in these precious materials, he continued, "this land ... doth abound most plentifully". (Jacob 2:12). In the same vein, Mormon reported: "Both the Lamanites and the Nephites ... did have an exceeding plenty of gold, and of silver, and of all manner of precious metals". (Helaman 6:9). As had Jacob before him, Mormon characterized the hoarded materials as "precious metals".

We do know that the Eight Witnesses to The Book of Mormon testified that the plates they were shown and "hefted" had "the appearance of gold" and that Joseph Smith wrote in his History that Moroni told him that the book that was hidden in the Hill Cumorah was "written upon gold plates". (J.S.H. 1:34). But The Book of Mormon record itself does not corroborate Moroni's characterization of the gold composition of the plates. In the Church, however, it is commonly accepted that the records, other than The Plates of Brass, were "gold plates". Gold has always denoted value, and at the very least, the precious gift of The Book of Mormon is equivalent to the gifts of gold, frankincense, and myrrh, traditionally bestowed by the Wise Men of the East upon the Christ child in Bethlehem.

Interestingly, however, none of The Book of Mormon chroniclers describe their records as "gold plates," with the prominent exception of the Plates of Ether, that are specifically characterized as being of "pure gold". (Mosiah 8:9). Nephi's record was engraven upon "plates of ore". (1 Nephi 19:1). It was the record upon these plates that was pleasing to Mormon, and not the plates themselves. (The Words of Mormon, 1:4). As a matter of fact, when occasion arose, the various record keepers in The Book of Mormon almost pointedly described only the intrinsic quality of the plates entrusted to their care, while pointedly and characteristically ignoring the temporal value of the metals upon which the records were engraven.

The Testimony of the Prophet Joseph Smith is also interesting because his account of the initial appearance of the angel who delivered the plates is unique. (See J.S.H. 1:29-43). Joseph wrote that late one evening a light started to appear in his bedchamber and grew brighter and brighter until it was lighter than at noonday. Suddenly the Angel Moroni appeared before him, standing in the air. Clearly, Moroni came from another realm or dimension. He did not come through the door to enter the room. Rather, he just "appeared".

After he had delivered a detailed message, the light began to gather up around Moroni, and he ascended in a conduit right into heaven. This remarkable description is alien to our experience. None of us has ever seen light gather around an individual in this manner, presumably leaving the rest of the room in enveloping darkness, and none of us has ever seen such a light surround an individual who is then sucked up into the heavens as though the ceiling of the room were non-existent. The events of that evening are more remarkable when we realize that they were repeated, for emphasis, two more times.

On the following day, and in broad daylight, Moroni again appeared to Joseph in a field near his home. Once more, this resurrected being was described as being surrounded by an unearthly light that transcended the brilliance of the sun itself.

Just how important is it for us to read, understand, and apply the principles contained in this book that was heralded by this heavenly angel? Joseph Fielding Smith, Jr. stated: "No member of this Church can stand approved in the presence of God who has not seriously and carefully read The Book of Mormon". (C.R., 10/1961). The witness of the divinity of Jesus Christ gained through study of The Book of Mormon is an invaluable aid for those who desire to be valiant in the testimony of Jesus. Often, we marvel at the care with which the foundation was laid for the Restoration of the Gospel and the translation and publication of The Book of Mormon. Sometimes, however, we are guilty of carelessness in the diligence with which we actually study its pages. President Smith's statement is a reminder that we all need to sharpen our scholarship to a fine point.

Moroni's challenge, therefore, should be thoughtfully pondered. Every day, in fact, thousands put his promise to the test. When Heavenly Father placed His spirit children on the earth, he anticipated their initial ignorance of the saving principles of the Gospel. But His nurture of our spirits in the pre-earth existence had endowed each of us with a solid understanding of Gospel principles. It was only when we could learn no more in that setting, that we welcomed the opportunity to come to the earth to continue our education. (See Abraham 3:26, & Titus 1:2). We left our heavenly home with the assurance from our Father that, while on earth, we would have the Light of Christ and the influence of the Holy Ghost, and that heavenly power would help us to recognize the truth when we heard it. (See D&C 84:46, & 93:2). As Brigham Young declared: "Every Gospel principle carries within it a witness that it is true". In fact, Joseph Fielding Smith, Jr. who, like President Young, was a prophet, seer, and revelator, said that the witness of the Holy Ghost is more powerful than a vision or even the manifestation of heavenly messengers.

This concept is one of the beautiful simplicities of the Gospel. The Plan allows all of us to enjoy the same access to the simplest, and yet most powerful, witness to the truth. In an inarticulate voice softer than the faintest whisper of sweet breath on the cheek, the Holy Ghost gently testifies, or bears witness, of truth. As Moroni 10:5 teaches (in a verse that is often overlooked, in favor of the previous verse): "By the power of the Holy Ghost ye may know the truth of all things".

The Holy Ghost has revealed all that is true, and has illuminated every eternal principle that has guided the minds of men and women since the dawn of history. We constantly benefit from that which He reveals. In the Last Days, when the Spirit is "poured out upon all flesh, and when "young men see visions, and old men dream dreams", it will be the Holy Ghost Who provides the creative drive. (Joel 2:28). The irony is that many will fail to recognize the source of their inspiration. Job did not. He wrote: "For God speaketh once, yea twice, yet man perceiveth it not. In a dream, in a vision of the night, when deep sleep falleth upon men, in slumberings upon the bed; then he openeth the ears of men, and sealeth their instruction." (Job 33:14-16). We cannot help but think of the experience of Joseph Smith in his bedchamber, when we read Job's description of how Heavenly Father communicates with His children.

Of course, Jesus Christ wants us to have a testimony of the divine authenticity of The Book of Mormon. It has come to us through thousands of years of effort on the part of ancient prophets and after the personal sacrifice of countless individuals who have passed through the refiner's fire. The prophet Isaiah foresaw a "marvelous work and a wonder" that would not come to pass for another 2,700 years (Isaiah 29:14), and in the apocalyptic vision of John, another angel was seen "in the midst of heaven, having the everlasting Gospel to preach unto them that dwell on the earth, and to every nation, and kindred, and tongue, and people". (Revelation 14:6).

Precisely because The Book of Mormon is another testament, or second witness, of Jesus Christ, missionaries use it to great effect as a principal tool of conversion. The organization of the book is divinely inspired to assist Heavenly Father in His work to bring to pass our immortality and eternal life, by teaching us the principles of faith, repentance, baptism, and the ordinances of the priesthood. (See Moses 1:39).

All who desire to have a sure personal witnesses must carefully and prayerfully read The Book of Mormon, and then ask in faith if what they have studied is true. They will then receive the testimony of the Holy Ghost to motivate them to seek out the Priesthood and to enter into sacred covenants with God. It will be as it was on the Day of Pentecost, when Peter and others were preaching to a multitude whose hearts and minds were open and receptive to the truth. The words of the Apostles carried the weight of authority, and penetrated the hearts of their listeners to the end that they asked: "Men and brethren, what shall we do? Then Peter said unto them, Repent, and be baptized every one of you in the name of Jesus Christ for the remission of sins, and ye shall receive the gift of the Holy Ghost". (Acts 2:37-38). On that day, there were about 3,000 souls added to the kingdom of God on earth. (See Commentary Reference to 3 Nephi 15:21-24).

A similar scenario exists today. Since the Restoration of the Gospel, there has been a Pentecostal outpouring of the Spirit, and those with a sincere desire to understand the will of God bring the same humble petition to the doorstep of the missionaries: "Now that we have heard your message, have put it to the test of prayerful inquiry, and have received a witness of the Spirit, what shall we do?" The response of the servants of the Lord is unequivocal: "You must exercise saving faith that leads to the waters of baptism and to continuing commitment, dedicated discipleship, selfless service, and sustained spirituality".

Members of the Church believe they "must be called of God, by prophecy, and by the laying on of hands, by those who are in authority, to preach the Gospel, and to administer the ordinances thereof". (5th Article of Faith). The first ordinance of the Gospel following baptism is confirmation as a member of the Church together with the bestowal of the Holy Ghost. Even though many individuals receive their testimony of The Book of Mormon before becoming members of the Church, their expanding understanding will be further enhanced following their baptism as the Spirit unfolds to them the mysteries of the kingdom. As Joseph Smith wrote of his own experience almost two years after the organization of the Church: "By the power of the Spirit our eyes were opened and our understandings were enlightened, so as to see and understand the things of God". (D&C 76:12).

Critical to comprehension of the monumental themes contained within The Book of Mormon is familiarity with the underlying structure of the text. It is not too difficult to understand, as long as we remember that Mormon was the prophet who gathered all the records together and who then abridged certain of these into The Plates of Mormon. (See Mormon 1:1). This is the main reason why the text is called The Book of Mormon. In a larger sense, though, it is not really his book, alone.

The scope of its 531 pages is far-reaching, and its literary style was intentionally designed to focus on the core material rather than on its various authors. It is remarkable, however, that 15 major writing styles and personalities survived both abridgment and translation. The working vocabulary of 1 Nephi alone has 23% more words than comparable Old Testament sections, and although there are only 2,696 root words in the entire book, or only 10% of Shakespeare's working vocabulary, its depth is breathtaking. Sometimes, less is more.

Mormon said that he could not write "the hundredth part of the things of (his) people". (Words of Mormon 1:5, see Jacob 3:13, & Helaman 3:14). Even though Joseph Smith wrote in his history that the plates at the Hill Cumorah were deposited in the earth in a box fashioned out of stone, other sources indicate that there were many more plates in the collection at that site. (See Helaman 3:15). Brigham Young said that there was a whole room, with plates stacked high against the walls. Together, he said that they would comprise several wagon loads.

What we do have, swells in significance when we realize that the body of the records included in The Book of Mormon is a condensation of that which had been considered to be of most importance in the eyes of a long line of Nephite prophet-historians. High Nibley rightly called the book "a blueprint for survival in the Last Days". As such, it is a detailed and accurate representation of a much larger structure. He said: "The events and situations that not many years ago seemed to some as wildly improbable and greatly overdrawn, have suddenly become the story of our times, and we see and shall see the words of the prophets who speak to us from the dust fearfully and wonderfully vindicated". ("The World and The Prophets", p. 196).

Nephi only started writing 30 years after leaving Jerusalem, which might give solace to those of us who have trouble maintaining the continuity of our own personal journals. He had plenty of time, beforehand, to distill in his mind just what he would include and how he would do it. Writing from the perspective of middle age might also have been an advantage, for hindsight always seems to be 20 / 20, and maturity often gives us a mentally, emotionally, and spiritually stable perspective that is too frequently lacking in youth.

First, he abridged the writings of his father that were collectively called The Book of Lehi, and then he made his own carefully constructed record. It took Nephi 10 years just to write the first 25 chapters, possibly because he wrote in a very stylized Hebraic pattern, the first nine chapters of 1 Nephi comprising a complex chiasm. Then, in chapters 10-22 he worked out a second, parallel chiasm. Note that Chapter 9 and Chapter 22 each end with a formal "Amen", signifying the end of that distinctive Hebraic literary device.

The Small Plates of Nephi in their entirety include the First and Second Books of Nephi, the Books of Jacob, Enos, Jarom, and Omni, and the Words of Mormon. These plates were placed in the repository at Cumorah for a reason that was unclear to Mormon. The Small Plates included a duplication of The Book of Lehi, an abridgement of which was written on The Large Plates of Nephi. The reason for their preservation became obvious only when Martin Harris lost the initial 116 pages of manuscript translation, forcing Joseph Smith to turn to The Small Plates of Nephi in order to translate a parallel history of the early Nephite record to be used as a substitute for the missing and potentially corrupted text.

The Small Plates of Nephi are always called "these plates". They were translated in the first-person tense, inasmuch as they came, not from an abridgement, but directly from the record of Nephi and his descendants, up to and including Omni. The period of history covered by these plates is slightly less than half of the Nephite history, or 470 out of a total of 1,021 years.

The Words of Mormon that follows Omni is an editorial insert written by Mormon in 385 A.D. and inserted by him in the record, to bridge the gap between The Small Plates of Nephi and The Plates of Mormon (his abridgement of the balance of The Large Plates of Nephi) that follow.

The literary labor of Mormon, called The Plates of Mormon, comprises The Books of Mosiah, Alma, Helaman, Third Nephi - The Book of Nephi, Fourth Nephi - The Book of Nephi, and The Book of Mormon chapters 1-7. When reading from the translation of The Plates of Mormon, the text is generally in the third person tense, inasmuch as it is an abridgement from The Large Plates of Nephi. When Mormon inserted editorial comments throughout his abridgement, it was written in the first-person tense., often accompanied by the phrase "and thus we see." When reading 1 Nephi through Omni, "those plates" means The Large Plates of Nephi that follow The Words of Mormon in the format of The Book of Mormon. The Plates of Mormon also included writings of Mormon's son Moroni. These are found in The Book of Mormon Chapters 8 & 9, and in The Book of Moroni.

The Book of Ether is an abridgment from an ancient record that was written upon 24 gold plates found by the people of King Limhi in the days of King Mosiah. At least a portion of these plates was abridged by Moroni, either from Mosiah's earlier translation or directly from The Plates of Ether. Moroni inserted editorial comments of his own, and included this record in a general history under the title "The Book of Ether". (See Ether 1:1-2).

At great expense and personal risk, Lehi's sons retrieved The Plates of Brass from Jerusalem. They contained "the five books of Moses (or the first five books of the Old Testament), and also a record of the Jews from the beginning down to the commencement of the reign of Zedekiah, king of Judah; and also, the prophecies of the holy prophets". (1 Nephi 5:11-13). Consequently, many of the writings of the prophet Isaiah are prominently found upon The Plates of Brass.

"The version of Isaiah in the Nephite scripture hews an independent course for itself, as might be expected of a truly ancient and authentic record. It makes additions to the present text in certain places, omits material in others, transposes, makes grammatical changes, finds support at times for its unusual readings in the ancient Greek, Syriac, and Latin Versions, and at other times no support at all. In general, it presents phenomena of great interest to the student of Isaiah". (Sydney B. Sperry, "Book of Mormon Compendium", p. 512).

"The text of Isaiah in The Book of Mormon is not word for word the same as that of the King James Translation. Of 433 verses of Isaiah in the Nephite record, Joseph Smith modified 234. Some of the changes were slight, while others were radical. However, 199 verses are word for word the same as the K.J.T. We, therefore, freely admit that Joseph Smith may have used the K.J.T. when he came to the text of Isaiah on the plates. As long as the K.J.T. agreed substantially with the text on the plates, he let it pass; when it differed significantly, he translated the Nephite version and dictated the necessary changes". (Sydney B. Sperry, "Book of Mormon Compendium", p. 507-508).

As Hugh Nibley has pointed out: "Resemblances between the Bible and The Book of Mormon are not hard to explain and are confirmation of authenticity. If The Book of Mormon is what it says it is, we should expect to find within its pages a strong biblical influence. Its prophets sound like those of the Old Testament because they studied and consciously quoted the words of those prophets, and all prophets moreover are programmed to sound alike, being called for the same purpose, under much the same conditions". ("Churches in The Wilderness").

The Plates of Brass were the Nephite scriptures, and included therein was the written record of their family histories and genealogies. They were revered by the Nephites, as evidenced by frequent quotations from and references to them throughout The Book of Mormon. As Nephi explained: "And I did read many things unto them which were written in the books of Moses; but that I might more fully persuade them to believe in the Lord their Redeemer I did read unto them that which was written by the prophet Isaiah; for I did liken all scriptures unto us, that it might be for our profit and learning". (1 Nephi 1:23).

The "books of Moses" to which Nephi referred concern the Pentateuch, Torah, or The Law. These are not to be confused with The Book of Moses in The Pearl of Great Price. Nephi's books of Moses were, in fact, the principal scriptures of the Jews. From these books of The Law, there sprang up an encyclopedic interpretation by the Jews at Jerusalem called The Talmud.

Readers of The Book of Mormon will repeatedly encounter direct references to Isaiah in its text. As a matter of fact, 32% of The Book of Isaiah is quoted in The Book of Mormon, while 3% is paraphrased. Following the pattern established earlier in The Book of Mormon, in the New Testament there are more quotations attributable to Isaiah than to all other Old Testament prophets combined. It is little wonder that The Book of Mormon should rely so heavily on Isaiah, however, since his prophecies not only reflect Old World religious philosophy, but also a latter-day world view and testament of Jesus Christ.

Nephi delighted in the words of Isaiah, and recorded 2 Nephi Chapters 12-24 in an effort to prove the truth of Christ's coming, and that save He should come, we must perish. Isaiah was what we call a "Messianic Prophet" whose principal mission was to point us toward the Savior, to His teachings, and to salvation through obedience to the principles of His Gospel.

During the ministry of Isaiah, the Ten Tribes were taken captive and later fled to the north where they were swallowed up and lost to history. But they carried with them the words of Isaiah, just as Lehi did in his journey to the Promised Land. (See D&C 133:26 & 2 Nephi 29:13-14). The Jews also retained Isaiah's words, and today, Covenant Israel, or the Church, has them. His is a very diversified audience.

Nephi knew that the words of Isaiah would be as a pearl of great price in the Last Days, and to those who would suppose that they are not, he said "I (will) speak particularly, and confine the words unto mine own people; for I know that they shall be of great worth unto them in the last days; for in that day shall they understand them; wherefore, for their good have I written them". (2 Nephi 25:8). Nephi considered the writings of Isaiah, who had lived just over a century earlier, to be scripture. Clearly, he understood that whatsoever the prophets speak when moved upon by the Spirit, "shall be the will of the Lord, shall be the mind of the Lord, shall be the word of the Lord, shall be the voice of the Lord, and the power of God unto salvation". (D&C 68:4).

Today, it is the clear responsibility of members of the Church to carefully and prayerfully study the prophecies of Isaiah, for they were meant for our generation. His language might be veiled in symbolism and shadows of meaning with which we are not superficially familiar. Nevertheless, we have been commanded by the Savior Himself: "Seek ye out of the best books words of wisdom; seek learning, even by study and also by faith" (D&C 88:118) and "live by every word that proceedeth forth from the mouth of God". (D&C 84:44).

Nephi recognized Isaiah's witness of the Lord Jesus Christ as pre-eminent among the testimonies of the prophets. It should be no surprise that the Savior declared to the Nephite Saints: "And now, behold, I say unto you, that ye ought to search (his teachings). Yea, a commandment I give unto you that ye search these things diligently; for great are the words of Isaiah". (3 Nephi 23:1). The main reason for the scriptures, after all, is to persuade us to believe in Christ. This is why the prophets all seem to sound alike. They all draw upon the same eternal truths to prove their points. Theirs is not vain repetition, but rather theatrical encore. "The prophets do have much the same message, and the now recognized practice by the prophets of giving out the words of their predecessors as their own receives its first clear statement and justification in The Book of Mormon". (Hugh Nibley, "Since Cumorah", p. 40-41).

Shakespeare wrote: "The past is prologue". ("The Tempest", Act 2, scene 1, 245-254). The phrase was intended to imply that our past is merely a prologue, or an introduction, to the great adventure upon which we will embark if we follow through on our plans. This original interpretation teaches that what has come before on our journey through life doesn't matter in the grand scheme of things, because a new future lies before us, subject to the choices we will yet make. The human condition does not change much over time, which is one reason why the Lord has revealed The Book of Mormon in the Last Days, so that we might profit from the experiences of the Nephites who are distant from us in time and yet are so like us.

Hugh Nibley observed: "The tragedy of the Nephites, who brought destruction by war upon their own heads, was not what became of them, but rather what they themselves became". ("Since Cumorah", p. 425). "A man's character is his fate", wrote the Greek philosopher Heraclitus. The Nephite scriptures are a study in human frailties, and the epic drama that unfolds before our minds' eye strengthens and clarifies our moral and ethical values.

In The Book of Mormon, "we are not laying down ground rules for taste, or saying that it is good because some people like it, or bad because others do not. What we are saying is that whatever one may think of it, is one of the great realities of our time, and that what makes it so is that millions of people believe it. Its literary or artistic qualities do not enter into the discussion. It was written to be believed. It's one and only merit is truth. Without that merit, it is all that non-believers say it is. With it, it is all that believers say it is". (Hugh Nibley, "Of All Things", p. 93). With this historical perspective, an abiding testimony in the divinity of the work, and an anticipation of enlightenment throughout the journey, let us commit and re-commit ourselves to a lifetime study of this keystone text.

The Book of Mosiah
130 B.C - 91 B.C.

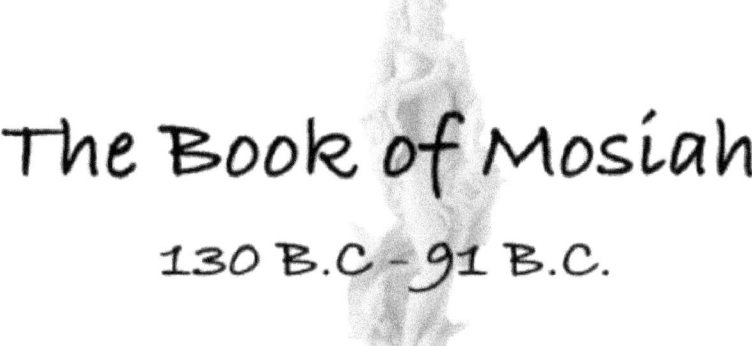

Mosiah
Chapter 1

Mosiah was the third king to rule in Zarahemla, following in the footsteps of his father, Benjamin, and grandfather, Mosiah. After the elder Mosiah had led the righteous Nephites out of the Land of Nephi two generations earlier, he "was made king over the land of Zarahemla". (Omni 1:12). With conspicuous order, "the people of Zarahemla and of Mosiah did unite together; and Mosiah was appointed to be their king". (Omni 1:19). Thus, "all the people of Zarahemla were numbered with the Nephites, and this because the kingdom had been conferred upon none but those who were descendants of Nephi". (Mosiah 25:13). Clearly, then, Mosiah was a descendant of Nephi.

Centuries earlier, when Nephi died, the people had been "desirous to retain in remembrance his name. And whoso should reign in his stead were called by the people, second Nephi, third Nephi, and so forth, according to the reigns of the kings; and thus, they were called by the people, let them be of whatever name they would". (Jacob 1:11). Perhaps, after Jacob died, the practice was discontinued, or it might be that Mosiah shed the title by which he was known in the Land of Nephi, when he departed into the wilderness,, bound for Zarahemla.

Just before his death, Nephi had "anointed a man to be a king and a ruler over his people". (Jacob 1:10). It is likely, especially in light of Mosiah 25:13 cited above, that this individual was one of Nephi's own sons. If this was the case, then Mosiah could have been last in a line of Nephi's direct descendants who reigned over the Nephites in the Land of Nephi. (See 1 Nephi 2:22). Following his rule, the Nephites adopted a government of judges, and for all practical purposes the monarchy was discontinued. (See Mosiah 29:47). But years later, memories of the royal line persisted, for "those who were in favor of kings were those of high birth, and they sought to be kings". (Alma 51:8).

Before the death of Nephi, his younger brother Jacob was entrusted with the care of the Small Plates of Nephi that contained the religious history of the Nephites. See 1 Nephi 19:1-2, & Jacob 1:1-2). These plates passed from Jacob to his son Enos, grandson Jarom, great grandson Omni, great-great grandson Amaron, and then to Amaron's brother Chemish. Chemish entrusted these records to his son Abinadom, who finally conferred the sacred responsibility upon his son Amaleki.

The Large Plates of Nephi, upon which was recorded the secular history of the Nephites, had always remained in the possession of the king. (See 1 Nephi 19:4, & Jacob 1:3). When Mosiah was "warned of the Lord that he should flee out of the land of Nephi," as the king, he would have taken the Plates of Brass and the Large Plates of Nephi, as well as the various other emblems of authority, with him. (Omni 1:12, see Commentary Reference to Mosiah 1:15).

If these had been in the possession of an apostate Nephite king, it might have been as difficult for Mosiah to obtain them as it had earlier been for Nephi. (See 1 Nephi Chapters 3, & 4). But there is not the slightest hint in The Book of Mormon that intrigue or stratagem was employed regarding the removal of these treasures from the Land of Nephi. The inference is clear; Mosiah simply gathered up those things that had been entrusted to his care in his capacity as king.

The record reveals that Amaleki had no children, and so before his death he delivered the Small Plates to Mosiah's son King Benjamin. (Omni 1:25). Thus, the care of both The Small and Large Plates of Nephi became the sole responsibility of the king.

Later, when Alma became the Presiding High Priest in Zarahemla, he was authorized by Benjamin's son Mosiah II to "establish Churches throughout all the land of Zarahemla". (Mosiah 25:19). This is the first time in The Book of Mormon that a formal Church organization is mentioned. It is likely that at this same time, Mosiah II entrusted Alma with the care of all of the plates and the other emblems of ecclesiastical authority. From this time on, the sacred records would be maintained by religious, rather than by civil, leaders.

In addition to Mormon Chapters 1-7, the literary labor of Mormon comprises Mosiah, Alma, Helaman, 3 Nephi, and 4 Nephi, all abridged from the Large Plates of Nephi and written on the Plates of Mormon. The Book of Mosiah spans 33 years of history, from 125 B.C. (Mosiah 1:10) to 92 B.C. (Mosiah 29:46). But only Chapters 25-29 concern the reign of Mosiah himself. (See Commentary Reference to Mosiah 29:47).

This book is an excellent example of literature that, at first glance, seems to have a very difficult structure. It is not structured chronologically, and can be very confusing if one tries to understand it according to the wrong organizational scheme. However, when its underlying 28-part chiastic order is appreciated, it makes sense. (See Commentary Reference to Mosiah 29:33).

A King Benjamin exhorts his sons. (Mosiah 1:1-8).
B Mosiah is chosen to succeed his father. (Mosiah 1:10).
C Mosiah receives the records. (Mosiah 1:16).
D Benjamin's speech and the words of the angel. (Mosiah 2:9-5:15).
E The people enter into a covenant. (Mosiah 6:1)
F Priests are consecrated. (Mosiah 6:13).
G Ammon leaves Zarahemla for the Land of Nephi. (Mosiah 7:1-6).
H The people are in bondage; Ammon put in prison. (Mosiah 7:15).
I The 24 Gold Plates of Ether. (Mosiah 8:9).
J The record of Zeniff begins as he leaves Zarahemla. (Mosiah 9:1).
K Defense against the Lamanites. Mosiah 9:14-10:20).
L Noah and his priests. (Mosiah 11).
M Abinadi is persecuted and thrown into prison. (Mosiah 11-12).
N Abinadi reads the old law to the priests. (Mosiah 13-14).

N_1 Abinadi makes his own prophecies. (Mosiah 15-16).
M_1 Abinadi is persecuted and is killed. (Mosiah 17:5-20).
L_1 Noah and his priests. (Mosiah 18:32-20:5).

K₁ The Lamanites threaten the People of Limhi. (Mosiah 20:6).
J₁ The Record of Zeniff ends as he leaves Lehi-Nephi. (Mosiah 22).
I₁ The 24 Gold Plates of Ether. (Mosiah 21:27-22:14).
H₁ The people of Ammon are in bondage. (Mosiah 23).
G₁ Alma leaves the land of Nephi for Zarahemla. (Mosiah 24).
F₁ The Church is organized by Alma. (Mosiah 25:14-24).
E₁ Unbelievers refuse to enter into the covenants. (Mosiah 26:1-4).
D₁ The words of Alma and of the angel of the Lord. (Mosiah 26-27).
C₁ Alma the Younger receives the records. (Mosiah 28-30).
B₁ Judges are chosen instead of a king. (Mosiah 29:5-32).
A₁ Mosiah exhorts his people. (Mosiah 29:5-32).

Beginning with The Book of Mosiah, The Book of Mormon is written in the third person, inasmuch as it is an abridgment by Mormon of the records of other prophets. The only exceptions are where Mormon inserted his own editorial comments or quoted directly from the plates from which he was making the abridgement, The Book of Mormon Chapters 8 & 9, and the Books of Ether and Moroni.

The Book of Mosiah is a carefully constructed combination of Nephite royal and priestly records and histories condensed into a symbolic complex. We cannot hope to understand this book, or any other in The Book of Mormon for that matter, unless we try to understand Nephite culture. We do not have the benefit of a narrator to tell us about the thoughts and motives of the characters in this drama. We can only learn about these great personalities by reading about them in their own scriptures. As we gain valuable insights from their recorded actions and words, we come to a greater understanding of the pivotal roles they played in the history of the New World.

King Benjamin, "by laboring with all the might of his body and the faculty of his whole soul, and also the prophets," was able to "establish peace in the land". (Words of Mormon 1:18). The Nephites had been able to withstand the onslaught of the Lamanites, and had "slain many thousands" of them, in order to protect their sacred rights and privileges. (Words of Mormon 1:14). For "all the remainder of his days" then, Benjamin and his people enjoyed peace in Zarahemla. (V. 1).

Benjamin had three sons, named Mosiah, Helorum, and Helaman. These were the grandchildren of Mosiah, who had fled with the righteous Nephites from the Land of Nephi many years earlier. Benjamin recognized that his finest hour as a teacher and leader would first be realized as he labored with the members of his own family. Therefore, he taught his sons "in the language of his fathers" (v. 2), or "in the language of the Egyptians" (v. 3), so that they could read the scriptures recorded in that language on the plates. (See Commentary Reference to Enos 1:1). It was necessary that they have this knowledge "that thereby they might become men of understanding, and that they might know concerning the prophecies". (V. 3).

"The reformed Egyptian" was probably the written language only of the plates and of the royal and priestly minority among the Nephites, since it was an abbreviated shorthand particularly suitable for use when engraving upon metal plates. The Nephites were surely literate, for written communications were used and the scriptures were available among them, but the common people probably spoke and wrote in Hebrew. (See Jacob 4:2, Mosiah 2:7-8, 12:20, 13:11, 24:4-6, 29:5-36, & Alma 63:12).

Benjamin bore his testimony to his sons (V. 3-8), and taught them the value of the Plates of Brass, explaining that were it not for them, the Nephites would not have known "the mysteries of God" which are the saving principles of the Gospel of Jesus Christ. (V. 3, see v. 5). They are referred to as mysteries since they are unavailable to the natural man because they must be revealed by God on condition of faith and obedience. The mysteries are designed to lead God's children, who see with the eye of faith, to eternal life. (See Mosiah 2:9).

The Lamanite stumbling block (the mysteries) that Benjamin described parallels that of the ignorant in the world today, who "know nothing concerning these things, or even do not believe them when they are taught them, because of the traditions of their fathers, which are not correct". (V. 6).

Benjamin bore testimony to his sons that the records were true, and he indicated that they could know these things of a surety because they had the plates in their possession. (V. 6). But would our possession of the plates ever prove that they were of God? If we had them today, could they take the place of testimony? No, "the presence of the plates would only prove that there are plates, and no more. It would not prove that Nephites wrote them, or that an angel brought them, or that they had been translated by the gift and power of God. A far more impressive claim is put forth when the whole work is given to the world as a divinely inspired translation". (Hugh Nibley, "An Approach to The Book of Mormon," p. 17-18).

We can have the same witness today that the people of Zarahemla had in the days of King Benjamin. On one occasion, the Lord told Joseph Smith: "This generation shall have my word through you". (D&C 5:10). On another, He said: "And I, Jesus Christ, your Lord and your God, have spoken it. These words are not of men nor of man, but of me; wherefore, you shall testify they are of me and not of man; For it is my voice which speaketh them unto you; for they are given by my Spirit unto you, and by my power you can read them one to another; and save it were by my power you could not have them; Wherefore, you can testify that you have heard my voice, and know my words". (D&C 18:33-36). When we read the words of The Doctrine and Covenants, or of The Book of Mormon, we are hearing the voice of the Lord, as well as reading His words, if we do so by the Spirit. The Savior said: "Learn of me, and listen to my words; walk in the meekness of my Spirit, and you shall have peace in me". (D&C 19:23).

In verse 7, Benjamin finished bearing his testimony to his sons by reiterating the theme of The Book of Mormon: "I would that ye should keep the commandments of God, that ye may prosper in the land". (See V. 17).

Verses 9-18 describe the preparations for a large meeting to be held the next day. Initially, Benjamin made a distinction between the People of Zarahemla and the People of Mosiah, who lived in the land, but he promised that all would soon be given "a new name, that thereby they (might) be distinguished above all the people which the Lord God hath brought out of the land of Jerusalem". (V. 10-11). That new name was to be the name of Christ. (See Mosiah 5:8). A central purpose of the sermon known today as "The King Benjamin Discourse" in Mosiah Chapters 2-5 was to bring the people to the point where they would be willing to make commitments preparatory to entering into a covenant with God, or preparatory to renewing their existing covenants with God, in which they would take upon themselves the name of Christ.

Benjamin gave Mosiah "charge concerning all the affairs of the kingdom," and he was consecrated king. (V. 15, see Mosiah 2:11). Mosiah was also given the "types" of national treasures that a real king was anciently required to possess. (V. 16). First, he received the Plates of Brass, that included much of the Old Testament, a Book of Joseph (1 Nephi 5:14), and Lehi's genealogy. These records, together with the genealogy of the Nephite kings kept on the Large Plates of Nephi, established the tangible lineal legitimacy of Mosiah's right to rule as king in Zarahemla. (See 1 Nephi 6:1, & 9:4).

Secondly, Mosiah was given the sword of Laban, that in addition to being a fine weapon much copied by the Nephites, was also a symbol of power and rule. Even today, in the pomp and circumstance of ceremonial military review, and in the bestowal of monarchial rights and privileges, the sword retains the symbolism of temporal authority.

Lastly Mosiah took possession of the Liahona that was a true royal treasure, having been passed from father to son by Lehi's descendants. Of all the symbols of authority, it is the most authentic. We do not know exactly what it looked like, but orbs, spheres of the firmament, crystal balls, and the like have survived in religious art, although they are stylized almost beyond recognition, and understanding of the underlying power behind the operation of the Liahona has been completely lost.

It is likely that Mosiah was also given the Urim & Thummim that eventually passed into the hands of the latter-day seer, Joseph Smith. (See Omni 1:20-21, & Mosiah 8:13). In his history, it is recorded that "there were two stones in silver bows - and these stones, fastened to a breastplate, constituted what is called the Urim and Thummim - deposited with the plates; and the possession and use of these stones were what constituted seers in ancient or former times". (J.S.H. 1:35).

Verse 17 alludes to the major theme of The Book of Mormon: "Therefore, as (those in Lehi's party) were unfaithful they did not prosper nor progress in their journey, but were driven back, and incurred the displeasure of God upon them; and therefore, they were smitten with famine and sore afflictions, to stir them up in remembrance of their duty". (V. 7).

The people gathered at a temple that had been constructed in Zarahemla to listen to King Benjamin's discourse. (V. 18). This is the first reference to a temple in the Land of Zarahemla. In chapels, we organize stakes, wards, quorums, relief societies, and so on. King Benjamin's desire was to consummate the organization of the celestial family unit in the temple, and so the setting that was chosen for his instruction was ideal.

In all circumstances, the Church is commanded to build temples to the Holy Name of God in order to accomplish this purpose. Josephus provided us with a view of temple construction 2,100 years before his own day, in the ancient city of Salem. "He who first built (the city) was a potent man among the Canaanites," wrote the Jewish historian, "and is in our tongue called Melchizedek, the Righteous King, for such he really was; on which account he was there the first Priest of God, and first built a temple there, and called the city Jerusalem, which was formerly called Salem". ("Wars of the Jews," p. 588).

Soon after the righteous left the Land of Their First Inheritance, they built a temple in the Land of Nephi. (2 Nephi 5:16). Now we find that there was such a house of worship already in existence in the Land of Zarahemla, likely built by the People of Zarahemla, who had come out from Jerusalem with Mulek 400 years earlier, and who had been responsive to the Lord's command that His people always build temples to His holy name. (See D&C 124:39).

Mosiah was the third king to rule in Zarahemla, following in the footsteps of his father, Benjamin, and his grandfather, Mosiah. After the elder Mosiah had led the righteous Nephites out of the Land of Nephi two generations earlier, he "was made king over the land of Zarahemla". (Omni 1:12). With conspicuous order, "the people of Zarahemla and of Mosiah did unite together; and Mosiah was appointed to be their king". (Omni 1:19). Thus, "all the people of Zarahemla were numbered with the Nephites, and this because the kingdom had been conferred upon none but those who were descendants of Nephi". (Mosiah 25:13). Clearly, then, Mosiah was a descendant of Nephi.

Mosiah
Chapter 2

This chapter begins The Book of Mormon equivalent of The Sermon on the Mount. (See 3 Nephi 12). The counsel that King Benjamin gave is one of the greatest sermons in the scriptures, and is a practical statement of religious conduct applicable to all times. The gathered multitude offered sacrifice according to the Law of Moses and gave thanks for their great blessings. (V. 2). Their fathers had been guided from the land of Jerusalem and had been delivered from the hands of the Babylonians. Through the years, they had been blessed with righteous priests and teachers, and now they were fortunate to have a "just man to be their king, who had established peace in the land". Furthermore, they had been taught to keep the laws of the Gospel. Consequently, in obedience to the first two great commandments, they were "filled with love towards God and all men". (V. 4).

The multitude consisted of a family-oriented society gathered in its individual groups in and around the temple. (V. 5-6). Benjamin spoke from a high tower so that more people could hear him, and for those who were not within the sound of his voice, a written record of what he said was passed around. (V. 7-8). One is reminded of Joseph Smith, who on one occasion spoke to the Saints in Nauvoo. He began by saying: "I have three requests to make of the congregation: The first is, that all who have faith will exercise it and pray the Lord to calm the wind; for as it blows now, I cannot speak long without seriously injuring my health; the next is that I may have your prayers that the Lord will strengthen my lungs, so that I may be able to make you all hear; and the third is, that you will pray for the Holy Ghost to rest upon me, so as to enable me to declare those things that are true".

In the case of Benjamin, his address had been carefully thought out, stylistically composed, and prepared well ahead of time, with copies available for general distribution at the time of its delivery. Clearly, the writing of the Nephites was not confined to plates; individuals and families had their own copies of the scriptures. (See Mosiah 29:5-36, & Alma 63:12).

That which follows, Mosiah 2:9 to 5:15, is a discussion of some of the most important mysteries of God. (See Commentary Reference to Mosiah 1:5). Benjamin was concerned that the people might trifle with the words that he should speak. He recognized the serious nature of his topic, and wanted his people to hearken to him, or pay strict attention, and to open their ears that they might listen carefully, and their hearts, that they might feel the Spirit of his message, and their minds, in order to understand. (V. 9).

When we approach a Gospel discussion from this level of preparation or listen to a General Authority speak, the mysteries of God are unfolded to our view. (See D&C 71:1, Alma 12:9, 37:4, & D&C 76:7). Joseph Smith described one of his own experiences in these words: "Our minds being now enlightened, we began to have the scriptures laid open to our understandings, and the true meaning and intention of their more mysterious passages revealed unto us in a manner which we never could attain to previously, nor ever before had thought of". (Joseph Smith, after his baptism, May 15, 1829. J.S.H. 1:74).

Benjamin's desire was to communicate with his people on a similar plane that was beyond the mere cognition level to one of deep spiritual understanding. He used a wide range of teaching techniques: rapport and example (2:11, 14-15), analogy (2:19), questions (2:18, 4:19), scripture (2:34), personal experience (3:2), literary devices (2:38, 5:10-12), cause and consequence (4:11-16), testimony (2:35, 41), admonition (4:9-10), and challenge (4:30). His teachings were structured so that his people would receive his message in a hierarchy based first on understanding (2:9), next acceptance (5:1), then commitment (6:1), and finally recommitment (6:3).

In verses 11-21, "service" is mentioned 12 times. Benjamin was old and frail when he gave this sermon, but he was strong in spirit and delivered his message "with all the might, mind and strength which the Lord" had granted to him. (V. 11). He had not allowed age or infirmity to be factors in the quality of service he had rendered, and so no excuse his people might now make would be acceptable. He was as Spencer W. Kimball, who once declared: "I am like an old shoe, to be worn out in the service of the Lord".

Benjamin had received no pay for his labor; he had "not sought gold nor silver nor any manner of riches". (V. 12). He had no personal agenda, and so his rule had been much less likely to lead the people into unrighteousness. "Neither have I suffered that ye should be confined in dungeons," he reminded them, "nor that ye should make slaves one of another, nor that ye should murder or plunder, or steal or commit adultery; nor even have I suffered that ye should commit any manner of wickedness". (V. 13). Rather, he had constantly guided them to exercise obedience to God in all things. He had set the example by working shoulder to shoulder with his people, that he might not be a burden to them, and that they might not be grievously taxed. (V. 13-14). Few leaders of nations can say, as he did: "I tell you these things that ye may know that I can answer a clear conscience before God this day". (V. 15, see V. 27).

The Hokmah then invoked by Benjamin touches us deeply: "When ye are in the service of your fellow beings," he said, "ye are only in the service of your God". (V. 17). The Creator does not generally intervene personally in our affairs, nor is He typically served directly. The Savior set the pattern when He declared: "Verily I say unto you, Inasmuch as ye have done it unto one of the least of these my brethren, ye have done it unto me". (Matthew 25:40). We all should focus on what C.S. Lewis called "acts of quiet Christianity," that are charitable acts of service for which there is no recognition, recompense, or thought of reciprocation.

Verses 19-26 constitute a discourse on true humility. Benjamin urged his people to thank God, and not him, for their peace and prosperity. (V. 19). He said that if they praised Him, and served Him "with all (their) whole souls, yet (they) would remain unprofitable servants. (V. 20-21). That is because our debt to God is completely beyond our ability to pay. We can do nothing that tips the scales in our favor. (See 2 Nephi 25:23). But God does not ask us to settle our account with Him; He only asks that we keep His commandments. The marvel of His love is that the more we try to serve Him, the more He blesses us. Therefore, we become even more deeply indebted to Him and remain so forever. (V. 24). When, ultimately, the precious blood of Christ redeems us, it is by grace alone that we enjoy salvation.

One of the greatest sins, therefore, is that of ingratitude. Gratitude is deeper than thanks which is the beginning of gratitude, and may consist merely of words, but gratitude is shown in action. It is independent of circumstances, penetrates the deepest undercurrents of life, and is founded upon God. (V. 24). We demonstrate ingratitude to God by our willful disobedience to His commandments. Ingratitude, then, is the companion of sin.

In verse 25, Benjamin compared us to the dust of the earth, trying to relate our "nothingness" to our debt to God. (See Mosiah 4:2, & Moses 1:10). In this sense, Brigham Young declared: "There is no one who ever made a sacrifice on this earth for the kingdom of heaven except the Savior. I would not give the ashes of a rye straw for those who feel they are making a sacrifice for God. We are doing this for our own happiness, welfare, and exaltation, and for nobody else's. What we do, we do for the salvation of the inhabitants of the earth, not for the salvation of the heavens, the angels, or God". (J.D., 16:114).

Benjamin had a "clear conscience before God". (V. 27). Marion D. Hanks observed: "At the banquet of consequences, when we go with our loved ones, there will not be much that is satisfying at the table unless we are able to bow our heads in reverence, rather than hang them in shame, in the presence of God who will be there". (B.Y.U. Speeches of The Year, 10/3/1967).

Because he had fulfilled the mandate of his royal office, Benjamin declared to his people that their blood "should not come upon" him. (V. 27-28). He used this metaphor to illustrate that he could not be held accountable for the behavior of the people, precisely because he had properly instructed them in every point of doctrine. (See Jacob 1:19). He would go down to his grave in peace, with a spark of celestial fire glowing brightly within his bosom.

He announced publicly the consecration of his son Mosiah as "a king and a ruler" over the people. (V. 30). In verse 31, Benjamin made no distinction between his own words, those of his father, of his son Mosiah, or those of the Savior, declaring: "As ye have kept my commandments, and also the commandments of my father ... even so ... ye shall keep the commandments of my son, or the commandments of God which shall be delivered unto you by him". The Lord Himself explained: "What I have spoken, I have spoken, and I excuse not myself; and though the heavens and the earth pass away, my word shall not pass away, but shall all be fulfilled, whether by mine own voice or by the voice of my servants, it is the same". (D&C 1:38, see D&C 18:35, & 21:5).

Warning against those who would bind themselves to the voice of evil, Mosiah said that such individuals must suffer "everlasting punishment". (V. 33, see Mosiah 1:1). Everlasting or endless punishment does not mean that those who partake of it must endure it forever. (See D&C 19:6-12). Rather, it means that they must suffer God's punishment for the transgression of law, and when they have paid the penalty, they will be released, but the punishment itself will remain as it awaits the next guilty party, and so on. "To hell there is an exit as well as an entrance. It is a place prepared for the teaching and disciplining of those who failed to learn here on earth what they should have learned. No one will be kept in hell longer than is necessary to bring them to a fitness for something better". (James E. Talmage, C.R. 4/1930).

By Joseph Smith's time, when The Book of Mormon was first published, the Christian world had lost the knowledge of the parent-child relationship between God and mankind, and instead taught a very different doctrine. The understanding of the character of God had been perverted by a distorted concept of His Plan for His children. Since the Restoration of the Gospel, people have revolted against God by denying altogether the very existence or power of Satan in the world. It is only natural that they would also deny the reality of hell as a place of correction reserved for the disobedient. (See 2 Nephi 28).

Verses 36-40, however, identify the consequences of sin in very plain language. Its effect on those who have "been taught in all these things" is that when the guidance of the Spirit is withdrawn they are left alone to grope in darkness. Guilt causes them to shrink from Church activity, and in the poverty of the Spirit, the sinner has no claim on priesthood power, prosperity, protection, or preservation. (V. 36). While yet in mortality, such individuals may descend into a pit of despair, despondency, dejection, depression, and desolation that feels very much like "hell".

Tragically, feeling uncomfortable in any proximity whatsoever to spiritual experiences, those individuals withdraw to lifestyles devoid of such associations. Thus, begins a downward spiral that gains momentum and spins out of control as sinful practices, more easily committed, become entrenched. (See 2 Nephi 26:22, & Commentary Reference to Mosiah 5:10-11). Even worse, "those "that doeth this, the same cometh out in open rebellion against God". (V. 37). "Thus saith the Lord concerning all those who know my power, and have been made partakers thereof, and suffered themselves through the power of the devil to be overcome, and to deny the truth and defy my power. They are they who are the sons of perdition". (D&C 76:31-32). Perdition is "utter ruin".

However, "the sin against the Holy Ghost requires such knowledge that it is manifestly impossible for the rank and file to commit such a sin". (Spencer W. Kimball). Thru the Holy Ghost, the truth must be woven into the very fiber and sinews of the body so that it cannot be forgotten". (Joseph Fielding Smith, Jr.). To sin against such a manifestation of light puts these individuals outside the redemptive powers of Christ. They cannot partake of His mercy, because they have lost the Spirit of God and can no longer suffer themselves to repent.

One who puts Christ to open shame "thereby commits murder, by assenting unto the Lord's death, that is, having a perfect knowledge of the truth, he comes out in open rebellion and places himself in a position wherein he would have crucified Christ knowing perfectly the while that He was the Son of God. Christ is thus crucified afresh, and put to open shame". (Bruce R. McConkie, "Mormon Doctrine," p. 816, see D&C 76:35).

In any event, one who has been taught in all the ways of truth and who then turns from the light "becometh an enemy to all righteousness". (V. 37). Joseph Fielding Smith wrote: "When the Spirit is withdrawn, darkness supersedes the light, and apostasy will follow. This is one of the greatest evidences of the divinity of the Latter-day work. In other organizations, men may commit all manner of sin, and still retain their membership, because they have no companionship with the Holy Ghost to lose, but in the Church, when a man sins and continues without repentance, the Spirit is withdrawn, and when he is left to himself the adversary takes possession of his mind, and he denies the faith". ("Doctrines of Salvation," 3:309, see Alma 47:36, & 52:33). Those who break windows not only enjoy throwing stones, but also the sound of shattering glass, more than they do fresh air.

Critics who would attempt to highlight perceived shortcomings of the Church or its members are sucking on pickles rather than savoring a delicious multiple course feast. At a well-planned and meticulously prepared banquet, the food is designed to satisfy the palates of those who have come with eager anticipation and an expectation of being satiated. But a Master Chef knows how to blend together all His preparations into a perfectly homogenous, nutritious, and complimentary whole.

Verse 38 describes the state of the unrepentant in the spirit prison of the unjust, and is a graphic reminder that hell is more than the mere recognition of lost opportunities. (See Commentary Reference to 2 Nephi 4:32, & D&C 76:73, 138:8 & 28, Isaiah 61:1, 1 Peter 3:19 & Moses 7:57). The guilt, pain and anguish of unresolved sin are "like an unquenchable fire". (V. 38). Mercy has "no claim on that man" (V. 39), even as Justice demands a "never-ending torment". For those individuals, it is as if no Atonement had been made, and they are thus required to pay for their own sins. They will be redeemed from hell only after the demands of Justice have been satisfied. Therefore, urged Benjamin: "Awake to a remembrance of the awful situation of those that have fallen into transgression". (V. 40). Contrast their situation with "the blessed and happy state of those that keep the commandments "(V. 41). ""Happiness is the object and design of our existence and will be the end thereof, if we follow the path that leads to it. And this path is virtue, uprightness, faithfulness, holiness, and keeping all the commandments of God. In obedience there is joy and peace ... and as God has designed our happiness ... He never has, He never will, give a commandment to His people that is not calculated in its nature to promote that happiness which He has designed."" (History of the Church, 5:134-135, see Commentary Reference to 2 Nephi 2:13).

Every law has both a blessing and a punishment affixed to it. When the law is obeyed a blessing is given that results in happiness or joy. When the law is disobeyed, punishment is given that results in unhappiness or misery. Benjamin now sealed those principles that he had taught with the indelible stamp of divine authenticity and approval, by declaring: "Thus saith the Lord". (V. 41).

"I tell you these things that ye may learn wisdom; that ye may learn that when ye are in the service of your fellow beings ye are only in the service of your God." (Mosiah 2:17).

Mosiah
Chapter 3

Benjamin reserved counsel of the highest importance for the second division of his address. The effect on the people was bound to be impressive, for in this chapter Benjamin recounted a revelation from an angel of God. The first 18 verses comprise a crystal-clear prophecy and testimony of the Savior, His name, mission, and character. This is another example where The Book of Mormon is a powerful witness of Christ.

The angel came to "declare glad tidings of great joy". (V. 3, see Luke 2:10). Benjamin's prayer had been to know that the revelations concerning the Coming of The Lord were true. (V. 4). In a most impressive and powerful manner, the angel now declared that the Lord would indeed come, clothed with power and authority, \to work out the final details of the Infinite Atonement. (V 5, see V. 6-9, & Commentary Reference to Alma 5:50).

The Atonement redeemed all mankind from the effects of the Fall of Adam and Eve, conditioned only on repentance; it also redeemed those who are not accountable, who "died not knowing the will of God concerning them, or who (had) ignorantly sinned". (V. 11, see Commentary Reference to Mosiah 15:22). "They are the irresponsibles, who know not good from evil, and are therefore blameless. They who die without law are redeemed without law and are those who shall have part in the First Resurrection". (Orson F. Whitney, "Whitney on Doctrine," p. 442).

Many persons have been faithful to the doctrines that they have been taught, however flawed they may be. They cannot be held accountable for that which they did in obedience to the principles they devoutly believed. The Lord will judge us by the intent of the heart as well as by our understanding. (See Joseph Fielding Smith Jr., "Answers to Gospel Questions," 4:77 & D&C 29:50).

Those who have died "in their ignorance" are they who would evidently have accepted the Gospel while in mortality had they had the opportunity to do so. "All who have died without a knowledge of this Gospel, who would have received it if they had been permitted to tarry, shall be heirs of the celestial kingdom of God; Also all that shall die henceforth without a knowledge of it, who would have received it with all their hearts, shall be heirs of that kingdom; For I, the Lord, will judge all men according to their works, according to the desire of their hearts". (D&C 137:7-8). According to the law, they may be resurrected after accepting the Gospel, after it has been preached to them in the Spirit World, and when the ordinances typifying their obedience to eternal covenants have been performed vicariously in the temple. (See Commentary References to Mosiah 5:5-15, & Mosiah Chapter 16).

In Mosiah 15:25, Abinadi explained: "Little children also have eternal life". They are "redeemed from the foundation of the world through (the) Only Begotten". (D&C 29:46). "All children who die before they arrive at the years of accountability are saved in the celestial kingdom of heaven". (D&C 137:10). In other words, provision for their exaltation was made at the Grand Council in Heaven even before the world was, in conformity with the infinite nature of the Atonement. "Little children cannot (or need not) repent; wherefore, it is awful wickedness to deny the pure mercies of God unto them, for they are all alive in him because of his mercy". (Moroni 8:19).

Additionally, those who do not have the mental capability to understand the laws of God are redeemed regardless of their obedience to those laws. As Joseph Fielding Smith, Jr. wrote: "Mentally deficient persons are classed among those who are redeemed as little children". ("Doctrines of Salvation," 2:55, see Commentary Reference to Mosiah 15:22).

As stated above, the Atonement redeemed little children from the effects of the Fall. (V. 16, see Mosiah 15:25). As children advance in years, they become accountable. This suggests developing accountability, as they gradually assume complete responsibility for their actions. "Heaven lies about us in our infancy," wrote William Wordsworth. "Shades of the prison house begin to close upon the growing boy, but he beholds the light and whence it flows. He sees it in his joy. The youth, who daily farther from the east must travel, still is nature's priest, and by the vision splendid, is on his way attended. At length the man perceives it die away, and fade into the light of common day". The Atonement has the power to reverse that process.

Benjamin taught that people other than the Jews and the Nephites also knew of the Coming of Christ. "The Lord God hath sent his holy prophets among all the children of men, to declare these things to every kindred, nation, and tongue, that whosoever should believe that Christ should come, the same might receive remission of their sins". (V. 13, see V. 20). His Atonement was Infinite, that is to say, it spans all time, places, and circumstances. All who have or who will ever live on the earth have a claim on the redemptive power of the Atonement. The ancients "rejoice(d) with exceedingly great joy, even as though he had already come among them". (V. 13, see V. 17-18, & Jacob 4:4-6). As the Savior told the Jews at Jerusalem: "Your father Abraham rejoiced to see my day: and he saw it, and was glad". (John 8:56).

Verse 17 is an unequivocal statement of profound doctrinal certainty: "There shall be no other name given nor any other way nor means whereby salvation can come unto the children of men, only in and through the name of Christ". (See Mosiah 5:7-10). The Law of Justice made the Atonement of Jesus Christ necessary, while the Law of Mercy made it possible. The two Laws are in complete harmony, with Mercy introducing the condition of vicarious payment for the laws that have been transgressed and for which Justice rightfully has demanded a penalty.

Boyd K. Packer dramatically illustrated these principles: "There was once a man who wanted something very much," he said. "It seemed more important than anything else in his life. In order for him to have his desire, he incurred a great debt. He had been warned about going into that much debt, and particularly about his creditor. But it seemed so important for him to do what he wanted to do, and to have what he wanted, right now. He was sure he could pay for it later.

So, he signed a contract. He would pay it off some time along the way. He didn't worry too much about it, for the due date seemed such a long time away. He had what he wanted now, and that was what seemed important. The creditor was always somewhere in the back of his mind, however and he made token payments now and again, thinking somehow that the day of reckoning would never come. But as it always does, the day came, and the contract fell due. The debt had not been fully paid. His creditor appeared and demanded payment in full. Only then, did the man realize that his creditor not only had the power to repossess all that he owned, but the power to cast him into prison, as well.

"I cannot pay you, for I have not the power to do so," he confessed. "Then," said the creditor, "we will exercise the contract, take your possessions, and you shall go to prison. You agreed to that. It was your choice. You signed the contract, and now it must be enforced". "Can you not extend the time, or forgive the debt," the debtor begged. "Arrange some way for me to keep what I have, and not go to prison. Surely, you believe in mercy. Will you not show mercy?"

The creditor replied, "Mercy is always so one-sided. It would serve only you. If I show mercy to you, it will leave me unpaid. It is justice that I demand. Do you believe in justice?" "I believed in justice when I signed the contract," the debtor said. "It was on my side then, for I thought it would protect me. I did not need mercy then, nor think I should ever need it. Justice, I thought, would serve both of us equally as well". "It is justice that demands that you pay the contract, or suffer the penalty," the creditor replied. "That is the law. You have agreed to it, and that is the way it must be. Mercy cannot rob Justice".

There they were. One demanding justice, the other pleading for mercy. Neither could prevail, except at the expense of the other. "If you do not forgive the debt there will be no mercy," the debtor pleaded. "If I do, there will be no justice," was the reply. Both laws, it seemed, could not be served. They are two external ideals that appear to contradict one another. Is there no way for justice to be fully served, and mercy also? There is a way! The Law of Justice can be fully satisfied, and mercy can be fully extended - but it takes someone else, a third-party. And so did it happen this time.

The debtor had a friend. He came to help. He knew the debtor well. He knew him to be shortsighted. He thought him foolish to have gotten himself into such a predicament. Nevertheless, he wanted to help because he loved him. He stepped between them, faced the creditor, and made this offer. "I will pay the debt, if you will free the debtor from his contract so that he may keep his possessions and not go to prison".

As the creditor was pondering this offer, the mediator added, "You demanded justice. Though he cannot pay you, I will do so. You will have been justly dealt with and can ask no more. It would not be just". And so, the creditor agreed. The mediator turned then to the debtor. "If I pay your debt, will you accept me as your creditor?" "Oh, yes, yes!" cried the debtor. "You saved me from prison and showed mercy to me". "Then," said the benefactor, "you will pay the debt to me, and I will set the terms. It will not be easy, but it will be possible. I will provide a way. You need not go to prison".

And so it was that the creditor was paid in full. He had been justly dealt with. No contract had been broken. The debtor, in turn, had been extended mercy. Both laws stood fulfilled. Because there was a mediator, justice had claimed its full share, and mercy was fully satisfied. ("Ensign," 5/1977, p. 54-55).

Elder Packer went on to say: "Each of us lives on a kind of spiritual credit. One day, the account will be closed, and a settlement demanded. However casually we may view it now, when that day comes and the foreclosure is imminent, we will look around in restless agony for someone, anyone, to help us. And by eternal law, mercy cannot be extended save there be one who is both willing and able to assume our debt, and pay the price, and arrange the terms of our redemption".

Verse 18 declares that God's "judgment is just," that is to say, the Law of Justice requires impartiality. (See D&C 82:10, & 130:20-21). We must become as little children, and have their quality of faith, because the natural man is an enemy to God, suffering from congenital shortsightedness, mechanically and repetitively giving in to selfishness and physical appetites. "For the natural man is an enemy to God, and has been from the fall of Adam, and will be, forever and ever, unless he yieldeth to the enticings of the Holy Spirit, and putteth off the natural man, and becometh a saint through the Atonement of Christ the Lord, and becometh as a child, submissive, meek, humble, patient, full of love, willing to submit to all things which the Lord seeth fit to inflict upon him, even as a child doth submit to his father". (V. 19).

In particular, when pride swells in our bosom, it occupies such a volume that it squeezes out our capacity for meaningful happiness. N. Eldon Tanner observed: "The craving for praise and popularity too often controls actions, and as a people succumb, they find themselves bending their character, when they think they are only taking a bow". As a result, many become disillusioned when their search for happiness through acquisition, accumulation, and even achievement rings hollow, and leaves a sour aftertaste imprinted on the spirit.

David O. McKay taught: "Spirituality is the consciousness of victory over self, and of communion with the infinite". The invitation of the Spirit leads us to sainthood through repentance and forgiveness because of the Atonement of Christ. (V. 19). As we "submit to all things," we develop the nature and character of the Savior. In effect, He counsels us: "All that I have I could give to you, but what I am, you must earn for yourself, line upon line, and precept upon precept".

The following story, also attributed to Elder Packer, illustrates this principle: "A kind and beloved nobleman had been blessed with great riches. Through years of generous but wise use of his wealth, he had been able to strengthen both his country and his fellowmen. As his son approached manhood, the nobleman desired that the son might inherit his fortune. He knew well, however, that if he were to bestow his wealth upon the lad, who as yet had developed little wisdom or stature from the lessons of life, the treasure would in all likelihood be misused. The father's chief concern was that of building character in his son. Then the blessing of wealth could make his son a power for good.

Accordingly, the father called his son to his side and made him a promise. "My son," said the father, "all that I have I desire to give to you - not only my wealth, but also my position and standing among men. That which I have, I might easily give to you, but that which I am, you must earn for yourself. I shall make obtaining my fortune dependent upon your living as I have lived, and learning the things I have learned. Thereby, my son, shall you gain the greatest of inheritances. I shall give you the laws and principles by which my wisdom and stature have come to me. You shall also receive a charge and a promise: Follow my example, mastering as I have mastered, and I will make you equal to me. All that I have shall be yours. You are free to choose, my son. Will you not promise me your devotion to these things?"

With pure desire and true gratitude, the son promised to follow the noble pattern of his father's life. With guidance and encouragement, he discovered for himself the sweetness of nobility. The son, in harmony with the prescribed conditions, thereby obtained his legacy".

The Gospel of Jesus Christ categorically and unequivocally rejects the doctrine of the natural and inherent depravity of man, and the equally destructive doctrine that man does not need a Redeemer. "Every spirit of man was innocent in the beginning; and God having redeemed man from the fall, men became again, in their infant state, innocent before God. And that wicked one cometh and taketh away light and truth, through disobedience, from the children of men, and because of the tradition of their fathers". (D&C 93:38-39). We can reach our celestial potential only if we follow the established pattern and example of the Master. The Gospel gives us the tools to raise our "children in light and truth" and our religion is more involved with recovery than discovery. (D&C 93:40). Our destiny is not union, but reunion with divine realities. As an institution, and on a personal level, religious recognition is a relearning of that which we have already understood. Hence, Brigham Young's statement: "Every Gospel principle carries within itself a witness that it is true". It has the ring of truth because we have heard it before.

One day, the Gospel will be carried to every corner of the earth. (V. 20). At that time, the only hope for the world will be to be found blameless through faith and repentance. Benjamin warned his people that, having been taught correct principles, now that they understood the true doctrine of Christ, they were accountable for their actions. This is the Gospel pattern.

The message delivered by the angel would "stand as a bright testimony against this people," said Benjamin. (V. 24). His sermon, central to the message of The Book of Mormon, will likewise stand as a testimony against faithless members of The Church of Jesus Christ of Latter-day Saints at the Day of Judgment. Perhaps this is why several of the Nephite prophets have reminded us that they will be present with Jesus Christ when we meet Him at the Judgment Bar. (See 2 Nephi 33:11, Jacob 6:13, & Moroni 10:34).

When Benjamin characterized the wicked as having "drunk out of the cup of the wrath of God," he was not just using poetical metaphor. (V. 26). Rather, he was alluding to the symbolism of water that communicated a very powerful message to the mind of the ancients. Ordeals by water are mentioned several times in The Book of Mormon. (See 2 Nephi 8:17, & 3 Nephi 11:11). We may dismiss them as superstitious indulgences, but there is a wealth of symbolism associated with water, and its power to save or to destroy.

In any event, Mercy has no claim on the wicked who have chosen to deny themselves the blessings of the Atonement. That "their torment is as a lake of fire and brimstone" should not be taken literally. (V. 27). However, at the Judgment and immediately thereafter, the cheeks of such individuals will burn with guilt, and they will have a bright recollection of their sins. It will be a very unpleasant experience as the awful avalanche of consequences overwhelms them and smothers any hope of foreseeable deliverance.

"And many signs, and wonders, and types, and shadows showed he unto them, concerning his coming." (Mosiah 3:15).

Mosiah
Chapter 4

Having preached so persuasively about the absolute necessity of obedience to Law as the requirement of salvation, King Benjamin next focused on the way to obtain a remission of sins. (V. 1-3, & 9-10). He finished quoting the angel and again spoke his own words. The things that he had declared to the people by the mouth of the angel were so powerful that thousands fell to the earth, for "the fear of the Lord had come upon them". (V. 1). They confessed their faith in Christ even though He had not yet come to the world. The word "fear" has several shades of meaning in the Hebrew language. One is "reverence". So, the "fear of the Lord" can mean to have reverential awe. Also, to fear the Lord is to obey the greatest of all the commandments, or to love Him.

The people viewed themselves as "less than the dust of the earth" because even the elements are obedient to the will of God. (V. 2). Their faith had convicted them of their sins and motivated them to seek forgiveness. They also cried "aloud with one voice, saying: O have mercy, and apply the atoning blood of Christ that we may receive forgiveness of our sins, and our hearts may be purified; for we believe in Jesus Christ, the Son of God, who created heaven and earth, and all things; who shall come down among the children of men". (V. 2).

Then, in verse 5, Benjamin confirmed that with the mysteries of God unfolded to their understanding, they would be able to recognize that without redemption through the Atonement, they would be as nothing, or in a "worthless and fallen state". (See Mosiah 1:3). How did they know that a forgiveness of sins had been granted? Benjamin identified three key factors.

First, the Spirit of the Lord came upon them. The Light of Christ is the light of truth. (See Essay: "The Light of Christ"). It is the Spirit that is impersonal and fills the immensity of space, the Spirit that is the agency by which God governs and controls all things. Christ is the Light of the world, and when His Spirit quickens man, he is like a white-hot spark struck off the divine anvil of God. "I said to the man who stood at the gate of the year, 'Give me a light, that I may tread safely into the unknown.' And he replied, 'Go out into the darkness, and put your hand in the hand of God. That shall be to you better than a light, and safer than the known way.' (Minnie Haskins, "A Dialogue Between a Man, and the Keeper of The Gate of The Year").

"Faith in Christ," then, "is not a leap in the dark. It is, instead, trust in what the spirit learned eons ago, and religious recognition is just that - re-cognition, a re-knowing". (Truman Madsen, "The Truth, The Way, The Life: B.H. Roberts' Masterwork," B.Y.U. Studies, V. 15, N. 3, p. 263). "Intelligence cleaveth unto intelligence, truth embraceth truth, light cleaveth unto light". (D&C 88:40).

Christ is the Life of the world. He said: "I am the resurrection and the life; he that believeth in me, though he were dead, yet shall he live. And whosoever liveth and believeth in me shall never die". (John 11:25-26). "God so loved the world," in fact, "that He gave his Only Begotten Son, that whosoever believeth in Him should not perish, but have everlasting life". (John 3:16, see 3 Nephi 27:13-14). Heavenly Father intervened in our lives in the most intensely personal way that was possible when He sent His Only Begotten Son to be the Savior of the world.

If we are to love the way Heavenly Father and Jesus Christ love, if we are to have the pure love of Christ in our own lives, we must become involved in the lives of others in ways that are equally intense and personal. We must find ways to influence for good the lives of our brothers and sisters, even if these ways require an uncomfortable and selfless personal sacrifice. We must never forget the two greatest commandments are to love the Lord, and to love our fellowmen.

The Spirit of man is the candle of the Lord. "The Life of Christ may envelop all of man's life, (which) even in its most secular details, may be sacramental". (Truman Madsen). It is a serious thing to live in a society of possible Gods and Goddesses" wrote C.S. Lewis, "to remember that the dullest and most uninteresting person you talk to may one day be a creature which if you saw it now, you would be strongly tempted to worship. It is in the light of these overwhelming possibilities, it is with the awe and the circumspection proper to them, that we should conduct all our dealings with one another; all friendships, all loves, all play and politics. There are no ordinary people. You have never talked to a mere mortal - it is immortals with whom we joke, work, marry, snub and exploit. Our charity must be a real and costly love. Next to the blessed sacrament itself, your neighbor is the holiest object presented to your senses. If he is your Christian neighbor, he is holy in almost the same way, for in him also Christ is truly hidden and glorified". ("The Weight of Glory," p. 14-15).

The second evidence of forgiveness came as the people were filled with joy. Lehi taught: "Adam fell that men might be, and men are that they might have joy". (2 Nephi 2:25). This simple aphorism speaks volumes, and is one of the basic messages of the Restoration. When the Fall of Adam is considered in conjunction with the Atonement of Christ, it is clear that both are part of God's Plan of Happiness, for we can only attain a fulness of joy in a personal, tangible, resurrection. "For man is spirit, the elements are eternal, and spirit and element, inseparably connected, receive a fulness of joy". (D&C 93:33)

Lastly, they had peace of conscience. (V. 3). In his last hours of mortality, Joseph Smith was able to declare that he had a "conscience void of offense towards God, and towards all men". (D&C 135:5). He gave the rest of us the confidence to walk in the valley of the shadow of death and yet to fear no evil. (See Psalms 23:4). "Life actually has no significance except as a preparation for the ultimate goal of death," wrote Carl Jung. "In Christianity, the meaning of existence is consummated in its end". For Latter-day Saints, "one of the greatest contributions of Joseph Smith was his knowledge of what is to come after death. He did much to clarify our understanding of heaven, and to make it seem worth working for". ("My Religion and Me" Lesson Manual).

In his discourse, Benjamin did not specifically mention baptism by water and of the Holy Ghost, since his listeners were likely already members of the Church. After all, many who attended King Benjamin's Discourse stood within the sacred precincts of the temple. (See Mosiah 1:18). Hundreds of years earlier, Nephi had taught: "The gate by which ye should enter is repentance and baptism by water; and then cometh a remission of your sins by fire and by the Holy Ghost". (2 Nephi 31:17). Later in the record, Alma would urge his congregation of expatriates from the Land of Nephi to be baptized, as well. (Mosiah 18:10). It seems clear that their manner of baptism was in doctrinal harmony with its purpose in the latter days, although before the ministry of Christ in the New World the ordinance was administered by virtue of the authority of the Melchizedek Priesthood.

Again, Benjamin addressed the reality of our utter dependence upon God for salvation. If we come to a knowledge of God, and diligently keep His commandments, "all mankind, which ever were since the fall of Adam, or who are, or who ever shall be, even unto the end of the world" shall receive salvation. (V. 6-7). The Atonement is infinite in both time and space, and eternal in its scope. Christ was the Lamb slain from before the foundation of the world. (Revelation 13:8). That is to say, the power of the Atonement was initiated and set in motion before the creation of the Earth. His way was, is, and forever will be, the only way. (See V. 8).

We would do well to think of the following two verses as we regularly review and renew our own baptismal covenant through the ordinance of the Sacrament: "Believe in God; believe that he is, and that he created all things, both in heaven and in earth; believe that he has all wisdom, and all power, both in heaven and in earth; believe that man doth not comprehend all the things which the Lord can comprehend. And again, believe that ye must repent of your sins, and forsake them, and humble yourselves before God; and ask in sincerity of heart that he would forgive you, and now, if you believe all these things see that ye do them". (V. 9-10).

King Benjamin was vitally concerned about the depth of the people's spirituality. Having opened the eyes of their understanding to the mysteries of God concerning their salvation, he urged them to remember Him, retain humility in their relationship with Him, call on Him in daily prayer, and endure in righteousness for Him. (See V. 11).

If they did this, they would be entitled to enter into His Rest, to gain a perfect knowledge of the divinity of the work. Consequently, they would rest from fear, doubt, and the apprehension of danger, as well as from the religious turmoil of the world and from the vagaries of men. (See Alma 12:34, 13:16, 16:17, Moroni 7:3, & D&C 84:24). They would enjoy the peace that follows obedience to celestial principles.

King Benjamin taught that other blessings would also follow obedience. (V. 12-16). His people would have joy, being "filled with the love of God," and would retain a remission of their sins. This is important, because, as Brigham Young warned: "When an individual refuses to comply with the further requirements of heaven, the sins he had formerly committed return upon his head and his former righteousness departs from him". (J.D., 8:124). Also, the people would grow in the knowledge of God, and would live together in peace, harmony, and plenty. Their children would benefit from their righteous example, and would "walk in the ways of truth and soberness (and would) love one another, and serve one another". (V. 15).

Verses 17-26 address the necessity caring for the poor. After the people had made a public declaration of their commitment to personally live in obedience to Gospel principles, their next logical focus of concern would be to address the needs of the poor among them. (See Commentary Reference to Mosiah 29:21).

Benjamin reminded his listeners that they had been pleading, even begging, for a remission of their sins, so in a sense, they were all beggars. (V. 19-20). The Lord had answered their petition in a marvelous way, and so Benjamin chose to focus on the intensity of that powerful personal epiphany to motivate his people to impart of their substance one to another, according to their need. "And remember in all things the poor and the needy, the sick and the afflicted," taught the Savior, "for he that doeth not these things, the same is not my disciple". (D&C 52:40).

While yet in mortality, we "may walk guiltless before God," retaining a remission of our sins from day to day. (V. 26). We can be holy people, celestial people, even a society of Saints. We need to use common sense, though, in our charitable endeavors. Verse 27 provides the practical advice: To "see that all ... things are done in wisdom and order; for it is not requisite that a man should run faster than he has strength". (See D&C 10:4). Overzealous efforts, without wisdom and patience, and discernment, lead to errors in judgment.

Benjamin told his audience that there are many ways to commit sin. (V. 29). There is a rule, however, that is the foundation for purposeful living, and the order of counsel is significant: Having been taught the truth, and with a firm knowledge of that which is good, we must take care first to watch our thoughts, then our words, and finally our deeds. (V. 30). Having been taught correct principles, the people were left to govern their own behavior according to the light and knowledge they had received. (See D&C 58:26). Usually, the Lord gives us the overall objectives to be accomplished and some guidelines to follow, but He expects us to work out most of the details and methods ourselves. These are developed through study, prayer, and the promptings of the Spirit, things which Benjamin now expected of his people, inasmuch as they had been carefully taught. As Joseph Smith famously declared: "I teach people correct principles, and they govern themselves." (John Taylor Quote In "The Organization of the Church", "Millennial Star", 11/15/1851, p. 339).

Mosiah
Chapter 5

Benjamin went beyond the understanding level of teaching to that of acceptance, when "he sent among them, desiring to know of his people if they believed the words which he had spoken unto them". (V. 1). With one united voice, they answered with a resounding "Yes!" They had been born again. The desired result of all Gospel oriented teaching had been achieved. A mighty change had been wrought in the hearts of the people, and they had no more disposition to do evil. (See V. 2). They had the spirit of prophecy, the testimony of Jesus, and great knowledge of the mysteries, gained by personal revelation. (See V. 3-4). A careful reading of verses 2-4 will help us to know if we have been "born again", as well.

With such intensity of commitment, the people were "willing to enter into a covenant" with God. (V. 5). Verses 5-15 are of the greatest significance to Latter-day Saints, whose religious teachings stress the importance of their covenant relationship with God. King Benjamin's congregation consisted of members of the Church who did not fully appreciate the significance of their baptism, and therefore they now needed to renew that covenant. (See Alma 5:14 & 26). Today, the Church emphasizes its importance, and rather than drinking "out of the cup of the wrath of God" (v. 5), its members drink from the sacrament cup in token of their remembrance of the sacrifice of the Son of God and their baptismal covenant. Among King Benjamin's people, so universal was the rededication of the multitude's resolve, "that there was not one soul, except it were little children, but who had entered into the covenant and had taken upon them the name of Christ". (See Mosiah 6:2).

Covenants are binding contracts, and since God is a party to every Gospel covenant, they must come through revelation. No person enters into such covenants except on the basis of direct revelation from God. It follows that the only ones who can enter into covenants are members of the Church of Jesus Christ who believe in revelation as a tenet of their faith!

The covenants we make with God reflect His attributes. God is moral, so He gives us the Covenant of Chastity; He has charity, so He commands us to love Him and each other. God is disciplined, so He gives us the Law of Obedience. Because He is a righteous steward, He gives us the Law of Consecration. Because He loves His less fortunate children, He gives us the Law of the Fast. Because His is a perfected, resurrected body, He gives us the Word of Wisdom. Because He is omniscient, He gives us the commandment to seek knowledge. In consequence of the Gift of His Son, He gives us the Law of Sacrifice. Because He rested from His labors on the seventh day, He gives us the Law of the Sabbath.

God is our Father, and He is perfect in every way. He could give us everything He has, but what He is, we must earn for ourselves, as we struggle to overcome adversity and achieve self-mastery. The purpose of the covenants we make with Him is to help us to more clearly focus our efforts to become as He is. If it were not possible to become as God is, covenants would be unnecessary. (See Commentary Reference to Mosiah 3:19). Keeping covenants puts us beyond the power of the adversary, as obedience endows us with the priesthood and spiritual power necessary to overcome evil and obtain exaltation. The Prophet Joseph Smith said: "Salvation consists of our being placed beyond the power of our enemies, meaning the enemies of our progression, such as dishonesty, greediness, lying, immorality, and other vices". ("The Words of Joseph Smith: The Contemporary Accounts of the Nauvoo Discourses of the Prophet Joseph", 5/21/1843).

"For by doing these things (entering into covenants) the gates of hell shall not prevail against you; yea, and the Lord God will disperse the powers of darkness from before you, and cause the heavens to shake for thy good, and His name's glory". (D&C 21:6). The gates of hell mark the entrance to the spirit world of the unjust, where disobedient spirits who could not abide their covenants are allowed to work out their own salvation on their own while they await the day of their redemption from the Satan's stranglehold. (See Commentary Reference to 2 Nephi 4:32, D&C 76:73, & 138:8 & 28, Isaiah 61:1, 1 Peter 3:19 & Moses 7:57).

Although in the Last Days we live in spiritual Babylon, keeping our covenants made with God guarantees that we can live with confidence and high hopes for the future. We can be the happiest people on the face of the earth. In 1830, the Lord declared "The day speedily cometh; the hour is not yet, but is nigh at hand, when peace shall be taken from the earth, and the devil shall have power over his own dominion". (D&C 1:35). But, at the same time, He promised: "If ye are prepared, ye shall not fear". (D&C 38:30). We take our cue from Father Abraham, who lived in his youth in the land of the Chaldeans, at the residence of his fathers, and "saw that it was needful ... to obtain another place of residence; And, finding there was (the promise of) greater happiness and peace and rest" with a change in his physical surroundings, he "sought for the blessings of the fathers," or in other words, the protection of the covenant God had made with his righteous ancestors. (Abraham 1:1-2).

"My peace I give unto you," promised the Savior, "not as the world giveth, give I unto you". (John 14:27). He was referring to a gift the world cannot bestow, that cannot be purchased with money, that cannot be expensively wrapped or tangibly handled. His gift of peace is not "the peace of the world, of ease, of luxury, idleness, absence of turmoil, and strife, but the peace born of the righteous life, the peace that lifts the soul, that day by day brings us closer to the home of Eternal Peace, the dwelling place of our Father". (J. Reuben Clark, Jr.)

King Benjamin told his people that because of their covenant with God, they would "be called the children of Christ, his sons and his daughters". (V. 7, see Commentary Reference to Mosiah 15:7). Even well-meaning individuals use the term "Christian" in ways that are much less powerful than its true meaning would suggest. Christians recognize that "Jesus Christ (is) the Son of God, the Father of heaven and earth, the Creator of all things". (Mosiah 3:8). And so, they humbly take His name upon themselves. (See Essay: "Name-titles of Jesus Christ").

Just as we are known by the name of our mortal parents, so too are we called by the name of Christ in a familial way. We are His children in the sense that He united our body and spirit through the Resurrection: "For this day He hath spiritually begotten you," explained Benjamin. (V. 7). There is a special family relationship reserved for the faithful that is in addition to the reality that we are all spirit children of our Father. (See D&C 34:3, & 121:7).

Benjamin taught that those who enter into the Covenant "are born of him". (V. 7). In our day, we hear a lot about "Born Again Christians". From Benjamin's perspective, these are they who are in a covenant relationship with the Lord. Since only members of Christ's true Church can have that bond through the authority of the priesthood vested in its administrators, if follows that the only real Born-Again Christians are Latter-day Saints! (See Mosiah 27:25,

Alma 5:14, & 7:14, then Mosiah 15:10-11, Alma 22:15, & 36:24). As the Lord unambiguously revealed to Joseph Smith, the "greater priesthood administereth the Gospel and holdeth the key to the mysteries of the kingdom, even the key of the knowledge of God. Therefore, in the ordinances thereof, the power of godliness is manifest. And without the ordinances thereof, and the authority of the priesthood, the power of godliness is not manifest unto men in the flesh". (D&C 84:19-21).

Only by making covenants with God and Christ can we break the bands of death, and are we made free. "There is no other name given whereby salvation cometh," said Benjamin; "therefore, I would that ye should take upon you the name of Christ, all you that have entered into the covenant with God". (V. 8). Is it any wonder that the Church of Jesus Christ of Latter-day Saints is a missionary oriented Church, and that the Savior proclaims that it "is the only true and living Church upon the face of the whole earth, with which I, the Lord, am well pleased?" (D&C 1:30). No other Church has the authority of the priesthood, that is necessary to bind and ratify the covenants we make with God. The reality of the apostasy and the subsequent restoration of priesthood authority are well documented in the scriptures and in the history of the Church. No other organization has the power to break the death grip of Satan, who would drag our souls down to hell in an instant, if he were given the opportunity to do so. Without the power of covenants, his capacity to thwart the Plan is compounded.

The attitude of the subjects of King Benjamin following his discourse was the same as that of true believers 50 years later, who "took upon them, gladly, the name of Christ, or Christians, as they were called, because of their belief in Christ who should come". (Alma 46:15). They recognized the source of the only legitimate authority on earth with the power to sanctify us so that we can be brought into the presence of God. So, too, on the Day of Pentecost, over three thousand people "were pricked in their heart, and said unto Peter and to the rest of the apostles, Men and brethren, what shall we do? Then Peter said unto them, Repent, and be baptized every one of you in the name of Jesus Christ for the remission of sins, and ye shall receive the gift of the Holy Ghost." (Acts 2:37-38). "And they continued steadfastly in the apostles' doctrine and fellowship, and in breaking of bread, and in prayers." (Acts 2:42, see Commentary Reference to 3 Nephi 15:21-24).

In fulfillment of Benjamin's promise to his people, (see Mosiah 1:11), they were no longer "the people of Zarahemla" or "the people of Nephi," but "Christians". Those who would take upon themselves the name of Christ would be found "at the right hand of God, for (they would) know the name by which (they would be) called; for (they would) be called by the name of Christ". (V. 9). As the Savior said: "My sheep hear my voice, and I know them, and they follow me". (John 10:27). The covenant relationship He has with His sheep brings them together into an intimacy that only comes through a close personal connection.

Benjamin pointed out that those who would not take upon themselves the name of Christ would find themselves in His disfavor, for their misplaced fealty would be manifest. "Whosoever shall not take upon him the name of Christ," Benjamin declared, "must be called by some other name; therefore, he findeth himself on the left hand of God". (V. 10). About 40 years later, Alma asked the people of Zarahemla: "If ye will not hearken unto the voice of the good shepherd, to the name by which ye are called, behold, ye are not the sheep of the good shepherd. And now if ye are not the sheep of the good shepherd, of what fold are ye? Behold, I say unto you, that the devil is your shepherd, and ye are of his fold; and now, who can deny this? ... Whosoever bringeth forth evil works, the same becometh a child of the devil, for he hearkeneth unto his voice, and doth follow him". (Alma 5:38-41). In this sense, Benjamin warned his people that through transgression the name of Christ would be blotted out of their hearts. If this were to occur, they would no longer feel like Christians. (V. 11, see Mosiah 2:37). It seems that, sooner or later, we will all be given the opportunity to declare our genealogy, and to establish our lineage either back to the Father of our Spirits, or to Satan. What a tragedy it would be, if we were to turn our backs on the Living God, and to instead settle for the illegitimacy of the great imposter.

Today, an invitation to come unto Christ is extended by the missionaries to those who are pure in heart: Deny the cares of the world and respond to a nobler calling. The discipline required of those who follow the Royal Law is alien to the natural man. "Urging self-restraints on hedonists is like asking Dracula to avoid hanging around the blood bank". (Neal Maxwell, C.R. 4/1995). But Christians know that it is only the redeeming blood of Jesus Christ that can sanctify our souls, and transfusions of Type Joseph blood is offered free of charge to all who would have a change of heart.

We must both hear and know "the name by which (Christ) shall call (us)". (V. 12). Many hear, yet do not comprehend, "for how knoweth a man the master whom he has not served, and who is a stranger to him, and is far from the thoughts and intents of his heart?" (V. 13, see K.J.T. & J.S.T. Matthew 7:23).

Baptism alone does not assure us of eternal life. Committed and recommitted members of the Church also need to be "steadfast and immovable, always abounding in good works". (V. 15). They need to be sealed to the Savior by the ratifying power of the Holy Spirit of Promise that is the Holy Ghost. (See D&C 88:3-4). Our calling and election is made sure only after the Lord has fully proven us. Then, when we receive "the other Comforter," Christ will appear and personally teach us the visions of eternity.

Mosiah
Chapter 6

The people had both understood and accepted King Benjamin's message. Now, the final element of effective teaching required a binding behavioral commitment and public declaration. "King Benjamin thought it was expedient, after having finished speaking to the people, that he should take the names of all those who had entered into a covenant with God to keep his commandments". (V. 1). Every soul in his audience beyond the age of accountability was given the opportunity to make such a commitment. "And it came to pass that there was not one soul, except it were little children, but who had entered into the covenant and had taken upon them the name of Christ". (V. 2).

Joshua had required the same declaration from his people a thousand years earlier in the Promised Land of Israel. "Fear the Lord," he had demanded, "and serve him in sincerity and in truth; and put away the gods which your fathers served on the other side of the flood, and in Egypt; and serve ye the Lord ... Choose ye this day whom ye will serve ... but as for me and my house, we will serve the Lord". (Joshua 24:14-15).

Choice is at the heart of the Gospel of Jesus Christ. "There are many called, but few are chosen," wrote Joseph Smith from Liberty Jail. "And why are they not chosen? Because their hearts are set so much upon the things of this world, and aspire to the honors of men, that they do not learn this one lesson: That the rights of the priesthood are inseparably connected with the powers of heaven, and that the powers of heaven cannot be controlled nor handled only upon the principles of righteousness". (D&C 121:34-36). When our hearts are set only upon temporal things, the spiritual glue that binds together the fabric of our daily lives is irreparably compromised.

It was against this danger that King Benjamin now wished to protect his people. Therefore, he provided for follow-up and accountability by calling ministers to see to the needs of the people on an ongoing basis. He "appointed priests to teach the people, that thereby they might hear and know the commandments of God, and to stir them up in remembrance of the oath which they had made". (V. 3). As the Lord reminded the Saints: "There has been a day of calling, but the time has come for a day of choosing; and let those be chosen that are worthy". (D&C 105:35).

We are called when we become members of the Church of Jesus Christ, and are chosen when we have endured to the end in righteousness. In a pattern reminiscent of that which was established in Zarahemla, the Lord has again provided young men of the Aaronic Priesthood to "watch over the Church always, and be with and strengthen them; And see that there is no iniquity in the Church, neither hardness with each other, neither lying, backbiting, nor evil speaking; And see that the Church meet together often, and also see that all the members do their duty". (D&C 20:53-55).

Around 124 B.C., having set in order the affairs of his kingdom, Benjamin died, probably as well prepared as anyone could be to meet their Savior and their God. He had served by properly training his own sons, by teaching the commandments to all his people, by ministering to the needs of his countrymen unselfishly, and by preparing all who would listen to make holy covenants that they might be ready to meet Christ at the Judgment Bar. He was one of the few truly righteous, noble, and benevolent monarchs in all of history, and was a ruler whom his subjects could properly emulate.

His son followed in his righteous footsteps and "did walk in the ways of the Lord, and did observe his judgments and his statutes, and did keep his commandments in all things whatsoever he commanded him". (V. 6). Mosiah did "that which his father had done in all things. And there was no contention among all his people". (V. 7).

Mosiah
Chapter 7

Mormon's abridgment briefly tells, in chapters 7 & 8, how a search party from the Land of Zarahemla found the colony established by a Nephite named Zeniff in the Land of Nephi that was his ancestral homeland. To help us to understand how his own descendants came into bondage to the Lamanites, Mormon inserted into the record Zeniff's own narrative, in Mosiah chapters 9-22.

Those chapters also explain the manner in which the people were finally delivered from bondage and how they returned to Zarahemla. Chapters 9-17 deal primarily with the mission of the great prophet Abinadi to Zeniff's son, who was named Noah. In chapters 23 and 24, Mormon explained how a group from the original colony who followed Alma the Elder was also delivered from bondage.

In verse 1, Mormon related that King Mosiah was interested in knowing what had happened to the people of Zeniff, who had left Zarahemla almost 80 years earlier, to dwell in the City of Lehi-Nephi. (See Alma 24:19). A search party set out under the leadership of Ammon, who was a descendant of Zarahemla and not to be confused with the son of Mosiah by the same name. (V. 3). This group traveled for 40 days in the wilderness before reaching the Land of Nephi.

A parallel account of what happened next is found in Mosiah 21:19. Outside the walls of the fortified City of Lehi-Nephi, the party was mistakenly identified as a group of the wicked priests of King Noah. Ammon was arrested by the guards of Noah's son Limhi, and presently brought before him to answer charges. (V. 7-11).

When Ammon explained to Limhi who he really was and the purpose of his journey, Limhi rejoiced in a newfound opportunity to throw off the yoke of bondage to the Lamanites. (V. 13-14). Interestingly, part of their bondage was "a tax which (was) grievous to be borne". (V. 15). In reality, they were in a 50% tax bracket which is not unusually high by our standards today. (V. 22). However, any tax is grievous if those paying it do not derive benefit from their sacrifice, as was the case with the people of Limhi. (V. 23).

Limhi desired to speak to his people, and so, at his command, they gathered at the temple. (V. 17). We know that Nephi had built a temple in the Land of Nephi hundreds of years earlier. (See 2 Nephi 5:16). We do not know whether or not the temple referenced here was the same building, but it is unlikely that it was a temple in the traditional sense, since by the time of Limhi's reign, the people were in a general state of apostasy. For some time, since they had no legitimate priesthood authority, they had not entered into temple covenants as we understand them today. (See Commentary References to 2 Nephi 5:16, & Mosiah 1:18).

Limhi suggested that, with newfound faith and enthusiastic participation, their ongoing struggle with the Lamanites would be "effectual". (V. 18). That is to say, their effort would adequately answer its purpose, which was the liberation of the Nephites in the Land of Nephi from bondage.

In verses 18-33, Limhi preached to his people. Although his message was basically sound for one who was not well-founded in Gospel doctrine, he tended to be a little long-winded, especially considering that Mormon only included "a few" of his remarks in his abridgment of the sermon. (See Mosiah 8:1).

Limhi portrayed his grandfather Zeniff as one who had been overzealous in his eagerness to settle in the Land of Nephi, and who had consequently been seduced by the "cunning and craftiness of King Laman". (V. 21, see Mosiah 9:3, & 10). This Lamanite king had only wanted to bring the Nephite immigrants into bondage. (For background on these circumstances, see Mosiah 19:15).

Limhi suggested that his people had fallen into temporal bondage to the Lamanites due to transgression of the laws of God. (V. 25). This is often the pattern. (See v. 29). The effect of transgression on the people in any circumstance is "poison," or spiritual death. (V. 30). When men and women walk in darkness, they often stumble over hidden obstacles intentionally designed to bring them into subjection to powerful adversaries. Pride goeth before a fall, when "Me" and "Mine" become more important than "Thee" and "Thine".

The Lord had said: "If my people shall sow filthiness they shall reap the east wind, which bringeth immediate destruction". (V. 31). In Hebrew, one would say the winds were oriented relative to the land of Israel, and they were designated by the four cardinal points of the compass. Cool winds came from the north, moist winds from the western sea, warm winds from the south, and dry winds, often laden with sand, from the eastern deserts. These last winds were devastating and so the metaphor was not only personal, but also powerful, predictive, and even prophetic. (See Commentary Reference to Mosiah 12:6).

The iniquity of Limhi's people had been so great that the wicked priests of his father King Noah had slain a prophet of God named Abinadi. (V. 26, see Mosiah 11:20). Limhi had evidently been favorably touched by this prophet's teachings, however, for he characterized Abinadi as "a just man". (See Mosiah 19:17). Although not converted at that time, as was a priest of King Noah named Alma (See Mosiah 17:2), Limhi and his people were now prepared and eager to be taught true Gospel principles by Ammon, and as a result, they requested baptism. (See Mosiah 21:33). Their zealous petition was a bit premature, for they required significant additional Gospel instruction before it could be granted.

Limhi finished speaking to his people by giving to them a formula for their deliverance. (V. 32). They would be required to turn to the Lord, put their trust in Him, and serve Him. Mosiah Chapter 21 reveals what kind of binding covenants the people were required and willing to make.

Today, in addition to the bondage of sin, many who desire to come to the waters of baptism have experienced physical, financial, social, intellectual, emotional, or psychological trauma. The protection they receive, or the comfort they are given, is determined by how carefully they listen to the promptings of the Holy Ghost and to the counsel of the prophet, by how faithfully they read the scriptures, by how righteously they determine to conduct their lives, and by how humbly they "bring forth fruit meet for repentance, that (they) may also enter into (His) rest. (Alma 13:13).

Mosiah
Chapter 8

Limhi invited Ammon to recount to his people the message that had been delivered by King Benjamin in his last great sermon in Zarahemla. (V. 1-3, see Mosiah Chapters 2-6). Then, Limhi showed Ammon metal plates upon which his people had been recording their history since the departure of his grandfather Zeniff from Zarahemla. (V. 5). It was an abridgment of these records that Mormon later inserted into the Plates of Mormon, and that comprise Mosiah Chapters 9-22 of The Book of Mormon.

Limhi then asked Ammon if he could interpret languages. His reason was explained in verses 7-11. It seems that he had dispatched a search party into the wilderness, to see if it might be able to contact his ancestral Nephites living back in the Land of Zarahemla. Its mission was to seek assistance for relief from their bondage to the Lamanites in the Land of Nephi. This party had become "lost in the wilderness for the space of many days," and finally stumbled upon a land to the northwest of Zarahemla "covered with bones of men, and of beasts, and with ruins of buildings". (V. 8, see Omni 1:22). They had found the remains of the Jaredite civilization, but mistakenly thought it to be that of Zarahemla. (See Mosiah 21:26).

How far did this party travel before finding the last great battlefields of the Jaredites? In close proximity was the hill called Ramah, and later Cumorah. (See Mormon Chapter 6). Surely, they had not wandered 3,000 miles through the wilderness to what is now Palmyra, New York, and then back again. The likelihood is that, either Zarahemla was somewhere in the northeast of the North American Continent, or the Land of Cumorah was in Meso-America. In either case, Cumorah would probably be within a few hundred miles of both the Land of Nephi and the Land of Zarahemla. A third possibility is that there were two Cumorahs. (See Commentary Reference to Mosiah 23:3, and Essay: "Were There Two Cumorahs?").

In any event, when the group of 43 explorers returned home to the Land of Nephi, they produced "24 plates, which (were) filled with engravings, and they (were) of pure gold". This is the first mention in The Book of Mormon of the Plates of Ether, and is the first time any plates were described as being made of "gold". (See Mosiah 28:11, and 1 Nephi 19:1, which describes "plates of ore"). The discovery of these plates was no accident. (See V. 19). Moroni, in his abridgment of the Plates of Ether on the Plates of Mormon, wrote that Ether "finished his record and he hid them in a manner that the people of Limhi did find them". (Ether 15:33).

In The Book of Omni is an account of Coriantumr, who was the last survivor of the Jaredite battles, and who was found by the People of Zarahemla. (See Omni 1:20-22). Therefore, the Jaredite civilization could not have been destroyed until some time after 600 B.C., when Mulek and his band, who were the progenitors of the People of Zarahemla, arrived in the New World.

The group sent out by Limhi returned to the Land of Nephi not many days before the coincident arrival of Ammon there. This would place the time of the discovery of the Land of Desolation at about 121 B.C. (See Alma 22:30-31).

It was the record engraven upon these plates of gold that had been brought back to Limhi that intrigued the king, and he was desirous to know their interpretation. (V. 12). Ammon told Limhi that, back in Zarahemla, King Mosiah could translate the record by means of "interpreters" in his possession, because by the authority of God he was a qualified "seer". (V. 13-16, see Commentary Reference to Mosiah 28:11-15). These "interpreters" were the ancient Urim and Thummim, first mentioned in Exodus 28:30. (V. 13). Joseph Smith described this instrument as "two stones in silver bows and these stones, fastened to a breastplate, constituted what is called the Urim and Thummim. The possession and use of these stones were what constituted 'seers' in ancient or former times". (J.S.H. 1:35).

"A seer is one who may see, talk, and receive personal instruction from God. Our prophet is a seer and a revelator. There must be someone to whom the people can turn and trust, who can speak for God. God must have someone on earth who can point the way and say: 'This is true.' God has given us a living seer and prophet (who) reveals personal testimony that Jesus is in very deed the Risen Savior, the Living God". (Theodore Burton, C.R. 10/1961). A seer is an interpreter and clarifier of eternal truth; one who walks in the Lord's light with open eyes. (See D&C 21:1). A seer is literally a 'see-er,' one who has the right to use the Urim and Thummim.

By seers "shall all things be revealed". (V. 17). Helen Keller once observed: "There is one tragedy in life worse than to be born without sight, and that is to be born with sight, but without vision. "Our loving God has "provided a means that man, through faith, might work mighty miracles; therefore, he becometh a great benefit to his fellow beings". (V. 18). A seer can see the storm clouds before they appear on the horizon.

With awakening recognition, Limhi now understood that only the authorized servant of the Lord could interpret the 24 gold plates of Ether, and he was convinced that Mosiah's Urim and Thummim was the key that would unlock the messages hidden within the characters on the plates. "A great mystery is contained within these plates," he declared, "and these interpreters were doubtless prepared for the purpose of unfolding all such mysteries to the children of men". (V. 19).

Two thousand years later, the spiritual illumination of our minds is still the key to an understanding of the mysteries of God. On the subject of secular Christianity and the New Dispensation, B.H. Roberts wrote: "In their efforts to clarify (their consideration of Christ) they were often simply multiplying mirrors and studying angles without increasing the light. The New Dispensation brought a flood of light that did not simply replace the darkness, but illuminated elements and principles, and their relationships, that heretofore had been (only) dimly perceived". ("The Truth, The Way, The Life," p. 263).

With a much clearer understanding of the blessing that a living prophet. seer, and revelator could be to his people, Limhi expressed his dismay that those who are stubborn "will not seek wisdom, neither do they desire that she should rule over them!" Under those circumstances, "how blind and impenetrable are the understandings of the children of men". (V. 20).

On the college portals in Moorish Granada (1300-1492) were inscribed these lines: "The world is supported by four things, the learning of the wise, the justice of the great, the prayers of the good, and the valor of the brave". The casualties of every dispensation are those who substitute intellect for intelligence. These learned ones suppose that, by raw brainpower, they can judge both the truth and the morality of the word of the Lord and of His prophets. In a society of Saints, however, people will gain knowledge by study and by faith, and will not confuse the two.

"And Ammon said
that a seer is a revelator
and a prophet also; and a gift
which is greater can no man have."
(Mosiah 8:16).

Mosiah
Chapter 9

Chapters 9 and 10 in The Book of Mosiah are a verbatim account from Zeniff's record, and concern events that took place about 80 years before the arrival of Ammon in The Land of Nephi. (See Mosiah 8:5). Mormon recorded these verses in the first-person tense because they constitute the personal memoir of Zeniff. Then, chapters 11-22 are Mormon's abridgement of the record of Zeniff, while chapters 23-24 concern Alma and his people, who were driven into the wilderness by king Noah.

An expedition had bean mounted in Zarahemla to return to the land of the Nephites' first inheritance. (See Omni 1:27-30). This land was called The Land of Nephi, as well as The Land of Lehi-Nephi which seems to have been a limited district immediately surrounding a city of the same name. (See V. 6). The land of Nephi was south of the great wilderness and the narrow neck of land. (See Alma 22:32, 63:5, Ether 10:20, & Mormon 2:29). For all practical purposes, when considering all the clues within The Book of Mormon relating to geography, the narrow neck of land may have been the Isthmus of Tehuantepec in southern Mexico that is the shortest distance between the Gulf of Mexico and the Pacific Ocean. Interestingly, the isthmus runs in a north – south direction. It is 125 miles across, which is four times wider than the Isthmus of Panama that connects the Caribbean Sea with the Pacific Ocean far to the south. The Land of Nephi to the south of the narrow neck of land was the land of promise for the Nephites.

The first expedition from Zarahemla had ended in failure, in the sense that it had not established contact with Zarahemla, and so Zeniff determined to try again. (V. 2, see Omni 1:28). He admitted that he had been "over-zealous" in his efforts, and he noted with regret and self-deprecation that he had been "slow to remember the Lord." (V. 3). He had acted contrary to His counsel by returning to The Land of Nephi and re-establishing a Nephite colony there, that ultimately failed after 80 difficult years. (See Omni 1:12-13).

And yet, we can empathize with Zeniff, who was consumed by a desire to return to the land of his fathers. "Breathes there a man with soul so dead, who never to himself hath said 'This is my own, my native land!' Whose heart hath ne'er within him burned, as home his footsteps he hath turned from wandering on a foreign strand? If such there breathe, go, mark him well, for him no minstrel raptures swell. High though his titles, proud his name, boundless his wealth as wish can claim, despite these titles, power, and pelf, the wretch (is) concentered all in self." (Sir Walter Scott, "The Lay of The Ancient Minstrel").

And so, the colony was established on a hopeful note, with the approval of the Lamanites then living in the land. (V. 6). Its location was identified as "the land of Lehi-Nephi, and the land of Shilom." (V. 6), and later as the "Land of Nephi." (V. 10). No note seems to have been taken of the ominous fact that the City of Lehi-Nephi lay in ruin, and there was not a trace of its former Nephite inhabitants who had been those who had stayed behind when the Elder Mosiah had left The Land of Nephi many years earlier.

Zeniff should have been wary of the intentions of the Lamanite king, though, who had all too readily "yielded up the land", that the Nephites might possess it. (V. 10). We are reminded of the spider who said to the fly: "Will you walk into my parlour? Tis the prettiest little parlour that ever you did spy. The way into my parlour is up a winding stair, and I have many curious things to shew when you are there. Oh no, no, said the little fly. To ask me is in vain, for who goes up your winding stair can ne'er come down again. I'm sure you must be weary, dear, with soaring up so high; Will you rest upon my little bed? said the spider to the fly. There are pretty curtains drawn around; the sheets are fine and thin, and if you like to rest awhile, I'll snugly tuck you in! Oh no, no, said the little fly, for I've often heard it said, they never, never wake again, who sleep upon your bed! Said the cunning spider to the fly, dear friend what can I do, to prove the warm affection I've always felt for you? I have within my pantry, good store of all that's nice; I'm sure you're very welcome—will you please to take a slice? Oh no, no, said the little fly, kind sir, that cannot be, I've heard what's in your pantry, and I do not wish to see! Sweet creature! said the spider, you're witty and you're wise. How handsome are your gauzy wings, how brilliant are your eyes! I've a little looking glass upon my parlour shelf. If you'll step in one moment, dear, you shall behold yourself. I thank you, gentle sir, she said, for what you're pleased to say, and bidding you good morning now, I'll call another day. The spider turned him round about, and went into his den, for well he knew the silly fly would soon come back again. So, he wove a subtle web, in a little corner sly, and set his table ready, to dine upon the fly. Then he came out to his door again, and merrily did sing, come hither, hither, pretty fly, with the pearl and silver wing. Your robes are green and purple; there's a crest upon your head. Your eyes are like the diamond bright, but mine are dull as lead! Alas, alas! how very soon this silly little fly, hearing his wily, flattering words, came slowly flitting by. With buzzing wings, she hung aloft, then near and nearer drew, thinking only of her brilliant eyes, and green and purple hue; thinking only of her crested head. Poor foolish thing! At last, up jumped the cunning Spider, and fiercely held her fast. He dragged her up his winding stair, into his dismal den, within his little parlour, but she ne'er came out again! And now dear little children, who may this story read, to idle, silly flattering words, I pray you ne'er give heed. Unto an evil counsellor, close heart and ear and eye, and take a lesson from this tale of the spider and the fly." (Mary Howett, "The Spider and The Fly" 1829).

For 12 years, the Nephite colonists prospered. (V. 9-11). Then, the Lamanites began to covet the fruits of their labor, and armed conflict followed. But the Nephites had a "secret weapon" that was incomprehensible to the Lamanite military commanders. They went forth to battle "in the strength of the Lord." (V. 17, see Mosiah 10:10-11, & Commentary Reference to Mosiah 18:21). This was the same plan that had been so effective against the Lamanites when they had attacked the Nephites under the Elder Mosiah who were living in The Land of Zarahemla. (See Words of Mormon 1:14). Nevertheless, the cost due to this conflict was 279 Nephite and 3,045 Lamanite dead. (V. 18-19).

Mosiah
Chapter 10

For nine years following their initial conflict with the Lamanites, the colony of Zeniff lived in relative temporal security. Then, following the death of King Laman, his son raised a new army to attack the Nephites. (V. 1-7). We learn in these verses that the Lamanites shaved their heads and were naked except for a leather girdle. They must have presented a formidable sight. "They were a wild, and ferocious, and a bloodthirsty people". (V. 12). Nevertheless, the Nephites went into battle "in the strength of the Lord" and again prevailed over the Lamanites. (V 10, see v. 20).

Zeniff observed that "the Lamanites knew nothing concerning the Lord, nor the strength of the Lord". (V. 11). Even though the Nephite colony had been in physical bondage for around 30 years, their Lamanites overseers were themselves in the bondage of spiritual darkness, which is an all-encompassing, overwhelming, and frequently irreversible disability with much more damaging consequences than physical servitude.

Verses 12-17 chronicle the misguided traditions of the Lamanites, which contribute to our understanding of their resentment of the Nephites. They believed that their fathers had left Jerusalem under duress, and that while in the wilderness of the Arabian Peninsula, they had been wronged by Nephi. They also believed that during their dangerous passage upon the sea, as well as after they had arrived in the Promised Land, that Nephi had wrested power from Laman, to whom leadership rightfully belonged. They even felt betrayed because Nephi had finally departed into the wilderness, taking with him the records of his people. In consequence of these misunderstandings and for the misconstrued and inaccurate perceptions of the Nephites upon which the Lamanites had built mistrust over the next 400 years, the present generation harbored "an eternal hatred towards the children of Nephi". (V. 17). As Mormon said, it was only the "incorrect or false traditions" of the Lamanites that kept them from a knowledge of the truth, and when diplomacy failed, weapons took the place of words. (See Alma 3:8 & 37:9).

About 40 years after leading his band of expatriates from the Land of Zarahemla to the Land of Nephi, Zeniff conferred the kingdom upon one of his sons, named Noah. (V. 22). It was his prayer that the Lord might continue to bless his people. Little did he know what was really in store for them!

"Now, the Lamanites knew nothing concerning the Lord, nor the strength of the Lord ... They were a wild, and ferocious, and a blood-thirsty people, believing in the tradition of their fathers." (Mosiah 10:11-12).

Mosiah
Chapter 11

Chapters 11-22 of The Book of Mosiah comprise Mormon's abridgement of the record of Zeniff. (See Mosiah 8:5). Chapters 11-17 concern the reign of Zeniff's son named Noah, who "did not walk in the ways of his father". (V. 1).

God will never compel us to do right, and Satan has no power to force us to do wrong. God always casts his vote for us, and Satan always votes against us. Then, we vote to break the tie. It is our choice that gives significance to our lives. In Noah's case, he elected to go with Satan. (V. 2).

The first few verses of Chapter 11 express the Nephites' sensitivity to unjust taxation. The oppressive tax laid upon the Nephites by Noah was 20% "of all they possessed," which is not oppressive by today's standards. (V. 3). However, the revenue thus created was used only to support the wickedness of Noah and his burgeoning governmental bureaucracy. (V. 4, 6, 12-13, see Commentary Reference to Mosiah 7:13-15). This made the tax oppressive in the eyes of the Nephites upon whose shoulders the financial burden lay.

Noah summarily released all those priests "that had been consecrated by his father" Zeniff, and installed new ones who practiced priestcraft and engaged in idolatry. (V. 5, & 7, see 2 Nephi 26:29). The focus of their worship became their "elegant and spacious buildings and fine work of wood, and all manner of precious things". (V. 8-11).

One is reminded of the Emperor Justinian, who "began a new St. Sophia. He summoned the most famous of living architects to plan and superintend the work. Abandoning the traditional basilican form, they conceived a design whose center would be a spacious dome resting not on walls but on massive piers, and buttressed by a half dome at either end. Ten thousand workmen were engaged, and 320,000 pounds of gold were spent on the enterprise. In five years and ten months the edifice was complete, and on December 26, 537 A.D., the Emperor led a solemn inaugural procession to the resplendent cathedral. Justinian walked alone to the pulpit, and lifting up his hands, cried out: "Oh Solomon! I have vanquished you!" (Will Durant, "The Lessons of History," 4:130).

Today, when we study the archaeological evidence of ancient Meso-American cultures, we may be witnessing the remnants of apostate Lamanite civilizations, since it was they who worshipped gods of wood and of stone, and who focused their attention on temporal monuments to their profane deities. (See Ezekiel 20:32). Jeremiah might have asked of these apostates: "Shall a man make gods unto himself, and they are no gods?" (Jeremiah 16:20). The answer is "Yes," for as Ben Jonson observed 400 years ago: All virtue, and almost any vice, is sold for almighty gold! Some things never change, for the Lord observed of our own day: "Every man walketh in his own way, and after the image of his own god, whose image is in the likeness of the world, and whose substance is that of an idol". (D&C 1:16).

What are these caricatures of the Savior in powerless forms? Can we identify these counterfeit versions of the divine model, and beware? Whether it is an entertainment or sports figure, the almighty dollar or eternal youth, government paternalism, the ivory towers of secular learning or the robes of the false priesthood, these idols of wood and stone have no power to save, but instead divert our attention from the "light of the world". The Savior said: "He that followeth me shall not walk in darkness, but shall have the light of life". (John 8:12, see Commentary Reference to Mosiah 16:9).

The center of Noah's attention is revealed when we read that "he placed his heart upon his riches, and he spent his time in riotous living with his wives and his concubines; and so did also his priests spend their time with harlots". (V. 14). In the Last Days, both secular and religious leaders sometimes follow similar patterns and ignore Isaiah's warning: "Come down, and sit in the dust, O virgin daughter of Babylon, sit on the ground, for thou shalt no more be called tender and delicate. Thy nakedness shall be uncovered; yea, thy shame shall be seen: (but) I will take vengeance". (Isaiah 47:1-3).

Noah and his priests were drunkards, as well, who were "lifted up in the pride of their hearts (and) did boast in their own strength". (V. 15-19). Thus, is described the world's philosophy of self-sufficiency. Devoid of humility, it is highly egotistical. It makes men and women the arbiters of all things, when they look to no source higher than themselves for the solution to every problem and the answer to every question. Such a philosophy is diametrically opposed to that of the divine model that is expressed in humility, selflessness, and child-line faith.

It was within this religious vacuum that a prophet named Abinadi appeared in the Land of Nephi. We do not know where he came from, or from whom he received his priesthood authority, but from the account provided by Mormon we know that his life was a study in commitment, and that he spoke with the power of God. (V. 20)

But Noah and the other Nephites of the people of Zeniff were zealots, who embraced the tribal and related customs and institutions of an earlier time. As such, they were particularly unreceptive to the total condemnation of their apostate practices by Abinadi since they prided themselves on their separatism and in their reestablishment of what they saw as a plausible system.

Moreover, Noah was a charismatic leader, and "the eyes of the people were blinded; therefore, they hardened their hearts against the words of Abinadi". (V. 29). From this time on, Abinadi found himself in circumstances similar to those of Lehi in Jerusalem, when the people had sought to take his life.

His message would provide a text for all the great religious activists, who, like Martin Luther "sought nothing beyond reforming the Church in conformity with the Holy Scriptures". He wrote: "The spiritual powers have been not only corrupted by sin, but have been absolutely destroyed; so that there is now nothing in them but a depraved reason and a will that is the enemy and opponent of God. I simply say that Christianity has ceased to exist among those who should have preserved it". (Ernest Schweibert, "Luther and His Times: The Reformation from a New Perspective," 1950, p. 509).

Mosiah
Chapter 12

Because of the persecution he experienced in the Land of Nephi, Abinadi went into hiding for two full years before returning at the Lord's command to preach to the people of Noah. (V. 1). In verses 2-7, Abinadi outlined how the Lord would deal with the wicked Nephites. They would suffer from the terrible effects of bondage, and from famine and pestilence. (V. 2, & 4). In sum, they would "be smitten with the east wind". (V. 6, see Commentary Reference to Mosiah 7:31). This symbolized disaster to the Nephites, because in the Holy Land, east winds brought crop-destroying sandstorms. (See Commentary Reference to Mosiah 7:31). Noah's own fate was foretold in verse 2. His life would "be valued even as a garment in a hot furnace". This was a reference to the manner of his death. (See Mosiah 13:10).

Even so, God's unconditional love for His children was illustrated when Abinadi quoted the Master, saying of this people hardened in iniquity: "Except they repent, I will utterly destroy them". (V. 8). No matter how determinedly they had turned their backs on Him; God still extended His hand, and offered them mercy conditioned only on repentance.

Instead, the infuriated populace took Abinadi, bound him, and carried him to the king, there to be judged for his supposed crimes. Under ancient Israelite law, the general population was primarily obligated to enforce the law. Abinadi's apprehension by the people and the ensuing deliberation over their accusations constituted a legitimate trial.

There can be little doubt that one of the basic charges brought against Abinadi was that of false prophecy. The people reported to the king: "He saith that thou shalt be as a stalk, even as a dry stalk of the field, which is run over by the beasts, and trodden under foot". (V. 11). These are classic Near Eastern curses, or "oaths of adjuration," and the charge was that Abinadi had pretended that the Lord had spoken them. (V. 12). The claim of the people was that Abinadi had "prophesied in vain". (V. 13). Inasmuch as false prophecy was a crime in ancient Israel, Abinadi was delivered into the hands of Noah, setting the stage for the king and his priests to render judgment in the case. (V. 16).

First, Abinadi was cast into prison. (V. 17). Prisons had limited use in the administration of justice in ancient Israel, and their purpose was basically to hold the accused pending their trial. Very few punishment alternatives existed under Israelite law. Either Abinadi had to be freed, or the ultimate penalty had to be imposed, inasmuch as death was the most common punishment for serious offenses under Israelite law.

The prophet was brought before the king and his priests so that "they might have wherewith to accuse him". (V. 18-19). Israelite law preferred not to sentence anyone to death without first extracting from that person a confession of his own guilt. Noah and his priests constructed their questions in order to trap Abinadi, so that he might speedily acknowledge his guilt, so they could be done with the matter. But to their surprise, "he did withstand them in all their questions". (V. 19). He had a message, and he was not about to let the cunning of Noah prevent him from delivering it.

In verses 20-24, the priests asked Abinadi why he bore tidings of doom and destruction, whereas Isaiah had declared that a true prophet is one who brings good tidings and publishes peace: "How beautiful upon the mountains are the feet of him that bringeth good tidings," quoted the priests, "that publisheth peace; that bringeth good tidings of good, that publisheth salvation; that saith unto Zion, Thy God reigneth". (Isaiah 52:7-10). But their very question provided Abinadi with an ideal foundation for his intended presentation. It was not something the priests wanted to hear.

The prophet refrained from specifically interpreting this prophecy until after he had derided Noah and his priests for their ignorance of the Law of Moses and for their failure to teach it to the people. (See Mosiah 15:11-19). "Are you priests," he asked, "and pretend to teach this people, and to understand the spirit of prophesying, and yet desire to know of me what these things mean?" (V. 25). He powerfully denounced the priests, who were all form and no substance, who had a form of godliness, and yet denied the power thereof.

In verses 25-32, Abinadi probed the depth of knowledge of the priests and their commitment to the Law. He turned the tables on them, he becoming the inquisitor, and they the defendants. His questions had great depth: "If ye teach the law of Moses, why do ye not keep it?" he asked. (V. 29). He appealed to the priests themselves and to God as his Witness, declaring, "Ye know that I speak the truth; and you ought to tremble before God". (V. 30). He pressed the priests to acknowledge that salvation came by the Law of Moses. (V. 32). In Mosiah 13:27-35, Abinadi would build upon this admission, to bear powerful witness that the Law itself was a type of the Messiah to come. In verses 33-34, and in Mosiah 13:13-24, Abinadi outlined the Ten Commandments and asked if the priests were obedient to them.

Mosiah
Chapter 13

King Noah's reaction to the boldness of Abinadi was to pronounce him mad, that anciently was a term used to describe false prophets. (V. 4). Then, Noah attempted to have him slain, having established to his own satisfaction justification for doing so. (V. 1). However, it was typical in antiquity to appeal to Deity to verify one's innocence, and this was Abinadi's response to the immediate threat from Noah. (V. 3).

The Spirit of the Lord came upon him, and his face "shone with exceeding luster". (V. 5). When Moses returned from Mt. Sinai, his face also had shone with the glory of the Lord. (See Exodus 34:30). Abinadi spoke with "authority from God" (V. 6), and King Noah and his wicked priests were powerless to intervene as he recited the rest of the Ten Commandments and expounded the scriptures. (V. 7-9).

Here in the 13th chapter of Mosiah, in Exodus Chapter 20, and in Deuteronomy Chapter 5, are the only places in the entire Standard Works where the Ten Commandments are listed in sequence. Some people have the idea that they were first given to Moses on Sinai, but this is not the case. They are from the beginning, and were understood in righteous communities from the days of Adam, to whom the Fulness of The Gospel had first been given. Spencer W. Kimball taught: "The Ten Commandments even antedated earth life, and were part of the test for mortals established in the Council of Heaven". The Law and the Prophets form the basis of our moral and ethical beliefs, and lie at the foundation of the Gospel Plan.

The Nephites carried the Decalogue upon the Plates of Brass to the Promised Land, and we know that Abinadi had a written copy of these scriptures, because he referred to them during his discourse. "And now I read unto you the remainder of the commandments of God," said Abinadi, "for I perceive that they are not written in your hearts; I perceive that ye have studied and taught iniquity the most part of your lives". (V. 11, see 2 Corinthians 3:3). This verse and Mosiah 15:26-27 suggest that King Noah and his priests had sunk to such depths of apostasy that they were breaking all ten of the commandments.

The Law of Moses was a Law of Carnal Commandments including the Ten Commandments and basic principles of the Gospel such as faith, repentance, baptism, and the gift of the Holy Ghost. It was a preparatory Gospel, and its outward ordinances were "types of things to come". Their purpose was to point the people toward Christ. (V. 31). "For this end," wrote Nephi, "hath the law of Moses been given; and all things which have been given of God from the beginning of the world, unto man, are the typifying of him". (2 Nephi 11:4). Paul would teach the same principles to the Galatians that Abinadi had taught to the wicked priests of Noah. Salvation does not come through obedience to the Law of Moses alone, but rather through Christ. (V. 27).

"The Law was our schoolmaster to bring us to Christ". (Galatians 3:24-26, see Mosiah 3:14-15, Alma 25:15-16, 34:14, 37:38-45, & Helaman 8:14-16). It was fulfilled at the time of the Resurrection of the Savior. (See 3 Nephi 15:8). Our own dispensation contains the Fulness of the Gospel, meaning every Gospel law, ordinance, and covenant necessary for salvation and exaltation has been revealed and is currently available to the faithful through the Lord's authorized servants.

Abinadi painted a powerful portrait heavy with symbolism that should have penetrated even the hardened hearts of these apostate Nephites, especially when Noah himself was again warned that the fate of the prophet would be tied to the king's, and that it would be "as a type and a shadow of things which are to come". (V. 10, see Mosiah 17:18 & Alma 25:10).

Mosiah
Chapter 14

In chapters 12 and 13, Abinadi had taught King Noah and his priests about the Mosaic Law, or Law of Carnal Commandments, and its relationship to the Promised Messiah. This chapter in Mormon's abridgement is a continuation of his discourse. Here Abinadi commenced an extensive quotation from the Plates of Brass, reading from Isaiah Chapter 53 because of that prophet's clear understanding of the mission of the Savior.

Isaiah asked: "To whom is the arm (or power) of the Lord revealed?" (V. 1). The answer is to no-one, for the Jews did not believe in Christ, His mighty works notwithstanding. "But though he had done so many miracles before them," wrote the Apostle John, "yet they believed not on him; that the saying of Esaias the prophet might be fulfilled, which he spake, Lord, who hath believed our report? and to whom hath the arm of the Lord been revealed? (John 12:37-38).

Instead, the Mortal Messiah would bring new life to a spiritually dead world, although He would appear as other men, and would humbly avoid the limelight. (V. 2). During His mortal ministry He would never command center stage. As a matter of fact, it would have been counterproductive to the purpose of His ministry to do so. Instead, He would be "despised and rejected of men," and many who witnessed the events of His ministry would incorrectly assume that He suffered because He had done wrong. (V. 3, see 1 Nephi 19:14). But it was He who "has borne our griefs, and carried our sorrows." (V. 4).

Verses 5 and 6 make clear that the Lord is our Redeemer. "With his stripes (or bruises) we are healed". He made possible our redemption. Even though all have transgressed the law, He has quietly borne all our sins. Even during the mockery of His trial, He maintained a dignified silence. (V. 7). By oppression and a miscarriage of justice, His life was taken, and now "who shall declare his generation," or, in a very special sense, who shall be His posterity? (V. 8, see Commentary Reference to Mosiah 5:7 & to Mosiah 15:7).

While His body lay in the borrowed tomb of Joseph of Arimathea, He opened the door to the Spirit

Prison. (V. 9). Our Father knew that His Son must suffer, to bring to pass our immortality and eternal life: "Yet it pleased the Lord (or the Father) to bruise him." (V. 10, see Mosiah 15:7-8).

When the Father allowed the sacrifice of His Son to satisfy the demands of Justice, which required punishment as the consequence of the violation of eternal law, the way was opened for the obedient to be born again and to become His spiritual posterity. To the extent that the faithful would partake of the fruit of the Tree of Life, which is eternal life, the purpose of the Lord would be accomplished. (V. 10, see 1 Nephi 8:30, & Mosiah 5:7).

Verses 11 and 12 illustrate the triumph of the Lord through His suffering. He shall see His efforts bear fruit, and because of His affliction, His disciples will bear the message of salvation to many. Our Father will see to it that His Son's suffering satisfies the requirements of the Law of Justice, that all who repent may be saved as a result of His Atonement.

Abinadi's powerful presentation of Isaiah's teachings should have been of great significance to the wicked Nephites in his audience. Had they taken his message literally and personally, it would have changed the course of their lives. As a matter of fact, only one of the priests of Noah was touched, and he prostrated himself upon the altar of sacrifice before the Lord with a broken heart and a contrite spirit. His name was Alma. (See Mosiah 17:2).

Mosiah
Chapter 15

Abinadi expounded upon Isaiah Chapter 53 in the first 13 verses of this chapter. He said that the God of the Old Testament should "come down among the children of men". (V. 1). We know that this is Jesus Christ, for He declared to the Nephites: "Behold, I am he that gave the law, and I am he who covenanted with my people Israel". (3 Nephi 15:5).

Many Book of Mormon names have linguistic roots, and Abinadi is one of them. It means "My Divine Father is present". This subtle stylistic feature of The Book of Mormon is called "metonymy," which is "the practice of giving a person or place a name whose meaning reflects an event or trait associated with that person or place. A closely related practice sees a person's name become symbolic of some phenomenon". (FARMS Preliminary Report). Many examples of metonymy can be documented in The Book of Mormon.

Jesus Christ is properly called both the Father and the Son. (V. 2). Heavenly Father and His Son "are one God, yea, the very Eternal Father of heaven and of earth". (V. 4). Latter-day Saints understand that there is a physical and spiritual rapport between the Father and the Son, and between Them and the true believer. Through this rapport that is effected by the Holy Ghost, we become "one" in a spiritual sense. (See Commentary Reference to Mosiah 5:6-7).

This is a unique teaching of The Church of Jesus Christ of Latter-day Saints. It derives from doctrine found in the Standard Works and in the teachings of Latter-day prophets. Stephen Robinson, in his very insightful book entitled "Are Mormons Christian?" has written: "Non-LDS Christians usually think of the Godhead (the Trinity) in ambiguous terms. They habitually, and most often unconsciously, equate the biblical teaching on the nature of the Godhead with the later philosophical statement formulated at the Council of Chalcedon in A.D. 451 - the Nicene Creed. But these two ways of perceiving God are simply not equivalent.

Biblical theology, like LDS theology, affirms the threefold nature of the Godhead; but also, like LDS theology, biblical theology lacks any indication of a Nicene understanding. Ultimately, being Christian is less a matter of perceiving God in the same Nicene or Chalcedonian terms as other Christians do, and more a matter of perceiving God in the same biblical terms as the first Christians did.

The Latter-day Saint concept of God differs from that of Nicene orthodoxy in more than just the latter's Trinitarian doctrine. The Latter-day Saints teach that God the Father is an anthropomorphic being - that is, that he has a tangible body: "The Father has a body of flesh and bones as tangible as man's; the Son also; but the Holy Ghost has not a body of flesh and bones, but is a personage of Spirit. Were it not so, the Holy Ghost could not dwell in us". (D&C 130:22.)

Some critics of the Latter-day Saints have argued that belief in an anthropomorphic Deity represents a departure not merely from the Nicene conception of God but from the biblical teaching as well, since John 4:24 teaches very clearly that "God is a Spirit: and they that worship him must worship him in spirit and in truth". But the Latter-day Saints do not dispute this passage at all, unless it is interpreted as limiting God to being merely a spirit.

The Latter-day Saints accept unequivocally all the biblical teachings on the nature of God, but they reject the extra-biblical elaborations of the councils and creeds. A doctrinal exclusion applied to the Latter-day Saints for rejecting the Nicene doctrine of the Trinity is invalid because that doctrine was not taught in the Bible or in the early Christian Church. It is not found in the teachings of the Apostolic Fathers or those of the Greek Apologists.

Latter-day Saints agree that God the Father is spirit in the highest sense of the word, but they deny that this limits him to incorporeality. God is a spirit in the person of the Holy Ghost, but in the person of the Son, God has a tangible body. On the grounds of modern revelation, Latter-day Saints believe that God the Father also has a tangible body, but they grant that this cannot be proved or disproved from the Bible. Still, given their philosophical assumptions, it is the orthodox who must, without biblical warrant, dismiss the biblical anthropomorphisms applied to God as merely figurative, while the Latter-day Saints accept them at face value. The anthropomorphic view of God is compatible with biblical imagery, but conflicts with the Greek philosophical definition of God. If conceiving of God in anthropomorphic terms, as the Latter-day Saints do, excludes one from being a Christian, then most Christians, both ancient and modern, must also be excluded, for most are guilty in some degree of conceiving of God in anthropomorphic biblical terms rather than in the abstract terms of philosophical theology. Moreover," concluded Brother Robinson, "since the Bible itself describes God in anthropomorphic language, even if such descriptions are understood merely as helpful symbolism or allegory, it cannot be seriously argued that perceiving God in anthropomorphic terms is an un-Christian practice".

Members of the Church understand this concept because it is spiritually discerned by direct experience. "But the natural man receiveth not the things of the Spirit of God: for they are foolishness unto him: neither can he know them, because they are spiritually discerned". (1 Corinthians 2:14).

Elohim is our Heavenly Father. We were born of Him as His spirit children. We acquired His spiritual qualities and characteristics, and were raised by Him to spiritual maturity until we could progress no more. There were some laws that pertain only to mortality that we could not have the opportunity to obey as spirit children, and so there were some blessings that were unavailable to us. Therefore, we left His presence to fulfil a mission on earth. Even now, living in a foreign land, we are yet His spirit sons and daughters who enjoy a measure of His divine nature. If we continue to develop His characteristics during this period of probation we will eventually become as He is. We will assume both the image and likeness of God. (See Ether 3:15-17, Genesis 1:26-27, & 5:3, D&C 20:18, Moses 2:26, & 6:8-9, & Abraham 4:26).

Our earthly fathers have given us mortal life, and, in general, we have acquired their qualities and characteristics that pertain to mortality. We bear their names and reflect their nature. If they have been honorable, we may choose to emulate them, and become as they are. Jesus Christ gave all mankind immortality or life beyond the grave, through the Resurrection. Thus, He is the Father of all the family of man. Through the sanctifying influence of His Atonement, we may all be spiritually reborn as well. Thus, He becomes the Father of all who follow His example and subordinate their will to His.

Through this rebirth, we acquire the distinctive characteristics of Christ, become partakers of His divine nature, and become His sons and daughters. By the covenant of baptism, we take upon ourselves a new name, which is His name, and by our obedience to the principles of the Gospel, we enjoy the companionship of His Spirit. This rebirth permits a mighty change in our nature, so that we may become as He is.

Christ is the Father in the sense that He is the Creator of heaven and earth, and because He has assumed the full stature of His Own Father, inasmuch as He possesses the gifts and power by which we may be brought to perfection. Thus, Jesus taught: "He that hath seen me hath seen the Father". (John 14:9, see John 1:18, & 12:45).

He is the Son, inasmuch as He was the Firstborn in the Spirit and is "the firstborn of every creature". (Colossians 1:15-19, see D&C 93:21). He is also the Son because He submitted to the will of the Father. (See Hebrews 12:9). The Apostle John recorded that Jesus "received not of the fulness at the first, but received grace for grace". (D&C 93:12). Through His obedience, more and more power was given, until a fulness of power was received. (See Ether 12:27). The conditions by which all of God's children may receive this power are submission to His will and obedience to His commandments.

Jesus was the perfect example of submission and obedience. "And it came to pass that Jesus grew up with his brethren, and waxed strong, and waited upon the Lord for the time of his ministry to come. And he served under his father, and he spoke not as other men, neither could he be taught, for he needed not that any man should teach him. And after many years, the hour of his ministry grew nigh". (J.S.T. Matthew 3:22-25).

We are not capable of perfection through our own efforts. A greater endowment, or gift of power beyond our own capabilities, is required. The Savior is able to provide that gift for us, for He has been divinely invested with the power of God the Father. Through the Atonement, we are spiritually born of Him.

Abinadi made a very interesting observation in verse 5, suggesting that when the Son of God became mortal, His flesh, or his earthly inclinations and characteristics, were at all times subject to his Spirit. We are, after all, spiritual beings having mortal experiences.. As a result, Jesus did not yield to temptation, but led a sinless life. The key, then, is to develop the same sense of discipline, by making the flesh at all times subject to the Spirit. The Savior commanded: "Therefore, I would that ye should be perfect even as I, or your Father who is in heaven is perfect". (3 Nephi 12:48).

In spite of His innocence, He was crucified, and He suffered death when His mortal body "gave up the ghost". (V. 7). However, having been born of a mortal mother and an immortal father, Jesus had inherited power over death. He was never subject to death; therefore, He was not under the curse of Adam's transgression. "For as in Adam all die, even so in Christ shall all be made alive". (1 Corinthians 15:22, see 2 Nephi 25:25, & Mosiah 3:11).

He declared that He had life in Himself so that He could lay down His life and take it again. "For as the Father hath life in himself; so hath he given to the Son to have life in himself; And hath given him authority to execute judgment also, because he is the Son of man" of Holiness. (John 5:25-27). "Thus, He became the Resurrection and the Life, with power to open the door to eternity, and redeem from Satan's power every living creature". (Joseph Fielding Smith, "Man: His Origin & Destiny," p. 379 see V. 8).

Again, Abinadi echoed King Benjamin, asking Noah and his wicked priests: "And now I say unto you, who shall declare his generation? Behold, I say unto you, that when his soul has been made an offering for sin he shall see his seed. And now what say ye?. And who shall be his seed? (V. 10). In other words: "Because of the covenant of baptism which you have made, can you call yourselves the Children of Christ, His sons and His daughters? Has He spiritually begotten you? Are your hearts changed through faith on His name because you are born of Him? Therefore, can you look forward to the day of your redemption?" (See Mosiah 5:7).

The priests of Noah did not qualify to be the spiritual posterity of Christ, or "his seed". (V. 11, see Mosiah 14:8). In Mosiah 12:21-24, the priests had mistaken Isaiah's prophecy of the message and mission of the Messiah, who was the official herald of the Gospel, for a criterion of the appropriate behavior of a true prophet. Abinadi had refrained from interpreting this prophecy until after he had derided the king and his priests for their ignorance of the Law of Moses, and for their failure to teach it to the people.

But in verses 14-19, Abinadi provided the answer to the initial question that had been posed by the priests: "What meaneth the words which are written, and which have been taught by our fathers, saying: How beautiful upon the mountains are the feet of him that bringeth good tidings (and) that publisheth salvation; that saith unto Zion, Thy God reigneth?" (Mosiah 12:21-24)

"The seed of Christ" or "the heirs of the kingdom of God" are "they who have published peace". (V. 11 & 14). The Lord is "the founder of peace". (V. 18). "My peace I give unto you," promised the Savior, "not as the world giveth, give I unto you". (John 14:27). His peace "is not the peace of the world, of ease, of luxury, idleness, absence of turmoil, and strife, but the peace born of the righteous life, the peace that lifts the soul, that day by day brings us closer to the home of Eternal Peace, the dwelling place of our Father". (J. Reuben Clark, Jr.).

Redemption was conceived and set in motion even before the creation of the dwelling place of mortal man. (V. 19). When the time of His ministry drew nigh, He had already proven Himself capable and worthy of exercising the power manifested in the priesthood Keys of Resurrection for all mankind. (V. 20, see John 11:25). He is the Christ, the Anointed One, the Great Jehovah, and the Messiah of the Old Testament. (V. 21, see 3 Nephi 15:5).

Those who will participate in the First Resurrection and who will inherit eternal life, will be those who have kept the commandments of God, as well as those who have died "in their ignorance, not having salvation declared unto them". (V. 22-24). Many persons have been faithful to the doctrines that they have been taught. They cannot be condemned for that which was done in faith and obedience to the principles that they devoutly believed. The Lord will judge us by the intent of our hearts, as well as by our understanding. (See Joseph Fielding Smith, Jr., "Answers to Gospel Questions," 4:77). "And he that hath no understanding, it remaineth in me to do according as it is written". (D&C 29:50).

Those who have died "in their ignorance" are they who would evidently have accepted the Gospel while in mortality, had they had the opportunity to do so. "All who have died without a knowledge of this Gospel, who would have received it if they had been permitted to tarry, shall be heirs of the celestial kingdom of God; Also all that shall die henceforth without a knowledge of it, who would have received it with all their hearts, shall be heirs of that kingdom; For I, the Lord, will judge all men according to their works, according to the desire of their hearts". (D&C 137:7-8). According to the law, they may be resurrected after accepting the Gospel, after it has been preached to them in the Spirit World, and when the ordinances typifying their obedience to eternal covenants have been performed vicariously in the temple. (See Commentary References to Mosiah 5:5-15, & Mosiah Chapter 16).

Abinadi explained: "Little children also have eternal life". (V. 25). They are "redeemed from the foundation of the world through (the) Only Begotten". (D&C 29:46). "All children who die before they arrive at the years of accountability are saved in the celestial kingdom of heaven". (D&C 137:10). In other words, provision for their exaltation was made at the Grand Council in Heaven even before the world was. "Little children cannot (or 'need not') repent; wherefore, it is awful wickedness to deny the pure mercies of God unto them, for they are all alive in him because of his mercy". (Moroni 8:19).

Having clearly established the conditions by which the Saints might enjoy resurrection, Abinadi turned his attention to those who would come forth in the Second Resurrection of the Unjust. (V. 26-27, see John 5:28-29, Acts 24:15, Revelation 20, D&C 76:17, 88:22-31, & 97:102). He knew this subject would strike a sensitive chord in the hearts of the unrepentant priests and so he declared: "Therefore, ought ye not to tremble?" (V. 27).

Abinadi delivered his warning with boldness. He knew that the impact should cause his apostate listeners, clothed in the robes of the false priesthood, to quake and tremble. It mattered not at all to him that his temporal welfare hung in the balance. He fearlessly broke forth into a psalm of thanksgiving in verses 29-31. In spite of the stark reality of his imprisonment, the mockery of his trial before King Noah, and the probability of his imminent martyrdom, Abinadi's rapture was itself evidence of the validity of his message.

He had previously stood before his accusers and declared: "The holy prophets are they who have published peace, who have brought good tidings who have published salvation; and saith unto Zion: Thy God reigneth!" (V. 13-14). Now, in the midst of the turmoil and tension of his trial, he exhibited the intrinsic majesty with which his Father had endowed him. The declaration of the Master is universally applicable, but was particularly appropriate to Abinadi's circumstances: "Peace I leave with you, my peace I give unto you," He promised, "not as the world giveth, give I unto you. Let not your heart be troubled, neither let it be afraid". (John 14:27).

When reading the account of Abinadi standing in chains before the court of King Noah, we are reminded of the similar experience of the Prophet Joseph Smith. On the occasion just after his acquittal of false charges before Missourians, he declared: "All is well between me and the heavens; I have no enmity against anyone; and as the prayer of Jesus, so I pray - 'Father, forgive me my trespasses as I forgive those who trespass against me,' for I freely forgive all men. If we would secure and cultivate the love of others, we must love others, even our enemies as well as our friends". (H.C., 5:498).

On another occasion, just before his own martyrdom, he said: "I am calm as a summer's morning; I have a conscience void of offense towards God, and towards all men". (D& C 135:4). Joseph Smith and Abinadi have given each of us the courage to walk in the valley of the shadow of death, and yet to fear no evil. (See Psalms 233, & Commentary Reference to Mosiah 17:18). Even in the midst of the "evils and designs which do and will exist in the hearts of conspiring men in the last days," the Saints may take comfort in the word of the Lord, that He will support us "against all the fiery darts of the adversary," and be with us "in every time of trouble". (D&C 80:4, & 3:8).

When Joseph was a prisoner in Liberty Jail, incarcerated for months on false charges and the subject of the repeated verbal abuse of the guards, he was finally moved to stand and exclaim: "Silence, ye fiends of the infernal pit. In the name of Jesus Christ, I rebuke you, and command you to be still. I will not live another minute and hear such language. Cease such talk, or your or I die this instant". He ceased to speak. "He stood erect in terrible majesty, chained, and without a weapon, calm, unruffled, and dignified as an angel. He looked down upon his quailing guards, whose knees smote together, and who, shrinking into a corner, or crouching at his feet, begged his pardon, and remained quiet until an exchange of guards. I have seen ministers of justice," recalled Parley P. Pratt, who was a witness to this scene, "clothed in ministerial robes and criminals arraigned before them, while life was suspended upon a breath in the courts of England. I have witnessed a Congress in solemn session to give laws to nations. I have tried to conceive of kings, of royal courts, of thrones and crowns, and of emperors assembled to decide the fate of kingdoms, but dignity and majesty have I seen but once, as it stood in chains, at midnight, in a dungeon, in an obscure village in Missouri". (Parley P. Pratt, "Autobiography," p. 210-211).

Jacob Bronowski wrote: "We are all afraid - for our confidence, for the future, for the world. That is the nature of the human imagination. Yet, every man and woman, every civilization, has gone forward because of its engagement with what it has set itself to do. Our personal commitment to our skills, our intellectual and emotional commitment working together as one, has made the Ascent of Man". ("The Ascent of Man," p. 438).

The religious commitment of the servants of God sheds new light on our potential and opens up to our minds a profoundly deeper perspective. Someone once said of Joseph Smith: "One of his greatest contributions was his knowledge of what is to come after death. He did much to clarify our understanding of heaven, and to make it seem worth working for". The same could be said of the Prophet Abinadi.

The prophet Abinadi expounded upon Isaiah Chapter 53 in the first 13 verses of this chapter. He said that the God of the Old Testament should "come down among the children of men". (V. 1). We know that this is Jesus Christ, for He declared to the Nephites: "Behold, I am he that gave the law, and I am he who covenanted with my people Israel". (3 Nephi 15:5).

Mosiah
Chapter 16

Abinadi prophesied: "The time shall come when all shall see the salvation of the Lord; when every nation, kindred, tongue, and people shall see eye to eye and shall confess before God that his judgments are just". This shall take place as a result of the universality of the resurrection just before, during, and at the end of the Millennium. Still, we must do more to obtain eternal life in the Celestial Kingdom than just acknowledge that Jesus Christ is Lord. There is a difference between accepting Jesus Christ, and accepting the Gospel.

If, as Joseph Fielding Smith, Jr. taught: "The vast majority of mankind will go into the telestial kingdom," the question of eternal progression becomes vitally important to those billions of souls whose improvement would seem to halt at the Last Judgment. Was Heavenly Father's perfect Plan designed to save only a small percentage of His spirit children in the Celestial Kingdom? Is agency during mortality so significant that our actions here will forever determine our status? Before the Fall, Adam lived in the Garden of Eden in a morally static, vegetative state. Will his posterity repeat that scenario and do so again?

The question whether we may add to our glory to such a degree that we can eternally progress not only within kingdoms, but also from one degree of glory to another, remains unsettled in the Church. As a matter of fact, the position of the First Presidency is one of neutrality. It says: "The Church has never announced a definite doctrine upon this point. Some of the Brethren have held the view that it was possible in the course of progression to advance from one glory to another, involving the principle of eternal progression; others of the Brethren have taken an opposite view. But, as stated, the Church has never announced a definite doctrine on this point". (Joseph Anderson, Secretary to the First Presidency, 3/5, 1952).

D&C 76:112 has been quoted as one evidence that progression between degrees of glory is not possible: "And they (referring to those who inherit telestial glory) shall be servants of the Most High; but where God and Christ dwell they cannot come, worlds without end".

It has been argued that the time when we may elect to live a celestial law has passed when we are judged and assigned to a lesser kingdom of glory. Thereafter, it is said that we may progress only within the limitations of whichever kingdom within which we find ourselves. Our progression is not to the extent that would ever lead us to live a celestial law. To put it another way, we lose the ability to exercise our capacity to become as God is because we have neglected to do so when the opportunity was available to us.

However, the statement by the Secretary to The First Presidency quoted above recognizes that there are faithful members of the Church who believe that it may be possible to progress from one degree of glory to another. They point out that D&C 76:112 does not talk about progression from one degree of glory to another but only states that those who persist in exhibiting telestial characteristics cannot come where God and Christ dwell. This passage refers to qualities of general classes of people rather than to individuals, and does not say what will happen to those who change their nature. In other words, those with the described characteristics obviously cannot come where Christ is, but if they are able to make changes, they may no longer be prohibited from dwelling with God.

The general feeling of the message of D&C 76 may favor the idea of possible progression between kingdoms. Those in the telestial degree of glory are described as heirs of salvation through the ministration of angels who shall be servants of the Most High. (D&C 76:88 & 112). But the Lord revealed to Moses that His whole focus of attention, His very work and glory, is to bring about our immortality and eternal life. (Moses 1:28-29). Even David rejoiced that his soul would not be left in hell for all of eternity. (See Psalms 16:10).

Misunderstanding has arisen from D&C 76:73-74. "And again, we saw the terrestrial world, and behold and lo, these are they who are of the terrestrial ... Behold, these are they who died without law; and also, they who are the spirits of men kept in prison, whom the Son visited, and preached the Gospel unto them, that they might be judged according to men in the flesh; Who received not the testimony of Jesus in the flesh, but afterwards received it".

Some misinterpret these verses by erroneously thinking that they teach a doctrine that those who accept the Gospel after leaving this life will only be eligible for a terrestrial degree of glory. If that were true, then most of the work done in the temple would be ineffectual in accomplishing the end for which it was designed.

The difficulty arises out of a failure to recognize that there is a distinction between acceptance of the Gospel and acceptance of Jesus Christ. Those "who shall come forth in the resurrection of the just (are) they who received the testimony of Jesus, and believed on his name and were baptized ... That by keeping the commandments they might be washed and cleansed from all their sins, and receive the Holy Spirit by the laying on of the hands of him who is ordained and sealed unto this power; And who overcome by faith, and are sealed by the Holy Spirit of promise ... They are they who are the Church of the Firstborn". (D&C 76:51-54).

The acceptance of Jesus does not qualify us for the celestial kingdom. Many fine Christians accept Jesus, and they will still go to the terrestrial kingdom. These are they who "received not the Gospel, neither the testimony of Jesus, neither the prophets, neither the everlasting covenant. Last of all, these are all they who will not be gathered with the saints, to be caught up unto the Church of the Firstborn, and received into the cloud". (D&C 76:101-102).

Only those who embrace the Gospel may go to the highest degree of glory. "These are they who are priests and kings, who have received of his fulness, and of his glory; and are priests of the Most High, after the order of Melchizedek, which was after the order of Enoch, which was after the order of the Only Begotten Son. Wherefore, as it is written, they are gods, even the sons of God". (D&C 76:56-58, see John 10:34).

The Vision teaches that the Gospel was taught to the spirits kept in prison. If they accept Christ, and not the fulness of the Gospel, they will inherit the terrestrial kingdom. We might reasonably conclude that those who also accept the Gospel and have the necessary ordinances performed vicariously in the temple will be heirs of the celestial kingdom of glory. "These shall dwell in the presence of God and his Christ forever and ever". (D&C 76:62). And "the presence of the Lord shall be as the melting fire that burneth, and as the fire which causeth the waters to boil". (D&C 133:41). Those of His children who have grown to the stature of their Father and approach His dwelling place shall see "the transcendent beauty of the gate through which the heirs of that kingdom will enter, which (is) like unto circling flames of fire; also, the blazing throne of God, wherein (shall be) seated the Father and the Son". And the "beautiful streets of that kingdom, (that have) the appearance of being paved with gold". (D&C 137:2-4).

Some of the Brethren of the leadership of the Church have expressed tolerant views on this subject. A sampling of these is as follows:

1). "Environment will correspond to nature, with always the possibility present of improving both the environment and nature, until a fulness of joy is attained by each intelligent entity". (B.H. Roberts, "Joseph Smith the Prophet-Teacher," p. 27-28).

2). J. Reuben Clark, Jr. reasoned: "I am not a strict constructionist, believing that we seal our eternal progress by what we do here. It is my belief that God will save all His children that He can; and while, if we live unrighteously here, we shall not go to the other side in the same status, so to speak, as those who live righteously; nevertheless, the unrighteous will have their chance, and in the eons of the eternities that are to follow, they, too, may climb to the destinies to which they who are righteous and serve God, have climbed". (Church News, 3/23/1960).

3). "Everlasting blessedness is thoroughly consistent with justice," concluded James E. Talmage. "The souls that attain to salvation and eternal life shall have glory added upon their heads forever and ever. But the thought of never-ending punishment as the fate of all who die in their sins is repugnant, and rightly so. As reward for righteous living is to be proportionate to desserts, so punishment for sin must be graded according to the offense. The purpose of punishment is disciplinary, reformatory, and in support of justice. God's mercy is as truly manifest in the suffering which He allows, as in the joy of salvation which He bestows. As to the duration of punishment, we may take assurance that it shall be measured to the individual in just accordance with the sum of his iniquity. That every sentence for sin must be interminable is as directly opposed to a rational conception of justice as it is contradictory to the revealed Word of God.

It was mercifully foreordained that even the prisoners thronging the pit should in due time be visited (See Isaiah 24:21-22), and be offered means of amelioration. (See Isaiah 42:7). As has been noted above, David sang rapturously, 'Thou wilt not leave my soul in hell.' (Psalms 16:10). True, the scriptures speak of endless punishment, and depict everlasting burnings, eternal damnation, and the sufferings incident to unquenchable fire, as features of the Judgment reserved for the wicked. But none of these awful possibilities are anywhere in scripture declared to be the unending fate of the individual sinner.

Blessing or punishment ordained of God is eternal, for He is eternal, and eternal are all His ways. His is a system of endless and eternal punishment, for it will always exist as the place or condition provided for the rebellious and disobedient, but the penalty as visited upon the individual will terminate when through repentance and excipiation the necessary reform has been effected and the uttermost farthing paid.

Even to hell there is an exit as well as an entrance; and when sentence has been served, commuted perhaps by repentance and its attendant works, the prison doors shall open, and the penitent captive be afforded opportunity to comply with the law which he aforetime violated. But the prison remains, and the eternal decree prescribing punishment for the offender stands unrepealed. So it is even with the penal institutions established by man". (James E. Talmage, "The Vitality of Mormonism," pp. 264-265).

4). Brigham Young felt: "All organized existence is in progress either to an endless advancement in eternal perfections, or back to dissolution. There is no period in all the eternities wherein organized existence will become stationary, that it cannot advance in knowledge, wisdom, power, and glory". (J.D., 1:349).

5). There are certain points of doctrine that simply are not clear. To his son, Alma once declared: "Now these mysteries are not yet fully made known unto me; therefore, I shall forbear". (Alma 37:11). He felt that it was always better to keep one's opinion to oneself, rather than to speculate without the foundation of fact or specific revelation. Sometimes, it is better to remain silent and be thought a fool, rather than to speak and remove all doubt.

6). Joseph Smith declared to an assembly of the Saints: "I could explain a hundred-fold more than

I ever have of the glories of the kingdoms manifested to me in vision, were I permitted, and were the people prepared to receive them". (Joseph Smith, Jr., H.C., 5:402). The fact remains that we have not been given the revelation that answers the question regarding progression between kingdoms of glory.

With a greater appreciation of the concepts relating to resurrection to kingdoms of glory, let us return to Abinadi's discourse, wherein he stated that at the time of the Final Judgment, those who have not hearkened to the voice of the Lord will "have cause to howl, and weep, and wail, and gnash their teeth". (V. 2). The character of such people is that they "are carnal and devilish". (V. 3). For such individuals, it is "as though there was no redemption made," so far as regaining the presence of God is concerned. (V. 5).

Abinadi was so sure of the mortal mission of the Savior, that he spoke of it in the past tense. "And now, if Christ had not come into the world, speaking of things to come as though they had already come, there could have been no redemption. And if Christ had not risen from the dead, or have broken the bands of death that the graves should have no victory, and that death should have no sting, there could have been no resurrection. But there is a resurrection, therefore the grave hath no victory, and the sting of death is swallowed up in Christ". (V. 6-8). These verses remind us of Paul's teachings on the same subject wherein he quoted the same scriptures that were available to Abinadi. "So, when this corruptible shall have put on incorruption, and this mortal shall have put on immortality, then shall be brought to pass the saying that is written, Death is swallowed up in victory. O death, where is thy sting? O grave, where is thy victory?" (1 Corinthians 15:54-55)

Paul said that the sting of death, which is sin (1 Corinthians 15:56) "is swallowed up in Christ" since He accepted the responsibility to deal with physical and spiritual death through His Atonement and the Resurrection. (V. 8). Abinadi characterized Christ as "the light and the life of the world; yea, a light that is endless, that can never be darkened; yea, and also a life which is endless; that there can be no more death". (V. 9).

Christ is the Light of the world, and when His Spirit quickens us, we are like white-hot sparks struck off the divine anvil of God. "I said to the man who stood at the gate of the year, 'Give me a light, that I may tread safely into the unknown.' And he replied, 'Go out into the darkness, and put your hand in the hand of God. That shall be to you better than a light, and safer than the known way.' (Minnie Haskins, "A Dialogue Between a Man, and the Keeper of The Gate of The Year"). "Faith in Christ is not a leap in the dark. It is, instead, trust in what ours spirits learned eons ago, and religious recognition is just that - re-cognition, a re-knowing. ("The Truth, The Way, The Life: B.H. Roberts' Masterwork," B.Y.U. Studies, V. 15). "Intelligence cleaveth unto intelligence, truth embraceth truth, (and) light cleaveth unto light". (D&C 88:40).

Christ is the Life of the world. He said: "I am the resurrection and the life; he that believeth in me, though he were dead, yet shall he live. And whosoever liveth and believeth in me shall never die".

(John 11:25-26). "God so loved the world, that He gave his Only Begotten Son, that whosoever believeth in Him should not perish, but have everlasting life". (John 3:16, see 3 Nephi 27:13-14). We sometimes fail to remember that Heavenly Father intervened in our lives in an intensely personal way when He sent His Son to be the Savior of the world. If we are to love the way Heavenly Father and Jesus Christ love, if we are to have the pure love of Christ in our own lives, we must become intertwined within the lives of others in ways that are equally intense and personal. We must find ways to influence others for good, even at the cost of personal sacrifice. We must never forget the two greatest commandments are to love the Lord, and to love our neighbors.

The Spirit of men and women is the candle of the Lord. "The Life of Christ may envelop our lives, (which) even in their most secular details, may be sacramental". (Truman Madsen). C.S. Lewis said: "It is a serious thing to live in a society of possible Gods and Goddesses, and to remember that the dullest and most uninteresting person you talk to may one day be a creature which if you saw it now, you would be strongly tempted to worship. It is in the light of this overwhelming possibility, it is with the awe and the circumspection proper to it, that we should conduct all our dealings with one another. There are no ordinary people. You have never talked to a mere mortal; it is immortals with whom we joke, work, marry, snub and exploit. Our charity must be a real and costly love. Next to the blessed sacrament itself, your neighbor is the holiest object presented to your senses, for in him also Christ is truly hidden and glorified". ("The Weight of Glory", p. 14).

Our progression is boundless. "The command to be perfect is not idealistic gas. "Nor is it a command to do the impossible," wrote Lewis. "He is going to make us into creatures that can obey that command. In the Bible, He said that we were 'gods', and He is going to make good His words, if we let Him. He will make the feeblest and filthiest of us into a god or goddess, dazzling, radiant, immortal creature, pulsating all through with such energy and joy and wisdom and love as we cannot now imagine, a bright stainless mirror which reflects back to God perfectly His own boundless power and delight and goodness. The process will be long and in parts very painful; but that is what we are in for. Nothing less. He meant what He said". (The Weight of Glory," p. 14-15). We were created in His image. There is a divine center in the human genome, and to be fashioned in His likeness will take us to an entirely different dimension. Conformity to the will of God will be manifest in spiritual power. Truly, our potential will be expressed in lives that are in harmony with God's Plan that is a roadmap to the stars, and that will guide us safely Home.

As the Lord's servant, Abinadi delivered His message with clarity, echoing the words of the Master, Who declared: "I am the way, the truth, and the life; no man cometh unto the Father, but by me". (John 14:6). Now, he vividly described the ultimate state of the righteous, contrasting it with that of the wicked. "Even this mortal shall put on immortality, and this corruption shall put on incorruption, and (all mankind) shall be brought to stand before the bar of God, to be judged of him according to their works whether they be good or whether they be evil. If they be good, to the resurrection of endless life and happiness; and if they be evil, to the resurrection of endless damnation, being delivered up to the devil, who hath subjected them, which is damnation". (V. 10-12).

Abinadi again asked the priests: "Ought ye not to tremble and repent of your sins, and remember that only in and through Christ ye can be saved". (V. 13). He urged them to look to Christ, who is "the very Eternal Father" by divine investiture of authority from Elohim and in the sense that He is Creator of the Earth and the Father of the faithful. (V. 15).

Because of the testimony of the Spirit and those powerful written and spoken testimonies of men and women like Abinadi, members of The Church of Jesus Christ of Latter-day Saints may claim, as no other people, that they believe in Christ. They belong to His Church. The Book of Mormon is Another Testament of Jesus Christ. They are Saints of the Most High God!

Members of His Church speak and testify of His ante-mortal existence, and His foreordination to be the Redeemer of the world. They speak in reverential awe of the scriptures that describe His relationship with our Father, and of His divine investiture of authority. His appearances to His servants throughout history were many. The Book of Mormon, particularly, explains His condescension in taking a mortal body. Thus, all those children whom He has spiritually begotten can better understand the relationship between His power, might, dominion, and authority and the temptation to which He was subjected.

In His baptism, He demonstrated by example the way for us to follow. In His ministry, He taught the truths of the Gospel in simplicity. In the Garden of Gethsemane, He demonstrated His strength and compassion. The crucifixion, then, was only an apostrophe, His death but a pause for reflection, to permit us to re-focus our attention on His resurrection and ascension into heaven.

When He comes again, it will be in the clouds. The Church of the Firstborn will accompany him, and His Second Coming will usher in His millennial reign. For a thousand years, His Gospel will penetrate every soul and burn brightly in every bosom.

He is our Advocate with the Father and the Bread of Life. He is the Cornerstone of our creation, the Foundation of our existence. He is the Creator of worlds without number, and the Deliverer of the Covenant to all the children of our Father.

He is Emmanuel: truly, God is with us. The Firstborn of the Spirit Children of the Father, He is perfect in every detail. He is the Good Shepherd, and the Judge of both the quick and the dead. As Lord, King, and Jehovah, He has all power to act as Mediator and as the Messenger of the Covenant.

The Lamb of God, He is the Messiah, the Anointed One, and our anticipated Redeemer. He is our Rock, and our Savior, the Only Begotten Son of God in the flesh. He is the Son of Man of Holiness, and our Second Comforter as we learn to trust completely in His Holy Name.

"There is a resurrection,
therefore, the grave hath no
victory, and the sting of death
is swallowed up in Christ. He is the
light and the life of the world; yea, a light
that is endless that can never be darkened; yea,
and also, a life which is endless, that there can be no
more death. Even this mortal shall put on immortality,
and this corruption shall put on incorruption, and
shall be brought to stand before the bar of God, to
be judged of him. (Mosiah 16:9-10).

Mosiah
Chapter 17

Even after hearing such powerful testimony, King Noah still commanded that his priests should put Abinadi to death. (V. 1). But rather than immediately carrying out the order, they first had to deal with a maverick in their own ranks who would not participate in that travesty of justice. This man's name was Alma. A possible meaning of "Alma," derived from the Aramaic, is "eternity". (See Commentary Reference to Mosiah 15:1). This fits in neatly with the concept of eternal life that would prove to be a recurring element throughout Alma's teachings.

Alma was "a young man" and he might have been the first of the priests to cast his vote in the case of Abinadi. (V. 2). According to Jewish law, the youngest member of the Sanhedrin, or ruling body, voted first, in order to protect him from being unduly influenced by the senior members of the court. In this case, Noah and the other priests would have clearly exerted a strong negative influence on an impressionable youth.

The problem for Noah was that Alma had "believed the words which Abinadi had spoken". (V. 2, see Mosiah 26:15). His conversion was based on the teachings of one man alone. Abinadi may have felt that he had failed as a missionary. As far as we know, his only convert was Alma. But much of the religious history of the Nephites during the next three hundred years revolves around this man and his descendants. He not only began a religious revival among his own people, but he was later given power by his new sovereign King Mosiah to establish Churches throughout all his adoptive Land of Zarahemla.

As a member of the Church court trying Abinadi, Alma might have been appointed as defense counsel. If so, perhaps the notes he kept of the proceedings formed the substance of the account of Abinadi's teachings that were preserved in The Book of Mormon. In any event, when Alma "began to plead with the king that he would not be angry with Abinadi," Noah became even more so, and cast Alma out of the courtroom. (V. 2-3).

Perhaps Alma's impassioned plea enraged Noah because there were now two witnesses (Abinadi and Alma) testifying against him and his practices, which was sufficient for the court to indict him for crimes, as well. The accuser was about to become the accused. To prevent this, Noah sent servants after Alma to silence his protests by slaying him. (V. 3).

Alma fled, and hid for many days, taking that opportunity to write down all the things that he had witnessed, and "all the words which Abinadi had spoken". (V. 4). It is very probable that, in The Book of Mormon, the account of Abinadi is due to the foresight and industry of Alma, as well as to the editorial skills of Mormon.

Noah waited three days before again bringing Abinadi before the court. (V. 6). It was improper, in the Jewish judicial system, to render a guilty verdict on the same day that testimony was heard. Noah took this opportunity during the lull in the proceedings to announce that he would being a new accusation against Abinadi that was a capital offense. (V. 7). The lying and false prophecy charges were summarily dropped, and Abinadi was instead charged with blasphemy.

This is the typical reaction to the prophets of the people in all ages. As Nephi said: "The guilty take the truth to be hard, for it cutteth them to the very center". (1 Nephi 16:22). This is why false prophets and corrupt priests so often flourish among the people. They salve the conscience, not only telling the people there is no wickedness in their actions, but also claiming that their behavior is acceptable to, and sanctioned by, God. (See Alma 14:7).

Abinadi's stated crime was that he had "said that God himself should come down among the children of men". (V. 8). But this charge was contrived. The real reason Noah sought his life was that he had "spoken evil" concerning him and his people. (V. 8). Abinadi was given the opportunity to recant in order to save his own life. The function of a court like the Sanhedrin was to preserve the purity of religion. If the accused were willing to recant, or repent, the main function of the court would have been fully satisfied.

But Abinadi refused to do so, and instead declared his willingness to suffer death, for it would "stand as a testimony" against Noah and his priests at the last day. (V. 9-10). The last hope of an accused to authenticate his innocence was to submit to an ordeal. In this case, Abinadi offered to suffer whatever pain Noah desired to inflict upon him.

Upon hearing this, Noah uneasily shifted his position, and was about to release Abinadi. (V. 11). He feared the testimony or the witness of the words of Abinadi and Alma, as well as the new element introduced by Abinadi at this time, that would prove to be the witness of his innocent blood. But independently, the priests raised yet another accusation, saying that Abinadi had "reviled the king". (V. 12, see V. 10). Truly, "it is the wicked that stir up the hearts of the children of men unto bloodshed". (Mormon 4:5). Therefore, the king delivered Abinadi into the hands of the priests, for under Israelite Law the accusers were required to carry out the execution. He was taken outside the city walls, and preparations were made to burn him to death. (V. 12-13).

The final words of the Prophet Abinadi in verses 15-19 may have been recorded by a future convert or by Alma who may have been secretly present at the martyrdom. As the flames licked around his feet, Abinadi cried out that his accusers would inflict the same pains on others who would "believe in the salvation of the Lord their God". (V. 15). Not only that, but he also prophesied that his executioners would themselves "suffer the pains of death by fire". (V. 18, see Alma Chapter 25). This might have reference to the practice in ancient Near Eastern Law of a false accuser being given the same punishment that would have befallen the accused, when convicted.

Thus, Abinadi died as a martyr to the truth. His message benefited not only the Nephites, but it has also been an inspiration to Latter-day Israel and to the Lamanite peoples to whom The Book of Mormon has been carried. "Greater love hath no man than this," declared the Savior, "that a man lay down his life for his friends "(John 15:13).

The greatest points of contrast between Abinadi and the priests of Noah were the prophet's clear understanding of the Atonement and his willingness to keep the commandments, while the wicked priests did not understand and rebelled against the Law. The depth of their depravity matched their darkened and confused thinking. Sin is always ultimately responsible for such decadence. (See D&C 88:67-68 & Commentary Reference to Mosiah 15:29-31).

Abinadi joined the ranks of all those who have clarified our understanding of heaven, and have made it seem worth working for. Quite commonly, we think of mortal life and death as being opposite to each other, or mutually exclusive. In fact, as our insight deepens with the eternal perspective provided by the martyrdom of Abinadi, we come to think of the two as matters of degree. Because Mormon included the account of Abinadi in his abridgment of the Large Plates of Nephi, we have been more easily able to come to an understanding and appreciation of life and death, even under trying circumstances.

The counsel of Moroni to Joseph Smith was: "Wherever the sound (of the marvelous work) shall go it shall cause the ears of men to tingle, and wherever it shall be proclaimed, the pure in heart shall rejoice, while those who draw near to God with their mouths, and honor him with their lips, while their hearts are far from him, will seek its overthrow, and the destruction of those by whose hands it is carried. Therefore, marvel not if your name is made a derision, and had as a by-word among such, if you are the instrument in bringing it, by the gift of God, to the knowledge of the people". (Oliver Cowdery, "The Gathering of Latter Day Israel," "Messenger and Advocate," 1:79-80; 109-112, see Ivan J. Barrett, "Joseph Smith & The Restoration," p. 14).

"Martyrdom is not a thing of the past only," cautioned Bruce R. McConkie, "but of the present and of the future, for Satan has not yet been bound, and the servants of the Lord will not be silenced in this final age of warning and judgment. There are forces and powers in the world today, that would silence the tongues and shed the blood of every true witness of Christ in the world, if they had the power and means to do it". ("Mormon Doctrine," p. 469.)

"There was one
among them whose name was Alma,
he also being a descendant of Nephi. And
he was a young man, and he believed the words
which Abinadi had spoken ... But the king was...
wroth, and caused that Alma should be cast out ... and
sent his servants after him, that they might slay him.
But he fled before them and hid himself that they
found him not. And he, being concealed for
many days, did write all the words
which Abinadi had spoken."
(Mosiah 17:2-4).

Mosiah
Chapter 18

This chapter forms a literary unit all by itself, and might have been inserted into the record in order to give an account of certain unusual historical facts relevant to the flowing narrative. It is also one of the best sources in the Standard Works for information on the ordinance of baptism.

Alma repented of the sins he had committed as a corrupt priest on Noah's payroll, and he went through the Land of Nephi preaching the "words of Abinadi," utilizing as his text the record he had made of the prophet's teachings. (V. 1, see Mosiah 17:4).

He went to a place that was called "Mormon". This is the first geographical use of the name, but it must have been known to the people as a refuge from the winds of war, the sandstorms of strife, and the calamity of contention that were sweeping the Land of Nephi. The events that took place here were spiritually impressive and far-reaching in their consequences. Five hundred years later, the great prophet into whose care was entrusted the record of the Nephites was given this same name.

The "waters of Mormon" were pure and clean and were thus ideally suited to the ordinance of baptism. (V. 5, & 8). These waters stood in sharp contrast to the river of filthy water in Lehi's dream, that represented the sins of the world. (See 1 Nephi 15:28)

Alma taught the first principles of the Gospel beside the waters of Mormon. "And he did preach unto them repentance, and redemption, and faith on the Lord". (V. 7). Then he explained to his congregation the covenant of baptism, that in our day we reaffirm when we partake of the sacrament. (V. 8).

This account from the ministry of Alma offers plain counsel concerning the proper attitude of those who desire baptism, and it should be studied by all those who desire to take upon themselves the name of Christ. "And it came to pass that he said unto them: Behold, here are the waters of Mormon (for thus were they called) and now, as ye are desirous to come into the fold of God, and to be called his people, and are willing to bear one another's burdens, that they may be light; Yea, and are willing to mourn with those that mourn; yea, and comfort those that stand in need of comfort, and to stand as witnesses of God at all times and in all things, and in all places that ye may be in, even until death, that ye maybe redeemed of God, and be numbered with those of the first resurrection, that ye may have eternal life - Now I say unto you, if this be the desire of your hearts, what have you against being baptized in the name of the Lord, as a witness before him that ye have entered into a covenant with him, that ye will serve him, and keep his commandments, that he may pour out his Spirit more abundantly upon you?" (V. 8-10, see Moroni 6:1-3).

When we "come into the fold of God" we are "called his people" as we become members of a Church that is the ultimate auxiliary organization to the family. Its purpose is to aid those who have participated in the initial and introductory ordinance of baptism, thereby making possible their further progression.

There is only one way, one fold, and one true Church. Paul explained to the Ephesians that there is "one Lord, one faith, one baptism". (Ephesians 4:5). If all Churches were equal, then the Lord's true Church would not exist anywhere. If, in education, any program were the equal of any other, then receiving a degree would be based on an indiscriminate and uniformly mediocre course of study that would somehow qualify the recipient in all fields of study. But this is contrary to the natural order of things. Only by the power of specific priesthood ordinances and by making sacred covenants with God, may we truly be called "Christians". (See Mosiah 5:7). A sobering question that we should all periodically ask ourselves is this: 'If I were on trial for being a Christian, would the evidence for my conviction be overwhelming?'

Alma asked those who stood near the waters of Mormon if they were "willing to bear one another's burdens, that they may be light". Harold B. Lee once said that the heaviest burdens that we have to carry are our own sins. In contrast, the Savior declared that His yoke was easy, and His burden was light, precisely because He did not carry the burden of sin. (See Matthew 11:29-30). We might ask ourselves, as Alma had asked these baptismal candidates: "How can we help each other as we all struggle in sin?"

Intense interpersonal involvement by the members of the Lord's Church can do much to relieve suffering. It sometimes seems to be a full-time job. But as President Gordon B. Hinckley said: "The Church cannot hope to save a man on Sunday, if during the week it is a complacent witness to the destruction of his soul". (C.R. 10/2012).

Alma went on to describe those who would enter into the covenant of baptism as the kind of persons who would "mourn with those that mourn; yea, and comfort those that stand in need of comfort". The Lord Himself declared: "Thou shalt live together in love, insomuch that thou shalt weep for the loss of them that die". (D&C 42:45). Grief is good ("Good grief") when we mourn for those who have died in full faith and fellowship in the Church and Kingdom of God, with the secure hope of eternal life. As Joseph Fielding Smith said: "They shall never die the second death, and feel the torment of the wicked, when they come face to face with eternity". ("Church History and Modern Revelation", 1:186.)

However, mourning also describes the sense of loss that is felt by those who carry with them the burden of sin. When we mourn together, we help our brothers and sisters overcome the negative consequences of sin. To the extent that we can, we facilitate the process of repentance and help them to feel the joy of forgiveness.

Covenant individuals are "witnesses of God" to whomever they meet, in whatever circumstances they might find themselves, and wherever they might be. Heaven's admission policy is this: "Persons of any race, creed, color, or national origin are accepted for admission to heaven provided they maintain ideals and standards in harmony with those of The Church of Jesus Christ of Latter-day Saints, and meet heaven's requirements. These are baptism, and the ordinances of the Melchizedek Priesthood".

Zion comes in many different colors. It speaks Aymara, Zulu, and dozens of other languages. It lives in thousands of stakes, in practically every country in the world, from Argentina to Zimbabwe. It has millions of members who are red, yellow, brown, black, and white. Zion wears a sarong, a grass skirt, a blue collar, a tupeno, a business suit, and a kilt. It lives in igloos, huts, and high-rises. Most important of all, it shares a common testimony that Jesus is the Christ, and that His love, indeed, makes the world go round. Today it is more important than ever to remember the words attributed to Harold B. Lee: "There is no United States of America in heaven". The great equalizer in the sight of God is our obedience to His will.

It is impossible to overestimate the power inherent in the ordinance of baptism. "No man of himself can lift himself to celestial glory. Our growth depends on the light of Christ, guidance of the Holy Ghost, and the power of the priesthood that is given us by God and his Son. The religion of Jesus Christ is not just a philosophy of life; it is the generator of life. If you go it alone, you cannot succeed. If you receive His power, you will increase and make it. There is no other way". ("My Religion and Me," Sunday School Course Manual).

Whether in Alma's day or in our own, the power of the Church rests in the vitality of its members. The Church rises and falls on the tide of their personal witnesses. Alvin R. Dyer warned: "We must not be caught in the bind of building a Church and killing the articles of its faith, or permitting form to triumph over spirit. The Church and Kingdom of God is built by the ardor and conviction of its members. We must be alert to the expansion of its assets at the cost of lost conviction. When buildings or institutions grow bigger and bigger, let us be fearful lest the Spirit will thin out". ("A Foundation for Education").

As members of the Church continue to "witness of God at all times and in all things, and in all places," the foundation of the Kingdom of God will be anchored in bedrock. A story illustrates the point: An Irishman built a wall around his farm that was five feet high and eight feet thick. When asked why he built it so thick, he replied that if the wind ever blew so hard that it toppled the wall, it would still be five feet thick. The Church is such an organization.

Alma compared the fountain at the waters of Mormon to the attitude of the righteous who stand beside the waters of baptism, contemplating the ordinance and its associated covenants. "These currents and many more are part of the flowing fountain of the Church. If we do not drink, if we die of thirst while only inches from the fountain, the fault comes down to us. For the free, full, flowing, living water is there". (Truman Madsen, "Christ & The Inner Life," p. 31).

Therefore, Alma urged his congregation to be baptized. "Now I say unto you," he asked, "if this be the desire of your hearts, what have you against being baptized in the name of the Lord, as a witness before him that ye have entered into a covenant with him, that ye will serve him and keep his commandments, that he may pour out his Spirit more abundantly upon you?" (V. 10). It seems clear from this verse that the ordinance was the same then as now, and was well-understood by his congregation. (See Commentary References to 2 Nephi 9:24, & Mosiah 4:3, & D&C 20:37). From Qumran, we read in The Manual of Discipline from The Serek Scroll, which contains texts from the Old World that roughly parallel the missionary efforts of Alma: "His sin is forgiven him and in the humility of his soul he is for all the Laws of God; his flesh is cleansed shining bright in the waters of purification, even in the waters of baptism, and he shall be given a new name in due time to walk perfectly in all the ways of God". (Cited in Hugh Nibley, "An Approach to The Book of Mormon," p. 149).

In just the same way that King Benjamin's people had reacted, (see Mosiah 5:2-5), the people of Alma "clapped their hands for joy, and exclaimed: This is the desire of our hearts". (V. 11, see Alma 46:15). For many years, the spirit of these people had been stifled by the oppressive rule of Noah. Now they yearned for the opportunity to find expression for the wonderful feelings that were welling up inside them. These individuals wished to put to death the old sinful persons they had been, the font being symbolic of the grave. In the dual symbolism of baptism, they would be reborn as a new creature in Christ. (See Mosiah 5:7).

Alma took a young man named Helam into the waters, and stated his authority to perform the ordinance: "Helam," he said, "I baptize thee, having authority from the Almighty God, as a testimony that you have entered into a covenant to serve him until you are dead as to the mortal body; and may the Spirit of the Lord be poured out upon you; and may he grant unto you eternal life, through the redemption of Christ, whom he has prepared from the foundation of the world". (V. 13). Where he received the authority to baptize we do not know, (see Verse 18), but as Joseph Fielding Smith, Jr. taught: "We may conclude that Alma held the priesthood". ("Answers to Gospel Questions," 3:203, see Commentary Reference to Mosiah 26:15-32). Possibly Alma received his authority from Abinadi, but we do not know. Joseph Smith simply taught that after Moses, "All the prophets had the Melchizedek Priesthood, and were ordained by God Himself". ("Teachings," p. 181).

Curiously, "both Alma and Helam were buried in the water". (V. 14). Joseph Fielding Smith, Jr. believed that "Alma was baptized and held the priesthood before the coming of Abinadi, but he became involved with other priests under the reign of the wicked King Noah, and when he baptized Helam, he felt he needed a cleansing himself, so he buried himself in the water as a token of full repentance". It may be significant that Alma did not repeat his own immersion during any subsequent baptisms at the waters of Mormon. (V. 15).

By the time Alma had finished the baptisms, there were about 204 members, and it was thus necessary to organize a Church among them. (V. 17). This is the first time in The Book of Mormon that any mention is made of a formal Church organization among the Nephites. From the days of Lehi, there had been many inspired prophets who had power and authority of the Holy Priesthood. Remarkably, however, no Church organization is mentioned until Mosiah 18:17. The Nephites surely had some type of institutionalized body from the time of Lehi until the reign of the Elder Mosiah. (See Omni 1:12). But after Mosiah led the faithful out of the Land of Nephi in the days of their transgression, there was evidently no formal organization until Alma set one up. As we understand it today, the Church is a vehicle to bring people closer to God, through the ordinances of the Gospel. Because its programs help us to keep the covenant of baptism, it would be natural for Alma to desire the formality of Church programs to accomplish the same purposes.

Mormon took pains to validate the authority of Alma to administer other Gospel ordinances. "And it came to pass that Alma, having authority from God, ordained priests; even one priest to every fifty of their number did he ordain to preach unto them, and to teach them concerning the things pertaining to the kingdom of God". (V. 18). When he reported that Alma had ordained priests to minister to the people, he was referring to offices within the Melchizedek Priesthood, inasmuch as the Nephites did not hold the authority of the Aaronic Priesthood until the post-mortal ministry of the Savior. (See Commentary Reference to 2 Nephi 5:26). Joseph Smith taught: "Wherever there is a righteous man on the earth unto whom God revealed His word and gives power and authority to administer in His name, and wherever there is a priest of God, a minister who has power and authority from God to administer in the ordnances of the Gospel and officiate in the Priesthood of God, there is the Kingdom of God". (H.C., 5:256).

Alma expressly commanded that nothing but the true Doctrine of Christ should be taught among the people. "And he commanded them that they should teach nothing save it were the things which he had taught, and which had been spoken by the mouth of the holy prophets". (V. 19, See Commentary Volume One: Chapters on 1 Nephi 19 & 29 - 31). Speakers and teachers are obligated to confine their expressions to the doctrines that have been revealed in plainness. They are to preach Jesus Christ and Him crucified and to declare the first principles of the Gospel. "Yea, even (Alma) commanded them that they should preach nothing save it were repentance and faith on the Lord, who had redeemed his people". (V. 20, see "Teachings," p. 109 & 292).

Those who speak in the various conferences of the Church illustrate by their example this practice.

As Spencer W. Kimball taught: "The great objective of all our work is to build character and increase faith in the lives of those whom we serve. If one cannot accept and teach the programs of the Church in an orthodox way, without reservation, he should not teach". (C.R. 4/1948). As the Savior Himself commanded: "And they shall observe the covenants and Church articles to do them, and these shall be their teachings, as they shall be directed by the Spirit. And the Spirit shall be given unto you by the prayer of faith; and if ye receive not the Spirit ye shall not teach". (D&C 42:13-14).

President Joseph Fielding Smith stated that "no one should be called upon to teach and no one should attempt to teach the doctrines of the Church unless he is fully converted and has an abiding testimony of their truth. This testimony can only be received through prayerful study and obedience to all the commandments of the Lord. No man or woman can teach by the Spirit what he or she does not practice. Sincerity, integrity, and loyalty are essential factors, and these will be accompanied by the spirit of prayer. The Comforter, 'who knoweth all things,' we should rely on, and then our teachings shall be approved of our Father in Heaven." ("Church History and Modern Revelation", 1:184-85.)

Thus, were the people to be unified. "And (Alma) commanded them that there should be no contention one with another, but that they should look forward with one eye, having one faith and one baptism, having their hearts knit together in unity and in love one towards another". (V. 21, see Ephesians 4:5). "God was their radar and warning system that saved them the need of constant and costly vigilance on all fronts, to say nothing of expensive and wasteful war plans and war games. This was their policy of preparedness. The keystone of their defense was unity at home". (Hugh Nibley, "The World & The Prophets," p. 195-196, see Mosiah 9:17, 21:6-7, & Helaman 6:37).

The Dead Sea Covenantors of Qumran provide a parallel view of the unity of the faithful. The writers of the Scrolls called their organization a "Yanad" or "Church," and the name they gave themselves was "Latter-day Saints". Their emphasis on oneness is a reminder that these churches in the wilderness thought of themselves as scale models of Enoch's City of Zion, because they were of one heart and one mind. There is incredible power in unity. The whole is truly greater than the sum of its parts. We can take an analogy from simple mechanics. One two by four board, eight feet long and standing on end, will support a weight of 600 pounds. Two identical boards, standing unitedly on end, will support a weight of 2,400 pounds. One two by six, ten feet long and laying horizontally, will support a weight of 400 pounds. Two identical boards will together support a weight of 1,600 pounds.

"And the Lord called his people Zion, because they were of one heart and one mind, and dwelt in righteousness". (Moses 7:18). What kind of power or strength is there in being unified? There is power to "break mountains, to divide the seas, to dry up waters, to turn them out of their course; to put at defiance the armies of nations, to divide the earth, to break every band, (and) to stand in the presence of God". (J.S.T. Genesis 14:30-31).

Alma saw to it that the priests whom he had ordained did not stray from their mandate to teach the people. Under his tutelage, they would "wax strong in the Spirit, having the knowledge of God". (V. 23-26). On one occasion, Brigham H. Roberts "said after a coherent and vigorous presentation that he loved books; indeed, that in some degree books had made him. But then in a most vehement way he said, 'But I am not dependent on books. I am dependent for what I really know and really trust, on the direct experience of God.'" (Truman Madsen, "Defender of The Faith," p. 374).

After the baptismal service had concluded beside the waters of Mormon, Alma taught some of the basic principles of the Law of Zion, which today we call the Law of Consecration. While there is no evidence that the Nephites formally adopted this law, it is evident that Alma's little group of converts had the spirit of Zion in their minds and hearts. These verses effectively outline Alma's welfare plan. "And again, Alma commanded that the people of the Church should impart of their substance, every one according to that which he had; if he have more abundantly he should impart more abundantly; and of him that had but little, but little should be required; and to him that had not should be given. And thus, they should impart of their substance of their own free will and good desires towards God, and to those priests that stood in need, yea, and to every needy, naked soul. And this he said unto them, having been commanded of God; and they did walk uprightly before God, imparting to one another both temporally and spiritually according to their needs and their wants ". (V. 27-29).

There follows a beautifully constructed and poetically pleasing formal conclusion to all that had come to pass by the waters of Mormon. It was evidently written by Mormon himself. "All this was done in Mormon, yea, by the waters of Mormon, in the forest that was near the waters of Mormon; yea, the place of Mormon, the waters of Mormon, the forest of Mormon, how beautiful are they to the eyes of them who there came to the knowledge of their Redeemer". (V. 30). In this verse, as he summed up the achievements of Alma's holy band, who were struggling to be real Saints, and to a degree succeeding in their efforts, Mormon broke out into a hymn of joy. These verses are a hymn with a melody that hovers about the word 'Mormon.' "The imagery is that of a wanderer saved by the water and the tree of life; saved from spiritual death to find redemption and salvation. The trees and water provide life giving knowledge as sustenance". (Hugh Nibley, "Churches in The Wilderness", see 1 Nephi 2:9, & Ether 8:26).

In many instances, Churches in the Wilderness have prepared those who would be called Saints for holy missions. "We see the same thing happening in the cases of Lehi and his sons, Mosiah, Ether, Moses, John the Baptist, and the Lord Himself. In typical fashion, Alma came out of hiding to do his work among the people. But so much activity at Mormon eventually attracted the attention of the king's spies. (V. 32). Like others before him, and foreshadowing those who would follow, Alma "departed into the wilderness" with his band that had now grown to about 450 souls. (V. 34). We find out what happened to these of God's wandering people in Mosiah Chapters 23, & 24.

The fate of Alma's colony was similar to that of Qumran. What happened in The Book of Mormon quite sensibly suggests what could have happened at Qumran, with a jealous monarch (Herod) keeping the place under surveillance until deciding that it would have to go. With external evidence for the divine authenticity of The Book of Mormon accumulating, we find that it is not the Prophet Joseph Smith, but his critics, who find themselves with a lot of explaining to do.

Mosiah
Chapter 19

In this chapter, we return to the account of King Noah and his people, that continues through chapter 22. An army of Noah that had been mobilized had been unsuccessful in finding Alma's people, so they returned to the City of Lehi-Nephi, and to Shilom. (V. 1, see Mosiah 9:8). There they found a rebellion brewing among the people, and "there began to be a great contention among them". (V. 2-3). One cannot help but contrast this division with the unity of Alma's people, that is described in Mosiah 18:21.

A man named Gideon, who was a great patriot, appeared upon the scene. He was one who could not stand idly by while his nation fell apart because of governmental corruption. Gideon was destined to become a leader in the Church who would serve faithfully for 54 years before his eventual martyrdom. (V. 4, see Alma Chapter 1).

Now, however, Gideon fought against Noah in the strength of his youth. (V. 5-7). In the midst of their personal combat, it was discovered that an army of the Lamanites had appeared in the border of the land. Completely rotten from within, Noah's kingdom was about to crumble before his eyes. With this external threat looming on the horizon, he begged Gideon to spare his life, professing a concern for his people. Gideon did so, that Abinadi's prophecy concerning the fate of Noah might be fulfilled. (V. 8, see Mosiah 12:3, & 10 & 13:10).

Lacking the defense plan founded on personal righteousness that had been adopted by Alma, the spiritually bankrupt people of Noah fled in disarray into the wilderness. (V. 9 see Commentary Reference to Mosiah 18:21). As Dag Hammarskjöld observed: "The longest journey is the journey inward". Due to the Nephites' complete lack of organization, the Lamanites were easily able to overtake them, and they "began to slay them". (V. 10). Thus, the apostate Nephites suffered both physical and spiritual death in the wilderness of sin. Showing his true colors, Noah, and a number of men that included the body of his priests, abandoned their slower moving families in order to make good their own escape. "Now it came to pass that the king commanded them that all the men should leave their wives and their children, and flee before the Lamanites". (V. 11).

"Now there were many that would not leave them, but had rather stay and perish with them. And the rest left their wives and their children and fled". (V. 12). Those who would not leave their families included Limhi and Gideon. They were able to sue for peace with the Lamanites under the same terms described in Mosiah 7:22, namely, that the Nephites would pay an annual tribute to their oppressors amounting to one-half of their property. In addition, the Lamanites demanded that Noah be delivered into their hands. Even they recognized his wickedness, and that he posed a threat to both the Nephites and the Lamanites in the Land of Nephi.

"And now there was one of the sons of the king among those that were taken captive, whose name was Limhi". (V. 16). So, he dispatched his faithful servant Gideon into the wilderness to find Noah. (V. 17-18). There, they found those who had earlier deserted their families. These had experienced a change of heart, and "had sworn in their hearts that they would return to the land of Nephi, and if their wives and their children were slain, and also those that had tarried with them, that they would seek revenge, and also perish with them". (V. 19).

When Noah had tried to prevent their departure, they had seized him, and "caused that he should suffer, even unto death by fire" in fulfillment of Abinadi's prophecy. (V. 20, see Mosiah 17:18). Only the priests in company with Noah had been able to escape a similar fate. When the people "were about to take (them) also and put them to death ... they fled before them". (V. 21). For many years to come, these priests and their descendants would be responsible for much mischief among both the Nephites and the Lamanites.

Limhi then became a tributary ruler under Lamanite control, and there was again "peace in the land". (V. 25-29). Peace, as the world defines it, has many faces. Truly, Satan patronizes principles and distorts their definition into cartoon-like caricatures that are pleasantly palatable to carnal cravings. His peace is the absence of armed conflict. It is the complacency that is born of indifference and apathy. It is the misguided sanctuary of promising economic growth factors. It is the inherent instability of full employment statistics. It is the sham of selfish satisfaction at the expense of selfless service. It is "business as usual" and "don't rock the boat". It is blissful ignorance, as the party atmosphere blithely teeters on the brink of the precipice of self-destruction. It is pacification through a false sense of carnal security, as the devil whispers into patronizing ears: "All is well in Zion; yea, Zion prospereth, all is well," even as he "cheateth their souls, and leadeth them away carefully down to hell". (2 Nephi 28:21).

The Snake River in Southeastern Washington is navigable thanks to the efforts of the Army Corps of Engineers that has overseen the construction of several dams and maintains a variety of aids to navigation along the course of the river. One such dam is the Little Goose; at this point in the rivers' journey to the sea, the water level drops 95 feet, and in the spring flood up to 200,000 cubic feet of water per second drops over the spillway.

Approaching the dam from downriver, one is first aware of the noise, and of a low rumble from the as yet invisible waterfall. Then, debris in the water, foam, and turbulence become apparent. When the dam itself comes into view, because of the churning whitewater, it appears that progress is effectively blocked, and that all boat traffic must halt. But a way to continue has been provided, on condition that the appropriate principles are followed. A lock has been prepared to avoid destruction by the cascading water, and to allow boaters to ascend beyond the danger to the safety of calm water upriver from the falls.

First, using knowledge of the proper use of radio equipment, the lock operator needs to be contacted. The correct frequency and call sign must be known in order to be heard. The VHF radio used is really a transceiver; it has the capacity to both send and to receive messages. When the plea "Help me" is sent, the reply is quickly received: "Follow my instructions, and also the signals I will prominently display as aids to navigation, and all will be well."

At this point, massive steel gates 100 feet high open like huge jaws, revealing calm water stretching a thousand feet into the distance. When a boat enters the lock, and the gates close behind, it does not matter whether one boat or 20 enter the lock; the same volume of water is used each time the lock is operated. The water that had been uselessly spilling over the dam is now diverted to the lock, and the power and weight of that water lifts the boat 95 feet to the level of the upper lake. Metal gates again open onto a serene and peaceful expanse of water stretching in a mirror-like calm for 20 miles to the horizon.

From a new perspective one can see with greater clarity the rationale of the controlled release of water, the engineering principles that have made the river navigable, and the wisdom of communicating with the operator of the lock.

"And now,
there was one of the
sons of the king among
them that were taken captive,
whose name was Limhi."
(Mosiah 19:6).

Mosiah
Chapter 20

In this chapter, we read the account of two dozen young Lamanite women who were abducted by the priests of Noah. These lackeys were the same cowards who had bolted like frightened rabbits before the invading Lamanite armies, leaving their wives and children behind to fend for themselves. (See Mosiah 19:11). They had later avoided the fate of King Noah by fleeing further into the wilderness. (See Mosiah 19:21). Actually, their retreat only took them deeper into the spiritual vacuum of their own shallow lives that had been sucked dry by their wickedness. In contrast, their families had been spared temporal destruction at the hands of the Lamanites, and ultimately were able to join the Nephites in the Land of Zarahemla, where they were able to reconstruct their spiritual lives as well. (See Mosiah 19:14, & 25:12).

But having abandoned their own families, these thoroughly debauched priests "came forth out of their secret places" and kidnapped the Lamanite women, with the intention of first seducing them, and then taking them to wife in a charade of propriety. (V. 4-5). Mosiah 23:31-39 describes the ultimate fate of these individuals.

When the Lamanites realized that their young women were missing, they mistakenly assumed that Limhi and his people were responsible, and that they had broken the oath of fealty made after their recent subjugation. (V. 6, see Mosiah 19:26). "Therefore, they sent their armies forth; yea, even the king himself went before his people; and they went up to the land of Nephi to destroy the people of Limhi". (V. 7).

The Nephites were forced to fight like dragons "for their lives, and for their wives, and for their children". (V. 11). Fortunately for them, the wounded king of the Lamanites was captured and interrogated. The Nephites learned from him the reason for the renewed hostilities. "And now the king said: I have broken the oath because thy people did carry away the daughters of my people; therefore, in my anger I did cause my people to come up to war against thy people". (V. 15).

Gideon was perceptive enough to realize that the priests of Noah must be responsible. "Do ye not remember the priests of thy father," he asked Limhi, "whom this people sought to destroy?. And are they not in the wilderness? And are not they the ones who have stolen the daughters of the Lamanites?" (V. 17-18). He was also humble enough to recognize that his people were receiving the wages of their sins, just as Abinadi had prophesied they must. "For, are not the words of Abinadi fulfilled, which he prophesied against us - and all this because we would not hearken unto the words of the Lord, and turn from our iniquities?" (V. 21, see Mosiah 12:1-8).

Gideon's advice to Limhi was to pacify the Lamanites, whose army was numerically superior to their own, so that they might avoid destruction. "For it is better that we should be in bondage," he reasoned, "than that we should lose our lives". (V. 22). This is not the heady "Give me liberty or give me death!" rhetoric of the American Revolution, still so fresh in the minds of Joseph Smith's generation. (See Commentary Reference to Mosiah 29:24). Both Gideon and Limhi would live to see the day when the chastening hand of the Lord would soften the hearts of the Nephites living in the Land of Nephi sufficiently to bring them to such a condition of reliance upon the Lord that He would dramatically intervene in their behalf.

Gideon's counsel was adopted, and the wounded king of the Lamanites made an oath to Limhi that his people should not slay the Nephites. So tremendous was their respect for an oath sworn before God, that the Nephites went to meet the Lamanites unarmed and defenseless. The king "did plead in behalf of the people of Limhi, and when the Lamanites saw the people of Limhi, that they were without arms, they had compassion on them and were pacified toward them, and returned with their king in peace to their own land". (V. 25-26).

Less than 50 years later, the Sons of Mosiah would embark on a mission of mercy to this same Land of Nephi. There, they would encounter formidable obstacles, but would also enjoy phenomenal success among the Lamanites. In the compassion with which these Lamanites treated the People of Limhi, we may see a glimmer of the humility with which some of their descendants would later accept the message of salvation delivered by Ammon, Aaron, Omner, and Himni.

Mosiah
Chapter 21

Relationships between the Nephites and Lamanites remained on an even keel "for many days". (V. 1). But Satan kept working on the Lamanites, and eventually they were once again "stirred up in anger against the Nephites". (V. 2). The devil is an incurable, insufferable, insomniac. He never sleeps, and is ever observant. He cannot read our hearts and our thoughts, but he knows us, for our words and our deeds betray us. Then he moves in, and "has power to place thoughts in our minds and to whisper to us in unspoken impressions, and in other ways, he plays upon our weakness". (Joseph Fielding Smith, Jr., 1972-3 Melchizedek Priesthood Personal Study Guide, p. 298).

One of the principal points of vulnerability of the Lamanites throughout Nephite history was that they were particularly susceptible to the spirit of contention. Allowing this influence in their homes, they opened the door to Satan's missionaries and beckoned them to enter as invited guests. An effective counter measure to contention is love, because it is alien to Satan. When it is the language spoken in the home and in society, Satan and his disciples must uncomfortably slink away in confusion.

"I love everybody, even though some people make misteaks," said five-year-old Kathryn Hudson. "Where did you learn that?" she was asked. "In Church?" "No. When I was up in Heaven. Heavenly Father told me that". She learned very early in life that the best way to conquer our enemies is to make friends out of them. "He drew a circle that shut me out, "wrote the poet. "Heretic, rebel, a thing to flout. But love and I had the wit to win. We drew a circle that took him in". (Edwin Markham)

Relationships between individuals and societies can work for both good and evil. "When we sow a thought, we reap an act. When we sow an act, we reap a habit. When we sow a habit, we reap a character. When we sow a character, we reap an eternal destiny." (David O. McKay). Our fate, then, is ultimately in our own hands. The judgment will be eminently fair, because we will have fashioned our own heaven or the chains of hell from the sum total of our thoughts, words, and deeds that define our character.

"You may know me," he said. "I'm your constant companion, your greatest helper, and your heaviest burden. I will either push you onward and upward or drag you down to failure. I will follow your commands quickly and the same, every time, if that's what you want. I'm easily managed. All you have to do is be firm with me. Show me exactly how you want it done, and after a few quick lessons I'll do it automatically. I'm the servant of all great men and women, and the servant of failures, too. I work with all the precision of a marvelous computer. You may run me for profit, or you may run me to ruin. It really makes no difference to me. So, work with me. Be easy with me and I will destroy you. But be firm with me, and the world will be your oyster. Who am I? I'm Habit!" (Anonymous).

The Lamanites had made an oath that they would not slay the people of Limhi. (See Mosiah 20:25). They observed the letter of the law concerning that oath, but not the spirit thereof, and they began to make life miserable for the Nephites, for they "would smite them on their cheeks, and exercise authority over them; and began to put heavy burdens upon their backs, and drive them as they would a dumb ass," in further fulfillment of the prophecy of Abinadi. (V. 3, see V. 4, & Mosiah 12:2).

Their exercise of authority over the Nephites is an example of the unrighteous dominion spoken of in the Doctrine and Covenants. In a letter to the Saints from Liberty Jail, Joseph Smith wrote that he had learned "by sad experience that it is the nature and disposition of almost all men, as soon as they get a little authority, as they suppose, they will immediately begin to exercise unrighteous dominion". (D&C 121:39).

The exercise of authority through the use of violent means is a poor substitute for leadership or power. As a matter of fact, power and violence are mutually exclusive; where one is present the other is absent. Many of us are inclined to abuse authority, especially those who are least prepared for positions of trust and responsibility.

The people of Limhi were about to learn the lesson that when people murmur, the Lord often chastens them in order to give them the opportunity to repent. "Verily, thus saith the Lord unto you whom I love, and whom I love I also chasten that their sins may be forgiven, for with the chastisement I prepare a way for their deliverance in all things out of temptation". (D&C 95:1). That punishment follows sin natural, but it can be a positive consequence when it is the very thing that brings one to repentance. Truly, the Lord is merciful to His disobedient children, and His course is one eternal round. All of the experiences of mortality may work to our benefit. There must needs be opposition in all things, else God would cease to be God.

In the case of the people of Limhi, however, because of the weight of their afflictions their resolve weakened. As the breastwork of their spiritual fortress was breached, fear supplanted faith, and they lost both their perspective and their focus on the proven battle plan that centered on reliance on the Lord and trust in His strength. (See Mosiah 9:17 & 18:21).

They followed the path of expediency, sought a military solution to their problems, and so "put on their armor, and went forth against the Lamanites". (V. 7). They would have been much better off if they had instead put on the whole armor of God: "Wherefore, lift up your hearts, and rejoice," said the Lord, "and gird up your loins, and take upon you my whole armor, that ye may be able to withstand the evil day, having your loins girt about with truth, having on the breastplate of righteousness and your feet shod with the preparation of the Gospel of peace, taking the shield of faith wherewith ye shall be able to quench all the fiery darts of the wicked. And take the helmet of salvation, and the sword of my Spirit, which I will pour out upon you, and my word which I reveal unto you". (D&C 27:15-18).

The people of Limhi had not yet learned that righteousness begins with internal attitude control and is not just an outward observance of the rules of conduct. They needed to experience a mighty change in their hearts in order to hope for an improvement in their physical circumstances. Consider an analogy from our own day: If living a righteous life were simply a question of following the rules, then we could program a computer to be righteous! It is the desire and effort required to be righteous in the face of obstacles and opposition that gives nobility to our character.

Therefore, ill prepared to face their enemies, the People of Limhi were soundly defeated in three great battles, by the Lamanites. (V. 8-12). Finally, they began to get the message. The scriptures say they "did humble themselves even to the dust, subjecting themselves to the yoke of bondage, submitting themselves to be smitten, and they did cry mightily to God". (V. 13-14). The Lord heard their petitions, but because of their iniquities, He "did not see fit to deliver them out of bondage" just yet. (V. 15). Nevertheless, He began to soften the hearts of their oppressors, so "that there was no more disturbance between the Lamanites and the people of Limhi". (V. 22).

In these circumstances, the Nephites prudently kept together in groups, lest the Lamanites fall upon them. (V. 18-19). In addition, they were on the lookout for those elusive priests of Noah who had caused such great problems for the people of Limhi, for they had returned to the land to plunder the Nephite fields and storehouses and carry off "their grain and many of their precious things". (V. 20). Therefore, when Limhi traveled outside the walls of the city, armed guards always accompanied him. If he were lucky enough to capture Noah's priests, it was his intention to cast them into prison, and then put them to death as punishment for all the trouble they had caused his people in the Land of Nephi. (V. 23).

It was into this seething cauldron of disorder that Ammon and his brethren from Zarahemla were unknowingly thrust. (V. 23-24, see Mosiah chapters 7 & 8). After their capture and subsequent interrogation, it was established who they were and from whence they had come. Limhi rejoiced because he had supposed that Zarahemla lay in ruin. (V. 26). It is understandable that after 80 years of struggle in the Land of Nephi, when so many of their number had been slain in battle with the Lamanites, Limhi was overjoyed to re-establish contact with Nephites from Zarahemla. He may have seen in them the key to the temporal salvation of his people.

Before Ammon's arrival in Nephi, a search party had been dispatched to find Zarahemla. (V. 25). It had become hopelessly lost in the wilderness, and had instead stumbled upon "a land which was covered with dry bones". (V. 26). They called this the Land of Desolation. "No part of the land was desolate, save it were for timber; but because of the greatness of the destruction of the people who had before inhabited the land it was called desolate". (Helaman 3:6). The party made its way back home, bringing with it the 24 Gold Plates of Ether. This all occurred shortly before Ammon's arrival in the Land of Nephi. Both Ammon and Limhi were filled with joy to realize that, with the aid of the Urim and Thummim, Mosiah would be able to interpret the engravings. (V. 27-28, see Mosiah 8:12-15, & Commentary Reference to Mosiah 28:11-12).

At the same time, Ammon was filled with sorrow to learn that Noah and his priests had been responsible for so much iniquity and conflict with the Lamanites. He also mourned the death of Abinadi, and "for the departure of Alma and the people that went with him, who had formed a Church of God through the strength and power of God, and (through) faith on the words which had been spoken by Abinadi". (V. 29-30). Ammon would have gladly welcomed Alma and his brethren to join the larger body of the Church, for Alma's little flock itself "had entered into a covenant with God to serve him and keep his commandments". (V. 31).

After their instruction in the first principles of the Gospel, namely faith on the Lord Jesus Christ and repentance for the sins they had committed, "Limhi and many of his people were desirous to be baptized". (V. 33). But because of apostasy, no one then living in the Land of Nephi had the authority to perform this ordinance of the Gospel. For his part, Ammon declined the honor, considering himself to be unworthy. (V. 33). This implies that Ammon did hold the priesthood, since his refusal was based on worthiness, and not on authority. But more importantly, there were lessons yet to be learned, and experiences to be had, that would complete the necessary preparation of the people of Limhi for baptism.

Nevertheless, the people of Limhi yearned for that same peace enjoyed by Alma and the Church he had established in the wilderness. (V. 34). "They were desirous to be baptized as a witness and a testimony that they were willing to serve God with all their hearts". At this point, Mormon inserted an editorial comment into the record, assuring us that "an account of their baptism (should) be given hereafter". (V. 35, see Mosiah 25:17-18).

These people had begun to experience the mighty change of heart that had been described by King Benjamin. (See Mosiah 5:7). The recorded history of their struggles in the Land of Nephi illustrates the contrast between the spiritual and the natural man, that is a difference of generation and not just of degree. Having tasted the fruit of the Tree of Life, they now wanted to partake fully, and enter into the Fold of God by the strait and narrow gate of baptism, in order to enjoy companionship in the household of the faithful, and to be born again into the Church and Kingdom of God.

They were about to experience the peace that comes through integrity, and they would soon enjoy the blessings that follow obedience. (See D&C 130:20-21). "Until one is committed there is hesitancy, the chance to draw back, and always ineffectiveness. Concerning all acts of initiative, there is one elementary truth, the ignorance of which kills countless ideas and splendid plans, and it is this: The moment one definitely commits oneself, then Providence moves too. All sorts of things occur to help one that would never have otherwise occurred". (Thomas Hornbein, "Everest - The West Ridge").

Now Ammon and the people of Limhi focused their attention on escape from Lamanite bondage. The People of Limhi desired to be schooled in the first principles and ordinances of the Gospel, so that they might be baptized and enjoy fellowship with the Church, and to have the Plates of Ether translated by the Prophet Mosiah. They yearned to be "no more strangers and foreigners, but fellowcitizens with the saints, and of the household of God, (and to be) built upon the foundation of the … prophets, Jesus Christ himself being the chief corner stone." (Ephesians 2:19). Their humility and repentance would shortly bring them the deliverance for which they prayed.

Our careful study of
The Book of Mormon suggests that one of the
principal points of vulnerability of the Lamanites
throughout Nephite history was that they were nearly
always susceptible to the spirit of contention. Allowing
this influence in their homes opened the door to Satan's
missionaries and beckoned them to enter in as invited
guests. An effective counter measure to contention,
both then and now, is love, because it is alien to
Satan. When it is the language spoken in the
home and in society, and words are softly
spoken, when charity never faileth, he
and his disciples are compelled to
uncomfortably slink away
in uncomprehending
confusion.

Mosiah
Chapter 22

It was Gideon who devised a stratagem whereby the people of King Limhi might be delivered, without bloodshed, from bondage. (V. 3-6). The Lamanite guards at the city gates were typically drunken in the evenings, and when an extra measure of wine was delivered as tribute, they were soon completely out of touch with reality. (V. 7).

It must have caused quite an uproar when the Nephites left the city with their flocks and herds, but they were able to do so without alerting the intoxicated guards. (V. 11). Ammon guided them, for he knew the way back, "and after many days in the wilderness, they arrived in the land of Zarahemla". (V. 11-13). Their journey may have lasted around two weeks. When Alma's party reached Zarahemla some time later, it had taken them as little as 12 days. (See Mosiah 24:25).

The Book of Mormon records that the people took with them "all their gold, and silver, and their precious things". (V. 12). With this documentation, Mormon candidly recorded that the hearts of the people of Limhi were still influenced by their telestial trinkets, when they should have been set upon celestial sureties. (See Commentary Reference to Mosiah 25:15-16). Perhaps this is why Ammon had earlier declined the request of the people of Limhi to be baptized. (See Mosiah 21:33). Their hearts were not yet in the right place.

Later, after the people of Limhi had reached Zarahemla, Alma would preach "repentance and faith on the Lord" in the inaugural sermon of his ministry there. (Mosiah 25:15). At that time, he would exhort the People of Limhi to remember that it was the Lord who had delivered them, and not Gideon's plan, or the deleterious effect of wine on the Lamanites. (Mosiah 25:16, see Mosiah 22:3-7). Limhi's people had not completely put their welfare in the hands of the Lord the way Alma's people had done, and it would be necessary for them to be taught further in the first principles and ordinances of the Gospel, as a qualification for their baptism.

Alma's teaching would help to rekindle the desire of Limhi and his people to be baptized. Back in the Land of Nephi, during the infancy of their faith, they had wished to be baptized. (See Mosiah

21:35). At that time, the ordinance would have been premature; now they would be prepared, "because of their belief on the words of Alma". (Mosiah 25:18). Accordingly, Alma did baptize them, "and as many as he did baptize did belong to the Church of God". (Mosiah 25:18). When the people of Limhi arrived in Zarahemla, they were received with open arms and willingly became the subjects of King Mosiah, to whom they delivered "their records". (V. 13-14). These consisted of The Record of Zeniff and the Plates of Ether.

When the Lamanites in the Land of Nephi discovered that the people of Limhi were gone, they assembled an army to pursue them. But after two days, they "could no longer follow their tracks; therefore, they were lost in the wilderness". (V. 16). It was this army that, while they were looking for the way back to the Land of Nephi, would first stumble upon the priests of Noah, and then upon the people of Alma. (See Mosiah 23:31 & 35).

Mosiah
Chapter 23

Chapters 23 and 24 take up the story where Mosiah Chapter 18 left off, and comprise the account of Alma and his people after they had left the "place of Mormon".

When they fled from before the advancing armies of King Noah, they traveled 8 days into the wilderness. (V. 3). It is unclear in what direction they were headed, but when they finally left the Land of Helam it took them another twelve days before they finally arrived in Zarahemla. (See Mosiah 24:25). It had taken Ammon 40 days to reach the Land of Nephi from Zarahemla. (See Mosiah 7:5). On his return, guiding Limhi's people, he spent "many days" in the wilderness between Nephi and Zarahemla. (See Mosiah 22:11-13). Analyzed as a whole, these indirect geographical references indicate that the two were temporally separated from each other by no more than a journey of three weeks.

These geographical footnotes in The Book of Mormon also provide clues to possible locations for the Hill Cumorah. (See Mormon Chapter 8). Taking these into account, it is reasonable to assume that the hill called "Cumorah" in which Mormon hid the records of the Nephites may not have been the hill by that same name in western New York State, in the United States of America.

When King Limhi's search party found a land covered with bones of men and beasts, ruins of buildings, and remains of weapons of war, they did not yet realize that they had discovered the last battlefields and remains of the Jaredite civilization. (Mosiah 8:7-11). That this is the case is sealed by the fact that they found the twenty-four gold Plates of Ether which were expressly hidden by that Jaredite prophet in such a way that the men of Limhi might find them. (See Mosiah 8:9, & Ether 15:33).

The last battlefield of the Jaredites was in the vicinity of the Hill Ramah / Cumorah. (Ether 15:11). If it were located in what is now the state of New York, it would have been necessary for Limhi's men to have traveled about six thousand miles altogether in their attempts to find the Land of Zarahemla (if Zarahemla were in Meso-America). This is a completely unreasonable distance, considering that the elder Alma brought his group of Zeniff's people to the Land of Zarahemla in just twelve days. (See Mosiah 24:23-25).

Considering that it had taken Alma's group twenty days, to make up for any difference in position as compared with Limhi's people, they would only have traveled about four hundred miles, at the rate of twenty miles per day, to reach Zarahemla. (See Mosiah 23:3).

In view of these facts, it is reasonable to assume that the Hill Cumorah (Ramah to the Jaredites) around which the last great battles of the Nephites and Jaredites took place was in Meso-America, somewhere in the conservative range of 400 to 500 miles from Zarahemla. Wherever the hill was where Moroni deposited the records of the Nephites around 421 A.D., the Lord arranged for Joseph Smith to find them at a hill conveniently located near his home in Palmyra, New York, 1,400 years later.

Joseph Smith said that "Cumorah" in the Nephite language means "The place of light and truth". The history of the Church since the Restoration completely validates that translation. (Sydney B. Sperry, "Book of Mormon Compendium," p. 298-299).

After their flight before the army of King Noah, the people of Alma had found "a very beautiful and pleasant land of pure water" in the wilderness, which they called Helam. (V. 4, § 19). The people wanted Alma to be their king, but he declined. (V. 6-7). When we examine more closely the attitude of the Nephites toward kings, principled opposition to monarchy is hardly in evidence. They do not rise up to topple the thrones of their kings, as Fourth of July scenarios would have it. There are no farmers gathering at Lexington Green to send messages around the world. In every instance, it is the people themselves who desire a king, and the aversion to kingship comes from their leaders.

Not even Mosiah was reluctant to give up his crown when monarchy finally came to an end in Zarahemla. In fact, he willingly abdicated the throne. (See Mosiah 29:44). In the American view, despot kings held their people in bondage through superstition and ignorance until true principles of government inspired resistance. The Book of Mormon nearly reverses the roles. The people delighted in their subjection to their kings; and it was their rulers who were enlightened.

Alma counseled his people that "if it were possible that ye could always have just men to be your kings it would be well for you to have a king". (V. 8, see Mosiah 29:21). Apparently, there is nothing wrong with a monarchy. After all, Jesus will reign as King of Kings. A monarchy with a righteous king at its head is probably as good a form of government as any, as long as there is equality and "every man may enjoy his rights and privileges alike". (Mosiah 29:32, see Commentary References to Mosiah 29:13, 29:32, & 29:44).

In light of their miserable experience under the rule King Noah, however, Alma's counsel was to "stand fast in this liberty wherewith ye have been made free, and trust no man to be a king over you". (V. 13). As a matter of fact, he even warned his people to "trust no one to be your teacher nor your minister, except he be a man of God, walking in his ways, and keeping his commandments". (V. 14).

In the Church, the greatest qualifications required of teachers or leader are that they have faith in the principles of the Gospel, belief in revealed truth, and that they exercise their privileges in the spirit of fasting and prayer. When we have a knowledge of Gospel principles, we have the tools to weigh the qualities of our leader, measure what is being taught against the criterion of truth, and compare them to the standard of the scriptures and the prophets.

Alma taught his people "that every man should love his neighbor as himself," which is truly a Christ-like teaching. (V. 15). Furthermore, he saw to it that only just men were consecrated under his own hands to be priests and teachers, and this only after he had received a personal witness from the Lord confirming the anticipated action. (V. 17, see 5th Article of Faith).

Alma was the founder of the Church that had been established in the wilderness. (V. 16). He held the office of Presiding High Priest and was its ecclesiastical or spiritual leader. The establishment of this Church constituted a Dispensation of the Gospel, as sacred and significant as any other.

The Church had an effective ministering program and the people "began to prosper exceedingly". (V. 18-19). Nevertheless, the Lord saw fit to chasten his people (v. 21) for, said He, those "whom I love I also chasten that their sins may be forgiven, for with the chastisement I prepare a way for their deliverance in all things out of temptation". (D&C 95:1). This special form of punishment is the natural consequence of sin, but it is a positive influence when it brings a person or nation to repentance. (See Alma 42:16).

Mormon observed that only the Lord had the power to deliver the people of Alma. "None could deliver them, but the Lord their God". (V. 23). They would discover that his word "is quick (living or alive; quickened by the Spirit, or given spiritual life) and powerful (a source of life and energy), sharper than a two-edged sword, (separating truth from error) to the dividing asunder of both joints and marrow" (penetrating to the innermost parts of man). (D&C 6:2).

It must have been a thrill for Mormon to abridge the record of Alma, and to relive through the scriptures the deliverance of his forefathers. For "he did deliver them, and he did show forth his mighty power unto them". (V. 24, see Mosiah Chapter 24). It came about in the following way. We have previously learned that the Lamanites who had been in pursuit of the people of Limhi had become lost in the wilderness, and while wandering about had stumbled upon the Land of Helam. (V. 25, see Mosiah 22:15-16). The appearance of an army in the borders of their land terrified the People of Alma. (V. 26). To see a hostile force "with their numerous hosts, men armed with bows, and with arrows, and with swords, and with cimiters, and with stones, and with slings; and they had their heads shaved that they were naked; and they were girdled with a leathern girdle about their loins" would be frightening indeed. (Mosiah 10:8, see Enos 1:20).

Alma's strategy was to hush the fears of his people, and to "cry unto the Lord". (V. 28). His prayers were immediately answered, in sharp contrast to those of Limhi's people. (See Mosiah 21:18). The hearts of the Lamanites were softened, and the lives of Alma's people were spared.

While this army of Lamanites had been wandering about in the wilderness, trying to find their way home again, they had also encountered the shadowy priests of Noah, in a place which they called Amulon, so named after their leader, who was one of the most hardened apostates. (V. 31-32). It was the Amulonites who had kidnapped and then taken the daughters of the Lamanites in adultery. They now sent out these women to pacify the army. (V. 33).

The Amulonites and Lamanites joined forces, as a result, and again took up the march through the wilderness looking for the Land of Nephi, when, as noted above, they accidentally discovered Alma and his people in the Land of Helam. (V. 35). Alma was promised that, if he would direct them to the Land of Nephi, his people would be granted their lives and liberty. (V. 36). We can only assume it was the Lamanite women accompanying the Lamanites and Amulonites who asked for directions. It certainly never would have crossed the minds of the men to do so. (Suddenly it dawns on us why Moses and Joshua wandered for forty years in the wilderness of Sinai, maddeningly close to the Promised Land. Some things never change.)

Anyway, the promise evidently did not carry the weight of an oath, because after Alma had done as the Lamanites wished, guards were posted about in the Land of Helam, when their main body left for the Land of Nephi. (V. 38). Worst of all, Alma's former colleague Amulon was established by the king of the Lamanites as a puppet ruler over Alma and his people in the vassal state of Helam. (V. 39).

The people of Alma were in a precarious position, because their ruler was not a Lamanite who acted only in ignorance of the truth, but an apostate who had willfully renounced all that is good and true. (See Commentary Reference to Mosiah 2:37, Alma 24:30, & Moses 8:21). In reality, Amulon was a false priest, a counterfeit version of the divine model, and a caricature of the Savior in powerless form. (See Mosiah Chapter 24). As such, he was a very dangerous adversary.

The people of Alma had taken advantage of the life-generating power of the ordinances of the Gospel of Jesus Christ, and they could not be discouraged, even though their circumstances were straitened. Abraham Lincoln echoed their attitude. Said he: "I will prepare myself, and someday my time will come". Truly, discouragement is not the result of inadequacy, but is rather the result of a lack of preparation and courage. The people of Alma fortunately had both strong hearts and deep spiritual reserves.

Mosiah
Chapter 24

Amulon gained "favor in the eyes of the king of the Lamanites," whose name was Laman. (V. 1 & 3). Amulon persuaded Laman to appoint him and his cronies to be teachers over his people. Whereas Alma had consecrated priests and teachers after receiving divine confirmation, Amulon was "appointed" to the position through political patronage and influence peddling. (V. 4,5). Just what kind of teachers did Laman expect Amulon and his fellow priests to be?

The Lamanites living in the land of Shemlon, and in the land of Shilom, and in the land of Amulon were taught nothing concerning the Gospel. "They knew not God; neither did the brethren of Amulon teach them anything concerning the Lord their God, neither the law of Moses; nor did they teach them the words of Abinadi". (V. 5). However, "the language of Nephi began to be taught among all the people of the Lamanites". (V. 4). The fact that the Nephites and Lamanites began to speak the same language became more significant later on, when missionary efforts by the Sons of Mosiah commenced among the Lamanites. Amulon and his brethren had unwittingly taught the Lamanites the language of the missionary discussions! They were also ignorantly taught a Gospel principle when they instructed the Lamanites, for they were told to "keep their record ... that they might write one to another". (V. 6).

"And thus, the Lamanites began to increase in riches, and began to trade one with another and wax great, and began to be a cunning and a wise people, as to the wisdom of the world, yea, a very cunning people, delighting in all manner of wickedness and plunder, except it were among their own brethren". (V. 7).

Alma's conduct in the council chambers of King Noah had either shamed or angered Amulon, who now bore a personal grudge, and he "began to exercise authority" over his former colleague. (V. 8). "For Amulon knew Alma, that he had been one of the king's priests, and that it was he that believed the words of Abinadi, and was driven out before the king, and therefore he was wroth with him ... and put tasks upon them, and put taskmasters over them". (V. 9).

Even Amulon's children were encouraged to persecute the Nephite children. Truly, Alma and his people suffered in their bondage, but not because of wickedness. Mormon used the experience of Alma to teach us why the Lord allows His people to be chastened. (See Commentary Reference to Mosiah 23:21-23).

What Amulon hadn't anticipated was that the greater their afflictions, the more the people of Alma would "cry mightily to God". (V. 10). At least by association, he knew the power of prayer, and so he commanded "that they should stop their cries; and he put guards over them to watch them, that whosoever should be found calling upon God should be put to death". (V. 11). Prayer had evidently not been a part of Amulon's personal experience, though, because he was unaware that the people of Alma could outwardly comply with his decree, and still "pour out their hearts" to God. (V. 12). They did just that. "The effectual fervent prayer of a righteous man availeth much". (James 5:16). One need not pray with eloquence, but only with fervor. Two examples illustrate the point.

Elaine Cannon related the following story. She said that in her ward fast meeting a young woman stood up under great difficulty, the first time she had been able to do so since her husband had passed away. They hadn't been married very long before he fell terminally ill. She said that in his final days, he was suffering beyond belief, and she was really desperate. She knelt by the side of his bed, and cried out to the Lord as only a woman can do, full of anxiety, full of demands, pleading, almost scolding the Lord to hear her and answer her prayers and help her husband, to heal him. She was near hysteria. Then she felt a touch on her shoulder, and it was her husband trying to calm her. He said to her, "Just pray that I may be able to sleep through the night". As she spoke in that fast meeting, she said, "That sweet sustaining lesson taught me that you don't ask for the whole world, you don't demand that your will be done, you just pray that you can meet the challenges of the day. And that lesson from my husband just before he died has helped me to sleep through the night, too".

The second illustration comes from the life of Enzio Busche. While still a young man and before joining the Church, he found himself lying in a hospital bed near death. He asked a nun: "Is the Catholic Church the true Church of Christ?" The nun hesitatingly replied, "My Church is not the Church you are seeking. Mine is a Church of tradition". He asked, "How many Churches are there?" and she said there were at least 700 in the world. He thought, "That's not so bad. If I get out of this hospital, I'll investigate one a month until I find the true Church of Christ". He recovered from his illness, and began to investigate the Churches. But after many months, he and his wife despaired of ever finding Christ's true Church. They cried unto the Lord "until the ceiling shook". Two days later, the missionaries knocked on their door. The rest is history. (Notes from a Fireside Address, Washington Spokane North Stake, 10/18/1980).

Without doubt, the people of Alma also "shook the ceiling" with their prayers, "and it came to pass that the voice of the Lord came to them in their afflictions, saying: Lift up your heads and be of good comfort, for I know of the covenant which ye have made unto me; and I will deliver (you) out of bondage". (V. 13, see V. 16). The Lord also gave them a remarkable promise, that He would ease their burdens in order that they might witness and know of a surety that He was with them. They were promised that they would not even be able to feel their burdens upon their backs. (V. 14). "And they did submit cheerfully and with patience to all the will of the Lord". (V. 15).

An important observation is that it would be wrong to assume that the more righteous we are, the less we will suffer. The promise is that we will be blessed, even though our blessing may be the strength to endure suffering. All suffer. The difference is that the wicked must suffer the consequences of sin, in addition to the suffering that is a part of our mortal experience. (See D&C 121:7). Marion G. Romney once said: "If we can bear our afflictions with understanding, faith, and courage, we shall be strengthened and comforted and spared the torment that accompanies the mistaken idea that all suffering comes as a chastisement for transgression". (C.R. 10/1964).

In Helam, the Lord showed forth His power by causing a deep sleep to come upon the Lamanites and the Nephite taskmasters. (V. 19). It was not necessary to make the guards drunk with wine, as had been the case with the People of Limhi. The Lord merely said the word, and it was so. "Behold, I am God and have spoken it". (D&C 1:24).

Fearlessly, "Alma and his people departed into the wilderness". (V. 20). Conspicuously absent in the record is any mention that they took any earthly treasures with them. They traveled only a day before pitching their tents in the valley they called Alma, where "they poured out their thanks to God because he had been merciful unto them, and eased their burdens, and had delivered them out of bondage; for they were in bondage, and none could deliver them except it were the Lord their God". (V. 20-21). As a man of the Pharisees named Nicodemus, a ruler of the Jews, told Jesus: "Rabbi, we know that thou art a teacher come from God: for no man can do these miracles that thou doest, except God be with him". (John 3:2).

Then, the voice of this same God of miracles came unto Alma, encouraging him to make haste, for the Lamanites had awakened from their sleep. Thus, we are taught that the Lord will bring about the means of deliverance, but then it is up to us to pull it off. The Lord assured Alma that He would not abandon them, however. He declared His intention to "stop the Lamanites in this valley that they come no further in pursuit of this people". (V. 23). We do not know how the Lord accomplished this, but only that He said it would be done. And so, it was.

After twelve days, the people of Alma arrived in Zarahemla, establishing the distance to that land from the Land of Nephi at no more than 20 days' travel time. (See Mosiah 23:3). There, "king Mosiah did also receive them with joy". (V. 25). Finally, the people of Limhi and of Alma were reunited in Zarahemla. They were the only remaining Nephites from Zeniff's colony who were still faithful to teachings of the Gospel.

"And Amulon commanded them that they stop their cries; and he put guards over them to watch them, that whosoever should be found calling upon God should be put to death. And Alma and his people did not raise their voices to the Lord their God, but did pour out their hears to him; and he did know the thoughts of their hearts."
(Mosiah 24:11-12).

Mosiah
Chapter 25

In chapters 25-29, we return to a consideration of the affairs of King Mosiah in the Land of Zarahemla. This chapter opens with an account of a large gathering of the people, ordered by the king. (V. 1). The group as a whole was comprised of the People of Zarahemla, the Nephites who lived in Zarahemla, and the People of Limhi and of Alma who had recently arrived there from the Land of Nephi, by way of the Land of Helam.

Mormon recorded: "There were not so many who were descendants of Nephi, as there were of the people of Zarahemla, who was a descendant of Mulek," or more specifically, of those who had fled Jerusalem with Mulek at the time of its fall to the Babylonians, around 588 B.C. (V. 2).

The Bible does not identify a son of Zedekiah named Mulek, but it does say: "Thus saith the Lord God; I will also take of the highest branch of the high cedar, and will set it. I will crop off from the top of his young twigs a tender one, and will plant it upon an high mountain and eminent and it shall bring forth boughs, and bear fruit, and be a goodly cedar, and under it shall dwell all fowl of every wing, in the shadow of the branches thereof shall they dwell. And all the trees of the field shall know that I the Lord have brought down the high tree, have exalted the low tree, have dried up the green tree, and have made the dry tree to flourish". (Ezekiel 17:22-24).

The meaning is clear. A child of Zedekiah, the 31-year-old king, was to be cropped from the family tree and planted in another land. The name "Muleq" (Hebrew variant "to break or nip off") reminded his followers that he was both their king and the plucked off twig of Ezekiel's prophecy, fulfilled in the grim fall of Jerusalem, and in the transplanting of Judah's ruling house to another land. This land was the South Wilderness. (See Alma 22:31).

Mormon then recorded that even the combined ranks of the Nephites and People of Zarahemla were not half as numerous as the Lamanites. (V. 3). The Lamanites had destroyed the main body of the Nephites left behind in the Land of Nephi after the Elder Mosiah had departed into the wilderness. Other Nephites died during Zeniff's, Noah's, and Limhi's recolonization efforts in the

Land of Nephi. Additionally, the number of Lamanites was bolstered by defections of Nephites over the years, dating back even to the time of Jacob. (See Jacob 1:4, & Mosiah 23:25). Finally, it is possible that non-Israelites coincidentally living in the land also joined the Lamanites.

When the people were gathered into two groups (V. 4), Mosiah read to them from the records of Zeniff (V. 5), and from records kept by the people of Alma. (V. 6). For some reason, Mosiah did not translate the 24 Gold Plates of Ether at this time. Remarkably, he waited another 28 years to do so. (See Mosiah 28:11). But the records that he did share at this time "enlarged the memory of this people" (Alma 37:8), and they "were struck with wonder and amazement". (V. 7).

They had greatly contrasted feelings. The People of Zarahemla were joyful that their brethren had been delivered from bondage. (V. 8). At the same time, they were filled with sorrow that so many had been slain. (V. 9). They gave thanks to God for His goodness (V. 10), and yet were "filled with pain and anguish" for the welfare of the souls of the Lamanites, who were also "their brethren". (V. 11). We encounter these recurring feelings throughout The Book of Mormon. However, it was these same Nephites who later thought the Sons of Mosiah foolish for their desire to undertake a missionary journey to the Lamanites. (See Commentary References to Mosiah 26:1, 28:4, & 29:4-6).

Among those in Mosiah's audience were the abandoned wives and children of Amulon and his brethren, who had been the wicked priests of Noah. They were naturally "displeased with the conduct of their fathers," who not only had displayed cowardice, but who had later taken the daughters of the Lamanites in adultery, and in so doing had further shamed their families. (V. 12). Consequently, they "would no longer be called by the names of their fathers" who were now cultural Lamanites. (See Jacob 1:14). They successfully petitioned Mosiah to allow them to be "called the children of Nephi, and be numbered among those who were called Nephites". (V. 12).

The people as a whole, including the People of Zarahemla, were also to be "numbered with the Nephites". (V. 13). Mormon reiterated the point that "Nephite" was the correct appellation of this people, inasmuch as every king had been a direct descendant of Nephi himself.

When Mosiah had finished, he directed that Alma should speak to the people. (V. 14). Mosiah recognized Alma's great oratorical talents, as well as his priesthood. He took steps to effectively separate political and ecclesiastical authority in the Land of Zarahemla by giving Alma authority over the Church and its affairs, while he retained political leadership. (See Mosiah 25:19 & 26:8).

During this inaugural sermon of his ministry in Zarahemla, Alma preached "repentance and faith on the Lord" to the people. (V. 15). He exhorted the People of Limhi to remember that it was the Lord who had delivered them, and not Gideon's Plan or the effect of wine on the Lamanites. (V. 16, see Mosiah 22:3-7). Limhi's people had not completely put their welfare in the hands of the

Lord the way Alma's people had done, and it was now necessary that they should be taught the first principles and ordinances of the Gospel. (See Commentary Reference to Mosiah 22:12).

Alma's teaching rekindled the desire of Limhi and his people join the fold of God. (V. 17). About a year earlier in the Land of Nephi during the infancy of their faith, they had wished to be baptized. (See Mosiah 21:35). Then, the ordinance would have been premature; but now they were prepared, "because of their belief on the words of Alma". (V. 18). Accordingly, they were baptized by Alma, "and as many as he did baptize did belong to the Church of God". (V. 18). The word "Church" does not occur in the Old Testament, but is found 77 times in the New Testament, and 227 times in The Book of Mormon. To understand the concept of "Church" as it is used in The Book of Mormon, we need to carefully study the remaining verses of this chapter, as well as Alma 16:13.

The "Church" would continue to play a significant role in the lives of the righteous people throughout Book of Mormon history. The text invariably uses the term "synagogue," that is a Greek word, to designate early Jewish assemblies, and "Church," from the Greek "ecclesia," to designate such assemblies after they had become Christian. It is hard to think of more appropriate terms, bearing in mind that this is a translation, and the purpose of the words is not to convey what the Nephites called their communities, but only how we are to picture them in our own minds. (See D&C 66:7, Mosiah 25:13, Alma 19:34, 21:16, 23:4, & 32:1-4).

Mosiah "granted unto Alma that he might establish Churches throughout all the land of Zarahemla, and gave him power to ordain priests, and teachers over every Church". (V. 19). These Churches were the first in the Land of Zarahemla since the Elder Mosiah had left the Land of Nephi two generations earlier.

In light of his background as one of the priests of Noah, it is not hard to understand why Alma now took the ordination of priesthood leaders very seriously. They were to preach orthodox doctrine as it had been delivered to them by his own mouth. (V. 21). "There was nothing preached in all the Churches except it were repentance and faith in God". (V. 22, see V. 15). Therefore, even though there were many Churches established in the land, "they were all one Church, yea, even the Church of God". (V. 22). They confined their instruction to the doctrine of Christ.

All who were desirous to be baptized into the Church were called "the people of God" who "were blessed and prospered in the land". (V. 24). Because of the covenant that they had made, they were called the Children of Christ, his sons and his daughters, for that day he had spiritually begotten them. (See Mosiah 5:7).

"When
they thought
upon the Lamanites,
who were their brethren,
of their sinful and polluted
state, they were filled with
pain and anguish for the
welfare of their souls."
(Mosiah 25:11).

Mosiah
Chapter 26

During the next twenty years in the Land of Zarahemla, there were many of the rising generation who were sorely tempted, yielded to Satan's influences, and who then fell into apostasy. (V. 1-4). As Brigham Young said: "Though our children are begotten in righteousness, and brought forth in holiness, they must be tried and tempted, for they are agents before our Father, the same as you or I". It is inevitable that some will stumble as they make their way along the path leading to the Tree of Life.

The order in which these difficulties were enumerated by Mormon is significant. Because of unbelief, they could not understand the word of God. This resulted in spiritual sclerosis or a hardening of the heart. As a result, they would not hearken to the commandment to be baptized and to join the Church, or if they were already members, they would not remain faithful to their covenants.

"They were a separate people as to their faith". (V. 4). In effect, they became cultural Lamanites. They had committed sins that required repentance, but they could not muster the faith necessary to call upon God, which is the pathway leading to forgiveness. (See V. 22). Therefore, they were in a tailspin, spiraling downward in a sustained stall from which it was becoming increasingly difficult to regain control.

Even though these people were identifiable by their faithlessness, they mingled socially with the members of the Church and exerted influence over them. Those members who consequently committed sin were "admonished by the Church". (V. 6). As Alma the Younger later taught, "Come ye out from the wicked, and be ye separate, and touch not their unclean things". (Alma 5:57). The situation is not so different today.

It was necessary for those who had violated the most serious covenants to work out the details of their repentance before the Presiding High Priest of the Church. King Mosiah had previously "given Alma the authority over the Church". (V. 8, see Mosiah 25:19). Alma presided by the authority of the "priesthood," a word that is used only 6 times in The Book of Mormon. In each case, it is Alma who is speaking, and 5 of these citations occur in Alma chapter 13 when he was preaching in the wicked City of Ammonihah. (See Alma 4:20, 13:6, 7, 10, 14, & 18). Priesthood "is the legitimate rule of God whether in the heavens or on the earth, and it is the only legitimate power that has a right to rule upon the earth; and when the will of God is done on earth as it is in the heavens, no other power will bear rule". (John Taylor, J.D., 5:187).

In spite of his authority, Alma had never been in a position that required the trial of a person for his Church membership. "There had not any such thing happened before in the Church; therefore, Alma was troubled in his spirit". (V. 10). He would have felt a whole lot better had King Mosiah taken charge. But recognizing that this was a religious and not a civil complaint, Mosiah refused to allow the state to become involved. To do so would have usurped Alma's authority as Presiding High Priest of the Church and would have undermined his ecclesiastical leadership. (V. 12).

Without a General Handbook of Instructions, Alma could only turn to the Lord for direction. Therefore, "he went and inquired of the Lord what he should do concerning this matter". (V. 13). When the extremity of the situation offers no other solution, the Lord expects us to go to Him for guidance. However, great effort and spiritual energy are generally prerequisites in the supplication for help. Only "after he had poured out his whole soul to God, (did) the voice of the Lord" come to Alma. (V. 14). But this was as it should be.

The result of Alma's prayer was a revelation from God, comprising verses 15-32. In it, the Lord confirmed His acceptance of all that Alma had done, verified the legitimacy of his priesthood, and explained the need for forgiveness of the repentant and excommunication of the habitually and willfully rebellious. This policy has been reaffirmed in our day. Excommunication remains the most serious form of ecclesiastical punishment for sin. (See V. 32).

Abinadi had come into the Land of Nephi with none of the trappings of power save his authority. (See Mosiah 11:20, & Commentary Reference to Mosiah 28:16). Now the Lord commended Alma for his trust in that great prophet: "Thou art blessed because of thy exceeding faith in the words alone of my servant Abinadi". (V. 15). Many in Zarahemla would also develop saving faith only after hearing the words of Alma. (V. 16). It is commendable to believe the truth without being overwhelmed with tangible evidence or other proofs.

Faith is not to receive a sign from heaven. Instead, it precedes the miracle. During its genesis, it is necessary to take a few steps into the darkness, and then faith, that spiritual strong searchlight, will illuminate the way. This is why Alma taught the Zoramites: "if a man knoweth a thing he hath no cause to believe, for he knoweth it". (Alma 32:18). That is to say, in its initial stage of development, faith is not knowledge. No exercise of faith is necessary to receive a sign from heaven. If a sign is given, one might have a sure knowledge of the event, but no expenditure of faith has been necessary to produce it. Under proper circumstances, though, as we gain spiritual maturity "by doing our duty, faith increases until it becomes perfect knowledge". (Heber J. Grant, C.R. 4/1934). Initially, faith is to believe what we do not see, and the reward of faith is to see what we believe. Some things have to be believed to be seen.

But Heavenly Father will not leave us spiritually destitute, and He has not abandoned us in our mortal mission field. "Faith in Christ is not a leap in the dark. It is, instead, trust in what the spirit learned eons ago; and religious recognition is just that, a re-cognition, a re-knowing, the sum of existence. If we thwart or suppress that instinctive response, we are accountable, and to a degree, we condemn ourselves. We knew Christ before this life, we know Him here, and we will know Him hereafter. His sheep do indeed know His voice. And thus, the impact of truth on man is a test of man" and not of God. (Truman Madsen, Commentary on "B.H. Roberts, The Way, The Truth and The Life").

Thus, Alma taught: "How much more cursed is he that knoweth the will of God and doeth it not, than he that only believeth, or only hath cause to believe, and falleth into transgression?" (Alma 32:18). Belief is a mental assent to the truth or actuality of principle, without the moral element of responsibility that we call faith. To those to whom much is given, however, much is expected. The gift of faith requires action. Therefore, "faith without works is dead, being alone". (James 2:17).

To Alma, the Lord reiterated that His people were to be called after His name. (V. 18, see Mosiah 5:7, & 25:24). Then, He reconfirmed the personal covenant He had made with Alma by verifying that Alma's calling and election were made sure. "Thou art my servant", the Lord told Alma, "and I covenant with thee that thou shalt have eternal life; and thou shalt serve me and go forth in my name, and shalt gather together my sheep". (V. 20, see 2 Nephi 1:15). This is the "crowning event for the faithful. Perhaps it will not come until you have endured to the end of this life. Generally at that time, but sometimes earlier, your calling and election may be made sure when the Lord or one of his servants speaks that assurance to you". (C.E.S. "Book of Mormon Manual," p. 223).

"After we so devote ourselves to righteousness that our calling and election is made sure, then it will be our privilege to receive the Second Comforter, who is the Lord Jesus Christ Himself". (Joseph Smith, "Teachings," p. 150-1, see D&C 88:3-4). "Every one being ordained after this order and calling (of the Melchizedek Priesthood) should have power, by faith, to break mountains, to divide the seas, to dry up waters, to turn them out of their course; to put at defiance the armies of nations, to stand in the presence of God; to do all things according to his will, according to his command, subdue principalities and powers; and this by the will of the Son of God which was before the foundation of the world". (J.S.T. Genesis 14:30-31).

In the Land of Zarahemla, Alma had established seven Churches in the name of Christ for the purpose of receiving into fellowship those who had been baptized unto repentance. (V. 22). Those who believed that Christ would take upon Himself "the sins of the world" were those who had generated faith sufficient to salvation through forgiveness of sins. (V. 22-23). The Lord numbers

His children by their willingness to accept covenants. (See Commentary Reference to 2 Nephi 30:3). The missionary efforts of members of the Church in the conversion process are really quite simple. Just find those who are the elect, and teach them by the Spirit. "And ye are called to bring to pass the gathering of mine elect," declared the Lord, "for mine elect hear my voice and harden not their hearts". (D&C 29:7).

In contrast are those will not come forth until "the second trump shall sound". (V. 25). These are they who "never knew" the Lord, and who in consequence will come forth in the Second Resurrection, which is the Resurrection of the Unjust. (V. 25, see D&C 76:85). With such, the Lord will declare that He never "knew them". We never enjoyed the spiritual bond and closeness with the Savior that is typified by the marriage relationship. (V. 27). "And then will I profess unto them, I never knew you". (K.J.T. Matthew 7:23). The J.S.T. version of Matthew 7:23 reads: "And then will I say, Ye never knew me," that is more consistent with the scenario in Mosiah 26:25, and also with Mosiah 5:13, that states: "For how knoweth a man the master whom he has not served, and who is a stranger unto him, and is far from the thoughts and intents of his heart?"

The Lord told Alma that those who would not hear His voice should not be received into the Church. (V. 28). Those who hear the word of the Lord are blessed with His counsel so that they may testify to the world that He lives. "These words are not of men nor of man, but of me;" said the Lord Himself, "wherefore, you shall testify they are of me and not of man; For it is my voice which speaketh them unto you, for they are given by my Spirit unto you, and by my power you can read them one to another; and save it were by my power you could not have them; Wherefore, you can testify that you have heard my voice, and know my words". (D&C 18:34-36). "And you must preach unto the world," said the Lord, declaring: "Repent and be baptized, and not only men, but women, and children who have arrived at the years of accountability. And now, after that you have received this, you must keep my commandments in all things". (D&C 18:41-43).

Alma was instructed to act as a judge in Church tribunals, but to exercise mercy toward those who confessed and repented. He was told that it was proper that both he and the Lord should forgive such individuals. "Therefore, I say unto you," declared the Lord, "Go; and whosoever transgresseth against me, him shall ye judge according to the sins which he has committed; and if he confess his sins before thee and me, and repenteth in the sincerity of his heart, him shall ye forgive, and I will forgive him also". (V. 29). In like manner, the Lord spoke to His chief apostle, declaring: "Thou art Peter, and upon this rock I will build my Church; and the gates of hell shall not prevail against it. And I will give unto thee the keys of the kingdom of heaven: and whatsoever thou shalt bind on earth shall be bound in heaven: and whatsoever thou shalt loose on earth shall be loosed in heaven". (Matthew 16:19).

In our day, the Bishop and others in comparable positions extend forgiveness in the sense of waiving the penalty. In this capacity, the Bishop represents the Lord. This is why it is proper that members confess their sins to the Bishop, when those sins might jeopardize their Church standing.

Judicial action as it relates to members is required for three reasons: to preserve the good name of the Church, to help the sinner on the pathway to repentance and forgiveness, and to ensure impartiality when dealing with Church members.

However, it is only the Lord Who forgives sin. "The Son of man hath power on earth to forgive sins". (Matthew 9:6). He recognizes that his children do not become perfect overnight. Therefore, "as often as my people repent will I forgive them their trespasses against me". (V. 30). Of those who will not repent, he said, "the same shall not be numbered among my people". (V. 32). Excommunication is the extent of the penalty. (See V. 36).

"We believe that all religious societies have a right to deal with their members for disorderly conduct, according to the rules and regulations of such societies; provided that such dealings be for fellowship and good standing; but we do not believe that any religious society has authority to try men on the right of property or life, to take from them this world's goods, or to put them in jeopardy of either life or limb, or to inflict any physical punishment upon them. They can only excommunicate them from their society and withdraw from them their fellowship". (D&C 134:10).

When the revelation from the Lord closed, Alma was quick to write down what he had learned. (V. 33). In the infancy of the Church in Zarahemla, he was establishing a General Handbook of Instructions to guide his subsequent actions as the Presiding High Priest.

Unhappily, there were some individuals who would not repent of their sins. Accordingly, "their names were blotted out" by the authority of the priesthood. (V. 36, see Matthew 16:18-19). To blot out means as "to wipe out of existence and of memory". In the Gospel sense, excommunication is more than a withdrawal of fellowship and of the Spirit. It is to have one's name expunged from The Book of Life.

When the membership was purged of those individuals who would not repent, there again began to be peace and prosperity in the affairs of the Church. (V. 37). Alma continued to walk "circumspectly before God". He was cautious and attentive to every detail, for, while the internal affairs of the Church were peaceful, externally, there was still intense persecution. (V. 38). Nevertheless, the leaders continued to admonish their brethren and to counsel them that when they committed sin, they were to "pray without ceasing and to give thanks in all things". (V. 39).

"For behold, this is my church; whosoever is baptized shall be baptized unto repentance. And whomsoever ye receive shall believe in my name; and him will I freely forgive."
(Mosiah 26:22).

Mosiah
Chapter 27

The activity of the unbelievers increased during the next eight years to the point that the faithful members of the Church complained to Alma, who brought their case before the king. (V. 1). As a result of their petition, Mosiah "sent a proclamation throughout the land roundabout that there should not any unbeliever persecute any of those who belonged to the Church of God". (V. 2, see Alma 1:21 & Ether 7:24-25). Note that the command came from Mosiah, who was the civil leader responsible for maintaining peace and order among the people. It did not come from Alma, who was the ecclesiastical leader in Zarahemla.

Mosiah had consulted with priesthood leaders, whose consensus was that inequality, pride, haughtiness, lack of esteem, laziness, and idleness were threatening the integrity of the nation. (V. 3-4). They determined to set an example for the people, "and doing these things, they did abound in the grace of God". (V. 5). The people, especially those of Alma and Limhi, must have recalled in stark contrast the negative example set by the wicked priests of King Noah, back in the Land of Nephi, not many years earlier. (See Mosiah 11:6).

As they grew in grace, the People of Zarahemla enjoyed in greater abundance the gifts and power of God by which men and women can be brought to perfection. Even the Savior "received not of the fulness at first, but continued from grace to grace, until he received a fulness". (D&C 93:12). "And it came to pass that Jesus grew up with his brethren, and waxed strong, and waited upon the Lord for the time of his ministry to come. And he served under his father, and he spake not as other men, neither could he be taught, for he needed not that any man should teach him. And after many years, the hour of his ministry grew nigh". (J.S.T. Matthew 3:22-25). The conditions for receiving the gifts of God are submission to His will and obedience to His commandments. No one is capable of perfection through their own efforts. A greater endowment beyond our own capabilities is required.

"And the Lord did visit them and prosper them". (V. 7). In our day, He has reaffirmed to the

Saints: "Sanctify yourselves, that your minds become single to God, and the days will come that you shall see him; for he will unveil his face unto you". (D&C 88:68).

He said that He would do it in His own way, though. He tells us that when anyone repents, is baptized, keeps the commandments, prays to God, and listens to the Holy Ghost, they "shall see my face and know that I am". (D&C 93:1). "The veil shall be rent, and you shall see me, not with the carnal neither natural mind, but with the spiritual". (D&C 67:10, see V. 30).

Anyone who has obtained a witness of God has "seen" Him, in this sense. When a friend or teacher introduces us to a new concept and a light goes on in our brain, we often respond by saying "I see what you mean". This signifies that we have grasped the concept and are prepared to add it to our intellectual or spiritual data bank, where its presence enlarges our working fund of practical knowledge. When the righteous Nephites had thus "seen" God, their sure testimony enabled them to become "a large and wealthy people". (V. 7).

Fortunately, the temporal prosperity of the Nephites did not yet prove to be a corrupting influence. Too often, though, the recipients of God's blessings forget the source of their good fortune, lose their way, wander off and are lost. (See 1 Nephi 8:23). Today, lost souls in many cultures find themselves engulfed in an exceedingly great mist of darkness. "And the anger of the Lord is kindled, and his sword is bathed in heaven, and it shall fall upon the inhabitants of the earth ... For they have strayed from mine ordinances, and have broken mine everlasting covenant". (D&C 1:13-16). God is infinitely patient and long suffering, but when the world exceeds the limits of Justice, He can no longer forebear.

Newsweek Magazine reported that, long ago, "Europeans who investigated the phenomenon of a country without a titled aristocracy discerned that the pursuit of wealth would become the Americans' route to distinction, and that America would eventually develop an ideology founded on money: capitalism". With prophetic foresight, the Lord warned the Church: "If ye seek the riches which it is the will of the Father to give unto you, ye shall be the richest of all people, for ye shall have the riches of eternity; and it must needs be that the riches of the earth are mine to give; but beware of pride, lest ye become as the Nephites of old". (D&C 38:39, see D&C 1:4, & D&C 6:7).

Early in their history, the Prophet Jacob gave his Nephite brethren the antidote for pride. The formula consists of the Nephite version of the Golden Rule: "Think of your brethren like unto yourselves," and "before seeking for riches," seek the kingdom of God. (Jacob 2:17). This is our number one priority. Then, when we have shed ourselves of pride and other character crippling personality traits, and have obtained the kingdom, God will grant us the temporal blessings necessary to "clothe the naked, and to feed the hungry, and to liberate the captive, and administer relief to the sick and the afflicted". (Jacob 2:19). As we prepare to partake of the Sacrament each week, we should repetitively ask ourselves: "How do we accomplish these things today as individuals and as a Church?"

Unfortunately, in Zarahemla four of the Sons of Mosiah and one of Alma's sons named after his father "were numbered among the unbelievers". (V. 8). They had already traveled quite a distance down the road to apostasy. Alma the Younger, especially, was "in the gall of bitterness and the bands of iniquity (and) the darkest abyss". (V. 29). In effect, the light of Christ had been unsuccessful in its efforts to penetrate the barriers he had created, that surrounded him like a swirling mist of darkness.

Alma's son had substituted idolatry, or the worship of false gods, for worship of the only true and living God. He was "a very wicked and an idolatrous man. And he was a man of many words, and did speak much flattery to the people; therefore, he led many of the people to do after the manner of his iniquities". (V. 8). Satan is a skillful imitator, and he spreads the counterfeit coin of false doctrine. Beware this spurious currency; for it will purchase nothing but misery, disappointment, and spiritual death.

Men and women worship many false gods. But "shall a man make gods unto himself, and they are no gods?" (Jeremiah 16:20). Baal worshippers are as prevalent today as they ever were. It is, after all, in our day that "every man walketh in his own way, and after the image of his own god, whose image is in the likeness of the world, and whose substance is that of an idol". (D&C 1:16). Satan has no respect for the pseudo-sophistication of the Twenty First Century. In fact, our lifestyle has probably created even more opportunities for him to trash celestial sureties, and substitute them with telestial toys.

Alma the Younger became a great "hinderment" to the Church, (V. 9). This word is an interesting colloquialism of the Nineteenth Century, and is not found in the current edition of the Oxford English Dictionary. In any case, by dishonest means he stole the hearts of the people and went about in secret as an unwitting tool in the hand of Satan, whose desire it was "to destroy the Church and to lead astray the people of the Lord". (V. 10). In so doing, the young man violated the commandments of God, as well as the proclamation that had been recently issued by the king. (See v. 2).

As the Sons of Mosiah and Alma the Younger were going about the Land of Zarahemla spreading their mischief, an angel sent from God appeared to them. (V. 15). Laman and Lemuel had experienced a similar manifestation 500 years earlier, and yet it had not changed their behavior. (See 1 Nephi 3:29). This time, however, events were unfolding that would forever alter the course of Nephite and Lamanite history.

The angel "descended, as it were, in a cloud and he spake, as it were, with a voice of thunder". (V. 15). The Apostle John, who also witnessed the Lord's power, described Him in these terms: "His head and his hairs were white like wool, as white as snow, and his eyes were as a flame of fire; And his feet like unto fine brass, as if they burned in a furnace, and his voice as the sound of many waters". (Revelation 1:14-15)

Latter-day prophets have also reflected on their many revelations. Joseph Smith said: "Often times (the still small voice) maketh my bones to quake". (D&C 85:6, see N.B. Lundwall, "The Vision," p. 11). "The Holy Ghost is what every Saint needs, wrote Wilford W. Woodruff. "It is far more important than the ministration of an angel". "The impressions that come from the Holy Ghost are far more significant than a vision, declared Joseph Fielding Smith, Jr. "It is where spirit speaks to spirit, and the imprint upon the mind is far more difficult to erase".

Since faith precedes the miracle, then perhaps under normal circumstances the ministration of an angel to an ill-prepared youth like Alma the Younger would prove to be ineffectual. Note the futility of the angel's appearance to Laman and Lemuel, cited above. On the other hand, the testimony of garden-variety Latter-day Saints is the sure witness that comes from the Holy Ghost, Who is the third member of the Godhead, and Whose mission it is to testify of eternal truth. When God desires to "shew unto the heirs of promise the immutability of his counsel, (He) confirm(s) it by an oath." For example, "when God made promise to Abraham, because he could swear by no greater, he sware by himself." (Hebrews 6:13, & 17).

The Lord chose to touch Alma the Younger and the Sons of Mosiah through the medium of an angelic messenger specifically because of the faith and the fervent prayers of their loved ones. "And again, the angel said: "Behold, the Lord hath hearth the prayers of his people, and also the prayers of his servant, Alma, who is thy father; for he has prayed with much faith concerning thee that thou mightest be brought to the knowledge of the truth; therefore, for this purpose have I come to convince thee of the power and authority of God, that the prayers of his servants might be answered according to their faith". (V. 14, see Alma 8:15). It seems clear from this passage and others that angels do, indeed, watch over us.

In answer to the prayers of Alma the Younger's people, who would be to him as "saviors on Mount Zion," the angel's visit served to convince both him and the people of the omnipotence of God. After all, how could anyone dispute such power, wherein two witnesses had been provided?. After all, had not an angel from His presence appeared, and had not the very earth shaken at the sound of his voice? (V. 15, see 1 Nephi 17:54).

The angel asked Alma why he was persecuting the Saints, for he declared that the Church was Jesus Christ's, and nothing could overthrow it, except the transgression of its members. (V. 13). Heber J. Grant echoed these words when he said, "We can never be injured by any mortals, except ourselves". (C.R. 4/1909). The Lord Himself reassured us, saying: "It is not the work of God that is frustrated, but the work of men". (D&C 3:3). The enemies of the Church have never done anything that has injured the work of God, and they never will. Where are the men of influence, the men of power, and the men of prestige who have worked against the Church of Jesus Christ of Latter-day Saints?

The angel used the experience of the captivity of Alma and his people to teach his son a lesson on the power of God. (V. 16). He admonished Alma the Younger to spare the Church, asking him to do it "even if thou wilt of thyself be cast off". (V. 16). In other words, the angel said, "Destroy yourself if you must, but spare the Church". Then he departed. The effect of the visit of the angel was so powerful that Alma completely lost his strength for three days. (See Alma 36:10). During this time, his father rejoiced, and after a day had passed, he and the clergy fasted and prayed that young Alma might regain his faculties, "that the eyes of the people might be opened to see and know of the goodness and glory of God". (V. 23). Alma did regain his strength, and then declared that during his ordeal he had repented of his sins "nigh unto death". (V. 28). He later referred to this experience as his "conversion". (Alma 27:25).

The Lord had redeemed him, and he had been born of the Spirit. (V. 24). His sins had been grievous. Many years later he said: "I have murdered many of his children, or rather led them away unto (spiritual) destruction; yea, and in fine so great had been my iniquities, that the very thought of coming into the presence of my God did rack my soul with inexpressible horrors". (Alma 36:3).

He had been born again, "born of God, changed from (a) carnal and fallen state, to a state of righteousness, being redeemed of God, becoming his son". (V. 25, see Mosiah 5:7, & Alma 7:14). The covenant he had made with God was a binding contract founded on direct revelation.

The 9th Article of Faith states: "We believe all that God has revealed, all that He does now reveal, and we believe that He will yet reveal many great and important things pertaining to the Kingdom of God". What could be more important to us than to know by revelation that ordinances of the priesthood pertaining to salvation and exaltation may be performed in our behalf, and that they are binding on earth and in heaven? (See Matthew 16:19).

It is a principle central to the Plan that all are welcome to participate fully in Gospel ordinances. The invitation is extended to all to "Come unto Christ". (See Moroni 10:32). All the Lord requires is "the hearts of the children of men". (D&C 64:22). Truly, He is "no respecter of persons". (D&C 1:35). Holiness is not an office or a calling, but is living in harmony with the principles and ordinances of the Gospel of Jesus Christ.

In our day, beside the waters of baptism, the penitent receive the Holy Ghost, and are confirmed as members of The Church of Jesus Christ of Latter-day Saints. They take upon themselves the name of Christ. The Holy Ghost ratifies the administrators' authority. They are "Born Again Christians" in the true and proper sense of the word. By spiritual rebirth, they become new creatures in Christ. (See 2 Corinthians 5:17). But even card-carrying members of the Church "can in nowise inherit the kingdom of God" unless they experience a spiritual conversion. (V. 26). Every member of the Church would do well to ponder the conversion story of Alma the Younger. From "the gall of bitterness and bonds of iniquity," from out of "the darkest abyss," he came to behold "the marvelous light of God". (V. 29). Whereas his soul had been "racked with eternal torment," afterward there was "nothing so exquisite and sweet as was (his) joy". (Alma 36:21). In our day, the Lord has promised: "If your eye be single to my glory your whole bodies shall be filled with light, and there shall be no darkness in you, and that body which is filled with light comprehendeth all things". (D&C 88:67).

Alma foresaw the Last Days, when the wicked would "receive the judgment of an everlasting punishment". (V. 31). He had "seen the light," and understood by personal revelation that it is Christ Who is the Life and the Light of the world. Every man and woman in the world has a measure of that light. Daily living can be a process of detraction, in the sense that light can be lost through behavior that is inconsistent with eternal principles. The Judgment, then, may be a process of measuring the numbers of "foot-candles of light" that we bring to the Bar of Justice. In this sense, then, we will judge ourselves.

"The Book of Life is the record of our acts that are written in our own bodies. It is the record engraven on the very bones, sinews, and flesh of the mortal body. That is, every thought, word, and deed has an effect on the human body; all these leave their marks which can be read by Him who is Eternal as easily as the words of a book can be read". (Bruce R. McConkie, "Mormon Doctrine," p. 97). Carol Lynn Pearson wrote: "I don't fret as to where my soul will be assigned, whether I find myself with the Celestial, or not quite qualify. It's simple: Water meets its own level. So shall I". ("Beginnings," p. 53).

Having been "born again," Alma and the Sons of Mosiah now felt a burning desire to share the Gospel with their neighbors, and so they traveled "round about through all the land, publishing to all the people the things which they had seen, and preaching the word of God in much tribulation," suffering trials similar to those they had inflicted upon the members of the Church before their conversion. (V. 32-33, see Mosiah 26:38-39).

The Sons of Mosiah are identified in verse 34 as Ammon, Aaron, Omner, and Himni, although the order of their birth is never clarified in The Book of Mormon. Their mission with Alma the Younger throughout the land of Zarahemla among the Nephites did much to repair the damage they had done, "and thus they were instruments in the hands of God in bringing many to the knowledge of the truth". (V. 35-36).

So impressed was Mormon with these young men, that he was moved to declare in his abridgement of the records: "And how blessed are they! For they did publish peace". (V. 37). The only man in the scriptures that is identified as a prince of peace, besides the Savior, was the great High Priest Melchizedek. What better tribute could be paid to a servant of the Lord than to publish peace in a world filled with raucous contention?

Mosiah
Chapter 28

The first 7 verses of this chapter concern the entreaties of the Sons of Mosiah to their father on behalf of their brethren the Lamanites. They desired to take the Gospel message to them, "that perhaps they might bring them to the knowledge of the Lord their God," and at the same time, put an end to nearly 500 years of fratricidal conflict. (V. 1-2).

Their focus of concern was revealing, and was patterned after that of their ancestors Nephi and Enos. (See 2 Nephi Chapter 33, & Enos 1:9 & 11). We typically think first of our own welfare, and then of that of our friends. Finally, when the Spirit truly quickens us, we think of all mankind, friend and foe alike, as our brethren, and we labor selflessly in their behalf.

The Sons of Mosiah properly went to their father, who was the king, for permission to travel to the land of Nephi, rather than to Alma, who was the head of the Church. Mosiah had the responsibility to make decisions regarding relations with other sovereign nations. (V. 1).

Whenever the land of Nephi that lay to the south of the land of Zarahemla is mentioned in The Book of Mormon, it is characterized as being "up," or higher in elevation. (V. 1 & 6, see Mosiah 7:1-4, 9 & 13, 20:7, 28:1, 5, 6, 7 & 9). Book of Mormon history very likely took place primarily in Southern Mexico and Northern Central America. The land of Lehi's First Inheritance would then be along the Pacific Coast of Guatemala or El Salvador. For the Lamanites "lived in the wilderness, and dwelt in tents; and they were spread through the wilderness on the west, in the land of Nephi; yea, and also on the west of the land of Zarahemla, in the borders by the seashore, and on the west in the land of Nephi, in the place of their fathers' first inheritance, and thus bordering along by the seashore". (Alma 22:28).

Conflicts with the Lamanites would have soon forced Nephi and his followers inland up into the mountain valleys of Highland Guatemala, where they established the City of Nephi. The Book of Mormon consistently describes the land of Nephi as a highland region, (e.g., Words of Mormon 1:13, Mosiah 7:6, Alma 49:10 & 56:3). The elevation would have created a cool, mild climate more comfortable than the hot, humid coastal plain. About 250 B.C., Mosiah I led Nephite refugees from the land of Nephi down into Zarahemla, probably located in the Mexican State of Chiapas, which is lower in elevation than Highland Guatemala. Between the two lands is rugged, mountainous wilderness, in which both Nephite scouts and Lamanite armies might easily become lost, as indeed they did. (See Mosiah 22:15-16).

Ammon, Aaron, Omner, and Himni had been "the very vilest of sinners" for they had been despicable on moral grounds. (V. 4). Now, "the very thoughts that any soul should endure endless torment did cause them to quake and tremble," so they determined to take the Gospel to the Lamanites, precisely because they were "a wild and a hardened and a ferocious people ... who delighted in murdering the Nephites, and robbing and plundering them". (Alma 17:14).

The priesthood leaders in Zarahemla reacted dramatically to their request. Ammon related: "Our brethren laughed us to scorn". They said that the Lamanites were "a stiffnecked people, whose hearts delight in the shedding of blood, whose days have been spent in the grossest iniquity, whose ways have been the ways of a transgressor from the beginning". (Alma 26:23-25). This rejoinder was just as polarized as that of the Lamanites toward the Nephites, and was a far cry from the feelings of those pious Nephites barely a generation earlier, who had been "filled with pain and anguish for the welfare of the souls of their brethren the Lamanites". (Mosiah 25:11).

But "they did plead with their father many days that they might go up to the land of Nephi". (V. 5). Mosiah took the correct course of action in the face of a significant petition with dramatic political consequences. He went for instruction to the Lord, Who told Mosiah to let them go, and promised him three things. (V. 6). First, He said that many Lamanites would listen to their message. (See Alma 23:8-13, 26:4, & 26:31). Secondly, He said that, consequently, both Mosiah's sons and the Lamanites would have eternal life. (See Alma 26:13-15, & 26:20). Finally, He promised Mosiah that his sons would return home safely from their mission. (See Alma 26:27-30).

Greatly relieved, Mosiah granted their request, and they departed into the wilderness on what turned out to be a 14-year full-time mission in a foreign land, lasting roughly from 90 B.C. to 77 B.C. (V. 8-9). Mormon promised to give a full mission report later in the record. (V. 9). Alma Chapters 17-26 contain that account, which is, by any standard, an amazing story.

The Church refines courageous young men like the Sons of Mosiah who can stand the heat of telestial fire. It is their destiny to join the army of God and receive the enemy into its hands.. Ammon, Aaron, Omner, and Himni did not elect to postpone their mission so that they could finish other important business at home. We do not know if they had athletic scholarships, girl friends, or lucrative employment opportunities. We do not know if they set aside opportunities for formal education, and Mormon did not reveal the details of their personal circumstances or temporal goals. But a modern prophet of God has given counsel in a book entitled "Life's

Directions" to the youth of the Church today: "Secular knowledge, important as it may be, can never save a soul nor open the celestial kingdom, nor create a world nor make a man a god, but it can be most helpful to that man who, placing first things first, has found the way to eternal life and who can now bring into play all knowledge to be his tool and servant. Beloved youth, can you see why we must let spiritual training take first place? Why we must pray with faith, and perfect our own lives, like the Savior's? Can you see that spiritual knowledge may be complemented with the secular in this life and on for eternities, but that the secular without the foundation of the spiritual is but like the foam upon the milk, or the fleeting shadow? Do not be deceived. One need not choose between the two, but only as to the sequence, for there is opportunity for one to get both simultaneously, but can you see that the seminary courses should be given even preferential attention over the high school subjects, the institute over the college courses, the study of the scriptures ahead of the study of the man-written texts, the association with the Church more important than clubs, fraternities, and sororities, the payment of tithing more important than paying tuition and fees? Can you see that the ordinances of the temple are more important than the Ph.D. or any and all other academic degrees?" (President Spencer W. Kimball)

There are parallels in our society to the mission calls received by the Sons of Mosiah, that might be illustrated by the following adaptation of scripture: "And it came to pass that the prophet did plead with the members of the Church many days that they might have the desire to teach their neighbors the Gospel. But the members laughed him to scorn. For they said unto him: Do ye suppose that we can bring our neighbors to the knowledge of the truth? Do ye suppose that we can convince them of the incorrectness of the traditions of their fathers, as stiffnecked a people as they are; whose hearts delight in the practice of abortion; whose days have been spent smoking and drinking, and in adultery; whose ways have been the ways of wild partygoers from the beginning? Moreover, they did say; Instead, let us take up arms against them, that we destroy them and their iniquity out of the land, lest they overrun us and destroy us with their habits and practices that are inconsistent with Gospel principles. But the prophet went and inquired of the Lord if the members should go among their neighbors to preach the word. And the Lord said unto him: Urge them to go, for many shall believe on their words, and all of my children who believe shall have eternal life, and I will deliver thy brethren out of the hands of those of your neighbors who refuse to accept these glad tidings. And so, as a result of the renewed efforts of faithful member of the Church, millions were brought to the knowledge of the Lord. Behold, in how many nations are branches of the Church now organized; in every land that has been dedicated to the preaching of the Gospel and the gathering of the Saints, multitudes have been loosed from the pains of hell, and they are brought to sing the song of redeeming love, and this because of the power of His word which has always dwelt within the bosom of the members. It was only necessary that they unlock the repository of the gift, nurture the word, and be true to their baptismal covenants. Even though, at times, the members were ostracized, and made fun of, and spit upon, and physically abused; and were mugged, and unfairly accused, and imprisoned; yet through the power and wisdom of God they were delivered again". (See Alma 26:23-25).

"Now my brethren, we see that God is mindful of every people, whatsoever land they may be in; yea, he numbereth his people, and his bowels of mercy are over all the earth". (Alma 26:37). "And he inviteth them all to come unto him and partake of his goodness; and he denieth none that come unto him, black and white, bond and free, male and female; and he remembereth the heathen; and all are alike unto God, both Jew and Gentile". (2 Nephi 26:33)

At this point, 28 years after receiving them, Mosiah "translated and caused to be written" the 24 Gold Plates of Ether. (V. 11, see Ether 1:2). The only part of the translation that was withheld from the people was the vision of the Brother of Jared, which included "all their oaths, and their covenants, and their agreements in their secret abominations; yea, and all their signs and their wonders ... lest peradventure they should fall into darkness also and be destroyed". (Alma 37:27). This was not revealed until after the Savior's visit to the Nephites. (See Alma 63:12, & Ether 4:1). Verses 11 through 19 provide a parenthetical note in the record, which explains the reason for Mosiah's translation, and the effect it had upon the Nephites.

The People of Limhi had carried these plates to Zarahemla almost three decades earlier. At that time, Mosiah had incorporated into the body of the Nephite records those of Zeniff and of Alma, and had made them available to the people, but he had never turned his attention to the Plates of Ether. (See Mosiah 25:5-7, and Commentary Reference to Mosiah 27:18).

The people of Limhi knew that something tremendously significant had happened in the land of Desolation, and they were anxious to find out what it was, by having the records translated that were found there. (V. 11-12, see Mosiah Chapter 21). This, Mosiah did by "means of those two stones which were fastened into the two rims of a bow". (V. 13). This was the Urim and Thummim, or Lights and Perfections. (J.S.H. 2:35). The history concerning the Urim and Thummim, or the "interpreters," is unclear. The Lord gave a Urim and Thummim to the Brother of Jared that he brought with him to the American continent. That it was this Urim and Thummim that was in the possession of Mosiah is suggested from Book of Mormon teachings. These were separate and distinct from the Urim and Thummim possessed by Abraham, and that was carefully guarded by Israel in the days of Aaron.

There is no record of Lehi bringing a Urim and Thummim with him to the Americas. How Mosiah came into possession of the Urim and Thummim the record does not reveal, more than to say that it was "a gift from God". Mosiah had this gift before the People of Limhi discovered the Jaredite record of Ether. It may have been received when the large stone with engravings upon it was brought to the Elder Mosiah. (See Omni 1:20-21). The Lord may have given it to him, or to some other prophet before his day.

Verses 14 and 15 suggest that the Urim and Thummim was given first to earlier prophets, and was kept by the Lord for safekeeping: "These things were prepared from the beginning, and were handed down from generation to generation ... and they have been kept and preserved by the hand of the Lord".

Mormon explained that possession of the Urim and Thummim identifies one as a "seer". (V. 16, see Commentary Reference to Mosiah 8:13). A seer is literally a 'See-er,' or one who has the right to use the Urim and Thummim. "A prophet is a teacher. He teaches the body of truth, the Gospel, revealed by the Lord to man, and under inspiration explains it to the understanding of the people. A seer is one who sees with spiritual eyes; he is an interpreter and clarifier of truth. He foresees the future. He is one who sees, who walks in the Lord's light with open eyes. A revelator makes known, with the Lord's help, something before unknown. The revelator always deals with truth, and it always comes with the divine stamp of approval. In summary, a prophet is a teacher of known truth, a seer is a perceiver of hidden truth, and a revelator is a bearer of new truth". (John A. Widtsoe, see Commentary Reference to Mosiah Chapter 8).

The Plates of Ether contained a history of "the people who were destroyed" back to the time of the Tower of Babel, and from there to Adam. (V. 17). That tower had been the binding place of heaven and earth where it was hoped that one could establish contact with heaven. In fact, that ziggurat was a vain and corrupt counterfeit of the temple, where alone we get our bearings on the eternities.

The purpose of the confounding of languages that took place after the destruction of the tower was that men and women might gain fluency in the universal language of the Spirit. Primarily because of the faith of the brother of Jared, the language of the Jaredites had been left intact at that time. (See Ether 1:34-35, & "The World of The Jaredites," p. 164-166).

The account of the destruction of the Jaredites, written upon the gold plates of Ether, caused "the people of Mosiah to mourn exceedingly". (V. 18). However, the Lord had given the People of Zarahemla the translation of these 24 gold plates to teach them the contrasting lessons of freedom and captivity, in order to help them prevent their own temporal or spiritual bondage in the future. In this sense, the plates "gave them much knowledge in the which they did rejoice". (V. 18).

Mormon noted that the record of the Jaredites would be given later. We know that account as The Book of Ether in The Book of Mormon. He thought it expedient that "all people should know the things which are written in this account". (V. 19). Today, the Lord has given us The Book of Mormon, in just the same way that He gave the Nephites The Book of Ether. Our Book of Mormon, then, is comparable in value to the records of the Jaredites given to the People of Zarahemla. What we do with The Book of Mormon, whether we use it as a guide to help us through the perilous Last Days, is entirely up to us, just as it was up to the Nephites to learn sobering lessons from The Book of Ether.

Hugh Nibley observed: "The last generation did not make much of The Book of Mormon. But now with every passing year this great and portentous story becomes more and more familiar and more frighteningly like our own. It is an exciting thing to discover that the man Lehi was a real historical character ... but it is far more important and significant to find oneself in this Twentieth Century standing, as it were, in his very shoes. The events and situations of The Book of Mormon that not many years ago seemed wildly improbable to some and greatly overdrawn have suddenly become the story of our own times, when we see and shall see the words of those prophets who speak to us from the dust fearfully and wonderfully vindicated". ("The World and The Prophets," p. 196).

Ezra Taft Benson admonished the Saints, telling them that if a Church member does not study The Book of Mormon, "he is placing his soul in jeopardy and neglecting that which could give spiritual and intellectual unity to his whole life. In two ways, The Book of Mormon brings us to Christ. First, it speaks plainly of Him and His Gospel. It testifies of His divinity, of the necessity for a Redeemer, and of our need to put our trust in Him. It bears witness of the Fall, the Atonement, and the first principles of the Gospel, including our need of a broken heart, a contrite spirit, and spiritual rebirth. It proclaims we must endure to the end in righteousness and live the moral lives of Saints. Secondly, The Book of Mormon exposes the enemies of Christ. It confounds false doctrines and contentions. It fortifies the humble followers of Christ against the evil designs, strategies, and doctrines of the devil in our day".

"Oh, my brethren," President Benson continued, "let us not treat lightly the great things we have received from the hand of the Lord. His word is one of the most valuable gifts He has given us. I urge you to recommit yourselves to a study of the scriptures. Read them in your families and teach your children to love and treasure them. Then, prayerfully and in counsel with others. seek every way possible to encourage the members of the Church to follow your example". (C.R. 4/1986). When we do so, we will find that the word has a powerful effect on us and has a great tendency to lead us to do that which is just. (See Alma 31:5).

With his sons gone on a mission of indeterminate length, Mosiah "had no-one to confer the kingdom upon". (V. 10). In anticipation of the change from monarchial government to that of judges, Mosiah took the emblems of authority, and gave them to Alma the Younger, who was destined to be Zarahemla's first Chief Judge and High Priest. (V. 20, see Mosiah 29:42). These emblems were the "types" of national treasures that a ruler was required to possess to validate the legitimacy of his power. (Gordon C. Thomasson, "The Complex Symbolism and the Symbolic Complex of Kingship in The Book of Mormon" FARMS, 1985, & Commentary Reference to Mosiah 1:55).

Mosiah
Chapter 29

There is a consistent pattern running through the pages of The Book of Mormon. Although it is basically the record of a people inhabiting the New World, its style has Old World precedents. Against that background, these patterns come into focus. In the Old-World history of the Israelite nation, Book of Mormon prototypes are laid down perfectly, for its intrinsic structure is biblical. Early American political, historical, and social forms are conspicuously absent. The events chronicled in Mosiah Chapter 29 are faithful reflections of these ancient patterns.

When Mosiah had conferred upon Alma the Younger the emblems of authority, he sent representatives throughout the land of Zarahemla, desiring to know the will of the people "concerning who should be their king". Mosiah was at this time about 62 years old and felt the need to pass the torch to a younger man. The people preferred Aaron, the son of Mosiah first mentioned in the scriptures, (V. 2). He was probably the eldest, and so would have been the logical candidate. (See Mosiah 27:34). However, he was away on a mission to the Lamanites that he and his 3 brothers felt was a more important responsibility. (V. 3).

A potential crisis loomed in the developing political stalemate, and Mosiah feared that, should someone else be appointed king, Aaron might one day return to claim the throne, creating a division among the people that could be the catalyst for conflict. (V. 7). Additionally, Mosiah was concerned that his once wayward son might "turn again to his pride and vain things and claim his right to the kingdom, which would cause him and also this people to commit much sin". (V. 9). His was a literate society, and so he circulated a position paper among his subjects to justify to them his course of action and to educate them so that they might more responsibly exercise their agency in the future. (V. 5-37).

Mosiah decided to remain king "for the remainder of (his) days" that turned out to be just one more year. (V. 11). In anticipation of his demise, he said: "We will appoint wise men to be judges, that will judge this people according to the commandments of God". (V. 11).

It has always been important to have leaders whose rule is founded on eternal law. The great American statesman and orator Daniel Webster declared: "If we and our posterity shall be true to the Christian religion, and if we and they shall live always in the fear of God and shall respect His commandments, we may have the highest hopes for the future fortunes of our country. It will have no decline and fall, but it will go on prospering. But if we or our posterity shall reject religious instructions and authority, violate the rules of morality, and recklessly destroy the political constitution that holds us together, no one can tell how sudden a catastrophe may overwhelm us, that shall bury all of our glory in profound obscurity". ("The Dignity and Importance of History," 2/23/1852).

At the same time, after concluding an extensive tour of America, Alexis de Tocqueville is widely believed to have written: "I sought for the greatness and genius of America in her commodious harbors and her ample rivers, and it was not there; in her fertile fields and boundless prairies and it was not there; in her rich mines and her vast world commerce, and it was not there. Not until I went to the churches of America and heard her pulpits aflame with righteousness did I understand the secret of her genius and her power." Whether or not the 19th century French diplomat, political scientist, and historian who wrote "Democracy in America" was the author of these observations, the conclusion that "America is great because she is good, and if America ever ceases to be good, she will cease to be great", deserves our careful consideration.

Mosiah recognized the preeminence of divine justice when he said: "It is better that a man should be judged of God than of man, for the judgments of God are always just, but the judgments of man are not always just". (V. 12). He then vividly contrasted the reign of his righteous father Benjamin to that of wicked King Noah. (V. 13 & 18).

The earlier Nephite kings and the Chief Judges who were to follow were executive, legislative, and judicial branches all in one. We shall see, however, that there was a system of checks and balances built into both systems. (See V. 28-29). More basic than the type of government, though, was the obedience of the rulers to the unvarying laws and commandments of God. When conditions of obedience prevail, Mosiah said: "It would be expedient that ye should always have kings to rule over you". (V. 13). Under such conditions, he felt that autocracy was preferable to democracy.

This principle might be startling to those who have been taught that democracy is ordained of God and is the best form of government. Actually, that form of government is best that allows men and women to exercise their agency to achieve their potential within the framework of the Gospel of Jesus Christ. Theocracy is the best form of monarchy. Short of that, Mosiah believed that a righteous and God-fearing king is best. (See Commentary References to Mosiah 23:6-7, & 29:44). His own father, after all, had provided the classic example of enlightened leadership.

But in and of itself, a disciplined mind is not enough. "If rationalism wishes to govern the world without regard to the religious needs of the soul, the experience of the French Revolution is there to teach us the consequences of such a blunder". (Ernest Renan, "The Apostles"). Religion is necessary to morality. Despite his cynicism, Rousseau was close to the mark when he wrote: "I do not know what the heart of a rascal may be; I know what is in the heart of an honest man. It is horrible". The point is, that even in the best of circumstances, we cannot be left to our own devices without the guiding influence of the Spirit. "Power tends to corrupt, and absolute power corrupts absolutely". (Lord Acton). When our hearts are set upon temporal things only, spirituality is weakened until our moral compass spins wildly out of control. (See Commentary Reference to Mosiah 21:3, D&C 25:10 & 121:35-36).

Will and Ariel Durant wrote: "Since men love freedom, and the freedom of individuals in society requires some regulation of conduct, its first condition is its limitation; make it absolute and it dies in chaos". ("The Lessons of History," p. 68). In the beginning, the Lord declared: "We will prove them herewith, to see if they will do all things whatsoever the Lord their God shall command them". In other words, we will impose conditions and limitations upon the exercise of agency, so that men and women will be able to continue to progress. "And they who keep their second estate shall have glory added upon their heads for ever and ever". (Abraham 3:25-26).

When we engage our agency, we automatically limit our options. When we choose well, we avoid less attractive consequences. Heavenly Father gives us commandments that allow us to grow closer to our potential every time we exercise our agency.

Neal A. Maxwell wrote: "Freedom wisely used to interact with the principles of the Gospel of Jesus Christ, far from producing drabness and uniformity in disciples, produces not only more significant individuals but more interesting individuals". There is something about the Gospel that makes personality more luxuriant, whereas sin robs us of our individuality. He continued: "What a great adventure most men decline when they choose not to know their Father. What great folly for the amateur climbing the rugged and strait and narrow way to decline the services of such an Experienced Guide. The unconfronted individual who persists in walking after his own way is clearly headed for a personality precipice". ("Freedom: A Hard Doctrine").

Freedom and security are incompatible. Security is at its zenith in prisons and hospitals, where every physical need is met. But the liability of freedom is risk. Our tendency to look to the government for cradle-to-the-grave job security, social security, and so on, speaks for itself. It is the evidence of a desire to avoid risk. Caesar provides security, and assumes the risk. The danger lies with the power-hungry individual who is eager to step into a vacuum and assume control. All that is required is that the people give up their agency, that is generally done willingly, yet blindly and ignorantly.

"Beware the leader who bangs the drums of war in order to whip the citizenry into a patriotic fervor, for patriotism is indeed a double-edged sword. It emboldens the blood, but narrows the mind. For when the drums of war reach a fever pitch, the blood boils with hate, and when minds have closed, leaders will have no need to seize the rights of the citizenry. Rather, the citizenry, infused with fear and blinded with patriotism, will offer up all of its rights to the leader, and gladly so. How do I know? For this is what I have done. And I am Caesar". (Anonymous).

"When God made the oyster, He guaranteed its absolute economic and social security. He built the oyster a house for shelter and protection from enemies. When hungry, the oyster simply opens its shell and food rushes in. It has freedom from want. But when God made the eagle, He declared: "The blue sky is the limit! Build your own house!" So, the eagle built on the highest mountain. Storms threaten it every day. For food, it flies through miles of rain and snow and wind. But the eagle, and not the oyster, is the emblem of America". (Morris Mandel). Besides, whoever heard of an "Oyster Scout"?

To Mosiah, monarchy was a "type" of basic Gospel principles, and was the antithesis of its unrighteous dictatorial opposite. He taught that the ideal relationship of a king to his subjects is like that of parents to their children, and of God to all His children. The role of parents, kings, and gods is ultimately to allow those within the sphere of their influence to exercise agency in order to strengthen commitment to personal responsibilities, and ultimately to help them to become co-inheritors of all that eternity has promised to the faithful. This lesson is implicit in the entire Book of Mormon. It serves as a complex type of the Plan of Salvation itself.

Then, Mosiah used the example of King Noah as a "type" of Satan, and his reign as a reflection of Lucifer's counterfeit Plan. (V. 18). Noah's strategy was patterned after his mentor, the devil. It was to consciously avoid teaching correct principles, and to deny the people their freedom, thus leaving them ultimately disinherited, driven from their lands, and left to physical and spiritual destruction. "And thus we see that the devil will not support his children at the last day, but doth speedily drag them down to hell". (Alma 30:60).

Men and women who would be free recognize the awesome responsibility of their stewardship. The last official words of President John F. Kennedy that were to have been delivered at the conclusion of a speech he planned to give in Dallas, Texas, on the afternoon of November 22, 1963, reflect his appreciation of this responsibility: "We in this country, in this generation, are - by destiny rather than by choice - the watchmen on the walls of world freedom. We ask, therefore, that we may be worthy of our power and responsibility; that we may exercise our strength with wisdom and restraint, and that we may achieve in our time and for all time the ancient vision of peace on earth, good will toward men. That must always be our goal, and the righteousness of our cause must always underlie our strength. For as was written long ago: "Except the Lord keep the city, the watchman waketh in vain." (Psalms 127:1).

Lord Acton, a Nineteenth Century British observer of the American political scene, noted: "It was from America that the plain ideas that men ought to mind their business, and that the nation is responsible to Heaven for the acts of the State burst upon the scene like a conqueror upon the world they were destined to transform, under the title of the Rights of Man; and the principle gained ground, that a nation can never abandon its fate to an authority it cannot control".

Mosiah pointed out that it was only because of their sincere repentance that the People of Limhi had been delivered from bondage. "And thus, doth the Lord work with his power in all cases among the children of men, extending the arm of mercy towards them that put their trust in him". (V. 20). It is an extremely important principle that "when we obtain any blessing from God, it is by obedience to that law upon which it is predicated". (D&C 130:21). It is critical that we understand that blessings follow obedience to the specific laws upon which those blessings are predicated.

Mosiah then cautioned his people that it is very difficult to dethrone a wicked king. (V. 21). Verses 21-24 reiterate that categorical Book of Mormon opposition to monarchy is not a matter of fixed principle. Mosiah's opposition to it was not advocated as a fundamental political truth. It was simply based on the premise that wicked kings have a tremendous potential power to spread mischief. A good king, however, is quite another matter, (See Commentary Reference to Mosiah 23:6-8, 29:13 & 24).

Verse 21 is interesting because it suggests that King Mosiah condoned revolution as an acceptable alternative to corrupt government. "Ye cannot dethrone an iniquitous king," he said, "save it be thru much contention and the shedding of much blood". Even President Abraham Lincoln, who led the United States of America into its bloodiest conflict in order to preserve the Union, declared 13 years earlier that "any people, anywhere, being inclined and having the power, have the right to rise up and shake off the existing government, and form a new one that suits them better".

The issue of "independence" is charged with special emotion for Americans. The word "independent" occurs only once in the scriptures and that in the context of describing the Church as a body. (D&C 78:14). The Church, moreover, can "stand independent above all creatures" only because it is entirely dependent upon the providence of God. As King Benjamin taught, when we serve God with our whole heart and soul, we are free from dependence upon any other being. God transfers our indebtedness to Him to the poor, and it is through them that He asks us to pay our debt to Him. Thus, a Zion Society is created.

No other religious organization, however, stresses so much the meaning and worth of the individual soul, as does The Church of Jesus Christ of Latter-day Saints. It is the ultimate value, and the Church is the instrument for its development. Surprisingly, the family is the highest expression within the Church of individual life, is the foundation for individual and collective happiness on earth, and is the basic building block of eternal life.

Verses 22-23 typify world events in the Twenty-first Century. Unrighteous rulers have had "friends in iniquity" and maintain large armies and secret police forces to protect their illegitimate rule and their selfish interests. They have torn up or disregarded the established laws of the land and have trampled under their feet both the Constitution with its Bill of Rights, and the commandments of God. (V. 22). They enact laws to suit their own wicked and corrupt purposes, and whoever is so bold as to defy these laws risks public ridicule and private destruction. Organized resistance against wicked rulers may be violently suppressed. In this manner, have unrighteous rulers "perverted the ways of all righteousness". (V. 23, see Commentary Reference to Mosiah 21:3).

There is nothing intrinsically wrong with monarchy. It is not diametrically opposed to good government. It is inexpedient, or not suitable to most circumstances, however, simply because it is too easily subject to abuse. (V. 24).

The American patriot Patrick Henry delivered the following speech from the floor of the House of Burgesses, Williamsburg, Virginia, in March 1775. It is a stirring denunciation of abusive monarchy: "They tell us, Sir, that we are weak and unable to cope with so formidable an adversary. Sir, we are not weak, if we make a proper use of those means which the God of nature hath placed in our power. Three millions of people, armed in the holy cause of liberty, and in such a country as that which we possess, are invincible by any force which our enemy can send against us. Besides, Sir, we shall not fight our battles alone. There is a just God who presides over the destinies of nations, and who will raise up friends to fight our battles for us. The battle, Sir, is not to the strong alone; it is to the vigilant, the active, the brave. Besides, Sir, we have no election. If we were base enough to desire it, it is now too late to retire from the contest. There is no retreat but in submission and slavery! Our chains are forged! Their clanking may be heard on the plains of Boston! The war is inevitable, and let it come! I repeat, Sir, let it come!

It is vain, Sir, to extenuate the matter. Gentlemen may cry, 'Peace, Peace!' but there is no peace. The war is actually begun! The next gale that sweeps from the North will bring to our ears the clash of resounding arms! Our brethren are already in the field! Why stand we here idle? What is it that gentlemen wish? What would they have? Is life so dear, or peace so sweet, as to be purchased at the price of chains and slavery? Forbid it, Almighty God! I know not what course others may take; but as for me, give me liberty or give me death!"

Given their situation, Mosiah declared that in order to preserve their liberty they must renounce monarchy and choose judges "by the voice of the people". (V. 25). To many, this may seem to refer to the democratic form of government desired by Patrick Henry, but the Lord's meaning may be different. The vote of the Church is the voice of the people in Church matters. This is the law of Common Consent. Before officers may serve in their positions, they must receive a formal sustaining vote of the people over whom they are to preside.

Judges, however, (such as those proposed by Mosiah in Zarahemla) would provide for the people a pattern of rule compatible with democratic government. In ancient Israel, Judges had been more than legal advisers. They were "deliverers," or men and women who redeemed tribe and nation from subjection to their neighbors, and who became local or national rulers. This is the pattern that was to be established with the introduction of Book of Mormon Judges.

Abraham Lincoln said that "you can fool some of the people some of the time, and you can fool some of the people all of the time, but you cannot fool all of the people all of the time." Mosiah put it a little differently: "It is not common that the voice of the people desireth anything contrary to that which is right; but it is common for the lesser part of the people to desire that which is not right; therefore, this shall ye observe and make it your law - to do your business by the voice of the people". (V. 26).

The law of Common Consent recognizes that the righteous exercise of agency allows men and women to progress to ultimate salvation. (See D&C 26:2). This is the real value of a "democratic" system. Inherent in this law, however, is a warning. If the voice of the people chooses iniquity, the Lord will visit them with great destruction. (V. 27). Today, we recognize "iniquity" as legalized abortion, prostitution, pornography, gambling, Sabbath-breaking, irresponsible media, use of illicit drugs, corruption in the music industry, dishonesty in the marketplace, violence in society, a homogenization of standards in both the spoken and the written word, and so on.

"The world seeks not the Lord to establish his righteousness, but every man walketh in his own way and after the image of his own god, whose image is in the likeness of the world, and whose substance is that of an idol which waxeth old and shall perish in Babylon, even Babylon the Great, which shall fall". (D&C 1:16, see Judges 21:2).

"Freedom does not mean license to exploit law in order to destroy it. It is not freedom that permits the Trojan Horse to be wheeled within the gates, and those within it to be heard in the name of tolerating a different point of view". (Taylor Caldwell, "Pillar of Iron," p. 511). "No people can maintain freedom unless their political institutions are founded upon faith in God and belief in the existence of moral law. God has endowed men and women with certain inalienable rights, and no legislature and no majority, however great, may morally limit or destroy those". (Ezra Taft Benson, "The American Challenge"). With these concepts in mind, Mosiah stressed that with Judges sustained by the voice of the people, personal accountability would prevail, and "if these people (were to) commit sins and iniquities they (should) be answered upon their own heads". (V. 30).

One of the liabilities of monarchy is that the king must ultimately assume personal responsibility for many of the iniquities of his subjects. (V. 31). Unfortunately, these include "the wars, and contentions, and bloodshed, and the stealing, and the plundering, and the committing of whoredoms, and all manner of iniquities which cannot be enumerated". (V. 36). Mosiah was hopeful that, even in the absence of personal accountability, "this inequality should be no more in this land". (V. 32, see V. 38). Other scriptures reinforce the concept of individual responsibility. Mosiah 27:3 stresses the philosophy of the recognition of equality among all the members of the Church by command of the king. Alma 30:11 tells us that there was in his society no law against a man's belief. These scriptures focus on the philosophy of agency, accountability, individual liberty, and independence within the context of the Gospel. (See Commentary Reference to V. 21).

"And many more things did Mosiah write unto them". (V. 33). Due both to the difficulty of writing upon plates, and because the keepers of the records were trying to summarize countless narratives from a long and complex history, The Book of Mormon contains phrases that reveal the inclusion of editorial condensations and omissions. (See Commentary References to Jacob 4:1 & Mosiah 1:8). Yet, the book is thoughtfully structured, and The Book of Mosiah is the most carefully composed of all.

Mosiah knew well "all the trials and troubles of a righteous king," having personally experienced many challenges carrying out the stewardship responsibilities of his office. (V. 33). "And he told them that these things ought not to be; but that the burden should come upon all the people, that every man might bear his part". (V. 34). Even though righteous individuals might lead the government, personal accountability would rule supreme. These teachings, then, constituted the position paper Mosiah had sent forth among the people (See V. 4), and having read and studied it, "they were convinced of the truth of his words". (V. 37).

When Joseph Smith was asked how he managed to govern so many people, he responded: "I teach them correct principles, and they govern themselves". ("Life of Joseph Smith the Prophet," p. 496). Perhaps he was taught this valuable lesson by either Mosiah or Mormon, for he once told John Taylor that he "not only had the principles of the Gospel developed but was conversant with the parties who officiated as the leading men in former ages". (J.D., 20:174-175). He had communication "not only with the Lord, but (also) with the ancient apostles and prophets". (J.D., 21:94). "Nephi and others of the ancient prophets who formerly lived on this continent came to him". (J.D., 17:374). George Q. Cannon said: "If you will read the history of the Church from the beginning, you will find that Joseph was visited by various angelic beings. He doubtless also had visits from Nephi, and it may be from Alma and others". (J.D., 13:47).

As a result of the education in political science that Mosiah's people had received from him, "they relinquished their desires for a king, and became exceedingly anxious that every man should have an equal chance throughout all the land". (V. 38). They assembled in bodies to cast their votes "concerning who should be their judges". (V. 39, see V. 41).

They recognized the wisdom of Mosiah's counsel, and "rejoiced because of the liberty which had been granted unto them". (V. 39). The leadership crisis threatening the Nephites that had so troubled Mosiah had been met head on, and averted. (V. 41). As is so often the case, a potential stumbling block had been turned into a stepping-stone. A crisis had become an opportunity for the people to incorporate a wonderful Gospel principle into their lives. "Change comes like a flash of lightning and a clap of thunder. The people shrink in fear, but after the storm, flowers bloom". ("I Ching" - The Chinese "Book of Changes").

As Tom Paine wrote, in each of our lives there are "times that try (our) souls. Yet we have this consolation with us, that the harder the conflict, the more glorious the triumph. What we obtain too cheap, we esteem too lightly; 'tis dearness only that gives everything its value. Heaven knows how to put a proper price upon its goods; and it would be strange, indeed, if ... celestial article(s) ... should not be highly rated". ("The Political Works of Thomas Paine," p. 55).

The people loved Mosiah "beyond measure". (V. 40). He was esteemed for his uncompromising integrity. Another great prophet leader who has led the army of Israel during the battle for survival in the last Days was Ezra Taft Benson, who, quoting Laurence Gould, declared: "I do not believe the greatest threat to our future is from bombs or missiles. I do not think our civilization will die that way. I think it will die when we no longer care, when the spiritual forces that make us wish to be right and noble die in the hearts of men, when we disregard the importance of law and order, and the basic principles upon which this nation has been built. Great nations are never conquered from outside, unless they are rotten inside. Our greatest national problem today is erosion of the national morality". (Cited in: "The American Challenge", see Commentary Reference to Alma 4:19).

Woven throughout the teachings of the prophets of all ages is the desire to instill in their people a sense of integrity that shines like a light through the eyes. George Washington wrote: "I hope I shall always possess firmness and virtue enough to maintain what I consider the most enviable of all titles, the character of an 'Honest Man.'"

The prophets teach the principle that "you cannot believe in honor until you have achieved it. Better keep yourself clean and bright: You are the window through which you must see the world". (George Bernard Shaw). "This above all, to thine own self be true, and it must follow, as the night the day, Thou canst not then be false to any man". (Shakespeare, "Hamlet").

And so, Alma the Younger was appointed to be the first Chief Judge of the Nephite nation. As Senator Daniel Webster said of John Jay, the first Chief Justice of the Supreme Court of the United States, so could we say of Alma the Younger: "When the spotless ermine of the judicial robe fell on (him), it touched nothing less spotless than itself". ("The Writings and Speeches of Daniel Webster," V. 2, p. 51).

Alma also held the position of Presiding High Priest, "his father having conferred the office upon him, and having given him the charge concerning all the affairs of the Church". (V. 42-43). In the account of the ministry of Alma that follows, we find "the beginning of philosophy, a recognition of the conflicts between men, a search for their cause, a condemnation of mere opinion ... and the discovery of a standard of judgment". (Epictetus).

Once again, "there was continual peace through the land". (V. 43). The Church always enjoys prosperity when its members zealously live in harmony with Gospel principles. After carefully observing The Church of Jesus Christ of Latter-day Saints, Leo Tolstoy was moved to predict: "If Mormonism could be true to its foundations and remain unchanged for four generations, it might well become the most powerful social influence in the world". He also observed: "The Mormon people teach the American religion; their principles teach the people not only of Heaven and its attendant glories, but how to live so that their social and economic relations with each other are placed on a sound basis. If the people follow the teachings of this Church, nothing can stop their progress — it will be limitless." (From a third-hand account by Cornell student and L.D.S. Church member Thomas J. Yates, of a meeting between Tolstoy and Andrew D. White, President of Cornell University, published in "The Improvement Era", 2/1939).

"And thus commenced the reign of the judges throughout all the land of Zarahemla". (V. 44). But the Nephite government was no more resistant to monarchy in practice than it was in theory. The institution of judgeships, rather than beginning a republican era in Book of Mormon history, slid back immediately toward monarchy. The Chief Judge much more resembled a king than an American President. Once elected, he never again submitted himself to the people. After being proclaimed Chief Judge by the voice of the people, Alma enjoyed life tenure. When he chose to resign because of his preoccupation with internal difficulties in Zarahemla, he selected his own successor. (See Alma 4:16). Thus, a dynasty seems to have begun, the judgeship passing "by right" to the successive sons of the judges. (See Commentary Reference to Mosiah 23:67, Alma 50:39, & Helaman 1:13).

At this point, Mormon recorded that the elder Alma died, "having lived to fulfil the commandments of God". (V. 45). He was 82 years old. "How carefully most men creep into nameless graves, while now and again one or two forget themselves into immortality". (Philip Brooks). Such was the case with Alma, whom we remember as one of the great figures in The Book of Mormon. It could have been said of Alma: "When he is dead, seek not his tomb in the earth, but find it in the hearts of men." (Jalal al-Din al-Rumi, the 14th century Sufi poet who founded the order of Dervishes, the religious group whose members whirl and dance as part of their worship.)

"Thus ended the reign of the kings over the people of Nephi". (V. 47). The change in government initiated by King Mosiah was considered so significant that, from this point on, the Nephites recorded their time from the beginning of the Reign of the Judges rather than from the year that Lehi had left Jerusalem, as had previously been the case. The duty and responsibility of the government in Zarahemla would be "to restrain those who would interfere with the inalienable rights of the individual, among which are the right to life, the right to liberty, the right to the pursuit of happiness, and the right to worship God according to the dictates of one's conscience". (William Jennings Bryan).

At Mosiah's retirement, perhaps he had thoughts similar to those of Thomas Jefferson, who mused: "If, in my retirement to the humble station of a private citizen, I am accompanied with the esteem and approbation of my fellow citizens, trophies obtained by blood-stained steel or amidst the tattered flags of the tented field will never be envied. The care of human life and happiness, and not their destruction, is the first and only legitimate object of good government, and was my only objective". ("The Writings of Thomas Jefferson," 8:165)

Mosiah died that same year, at 63 years of age. Mormon's abridgment of the Large Plates of Nephi on the Plates of Mormon gives us a complete picture of what he accomplished. He drew upon more than 20 texts and oral sources to give us a broad perspective of the events during Mosiah's reign. Cicero wrote: "The first law for the historian is that he shall never dare utter an untruth. The second is that he shall suppress nothing that is true. Moreover, there shall be no suspicion of partiality in his writing, or of malice".

The accounts abridged by Mormon that we cherish as The Book of Mosiah were true to the mandate given by Cicero. Although, as Washington Irving brooded, it is the rule that "history fades into fable; fact becomes clouded with doubt and controversy; the inscription molders from the tablet; the statue falls from the pedestal," and that "columns, arches, and pyramids are but heaps of sand, and their epitaphs, nothing but characters written in the dust," yet The Book of Mormon stands as a shining example of the divine model.

Truly, The Book of Mormon "is the witness that testifies to the passing of time; it illumines reality, vitalizes memory, provides guidance in daily life, and brings us tidings of antiquity". It is "the evidence of time, the light of truth, the life of memory, the directress of life, and the herald of antiquity, committed to immortality". (Cicero, "De Oratore," ii, 36). Within its pages, "the centuries roll back to the ancient age of gold". (Horace, "Odes," IV, ii, 39)

Combining so many records suggests a great deal of concern with writing. Mormon included more material in his abridgement from the reign of Mosiah, save any other king except Nephi. Yet he blessed us with only a hundred verses dealing with Mosiah himself. This suggests that something very crucial took place at that time, that went beyond the person of the king himself. While Mosiah was at the center of much attention, it seems that Mormon's concern was the process of bringing people to Christ. Within The Book of Mosiah, we discern that "human history becomes more and more a race between education and catastrophe". (H.G. Wells, "The Outline of History," 2:594).

There is a consistent pattern
running through the pages of The Book of Mormon.
Though it is basically the record of a people inhabiting the
New World, its style has Old World precedents. Against that
background, these patterns come into focus. In the Old-World
history of the Israelite nation, Book of Mormon prototypes
are laid down perfectly, for its intrinsic structure is
biblical. Early American political, historical, and
social forms are conspicuously absent. The
events chronicled throughout Mosiah
Chapter 29 are faithful reflections
of these ancient patterns.

The Book of Alma
91 B.C. - 53 B.C.

Alma
Chapter 1

The Book of Alma comprises 30% of the text of The Book of Mormon, but only 3.9% of the time span, from 91 B.C. to 52 B.C. Clearly, Mormon felt that these particular records would be of tremendous value to those living in the Last Days, and so a disproportionate share of his abridgment concerns these 39 years before the Coming of The Lord. Students of the scriptures will draw close parallels between The Book of Alma and our own time and circumstances.

There were three abridged authors of this book. First was Alma the Younger, who was responsible for chapters 1 through 44. Then came Helaman (chapters 45-62) and finally Shiblon (chapter 63). Both were sons of Alma the Younger. Mormon also inserted very interesting and enlightening editorial comments relative to the abridged text, as was his custom throughout The Book of Mormon. (See Alma 12:21-22, 19:14 & 36, Alma 24:19 & 27, 28:13-14, 30:60, 42:4, 7 & 14, 46:8, 50:19, Helaman 3:27-28, 6:34-35 & 40, 12:1 & 3). As we read, care should be taken to ponder these asides, because they provide very perceptive and penetrating insights into the wide range of topics under discussion.

The focus of the first half of The Book of Alma is missionary work. Chapters 1-16 deal with Alma the Younger's retrenchment efforts among the Nephites in the Land of Zarahemla. These occurred at the same time that the Sons of Mosiah were on a mission to the Lamanites in the Land of Nephi, and whose experiences are detailed in chapters 17-28. Therein are recounted some of the most exciting and inspiring missionary experiences ever recorded. Those who participated in these events are among the great prototypical missionary examples in the scriptures, from whom we may draw daily inspiration.

The superscription at the beginning of The Book of Alma, and nine others like it throughout The Book of Mormon, are part of the original text. This one gives attention only to the record of Alma the Younger, and not to that of Helaman or Shiblon. The setting of chapters 1-4 is Zarahemla, and the text opens with a description of the rise of priestcraft in that city.

In the first year of the reign of the Judges, (92 B.C.), a man named Nehor was brought before Alma to be judged by him. Nehor had gone among the people, preaching what he termed to be the word of God. (V. 1-2, see V. 15). The same situation exists today. When self-appointed prophets and teachers wrest the scriptures, and especially when they twist their meaning to their own material advantage, we can be sure that the welfare of Zion is not their focus of concern.

In 1820, the Lord characterized such individuals as those who "draw near to me with their lips, but (whose) hearts are far from me. They teach for doctrines the commandments of men, having a form of godliness, but they deny the power thereof". (J.S.H. 2:19). They are all form and no substance because they do not have anything to contribute to the welfare of Zion. Madison Avenue, and not the Holy Ghost, is the driving force and power that propels their message. As a result, they often meet with success among those who have itching ears.

Specifically, Nehor's crime was "bearing down against the Church". (V. 3-4). He had attempted to turn the practice of religion into a cult of personality in which the Nephites would be converted to people rather than to principles. This would have been divisive, leading the Church into a fractional period, in which the resultant diluted doctrines would lack the power to promote orthodoxy or to sustain the process of the sanctification of the Saints.

Nehor also ignored the Lord's admonition that "every man be diligent in all things". (D&C 75:29). He had obviously neglected his own doctrinal scholarship, and the Spirit no longer illuminated his way. As he lost sight of his goals, he mistakenly thought it would do no harm to probe the limits of patience of the priesthood leaders of the Church.

Nine years later, in Ammonihah, Zeezrom echoed Nehor when he said to Amulek: "All mankind should be saved at the last day, (and) they need not fear nor tremble". (V. 4, see Alma 11:34). This was welcome news to those without the dedication to overcome the inertia of indecision, but Mormon articulated the divine directive when he counseled: "Work out your own salvation with fear and trembling" before the Lord. (Mormon 9:29).

Nehor's priorities were distorted and the particulars of his relationship with God had become perverted. He suggested that men and women should "lift up their heads and rejoice" in boasting and pride rather than bow their heads in humility, as King Benjamin had taught. (V. 4, see Mosiah 4:19). His message of self-sufficiency was congenitally shortsighted and fatally flawed.

He believed and taught others that the Lord would redeem everyone to eternal life, not realizing that redemption is conditional. (V. 4). It was Lucifer, after all, who had said: "I will redeem all mankind, that one soul shall not be lost. And he became Satan, yea, even the devil, the father of all lies, to deceive and to blind men, and to lead them captive at his will, even as many as would not hearken unto (God's) will". (Moses 4:1). Nehor became an influential supporter of Satan, effectively promulgating his damning heresies among those Nephites who were theological fence-sitters, as well as among those who were already seated in the Adversary's cheering section.

So persuasive was Nehor's misguided teaching, that "many did believe on his words, even so many that they began to support him and give him money". (V. 5). Flushed with the temporal success of his counterfeit priesthood, "he began to be lifted up in the pride of his heart". (V. 8). Nehor personified the definition of a true fanatic: As soon as he lost sight of his objective, he redoubled his efforts. If he had ever really had the desire to reform the Church, it was now lost forever, as he was overwhelmed by the potential for financial gain from his ministry.

It was Joseph Smith's experience that "it is the nature and disposition of almost all men, as soon as they get a little authority, as they suppose, they will immediately begin to exercise unrighteous dominion". (D&C 121:39). A classic illustration of this principle is Nehor's arrogance, contempt, and lack of respect and of civility, when the aged Gideon, a proven champion of righteousness, confronted him.

Verse 7 is a contrast in style. Nehor's approach was to argue abrasively, after the manner of the devil, who is the father of contention. (See 3 Nephi 11:29). Gideon, on the other hand, admonished Nehor with the word of God. (See Ephesians 6:17, & Commentary Reference to Helaman 6:37). He counseled against wrong practices, and gave authoritative or warning advice without coercion or undue influence.

Because the word of God, by itself, was so superior to his own weak efforts, Nehor quickly resorted to violence in a vain attempt to strengthen his position. (V. 9, see Alma 4:19 & 5:3). He did not realize that real power and violence are mutually exclusive, and that where one is present, the other is absent. Righteous and faithful Gideon, who had served the Lord for so many years, was summarily slain by the hand of Nehor. (See Mosiah Chapter 19). He fell as a martyr in defense of the Gospel. Priestcraft and murder of the physical body do not go hand in hand, although in this case killing Gideon was Nehor's final act of defiance. But priestcraft and spiritual murder are soul mates. It is sad, but true, that those acting in defiance of God damage not only their own eternal selves but also those innocents within the sphere of their influence.

When Nehor was subsequently brought before Alma, the prophet/judge lamented that for the first time, a perverted doctrine was being preached among the people by a paid professional clergy. (V. 12, see 2 Nephi 26:29). Even worse, Nehor had endeavored to enforce his doctrine with the sword. It was for this crime that he was sentenced to death, according to the established law of the people. (V. 14, see v. 1).

Nehor was taken to the hill Manti, and there suffered "an ignominious death" that was shameful, disgraceful, and discreditable. (V. 15). The whole episode was all-the-more tragic because it was so entirely avoidable, and because it ultimately destroyed the lives of so many who had been negatively influenced by Nehor's example.

One would think that this would have put an end to priestcraft, but it did not, because Nehor typified many Nephites who "loved the vain things of the world" that have no real value. (V. 16). Such "riches and honor" are merely telestial trash, but they appeal to the carnal mind. These individuals mistake the sizzle for the steak. They not only lack an eternal perspective, but they also have a distorted temporal view.

Contrast the conduct and rewards of these false teachers with those of the worthy priesthood bearers described in Alma 1:28-29. The priests of Nehor only desired a superficial theological titillation, rather than the solid foundation of a Gospel-oriented lifestyle. In contrast, the ennobling character of principled individuals is typified by righteous disciples of Christ, such as Gideon, and is illustrated by the following story.

One day in the Parliament of England, in the presence of a gentleman, stood two creditors. To the first, the debtor had given his note, and to the second he had given but his word. When these two men learned that the gentleman had received income sufficient to satisfy only one of the debts, both came to him for payment. The man who held the note was surprised when his Lordship said to the other creditor, "As I cannot pay both at the same time, I will pay you first".

The holder of the note protested, saying, "But sir, I lent you that money first. Therefore, I should be paid first". His Lordship replied, "You have my signed note that I will pay you. This man has only my promise, my word of honor. I will redeem my honor first". At that, the first lender tore the note that was in his possession to pieces, threw the shreds into a waste basket, and said, "There, sir, now I, too, have but your word of honor". "In that event," said the gentleman, "you shall be paid first".

The vanity of those who had followed the example of Nehor was so great that they first assumed that they could cover their sins by "pretend(ing) to preach according to their belief". (V. 17). But, it is obvious from their subsequent behavior that favorable public opinion of their actions drifted far from the center stage of their concerns.

The priests of Nehor were careful not to commit murder, although verse 18 indicates that they were prevented from doing so only because of the deterrence afforded by the penalty for the crime. In the Last Days, the First Presidency has stated: "The Church views the shedding of human blood with the utmost abhorrence. We regard the killing of human beings, except in conformity with the civil law, as a capital crime which should be punished by shedding the blood of the criminal, after a public trial before a legally constituted court of the land". (Statement of The First Presidency of The Church, 1890).

Although these apostates did not openly lie, steal, rob, or commit murder, they did persecute the

Church, in spite of the fact that in Zarahemla, freedom of worship was a right protected by law. Verses 19-25 detail the extent of both internal and external persecution of the members and the manner in which it was inflicted. Church members were characterized as those who "had taken upon them the name of Christ". (V. 19, see Mosiah 5:7). The apostates afflicted these true believers "with all manner of words". (V. 20, see Alma 46:13-15). In contrast, Church law forbade persecution of member and nonmember alike. (V. 21, see Mosiah 27:2, Alma 4:8, & Ether 7:24-25).

Joseph Smith once declared: "I am ready to die in defending the rights of a good man of any denomination, for the same principle which would trample upon the rights of the Latter-day Saints would trample upon the rights of any other denomination (that) may be unpopular, or too weak to defend (itself)". (H.C., 5:498).

Unhappily, many in the Church in Zarahemla began "to contend warmly with their adversaries" within and outside the Church. (See Alma 4:8). Contention, rather than persecution, began to be "the cause of much trial with the Church, for the hearts of many were hardened and many withdrew themselves" from membership. (V. 23-24). These individuals became cultural Lamanites, aligned with the enemies of righteousness. (See Alma 24:30). "This was a great trial to those that did stand fast in the faith". (V. 25). The Church, collectively, can weather the storm of external persecution, but it is a very disruptive thing when there is contention within its ranks. (See V. 28).

Verses 26-28 describe a Zion Society existing in the midst of deepening unrighteousness. Whereas priestcraft resulted in contention, apostasy, affliction, and persecution, the service of the faithful brought peace, prosperity, and unity. Most important to these righteous stewards was the quality of their service and their worthy deeds, and not their position or recognition within the Church. (V. 26).

The faithful members of the Church were neat in their appearance, and they were attractive without the adornment of "costly apparel". (V. 27). Contrast this conservative lifestyle with the vanity that was gaining a foothold within the apostatizing membership. (See Alma 4:5, & 4:8). Because of their righteousness, the faithful "began to have continual peace again, notwithstanding all their persecutions". (V. 28). They enjoyed the inner peace of those who are free of the burden of sin.

The next few verses identify the real key to prosperity and stand in stark contrast to verse 16. "Because of the steadiness of the Church they began to be exceedingly rich, having abundance of all things whatsoever they stood in need". (V. 29). "In their prosperous circumstances" they were generous to all, "whether out of the Church or in the Church, having no respect to persons as to those who stood in need". (V. 30). In a Zion society, there are no poor among the people, in part because God prospers those who are obedient to His commandments, and in part because His Plan provides that the poor be exalted in that the rich are made low. (See D&C 104:16). When the Laws of Stewardship and Consecration are practiced, those who have directly enjoyed these blessings benefit those who are without temporal abundance. These laws help us to understand why the Lord said: "It is more blessed to give than to receive". (Acts 20:35).

As they obeyed these celestial principles, they began "to prosper and become far more wealthy than those who did not belong to the Church". (V. 31). Verse 32 identifies over a dozen lifestyle characteristics of the nonmembers that disqualified them for the blessings often enjoyed by the faithful.

1). They indulged in sorcery, or the use of power gained through the assistance of evil spirits. In effect, a sorcerer worships Satan rather than God, and uses such power as Satan can give, in a vain attempt to imitate the power of God. Though one might do this in complete ignorance of the evil source of that worldly power, the negative effects will be the same. 2). They also engaged in idolatry, which is the worship of "gold, and silver, and brass, and stone, and of wood, which neither can see, nor hear, nor walk". (Revelation 9:20). When men and women substitute such idols for God as the focus of their attention, they forfeit any blessings that would have been received as a result of obedience. (See D&C 130:18-19). 3). They repeated the sin of idleness that had been committed by Nehor. With lack of purpose in their lives, they found the time to engage in 4) vain babblings, characterized by thoughtless or excessive talk, irreverent or loose language, and aimless or pointless conversation. When we are not anxiously engaged in good causes, and when we lack a worthwhile focus for our attention, we tend to drift off course into more dubious activities. We stray from the firm foundation of proven principles, and consequently lose the stability and sense of purpose that celestial coordinates provide. 5). This lack of direction led to "envying" and 6) "strife," 7) the "wearing of costly apparel" and 8) "being lifted up in the pride of their own eyes". When they began to feel that they were better than their neighbors, they more easily indulged in 9) "lying, 10) thieving, 11) robbing, 12) committing whoredoms, and 13) murdering". Soon, 14) "all manner of wickedness" became their habitual pattern, that was necessary to cover their deplorable behavior. (V. 32).

Only by the exercise of the civil law by those who still honored decency and morality was outward peace maintained among the people in Zarahemla for the space of three years. (V. 33).

Alma
Chapter 2

This chapter provides an account of the second test of the new system of Judges. It concerns an internal uprising initiated by a man named Amlici, who embraced the heretical teachings of Nehor. Amlici, who was of the "Order of Nehors," had become so popular and powerful that he had been able to draw away to his ideology many of the people of Zarahemla. (V. 1). "This was alarming to the people of the Church," for they knew that what Amlici had thus far done was "according to their law (for) such things must be established by the voice of the people". (V. 3, see V. 5-6).

Amlici was determined to convert a majority of those in Zarahemla to his viewpoint, so that he might deprive the members of their rights and privileges, and so "destroy the Church of God". (V. 4). One wonders whether Amlici was only practicing priestcraft, or had he descended even below the cult of personality to become Anti-Christ? He seems to have come out in open rebellion against the Savior and all that He stands for. (See Commentary Reference to Jacob 7:4).

In any event, the stage was set for a great confrontation; the people throughout the land "cast in their voices" concerning the matter. (V. 5-6). These events illustrate that the really great battles of life are fought within the minds of men and women and are ideological, and that the life of the eternal soul is at stake. This time, righteousness prevailed, and "the voice of the people came against Amlici, that he was not made king over the people". (V. 7).

This should have put an end to his troublesome activities, but since Amlici was of the "Order of Nehors," he did not abide by the rules of civilized conduct. Verses 7-10 record the illegal activities of the Amlicites that followed their rejection by the voice of the people. It is the devil who plants the seeds in "the hearts of men to contend with anger, one with another". (3 Nephi 11:29). Inspired by the Prince of Darkness, "Amlici did stir up those who were in his favor to anger against those who were not in his favor". (V. 8). In an attempt to exercise unrighteous dominion and in defiance of established law, his supporters went ahead and made Amlici to be their king". (V. 9, see D&C 121:39). It would have been easy for counterfeit officials, clothed in the robes of the false priesthood, to carry out the consecration. Time and again, history has witnessed similar events. It had happened in the Land of Nephi in the court of King Noah, and now again in the Land of Zarahemla. Wherever it occurs, it is always with pomp and circumstance that the participants carry out the charade.

Amlici knew that his sedition would result in civil conflict, so his first act as monarch was to seize the initiative and declare open warfare against the Nephites. (V. 10). The Amlicites sought to distinguish themselves from the Nephites by assuming the physical characteristics of the Lamanites. (See Commentary Reference to Alma 3:4-12). After 500 years, Jacob's definition was no less accurate: "I shall call them Lamanites that seek to destroy the people of Nephi," he had written, "and those who are friendly to Nephi I shall call Nephites, or the people of Nephi". (Jacob 1:14). Mormon further distinguished the Nephites who lived at this time by calling them "the people of God". (V. 11).

Warfare is necessary when commanded by God, but without His sanction it is difficult to justify. Verses 12-16, that chronicle the preparations for war, and verses 17-23, that describe the actual battle, confirm this. Initially, there were 12,532 Amlicite and 6,562 Nephite dead. (V. 19). These staggering numbers reflect the tragic waste of life that is the inevitable result of armed conflict, when communication breaks down and there seems to be no common ground for the exchange of ideas.

Things took an even more ominous turn when Nephite spies discovered that the Amlicites had joined forces with the Lamanites, who were "numerous almost, as it were, as the sands of the sea". (V. 27, see v. 35). We learned in Jarom 1:6 that the Lamanites "were exceedingly more numerous than were they of the Nephites". The fact that it had been the pattern for Nephite apostates to become "cultural Lamanites" during the previous 500 years probably contributed significantly to their numbers, as well. Nevertheless, the Nephites were "strengthened by the hand of the Lord, having prayed mightily to him that he would deliver them out of the hands of their enemies". Consequently, "the Lamanites and the Amlicites did fall before them". (V. 28).

Alma himself fought face to face with Amlici. In the midst of their personal combat, when Alma cried out "O Lord, have mercy and spare my life, that I may be an instrument in thy hands to save and preserve this people," Amlici panicked, and losing his concentration, was slain by the sword of Alma. (V. 30-31). With this turn of events, the battle turned into a rout, and the Lamanites and Amlicites fled "towards the wilderness which was west and north" of Zarahemla. (V. 36, see Alma 22:27-30). In the opposite direction, the South Wilderness lay in the direction of the Land of Nephi, but it was so rugged that it was not easily penetrated, and so the retreating Lamanites and Amlicites took the path of least resistance in their flight, even though it was in the opposite direction of sanctuary in the Land of Nephi.

The Nephites pursued their enemies all the way to that part of the wilderness "called Hermounts (which) was infested by wild and ravenous beasts". (V. 37-38). Interestingly, in the Egyptian language, "Hermonthis" is the god of wild places and things, so this Nephite place name fit quite nicely. We do not know who may have given it the name, but it may have been the Jaredites. Ether 10:21 reports that they "did preserve the land southward for a wilderness, to get game". Perhaps it was this same old overgrown Asiatic hunting park that was now infested with wild and ravenous beasts.

This chapter
provided an account
of the second test of the new
system of Judges. It concerned an
internal uprising initiated by a man
named Amlici, who embraced the heretical
teachings of Nehor. Amlici, who was of the
"Order of Nehors," had become so popular and
powerful that he had been able to draw away to
his ideology many of the people of Zarahemla.
(V. 1). "This was alarming to the people of the
Church," for they knew that what Amlici had
thus far done was "according to their law
(for) such things must be established
by the voice of the people".
(V. 3, see V. 5-6).

Alma
Chapter 3

This chapter documents the threat of ecclesiastical tyranny over the Nephite nation in the Land of Zarahemla. Not long before the drama unfolded, Aesop, in ancient Greece, had observed: "Any excuse will serve a tyrant". In this case, it all came about because Amlici had coveted power. Mormon commented later in the record about the tremendous disruption one individual "can cause to take place among the children of men". (Alma 46:9). In our Twenty-First Century world, we have seen these same circumstances recurring, with global conflict always a real possibility and sometimes a frightening reality.

Aristotle cautioned: We should "be on our guard against those who flatter and mislead the multitude. Their actions prove what sort of men they are. Of the tyrant, spies and informers are the principal instruments. War is his favorite occupation, for the sake of engrossing the attention of the people, and making himself necessary to them as their leader. The tyrant, who in order to hold his power, suppresses every superiority, does away with good men, forbids education and light, controls every movement of the citizens and, keeping them under a perpetual servitude, wants them to grow accustomed to baseness and cowardice, has his spies everywhere to listen to what is said in the meetings, and spreads dissension and calumny among the citizens and impoverishes them, is obliged to make war in order to keep his subjects occupied and impose on them permanent need of a chief". ("Politics" 5:131).

The Nephites who were killed in the power struggles that followed Amlici's quest for domination could not be counted "because of the greatness of their number". (V. 1). We do know that "in one year were thousands and tens of thousands of souls sent to the eternal world". (V. 26).

Verses 4-12 represent another aside into the background of the "Nephites" and "Lamanites," and the means of their differentiation. "The Amlicites were distinguished from the Nephites, for they had marked themselves with red in their foreheads after the manner of the Lamanites; nevertheless, they had not shorn their heads like unto the Lamanites". (V. 4, see Alma 2:10). Either the Lamanites had red skin, or applied red paint to their bodies; we do not know which. In any case, the Amlicites unwittingly participated in the Lamanite curse by marking their bodies. (V. 5-8). After the Lamanites had "dwindled in unbelief, they became a dark, and loathsome, and a filthy people, full of idleness, and all manner of abominations". (1 Nephi 12:23). The mark was then set, "that thereby the Lord God might preserve his people, that they might not mix and believe in incorrect traditions which would prove their destruction". (V. 8, see v. 11, & Alma 45:14).

This mark was upon "Laman and Lemuel, and also the sons of Ishmael, and Ishmaelitish women," that is to say, sisters of Nephi. (V. 7, see Alma 17:19). "And it came to pass that whosoever did mingle his seed with that of the Lamanites did bring the same curse upon his seed," since "Nephite" and "Lamanite" were by now cultural rather than hereditary terms of distinction. (V. 9, see V. 13-17, & Jacob 1:14).

Although the Amlicites ignorantly fulfilled "the words of God when they began to mark themselves in their foreheads," they deserved the curse because, like the first Lamanites, they were apostate members of the Church who "had come out in open rebellion against God". (V. 18, see Commentary Reference to 2 Nephi 2:29, Mosiah 2:27, Alma 24:30, & 4 Nephi 1:38).

Mormon wanted us to learn from his account of the Amlicite rebellion "that they brought upon themselves the curse; and even so doth every man that is cursed bring upon himself his own condemnation". (V. 19). "For every man receiveth wages of him whom he listeth to obey". (V. 27).

Bruce R. McConkie felt: "Apostates exhibit varying degrees of indifference and of rebellion, and their punishment, in time and in eternity, is based on the type and degree of apostasy that is involved. Those who become indifferent to the Church, who simply drift from the course of righteousness to the way of the world, are not in the same category with traitors who fight the truth, and with those whose open rebellion destines them to eternal damnation as sons of perdition. All apostates are turned over to the buffetings of Satan in one degree or another, with the full wrath of Satan reserved for those who are cast into outer darkness with him in that kingdom devoid of glory". ("Doctrinal New Testament Commentary," V. 3).

Alma
Chapter 4

The Book of Mormon is a chronicle of recurring cycles. When the people are righteous, the Lord blesses them, and they begin to prosper. Temporal security tends to lead the people, and especially the rising generation, to pride. Then apostasy brings a loss of spiritual power and God's protection. Resulting warfare and suffering humbles the people, who then turn to the Lord, and the cycle begins anew. Alma Chapter 4 deals with such events.

Because of their afflictions, the people had been "awakened to a remembrance of their duty". (V. 3). The purpose of their chastisement was to bring them to a condition of repentance. God wants all His children to rely on the Atonement of His Son, rather than on their own energies, intellect, or abilities, so that they might qualify for eternal life. That is why He reproves those whom He loves. (See Hebrews 12:6, D&C 95:1 & 121:43). As a result of their chastisements, the Nephites in Zarahemla "began to establish the Church more fully". (V. 4).

There is a timelessness to the question: "How can we help to establish the Church?" Neal Maxwell said: "In the Last Days, discipleship will be lived in crescendo". The actions of each individual member of the Church will swell the chorus of voices shouting "Hallelujah," and will hasten the millennial reign of the Lord. B.H. Roberts once said: "The Latter-day Saints are the white-hot sparks struck off the Divine Anvil of God," destined to kindle a fire that will burn so brightly that it will celestialize the earth as it receives its rightful King.

True disciples commit the 13th Article of Faith to life, as well as to memory, and actively practice their religion. John Taylor observed: "There are some Christian people in this world who, if a man were poor or hungry, would say, let us pray for him. I would suggest a little different regimen for a person in this condition; rather, take him a bag of flour and a little beef or pork. A few such comforts will do him more good than your prayers". (Daniel Ludlow, "Companion to The Old Testament," p. 192). A familiar aphorism suggest: "When a person is down in the world, an ounce of help is better than a pound of preaching". Socrates said, "Know thyself". Cicero said, "Control

Thyself". But the 'Gospel teaches, "Give thyself". (1 Timothy 4:15). In just this way, those who establish the Church actively embrace the demands of discipleship.

These require a revision of commonly accepted standards of qualification. In the Kingdom of God, it is not ability, or inability, but availability that is important when His servants are called to the work. Brigham Young once declared: "I never count the cost of anything. I just find out what the Lord wants me to do, and I do it". It is this kind of total commitment and dedication that establishes the Church.

Before Joan of Arc was carried to the stake in circumstances similar to that of the Prophet Abinadi, she was given the opportunity to obtain her freedom by denying her beliefs. Instead, she made this powerful statement: "I know this now. Every man and woman give their lives for what they believe. Sometimes, people believe in little or nothing, and so they give their lives for little or nothing. One life is all we have, and we live it as we believe in living it, and then it is gone. But to surrender what you are, and live without belief, is more terrible than dying, even more terrible than dying young". Resolutely, then, she faced death, still true to her faith and her beliefs. Her final acts on earth were consistent with her convictions. It is this quality of total commitment and dedication that establishes the Church.

In 1830, in Western New York State, as a spirit of religious revivalism flared brightly among the people, Joseph Smith sought diligently to establish the Church. His efforts are carried on today by those to whom the torch has been passed. In 85 B.C. in the Land of Zarahemla, that same spirit burned among the people of Nephi, "who sought diligently to establish the Church". In addition to those of the faith, there were surely many non-members living in Zarahemla, for in the 109 years since the reign of Mosiah I, People of Zarahemla, People of Limhi, and other descendants of Zeniff, might not yet have had the benefit of baptism. Additionally, Lamanites as well as groups of people not mentioned in The Book of Mormon might have co-existed in the land.

"Alma, who had been consecrated the high priest over the people of the Church by the hand of his father Alma," was personally responsible for the baptism of many converts in the waters of Sidon. (V. 4). Altogether, in one year, "there were about three thousand five hundred souls that united themselves to the Church". (V. 5). "And they who were baptized in the name of Jesus were called the Church of Christ". (3 Nephi 26:21, see Alma 2:11).

At the end of 2022, Latter-day Saint Church membership totaled 17,002,461. Convert baptisms had fallen off a Covid-cliff in 2021, but rebounded the following year to 212,172 There were also 85,059 new children of record. The combined total represents a 1.17% growth rate. (Statistical report, 2022, CR, 4/2022). This suggests a total core Church population of over 100,000 members in the Nephite Church, if it were growing at a similar rate.

Within two years, however, Mormon documented the subtle effects of encroaching pride among the

Nephites. Riches, silks, fine twined linen, flocks, herds, gold, and silver were the evidences of their prosperity. All these things "they had obtained by their industry". (V. 6). In other words, there was nothing intrinsically wrong with the way their material possessions were obtained, but their "very costly apparel" betrayed the pride associated with their acquisition of material possessions, even though they were obtained through hard work. (See Alma 1:16).

The reference to "silk" in verse 6 deserves attention, for critics of The Book of Mormon have claimed that this fabric was unknown in the Near East before the time of Christ. In fact, the oldest fragments of silk date from 2,700 B.C. in China. That country's monopoly of silk culture led to trade with the West beginning in the 2nd century B.C. Evidently, there was earlier contact, since the Nephites were familiar with silk culture as early as 600 B.C. (See 1 Nephi 13:7, Alma 1:9, Commentary References to Helaman 6:13, Ether 10:24, & "Smith's Bible Dictionary," p. 668). A study of mummies along the Silk Road dates to 1,600 B.C., suggesting ancient contacts between the East and the West, and remnants of Chinese silk dating from 1,700 B.C. have been found in Egypt.

Mention of pride is made more than sixty times in The Book of Mormon. Some call it the parent sin. The sad fact is that "I" and "Mine" are usually accompanied by the unbended knee. Pride robs us of the wide-eyed wonder of innocence, kills our inquisitive spirit, and substitutes teachability with callous arrogance. Dante, speaking of the souls in the hellfire of his vision of Inferno, revealed that Pride, Envy, and Avarice were the three sparks that set their hearts on fire. Indeed, "pride breakfasted with plenty, dined with poverty, and supped with infamy". (Benjamin Franklin).

We are given two of a lot of things, and can generally get along without one of them: for example, eyes, ears, arms, legs, lungs, and kidneys. But we are only given one heart. Everyone needs a heart, and it is best to keep it softened. Spiritual sclerosis, or hardening of the spiritual arteries, when left undiagnosed and untreated ravages our souls and can be an eternally terminal condition.

The chastening hand of the Lord had prompted the Nephites to repent of their sins and to focus on the infinite. (See Commentary Reference to Alma 4:3). But their ensuing prosperity soon distorted their vision, leaving them spiritually shortsighted. "To the humble, the simpleness and the easiness of the way are glad realities. To the crowded, ego filled minds of proud men, the sudden sunlight from a spiritual sunrise is irritating rather than awesome, and causes them to blink rather than to stare in reverent awe". (Neal Maxwell, "That My Family Should Partake", p. 82).

Alma and his faithful teachers, priests, and elders were "sorely grieved for the wickedness which they saw had begun to be among their people". (V. 7, see V. 20, Alma 5:49, 13:1 & 13:8). They had been trained to be physicians of the soul, and easily recognized the signs of spiritual anemia among their people. The members of the Church had suffered temporal trauma, as well, because their attention was fixed on telestial toys and trinkets, rather than on celestial sureties. Their myopia was the classic lack of vision that has so often inspired the observation: "Having eyes they do not see". (See Mark 8:18, Palms 115:5, & Moses 6:11).

Because the people set their hearts upon the vain things of the world, they scorned and persecuted those who did not believe as they did. (V. 8, see Mosiah 27:2, & Alma 1:21). The wicked have always had this tendency. As a result, contentions arose among them, and the conflict between Church members was even greater than between them and nonmembers. Malice, or the conscious desire to harm others, was conspicuously prominent among the sins of the people.

Worst of all, "the wickedness of the Church was a great stumbling block to those who did not belong to the Church". Consequently, "the Church began to fall in its progress". (V. 10, see v. 11). Joseph Fielding Smith, Jr. declared: "The greatest crime in all this world is to lead men and women away from the true principles". (C.R. 4/1951, see Commentary Reference to Alma 39:11). The following story illustrates the level of human decency and concern that is expected of each of us, and particularly of members of the Church.

Before Fiorello La Guardia became mayor of New York City, he was a magistrate. One day there appeared before him a man accused of stealing a loaf of bread. Upon questioning, the man explained that he'd committed the crime to feed his family, for they were starving. Whereupon, La Guardia dismissed the case, and sentenced all present in the courtroom to pay a fine for living in a city where a man must steal to feed his family. The Lord illustrated the Gospel principle of concern for the welfare of others when He said: "I am the bread of life: He that cometh to me shall never hunger; and he that believeth on me shall never thirst". (John 6:35). In the Eternal Court of Justice, what will be the penalty for failure to provide others with the Bread of Life, or for feeding them stale, or moldy, or otherwise unwholesome bread?

Lyman Abbott said: "The brotherhood of man is an integral part of Christianity no less than the Fatherhood of God, and to deny the one is no less infidel than to deny the other". Truly, without the fatherhood of God, there is no brotherhood of man, and its mystic bond makes us one. This mind-expanding concept makes "the universe one great city, full of beloved ones, divine and human, by nature endeared to each other". (Epictetus).

Alma "saw great inequality among the people, some lifting themselves up with their pride, despising others, turning their backs upon the needy and the naked and those who were hungry, and those who were athirst, and those who were sick and afflicted". (V. 12). The Doctrine of Christ that Alma preached tore down the dividing prejudices of race, rank, and even ability, and taught universal love without distinction. Our neighbor, he explained to the inhabitants of Zarahemla, is anyone that needs our help.

In contrast to the Zarahemla lifestyle, there are no poor in a Zion society, for those who have been temporally blessed by the Lord take their stewardship responsibilities seriously, and welcome opportunities to consecrate everything with which the Lord has blessed them to the building up of the Church and Kingdom. (See Alma 1:30). Truly, in Zion, all are their brothers' keepers. (See Genesis 4:9).

In only a few years, the Mortal Messiah would identify who were His real disciples: "Then shall the King say unto them on his right hand, Come, ye blessed of my Father, inherit the kingdom prepared for you from the foundation of the world: For I was an hungered, and ye gave me meat: I was thirsty, and ye gave me drink: I was a stranger, and ye took me in. Naked, and ye clothed me: I was sick, and ye visited me: I was in prison, and ye came unto me. Then shall the righteous answer him, saying, Lord, when saw we thee an hungered, and fed thee? Or thirsty, and gave thee drink? When saw we thee a stranger, and took thee in? Or naked, and clothed thee? Or when saw we thee sick, or in prison, and came unto thee? And the King shall answer and say unto them, Verily I say unto you, Inasmuch as ye have done it unto one of the least of these my brethren, ye have done it unto me". (Matthew 25:34-40).

Those who were righteous among the Nephites abased themselves to the benefit of those who needed both physical and spiritual nourishment. (V. 13). They retained a remission of their sins by looking forward to the mortal ministry of Jesus Christ and by conducting their lives in conformity to the eternally relevant teachings of His prophets. The details of the Atonement had already been worked out, and so those who remained faithful in Alma's day could exercise perfect, saving faith in the future "resurrection of the dead, according to the will and power and deliverance of Jesus Christ". (V. 14). Jesus offered Himself from the foundation of the world to be its Savior. He held the power of resurrection in reserve, and so controlled His own future deliverance, leading the way for all who would take up their cross and follow Him in innocence along the path leading through Gethsemane, to Calvary, and on to the Celestial Kingdom. (See Moses 1:39, & Commentary Reference to 2 Nephi 9:18).

In the midst of the suffering of his people at the hands of their less faithful brethren, Alma was guided unerringly by the Spirit. Verse 15 is a classic study, as it contrasts "the humble followers of God" with "the remainder of his people". Perhaps those Church members who were not faithful to their covenants had gotten caught up in the machinery of the Church, without making contact with the Savior and without being spiritually begotten of Him. For such, life can be a treadmill. However, for the faithful who followed Alma and were true disciples of Christ, Gospel ordinances were a springboard to new spiritual heights. Their Church experiences provided sunbursts of sensitivity that charged their spiritual batteries. With him, they could enjoy God's Rest, or "that peace which surpasseth understanding". (Philippians 4:7).

"The Spirit of the Lord did not fail" Alma. (V. 16). Because of his righteousness, he enjoyed the constant companionship of the Holy Ghost. The veil was almost transparent because he was spiritually sensitive. After all, the Spirit quickens all life, and the two materials, body and spirit, make up each of our souls. (D&C 88:15). Therefore, we owe our very being to the presence of the Spirit, and the direction our lives take depends upon how we respond to its whisperings. If we allow it to, the Spirit will guide us to know the truth of all things. Joseph Smith showed the way, when he said: "By the power of the Spirit our eyes were opened and our understandings were enlightened, so as to see and understand the things of God". (D&C 76:10, see D&C 88:67-68)

As our powers expand, we experience the glittering facets of the life of the Spirit. "To use the careful preparation and training we receive as a springboard, to be capable of disciplined, controlled procedure and to be receptive to flashes of insight, is what solid Latter-day Saints should have going for them in their inner lives. The Gospel sets us free to be creative, and sets us creative to become more free. It is the perfect law of liberty". ("My Religion & Me," Lesson #9).

With spiritual insight, Alma saw a solution to the challenges facing the Church in Zarahemla. It must have dawned upon him only after considerable fasting and prayer, for he saw that its consequences would be far-reaching and all-encompassing in his Nephite society. He selected a righteous man named Nephihah to take his place as Chief Judge among the people, who was then sustained by the voice of the people according to the Law of Common Consent. The authority to be vested in him would include executive, legislative, and judicial powers that were to be based on the established rule of law rather than on any selfish motive. (V. 16-17). That the Holy Ghost guided Alma through this process is apparent from a reading of Alma 50:37, that eulogized Nephihah about 16 years later, in these words: "Nephihah, the second chief judge, died, having filled the judgment-seat with perfect uprightness before God".

Here we see a rare and remarkable thing. Alma, a man of great political power and prestige, relinquished it all, in order to bless the people more comprehensively. "He did this that he himself might go forth among his people, that he might preach the word of God unto them". (V. 19). Moral decay within the Church had prompted Alma to give up the office of Chief Judge. His action showed that, above all else, he considered rock-solid spirituality to be critical to the success of the nation.

Laurence Gould declared: "I do not believe the greatest threat to our future is from bombs or guided missiles. I do not think our civilization will die that way. I think it will die when we no longer care - when the spiritual forces that make us wish to be right and noble die in the hearts of men, when we disregard the importance of law and order, and the basic principles upon which this nation has been built. Great nations are never conquered from outside unless they are rotten inside. Our greatest problem today is erosion of the national morality". (Quoted by Thomas S. Monson, "Ensign", 7/2001, see Commentary Reference to Mosiah 29:40).

Freed from the burden of his civil administrative responsibilities, Alma embraced his ministry wholeheartedly and sought to stir his people up "in remembrance of their duty" by the use of the scriptures, "seeing no way that he might reclaim them save it were in bearing down in pure testimony against them". (V. 19). Alma considered the scriptures to be the most powerful tool at his disposal. Again and again, he relied on them to teach correct principles to his people.

When he sensed that they had a sound doctrinal understanding, he used the scriptures to convict them of their sins and to encourage them to mend their ways, and when they were scripturally naïve, he used them to guide them toward greater obedience based on a clearer understanding. In every instance, he used the scriptures when bearing his testimony of the divinity of the work in which he was engaged.

"A word about testimony. In one sense, a testimony is a wholly private thing. It is part of your life, your conscience, your experience, but you cannot show it to anyone else. That, of course, is why it is valuable to you. It is your personal comfort and warrant for your faith. No matter what happens to anyone else, you have something you know for sure about spiritual matters. You and the Lord have a functioning, ongoing, relationship and companionship". (Chauncy Riddle, "The Pillars of Testimony," B.Y.U. Devotional, 6/30/1970).

But in another sense, a testimony lives to be "borne". In the initial stages of a spiritual awakening, a testimony is born in the classical sense, with physical and emotional struggle. Then it must be developed through constant labor and careful attention, with significant nurturing and careful pruning, so that it might have the strength to stand independently without external witness.

We bear our testimony by carrying it with us at all times. Thus, it establishes one unvarying standard of conduct for every circumstance within which we might find ourselves. When we bear our testimonies, others may know with certainty where we stand, and that we will take the Lord's side on all issues and uphold righteousness in every situation. We also bear testimony as we give it to others when the Spirit dictates such an action. Testimony, like love, can grow only by unconditionally giving it away. When we bear testimony to others, oft-times the name of one more soul is added to the membership rolls of the Church. Our testimony is a gift that is to be given today, for yesterday is history, and tomorrow is a mystery. But today we live in the "present".

Although testimony is born of foundation faith in Jesus Christ and the principles of the Gospel, it is itself the necessary prerequisite to sustained saving faith. It is the driving force behind acting on faith. We have a testimony that the Gospel is true. Knowing that, we can then exercise great faith by acting on the saving principles, and by participating in the ordinances of the Gospel, beginning with baptism. Faith, without the works of righteousness and obedience to the commandments, that are the tangible expression of testimony, is dead, being alone. (See James 2:17).

In order for his people to develop testimony and exercise saving faith, "Alma delivered up the judgment seat to Nephihah, and confined himself wholly to the high priesthood of the holy order of

God, to the testimony of the word, according to the spirit of revelation and prophecy". (V. 20). The term "priesthood" is used only eight times in the text of The Book of Mormon: once here in verse 20, and seven times in Alma Chapter 13, in verses. 6, 7, 8 (twice), 10, 14, & 18).

As President of the Church, Alma recognized that teaching is the primary function of the priesthood. "This is the order after which I am called, yea, to preach unto my beloved brethren, yea, and every one that dwelleth in the land". (Alma 5:49, see Alma 5:3). Alma did not define his responsibilities only in terms of what he could do to reclaim those who had been previously baptized. He also understood that his covenant of baptism and the Oath and Covenant of the Melchizedek Priesthood included standing as a witness of God to those who were not yet members of the Church, who also lived in the Land of Zarahemla.

"Priesthood" is only specifically mentioned 4 times in The Book of Mormon, but evidence of the power of God permeates all the canonized texts dealing with His relationship with mankind. (V. 4, see Alma 13: 6, 7, & 8). Karl G. Maeser illustrated our total dependency upon God, and the wisdom of relying on the power of His priesthood when he was leading a party of young missionaries on foot across the Alps. As they slowly climbed the steep slope, he looked back and saw a row of sticks thrust into the glacial snow to mark the one safe path through the treacherous mountains. Something about those sticks impressed him, and halting the company of missionaries, he gestured toward them and said, "Brethren, there stands the priesthood. They are just common sticks like the rest of us. Some of them may even seem to be a little crooked, but the position they hold makes them what they are. If we step aside from the path they mark, we are lost".

By righteously exercising his priesthood authority, Alma sought to influence the people of the Land of Zarahemla with the power of the word of God. He hoped that bearing testimony might fire their faith and create a spiritually self-sustaining chain reaction. Alma recognized that "seeing, even the Savior, does not leave as deep an impression in the mind as does the testimony of the Holy Ghost. The impressions on the soul that come from the Holy Ghost are far more significant than a vision. It is where spirit speaks to spirit, and the imprint upon the soul is far more difficult to erase". (Joseph Fielding Smith, Jr., "Improvement Era", 11/1966).

Heber C. Kimball echoed Alma, when he warned the Saints in 1856 that many trials would test their faith, and that the time would come when no man or woman would be able to endure on borrowed light. Our day is the time of which he spoke. But Heavenly Father has purposely stacked the deck in our favor. While allowing us our agency, He is not indifferent to our tests of faith, nor is He an impartial observer, distanced from our struggles in mortality, and indiscriminately throwing pop quizzes in our direction. He never requires us to walk alone, and if at times it seems that there is only one set of footprints on the sands of time, it is because Christ lifts us up upon His shoulders when our own burdens seem so heavy that we lose the desire to carry on.

"Every member of the Church is entitled to know that God our Heavenly Father lives. They are also entitled to know that our elder brother, Jesus Christ, is the Savior and Redeemer of the world, and that he has opened the door for us, that we, through our individual acts, may receive salvation and exaltation and dwell once again in the presence of our Heavenly Father". (Henry D. Taylor).

This assurance and witness must be earned. First, we must have the desire, or spiritual thirst that awakens "the true light that lighteth every man that cometh into the world". (D&C 93:2). Secondly, we must study and search the scriptures; for in them, Jesus assured us, "ye think ye have eternal life; and they are they which testify of me". (John 5:39). Thirdly, we must pray. Alma testified: "Behold, I have fasted and prayed many days that I might know these things of myself. And now I do know of myself that they are true; for the Lord God hath made them manifest unto me by his Holy Spirit; and this is the spirit of revelation which is in me". (Alma 5:46). Lastly, we must be obedient to principles, for the Savior said: "Unto him that keepeth my commandments I will give the mysteries of my kingdom". (D&C 63:23). It is of these "mysteries" that we regularly bear testimony. (See Commentary Reference to Mosiah 1:5).

When our lives conform to the pattern established by the Savior, and the scales of darkness fall away, the eyes of our spiritual understanding will be opened. Our ears will increasingly understand otherwise inaudible whisperings, as our spiritual fluency is developed, and our hearts will swell with the pure love of Christ, as we lose ourselves in compassionate service.

Alma 4 addresses a cycle that regularly recurs in The Book of Mormon. When the people are righteous, the Lord blesses them, and they begin to prosper. Temporal security tends to lead the people, and especially the rising generation, to pride. Then, apostasy brings a loss of spiritual power and God's protection. Resulting warfare and suffering humble the people, who then turn to the Lord, and the cycle begins anew.

Alma
Chapter 5

Alma Chapter 5 is the second longest chapter in The Book of Mormon, after Jacob Chapter 5, and reads very much like a General Conference address. Its careful study teaches us that it is easy to mechanically spit out pat answers, but it is more challenging to embrace good questions. In Alma's discourse to the People of Zarahemla, we find many such questions. They are summarized below.

Alma asked if his people had sufficiently retained in remembrance the hardships that their fathers had endured, due to their spiritual bondage. (V. 6) He meant that history is prologue and he longed for his people to learn from the experiences of their fathers. He knew from his own troubled youth the sadness that can result from ignoring or rejecting counsel from one's elders.

He questioned if his people remembered how merciful and long-suffering Heavenly Father is toward those who are groping about in spiritual darkness. (V. 6). Isaiah, in particular among the prophets of the Old Testament, reminded Israel: "His arm is stretched out still". He is always willing to forgive those who repent. Alma must have remembered the patience that his own father had exercised during the years of his rebellion.

Alma wondered if his people remembered that Heavenly Father's Plan will deliver from the Spirit Prison of the Unjust those who there accept the Gospel. (V. 6, see Commentary Reference to 2 Nephi 4:32, & D&C 76:73, 138:8 & 28, Isaiah 61:1, 1 Peter 3:19 & Moses 7:57). His mercy satisfies Justice, breaks the barrier of death, and offers the hope of eternal family life to all who have ever lived on the earth, for God is absolutely non-discriminatory as He deals with His children. Sooner or later, all will either accept or reject the invitation to enter into a covenant relationship with Him. Therefore, Alma asked if Heavenly Father would really destroy those who are spiritually ignorant. (V. 8). Because His patience is Infinite and Eternal, He would not.

Alma answered this question with another. Has God, then, broken the bands of death and the chains of hell, that have bound these unfortunate individuals, in contrast to Satan who is unable to support his disciples at the Day of Judgment? (V. 9). The answer is an absolute and unequivocal 'Yes!' God is the Master of all circumstances. Every provision of the Plan was carefully thought out before its implementation, and harmonizes perfectly with its companion principles, including that of the need for opposition in all things.

Continuing on this track, Alma asked on what condition are we saved? (V. 10). No matter that God makes the rules, for His judgments are just. On what grounds, then, do we have hope of salvation? V. 10). It is the Atonement that establishes the firm foundation. Any other conditions are only its corollaries.

How is it, Alma questioned, that we have been loosed from the bands of death, and the chains of hell? (V. 10). It is because the Lamb slain from the foundation of the world is the Author of Salvation and the very Savior of the world. He is our Mediator. His sacrifice is central to the Plan of Salvation. That sacrifice was infinite in its consequences because it required that God Himself, Who is Endless and Eternal, should suffer and die upon the cross.

Years earlier, the words of Abinadi had greatly impressed Alma's father. Did not this mighty prophet prove that the power of the word is mightier than the sword? Was not Abinadi a prophet of God? Did not Abinadi speak the words of God? (V. 10). The Spirit testifies that this is true. His message had touched the receptive heart of the Elder Alma, as well as the hearts of generations of Nephites and Lamanites to come, and it continues to inspire us in the Last Days, especially those of us who are still in the infancy of our faith.

So, Alma asked his people if they had been spiritually born of God. (V. 14). Mormon hoped that his efforts to abridge the words of Alma would not be in vain and that his message would span the centuries to touch the hearts of the readers of The Book of Mormon in the Last Days. The very last words that Mormon wrote were these: "For behold, this (book) is written for the intent that ye may believe ... And if it so be that be believe in Christ, and are baptized, first with water, then with fire and with the Holy Ghost, following the example of our Savior, according to that which he hath commanded us, it shall be well with you in the day of judgment". (Mormon 7:9-10).

Alma's next question penetrates the barriers of time and place. He asked if his people had received the image of the Lord in their countenances. (V. 14). When they had, he assured them, their faces would reflect the Light of Christ. He knew that when they had experienced a mighty change in their hearts, it would change their inward parts. The world seeks change from the outside and fails miserably. The Gospel changes us from the inside and succeeds brilliantly. We are thus created to reach our potential in both the image and likeness of God our Father.

He asked his people if they exercised faith in the redemption of Him who had created them. (V. 15). Their testimonies would be the foundation for sustained, saving faith. Then, they would look forward with an eye of faith to stand one day before God to be judged according to their works.

Saving faith gives us the confidence to stand in the presence of God, before His Pleasing Bar, without averting our eyes. (See Jacob 6:13).

Could they imagine, he asked, if they could hear the voice of the Lord speaking to them: "Come unto me ye blessed, for behold, your works have been the works of righteousness". (V. 16). Alma knew by personal experience that God's Rest is reserved for the righteous, and so this principle became a cornerstone of his message.

Alma wondered if his people thought that they could lie to the Lord in the Day of Judgment, saying that they had been righteous, so that God would thereby save them. (V. 17). Beware, he cautioned, lest they think that they could fool Him. During His mortal ministry, the Lord had particularly harsh words for such hypocrites.

He continued, asking if they could imagine themselves before the Judgment Bar of God, with their souls filled with guilt and remorse, and a remembrance that they had set themselves in defiance to the commandments. (V. 18). When our true nature is revealed and it is found wanting, the consequences will be frightening. Could his people hope to look up to God at that day with a pure heart and clean hands? (V. 18). The prophet Isaiah had unequivocally warned: "Be ye clean that bear the vessels of the Lord". (Isaiah 52:11).

Knowing that dedicated disciples assume the nature of their mentor, he asked if the image of God had been engraven upon their countenances. (V. 19). Contrast this description of permanence with the fickle visage of those characterized as hypocrites. We cannot be hypocritical when we follow the Savior. The word "hypocrite" is from the Greek, where it describes the mask used by actors. in the plays written by Aeschylus, Euripedes, Aristophanes, and others. The term has come to derisively characterize those who make false appearances with the intent to deceive. A hypocrite, then, is someone who professes to be one thing, when actually it is a charade; he is an entirely different person behind his mask. If we are not careful, hypocrites can get under our skin; they can worm their way right into our hearts, minds, and souls and compromise our barrier protection. (See 2 Nephi 31:13, D&C 121:37, & 41-42).

In the novel "The Picture of Dorian Grey," by Oscar Wilde, a particularly handsome young man's portrait degenerates over time in response to his moral depravity and self-indulgence, while at the same time his face retains its alabaster innocence. He adheres to the philosophy that the only way to eliminate a temptation is to yield to it. After many years of decadence have taken a mighty toll on his character, he loses his mind, grabs a knife, and attacks the picture that with such stark realism and accuracy has reflected his mounting debauchery. The servants of the house awaken to a cry from the locked room, and break down the door. before them lies the body of an unrecognizable old man, stabbed in the heart, his face withered and decrepit. Only by the ring on his finger are they able to identify the disfigured corpse as their master. Beside the emaciated figure is the picture of Dorian Gray that has reverted to its original loveliness.

In Book 2 of Plato's "The Republic," Glaucon and Adeimantus present the myth of the Ring of Gyges, by means of which Gyges is able to make himself invisible. They then ask Socrates: "If one came into possession of such a ring, why should he act justly?" Socrates replies that although no one could see their body, the soul would be horribly disfigured by the evils that had been committed behind the illusory shield of invisibility.

And so, Alma asked if his people could think of being saved when they had yielded themselves to become subject to the devil? (V. 20). The very thought defies all logic. "Here is the agency of man, and here is the condemnation of man; because that which was from the beginning is plainly manifest unto them, and they receive not the light". (D&C 93:31).

How might we feel, Alma asked, standing before the Bar of God, clothed in garments stained with filthiness? (V. 22). The stirrings of religious recognition within us would at that very moment convict us of our sins. How much better to have washed our garments in the blood of the Lamb?

Of what do these things testify, Alma asked? (V. 22). The record of our lives is engraven indelibly in our sinews. Might that record testify of our guilt for all manner of wickedness?. After all, the Holy Spirit cannot lie. Do you suppose, Alma wondered, that one such as this can comfortably sit down in the Kingdom of God?. (V. 24). Carol Lynn Pearson wrote: "I don't fret as to where my soul will be assigned, whether I find myself with the Celestial, or not quite qualify. It's simple: Water meets its own level. So shall I". ("Beginnings," p. 53, see Commentary Reference to Mosiah 27:31).

Alma knew that those who listened to his words had, at one time, experienced a change of heart. He wondered if they could feel so at this moment. (V. 26). He knew that the Word could penetrate their innermost parts to touch the tender chords of their spiritual sensitivities. His people should have felt indescribable stirrings, for every Gospel principle carries within itself its own witness of its truthfulness. Hugh B. Brown described his relationship with the Spirit in these words: "Sometimes during solitude I hear truth spoken with clarity and freshness. Uncolored and untranslated it speaks from within myself in a language original but inarticulate, heard only with the soul".

Alma knew that the Gospel Plan successfully addresses every challenge of mortality. He wondered if his people could say, if they were called to die at that moment, that they had been sufficiently humble. (V. 27). For it is the meek who shall inherit the celestialized earth. (See Matthew 5:5). Alma wanted his people to take advantage of the Atonement of Christ, which is of no power or effect for those who will not accept the Lord as their personal Savior. He hoped that his people were stripped of pride, for he knew that nothing would keep one out of Zion more surely than the feeling of superiority over a neighbor. (V. 28). Nothing will kill the Spirit faster than pride. In all of its insidiously and grotesquely mutated forms, such as envy, flattery, vanity, selfishness, haughtiness, and covetousness, it is equally damaging.

Alma asked if any of his people had mocked or in any other way persecuted their brothers and sisters. (V. 30). The Gospel teaches that the worth of souls is great in the sight of God, Who esteems all mankind as one and is no respecter of persons. (D&C 18:10). This means that He values all His children as equally precious. Therefore, there is no justifiable circumstance in which any one of them may be treated unkindly or unfairly.

C.S. Lewis observed: "It is a serious thing to live in a society of possible Gods and Goddesses - to remember that the dullest and most uninteresting person you talk to may one day be a creature which if you saw it now, you would be strongly tempted to worship. It is in the light of these overwhelming possibilities, it is with the awe and the circumspection proper to them, that we should conduct all our dealings with one another, all friendships, all loves, all play all politics. There are no ordinary people. You have never talked to a mere mortal. It is immortals with whom we joke, work, marry, snub and exploit. Our charity must be a real and costly love. Next to the blessed sacrament itself, your neighbor is the holiest object presented to your senses". ("The Weight of Glory").

Alma knew that we cannot serve two masters. The questions posed to each of us is: "If you are not of the fold of the Good Shepherd, of what fold are you? Who can deny that if you are not of His fold, you are of the devil's?" (V. 39).

Alma asked the congregation if it supposed that he knew these things of himself. (V. 45). He explained that he was just as they were, endowed with the same earthly gifts with which our Heavenly Father blesses each of His children. Without interfering with our agency, these gifts are sufficient to guide us to behavior consistent with celestial principles. God wants each of us to pass the individual tests of mortality, and then to move on, having satisfied the entrance requirements for admittance to the Celestial Kingdom.

Alma bore testimony of these principles to his people, asking in effect: "How do you suppose that I know of their surety? (V. 45). Can you withstand these sayings? Just how powerful is the voice of the Spirit? Can you lay aside these things, and trample the Holy One under your feet? Would you make a mockery of your own Savior? How can you be so puffed up in the pride of your hearts? Will the cares of the world, and your insatiable desire for worldly goods, cloud your vision? Will you still set your hearts upon the vain things of the world, and upon your riches? Do you not yet understand that all is vanity? Will you persist in supposing that you are better than other people? Do you think that your accumulation of worldly goods establishes your superiority over others of less substantial means? Will you continue to persecute your brethren who humble themselves and walk after the Holy Order of God? Will you turn your backs upon the poor? Will you withhold your substance from them?" Today, members of the Church are often prompted to consider these same questions, as they listen to the counsel of their ecclesiastical leaders.

True to his word, Alma carried the messages of the scriptures to all the people. The great reformation movement that began in the City of Zarahemla, then spread "throughout all the land". (V. 1-2, see V. 62). So important was this particular discourse that Mormon included it verbatim, in the first-person tense, in his abridgement. (V. 2).

Alma first established his authority to preach the Gospel by declaring that he had been consecrated a "high priest over the Church of God" by his father, who had "power and authority from God to do these things". (V. 3). Certainly, Alma the Younger had many opportunities to witness his father's administration of the affairs of the Church, and to recognize that authority comes by the laying on of hands, but power derives from worthiness.

The mercy and power of God had allowed the Elder Alma to establish a Church in the Land of Mormon, and to witness its deliverance from physical bondage to the wicked Nephite King Noah. (V. 4). Subsequently, when his people were in captivity to the Lamanites in the Land of Helam, they were again delivered from physical "bondage by the power of his word," and came into the Land of Zarahemla understandably zealous to "establish the Church of God". (V. 5).

The power of the Covenant that God had made with His people was responsible for their deliverance. (See Mosiah 24:13-16). Now Alma the Younger wished to make the principles and promises of that Covenant the foundation of his Gospel message to the members of the Church in Zarahemla. Alma taught his people that whereas their fathers had been in physical bondage to Noah and to the Lamanites, now they were in spiritual bondage, and it was his desire to deliver them once again by the same power of the word of God. (See V. 6-13).

Alma may have remembered the story often told to him by his father, how Lehi had received a seemingly impossible commandment from the Lord. To his son Nephi, Lehi said: "Behold I have dreamed a dream, in the which the Lord hath commanded me that thou and thy brethren shall return to Jerusalem, (to) go unto the house of Laban, and seek the records, and bring them down hither into the wilderness". (1 Nephi 3:2, & 4).

In their subsequent efforts to obtain the records, Lehi's sons were stripped by Laban of all their gold and silver and precious things. (1 Nephi 3:22). The Lord does not need to purchase spiritual gifts with the treasures of the earth. As Nephi had declared to his unbelieving brethren: "I know that the Lord giveth no commandments unto the children of men, save he shall prepare a way for them that they may accomplish the thing which he commandeth them". (1 Nephi 3:7).

The angel had told Nephi, Laman, and Lemuel: "Behold, ye shall go up to Jerusalem again, and the Lord will deliver Laban into your hands". (1 Nephi 3:29). It was to be done the Lord's way, by the power of His mighty arm that is great in the sight of the faithful, but has a terrible effect upon the wicked.

That which Alma asked his brethren in verse 6 is particularly poignant because it was essentially the same thing asked of him by the angel at the time of his youthful rebellion. "Can ye dispute the power of God?" (Mosiah 27:16). It was that angel who had literally knocked sense into Alma and who had been the catalyst responsible for the deliverance of his soul from hell.

After several additional penetrating questions, Alma again relied on "the testimony of the word" (see Alma 4:20) and declared "Behold, I can tell you that this is all true". (V. 11-12). Speaking from experience, he asked his listeners if their hearts were changed, as had been their fathers'. (V. 13).

Verse 14 sets the stage for another round of questions in verses 15-26 and is a checklist of our spiritual well-being. Alma directed his questions to the "brethren of the Church" which is an indication that the baptism of water had qualified them for membership in the Church but had not assured them of the total spiritual transformation necessary to regain the presence of God. This comes through the baptism of fire and the Holy Ghost. (See Mosiah 5:7, 27:25-26, Alma 7:14, & 3 Nephi 27:20).

Alma asked his brethren: "Have ye spiritually been born of God?" (V. 14, see Mosiah 5:7, & Alma 7:14). He wanted to know if they had experienced the pure and unconditional love of Christ and if they had charity for all men. (See 2 Nephi 33). Mahatma Gandhi once said: "If a single man achieves the highest kind of love, it will be enough to neutralize the hatred of millions". Alma knew that the pure love of Christ in the hearts of his people would be a dynamic influence for good.

Later in The Book of Mormon, Moroni would urge his brethren: "Pray unto the Father with all the energy of heart, that ye may be filled with this love, which he hath bestowed upon all who are true followers of his Son, Jesus Christ". (Moroni 7:48). Both Alma and Moroni knew that love is a mighty conqueror: "He drew a circle that shut me out; heretic, rebel, a thing to flout. But Love and I had the will to win. We drew a circle that took him in". (Edward Markham)

We are richer today than we were yesterday, if we have laughed often, given something, forgiven even more, made a new friend, changed stumbling blocks into steppingstones, if we have thought more in terms of "thyself" than "myself," or if we have managed to be cheerful even when we were weary. Alma suggested that such individuals have received His image in their countenances, and have experienced a mighty change in their hearts. (V. 14, see V. 26). "This changed feeling is indescribable, but it is real. Happy is the person who has truly sensed the uplifting, transforming power that comes from this nearness to the Savior, this kinship to the Living Christ". (David O. McKay).

Alma then asked the congregation if they had faith in the atoning power of Christ, and more specifically, if they possessed the resolve to do whatever was necessary to activate its power in their own lives. When we have faith in the power of Christ to save us from, and not in, our sins, we will be profoundly motivated to live in accordance with His will. We will "look forward with an eye of faith," or with an eternal perspective. (V. 15). We will not only believe in Christ, but we will believe Christ, when He says that we can become celestial material.

In verses 16-18, Alma asked his listeners to vividly role-play, for successful experiences must be pre-played before they can be re-played. We are responsible for our own effects. If we don't stand for something, we will fall for anything. If we don't know where we are going, we will end up somewhere else, and we probably won't even care if we made the trip.

When we have a "pure heart and clean hands" we have the "image of God" engraven upon our countenances, which implies permanence. (V. 19). "Who shall ascend into the hill of the Lord," asked the Psalmist, "or who shall stand in his holy place: He that hath clean hands and a pure heart, who hath not lifted up his soul unto vanity, nor sworn deceitfully". (Psalms 24:4-5). Both Alma and the Psalmist used the literary device of parallelism to underscore the significance of clean hands and a pure heart.

On the other hand, if we have yielded, or given up and surrendered ourselves to the devil, we cannot be saved. Only when our "garments are washed white," or are "purified until they are cleansed from all stain" through the Atonement, can we be saved. (V. 21 & 24, see 1 Nephi 30:6). As far as the Atonement is concerned, the symbolism of blood equals cleanliness for "by the blood, (we) are sanctified". (Moses 6:60, see D&C 20:30-31). The spilled blood of the innocent, however, will condemn the guilty at the last day, while the holy prophets and all who follow their counsel will have "garments (that) are cleansed and are spotless, pure and white" in the redeeming blood of Christ. (V. 22-24)

Verse 26 emphasizes the question asked initially in verse 14: "If ye have experienced a change of heart, and if ye have felt to sing the song of redeeming love, I would ask, can ye feel so now?" This question probes the depths of our souls, for the song of redeeming love is an invitation to all men and women, everywhere, to "repent and (Christ) will receive (them)". (V. 35, see Alma 26:13).

"Men are that they might have joy," Lehi had declared. (2 Nephi 2:25). Repentance is essential since "the first condition of happiness is a clear conscience". (David O. McKay). As Abraham said: "Finding there was greater happiness and peace and rest for me, I sought for the blessings of the fathers" through the ordinances of the Gospel. (Abraham 1:1). Before a wound can heal, it has to be clean. The Savior provided the way through faith on His name, repentance because of His Sacrifice, and forgiveness because the antiseptic of the Atonement satisfied the demands of Justice. (See Moses 6:60).

As we participate in the ordinance of the Sacrament in renewal of our baptismal covenant, and so live that the Holy Ghost will be our Companion, we will be guided unerringly to do that which is right. "Every individual that lives according to the laws that the Lord has given to His people, and has received the blessings that He has in store for the faithful, should be able to know the things of God from the things which are not of God, the light from the darkness, that which comes from heaven and that which comes from somewhere else. This is the satisfaction and the consolation that the Latter-day Saints enjoy by living their religion. This is the knowledge which every one who thus lives possesses". (Brigham Young).

Verses 27-31 indicate that there is a great deal more involved in gaining salvation than the initial expression of faith or even the act of baptism for admission into the Church would suggest. Alma warned those in Zarahemla that "the kingdom of heaven is soon at hand" (v. 28); "the hour is close at hand" (v. 29); and "the time is at hand". (V. 30). One hundred sixteen years later, Zarahemla was, in fact, destroyed by fire at the crucifixion of Christ. (See 3 Nephi 8:8). Alma's point was that we should never procrastinate the day of our repentance. (Alma 13:27). To do so, for even a moment, entails the risk that we might become subject to the spirit of the devil. (Alma 34:35).

Following his searching questions, Alma extended God's invitation: "Repent, and I will receive you". (V. 33, see 2 Nephi 15:25). This declaration is so important that it is repeated 6 additional times, in verses 49, 50, 51, 54, 56, and 62.

Those who come unto Christ are invited to "eat and drink of the bread and the waters of life freely". (V. 34). Alma's audience had the scriptures and was invited to study them carefully: "Search the scriptures," commanded the Savior, "for in them ye think ye have eternal life. And they are they which testify of me". (John 5:39). "None of the prophets have written, nor prophesied, save they have spoken concerning ... Christ". (Jacob 7:11).

The next few verses are addressed to those who "have professed to have known the ways of righteousness, (but) nevertheless have gone astray". (V. 37). Professors of religion often "teach for doctrines the commandments of men, having a form of godliness, but they deny the power thereof". (J.S.H. 1:19). Creeds are an abomination in the sight of God and are corrupt when they lead people away from the truth. Insult is added to injury when hypocrisy further perverts humanized, spiritually impotent dogma, when people do not really believe, but are only "professors" of religion.

"Whatsoever is good cometh from God, and whatsoever is evil cometh from the devil". (V. 40). "We have no excuse to err in our knowledge and understanding of right and wrong. By inquiring of the Lord and listening to the voice of His Spirit, and having a willingness to be guided thereby, we will always find ourselves on the Lord's side of every issue, and be strengthened to hold fast to that which is good". (Delbert Stapeley, C.R. 4/1965)

Alma was a prophet of God who had been "called to speak after this manner, according to the holy order of God which is in Christ Jesus". (V. 44, see Alma 13:6-7 & 14). He preached with the power and authority of the Holy Melchizedek Priesthood. (See Alma 4:20). He taught that which had been made known unto him "by the Holy Spirit of God". (V. 46). It was not just the angel who had appeared to him years earlier who had taught him, but more powerfully, it was the Holy Ghost. Of Alma's developmental experiences, David O. McKay wrote: "Even the manifestation of God's power and the presence of His angels came, but when it did, it was simply a confirmation, it was not the testimony". ("True to The Faith," p. 262).

He had "fasted and prayed many days that (he) might know these things of (himself)," that he might have a strong, independent testimony of the Gospel. As the Savior taught: "I will tell you in your mind and in your heart by the Holy Ghost which shall come upon you, and which shall dwell in your heart. Now, behold, this is the spirit of revelation". (D&C 8:2-3, see V. 46).

In his youth, before he had paid the price by laying his life on the altar of sacrifice, he could not comprehend the language of the Spirit, for it was foreign to him. He had never made the journey to Christ; he had not traveled the path leading to the tree of life, let alone partaken of the delicious fruit of that tree. He had been a "natural man (who had received) not the things of the Spirit of God, for they (were) foolishness unto him, neither (could) he know them, because they are spiritually discerned". (1 Corinthians 2:14-15). Faith precedes the miracle, and Alma's experience was no exception.

"Having a testimony and being converted are not necessarily the same thing. A testimony comes when the Holy Ghost gives the earnest seeker a witness of the truth. A moving testimony vitalizes faith, that is, it induces repentance and obedience to the commandments. Conversion, on the other hand, is the fruit or the reward for repentance and obedience". (Marion G. Romney, C.R. 10/1963).

As one converted to the Gospel, Alma unflinchingly testified that Jesus Christ was "the Son, the Only Begotten of the Father, full of grace, and mercy, and truth". (V. 48). "Either this man was, and is, the Son of God, or else a madman, or something worse. But don't let us offer any patronizing nonsense about His (only) being a great human teacher!" (C.S. Lewis, "Mere Christianity," p. 40-41).

Alma reiterated that preaching the Gospel is the responsibility of those who bear the priesthood of God. "This is the order after which I am called, yea, to preach unto my beloved brethren, yea, and every one that dwelleth in the land". (V. 49). He did not make any distinction between member and non-member. Rather, he felt that it was his duty to teach the Gospel to everyone, and his message was the same, that all "must repent and be born again". (V. 49, see V. 33).

The Son of God was soon to come "in his glory". (V. 50). God's Rest "is the fulness of His glory". (D&C 84:24, see Alma 13:13, 16, & 29, & Commentary Reference to Alma 7:27). "Come unto Christ," Jacob had urged, "and partake of the goodness of God, that (you) might enter into his rest." (Jacob 1:7 see Alma 12:34-37). In this sense, Jesus came to the Earth in His glory, that is, as a lamb without spot or blemish, worthy at all times throughout His mortal life of the inner peace that righteousness brings. "The glory of God," after all, "is light and truth". (D&C 93:36). "Man (himself) is glorified in truth (until he) knoweth all things". (D&C 93:26).

The Son of God was soon to come "in his might". (V. 50). The scriptures tell us that Mosiah was "subject to all manner of infirmities in body and mind" nevertheless, he served with "might, mind, and strength". (Mosiah 2:11). Therefore, might does not necessarily mean "of unusual strength". It may mean "sufficient to the task at hand". In this sense, Alma later exhorted his brethren: "Cry unto God for mercy, for He is mighty to save". (Alma 34:18).

The Son of God was soon to come in "majesty". (V. 50). His majesty suggests that He is King of all the earth, and that He wields all power and is in control. The Psalmist asked: "Who is this King of Glory? The Lord strong and mighty, the Lord mighty in battle ... The Lord of hosts, he is the King of glory". (Psalms 24:8 & 10). As He said through His prophet Isaiah: "I am the Lord, your Holy One, the creator of Israel, your King". (Isaiah 43:15). Truly did John call Him "Lord of lords, and King of kings". (Revelation 17:14). To Joseph Smith, the Lord revealed that the heavens and the earth "are kingdoms, and any man who hath seen any or the least of these hath seen God moving in His majesty and power". (D&C 88:47).

The Son of God was soon to come in "power". (V. 50). The hallmark of the ministry of Jesus was the manifestation of the priesthood power that was intrinsic to His Person. Priesthood authority comes by the laying on of hands, but Priesthood power, that is God's Own power, is exercised on condition of personal righteousness or worthiness. (See Helaman 10:6, and D&C 128:11-12). Christ was the personification of these qualities. As He said to His disciples: "All power is given unto me in heaven and in earth". (Matthew 28:18).

The Son of God was soon to come in "dominion," in the sense that He held priesthood authority. (V. 50). All the earth is the dominion of Jesus Christ. "The heavens he made; the Earth is his footstool; and the foundation thereof is his". (Moses 6:44). Thus, we are given the admonition to avoid "unrighteous dominion," or to in any way curtail another's agency, by the exercise of profane authority, or worldly influence. (See D&C 121:37).

Alma warned the people of the City of Zarahemla that if they did not repent, they would risk being "hewn down and cast into the fire, yea, a fire which cannot be consumed, even an unquenchable fire". (V. 52, see V. 56). He uttered this prophecy in the name of the Lord: "Behold, and remember, the Holy One hath spoken it". (V. 52). In its dualistic fulfillment, The Book of Mormon does, in fact, record that the City of Zarahemla was burned at the crucifixion of Christ. (3 Nephi 8:8).

Verses 53-55 describe those things that cause the testimony of some to fail, and that place their eternal welfare in great jeopardy. To trample the Holy One under your feet" (V. 53), or to "set him at naught" (1 Nephi 19:7), or to have "crucified Him and put Him to an open shame" (D&C 76:35), is to deny the faith, repudiate testimony, forsake covenants, mock the Oath and Covenant of the Priesthood, persecute the Church, all at the risk of spiritual death as a Son of Perdition.

Individuals become enemies to righteousness when they are carried away in pride and vanity, as evidenced by "the wearing of costly apparel and setting (their) hearts upon the vain things of the world, upon (their) riches". (V. 53). These things have no lasting value, and it is when they become our focus of attention that we are guilty of the worship of false gods and idols. (See D&C 1:16).

If we have a one-dimensional view of the world, we will surely yield to the persuasions of the moment. The Gospel develops the whole individual as it gives us a multidimensional view of existence, providing a more accurate milieu within which we may exercise our agency. In this sense, the glory of God is intelligence, which is the ability to perceive both the physical and spiritual world around us, and engage in appropriate activities based on that which is true, and founded on a realistic appreciation of both cause and effect within the petri dish of opposition in all things.

Alma taught a doctrine of absolute equality within the Church, recognizing that those who derive the benefits of membership do so because of the "holy order of God" that makes the ordinances of baptism and receipt of the Holy Ghost available to all. Faith then matures "unto salvation" wherein we may "bring forth works which are meet for repentance". (V. 54). Works that qualify us for repentance go beyond recognition of our sins, remorse for our sins, a resolve to make a change, a reformation in our behavior, and restitution where possible.

In fact, when we fall short of obedience to any of God's laws, the Atonement stipulates that we travel the Royal Road of Repentance. This Requires that we act with Responsibility, as we Recognize the Reality of our transgression and view it with Revulsion, and experience Remorse that drives us to our knees. In our heart-felt prayers, we Relate to our Heavenly Father how we feel, in a process of confession that is the most painful example of Revelation. This demands that we Renounce our self-defeating behaviors, make Restitution to injured parties where possible, and then do whatever is necessary, as the Spirit directs us, to submit ourselves to a Refiner's fire that will help us to Re-establish a Reconciliation with heaven and Regain the Rapport with Jesus Christ that had formerly been our hope and our joy. As we Renew our Resolve to Recommit ourselves to walk the covenant path, it will be through the miracle of the grace of Him Who is our Redeemer, that we will Receive a Remission of our sin. Only then, will it become possible to move forward with purpose toward our Reward in heaven.

Our works may include participating worthily in the ordinance of the Sacrament and those of the temple. But we cannot "work" our way into heaven; it is completely beyond our power to do so. Nevertheless, "it is by grace that we are saved, after all we can do". (2 Nephi 25:23).

Brigham Young once said: "There is no man who ever made a sacrifice on this earth for the kingdom of heaven except the Savior. I would not give the ashes of a rye straw for that man who feels that he is making sacrifices for God. We are doing this for our own happiness, welfare, and exaltation, and for nobody else's. What we do, we do for the salvation of the inhabitants of the earth, not for the salvation of the heavens, the angels, or God". (J.D., 16:114).

Martin Luther agreed. By faith, he meant "no merely intellectual assent to a proposition, but vital, personal self-committal to a practical belief. He heartily approved of good works; what he denied was their efficacy for salvation. 'Good works,' he said, "do not make a good man, but a good man does good works'. And what makes a man good? Faith in God, and Christ". (Wil Durant, "The Reformation," p. 374-375). What really matters to God are those things that have eternal significance, and especially those activities that are associated with the priesthood.

Alma assured his people that the names of those who "persist in wickedness shall be blotted out". (V. 55-56). Church members who do not live according to Gospel standards generally excommunicate themselves by their actions, as they withdraw themselves from fellowship with the Saints. Water seeks its own level. (See Commentary Reference to Mosiah 27:31).

"The names of the righteous," on the other hand, "shall be written in The Book of life", which is a record kept in heaven that contains the names of the righteous, along with an account of their covenants and their good deeds. (V. 58). "We are not going to be saved in the Kingdom of God just because our names are on the records of the Church," explained Joseph Fielding Smith, Jr. We will have to have our names written in the Lamb's Book of Life. Therein is the evidence that we have kept the commandments. Every soul who will not keep the commandments shall have his name blotted out of that book". (Sydney Sperry, "Doctrine & Covenants Compendium," 2:28). Our lives are like diaries. Most people write one story, intending to write another. Their most humbling moment comes when they compare the two. With God's help, the record can be edited if necessary, with a fairy tale ending. We can all live happily ever after in a magical kingdom where the enchantment never ends.

If we speak against this doctrine, or this record, "it matters not, for the word of God must be fulfilled". (V. 58). "What does it matter that a few barking dogs snap at the heels of weary travelers, or that predators claim those few who fall by the way," asked Bruce R. McConkie? "The caravan moves on". (C.R. 10/1984). We must not let those who currently star in dime store pulp novels or "B" movies to influence us to compromise our high standards and accept the mediocrity with which they are apparently satisfied.

Alma closed his address in a way familiar to those who have listened through the years to ecclesiastical leaders in General Conference. He bore testimony "in the language of him who (had) commanded (him)". (V. 61). Lives can be changed by the power of the Word of God. Alma found his teaching to be most effective when it was accompanied by his testimony of the Word. (V. 61, see Alma 4:19-20, 5:1 & 44, & Helaman 6:37). Later, Mormon would effusively write of Alma's teaching style: "And now, as the preaching of the word had a great tendency to lead the people to do that which was just - yea, it had had more powerful effect upon the minds of the people than the sword, or anything else, which had happened unto them - therefore Alma thought it was expedient that they should try the virtue of the word of God". (Alma 31:5).

Joseph Smith taught: "A person can get nearer to God by reading The Book of Mormon than by reading any other book". There is great motivating and sanctifying power in the words of The Book of Mormon, precisely because, as a companion to the Bible, it is Another Testament of Jesus Christ. President Ezra Taft Benson counseled the young men of the Church: "The Book of Mormon will change your life. It will fortify you against the evils of our day. It will bring spirituality into your life, as no other book will. It will be the most important book you will read in preparation for a mission and for life. A young man who knows and loves The Book of Mormon, who has read it several times, who has an abiding testimony of its truthfulness, and who applies its teachings will be able to stand against the wiles of the devil and will be a mighty tool in the hands of the Lord". (C.R. 4/1986).

Later in the same address, he said: "Oh, my brethren, let us not treat lightly the great things we have received from the hand of the Lord. His word is one of the most valuable gifts He has given us. I urge you to recommit yourselves to a study of the scriptures. Read them in your families, and teach your children to love and treasure them. Then, prayerfully and in counsel with others. Seek every way possible to encourage the members of the Church to follow your example". (C.R. 4/1986).

Finally, Alma urged his listeners to come unto Christ and to participate in the ordinances administered by the priesthood. (See Moroni 10:32). Alma desired that the people be "convicted by their own conscience." (John 8:9). He knew that there is great motivating power to do good when we have the desire to enter into a covenant relationship with God. As we come to understand how we fit into God's Plan, our divine potential finds an avenue for expression, and eternal life becomes a realistic goal for which no effort expended seems too great. Alma's message was universal, for He spoke by commandment not only to the members of the Church, but also to those who had not yet united themselves with the Fold of God, as well as to both member and non-member in the Last Days. (V. 62).

Alma
Chapter 6

After Alma had spoken to the assembled members of the Church in the City of Zarahemla, "he ordained priests and elders, by laying his hands on their heads according to the order of God". (V. 1). "These priests and teachers held the Melchizedek Priesthood, (for) in general terms, a priest is a minister, and has no reference to any particular office in the priesthood". (Joseph Fielding Smith, Jr., "Doctrines of Salvation," 3:87, see Jacob 1:18).

Thus, the "order of the Church" began to be established in Zarahemla. (V. 4). That is to say, a priesthood government was organized so that every member might have an equal opportunity to come unto Christ. The world seeks to change mankind with legislation, social programs, and sometimes through overt coercion. The Lord's way is centered on an inner change facilitated by those who bear the priesthood.

David O. McKay once said at the close of a General Church Conference: "If we could be obedient to the counsel of the General Authorities that we have heard in this Conference, it would be sufficient to bring us into the presence of God". It was this order that Alma sought to establish in Zarahemla by the power of the priesthood.

The ordinances of the Gospel were "liberal unto all" in Zarahemla; in other words, they were available to member and nonmember alike. (V. 6). However, "the children of God" were under a special obligation to make efforts to bring both the temporal and spiritual blessings of the Gospel to nom-members. (See Mosiah 5:7, & 25:23-24).

Leaving the affairs of the Church in the City of Zarahemla in capable hands, Alma departed on a missionary journey, first going to the City of Gideon. (V. 7). The foundation of his teaching continued to be the scriptures, with reliance on the guidance of the Spirit and the power and authority of the priesthood. (V. 8). The people of the City of Gideon were better prepared to receive Alma's message than had been the hard-hearted people of Zarahemla. Therefore, the techniques

Alma used in his approach to the spiritual reformation of the Church changed when he left Zarahemla.

Bruce R. McConkie once wrote: "We save ourselves by our teaching, and we save those who will get in tune with the same spirit that we have, when we teach those truths. What a glorious and wondrous thing it is not to have to defend them and support them and uphold them. They are true, and they sustain and defend and uphold themselves. And they do it because the work is true. God be praised that we have the truths of salvation and that we are members of His Church and Kingdom of God on earth". ("The Foolishness of Teaching").

As we read in the coming chapters about Alma's missionary labors, we will continually marvel at the power of his testimony. One is reminded of "P.T.L.," which in the 1980s was associated with the "Praise the Lord" ministry. How much better to think of P.T.L. in the terms outlined by Thomas Monson when he said that we should "prepare with purpose, teach with testimony, and labor with love". (Aaronic Priesthood Commemoration Fireside, 5/17/1987). Remember, the scriptures say that it is "by works (that we are) justified, and not by faith only". (James 2:24). Those works that are driven by faith and emulate the example of the Master, who is the Divine Model, identify His disciples as profitable servants, worthy of their hire. To those, He has said: "Ye may eat and drink at my table in my kingdom, and sit on thrones". (Luke 22:30).

Alma
Chapter 7

The City of Gideon had been established around eight years earlier some distance from Zarahemla, and Alma had never visited the area, "having been wholly confined to the (governmental responsibilities of) the judgment seat" in the capital city. (V. 1, see Alma 6:7).

Alma's explanation to the people of Gideon that he had come to address them in his "own language" by his "own mouth," provides insight into Mormon's frequent usage of the word "language" in The Book of Mormon. (See Commentary Reference to 1 Nephi 1:2). Therefore, we should not generalize and assume that Book of Mormon peoples abandoned their Hebraic roots and spoke strange tongues.

As has been noted, because of the "awful dilemma" confronting the Church in Zarahemla, Alma had given up the judgment-seat in order to focus all his efforts on the ministry. (V. 2-3, see Alma 4:15-19). A "dilemma" is a situation that is faced with two equally unfavorable alternatives. For the Nephites in Zarahemla, their choice was either to lie to God regarding their state of righteousness or to face Him with an awful remembrance of their sins. (See Alma 5:17-18). Alma's role as their spiritual leader had been to help his people resolve this problem. That he had been successful in Zarahemla is attested by his expression of satisfaction to the people of Gideon: "They are established again in the way of his righteousness". (V. 4).

Alma taught the people of Gideon that the Savior would soon come "among his people". (V. 7). He cautioned them that this did not mean He would come to the Nephites during his mortal ministry. (V. 8). As a matter of fact, about 5 years later, the people were specifically taught that the Savior would visit them only after His resurrection. (Alma 16:20).

Alma 7:10 has been a source of confusion for some members of the Church as they have read The Book of Mormon, and has been identified by enemies of the Church as an error in the text. The first part of this verse, speaking of Jesus, reads: "And behold, he shall be born of Mary, at Jerusalem which is the land of our forefathers". In some early editions of The Book of Mormon, the rendering is "in Jerusalem". In any event, the term, "the land of Jerusalem," occurs forty-two times in the text of the current edition of The Book of Mormon, and so we might ask ourselves: 'What does this commonly used expression mean?'

The answer is quite simple. Bethlehem, just six miles from Jerusalem, is within the area designated by the Ancients themselves as "the land of Jerusalem". When The Book of Mormon text states that Jesus was born "at Jerusalem," or "in the land of Jerusalem," there is no conflict as long as one understands the ancient context. "Such a neat test of authenticity is not often found in ancient documents," wrote Hugh Nibley. "Therefore, what at first appears to be a textual error in The Book of Mormon instead powerfully supports its claim of authenticity". ("An Approach to The Book of Mormon," p. 82).

Verse 10 then declares that Mary conceived "by the power of the Holy Ghost". Evidently, no additional explanation was necessary. Suffice to say that Mary's conception would have been impossible without the overshadowing influence of the Holy Ghost.

The next few verses describe how the Atonement was made. With great clarity, Book of Mormon prophets taught principles that are elsewhere in scripture dealt with incompletely, but here, there is little room for confusion.

Verse 11 suggests that part of the Atonement was accomplished during the three years that the Savior labored among the Jews. "And he shall go forth, suffering pains and afflictions and temptations of every kind; and this that the word might be fulfilled which saith he will take upon him the pains and the sicknesses of his people". The description of the suffering of the Savior is particularly poignant in light of Alma's own suffering. (Alma 36:14, & 21. It seems that the work in which the Savior was engaged followed a natural progression, and was built "line upon line, and precept upon precept," until His preparation was complete, and every necessary detail had been worked out. Early in His ministry, Jesus said, "My time is not yet come". (John 7:6). But later, when all had been accomplished, He confirmed, "My time is at hand". (Matthew 26:18).

Verse 12 concerns the aspect of the Atonement that was completed upon the Cross. "And he will take upon him death, that he may loose the bands of death which bind his people; and he will take upon him their infirmities, that his bowels may be filled with mercy, according to the flesh, that he may know according to the flesh how to succor his people according to their infirmities". The crucified Christ is the primary focus of Christianity today, but if we fail to understand the Mortal Messiah, we risk relying upon only a one-dimensional view that ignores the wonderful harmony of both His humanity and His divinity. In the context of this verse, it is well to remember that people who have known hardship are usually better able to help others to meet adversity. This principle may help to explain why so many Church members, even after living Christ-like lives, are not spared challenges in their mortal lives. However, it would be wrong to assume that the more righteous we are, the less we will suffer. The promise is that we will be blessed even though the blessing may be the strength to endure suffering. All suffer. The difference is that the wicked must suffer the consequences of sin, in addition to the suffering that is a part of our mortal experience. (See D&C 121:7). Marion G. Romney once said: "If we can bear our afflictions with understanding, faith, and courage, we shall be strengthened and comforted and spared the torment that accompanies the mistaken idea that all suffering comes as a chastisement for transgression". (C.R. 10/1964).

Verse 13 focuses on the dimension of the Atonement that was fulfilled in Gethsemane. "Now the Spirit knoweth all things; nevertheless, the Son of God suffereth according to the flesh that he might take upon him the sins of his people, that he might blot out their transgressions according to the power of his deliverance". Latter-day Saints tend to emphasize Gethsemane as the pivotal experience attendant to the Savior's sacrifice, but we can see that it was really a many-faceted drama played out on different stages. It began even before the creation of the earth, for the scriptures identify Jesus Christ as "the Lamb slain from the foundation of the world". (Revelation 13:8).

Verses 14-16 then explain the effect that the Atonement can have upon our lives. First, Alma described the process by which we are "born again" or become alive to things of the Spirit. "Now I say unto you that ye must repent, and be born again; for the Spirit saith if ye are not born again ye cannot inherit the kingdom of heaven; therefore come and be baptized unto repentance, that ye may be washed from your sins, that ye may have faith on the Lamb of God, who taketh away the sins of the world, who is mighty to save and to cleanse from all unrighteousness".

Being born again was very much on the mind of Alma the Younger. "For, said he, I have repented of my sins, and have been redeemed of the Lord; behold I am born of the Spirit". (Mosiah 27:24-25). In his own life, he had given himself completely to the Savior, the only One who is mighty to save. It had been a harrowing ordeal as the refiner's fire had purged the effects of sin from the very marrow of his bones. (See Alma 14:6).

A modern-day Apostle described his similar experience: "I've never given my agency to anyone except Christ, and I want you to know that experience was akin to Gethsemane". (Boyd K. Packer). Perhaps each of us must ultimately follow the path to our personal and individual Garden of Gethsemane. It may be that we go unassisted, but if we are prepared, we need not fear. (See D&C 38:30). Joseph F. Smith declared: "No one need fear in their heart when they are conscious of having lived up to the principles of truth and righteousness as God has required it at their hands, according to their best knowledge and understanding".

One is reminded of the 1999 movie "Meet Joe Black". (A remake of the 1934 classic "Death Takes a Holiday"). In the final scene, the protagonist asks Death if he should be afraid of what lies in store for him. When Death gently answers and says: "Not a man like you, Bill", we know that, in the face of the inevitable, everything is going to be okay.

C.S. Lewis pondered Christ's suffering on the cross when He was left alone to conquer the world on His own merits. In His agony, as the sustaining influence of His Father's Spirit left Him, He cried out: "My God, my God, why hast thou forsaken me?" (Matthew 27:46). Perhaps the Savior's knowledge of this element of the Plan had been kept from Him precisely because it was critical to its execution. Perhaps eternal law required that He stand alone in one final test. In any event, Lewis wrote: "There is a mystery here which, even if I had the power, I might not have the courage to explore. Meanwhile, little people like you and me, if our prayers are sometimes granted beyond all hope and probability, had better not draw hasty conclusions to our own advantage. If we were stronger, we might be less tenderly treated. If we were braver, we might be sent, with far less help, to defend far more desperate posts in the great battle". ("The World's Last Night," p. 10-11).

When the Holy Ghost falls upon a worthy recipient, it has the effect of pouring out pure intelligence. All is calm and serene. The still small voice speaks to the spirit within, and a sanctifying, cleansing power begins to manifest itself. It was this quality of experience that Alma desired for the People of Gideon. "Yea, I say unto you come and fear not," promised Alma, "and whoso doeth this ... shall have eternal life, according to the testimony of the Holy Spirit, which testifieth in me". (V. 15-16).

The Spirit bore witness to Alma that his mission had been successful. (V. 17-20). Alma had preached, taught, expounded, and exhorted the people in order to awaken them to a sense of their duty to God. (See D&C 20:46). He challenged them to be baptized, and promised that after they had been received into the Church, they would be taught the true Order of the Priesthood. (V. 15, & 22). Knowledge of the doctrines of the kingdom does not automatically come with Church membership. A lifetime of learning is required.

Verses 23-24 describe the 13 key qualities necessary to walk blamelessly before God, that members can have as they come out of the waters of baptism. This beautiful admonition could be used to describe a true Latter-day Saint. "Be humble, and be submissive and gentle; easy to be entreated; full of patience and long-suffering; being temperate in all things; being diligent in keeping the commandments of God at all times; asking for whatsoever things ye stand in need, both spiritual and temporal; always returning thanks unto God for whatsoever things ye do receive. And see that ye have faith, hope, and charity, and then will ye always abound in good works". Joseph Smith might have been moved to compose the 13th Article of Faith because of his familiarity with this quotation from the Prophet Alma. (See Philippians 4:8).

Alma desired that "the peace of God" might rest upon the people of Gideon. (V. 27). God's Rest "is the fulness of His glory". (D&C 84:24, see Commentary Reference to Alma 5:50). The concepts of eternal life, God's Rest and the peace of God were strong elements throughout Alma's teachings. There are twelve references to God's Rest in The Book of Alma, more than anywhere else in The Book of Mormon. His path had not been easy, but after many struggles

Alma had found this supreme quality of satisfaction in his own life and he was single-minded in his desire to share with others the merciful Plan of Redemption, Salvation, and Happiness. (See Commentary Reference to Alma 13:6).

"Satan had gotten great hold upon the hearts of the people of the city of Ammonihah; therefore, they would not hearken unto the words of Alma. Nevertheless, Alma labored much in the spirit, wrestling with God in mighty prayer, that he would pour out his Spirit upon the people who were in the city, that he would also grant that he might baptize them unto repentance." (Alma 8:9-10).

Alma
Chapter 8

Sir Winston Churchill once said: "Men's and nations' finest hours are those when extraordinary challenge is met with extraordinary response". This chapter deals first with Alma's missionary labors in the Land of Melek, where he was well received (V. 3-5), and where he taught the people by the power of the Melchizedek Priesthood "according to the holy order of God" (V. 4), and "baptized throughout all the land". (V. 5). By all outward appearances, his mission in Melek was quite successful.

Then, in the City of Ammonihah, Alma and his missionary companion Amulek met a difficult challenge with a profoundly spiritual response that was initially disappointing because of the rejection of its message. These people had the same opportunities as those in Zarahemla, Gideon, and Melek, but full-scale apostasy and wickedness reigned supreme in Ammonihah. "Satan had gotten great hold upon the hearts of the people; therefore, they would not hearken unto the words of Alma". (V. 9).

Much of the world today reflects the attitude of those who lived in the Nephite City of Ammonihah. There is no end to pretense of being law abiding. Outward righteousness cloaks inner wickedness. Laws are designed to cover transgressions or to justify even the most abominable sins. Forms of murder, drug abuse, gambling, prostitution, pornography, sexual deviancy, and theft are already legitimized and legalized. On the one hand, there is general resistance to legislation that would enforce morality, while at the same time laws are passed that legalize immorality.

All is done in the name of due process and equal protection. The constraints of morality and ethics that society has traditionally placed on freedom have largely been eliminated, and our culture no longer regards the exercise of free will as an opportunity to do what is right. When license replaces freedom, carnality, sensuality, and the desire to do whatever one wants, become the baseline criteria for defining acceptable behavior. The resulting celebration of the senses actually dulls the perception of what is real, and what is only an illusion, or caricature of reality.

Without universally applicable standards, the very fabric of society begins to tear apart. Even as the world seems to be preoccupied with justice, a closer look reveals that this is so only superficially, since its administration is too often at the expense of truth. There may be "less injustice in this world than a century ago. But only a vile idiot would argue that there is less untruth. We are threatened not by the absence of justice, (but by the) fantastic prevalence of untruth. Truth responds to a deeper human need than does justice. We can live with injustice a long time, indeed, that is the human condition; but we cannot long live with untruth". (John Lukacs, "The Passing of The Modern Age").

In America, observed Gordon B. Hinckley, we have become "a people of contention with strident and accusatory voices heard in arguments across the nation. We rose from scratch to become the greatest industrial power in the history of the Earth. Now, we spend millions of our resources in litigation one against another. Our spiritual power is sapped by a flood tide of pornography, and by a debilitating epidemic of the use of drugs that destroys both body and mind. In all too many ways, we have substituted human sophistry for the Almighty". ("Church News," 7/2/1988).

In similar circumstances in Ammonihah, "Alma labored much in the spirit, wrestling with God in mighty prayer, that he would pour out his Spirit upon the people who were in the city; that he would also grant that he might baptize them unto repentance". (V. 10). Even though these people rudely rejected him and "reviled him, and spit upon him, and caused that he should be cast out of their city," their temporal and spiritual welfare continued to weigh heavily on his mind. (V. 12).

After his physical ejection from Ammonihah, while he was on the road to the city that was called Aaron, Alma had a marvelous experience. The very same angel who had visited him in his youth and had called him to repentance again appeared. (V. 13-14). Angels do watch over us, as the Lord testifies: "For I will go before your face. I will be on your right hand, and on your left, and my Spirit shall be in your hearts, and mine angels round about you, to bear you up". (D&C 84:88).

This time, the angel commended him for his faithfulness. (V. 15). Then, he commanded Alma to return to Ammonihah, "to preach again unto the people of the city". (V. 16). We shall see that afterward, some of the people did repent, and although many lost their physical lives as a result, they were nevertheless saved from ultimate spiritual destruction. (Alma 14:1, 8 & 11).

Understandably, "after Alma had received his message from the angel of the Lord, he returned speedily to the land of Ammonihah". (V. 18). There, he was befriended by a man named Amulek who identified himself as "a Nephite" in the cultural, religious, and hereditary sense. (V. 20, see Alma 10:2). We know little of Amulek's background, but he might have been one of those who had been touched by Alma's message before his earlier expulsion from Ammonihah. (See Commentary Reference to Alma 10:1-9). There is an interesting similarity between these events and the experiences of Alma's father years earlier in the Land of Nephi at the time that Abinadi was called to preach repentance to the wicked Nephites. (See Mosiah 17:2, and Commentary Reference to

Alma 9:6). After their fortuitous meeting, Alma "tarried many days with Amulek," instructing him in spiritual matters, and in other ways helping his newfound "Greenie" to prepare for his mission. (V. 27, see Alma 10:10).

Even though "the people did wax more gross in their iniquities," Alma and Amulek went forth and preached the word of God, being "filled with the Holy Ghost," exercising the authority and power of the priesthood. (V. 28-31, see Helaman 10:6). The Lord must have given Alma and Amulek the same promise He extended to those who bear the priesthood in the Last Days: "And it shall be given thee in the very moment what thou shalt speak and write". (D&C 24:6). "Behold," promised the Savior, "I will go before you and be your rearward; and I will be in your midst, and you shall not be confounded". (D&C 49:27).

Priesthood is the authority and the power to act for and on behalf of God. Authority, as the 5th Article of Faith defines it, comes from the laying on of hands, while power, as the endowment in the temple defines it, comes from righteousness.

In their wickedness, the people of Ammonihah blindly sought to destroy the very individuals who could teach them how to be saved both temporally and spiritually. This is a puzzling characteristic of the wicked, who, in their ignorance, place themselves beyond the vale of saving grace.

The wicked inhabitants of Ammonihah tried every means at their disposal to silence the missionaries. Similar circumstances exist in the world today, where irreligious imperialism seeks to disallow certain of people's opinions simply because they grow out of unpopular religious convictions. Under such conditions, all society suffers. "When irreligion becomes the state religion, a society has the worst of all possible combinations. Its orthodoxy is insistent, and its inquisitors inevitable. Its paid ministry is numerous beyond belief, and its Caesars are insufferably condescending. Its majorities, when faced with clear alternatives, make the Barabbas choice, as did a mob centuries ago when Pilate confronted them with the need to decide. If we let come into being a secular Church which is shorn of traditional and divine values, where shall we go for inspiration in the crises of tomorrow?" (Neal Maxwell, "B.Y.U. Today," 12/1978, p. 11).

In Ammonihah, though, despite every effort of the wicked, neither Alma nor Amulek could "be confined in dungeons neither was it possible that any man could slay them". (V. 31, see Alma 14:26-29). The personality precipice looming before the wicked inhabitants of Ammonihah was only a year away, and so Alma and Amulek preached with urgency, although their message of salvation largely fell on deaf ears. It is interesting that in the following chapters (Alma Chapter 9 to 14 inclusive) powerful doctrine was abridged from the journals of missionaries whose message was essentially rejected. For example, one of the most significant statements recorded in the scriptures on the subject of the Melchizedek Priesthood was given to the people of Ammonihah in Alma Chapter 13.

They were at a spiritual crossroads and their eternal destiny hung in the balance. Joshua had declared: "Choose you this day whom ye will serve, but as for me and my house, we will serve the Lord". (Joshua 24:15). Truly, we are all "free to choose liberty and eternal life or captivity and death". (2 Nephi 2:27). In every contest that shapes our fortunes, God unerringly casts His vote for us. The devil always casts his against us, for he "seeketh that all men might be miserable like unto himself". (2 Nephi 2:27). It is we, then, who cast the deciding vote. We shape our own destiny.

The Lord desired to give the people of Ammonihah the chance to make that ultimate choice. Before doing so, however, He saw to it that they would be given every opportunity to choose well. The Lord sent his ablest missionaries among them, and armed them with strong testimonies, the sure knowledge of Gospel principles, unwavering faith, and priesthood power. Not until the missionaries had made one last attempt to reach them, would He allow these people entrenched in wickedness to completely forfeit their agency, capitulate to the devil's will, and suffer destruction at the hands of the Lamanites.

Alma
Chapter 9

After Alma preached the Gospel to the people of Ammonihah, they responded by ridiculing his testimony, saying: "Suppose ye that we shall believe the testimony of one man?" (V. 2). Interestingly, the Lord had provided a second witness in the person of Amulek, who soon had the opportunity to add his testimony to that of Alma's, with significant effect. (See Alma 10:12)

The people also declared that even if Alma should prophecy that Ammonihah should be destroyed in one day, they would not believe him. This was an exaggerated statement that reflected the reliance of the people of Ammonihah on the arm of flesh, but it was nevertheless a prophecy that was literally fulfilled only one year later. (V. 4, see V. 18, & Alma 16:10). One wonders if the unrepentant former inhabitants of the doomed City of Ammonihah became any more receptive to the Gospel Plan after they found themselves in the Spirit Prison of the Unjust. (See Commentary Reference to 2 Nephi 4:32, Alma 48:23, D&C 76:73, & 138:8 & 28, Isaiah 61:1, 1 Peter 3:19 & Moses 7:57).

When the divine spark is dimmed by depravity, and smothered by the suffocating stench of sin, the wicked have eyes and yet do not see, and have ears and yet cannot hear. Of those in our day who labor under that crushing burden of sin, Truman Madsen wrote: "Writers have chosen up sides to see who can articulate the most sophisticated despair. They are not describing the broad spectrum of life, but only life without God". ("Are Christians Mormons?"). The atheistic viewpoint sees with a jaundiced eye, and yet it argues with such vehemence and self-righteousness that it is sometimes clothed with an unearned legitimacy. The unrelenting promulgation of its tenets finally bestows upon them a familiarity that is undeserved, but unquestioned. "Vice is a monster of so frightful mien, as to be hated needs but to be seen. Yet seen too oft, familiar with her face, we first endure, then pity, then embrace". (Alexander Pope).

The people of Ammonihah were strangers to God, and so they asked: "Who is God, that sendeth no more authority than one man among this people, to declare unto them the truth of such great and marvelous things?" (V. 6). In his own darkened state of mind, wicked King Noah had said the same thing of Abinadi about sixty-eight years earlier. "Who is Abinadi, that I and my people should be judged of him, or who is the Lord, that shall bring upon my people such great affliction?" (Mosiah 11:27).

Alma sought to help the people to correctly understand the traditions of their fathers, who had been delivered by God's matchless power, mercy, and long-suffering. (V. 11). He tried to teach them that failure to repent carries two distinct consequences. "Except ye repent, ye can in nowise inherit the kingdom of God," he declared. "But behold, this is not all. He has commanded you to repent, or he will utterly destroy you from off the face of the earth". (V. 12). They would soon find the answer to the question they had posed in verse 6. The day of the Lord is great for those who have endured to the end in righteousness, but it is terrible for those who have procrastinated the day of their repentance and have failed to change their wicked ways.

According to Lehi, "the days of the children of men (in the time of Adam) were prolonged, according to the will of God, that they might repent while in the flesh". (2 Nephi 2:21). "The reason that our lives are extended as they are beyond the age of reproduction is to allow us the fullest possible opportunity to repent. Therefore, when men have lost the capacity to repent, they forfeit any right to sojourn further upon the face of the earth; the very purpose of this extended span of life being to practice repentance. When men announce that they have no intention of repenting there is no reason why God should let them stay around any longer to corrupt the rising generation". (Hugh Nibley, "Beyond Politics," p. 294).

Alma illustrated his point by reminding the people of Ammonihah that the Lamanites had been "cut off from the presence of the Lord". (V. 14). Nevertheless, he cautioned: "It shall be more tolerable for them in the day of judgment than for you, if ye remain in your sins, yea, and even more tolerable for them in this life than for you, except ye repent". (V. 15). For clarification, he explained: "And now behold, I say unto you, that if this people, who have received so many blessings from the hand of the Lord, should transgress contrary to the light and knowledge which they do have ... it would be far more tolerable for the Lamanites than for them". (V. 23). As Brigham Young cautioned: "Those who do not know anything of the Lord are far better off than we are, unless we live our religion". (J.D., 16:111).

Verses 20-23 teach the principle of increasing accountability, and enumerate a few of the blessings the highly favored "people of Nephi" had enjoyed during the previous 500 years. Their prayers had been answered, the Spirit had visited them, and they had conversed with angels. The voice of the Lord had come to them, and they had the spirit of prophecy and of revelation, and many other gifts. They had been delivered by God from Jerusalem, and had been saved from famine in that land. Not only this, but in their New World home they were mighty in battle and had been delivered out of bondage many times, prospering both temporally and spiritually.

After all these blessings, and with the promises of the Lord yet extended to the repentant, Alma exhorted his brethren of the City of Ammonihah to "reap the salvation of their souls, according to the power and deliverance of Jesus Christ". (V. 28). The Savior's mission on Earth was principally to "redeem those who (would) be baptized unto repentance, through faith on his name". (V. 27). Ultimately, the Atonement has purpose and meaning only for those who enter into covenants that are administered by the priesthood.

As Amulek later explained to the Zoramites: "And thus mercy can satisfy the demands of justice, and encircles (the repentant) in the arms of safety, while he that exercises no faith unto repentance is exposed to the whole law of the demands of justice; therefore, only unto him that has faith unto repentance is brought about the great and eternal plan of redemption". (Alma 34:16). Faith, without works of repentance, is dead, because alone it has insufficient power to save. If the residents of Ammonihah hoped to prosper in the land, they would have to repent and endure to the end in righteousness.

On the other hand, those who have been evil "shall reap the damnation of their souls, according to the power and captivation of the devil". (V. 28, see Alma 12:7). Through his evil influence and persuasive abilities, Satan can rob us of liberty but not necessarily of agency. Our freedom to act independently must be given away voluntarily. But like a mess of pottage, once we have sold our agency, however cheaply, it cannot easily be reclaimed. When we have made a pact with the devil, that old miser is not likely to have a change of heart and surrender the prize he has fought so hard to win.

Initially, at least, we choose our own destiny and are responsible for our own outcomes. When agency is maintained, truth will prevail. Error will expose itself in the sunlight of correct principles and under the scrutiny of applied Gospel standards. One of the reasons why the Gospel Plan is perfect is because it is designed to provide course correction and positive feedback. It is not only inherently self-perpetuating, but with self-diagnostic capabilities, those who embrace it experience improvement over time, as it harmoniously integrates them into the fold. Its shield of protection strengthens those who practice what they preach. Detrimental input is categorically rejected. Every data stream that is potentially damaging is immediately identified and faithfully filtered out, while the Plan blueprints offer suggestions to countermand every anticipated attack against its firewall that can be nigh unto impregnable.

"I teach people correct principles and they govern themselves," declared Joseph Smith. (John Taylor Quote In "The Organization of the Church", "Millennial Star", 11/15/1851, p. 339). This is not the course of safety, but it is the appropriate way. God declared to Adam while he was yet in the Garden: "Nevertheless, thou mayest choose for thyself, for it is given unto thee". (Moses 3:17). If we use our agency incorrectly, we may forfeit it and lose our freedom. While we have our birthright, we may choose to give it away, but once it is gone, it is extremely difficult to recover.

The consequence of our unrighteous use of agency is the loss of both our freedom and our power to act. In fact, there are two freedoms - the false, where we are free to do what we like; and the true, where we are free to do what we ought. "When freedom is used to disengage from the divine, it seems to cause some to grasp for an 'idea-god.' More and more, one sees sincere, idealistic men and women who live out their lives in the clean, well-lit prison of one idea, in the celebration of a single concept or a single majestic solution for all that is wrong in the world". (Neal Maxwell, "Freedom: A Hard Doctrine").

Once again, the people of Ammonihah were angry that Alma had preached things that were difficult for them to understand, and this time they sought to silence him by casting him into prison. (V. 30-33). "The guilty take the truth to be hard, for it cutteth them to the very center". (1 Nephi 16:2). But the Spirit was powerful, and it protected Alma. Under its influence, Amulek was able to preach to the people, as well.

Alma
Chapter 10

This chapter records the message delivered by Amulek to the inhabitants of Ammonihah. He identified himself as a descendant of a man named Aminadi, "who interpreted the writing which was upon the wall of the temple". (V. 2). This is the sole reference in the scriptures to Aminadi, as well as to an incident in a Nephite temple that has no other documentation.

Evidently, the more complete account of Aminadi that was written upon the Large Plates of Nephi was not included in Mormon's abridgement of those records. In the 1981 English language edition of The Book of Mormon, the reference to Aminadi's experience "in the temple" is Daniel 5:16. This scripture is referenced only because Daniel, who was a Judean exile born about 605 B.C. at the court of Nebuchadnezzar, had a similar experience. Any account of his life there could not have been written upon the Plates of Brass because Lehi had taken those with him from Jerusalem about 600 B.C.

During the reign of Belshazzar, about the year 539 B.C. and 23 years after the death of Nebuchadnezzar, when Daniel was an old man, there "came forth fingers of a man's hand, and wrote over against the candlestick upon the pilaster of the wall of the king's palace: and the king saw the part of the hand that wrote. Then the king's countenance was changed, and his thoughts troubled him so that the joints of his loins were loosed, and his knees smote one against another". (Daniel 5:5-6). The biblical account then relates how Daniel was able to interpret the writing upon the wall, predicting the downfall of Belshazzar that very night. (See Daniel 5:17-31). Clearly, then, the writing upon the wall of "the temple" to which Amulek alluded concerned another entirely different experience, by some individual other than Daniel.

Only by this interpretation does verse 2 make sense, for Amulek identified Aminadi as "a descendant of Nephi, who was the son of Lehi". Aminadi was a Nephite. That there were temples in the Land of Nephi and of Zarahemla is well documented in The Book of Mormon. (2 Nephi 5:16, Jacob 1:17, Mosiah 1:18, Alma 16:13, 23:2, Helaman 10:8, & 3 Nephi 11:1). The experience of Aminadi must have taken place in one of these temples of the Lord.

We have learned that Lehi was of the tribe of Joseph, (1 Nephi 5:14), but it is only here that we discover he was a descendant of Joseph's son Manasseh. (V. 2). The Assyrians led the Ten Tribes of Israel, including Manasseh, away into the North Countries about 721 B.C. The Old Testament helps to explain how it was that remnants of Manasseh were still living in Jerusalem over a hundred years later. From the Ten Tribes of the Northern Kingdom in about 941 B.C., Asa, the king of the land, gathered at Jerusalem "all Judah and Benjamin, and the strangers with them out of Ephraim and Manasseh, and out of Simeon, for they fell to him out of Israel in abundance". (2 Chronicles 15:9). These strangers, who dwelt in the capital city of the Kingdom of Judah, may have included the forefathers of Lehi and Ishmael.

In spite of the fact that Amulek was well known among the people of Ammonihah, that he was powerful and wealthy, and that he was a Nephite by lineage, he had never "known much of the way of the Lord, and his mysteries and marvelous power". (V. 4-5). Even though he had been called many times, he had neglected to answer. Where there is no student, there is no revelation, and where there is no listening ear, there is no voice.

Amulek related to the people that only the appearance of an angel had the power to cause him to shelter Alma upon his return to the City of Ammonihah. (V. 7-9). Could the angel who appeared to Amulek be the same one who had appeared to Alma at about the same time, as he was journeying "toward the city which was called Aaron"? (Alma 8:13). We do not know.

What we do know, is that Amulek had an important mission to accomplish in Ammonihah, for he testified there as a second witness of the truths taught by Alma. "As the Lord liveth," he said, "the things whereof he hath testified are true". (V. 10). When Amulek uttered this solemn oath, "the people began to be astonished, seeing there was more than one witness". (V. 12).

Some among the people, principally the lawyers, recognized the difficulty created by the appearance of this second witness, and therefore sought to destroy Alma and Amulek by catching them in the crimes of blasphemy and false prophecy. (V. 13-16, see V. 24, & 28-29). Thomas Jefferson wrote of a similar scenario among the religious deconstructionists of his day, asserting that "they have so distorted and deformed the doctrines of Jesus, so muffled them in mysticisms, fancies and falsehoods, have caricatured them into forms so inconceivable, as to shock reasonable thinkers. Happy in the prospect of a restoration of primitive Christianity, I must leave to younger persons to encounter and lop off the false branches which have been engrafted into it by the mythologists of the middle and modern ages". ("Jefferson's Complete Works," 7:210 & 257).

Alma and Amulek had no choice but to confront such individuals as were described by Jefferson. Missionaries of all ages have been forced to recognize and deal with the craft, power, and profit of "lawyers", as well. Jefferson said: "Sweep away their gossamer fabric of factious religion, and they would catch no more flies". (Quoted by Milton Backman, "American Religions and The Rise of Mormonism," p. 202). Relying on the Divine model, the two missionaries sought to cleanse the inner vessel to effect lasting change. (See Alma 60:23).

In ancient Israel, both blasphemy and false prophecy were capital offenses under the Law of Moses. Any person found guilty of committing this crime, even in the heat of a brawl, was to be stoned to death. "Blasphemy embraced many forms of insolent or seditious speech, whether against God, against the king, against another man, or against holy places or things, including the law, and the test for whether a prophet had spoken truly or falsely was usually to see 'if the thing follow not, nor come to pass.' (Deuteronomy 18:22, see "Sherem's Accusation Against Jacob," FARMS Update 74, 1/1991).

The people of Ammonihah had thrown out the taunting challenge that they would not believe the words of Alma and Amulek even "if thou shouldst prophesy that this great city should be destroyed in one day". (Alma 9:4). It is ironic that the bodies of these very same people would shortly repose quietly in the streets of Ammonihah in silent witness of the fulfillment of this prophecy, and as a vindication of the words of those they had sought to condemn for the crime of false prophecy. (See Alma 25:2).

By the spirit of prophecy, Amulek perceived the thoughts of the lawyers, "and he said unto them: O ye wicked and perverse generation, ye lawyers and hypocrites, for ye are laying the foundations of the devil; for ye are laying traps and snares to catch the holy ones of God". (V. 17). He warned the people of Ammonihah: "Well did Mosiah say if the time should come that the voice of this people should choose iniquity, they would be ripe for destruction". (V. 19, see Mosiah 29:27). As we read these verses, we might well apply Amulek's caution to elements within our own society.

Then, as now: "If it were not for the prayers of the righteous, who are now in the land, ye would even now be visited with utter destruction. But it is by the prayers of the righteous that ye are spared". (V. 22-23). When the wicked slay the righteous, they unwittingly sever the last thread holding Satan in check, thus hastening their own destruction. (See Alma 14:8). Spencer W. Kimball confirmed that, in the Last Days: "There are many upright and faithful who live all the commandments and whose lives and prayers keep the world from destruction".

President Harold B. Lee once related the following story. "President Clark said something that startled folks years back. He said: 'It is my faith that the Gospel Plan has always been here, that His priesthood has always been here, and that it will continue to be so until the end comes.' When that conference session was over there were many who said: 'My goodness, doesn't President Clark realize that there have been periods of apostasy following each dispensation of the Gospel?' I walked over to the Church Office Building with Joseph Fielding Smith, and he said, 'I believe there has never been a moment of time since the creation but what there has been someone holding the priesthood on the earth to hold Satan in check.'. And then I thought of Enoch's city with perhaps thousands who were taken into heaven and were translated. You remember. They must have been translated for a purpose, and may have had sojourn with those living on the earth ever since that time. I have thought of Elijah, perhaps Moses, for all we know - they were translated beings; also John the Revelator. I have thought of the Three Nephites. Why were they translated, and for what purpose were they permitted to tarry?. An answer was suggested when I heard this man whom we have considered one of our well-informed theologians say: 'There has never been a moment of time when there hasn't been someone holding the priesthood on the earth with power to check Satan and to hold him within bounds.' Now that doesn't mean that the Kingdom of God was present, because these men did not have the authority to administer the saving ordinances of the Gospel to the world. But these individuals were translated for a purpose known only to the Lord. There is no question, but what they were here". ("The Place of The Living Prophet. Seer, and Revelator," B.Y.U. Address to Institute Directors, 7/8/1964).

The terrible warning still applies today: "If ye will cast out the righteous from among you then will not the Lord stay his hand, but in his fierce anger he will come out against you; then ye shall be smitten by famine, and by pestilence, and by the sword". (V. 23). Satan rules with blood and horror on the earth, and the persecution of the Saints satisfies his twisted desire in two ways, in that both the righteous and the wicked are destroyed, the former by the latter, and the latter by God.

In the City of Ammonihah, Amulek taught a sober lesson for both his day and ours, when he said: "The foundation of the destruction of this people is beginning to be laid by the unrighteousness of your lawyers and your judges". (V. 27, see Alma 46:4). One of the potential problems of those trained in the law was well articulated by Theodore Roosevelt a hundred years ago when he said: "To educate a man in mind and not in morals is to educate a menace to society". These denunciations are only directed against those public servants who would willfully violate their stewardship and the public trust. There are many honest men and women who practice law; nevertheless, the profession seems particularly prone to abuse, perhaps because it is largely self-governing. Even Dallin Oaks, a lawyer himself, could not resist quoting Robert Frost in an address before the B.Y.U. School of Law. "Why is there always a secret singing when a lawyer cashes in? Why does a hearse horse snicker hauling a lawyer away?" (B.Y.U. Studies, 16:4, p. 508).

The stage was set for a confrontation with Zeezrom, who was one of the craftiest of those lawyers who had brought accusations against the missionaries. (V. 31-32). In chapter 11, we shall also see that Mormon's purpose for a lengthy explanation of Nephite coinage was to illustrate Zeezrom's wealth and the significance of the bribe that he offered to Amulek. (See Alma 11:22).

Alma
Chapter 11

Egyptian culture had a significant influence on the Nephites. A great interest in numbers and an expertise in using them were typical of the Egyptian preoccupation with mathematics, and Mormon's abridgement suggests that the Nephites were similarly interested in numerical values, inasmuch as their monetary system employed a simple and ingenious 1 - 2 - 4 - 7 hierarchy of values. In contrast, those in use today in the Western world are essentially 1 - 5 - 10 systems.

This chapter opens with a 19-verse parenthetical aside that describes the remarkable mathematical sophistication of the Nephite monetary system. Mormon included this revealing description so that the text that follows would be more meaningful to the reader. In Chapter 10, we learned that the stage was set for a confrontation with Zeezrom, who was one of the craftiest of those lawyers who had brought accusations against the missionaries. (V. 31-32). Mormon's lengthy explanation of Nephite coinage illustrated Zeezrom's wealth and the significance of the substantial bribe that he offered to Amulek. For continuity of the narrative from chapter 10, however, one must skip to verse 20.

Note that in verse 7, "barley" is mentioned. "Science" magazine, in its December 1983 issue, reported the first discovery of evidence of pre-Colombian domesticated barley in the New World. Before that time, it was thought by experts that barley did not exist among the Maya. Once again, The Book of Mormon got a jump on the scholars, inasmuch as its reference to barley predated that media announcement by some 2,000 years!

When Mormon described the relative values of grain, gold, and silver in the Nephite monetary system in verses 3-19, there was a subtle consistency of word usage, so that when comparing weight, the terminology "as great as" was used. When comparing value, however, the terminology "is equal to" was used.

"Zeezrom began to question Amulek, saying: Will ye answer me a few questions which I shall ask you? Now Zeezrom was a man who was expert in the devices of the devil, that he might destroy that which was good". (V. 21). "There is," wrote Neal A. Maxwell, "a nomadic reflection of plastic freedom as seen in the drifts of our modern sophists - the intellectual guerillas who have no homeland. The sophist, who is often a carrier of cleverness, is really a forlorn man without a country who draws his delight and satisfaction from the process of verbal combat and encounter itself; he does not seek resolution, but disruption. He seeks always to fight his battles on the home front of the believer. The sophist has nothing to defend. He takes no real risks because he believes in nothing. Perhaps, in a strange and twisted way, he wants to create the condition of drift that he experiences, by using the sword of speciousness to cut men and women away from the eternal things that anchor them". ("Freedom, A Hard Doctrine").

Amulek's response to Zeezrom was safe ground for missionaries under any circumstances. "Amulek said unto him … I shall say nothing which is contrary to the Spirit of the Lord". (V. 22). This standard would seem to be particularly important when dealing with an antagonistic member of the legal profession.

Zeezrom not only ignored Amulek's statement of faith, but he even offered a bribe in the amount of six onties of silver, that, as Mormon had demonstrated, was the highest unit of currency in the Nephite monetary system. To become a wealthy man, Amulek only had to deny "the existence of a Supreme Being". (V. 22).

True to his promise, however, Amulek spoke according to the Spirit of the Lord when he declared: "The righteous yieldeth to no such temptations". (V. 23). Capitulating to the devil's will would have left a soul scar that only the plastic surgery of repentance could have removed, and Amulek would have no part of it. He had no desire to pay the exorbitant premium on that kind of health insurance coverage.

Instead, he informed Zeezrom that for the great evil he had conceived, he would receive his own just reward. Zeezrom thought of himself as Mahan, "a great destroyer" (See Moses 5:31), when actually he was following the dangerous path leading to Perdition or "utter ruin". The adversary finally betrays his followers, for he cannot deliver on the promises he has made to them. "The devil will not support his children at the last day, but (instead) doth speedily drag them down to hell". (Alma 30:60).

In the discussion that followed, Zeezrom never really denied the existence of God. We are left to wonder whether the wicked can ever really do that, for there are so many evidences of His existence. To have valid grounds upon which we could base a denial of the reality of God might actually compromise the great Plan of Salvation. (See Alma 12:1, 7, & 8).

Initially, it was verbal combat that pushed Zeezrom's hot button. He tingled with excitement in anticipation of the theological titillation that comes from intellectually sparring with a man of God. As Richard L. Evans once observed: "Those who break windows to let in fresh air do not love fresh air as much as the sound of tinkling glass". But this encounter was destined to be much more than just a stimulating conversation or a legal joust. The rush felt by this eager young lawyer would instead convict him of his sins and compel him to change the course of his life.

In verses 34-37, Amulek taught important Gospel principles, namely that we cannot be saved in our sins, and that the redemption of Christ is conditional. Only those who "believe on his name" overcome spiritual death, while "the wicked remain as though there had been no redemption made". (V. 40-41, see Mosiah 5:8 & Alma 34:35). These will inherit immortality but not eternal life, and they will enjoy redemption from physical death but not spiritual death. This is because their resurrection does not reflect the triumph and glory of Christ, since they fall short of the entrance requirements to the Celestial Kingdom. (See Moses 1:39). They cannot claim the Merits of Christ because they lack saving faith in the grace of God.

Verses 42-44 affirm the great truth, largely disputed in our day, that all mankind shall receive a physical resurrection from the dead. "The spirit and body shall be reunited again in its perfect form; both limb and joint shall be restored to its proper frame, even as we now are at this time". (V. 42, & 44, see Alma 41:23). Joseph Fielding Smith, Jr., taught: "All deformities and imperfections will be removed, and the body will conform to the likeness of the Spirit". ("Doctrines of Salvation," 2:289, see D&C 77:2). In other words, in the resurrection our appearance will be an accurate reflection of our true spiritual stature. Ideally, it will be in both the image and the likeness of God. Moreover, "in the restoration of all things, there shall come perfection. Physical defects are due to the mortal condition and are not an inheritance from the (pre-earth life)". (Joseph Fielding Smith, Jr., "Answers to Gospel Questions," 4:185-189).

Another Gospel principle was taught when Amulek declared: "We shall be brought to stand before God, knowing even as we know now, and have a bright recollection of all our guilt". (V. 43). Nothing shall be withheld from our remembrance. "My father focuses heart-gripping flashes across the wall screen. Family slides. I am small, my brother is smaller, my sister is smallest. Days now dead re-open like old storybooks from memory's heaped box. Pulling out pictures of cooking in Grandfather's Dutch oven; playing cheetah in our backyard monkey-jungle; being beautifully Easter-bested with my coat buttoned wrong; hugging a mommy minus grey hair. Soberly, I think of another Father, Who someday shall open my mind, and flash reeling remembering of every day's minute across my soul, across the heavens, and kindly ask me to narrate." (Lora Lyn Stucker, "New Era," 8/1973).

Finally, Amulek taught that after the resurrection, our bodies will be quickened by the Spirit and become immortal, that they "can no more see corruption". (V. 45). His testimony began to have a powerful effect on Zeezrom, for when he "had finished these words the people began again to be astonished, and also Zeezrom began to tremble". (V. 46). He was as Belshazzar, "whose thoughts troubled him so that the joints of his loins were loosed, and his knees smote one against another". (Daniel 5:6).

When Joseph Smith wrote: "The Son of Man hath descended below them all," he meant that His arm of mercy is extended even to the Zeezroms of this world. (See D&C 122:8). "I bear testimony that you cannot sink farther than the light and sweeping intelligence of Jesus Christ can reach," wrote Truman Madsen. "I bear testimony that as long as there is one spark of the will to repent, He is there. He did not just descend to your condition; He descended below it, 'that He might be in all and through all things, the light of truth'". ("The Commanding Image of Christ").

Alma
Chapter 12

Now Alma began to "establish the words of Amulek". It makes sense for missionaries to travel in pairs so that one can reinforce the principles taught by the other. It was Alma's special gift to unfold "the scriptures beyond that which Amulek had done". (V. 1, see D&C 20:59).

Zeezrom's scheme to lie and to deceive the people was, in the words of Alma: "A plan of thine adversary". (V. 5). He declared: "This was a snare which he hath laid to catch this people, that he might bring you into subjection unto him, that he might encircle you about with his chains, that he might chain you down to everlasting destruction". (V. 6, see Alma 30:60).

The only individuals over whom Satan has any power are the wicked, who can be just as cruel, insensitive, self-serving, and full of hatred as he is. He uses them as tools to lash out at anything that is good. They are as pawns in his hand, but he esteems them as nothing. His hatred is all-consuming, typified by complete and utter darkness. Ultimately, he has no use even for the wicked because they nag him with a reminder of his heavenly home, his rebellion, and lost associations. There is something, perhaps a spark of divinity, that lingers even in the nature of the wicked, with which the devil is extremely uncomfortable.

The righteous, however, avoid his influence. They are only his adversaries in the sense that they "yieldeth to no such temptations". (Alma 11:23, see Alma 16:18 & 21). Intentionally picking a fight with the devil is foolish because it requires that the righteous move off the secure foundation of Gospel principles onto unstable worldly turf. This, Alma and Amulek steadfastly refused to do.

Now, Zeezrom began to comprehend the counterfeit and deceitful nature of the power by which he was operating, and so he sought to discover for himself and understand the source of legitimate power. (V. 7, see Alma 8:31, 9:28 & Helaman 10:7). "And Zeezrom began to inquire of them diligently, that he might know more concerning the kingdom of God". (V. 8). Diligence implies a sense of duty and responsibility. It suggests purpose and perseverance, until the desired goal is achieved. Because of his diligence, Zeezrom himself would soon be teaching the People of Ammonihah the principles of the Gospel. (See Alma 15:12).

Alma began to expound the mysteries of God to Zeezrom. (V. 9-18, see Commentary Reference to Mosiah 2:9, J.S.H. 1:74, & D&C 42:61). To understand spiritual things, we must have discernment, or guidance from the Holy Ghost. The Spirit teaches those who are sincerely investigating the Church, and when they are confirmed as members, they receive by ordinance the special gift of the Holy Ghost. One of His objectives is to guide us from the covenant waters of baptism along the strait and narrow path leading to the ordinances of the Melchizedek Priesthood that are necessary for us to obtain eternal life. This is one reason why we may be initially given the Holy Ghost in a priesthood ordinance beside the waters of baptism.

"He that will not harden his heart, to him is given the greater portion of the word, until it is given unto him to know the mysteries of God until he know them in full". (V. 10, see Mosiah 2:9, D&C 88:67). Alma's sermon in chapters 12 and 13 teaches the principle that all men and women may have access to the mysteries of God, which are the saving principles of the Gospel of Jesus Christ. (See Alma 29:8, & 3 Nephi 26:9-10). When individuals harden their hearts to the truth, however, "to them is given the lesser portion of the word until they know nothing concerning his mysteries, and then they are taken captive by the devil, and led by his will down to destruction. Now this is what is meant by the chains of hell". (V. 11).

The terrible thing about hardening our hearts is that understanding of "the word" is withheld, leaving us vulnerable to the devil's influence. The scriptures identify the consequences of sin in very plain language. Its effect on those of us who have been taught the principles of the Gospel in plainness is that spiritual guidance is withdrawn, and we are left alone to grope in darkness. Guilt causes us to shrink from Church activity, and in the absence of the Spirit, we have no claim on blessings, prosperity, or preservation. Tragically, feeling uncomfortable in proximity to spiritual experiences, we withdraw to lifestyles devoid of such associations. Thus begins a downward spiral that gains momentum as sinful practices, more easily committed, become entrenched.

Even worse, those "that doeth this, the same cometh out in open rebellion against God". (Mosiah 2:37). "Thus saith the Lord concerning all those who know my power, and have been made partakers thereof, and suffered themselves through the power of the devil to be overcome, and to deny the truth and defy my power. They are they who are the sons of perdition". (D&C 76:31-32). Nephi put it well, when he observed that Satan "leadeth them by the neck with a flaxen cord until he bindeth them with his strong cords forever". (2 Nephi 26:22). After all is said and done, it is the wicked, and not the righteous, who are so horribly treated by the devil. The righteous remain largely immune to his influence.

"Except a man be born again, he cannot see the kingdom of God". (John 3:3). We can take this scripture literally as well as figuratively. "We receive assurance and knowledge due to our faithfulness and adherence to the commandments of Jesus Christ. Those who reject their Redeemer and refuse to keep the commandments cannot know and comprehend these eternal truths". (Joseph F. Smith, "Man: His Origin and Destiny," p. 358-360, see 1 Corinthians 2:14). They things are only seen with the eye of faith and with interpretation by the Spirit.

Alma stressed that we must not harden our hearts against the word, "insomuch that it has not been found in us". (V. 12). Rather, we must take upon ourselves the name of Christ, keep His commandments, and always remember Him. We ought to be even as He is. Our charge is to "come unto Christ". (Moroni 10:32).

At the Judgment Bar, "our words will condemn us, yea, all our works will condemn us, and our thoughts will also condemn us". (V. 14). "In the armory of thought, we forge the weapons by which we destroy ourselves. We also fashion the tools with which we build for ourselves heavenly mansions of joy, strength, and peace. Between these two extremes are all grades of character, and we are their maker. We are the masters of thought, the shapers of condition, environment, and of destiny". (James Allen, "As a Man Thinketh").

King Benjamin had told the people of Zarahemla that there are many ways to commit sin. (Mosiah 4:29). There is a rule, however, that is the foundation for purposeful living, and the order of counsel is significant. When we have been taught the truth, and with a firm knowledge of that which is good, we must take care to watch our thoughts, words, and deeds. (Mosiah 4:30). When people are taught correct principles, they are left to govern their own behavior according to the light and knowledge they have received. (See D&C 58:26). Usually, the Lord gives us the overall objectives to be accomplished and some guidelines to follow, but He expects us to work out most of the details and methods ourselves. These are developed through study, prayer, and the promptings of the Spirit.

If we stand condemned, "we would fain be glad if we could command the rocks and the mountains to fall upon us to hide us from his presence". (V. 14). "In the Last Days, an angel will sound his trump, and reveal the secret acts of men, and the thoughts and intents of their hearts". (D&C 88:109). The Last Judgment will have begun. Although we may stand unrepentant at the Bar, in the presence of God "in his glory, and in his power, and in his might, majesty, and dominion," we will still have to acknowledge His justice and mercy. (V. 15, see Commentary Reference to Alma 5:50).

If Justice is required because we cannot claim Mercy based on our repentance and reliance upon the Atonement of the Redeemer, "then cometh a death, which is spiritual death; then is a time that whosoever dieth in his sins, as to a temporal death, shall also die a spiritual death; yea, he shall die as to things pertaining unto righteousness". (V. 16).

The second or spiritual death is banishment from the presence of God and from the influence of righteousness. The Sons of Perdition are "the only ones on whom the second death shall have any power". (D&C 76:37). All others who are not heirs of the I of God shall be redeemed from spiritual death or hell, but only after they have atoned for their own sins by personally paying the penalty that is the natural and inevitable consequence of their disobedience to immutable law.

Then, they shall inherit glory in the Telestial or Terrestrial Kingdom, but before they do, "their torments shall be as a lake of fire and brimstone". (V. 17). While in the Spirit Prison of The Unjust, "they shall be chained down to an everlasting destruction, according to the power and captivity of Satan, he having subjected them according to his will". (V. 17. see D&C 76:73, 138:8, 28, Isaiah 61:1, 1 Peter, 3:19, & Moses 7:57).

There is a great gulf, or divide, in the world of spirits. The righteous will await the resurrection in Paradise, while the unrighteous and unrepentant will be turned over to the buffetings of Satan until the uttermost farthing has been personally paid. We can either claim mercy because of the Atoning Sacrifice of Christ, or we can pay for our own sins, according to the demands of Justice. If we choose the latter course, it "shall be as though there had been no redemption made". (V. 18, see Alma 11:41).

During the probation of mortality, while the test is being administered, repentance following the violation of the commandments is still possible. Mid-course correction for error, improvement in the quality and direction of our lives, and realignment toward eternal realities, describe our conscious efforts as we continue the challenging journey called eternal progression. Frequent debriefings after particularly stressful episodes on the carousel of life help us to re-establish our concentration and to maintain our focus on the brass ring.

As Alma continued to expound upon the teaching of Amulek, "the people began to be more astonished". (V. 19). Zeezrom's own reaction to this doctrine was vividly described by Mormon, who recorded that "his soul began to be harrowed up under a consciousness of his own guilt; yea, he began to be encircled about by the pains of hell". (Alma 14:6-7)

With the defection of Zeezrom to the Lord's side, Antionah, a chief ruler, took over. He was a child of the devil who used a misinterpretation of the scriptures to attack the missionaries. This predictable battle plan of Satan is one that is frequently employed by his disciples. The encounter with Antionah illustrates that even the wicked are familiar with the scriptures, but their understanding is amiss, and they wrest the scriptures in a twisted and perverted way. (See V. 10-11).

Stephen Robinson has very forthrightly addressed this phenomenon. He wrote: "Time and again the Latter-day Saints are denied the privilege of defining and interpreting their own doctrines. Quite frequently, a Latter-day Saint attempting to explain the tenets of his or her faith to non-Mormons will be interrupted by some self-styled expert who says: 'No, that's not what you believe; this is what you believe.' There generally follows a recital of some hocus-pocus that is certainly not taught by the LDS Church. The resulting fictions generally fall into one of three categories: outright fabrications, distortions of genuine LDS doctrines into unrecognizable forms, or the representation of anomalies within the LDS tradition as mainline or official LDS teachings". ("Are Mormons Christians," in the chapter entitled "The Exclusion by Misrepresentation". p. 9-10).

The question posed by Antionah was: "What does the scripture mean, which saith that God placed cherubim and a flaming sword on the east of the Garden of Eden, lest our first parents should enter and partake of the fruit of the tree of life, and live forever?" (V. 21, & Genesis 3:24). In the balance of Chapter 12, Alma answered Antionah, and then, in Alma chapter 42, he taught his son about these same principles because Corianton had been similarly excusing his own behavior, claiming that it was unjust to punish sinners. Alma addressed the concerns of both Antionah and Corianton, basing his remarks on the reality that Justice is the unalterable decree of God Who declares that both righteousness and sin dictate their own consequences.

Fortunately, Alma was more familiar with the scriptures and with the doctrine of the Kingdom than were either Antionah or Corianton. He was able to explain to both that there is another dimension to Genesis 3:24 that takes into consideration the pitfall that would have been created had Adam and Eve been permitted to stretch forth their hands and partake of the fruit of the tree of life. In Ammonihah, Antionah's shallow Gospel scholarship led him to the conclusion that the only way to live forever was to "partake of the fruit of the tree of life". (V. 21). Antionah reasoned that mankind had a justification for sinning because God had placed cherubim and a flaming sword on the east of the Garden of Eden to guard the way to the tree. He mistakenly thought that the key to eternal life was simply partaking of the fruit. It was his belief that with cherubim and a flaming sword blocking the way to immortality, there could be "no possible chance that they should live forever". (V. 21).

Antionah was too literal in his private interpretation of scripture. He did not take into consideration the ramifications of what would happen within the context of the Plan of Salvation should Adam in his fallen state have stretched forth his hand and partaken of the fruit of the tree of life. He did not consider that for having done so, Adam would have been forever alienated from God's presence. Thus, Antionah's question provided Alma with a perfect teaching moment to explain to the wicked people of Ammonihah that, rather than justifying wicked behavior, the referenced scripture should instead have provided for them a strong incentive to propel them to seek and embrace another way whereby they might live forever, not in sin, but in purity and glory. Antionah's ignorance gave Alma the opportunity to teach the people of Ammonihah about agency, justice, atonement, mercy, repentance, forgiveness, and redemption. It allowed Alma to reveal to Antionah and his brethren how to proactively deal with the unalterable decrees of God relating to the wicked.

Alma correctly taught that, subtle though the symbolism might be, working out our salvation has less to do with cherubim and more to do with redemption. In the absence of repentance for our sins and without the benefit of the Gospel Plan, we would ultimately be miserable, living forever in our sins. He told Antionah: "And now behold, if it were possible that our first parents could have gone forth and partaken of the tree of life they would have been forever miserable, having no preparatory state; and thus, the Plan of Redemption would have been frustrated, and the word of God would have been void, taking none effect". (V. 26).

Without the option of redemption from sin, if Adam and Eve were to have partaken of the fruit of the tree of life, that is eternal life or the highest expression of the love of God, it would not have been possible for them to sustain a celestial existence. If they had forever remained in their filthy condition, stained by sin, they would have been incapable of maintaining strict obedience to celestial principles. Thus, the Plan of Salvation would have been frustrated and God's very mission statement, to bring about not only our immortality, but also our eternal life, would have been nullified.

The scenario Alma outlined to the people of Ammonihah, and later to his own son Corianton, demonstrated that this was not to be the case. The transgression of Adam and Eve resulted in alienation from His presence, that is spiritual death, and their expulsion from the Garden resulted in mortality, making their eventual temporal death inevitable. But Adam and Eve and their posterity were not created to live forever in the morally static vacuum of the Garden. Mortality is really our only opportunity to become acquainted with evil as well as with good, with darkness as well as with light, with error as well as with truth, and with punishment for the infraction of eternal laws as well as with the blessings that follow obedience. Ralph Waldo Emerson once asked: "What is the use of immortality to one who cannot wisely use half an hour?" This is why Alma and so many other parents have invested so much time and energy teaching their children correct principles and training them in their proper execution.

Alma told Antionah: "This is the thing which I was about to explain". (V. 22). Alma then taught that we came into this world to die. This creates a host of potential problems, but the Plan confronts each one with elegant solutions. For "we see that Adam did fall by the partaking of the forbidden fruit, according to the word of God; and thus, we see that by his fall, all mankind became a lost and fallen people. And now behold, I say unto you that if it had been possible for Adam to have partaken of the fruit of the tree of life at that time, there would have been no death, and the word would have been void, making God a liar, for he said: If thou eat thou shalt surely die". (V. 23).

This would have voided the Plan of Salvation. Although death is our only exit from mortality, it is an integral part of the Merciful Plan of our Father that caused us to shout for joy when it was explained to us. When Adam was placed in the Garden of Eden, it was with the understanding that he would transgress a law in order to trigger the mortal condition. When he was later expelled from the Garden in consequence of his transgression, the cherubim and a flaming sword insured that he would be able to fulfil the mission he had accepted at the Council in Heaven before the world was.

Alma taught Antionah that the Fall was a key component of the Plan, inasmuch as it gave Adam and Eve and their posterity the opportunity to sojourn on the earth to prepare for a resurrection. "And we see that death comes upon mankind, yea, the death which has been spoken of by Amulek, which is the temporal death; nevertheless, there was a space granted unto man in which he might repent; therefore this life became a probationary state; a time to prepare to meet God; a time to prepare for that endless state which has been spoken of by us, which is after the resurrection of the dead". (V. 24).

The death of our physical bodies is a wonderful element of the Gospel Plan. In fact, "it was appointed unto men that they must die; and after death, they must come to judgment, even that same judgment of which we have spoken, which is the end". (V. 27). In The Book of Mormon, with broad strokes the prophets paint a wonderfully vibrant portrait of the Plan, and after carefully studying their teachings, the ultimate purpose of the Fall snaps into sharp focus. We can almost hear Father in Heaven explaining how Adam and Eve would transgress His law in order to become mortal so they and all of their posterity could die. We can clearly see how the Fall allows us to prepare for our glorious resurrection. The Spirit teaches us that through the Atonement, we may receive the kinds of immortal bodies that we will need in order to dwell in celestial fire. The beauty of it is that our judgment will not come until we have had the opportunity to conform our lives with exactness to the principles of the Plan of Redemption.

"And after God had appointed that these things should come unto man, behold, then he saw that it was expedient that man should know concerning the things whereof he had appointed unto them; Therefore, he sent angels to converse with them, who caused men to behold of his glory. And they began from that time forth to call on his name; therefore, God conversed with men, and made known unto them the Plan of redemption, which had been prepared from the foundation of the world; and this he made known unto them according to their faith and repentance and their holy works". (V. 28-30). Alma hoped that as he taught the people of Ammonihah these truths, they would receive this same spiritual confirmation.

Men and women were to be instructed sufficiently and then to have the opportunity to act for themselves. Satan's way is coercive, but the "perfect law of liberty" presupposes the exercise of free will. However, unless behavior is in harmony with the laws of the Gospel, unbridled freedom will lead to tyranny. We are free to choose, but we cannot choose to escape the consequences of our poor choices. If we violate the commandments, we must repent, for we have the power within ourselves to be "as Gods, knowing good from evil," and we are "in a state to act according to (our will) and pleasures, whether to do evil or to do good". (V. 31).

Adam and Eve were unequivocally taught about the penalty that would follow the violation of the commandments. "God gave unto them commandments, after having made known unto them the Plan of redemption, that they should not do evil, the penalty thereof being a second death, which was an everlasting death as to things pertaining unto righteousness; for on such the Plan of redemption could have no power, for the works of justice could not be destroyed, according to the supreme goodness of God". (V. 32). Because God respected agency, He could not nullify the demands of Justice as they bore down on Adam and Eve and their posterity. Nor would He desire to do so, because there was an elegant solution to Adam's quandary that had been built into the Plan itself.

God provided another way for man to partake of the fruit of the tree of life. He "did call on men, in the name of his Son, (this being the Plan of redemption which was laid) saying: If ye will repent, and harden not your hearts, then will I have mercy on you, through mine Only Begotten Son. Therefore, whosoever repenteth, and hardeneth not his heart, he shall have claim on mercy through mine Only Begotten Son, unto a remission of his sins; and these shall enter into my rest". (V. 33-34). Whoever would have faith in Christ and repent would gain a remission of their sins, because of their claim on Mercy through His Atonement. Those who refused to repent because of the hardness of their hearts would not be able to enter into the Rest of God or the Fulness of His Glory, for obvious reasons.

"And now, my brethren," Alma urged the people of Ammonihah, "behold I say unto you, that if ye will harden your hearts ye shall not enter into the rest of the Lord; therefore your iniquity provoketh him that he sendeth down his wrath upon you as in the first provocation, (when men suffer physical death) yea, according to his word in the last provocation as well as the first, (when, without repentance, men will die spiritually) to the everlasting destruction of your souls; therefore, according to his word, unto the last death, as well as the first". (V. 36). Alma was extending an olive branch to the wicked people of Ammonihah. It was their last and only opportunity to avoid complete physical and spiritual destruction.

Spencer W. Kimball taught that circumstance does not make the man. It reveals him to himself, because as the lord and master of his thoughts, man is the maker of himself, the shaper and author of his environment. Men imagine that thought can be kept secret, but it cannot. It rapidly crystallizes into habit and solidifies into circumstance.

Even in Ammonihah, where the missionaries were ill-treated, Alma understood that his call to repentance was like trying to straighten a bent nail. A pat on the back is better than a bop on the head. Therefore, he closed this portion of his response to Antionah and those who stood with him with the following tender remarks: "And now, brethren, seeing we know these things, and they are true, let us repent, and harden not our hearts but let us enter into the rest of God". (V. 37). He sincerely hoped that a soft answer would turn away wrath. (See Proverbs 15:1). Alma knew what the inevitable consequences of the rejection of his message by the people of Ammonihah would be, and he desperately wanted them to avoid that fate. Therefore, he persevered, giving them additional instruction that illuminated and clarified doctrine relating to the Holy Order after The Son of God as does no other scripture in the Standard Works.

Alma
Chapter 13

These verses are among the most comprehensive of the scriptural interpretations that deal with Melchizedek, King of Salem. In his description of the Melchizedek Priesthood, Alma used seven variations: "His holy order" (Alma 13:1), "The order of his Son" (Alma 13:2), "The high priesthood of the holy order of God" (Alma 13:5, & 18), "The high priesthood of the holy order" (Alma 13:8), "his order" (Alma 13:16), "The holy order of God" (Alma 7:22, 8:4), and "The order of God" (Alma 6:1).

The full name of the priesthood, "The Holy Priesthood after the Order of The Son of God," is mentioned only once in the scriptures, by Jesus Christ Himself, in Doctrine & Covenants Section 107:3. The term "priesthood" itself is used only eight times in the text of The Book of Mormon: once in Alma 4:20, and seven times in Alma Chapter 13. (V. 6. 7, 8 (twice), 10, 14, & 18).

In the first 6 verses of this chapter, Alma explained the procedure whereby men are ordained to the priesthood. When Alma said: "I would cite your minds forward to the time when the Lord God gave these commandments," he was saying: Remember, in the beginning, when "the Lord God ordained priests, after this holy order". (V. 1).

Verses 2 and 14 make clear that the order of the priesthood is not of Melchizedek, but of God. Entrance into the order is by ordination. Righteousness, and not lineage, is important to the Lord. As a matter of fact, neither the King of Salem nor his subjects were of the lineage of Abraham, or of the House of Israel, but they had nevertheless entered into the Covenant that God first made with Adam.

Verse 3 is probably the clearest affirmation in The Book of Mormon that we lived before our birth. It states that those who in mortality receive the Melchizedek Priesthood were foreordained from the foundation of the world, based on their direct experience with God. In that pre-mortal life, they chose the better part, and in mortality they "are called with a holy calling". For Alma,

Melchizedek epitomized the practical realization that, from the foundation of the world, each of us has potential that is activated when we recognize and respond to the voice of the Lord.

"And thus, they have been called to this holy calling on account of their faith," with history as well as prophecy as their foundation, perhaps in the way that one is called to a position within the Church today. (V. 4, see Mosiah 5:13). "I like to think," said J. Reuben Clark, Jr., "that perhaps in that grand council, something was said to us indicating what would be expected of us of lesser calling and lesser stature, and empowering us, subject to reconfirmation here, to do certain things in building up the Kingdom of God on earth". (C.R. 10/1950, see Commentary Reference to Alma 13:4). In fact, verse 5 teaches that righteousness and obedience gave all of Heavenly Father's spirit children an equal opportunity to progress in their pre-earth life, and that faithful men who held priesthood power and authority in that first estate, again hold it in mortality. Abraham was told: "And they who keep their first estate shall be added upon; and they who keep not their first estate shall not have glory in the same kingdom with those who keep their first estate; and they who keep their second estate shall have glory added upon their heads for ever and ever". (Abraham 3:26). Paul taught that "before the world began," God promised his spirit children that they would be provided the opportunity to have eternal life. (Titus 1:2).

"And thus, being called by this holy calling, and ordained unto the high priesthood of the holy order of God," perhaps being called by a new name in Christ, men were empowered "to teach his commandments unto the children of men, that they also might enter into his rest". (V. 6, see Mosiah 5:10-12, Alma 16:19, 60:13, & D&C 84:24). Through Gospel teaching directed by those who hold the priesthood, the Church fulfills a vital function as it leads men and women to make decisions that set them squarely on the path of eternal progress. As they continue to make correct choices, they will ultimately qualify for eternal life and God's Rest.

The order of the Son transcends time and is from before the foundation of the world; it is "from eternity to all eternity". (V. 7). Paul described the Melchizedek Priesthood as being "without father, without mother, without descent, having neither beginning of days, nor end of life; but made like unto the Son of God". (Hebrews 7:3). Only God and His priesthood order are worthy to be called eternal, "without beginning of days and end of years". (V. 9). Melchizedek, on the other hand, was a mortal man who "reigned under his father". (V. 18). Alma made a careful distinction between the Order of the Priesthood and Melchizedek. He honored the former, while acknowledging the righteousness of the latter.

Alma taught that those who anciently held the priesthood were called as a result of divine revelation given to their file leaders, and were ordained according to a holy ordinance, thereby taking upon themselves "the high priesthood of the holy order". (V. 8). Thus, they became high priests forever. (V. 9). The term "high" may have been used by Alma to indicate the divine derivation of the priesthood, or as a term of qualitative exaltation, rather than to denote superiority or dominance over either ecclesiastical affairs or over other priesthoods.

Most sources dwell on "from whom" Melchizedek received his knowledge of the priesthood, but Alma tells us "how" he received it. It was "on account of (his) exceeding faith and repentance, and (his) righteousness before God". (V. 10). "Therefore, (he was) called". (V. 11).

Our Heavenly Father wants all His children to enjoy the blessings of the priesthood. The third member of the Godhead, the Holy Ghost, sanctifies those who qualify by "their exceeding faith and repentance, and their righteousness before God," to hold priesthood offices. They become white, pure, and spotless before God, and cannot "look upon sin save it were with abhorrence". (V. 12, see Mosiah 5:12, Alma 19:33-36, & D&C 88:68).

With an eye single to the glory of God, the righteous enter "into the rest of the Lord their God". (V. 12). Blessed, indeed, are the pure in heart, for they shall see God. (See Matthew 5:8). In so many words, Alma taught that the blessing of priesthood greatly enhances the experience of all who seek the fulness of God's glory. Priesthood amplifies the quiet spiritual stirrings that underlie all mortal experience.

Alma pointed out that during the ministry of Melchizedek, "there were many, exceedingly great many, who were made pure and entered into the rest of the Lord". (V. 12). Other sources confirm: "Men having this faith, coming up into this order of God, were translated and taken up into heaven. And now, Melchizedek was a priest of this order; therefore, he obtained peace in Salem, and was called the Prince of Peace. And his people wrought righteousness, and obtained heaven". (J.S.T. Genesis 14:32-34). Through the righteous exercise of priesthood power, Melchizedek had become a savior on Mt. Zion to his people. (See D&C 103:9 & Obadiah 1:31). A similar accomplishment may be repeated by any people willing to pay the price.

There are no social, cultural, racial, economic, or genealogical prerequisites limiting entrance to the brotherhood of the priesthood, or defining who may enjoy its blessings. Bringing "forth fruit meet for repentance" is the only condition for receiving priesthood ordinances. (V. 13). Alma turned to Melchizedek in order to illustrate the doctrine that all men may obtain knowledge of the mysteries of God through humility and the ordinances of the priesthood.

The Book of Genesis refers to Melchizedek as a "priest of the Most High God," but Alma calls him a "high priest after the order of the Son". (V. 14, see J.S.T. Genesis 14:26-40, & Hebrews 7:3). It is the symbolic ordinances with which Melchizedek was associated that was important to Alma. Melchizedek was a man of peace because he had obtained the spiritual powers and knowledge necessary to lead his people into the Rest of the Lord, through the order of the Son. (V. 16).

The Joseph Smith Translation of Genesis 14:25-36 records: "Melchizedek was a man of faith, who wrought righteousness; and when a child he feared God, and stopped the mouths of lions, and quenched the violence of fire. And thus, having been approved of God, he was ordained an high priest after the order of the covenant which God made with Enoch, it being after the order of the Son of God; which order came, not by man, nor the will of man; neither by father nor mother; neither by beginning of days nor end of years; but of God.

And it was delivered unto men by the calling of his own voice, according to his own will, unto as many as believed on his name. For God having sworn unto Enoch and unto his seed with an oath by himself; that every one being ordained after this order and calling should have power, by faith, to break mountains, to divide the seas, to dry up waters, to turn them out of their course; To put at defiance the armies of nations, to divide the earth, to break every band, to stand in the presence of God; to do all things according to his will, according to his command, subdue principalities and powers; and this by the will of the Son of God which was from before the foundation of the world.

And men having this faith, coming up unto this order of God, were translated and taken up into heaven. And now, Melchizedek was a priest of this order; therefore, he obtained peace in Salem, and was called the Prince of Peace. And his people wrought righteousness, and obtained heaven, and sought for the City of Enoch which God had before taken, separating it from the earth, having reserved it unto the latter days, or the end of the world.

And this Melchizedek, having thus established righteousness, was called the king of heaven by his people, or, in other words, "the King of peace". (J.S.T. Genesis 14:25-36).

In the Alma text, the ordinances, and not Melchizedek, are types of Christ. "Now these ordinances were given after this manner, that thereby the people might look forward on the Son of God, it being a type of his order, or it being his order, and this that they might look forward to him for a remission of their sins, that they might enter into the rest of the Lord". (V. 16).

"Melchizedek was a king over the land of Salem; and his people had waxed strong in iniquity and abomination; yea, they had all gone astray; they were full of all manner of wickedness". (V. 17). Perhaps because of the Nephite conviction of the wickedness of "the Jews at Jerusalem," Alma made no attempt to equate Salem with Jerusalem. Melchizedek was, for Alma, not the king of a city as such, but of a "land of Salem". For Alma, Salem simply meant "peace". (V. 17, see 1 Nephi 7:13-14). He hoped that the association of Salem with peace would not be lost on the people of Ammonihah. Surely, Mormon intended a similar message for members of the Church living in the Last Days.

The order of the priesthood involves a specific commission to preach repentance and to teach certain commandments leading to God's Rest. "But Melchizedek having exercised mighty faith, and received the office of the high priesthood according to the holy order of God, did preach repentance unto his people". (V. 18, see V. 6, & Alma 5:49). Alma felt that teaching was the paramount responsibility of the priesthood. He hardly mentioned the bureaucratic, authoritarian, official, or sacrificial powers of the priesthood in his sermons or writings. To him, the fruits of repentance were typified by the experience of Melchizedek in Salem: "And behold, they did repent; and Melchizedek did establish peace in the land in his days". (V. 18).

Alma must have greatly admired the teaching style of Melchizedek, for he would employ it throughout his ministry, continually trying "the virtue of the word of God". (Alma 31:5). Because Melchizedek had been able to establish peace, "he was called the prince of peace". (V. 18). It would be impossible to assign a greater appellation, for this is a name title of Jesus Christ Himself. (See Isaiah 9:6).

Melchizedek was "the king of Salem; and he did reign under his father," that is to say, in his father's stead. (V. 18). Similarly, the Nephite head of state until the reign of the Judges had shouldered the highest responsibility for both Church and state, assuming the role of both priest and king.

Of Melchizedek, Alma declared "there were many before him, and also there were many afterwards, but none were greater". (V. 19). For Alma, Melchizedek did not typify some distant reality. He was a concrete example that we may all receive the same knowledge that made him great. He was the teacher of a course of action that showed how we can benefit from the Atonement of Christ. Alma's direct approach illustrates that too much typology, or dealing with Melchizedek only as a symbol of the righteous king and priest, diminishes contact with the real, in favor of the shadow.

What Alma told the people of Ammonihah is repeated for the Latter-day Saints within the pages of The Book of Mormon. He emphasized that earlier scriptures stood behind his own interpretations, declaring: "Now, I need not rehearse the matter. Behold, the scriptures are before you". (V. 20). Even from our distant perspective in the Last Days, the example of Melchizedek can be as real and as motivational as it was for the Nephites.

In the last verses of this chapter, Alma exhorted his brethren in the wicked City of Ammonihah to repent, declaring: "The day of salvation draweth nigh," the birth of the Savior being just 82 years hence. (V. 22). He must have yearned to have the same influence with his people that Melchizedek had enjoyed in Salem, for initially it had been a city as wicked as Ammonihah.

Furthermore, the Lamanite destruction of Ammonihah was just a year away. Therefore, with great anxiety, Alma urged that the people "not procrastinate the day of (their) repentance". (V. 27). One of the characteristics of a truly committed missionary is sorrow unto pain for the sins of a people who will not repent. He declared his message clearly and plainly to their understanding. They would then be free to heed his words and view them as keys to their salvation, or to reject them so that at the last day they might stand as an indictment of their wicked ways. In either case, they could not escape the consequences of their actions.

The path before them was simple: "Humble yourselves before the Lord," begged Alma, and submit to His will. "Call on his holy name, and watch and pray continually," in order to be aware of the dangers present just over the horizon, so that "ye may not be tempted above that which ye can bear". "Thus, be led by the Holy Spirit, becoming humble, meek, submissive, patient, full of love, and all long-suffering. (Have) faith on the Lord; having a hope that ye shall receive eternal life; having the love of God always in your hearts, that ye may be lifted up at the last day and enter into his rest". (V. 28-29).

We might ask why Alma chose the wicked City of Ammonihah as his forum to speak about subjects as sacred as the priesthood and the activities of Melchizedek. Perhaps the answer lies in the similarities between the cities of Salem and Ammonihah. The wickedness of their inhabitants had marked each for destruction. In both cities, the only hope lay in repentance, following recognition of sin. Both were given that opportunity, for each had a great teacher who held the authority and power of the High Priesthood of the Holy Order of God.

The great lesson from Genesis could not have been lost on the people of Ammonihah. Salem had repented, and such was their subsequent righteousness that they were then translated. Whatever fate lay in store for Ammonihah, responsibility could only lie with its inhabitants, for they had been warned of the consequences of disobedience and then properly taught what they ought to do to avoid those consequences. It is disconcerting to realize that in our day the world faces a similar challenge, but largely ignores, in ways that are eerily similar to the rejection of Alma's message to the people of Ammonihah, the voice of warning raised by the servants of God who bear the same holy priesthood.

Today, the wicked are marked for destruction as surely as were the people of Ammonihah. "And thus, with the sword and by bloodshed the inhabitants of the earth shall mourn; and with famine, and plague, and earthquake, and the thunder of heaven, and the fierce and vivid lightning also, shall the inhabitants of the earth be made to feel the wrath, and indignation, and chastening hand of an Almighty God, until the consumption decreed hath made a full end of all nations". (D&C 87:6). The only questions are: How soon will the sword of justice fall on the nations of the earth, and how many will repent before that great and dreadful day?" O repent ye, repent ye!" urged Nephi. "Why will ye die?" he asked. Turn ye, turn ye unto the Lord your God". (Helaman 7:17).

Alma
Chapter 14

As a result of Alma's exhortations to the people, "many of them did believe on his words, and began to repent" and, as true believers always do, "to search the scriptures". (V. 1). This verse is another of the many evidences in The Book of Mormon that the people in general had copies of the records that were found upon the various plates kept in the possession of the rulers. (See V. 8).

An important principle frequently illustrated in the scriptures and in our own experience is re-emphasized in verse 2. The guilty take the truth to be hard. (See 1 Nephi 16:2). Consequently, the majority of those in Ammonihah "were desirous that they might destroy Alma and Amulek". (V. 2). To do so, they accused the two missionary companions of false prophecy and of sedition, both of which were capital offenses. Then they sought to dispose of them "privily," or secretly, stealthily, and craftily. (V. 2, see Commentary Reference to Mosiah 17:7). This proved impossible, though, perhaps because the well-publicized street-meetings of Alma and Amulek had created such a sensation and had made celebrities of the dynamic duo. Therefore, they were taken to the Chief Judge of the land where "the people went forth and witnessed against them. (V. 4-5, see V. 16).

Zeezrom, meanwhile, "was astonished at the words which had been spoken, and his soul began to be harrowed up under a consciousness of his own guilt". (V. 6). Harrowing a field breaks up the hardened crust of earth that has formed through disuse and neglect, so that seeds may be planted that will grow in the fertile soil that lies beneath. After our hearts are broken with an awful realization of our guilt, or when we are "harrowed up" by culpability, there exists a condition conducive to change and growth. Thus, Webster defines the term "harrow" as "to lacerate feelings, or to torment".

His intense feelings caused Zeezrom to cry out that he, and not Alma and Amulek, was the party actually guilty of heresy, blasphemy, and preaching false doctrine. (V. 7). But the people would not listen to him, and instead cast him out of the city along with "all those who believed in the words which had been spoken by Alma and Amulek". (V. 7). These people literally fled for their lives to the Land of Sidom, and were thus spared from destruction in Ammonihah. (See Alma 15:1).

The families of these refugees, however, were not so fortunate. They were dragged from their homes by the wicked and were thrown into a blazing inferno, along with their scriptures, in the mistaken belief that both they and their records would be "destroyed by fire". (V. 8). In reality, they instead became martyrs to the cause of truth. We might ask how justice could have become so twisted and perverted in Ammonihah that it would allow the murder of innocent women and children. Part of the answer might lie in the fact that the Chief Judge was himself "after the order and faith of Nehor, who slew Gideon". (V. 16, see Alma 15:15, 16:11, 21:4, & 24:28-29).

The missionaries were forced to watch these executions, and Amulek "was pained; and he said unto Alma: How can we witness this awful scene?" (V. 10). He was anxious to exercise the power of the priesthood to put an end to the carnage. (See Helaman 10:7). Ammonihah was Amulek's home. (Alma 8:20). Perhaps one or two of his own family members had received the witness of the Spirit, and had embraced the Gospel message. (See Alma 15:16). The intensity of Amulek's feeling is better understood if it is granted that loved ones might have been among those so horribly persecuted. (See Commentary Reference to Alma 15:16).

But Alma exhibited forbearance, declaring that the Spirit had constrained him. (V. 11, see Helaman 10:5). The Lord, he explained, would receive in glory those who had been killed, while at the same time their deaths would stand as a witness against the wicked. (V. 11, see Commentary Reference to Alma 8:13, & Alma 60:13). Martyrs are witnesses slain for their testimonies and that alone. (See Commentary Reference to Mosiah 17:20). The physical discomforts endured by those who refuse to renounce their testimonies of the truth do not seem to be significant to God, Whose focus is ever on the preservation of the eternal life of the spirit.

Spencer W. Kimball taught: "If pain and sorrow and total punishment immediately followed the doing of evil, no soul would repeat a misdeed. If joy and peace and rewards were instantaneously given the doer of good, there could be no evil. All would do good, and not because of the rightness of doing good. There would be no test of strength, no development of character, no growth of powers, no agency, but only satanic controls. If all the sick were healed, if all the righteous were protected, and the wicked destroyed, the whole program of the Father would be annulled and the basic principle of the Gospel, agency, would be ended". ("Faith Precedes the Miracle," p. 97-98).

In verses 15, 20, and 24, Mormon reported how the wicked repeatedly abused Alma and Amulek, while ridiculing them that they had no power. God also exhibits forbearance, but in verse 25 is a description of how His power was finally manifest. Alma and Amulek had been confined in prison and physically bound with the strong cords of Satan. (V. 23). They had lost their liberty, but not their agency. Of similar circumstances, Holocaust survivor Viktor E. Frankel wrote: "We who lived in concentration camps can remember those who walked through the huts comforting others, giving away their last piece of bread. They may have been few in number, but they offer sufficient proof that everything can be taken from a man but one thing, the last of the human freedoms: to choose one's attitude in any given set of circumstances, to choose one's own way". ("Man's Search for Freedom," p. 104).

In a testimonial from a survivor of a concentration camp, a man tells of watching a fellow inmate praying. He asks why? His companion answers: "I am thanking God." The man is stunned. "For what could you be thanking God in this hellhole?" And the second calmly responds: "I am thanking God that He did not make me like them." (Holocaust Memorial Museum, Washington D.C.).

In Ammonihah, the Chief Judge declared: "If ye have the power of God, deliver yourselves from these bands, and then we will believe that the Lord will destroy this people according to your words". (V. 24). The missionaries did just that, for "the power of God was upon Alma and Amulek, and they rose and stood upon their feet". (V. 25). At this, the people "began to flee, for the fear of destruction had come upon them". (V. 26). Because they had seen, they were believers, but faith must precede the miracle, and it was too late for that. Even if they had a desire to repent, they had procrastinated for too long, and their fate had been sealed. So great was their astonishment that "they fell to the earth, and did not obtain the outer door of the prison". (V. 27). As the earth began to shake, the walls collapsed, killing everyone inside except Alma and Amulek, who walked unharmed out of the rubble.

Those in the city heard the noise associated with the destruction of the prison and of the people within, and they came running toward the rising cloud of dust. When they saw the missionaries stepping into the sunlight, they "were struck with great fear, and fled from the presence of Alma and Amulek". (V. 29). "Now this was done that the Lord might show forth His power in them". (Alma 8:31). But it did not change the attitudes of the remaining inhabitants of the city. The record does not tell what they subsequently did, but presumably they resumed their wicked lifestyle, after this irritating and inconvenient interruption. "As a dog returneth to his vomit, so a fool returneth to his folly". (Proverbs 26:11).

"And this is the manner after which they were ordained – being called and prepared from the foundation of the world according to the foreknowledge of God, on account of their exceeding faith and good works; in the first place being left to choose good or evil."
(Alma 13:3).

Alma
Chapter 15

After that manifestation of divine intervention while in captivity in prison, Alma and Amulek were commanded by God to travel to Sidom. (V. 1). The people in Ammonihah had been given every reasonable opportunity to repent, but they had proven beyond a doubt that they had no intention of doing so. That was the fatal symptom of their hard-heart disease. They were in the terminal stage of sclerosis of their spiritual arteries.

Hugh Nibley wrote an interesting dialogue on this subject: "We: Dear Father, whenever the end is scheduled to be, can't you give us a little extension of time? He: Willingly. But tell me first, what will you do with it? We: Well, ahh, we will go on doing pretty much what we have always been doing. After all, isn't that why we are asking for an extension? He: And isn't that exactly why I want it to end so soon - because you show no inclination to change? Why should I reverse the order of nature so that you can go on doing the very things I want to put an end to? We: But is what we are doing so terribly wrong? The economy seems sound enough. Why shouldn't we go on doing the things that have made this country great? He: Haven't I made it clear enough to you what kind of greatness I expect of my offspring? Forget the statistics; you are capable of better things. Your stirring commercials don't impress me in the least. We: But why should we repent when all we are doing is what each considers to be for the best good of himself and the nation? He: Because it is not you, but I, to decide what that shall be, and I have told you a hundred times what is best for you individually and collectively, and that is repentance, no matter who you are. We: We find your inference objectionable, Sir, and quite unacceptable. He: I know". ("Beyond Politics," p. 279-280)

It must have been extremely difficult for Alma and Amulek when they arrived in the Land of Sidom to relate all that had happened to the wives and children of those who had been cast out of Ammonihah. (V. 2). But, to a spiritually illiterate city, the martyrs had given "a great lesson in the grammar of the Gospel, including this one: Death is a mere comma, and not an exclamation point". (Neal Maxwell). It is not extinguishing the light, but rather putting out the lamp because the dawn has come. Now, that same light of the Gospel was beginning to illuminate the understanding of husbands and fathers in the Land of Sidom. In their anguish, they were comforted and reassured that "life is eternal, love is immortal, and death is only a horizon which is nothing save the limit of our sight". (Raymond W. Rossiter).

In Sidom, "Zeezrom lay sick with a burning fever, which was caused by the great tribulations of his mind on account of his wickedness". (V. 3). He had only briefly been taught about redemption and repentance, and thus he was engulfed in the torment of the damned. (See Alma 12:25). Therefore, "he began to be scorched with a burning heat". (V. 3, see Mosiah 2:38, & Commentary Reference to Alma 14:6).

Alma could empathize with Zeezrom. Later in his ministry, he would reflect on the years of his own rebellious youth. "So great had been my iniquities," he confessed, "that the very thought of coming into the presence of my God did rack my soul with inexpressible horror". (Alma 36:14). Therefore, he was sympathetic to the state of mind of his former adversary, and now taught him the saving principles of the Gospel. By the power of the priesthood, Zeezrom was granted the indescribable gift of the Spirit when Alma declared: "O Lord our God, have mercy on this man, and heal him according to his faith which is in Christ". (V. 10).

At this, to the great astonishment of all the people, Zeezrom "leaped upon his feet, and began to walk". He was baptized and "began from that time forth to preach unto the people as a witness of Jesus Christ". (V. 11-12). His faith and works drew him closer to the "rest of the Lord". The measure of our character is revealed in our behavior when we hear and recognize the truth. The critical question that determines our true worth is: "Can we consciously and willingly change the trajectory of our lives?"

The two most important days of our lives are the day we are born and the day we find out why. On this day, at the waters of baptism, Zeezrom was "born again," and he became a son of God. His life would never again be the same for he was changed through faith on the Lord Jesus Christ. (See Mosiah 5:7).

Zeezrom was the first convert baptized in the Land of Sidom according to the missionary journals of Alma and Amulek, but he was certainly not the last. A Church was established there, with priests and teachers consecrated to welcome and instruct all who desired to enter into the fold through the waters of baptism. "(And) they were many, for they did flock in from all the region round about Sidom". (V. 13-14).

Alma's resignation of the Chief Judgeship and his faith in the ability of the Gospel to change lives were thus powerfully vindicated. "A great check" had been placed on the power wrought by Satan to negatively influence the lives of the people, who now worshipped in their sanctuaries, "watching and praying continually". (V. 17, see Alma 16:13).

Amulek had lost all his worldly possessions in the City of Ammonihah, but he had traded these telestial trinkets for celestial sureties. (V. 16). With the affairs of the Church in good order in the outlying districts, Alma was able to return the favor of Amulek's hospitality in Ammonihah. (See Alma 8:27). He brought Amulek to his own house in Zarahemla, where he "did administer unto him in his tribulations, and strengthened him in the Lord". (V. 18).

The warmth and security of Alma's home was certainly joyful to Amulek, for his own family life in Ammonihah had ultimately proven to be bleak, for he had been "rejected by those who were once his friends and also by his father and his kindred". (V. 16). In contrast, the company of his brethren in Zarahemla must have been like the balm of Gilead, providing him with a glimpse of heaven on earth.

In Alma's home, Amulek may have thought that he was "stepping on shore, and finding it heaven! Of taking hold of a hand, and finding it God's hand. Of breathing a new air, and finding it celestial air. Of feeling invigorated, and finding it immortality. Of passing from storm and tempest to an unbroken calm. Of waking up, and finding it home". (Robert E. Selle, see Commentary Reference to Alma 16:17).

"It came to pass that Amulek (had) forsaken all his gold, and silver, and precious things, which were in the land of Ammonihah, for the word f God, he being rejected by those who were once his friends, and also by his father and his kindred."
(Alma 15:16).

Alma
Chapter 16

Verse 1 illustrates Mormon's care in documenting the exact date of the fulfillment of Alma's prophecy concerning the destruction of Ammonihah. Also vividly depicted is the contrast between the peace found in Zarahemla and the warfare and bloodshed in Ammonihah. (V. 1-2, see Alma 9:4, & 12).

"In the eleventh year of the reign of the Judges over the people of Nephi, on the fifth day of the second month ... there was a cry of war heard throughout the land. And the people of Ammonihah were destroyed; yea, every living soul of the Ammonihahites was destroyed, and also their great city, which they said God could not destroy. And it was called Desolation of Nehors". (V. 1, 9 & 11). The Commentary Reference to Alma 25:1-2 explains how it came to be that an army of the Lamanites, that included the extremely volatile and militant Amulonites and Amalekites, came in to the Land of Zarahemla to unleash their fury on the Nephites, beginning at the City of Ammonihah.

Interestingly, the commanding general of the armies of the Nephites in the Land of Zarahemla at this time was a man by the name of Zoram, who is only mentioned by name in two verses in this chapter. (V. 5, & 7). One of his sons was named Aha, which in Egyptian means "warrior". This is an appropriate name for a Zoramite, whose tribe was among the most militant in The Book of Mormon, and particularly for the son of a military leader. (V. 5).

After destroying Ammonihah, the invading Lamanite army had "taken others captive into the wilderness". (V. 3, think "Apocalypto"). It became Zoram's responsibility to pursue them with his own army, in order to obtain the freedom of his people. To his great credit, and following the ancient pattern, "knowing that Alma was high priest over the Church, and having heard that he had the spirit of prophecy, therefore (he) went unto him and desired of him to know whither the Lord would that they should go into the wilderness in search of their brethren, who had been taken captive by the Lamanites". (V. 5).

Alma gave Zoram and his sons specific intelligence information that enabled his army to come "upon the armies of the Lamanites, and the Lamanites were scattered and driven (further) into the wilderness; and they took their brethren who had been taken captive by the Lamanites". (V. 8). Mormon was careful to contrast these Nephites with the inhabitants of Ammonihah. Of the former, he wrote: "there was not one soul of them had been lost," but of the latter, he noted: "every living soul was destroyed". (V. 8-9, see Commentary References to 2 Nephi 33:5, & Alma 25:2, Mosiah 29:27, & D&C 63:33).

The fate of the inhabitants of Ammonihah typifies the ultimate destiny of those in any age who engage in priestcraft or relentlessly persecute the Saints. For years afterward, their destruction was remembered by the Nephites as "the Desolation of Nehors". (V. 11). "Desolation" accurately describes the physical condition of the city that was "deprived of inhabitants, devastated or laid waste, and ruined". (O.E.D.). Desolation can also mean "deprivation of companionship; the condition of being forsaken and also deprivation of comfort or joy, or to render wretched". These definitions certainly fit the description of the shattered City of Ammonihah, as well as the spiritual condition of its slain inhabitants.

Those who intentionally alienate themselves from the Spirit of the Lord must find their own way. Consequently, they grope about in darkness both in this life and later in the spirit world when they find themselves cut off from light and truth because of the great gulf that separates the righteous from the wicked.

Wickedness never was happiness, for the Spirit is an indispensable part of mortal experience if we are to have joy. The physical world provides an excellent example of the necessity of all the ingredients for an abundant life. Without air, that we cannot even see, we would all be brain-dead in just over four minutes. Likewise, without the Spirit, that we cannot see, we would just as quickly be spiritually dead.

After the destruction of Ammonihah, Alma and Amulek "went forth (out of Zarahemla) preaching repentance" throughout all the land surrounding the wasted city. Understandably, the people they taught were quite receptive to the message, having witnessed, or heard about, the wrath of God that had been reserved for the wicked. (V. 13).

Verse 13 implies that there was more than one temple in the Land of Zarahemla, and that "synagogues built after the manner of the Jews" were commonly used for worship. Today, Bible scholars believe that synagogues first arose as a principal place of worship during the Babylonian exile in the absence of the temple. This would place their initial use at the time of Ezra, about 590 B.C. Consequently, the word "synagogue" occurs only once in the Old Testament (Psalms 74:8); yet it appears 26 times in The Book of Mormon.

Since the departure of Lehi from Jerusalem preceded the Babylonian exile, the frequent use of the term in The Book of Mormon can be explained in several ways. First, synagogue worship could have quite simply predated the exile, and either Lehi's or Mulek's party could have brought with them the practice of synagogue worship. However, there is no mention of such worship in The Book of Mormon until Alma 16:13, 2 Nephi 26:26 notwithstanding. Secondly, other unidentified groups arriving in the New World after the Babylonian exile could have introduced the practice to the Nephites.

Thirdly, the Nephite word for "place of assembly" simply could have been translated into the English as "synagogue". This explanation is quite intriguing, and makes another powerful statement in support of the authenticity of The Book of Mormon for the following reason. The Book of Mormon invariably uses "synagogue," that is a Greek word, to designate early Jewish assemblies, and "Church," from the Greek "ecclesia," to designate such assemblies after they had become Christian. It is hard to think of more appropriate terms, bearing in mind that this is a translation, and the purpose of the words is not to convey what the Nephites called their communities, but only how the translation invites us to picture them in our own minds. (See D&C 66:7, Mosiah 25:13, Alma 19:34, 21:16, 23:4, & 32:1-4).

Alma and Amulek were true to their missionary callings and magnified their priesthood responsibilities. Each man who bears the priesthood of God must "learn his duty, and act in the office in which he is appointed, in all diligence". (D&C 107:99). After they had taught the Gospel to the people in their synagogues, or places of assembly, branches of the Church were established "throughout the land". (V. 13-15).

The events that unfolded at that time in the Land of Zarahemla parallel those of our own day. The wicked inhabitants of Ammonihah who turned a deaf ear to the voice of warning of the prophets suffered an incredibly swift and utterly complete destruction. Afterward, in order to ready the surviving Nephites for His post-mortal ministry, the Lord "did pour out his Spirit on all the face of the land to prepare the minds of the children of men". He also did this "to prepare their hearts to receive the word which should be taught among them at the time of his coming - that they might not be hardened against the word, that they might not be unbelieving, and go on to destruction, but that they might receive the word with joy, and as a branch be grafted into the true vine, that they might enter into the rest of the Lord their God". (V. 16-17).

The "rest of the Lord" is born of a settled conviction of the truth. Today, we may enter into God's rest by coming to an understanding of the truths of the Gospel and by internalizing celestial principles. As the Savior taught: "Peace I leave with you, my peace I give unto you; not as the world giveth, give I unto you. Let not your heart be troubled, neither let it be afraid". (John 14:27).

In addition to experiencing the fruit of the tree of life, or the love of God whose expression is eternal life, these faithful Nephites were also taught that the Savior "would appear unto them after his resurrection, and this the people did hear with great joy and gladness". (V. 20).

Alma and Amulek, and "those priests who did go forth among the people got the victory over the devil". (V. 18 & 21, see Commentary Reference to Alma 12:5). Once again, a blueprint is provided for those living in the Last Days. The Book of Mormon articulates a policy guaranteed to make God's people free from Satan's influence, as well as from all foreign nations under his evil control. "Behold, this is a choice land, and whatsoever nation shall possess it shall be free from bondage, and from captivity, and from all other nations under heaven if they will but serve the God of the land, who is Jesus Christ". (Ether 2:12).

"We live in a day and in a world full of doubts and confusion, where people do not know what to believe, where tensions are high, where the pace is frantic and progress in terms of righteousness is not a popular goal. Violence and crudity are everyday patterns all around us. What a blessing it is to know there is a haven, a place of rest from the turmoil of the world. The prophets and the Savior have called upon us to enter into the rest of the Lord, where life has purpose and direction, and where priesthood power is possible". ("Gospel Doctrine Manual," p. 79).

The ministry of Alma had taken five years, but the people of Nephi had been greatly blessed by his efforts. "The word of God (was now being) preached in its purity in all the land," by an army of priesthood brethren, and the Lord poured out His blessings upon the people. (V. 21). In his abridgement of the Large Plates of Nephi, Mormon was now ready to turn his attention to the parallel missionary efforts of the former companions of Alma, because the experiences of these Sons of Mosiah illustrate the great joy that comes from sharing the Gospel with others.

Alma
Chapter 17

Chapters 17-26 recount the missionary experiences of the Sons of Mosiah among the Lamanites in the Land of Nephi, and cover the same 14-year period during which Alma labored among the Nephites in Zarahemla. (See Alma chapters 1-16). Chapters 17-20 focus specifically on the labors of Ammon. The first four verses of chapter 17 are a powerful testimony of the value of the ministry as a catalyst for spiritual growth.

The account opens as Alma was "journeying from the land of Gideon southward". Fourteen years after he and his friends had bid each other farewell, he was astonished to meet the Sons of Mosiah who were returning to Zarahemla. (V. 1, see Commentary Reference to Alma 27:15-16). Alma rejoiced that after long years of separation from his companions, "they were still his brethren in the Lord". (V. 2). From about 91 to 77 B.C., Alma had been in the Land of Zarahemla working to bring about a spiritual rebirth among his own people. His thoughts must have frequently turned to Ammon, Aaron, Omner, and Himni, and their missionary companions, who had literally walked into the valley of the shadow of death, in order to bring the Gospel message to the Lamanites. (See Psalm 23).

It must have seemed altogether remarkable to Alma that his highest and best hopes for the welfare of his brethren were now confirmed. As he learned the details of their experiences during those years, he would have recognized and appreciated the unchangeable formula for success: "They had waxed strong in the knowledge of the truth; for they were men of a sound understanding and they had searched the scriptures diligently, that they might know the word of God". (V. 2). "Who shall ascend into the hill of the Lord?" David had asked. "Or who shall stand in his holy place? He that hath clean hands, and a pure heart; who hath not lifted up his soul unto vanity, nor sworn deceitfully. He shall receive the blessing from the Lord, and righteousness from the God of his salvation". (Psalm 24:3-5).

The scriptures had become their message and the tools of their trade. Their confidence, we shall see, was directly related to their knowledge of God's word. "But," Mormon explained, "this is not all.

They had given themselves to much prayer, and fasting; therefore, they had the spirit of prophecy, and the spirit of revelation, and when they taught, they taught with the power and authority of God". (V. 3, see D&C 4, 121:45-46, 130:20-21, & 132:5). Because of these qualities of greatness, they had conquered every obstacle that lay in the path of their progress.

At the outset, they had received legal authority from King Mosiah to travel to the Land of Nephi (See Mosiah 28:1), but their power to preach the Gospel came through priesthood channels and ultimately from the personal righteousness that was the key to the success of their ministry.

Even though they had been urged to remain in Zarahemla, they had determined to go up to the Land of Nephi. (V. 5, & 8, see Mosiah 28:1-9, & Alma 26:23-25). Subsequently, they had spent many days trekking through the wilderness on their way to the mission field. (V. 9).

In verse 6, note the Semitic use of the plural form of a noun of quality: "and also this was the minds of the people". (See Commentary Reference to 1 Nephi 16:21). That is to say, it was the expectation of the people that the Sons of Mosiah would remain in Zarahemla and fulfil what was generally perceived to be their destiny to accept "the kingdom which their father was desirous to confer upon them". (V. 6).

However, they had other plans. The Sons of Mosiah "departed out of the land of Zarahemla, and took their swords, and their spears, and their bows, and their arrows, and their slings; and this they did that they might provide food for themselves while in the wilderness". (V. 7). They had no hostile intentions. The weapons they would need to fight their battles with the Lamanites were their scriptures and powerful testimonies. (See Alma 18:36, & 30:5).

Mormon inserted into the record a geographical inference that as the party traveled southward toward the Land of Nephi, they gained elevation, as they left what was likely the State of Chiapas in Southern Mexico toward what is now Highland Guatemala. "And thus, they departed into the wilderness with their numbers which they had selected, to go up to the Land of Nephi, to preach the word of God unto the Lamanites". (V. 8). They made good use of their time, for they "fasted much and prayed much that the Lord would grant unto them a portion of his Spirit to go with them, and abide with them, that they might be an instrument in the hands of God to bring, if it were possible, their brethren, the Lamanites, to the knowledge of the truth". (V. 9). This is good advice for missionaries in any age, whose preparation should be equally purposeful and whose objectives should be just as clearly defined.

We can establish only geographical generalities regarding the distance from Zarahemla to Nephi, as we read the accounts of different parties making the trip. The Sons of Mosiah spent "many days" in the wilderness as had the People of Limhi. (See Mosiah 23:12). Thirty years earlier, it had taken the Elder Alma somewhere between 12 and 20 days to make the journey. (See Mosiah 24:25).

Charity for the Lamanites is repeatedly illustrated in the record. In verse 9, Mormon characterized them as his brethren, and gently softened his description of their repulsive way of life. (See v. 30). In a strikingly even-handed way, Mormon simply described "the baseness (or inferior quality) of the traditions of their fathers, which were not correct". (See V. 14-15). This is quite a conciliatory statement from a man who had both witnessed and personally endured indescribable suffering at the hands of the Lamanites. Perhaps, by 385 A.D. Mormon clearly understood the differentiation between Nephites and Lamanites established by his ancestor Jacob, who had clarified: "Now the people which were not Lamanites were Nephites. But I, Jacob, shall not hereafter distinguish them by these names, but I shall call them Lamanites that seek to destroy the people of Nephi, and those who are friendly to Nephi I shall call Nephites, or the people of Nephi". (Jacob 1:13-14).

An angel had taught Jacob's brother Nephi: "Behold there are save two Churches only; the one is the Church of the Lamb of God, and the other is the Church of the devil; wherefore, whoso belongeth not to the Church of the Lamb of God belongeth to that great Church, which is the mother of abominations; and she is the whore of all the earth". (1 Nephi 14:10). Even today, the "whore" survives as a corrupt or idolatrous community, in stark contrast to the body of the Church. Whatever their lineage, Mormon surely believed that the best course would be to pray for those who find fault with the Church. After all, the Lamanites were only behaving as those who say: "It ain't my ignorance that done me in, but what I knowed that warn't so".

In response to their prayerful supplications to God, the Sons of Mosiah were given advice that is applicable to all missionaries. They were told by the whisperings of the Spirit to go among the people, to testify of the truth, be patient in all their afflictions, and to exemplify what they taught. If they would do these things, they were promised that their harvest of souls would be great. (V. 11).

As they enjoyed the Spirit of the Lord, they were profoundly comforted. (V. 10). They certainly needed courage, for "they had undertaken to preach the word of God to a wild and a hardened and a ferocious people who delighted in murdering the Nephites, and robbing and plundering them". (V. 14). The Lamanites at that time were "an indolent (or slothful, lazy, and idle) people" who had turned to the worship of idols. (V. 15). Consequently, the curse of God was upon them. Nevertheless, on condition of repentance "his hand (was) stretched out still". (V. 15, see 2 Nephi 15:25). It was for this cause that the Sons of Mosiah had undertaken their mission in the first place. (V. 16, see Mosiah 28:2). They simply loved the Lamanites as their brethren, and they were as pliant clay in the hands of the Master Potter, determined to be pure vessels who would respond instinctively to His will.

Ammon seems to have been the ecclesiastical leader of the party, for prior to their separation he gave each of the missionaries a priesthood blessing. (V. 18). Then, trusting in the power of the Lord, they, "went forth among (the Lamanites), every man alone". (V. 17). Knowing as we do the disposition of the Lamanites to heap abuse upon the Nephites, this simple statement encompasses an almost incomprehensible dimension.

In the next four chapters, Mormon recounted many significant details of Ammon's mission. As we study these, perhaps we can apply the missionary principles contained therein to our own circumstances and individually tailored challenges, as we confront our own latter-day cultural Lamanites.

Ammon first went to the Land of Ishmael. Both sons and two of the daughters of Ishmael had married children of Lehi, and by following the rebellious example of Laman and Lemuel, they became Lamanites. (V. 19, see 1 Nephi 7:6, & Alma 3:7). After the departure of Nephi and his righteous brethren, it seems that the Ishmaelites moved into and settled in that portion of the Land of Nephi that is identified in this verse.

So, in contrast to the present practice of missionaries traveling two by two, Ammon struck off by himself. Before long, he was arrested and became a willing prisoner of the Lamanites, who took him to their king named Lamoni. (V. 20-21). King Lamoni might have mistaken Ammon for one of the many apostate Nephites who had forsaken a life of righteousness and come into the Land of Nephi to settle among the Lamanites with whom they felt more comfortable. When Lamoni extended to Ammon the invitation to live among his people, he was probably offering him political asylum to become a cultural Lamanite and the equivalent of a naturalized citizen. (V. 22).

Ammon told the king that it was his desire to remain with the Lamanites, for the rest of his life, if necessary. (V. 23). The king still did not know the real reason for Ammon's appearance in his land. He only knew that there stood before him an impressive young Nephite warrior who had boldly come alone into the stronghold of the Lamanite nation. Ammon may have mentioned his royal heritage, or presented to Lamoni the introductory credentials given to him by his father, for the king immediately offered to give him one of his daughters to wife, a princess for a prince. (V. 24). Of course, Ammon refused, saying, "Nay, but I will be thy servant". (V. 25). King Lamoni had no conception of the quality of service that Ammon desired to give to him and his people, but he must have been further impressed with this humble demonstration of his noble character!

His opportunity to prepare the king's heart for the message of the Gospel came soon enough. God set the stage and provided a golden teaching moment when a band of Lamanite ruffians came to the waters of Sebus to scatter the flocks of the king. (V. 26-27). Ammon had paid the price to spiritually prepare himself, and his heart swelled with the confidence that God would manifest his power. (V. 29, see Commentary Reference to Alma 24:19, D&C 121:45, & Mosiah 28:7). Therefore, he looked forward with joy to the same situation that caused the Lamanite shepherds of the flock to "weep exceedingly". Those to whom the king had entrusted the care of his sheep now had an immediate and urgent problem of their own. They knew that they would lose their lives if the sheep were lost.

Perhaps Mormon included this episode in his abridgement of the records because he knew that in our day we would face our own "Lamanites by the waters of Sebus" and be thrust into situations with more profound primal needs, namely, the protection of our eternal lives.

Perhaps our moments of greatest challenge will come when we are placed in compromising social situations and are tempted to homogenize our standards. Maybe it will be when we are climbing the ladder of success and are tempted to scramble over those who are supposedly in our way and impeding our progress. It might be that when we are alone with our computer and surfing the web, we are prone to visit sites of questionable value. It may come at the end of the month when we are reconciling our checkbook and balancing our budget, and we have not yet paid our tithing. It may be when we have been neglectful in our assignments to minister within our ward family, or when we have not attended the temple in a while, and worldly concerns compete for our time and attention.

The Lord said: "That which the Spirit testifies unto you, even so I would that ye should do in all holiness of heart, walking uprightly before me, considering the end of your salvation, doing all things with prayer and thanksgiving, that ye may not be seduced by evil spirits, or doctrines of devils, or the commandments of men". (D&C 46:7). The "Lamanites" standing in the way of our progress are those frightful things we see when we take our minds off our goals. They cause us to lose focus. "Lamanites" influence us to lower our sights and our standards, and to compromise the effort needed to reach our objectives. If we are gliding smoothly through life with little expenditure of energy, we are probably going downhill. Our personal progress requires that we face the "Lamanite" pressures in our paths and climb to new heights of achievement.

We have "the power of God unto salvation" and are the architects of our own fate, in a very real sense. (Romans 1:16). We have the skills and the materials to build either a shanty or a temple in which to live our lives. Which one it will be depends on us. The outcome depends largely on whether or not we face the "Lamanites" in our lives with faith and courage.

Sometimes bad things happen to good people, and life can be unpredictable. There are uncertainties with which each of us must deal, but if our foundation is solid and our footing secure, we will be able to successfully adapt to every circumstance and maintain our focus. Fanatics lose sight of their objectives and redouble their efforts. We, on the other hand, remember the counsel of Paul, who was familiar with adversity: "Work out your own salvation with fear and trembling". (Philippians 2:12)

As we develop the habit of work, we learn that it can be the most invigorating, satisfying, even relaxing and greatest blessing of our lives. We develop a testimony of the truth that "Work without vision is drudgery; vision without work is dreamery; but work with vision is destiny!" (Harold B. Lee).

As we face our own "Lamanites by the Water of Sebus," we remember that our triumphs will come, not by default, but by design, by the strength of our own will, and by our reliance on the Lord. In all our "Lamanite" encounters, we will think pro-actively, rather than retroactively. We will direct the course of the circumstances in which we find ourselves. We may not be able to control everything that unfolds in our lives, but we will at least be able to influence outcomes and personal consequences.

Failure to do so amounts to the capitulation of our destiny to forces we believe to be beyond our control. If we roll over and turn belly-up to "Lamanites" when they menacingly surround and threaten us, we have already guaranteed failure. Our flocks will be scattered and our King disappointed. "Now the king will slay us," wailed the servants of Limoni. (Alma 17:28). But our Lord and Master will not take our lives. Instead, it is we who will forfeit our eternal lives if we allow "Lamanites" to overcome us.

Life is enough of a pressure cooker as it is, without introducing unneeded additional stress. Many events "remain to (be) overcome through patience (in order to) receive a more exceeding and eternal weight of glory". (D&C 63:66). The Lord told Joseph Smith: "Be patient in afflictions, for thou shalt have many, but endure them, for, lo, I am with thee, even until the end of thy days". (D&C 24:8). Therefore, "in everything (we) give thanks, waiting patiently on the Lord," even in the face of destruction at the hands of fierce "Lamanites". (D&C 98:1-2). We "seek the face of the Lord always, that in patience (we) may possess (our) souls, and ... have eternal life". (D&C 101:38).

King Lamoni's people were astonished by Ammon's actions by the waters of Sebus, because in the Land of Nephi the Lamanites had not yet learned how to draw upon the power of God. When the king's servants returned to the king and testified to him of the things they had seen Ammon do, "he was astonished exceedingly, and said: Surely, this is more than a man. Behold is this not the Great Spirit?" (Alma 18:1-2). They knew that God was capable of mighty works, but they had never considered that He might transfer His power to man so that he might also perform miracles. They did not know that they were capable of withstanding the onslaughts of even the most formidable bands of "Lamanites" roaming the land and trolling for the flocks of unsuspecting shepherds.

Whether or not Ammon was aware of the Lord's promise to Mosiah, we do not know, but before their mission, He had assured the king: "I will deliver thy sons out of the hands of the Lamanites". (Mosiah 28:7). At the waters of Sebus, Ammon faced the first real test of that promise.

Strengthened by the Lord, he slew 6 members of the raiding party with his sling, and then their leader with his sword. (V. 35, & 38). "Every man that lifted his club to smite Ammon, he smote off their arms with his sword; for he did withstand their blows by smiting their arms with the edge of his sword, insomuch that they began to be astonished, and began to flee before him; yea, and they were not few in number; and he caused them to flee by the strength of his arm". (V. 36-37).

He carried these gruesome trophies to "the king for a testimony of the things which they had done". (V. 39). This may be shocking to the western mind, but the practice of cutting off the arms of enemies specifically as a testimony of the conquest of victims is attested in Yigal Yadin's "The Art of Warfare in Biblical Lands". The extreme left of Band Four of The Gates of Shalmaneser III (858 - 824 B.C.) shows Assyrian troops cutting off the head, hands, and feet of vanquished enemies. In other reliefs, scribes record the number of dead in accordance with the number of severed heads, hands, and feet that Assyrian soldiers hold up before them.

Coincidentally, the splendid murals on the walls of those buildings in Mexico City that house the offices of national government vividly display Aztec warriors holding up the severed arms of their enemies in precisely the same fashion as described by Mormon in Alma chapter 17. Add one more to the list of innumerable small coincidences that, taken as a whole, powerfully attest to the authenticity of the ancient text.

"And it came to pass that king Lamoni inquired of his servants, saying: Where is this man that has such great power? And they said unto him: Behold, he is feeding thy horses."
(Alma 18:8-9).

Alma
Chapter 18

When the servants of King Lamoni testified to him of the things they had seen Ammon do, "he was astonished exceedingly, and said: Surely, this is more than a man. Behold is this not the Great Spirit?" (V. 1-2). His admiration of Ammon's qualities was superlative. Because he had never been taught the Gospel, Lamoni did not have a correct concept of Jesus Christ, who was, in fact, "the Great Spirit of whom (his) fathers (had) spoken". He had been taught only a fragment of the truth, through "the tradition of (the Lamanites,) which he had received from his father". (V. 5).

Mormon continued: "Notwithstanding they believed in a Great Spirit, they supposed that whatsoever they did was right". The same situation prevails today. Jesus Christ is viewed from a distorted perspective and is seen not as the Divine Son of God, the Savior and Redeemer of the world, and as the Author of Salvation, but rather as an outstanding moral teacher. (See Commentary Reference to Helaman 10:17). Because His Godliness is denied, so is the universal applicability of His teachings. The baby must be thrown out with the bathwater. Consequently, the people believe that whatever they do is right.

Those who lack the Gospel Standard anchor their belief system on the shifting sands of expediency and circumstance. They are left to make critical moral and ethical value judgments based on endocrine secretions rather than on the unchanging and eternally validated laws of the Gospel. Some subscribe to the damnable doctrine that man is a light unto himself. (See D&C 76:79). This heresy may be promulgated by "the honorable men of the earth, who (have been) blinded by the craftiness of men," but whoever they are, they fit one mold, seeking the thrill of the moment while ignoring eternal consequences. (D&C 76:75). In contrast, those who are valiant in the testimony of Jesus take His side on every issue, think what He thinks, believe what He believes, say what He would say, and do what He would do.

Lamoni recognized special qualities in the actions of Ammon at the waters of Sebus, and so "he inquired of his servants, saying: Where is this man that has such great power?" (V. 8). A rare example of dry humor in The Book of Mormon follows: "And they said unto him: Behold, he is feeding thy horses". (V. 9, see Alma 18:9, 19:5, 30:59, 33:21, 46:35, & 5532).

Interestingly, there are only 14 direct references to horses in the entire Book of Mormon. (See Commentary Reference to 2 Nephi 15:20). Often these come in conjunction with mention of chariots. Only once in the Book is the word "wheels" used, and this is a quotation from Isaiah. (See Commentary Reference to 2 Nephi 15:28).

By now, King Lamoni was convinced more than ever that Ammon was the Great Spirit. (V. 11). When Ammon had finished his work in the stables, he went to the royal chambers and saw that "the countenance of the king was changed". (V. 12). Ammon was overjoyed to see that the process of conversion had begun. Alma had witnessed the same transformation in the lives of the inhabitants of Zarahemla. Of these people, he had inquired, "Have ye spiritually been born of God. Have ye received his image in your countenances? Have ye experienced this mighty change in your hearts?" (Alma 5:14).

One of the servants of the king addressed Ammon as "Rabbanah, which is, being interpreted, powerful or great king". (V. 13). This term is similar to the Hebrew "Rabboni," that means "My Master". (John 20:16). Remember that Moroni wrote: "If our plates had been sufficiently large, we should have written in Hebrew". (Mormon 9:33). This variant term seems to convey the same idea.

In what language was Mormon's abridgment written? The most obvious answer is some form of Egyptian. Moroni stated: "We have written this record ... in the characters which are called among us the reformed Egyptian". (Mormon 9:32). Nephi confirmed this at the very beginning when he said: "I make a record in the language of my father, which consists of the learning of the Jews and the language of the Egyptians". (1 Nephi 1:1). While the simplest interpretation of these statements (and others like them in The Book of Mormon) is that the language of The Book of Mormon is Egyptian, some have suggested a slightly different understanding. They posit that while the script (or the written characters) of the plates is likely a form of Egyptian, the underlying language of the plates may be Hebrew (as a tangible reflection of the "learning of the Jews"). (1 Nephi 1:2).

In any event, the servant continued: "The king desireth thee to stay". (V. 13). This Ammon did, "for the space of an hour, according to their time". (V. 14). How the Nephites measured time, we do not know. Before the invention of modern timepieces, the ancients used sundials, water clocks, and hour glasses. We only know from Joseph Smith's translation that Ammon remained in the presence of Lamoni for the equivalent of an hour.

"Being filled with the Spirit of God, (Ammon) perceived the thoughts of the king," and understood that he was in amazement that the Lamanite raiders had been vanquished. (V. 16). When he revealed Lamoni's own thoughts to him, the king began to marvel even more, and in what must have been reverential tones, he wondered aloud: "Art thou that Great Spirit, who knows all things?" (V. 18).

He wanted to know the source of Ammon's extraordinary powers, and declared "whatsoever thou desirest of me I will grant it unto thee". (V. 21). An opportunity like this doesn't come along very often. Like the Genie who has been released from his prison in a bottle, and who then gives his liberator three wishes, King Lamoni granted to Ammon his fondest desire. "Ammon, being wise, yet harmless, simply said unto Lamoni: Wilt thou hearken unto my words?" (V. 22). The king agreed, "and thus he was caught with guile". (V. 23). "Guile" in this sense means "a stratagem," rather than "with deceitfulness or treachery". Lamoni was caught in the sense that after making a commitment to Ammon, he could not reject what was then taught him and still act in honesty. Ammon had used wisdom in his request. In granting it, Lamoni could not be harmed or risk injury.

Having established a foundation for basic teaching, Ammon probed the depth of understanding of the king, and then taught him, beginning at that level. (V. 24). He first testified of the reality of God. (V. 26-28). It was obvious to Ammon that Lamoni knew nothing outside the personal experience of his physical senses, so Ammon tenderly introduced the basic metaphysical concept of heaven. (V. 28-30).

In latter-day revelation, heaven is described as "worlds without end" or "eternal lives". (D&C 132:55). It is thus defined in the context of home and family. Those in heaven enjoy a continuation of the best qualities of family life. In the temple endowment and in temple marriage, we are taught the principles of obedience, sacrifice, consecration, and love, all within the framework of the family. The basic priesthood unit of the Church is the family, composed of a father, mother, and children, sealed by the power of the priesthood. It is a quorum that will endure in the eternities as a "forever family". Both husband and wife will preside together, as king and queen, priest, and priestess, to rule and reign in the house of God forever. The Gospel gives the children of God equal opportunity to preside over family kingdoms in the eternities. King Lamoni's innocent confession: "I do not know the heavens," was an invitation to this faithful missionary to explain the Plan of Salvation as it related to eternal family happiness. (V. 29). Their Gospel discussion could not have begun on a more promising note.

King Lamoni asked if heaven is above the earth. (V. 31). This question illustrates his childlike faith, and the answer was given in equal simplicity. Ammon explained: "Heaven is a place where God dwells and all his holy angels," and he then taught Limoni that God "looketh down upon all the children of men; and he knows all the thoughts and intents of the heart; for by his hand were they all created from the beginning". (V. 31-32, see Alma 12:14).

Now the eyes of his understanding were beginning to open, and Lamoni recognized Ammon as a true messenger from God. (V. 33). "I believe all these things which thou hast spoken," He declared.

"Art thou sent from God?". Ammon responded in simple language that was easy to understand, by establishing his authority to teach the Gospel. "I am a man," he said, "and man in the beginning was created after the image of God, and I am called by his Holy Spirit to teach these things unto this people, that they may be brought to a knowledge of that which is just and true. And a portion of that spirit dwelleth in me, which giveth me knowledge, and also power according to my faith and desires which are in God". (V. 34-35, see Alma 17:29).

Then Ammon gave an overview of the religious history of the earth from the Fall of Adam down to the time that Lehi left Jerusalem. "He began at the creation of the world, and also the creation of Adam, and told him all the things concerning the fall of man, and rehearsed and laid before him the records and the holy scriptures of the people, which had been spoken by the prophets, even down to the time that their father, Lehi, left Jerusalem". (V. 36, see Alma 17:7).

Then, using his thumb-worn personal copy of the scriptures, he "rehearsed unto them concerning the rebellions of Laman and Lemuel, and the sons of Ishmael" who were the forefathers of Lamoni. (V. 38). Rather than relating the history of the Lamanites in a negative way, he used their example to illustrate the universal need for a Savior and for redemption by Christ from the Fall. (V. 39).

How quickly can we learn to repent? It can happen as soon as we are willing to believe and to put away our sins with a determination to forsake them. (See Alma 22:18). For Lamoni's part, he "believed all his words, and he began to cry unto the Lord, saying: O Lord, have mercy upon me, and my people". (V. 40-41). When Lamoni said this, "he fell unto the earth, as if he were dead". (V. 42). The explanation for this unusual behavior is given in chapter 19, in verse 6.

Alma
Chapter 19

King Lamoni lay "as if he were dead" for two days and nights. (V. 1, see Alma 18:42). Finally, his queen asked Ammon to come to her court and administer to her husband. (V. 2-5). She was one whose faith would prove to be instrumental in establishing missionary work among the Lamanites in the Land of Nephi.

Because he had witnessed the similar circumstances of the conversion of his own friend Alma, Ammon "knew that king Lamoni was under the power of God; he knew that the dark veil of unbelief was being cast away from his mind, and the light which did light up his mind ... was the light of the glory of God ... and that the light of everlasting life was lit up in his soul, yea, he knew that this had overcome his natural frame, and he was carried away in God". (V. 6).

Ammon assured the queen that her husband was not dead, saying, "he sleepeth in God, and on the morrow he shall rise again". (V. 8). She declared: "I have had no witness save thy word, and the word of our servants; nevertheless, I believe that it shall be according as thou hast said". (V. 9). This was a remarkable exhibition of faith. Reflecting on this, Ammon declared: "There has not been such great faith among all the people of the Nephites". (V. 10).

The following morning, when Lamoni rose from his bed as Ammon had promised, he blessed the name of God, and declared to his wife with a solemn oath, "as sure as thou livest," that he had seen the Redeemer. At that, both he and the queen collapsed, "being overpowered by the Spirit". (V. 12-13). Ammon was so overcome with joy that he too sank down to the earth. (V. 14). When the servants of the king witnessed this, even they fell to the earth. (V. 16).

At this point in the record, we are introduced to a Lamanitish woman, whose name was Abish. She is one of only three women, and the only Lamanite woman, identified by name in The Book of Mormon. The others are Sariah (1 Nephi 2:5), and Isabel. (Alma 39:3). "Abish" is possibly the shortened form of "Abishmael," which in Hebrew means "My ancestral father was Ishmael". (See

Alma 17:19-21). This would certainly be an appropriate name for a Lamanite living in the Land of Ishmael. (See Commentary Reference to Alma 18:38).

Abish had been converted to the Lord many years earlier as a result of a vision. The record is unclear whether this vision was one she had of her father, or whether it was one had by her father. (V. 16). In any event, only at this moment did she publicly announce her conversion. When she saw the power of God working on the king and queen, their servants, and Ammon, she "ran forth from house to house, making it known unto the people". (V. 17).

Initially, when the people rushed to the palace, there was a mixed reaction to the sight that greeted their eyes. Some were angry with Ammon, for they immediately recognized that "he was a Nephite". (V. 18). That simple statement speaks volumes regarding the feelings of the assembled Lamanites, who harbored a passionate hatred of everything associated with their former brethren.

In fact, one Lamanite attempted to slay Ammon as he lay helpless on the ground. But as he lifted his sword, he fell dead. (V. 22). Once again, the Lord's promise to Mosiah was fulfilled that his sons would be delivered out of the hands of the Lamanites. "For the Lord had said unto Mosiah, his father: I will spare him, and it shall be unto him according to thy faith - therefore, Mosiah trusted him unto the Lord". (V. 23, see Mosiah 28:7).

The assembled multitude lost all ability to inflict any harm upon Ammon, and it was as it had been in the days of Enoch, when "no man laid hands on him; for fear came on all of them ... for he walked with God". (Moses 6:39). "And it came to pass that when the multitude beheld that the man had fallen dead, who lifted the sword to slay Ammon, fear came upon them all, and they durst not put forth their hands to touch him or any of those who had fallen; and they began to marvel again among themselves what could be the cause of this great power, or what all these things could mean". (V. 24). Some thought Ammon was "the Great Spirit, and others said he was sent by the Great Spirit". (V. 25).

The Adversary put it into the hearts of others that he was "a monster, who had been sent from the Nephites to torment them". (V. 26). One of Satan's subtle tactics is to portray that which is of God as if it were of the devil. Even the ministry of Christ Himself has been thus characterized. Among the Nephites in Zarahemla at the time of Samuel's ministry, the conventional wisdom confidently declared: "Behold, we know that this is a wicked tradition, which has been handed down unto us by our fathers, to cause us that we should believe in some great and marvelous thing which should come to pass, but not among us but in a land which is far distant, a land which we know not; therefore they can keep us in ignorance, for we cannot witness with our own eyes that they are true. And they will, by the cunning and the mysterious arts of the evil one, work some great mystery which we cannot understand, which will keep us down to be servants to their words, and also servants unto them, for we depend upon them to teach us the word; and thus will they keep us in ignorance if we will yield ourselves unto them, all the days of our lives. And many more things did the people imagine up in their hearts, which were foolish and vain; and they were much disturbed, for Satan did stir them up to do iniquity continually; yea, he did go about spreading rumors and contentions upon all the face of the land, that he might harden the hearts of the people against that which was good and against that which should come". (Helaman 16:20-22).

This technique can be very effective in blinding the eyes of the people. It is a strategy that is even today employed by Satan to great effect. When Satan gets "great hold upon the hearts of the people upon all the face of the land," the fate of nations hangs in the balance. (Helaman 16:23).

Therefore, moved by the Spirit, Abish sought to quickly put an end to the contention among her people that "began to be exceedingly sharp". (V. 28). When she reached down and touched the queen's hand she "arose and stood upon her feet". In a very special way, she had been taught the true nature of God and of the Savior. She "cried with a loud voice, saying: O blessed Jesus, who has saved me from an awful hell! O blessed God, have mercy on this people!" (V. 29, see John 17:3). Her reaction was essentially the same as had been her husband's. She first expressed thanks to God for His mercy on her own behalf, and then sought to extend the influence of the Atonement to others.

She spoke in tongues, "and when she had done this, she took the king, Lamoni, by the hand, and behold he arose and stood upon his feet". (V. 30). After rebuking the people for their contention, he began to teach them the principles of the Gospel, as he had been taught them by Ammon. However, many "would not hear his words; therefore, they went their way". (V. 32). But others stayed, and Ammon arose and ministered to them.

For those who had invited the Spirit to attend them, the experience was Pentecostal. Many saw angels and conversed with them. (V. 34). The hearts of the people "had been changed, that they had no more desire to do evil". (V. 33, see Mosiah 5:2). This is one of the clearest explanations of conversion found in the scriptures, and it is all the more remarkable for having occurred among Lamanites.

Joseph Smith taught: "The nearer a man approaches perfection, the clearer are his views, and the greater his enjoyments, 'til he has overcome the evils of his life and lost every desire for sin". ("Teachings," p. 51). As they walked into the light, the scales of darkness fell from the eyes of the Lamanites who had embraced the Gospel message. They and their descendants would prove to be among the most devoutly faithful of the children of God.

Those who believed requested baptism, "and they became a righteous people, and they did establish a Church". (V. 35, see 2 Nephi 9:23-24, & Commentary Reference to Alma 16:13). The chapter ends with another insightful editorial comment from Mormon: "And thus, the work of the Lord did commence among the Lamanites; thus, the Lord did begin to pour out his Spirit upon them; and we see that his arm is extended to all people who will repent and believe on his name". (V. 36, see 2 Nephi 15:25). All are invited "to come unto him and partake of his goodness; and he denieth none that come unto him, black and white, bond and free, male and female; and he remembereth the heathen; and all are alike unto God, both Jew and Gentile," Nephite and Lamanite, member, and non-member. (2 Nephi 26:33). Later, in his missionary report, Ammon would reflect on the conversion of these Lamanites by reminding his brethren: "We see that God is mindful of every people, whatsoever land they may be in; yea, he numbereth his people, and his bowels of mercy are over all the earth". (Alma 26:37). Joseph Fielding Smith, Jr. pointed out to the Latter-day Saints: "Every soul coming into this world came here with the promise that through obedience he would receive the blessings of salvation. No person was foreordained to sin or to perform a mission of evil". ("Doctrines of Salvation," 1:61).

Alma
Chapter 20

With the Church established in the Land of Ishmael, King Lamoni wanted to take Ammon to meet his father, who was king over all the Land of Nephi. The Lord warned Ammon, however, not to go, for He knew that, in his ignorance, the king would exercise all the power at his command in his own court and kingdom to take the life of the Nephite missionary.

Instead, Ammon was commanded by the word of the Lord to go to the Land of Middoni, where his brother Aaron, and also Muloki and Ammah, the only two missionary companions of the Sons of Mosiah who are mentioned by name in The Book of Mormon, were being held in prison. (V. 1-2). The Lord knew that, even with this detour, Lamoni's desire that his father experience Ammon's righteous influence would yet be realized.

The vassal king in the Land of Middoni was a friend of Lamoni named Antiomno. Therefore, when Lamoni learned that Ammon was about to journey there, he volunteered to accompany him, and immediately made ready his horses and chariots. (V. 3-6).

It was fortunate that Lamoni went with Ammon, for the travelers unexpectedly encountered Lamoni's father on the highway. (V. 8). His reaction to Ammon was as the Lord had said it would be, and was typical of the Lamanites. "Whither art thou going with this Nephite," he asked, "who is one of the children of a liar?" (V. 10, see Commentary References to Mosiah 10:12-17, & Alma 19:18). Forget any pretense of civility between the Nephites and Lamanites. Good manners had long since been abandoned, being replaced by the knee-jerk reactions of rudeness, suspicion, and overt hostility.

Even after Lamoni had recounted the details of his conversion after Ammon's arrival in the Land of Ishmael, "to his astonishment, his father was (still) angry with him". He expressed the standard mechanically delivered Lamanite line: "Behold, (Nephi) robbed our fathers" Laman and Lemuel by taking the Plates of Brass, and by literally and figuratively taking the other emblems of authority that bestowed legitimacy on their claim to rule over the children of Lehi. (V.

13, see Mosiah 10:15-16). Lamoni was summarily commanded to slay Ammon. Were Ammon to have encountered the old king in his own stronghold, supported by his retainers, things might have turned out very differently, for Lamoni might have been intimidated and unable to resist the ruthless authority of his father.

When Lamoni refused to harm Ammon, his father turned on his own son. When Ammon intervened, the old Lamanite warrior sought to smite him, also! (V. 15-20). "But Ammon withstood his blows, and also smote his arm, that he could not use it". (V. 20). The king, "fearing that he should lose his life," cried out, "If thou wilt spare me, I will grant unto thee whatsoever thou wilt ask". (V. 23). Like father, like son. (See Alma 28:21).

Ammon requested the king to release his brethren from prison in the Land of Middoni, and to grant Lamoni autonomy in the affairs of state in the Land of Ishmael. The king not only agreed to do so, but being "greatly astonished at the words which he had spoken, and also at the words which had been spoken by his son Lamoni, therefore he was desirous to learn them". (V. 26-27). Having had some sense literally knocked into him, and with a great change of heart, he actually invited Ammon and his brethren to visit him in the Land of Nephi while he nursed his sore arm back to health.

Eagerly anticipating the chance to follow up on this invitation, Lamoni and Ammon continued on their way to the Land of Middoni. Through his connections with the king of that land, Lamoni secured the release of Ammon's brethren. (V. 28). It was none too soon, for "they were naked, and their skins were worn exceedingly because of being bound with strong cords. And they also had suffered hunger, thirst, and all kinds of afflictions; nevertheless, they were patient in all their sufferings". (V. 29).

They were in a sorry physical state because, after the missionaries had separated upon their arrival in the Land of Nephi, "it was their lot to have fallen into the hands of a more hardened and a more stiffnecked people (who) would not hearken unto their words". (V. 30). These were the Amulonites and Amalekites, apostates who always made things difficult for the Nephites. (See Alma 21:2).

The missionaries "had been driven from house to house and from place to place, even until they had arrived in the land of Middoni". (Alma 20:30). There, they had been imprisoned for many days. But their adversities had been as diamond dust that polished them to greater luster. Their persecution proved to be effective missionary training that had strengthened and prepared them for dramatic accomplishments yet to come among the Lamanite people.

Carol Lynn Pearson wrote an insightful poem entitled "Short Roots," with a message that relates to the challenges faced by the Sons of Mosiah in the Land of Nephi: "The tree at the Church next door to me turned up its roots and died. They had tried to brace its leaning, but it lowered and lowered, and then there it lay leaves in grass and matted roots in air, like a loafer on a summer day. "Look there," said the gardener. "Short roots - all the growth went up. Big branches - short roots". "How come?" I asked. "Too much water. This tree never had to hunt for drink". Especially in thirsty times, my memory steps outside and looks at the tree at the Church next door to me that turned up its roots and died".

One reason that Aaron and
his missionary companions encountered
immediate obstacles to the work in Jerusalem
was that this land was inhabited by Amalekites and
Amulonites who were more wicked than the Lamanites
among whom Ammon labored. (V. 2). "Now the
Lamanites of themselves were sufficiently
hardened, but the Amalekites and the
Amulonites were still harder".
(Alma 20:3).

Alma
Chapter 21

Following the initial separation of the group of missionaries from Zarahemla, Aaron had gone to "the land that was called by the Lamanites, Jerusalem". (V. 1, see Commentary Reference to Alma 7:10). Ever since Laman and Lemuel had left Jerusalem nearly 600 years earlier, their descendants had longed for the temporal security that they had left behind, as they supposed. As did the Nephites, the Lamanites felt that they were "a lonesome and a solemn people, wanderers, cast out from Jerusalem, born in tribulation, in a wilderness". (Jacob 7:26). But those of the Lamanite persuasion were always ready to "murmur in many things against (Father Lehi), because (they felt that he had been) a visionary man, and had led them out of the land of Jerusalem, to leave the land of their inheritance, and their gold, and their silver, and their precious things, to perish in the wilderness. And this they said he had done because of the foolish imaginations of his heart". (1 Nephi 2:11).

One reason Aaron and his companions encountered immediate obstacles to the work in Jerusalem was that this land was inhabited by Amalekites and Amulonites who were more wicked than the Lamanites among whom Ammon labored. (V. 2). "Now the Lamanites of themselves were sufficiently hardened, but the Amalekites and the Amulonites were still harder". (V. 3).

The Amalekites were of the Order of Nehors. (See v. 4, & Alma 24:18). They were a sect of Nephite apostates of unclear origin. In the Lamanite armies, the commanders were in the habit of placing Amalekites in positions of authority, because of their aggressiveness, their intense hatred of their former brethren, and also because of their more wicked and murderous dispositions. (See Alma 43:6). This is the first reference to them by name in The Book of Mormon. The Amalekites were like the SS (the Schutzstaffel) of Nazi Germany, the black-uniformed elite corps of fanatical political soldiers who became virtually a state within a state.

The people of Amulon were descendants of Amulon and his associate wicked priests of King Noah. They were Nephites on their fathers' side and Lamanites on their mothers' side, but by education and association they were of the latter persuasion. (See Mosiah 23:30 & 39, & Mosiah 24:1-5).

So hardened in their hearts were these two groups that none of the Amulonites and only one Amalekite repented after receiving the Gospel message preached by the Sons of Mosiah. (V. 3, see Alma 23:14). The rest exerted an extremely negative influence on the other Lamanites in the city of Jerusalem. (V. 3).

It was this city and these people that Aaron had the misfortune to visit first. (V. 4). He initially preached to them "in their synagogues". Since the people had not been baptized, their places of assembly were not called "Churches". (See Commentary Reference to Alma 16:13, also V. 15, & 20).

As Aaron was preaching, one of the Amalekites or Amulonites who was of the Order of Nehors arose to contend with him, using the same arguments that even today are heard by the missionaries. He justified the righteousness of his people by pointing out that they had built sanctuaries in which to worship God. He declared that God would save all men, by grace, regardless of their works. Finally, he denied that the Savior would come to redeem mankind from its sins, calling that doctrine a "foolish tradition". (V. 5-9).

This individual fell into the same snare that Satan would set for the wicked inhabitants of the City of Zarahemla almost a hundred years later. In response to Nephi's teaching of the anticipated mortal ministry of the Savior, they responded: "Behold, we know that this is a wicked tradition, which has been handed down unto us by our fathers, to cause us that we should believe in some great and marvelous things which should come to pass, but not among us, but in a land which is far distant, a land which we know not; therefore they can keep us in ignorance, for we cannot witness with our own eyes that they are true". (Helaman 16:20). Neither can the unbelieving of the Last Days witness with their own eyes that the ministry of the Savior 2,000 years ago was a glad reality. Some things have to be believed to be seen.

Nevertheless, Aaron "open(ed) the scriptures unto them concerning the coming of Christ," in much the same way that Christ taught His fellow travelers on the Road to Emmaus. "And beginning at Moses and all the prophets," the Savior had "expounded unto them in all the scriptures the things concerning himself". But whereas those disciples in Judea could afterward reflect: "Did not our hearts burn within us, while he talked with us by the way, and while he opened to us the scriptures?" (Luke 24:27 & 32), the people of the City of Jerusalem in the Land of Nephi became "angry with (Aaron), and began to mock him, and would not hear the words which he spake". (V. 10). These people were deaf to the message of the Gospel. Similar resistance to the truth by those who were of the Order of Nehor had also hardened the hearts of the people of Ammonihah, resulting in the Desolation of Nehors. (See Alma 16:11). When people close their minds and hearts to the truth, surely they are left desolate, which renders them wretched, and made joyless and comfortless.

Aaron saw that further missionary efforts among this people would be fruitless, so he departed from the city of Jerusalem, and went to Ani-Anti. There he found Muloki and Ammah and his brethren, who were not having any greater success than he'd had. Therefore, the party left Ani-Anti and went to the Land of Middoni. (V. 12).

In Middoni, "Aaron and a certain number of his brethren were taken and cast into prison," while the remainder fled from the land. It was there that Ammon and Lamoni later rescued them. After their liberation, they preached "the word of God in every synagogue of the Amalekites, or in every assembly of the Lamanites where they could be admitted". (V. 13-16, see Alma 16:13).

Ammon and Lamoni returned to the Land of Ishmael, where synagogues were established to preach the word of God. (V. 18-20). One of the purposes of government is to allow religious worship, and so Lamoni declared that his subjects should be free, "that they might have the liberty of worshipping the Lord their God according to their desires, in whatsoever place they were in". (V. 18-22, see the 11th Article of Faith).

Ammon continued on a daily basis to preach, teach, expound, and exhort the people to be obedient, and thus "they gave heed unto his word, and they were zealous for keeping the commandments of God". (V. 23, see D&C 20:46). In a similar fashion in the Church today, we study the scriptures, have personal and family prayer, attend seminary daily and our Church meetings weekly, provide service to our less fortunate brethren, and strive to keep the commandments while enduring to the end of our lives in righteousness. Only be maintaining a hope in Christ and by relying on His Atonement throughout our lives can we hope for a glorious resurrection in the Celestial kingdom.

It is not enough to believe in Christ, in an abstract and impersonal sense; we must believe Christ, when He says that He has the power to save. "The keeper of the gate is the Holy One of Israel; and he employeth no servant there" precisely because He is our Advocate with the Father and because, as the Redeemer of Israel, He pleads our case at the Bar of Judgment. Therefore, it will be Jesus Christ who will be there to welcome us with open arms as we approach the Celestial Kingdom of God. (See 2 Nephi 9:41).

"Now Aaron began to open
the scriptures unto them concerning
the coming of Christ, and also concerning
the resurrection of the dead, and that there could
be no redemption for mankind, save it were through
the death and sufferings of Christ, and the
atonement of his blood."
(Alma 21:8).

Alma
Chapter 22

Meanwhile, Aaron had the opportunity to go to the Land of Nephi, being led by the Spirit to the home of the father of Lamoni. (V. 12). The old king requested Aaron to "administer unto (him)". In other words, he wanted Aaron to apply the Balm of Gilead to his troubled soul, and to teach him about the Gospel.

This Aaron did, testifying of the reality of God with a solemn oath. (V. 8). The king said that he would believe all the words of Aaron, who consequently must have felt a great burden of responsibility. (V. 2). Therefore, he turned to his scriptures for the substance of his message, teaching all the basic Gospel doctrines, "how God created man after his own image, and that God gave him commandments, and that because of transgression, man had fallen. And Aaron did expound unto him the scriptures from the creation of Adam, laying the fall of man before him, and their carnal state and also the Plan of redemption, which was prepared from the foundation of the world, through Christ, for all whosoever would believe on his name. And since man had fallen he could not merit anything of himself; but the sufferings and death of Christ atone for their sins, through faith and repentance, and so forth; and that he breaketh the bands of death, that the grave shall have no victory, and that the sting of death should be swallowed up in the hopes of glory; and Aaron did expound all these things unto the king". (V. 12-14).

When the king expressed his desire to "be born of God," Aaron explained to him the first principles and ordinances of the Gospel. "If thou wilt repent of all thy sins," he was told, "and will bow down before God, and call on his name in faith, believing that ye shall receive, then shall thou receive the hope which thou desirest". (V. 15-16, see Mosiah 5:7, & Alma 19:35). God has planted in our hearts an instinctive desire to worship. The issue, then, is not whether or not we shall worship, but rather who or what and how we shall worship.

The king expressed the prayer of his heart, when he exclaimed to God: "I will give away all my sins to know thee". (V. 18,, see Alma 42:27). All the theology of the Gospel can be boiled down to making the journey to Christ, and being filled with His love, casting off our natural inclinations, and conducting ourselves in a Christ-like way.

Then, an event occurred that was similar to that which had taken place in the court of King Lamoni. (V. 18-22, see Alma Chapter 18-19). The old king lost his strength, and fell to the earth as if he were dead. After Aaron restored him, "the whole household (was) converted unto the Lord". (V. 23)

Then, Mormon related how a proclamation was sent out by the king "throughout all the land, amongst all his people who were in all his land, who were in all the regions round about, which was bordering even to the sea, on the east and on the west, and which was divided from the land of Zarahemla by a narrow strip of wilderness, which ran from the sea east even to the sea west, and round about on the borders of the seashore, and the borders of the wilderness which was on the north by the land of Zarahemla, through the borders of Manti, by the head of the river Sidon, running from the east towards the west - and thus were the Lamanites and the Nephites divided". (V. 27).

The Book of Mormon is not a cartographic primer written to teach geography. Such references are usually incidental remarks connected with historical elements of the work. (See Commentary Reference to Alma 46:40). Nevertheless, verses 27 thru 34 is a digression by Mormon into the geography of the land, for verse 35 reads: "And now I, Mormon, after having said this, return again to the account of Ammon and Aaron, Omner and Himni, and their brethren".

There is nothing wrong in attempting to establish a correlation between New World geography and Book of Mormon detail. Such is done routinely in the lands of the Bible. Latter-day Saints and countless other Christian pilgrims have traveled to the Near East, where the faithful visit biblical sites with tourist guidebooks in one hand, and Old and New Testaments in the other. Such excursions are faith promoting and generate excitement in the hearts of Church members, who find biblical scholarship enhanced by the correlation of the scriptures with identifiable Old-World landmarks.

Recent research also credibly establishes The Book of Mormon in its New World setting. With the work of Dr. John Sorensen of the B.Y.U. Department of Archaeology, "the process of spelling out an explicit geographical and archeological context has begun in earnest. He presents a credible model for an ancient American background for The Book of Mormon. This model takes notice of details given in descriptions of The Book of Mormon lands, of battle movements, of cities built and abandoned, and of demographic data. He suggests that highland Guatemala is a good candidate for the land of Nephi, that the Isthmus of Tehuantepec fits the requirements of the 'narrow neck of land,' and that hundreds of other facts fall into place as this theory is carried to its logical conclusions. "An Ancient American Setting for The Book of Mormon," for the first time, writes Nephite cultural and natural history in the context of American hemispheric reality.

While there may always be resistance and controversy surrounding The Book of Mormon, here is a solid invitation to continuing research and comprehension". (Leonard J. Arrington, Truman G. Madsen, John W. Welch, Foreword to John Sorenson's "An Ancient American Setting for The Book of Mormon").

Mormon continued his parenthetical digression by describing how "the more idle part of the Lamanites lived in the wilderness in the borders by the seashore". (V. 28). They were on both the east and west coasts, "and thus the Nephites were nearly surrounded by the Lamanites". (V. 29). Consequently, the Nephites were always vulnerable to Lamanite attack. (See V. 33).

In addition to Zarahemla, the Nephites occupied the Land Bountiful, which was to the north, and which "bordered upon the land which they called Desolation". (V. 29-30). Desolation was not far from the Hill Cumorah / Ramah, and "was discovered by the people of Zarahemla" or the so-called Mulekites, "it being the place of their first landing". (V. 30). "Now the land south was called Lehi, and the land north was called Mulek, which was after the son of Zedekiah; for the Lord did bring Mulek into the land north, and Lehi into the land south". (Helaman 6:10).

Mormon continued, stating that the People of Zarahemla had come from their landing point in the north, "up into the south wilderness" until they reached Zarahemla, where they settled. "Thus, the land on the northward was called Desolation, and the land on the southward was called Bountiful" because there was abundant vegetation and there were animals of every kind living there. (V. 31, see Alma 27:5).

In The Book of Ether, we learn that the Jaredites settled only the land north of the narrow neck of land, and that they were prevented from migrating southward because of an abundance of poisonous serpents infesting the isthmus. Only after many generations were these reptiles eliminated, whereupon the Jaredites went forth "into the land southward, to hunt food for the people of the land," who must have by this time become quite numerous, "for the land was covered with animals of the forest". (Ether 10:19). Because of the abundance of game there, this land was maintained by the Jaredites as a hunting reserve, in the best Asiatic tradition. "And they did preserve the land southward for a wilderness, to get game. And the whole face of the land northward was covered with inhabitants". (Ether 10:21).

This would explain why there were no traces of former civilizations in the Land Southward when the People of Zarahemla established their colony there or when the Nephites immigrants arrived. It would also explain why the Nephites found "animals of every kind living there" in great abundance. (V. 31).

The prophet Ezekiel, in the Old Testament, spoke of the forefathers of the people of Zarahemla: "Thus said the Lord God, I will also take of the highest branch of the high cedar, and will set it. I will crop off from the top of his young twigs a tender one, and will plant it upon an high mountain". (Ezekiel 17:22). Ezekiel meant that a child of Zedekiah, the king, was to be cropped from the family tree and planted in another land.

"Muleq" is Hebrew, and means "to break off," or "to nip off". Although "Muleq" or "Mulek" is not mentioned in the Bible as a son of King Zedekiah, it is logical that the faithful followers of Prince Mulek would have been reminded at every mention of his name that he was both their king and the plucked off twig of Ezekiel's prophecy. Mulek would thus remain a symbol of prophecy fulfilled in the grim fall of Jerusalem, as well as a symbol of the prophecy of promise in the transplanting of Judah's ruling house to another land.

Mormon's digression provides further insight into Book of Mormon geography. He stated: "It was only the distance of a day and a half's journey for a Nephite, on the line Bountiful and the land Desolation, from the east to the west sea". (V. 32). Evidently, there was a Nephite line of fortification running between the two lands, and from sea to sea. This verse might mean that it was some distance between these two seas, but that it took the Nephites, who were swift runners, only a day and a half to travel the distance. In The Book of Helaman we read that the Nephites "did fortify against the Lamanites, from the west sea, even unto the east; it being a day's journey for a Nephite, on the line which they had fortified and stationed their armies to defend their north country". (Helaman 4:7).

"Thus, the land of Nephi and the land of Zarahemla were nearly surrounded by water, there being a small neck of land between the land northward and the land southward". (V. 32). However, since Limhi's explorers had passed through the narrow neck without knowing they had done so, it must have been of substantial width. (See Mosiah 8:7-8, & 21:25-26). When the record says that it was a day and a half's journey "for a Nephite," we can infer that it was a significant test of endurance to cover the distance in only 36 hours.

Because the Nephites had occupied the Land Bountiful "even from the east unto the west sea," they had effectively "hemmed in the Lamanites on the south" so that they might not continue to spill over from the Land of Nephi northward into territories already settled by the Nephites. (V. 33). "Therefore, the Lamanites could have no more possessions only in the land of Nephi, and in the wilderness round about". (V. 34). As the Lamanite population swelled, pressure on the Nephites to yield land to them north of the line of fortification increased. At this, Mormon "return(ed) again to the account of Ammon, and Aaron, Omner and Himni, and their brethren". (V. 35).

Alma
Chapter 23

In chapters 23-24 is recorded a dramatic account of the power of the Gospel of Jesus Christ to change almost a whole nation from a blood-thirsty, indolent, warlike people into an industrious, peace-loving society. The king of all the Lamanites had proclaimed a policy of religious toleration toward the four Sons of Mosiah and their missionary companions. (V. 1, see Alma 22:27). Consequently, they were able to go into the synagogues, temples, and sanctuaries of the people and "preach the word according to their desires". (V. 2-3).

Without the protection of the king, the missionaries could have expected to have had hands laid on them "to bind them, or to cast them into prison". They likely would have been spit upon, smitten, cast out of the places of assembly, scourged, and stoned. (V. 2). So, it was very fortunate that "the king had been converted unto the Lord, and all his household". (V. 3). He had experienced a mighty change of heart. (See Alma 20:10-13). Whereas before his conversion he had believed in "the wicked traditions of (his) fathers," he was now taught "to believe in the traditions of the Nephites". (V. 3, & 5). Formerly, his people had freely committed murder, plundered, stolen, and engaged in adultery and all manner of wickedness. (V. 3). Now, the whole culture "became a righteous people; they did lay down the weapons of their rebellion," both literally and figuratively, "that they did not fight against God anymore, neither against any of their brethren". (V. 7).

In their missionary work, the Sons of Mosiah went from city to city, "establishing churches and consecrating priests and teachers throughout the land among the Lamanites, to preach and to teach the word of God among them". (V. 4, see Commentary Reference to Alma 16:13). The Sons of Mosiah equaled the success of Jonah in Nineveh, and "thousands were brought to the knowledge of the Lord". (V. 5, see Mosiah 28:7, & Jonah 3). As a true measure of the success of their mission, "as many of the Lamanites as believed in their preaching, and were converted unto the Lord, never did fall away". (V. 6). Their hearts had been changed, and they had no more desire to do evil. (See Mosiah 5:2, Alma 19:33, & 24:6).

After Mormon identified those who had been converted, he wrote: "And these are they that laid down the weapons of their rebellion, yea, all their weapons of war; and they were all Lamanites". (V. 13, see V. 8-12). In other words, "Isn't it truly remarkable, that of all people, Lamanites would do such a thing?" (See V. 26-33).

Unfortunately, only one Amalekite was converted, and none of the Amulonites. (V. 14, see Alma 24:1). But those who had been "born again" desired even to have a new name, "that thereby they might be distinguished from their brethren". (V. 16). Every day in the Church in the Last Days, converts do as the Ammonites of old. (See Alma 27:16). They leave behind their former lives, change their names, and become Saints, promising never again to return to their wicked ways.

"And it came to pass that they called their names Anti-Nephi-Lehies; and they were called by this name and were no more called Lamanites". (V. 17, see Alma 24:3). At this time, there were now three distinct cultural groups of people that we know of living in the lands of The Book of Mormon: Nephites, Lamanites, and converted Lamanites.

There are two possible meanings of the name "Anti-Nephi-Lehi". A Semitic root of "anti" is "one who imitates". Therefore, "Anti-Nephi-Lehi" could be one who imitates the teachings of the descendants of Lehi and Nephi. ("Companion To the Book of Mormon," p. 210-211). It could also mean, in a Western sense, "those who opposed the unconverted Lamanites in the Land of Nephi-Lehi. Later in the record, these people became known as "The People of Ammon". (See Alma 27:16).

The "Anti-Nephi-Lehies" embraced the cultural traditions and lifestyle of the Nephite missionaries, and opened "a correspondence with them". (V. 18). As the scales of darkness began to fall from their eyes, they became a pure and delightsome people. (See 2 Nephi 30:6). This remarkable transformation was accomplished in a very short time due to the influence and power of the Gospel of Jesus Christ. Given the chance, it would do the same thing today for all the peoples of the earth, for it is the power of God unto spiritual and temporal salvation. (See Romans 1:16).

Alma
Chapter 24

Now, the father of King Lamoni experienced the same problem that Alma had faced in the Land of Zarahemla when Amlici had stirred up the people against the legitimate government, and much blood had been shed as a result. Here in the Land of Nephi, the Amalekites and Amulonites stirred up the Lamanites who had not been converted "to anger against their brethren". (V. 1).

In the face of this challenge, the strength of the old king failed him, and so he conferred the kingdom upon his son, who was likely the eldest brother of Lamoni. This righteous man took upon himself the name "Anti-Nephi-Lehi". (V. 3). One of his first official acts was to hold a council, that he might reach a decision regarding an appropriate response to the threat of the rebellious Lamanites. (V. 5).

"Now there was not one soul among all the people who had been converted unto the Lord that would take up arms against their brethren, nay, they would not even make any preparations for war; yea, and also their king commanded them that they should not". (V. 6). This is the only instance in the entire Book of Mormon in which Church members refused to defend themselves when threatened with attack. Mormon explained in verses 10-13 why they took this unprecedented position.

Anti-Nephi-Lehi thanked God that He had sent the Nephite missionaries to them, to reveal the truth regarding "the traditions of (their) wicked fathers". (V. 7). He also thanked God that the hearts of his people had been softened to receive the Gospel message and that his people had sufficient faith to recognize their sins. (V. 8-9). Then he expressed his gratitude that they had been given the opportunity to repent and to receive forgiveness even for the murders that they had committed. (V. 10). Clearly, the power of the Atonement, which is infinite and eternal, may, in special circumstances, pay the penalty for murder.

But Anti-Nephi-Lehi warned his people: "Let us stain our swords no more with the blood of our brethren". (V. 12). The quality of their sins and the difficulty with which they had repented helps to explain why these people would never again take up arms. "For perhaps," reasoned Anti-Nephi-Lehi, "if we should stain our swords again they can no more be washed bright through the blood of the Son of our great God, which shall be shed for the atonement of our sins". (V. 13).

He suggested to his people: "Since it has been as much as we could do to get our stains taken away from us, and our swords are made bright, let us hide them away that they may be kept bright, as a testimony to our God at the last day, or at the day that we shall be brought to stand before him to be judged, that we have not stained our swords in the blood of our brethren since he imparted his word unto us and has made us clean thereby". (V. 15).

It was only the special circumstances of the People of Anti-Nephi-Lehi that warranted such pacifism. Mormon, who was himself a wartime commander, recorded that the Nephites typically fought with all the energy at their command, for they "were inspired by a better cause, for they were not fighting for monarchy nor power, but they were fighting for their homes and their liberties, their wives and their children, and their all, yea, for their rites of worship and their Church". (Alma 43:46).

Although freedom of individual action and defense of agency are eternal rights, and are behaviors that we see manifest from the dawn of pre-mortal existence, it was with a dramatic demonstration of faith that Anti-Nephi-Lehi urged his people to be obedient to a more compelling covenant on a higher spiritual plane. We shall "hide away our swords," he proposed. "Yea, even we will bury them deep in the earth, that they may be kept bright, as a testimony that we have never used them, at the last day; and if our brethren destroy us, behold, we shall go to our God and shall be saved". (V. 16). The people went and buried their weapons in the earth, as their righteous king Anti-Nephi-Lehi had asked them to do. (V. 17). Perhaps this is a source of the "bury the hatchet" tradition of the so-called American Indians.

They accomplished this as a testimony and covenant with God, "that rather than shed the blood of their brethren, they would give up their own lives and rather than take away from a brother they would give unto him; and rather than spend their days in idleness they would labor abundantly with their hands". (V. 18). God selects His disciples while they are busy serving their brethren, while Satan selects his when they are idle and dreaming up mischief.

In verse 19, Mormon editorially commented on the conversion of the Lamanites in the Land of Nephi: "And thus we see that, when these Lamanites were brought to believe and to know the truth, they were firm and would suffer even unto death rather than commit sin; and thus, we see that they buried their weapons of peace, or they buried the weapons of war, for peace". (See Alma 24:19, & 28:13-14, & 30:60). This is a quality of the truly committed that could be generally applied to life's experiences.

Verse 19 also provides a good illustration of the difficulty encountered by the prophets when engraving upon metal plates. In this verse, Mormon realized that he had not written exactly what he had intended. Therefore, he added clarification: "And thus we see that they buried their weapons of peace, or they buried their weapons of war, for peace". (See Commentary Reference to Alma 25:14). Numerous other examples of clarifications in the text of The Book of Mormon can be found. (See Mosiah 4:24, 7:1, 7:8, 15:22, Alma 1:15, 2:34, 4:19, 10:5, 11:46, 17:18, 23:6, 25:14, 30:9, 35:25, 36:14, 41:11, 43:38, 50:32, 53:3, 53:10, 56:14, Helaman 1:4, 2:13-14, 3:33, 10:17, 14:21, 14:31, 3 Nephi 2:8, 9:1, 16:4, Commentary Reference to Jacob 4:1, & Essay: "Writing on Plates Was a Pain").

The expected threat materialized when a Lamanite army arrived in the borders of the land. "Now when the people saw that they were coming against them, they went out to meet them, and prostrated themselves before them to the earth, and began to call on the name of the Lord; and thus, they were in this attitude when the Lamanites began to fall upon them, and began to slay them with the sword". (V. 21).

Only after a thousand perished did the Lamanites "forebear from slaying them," and there were many who "repented of the things which they had done". (V. 24). Significantly, more than a thousand converts were added to the Fold as a result. (V. 26). "Thus, we see that the Lord worketh in many ways to the salvation of his people". (V. 27). Sometimes, even warfare and other satanic acts work to the benefit of God's purposes.

The most vicious of the Lamanite aggressors had been Amalekites and Amulonites, who were apostate Nephites of the Order of Nehors. (V. 28). None of these were among those who repented or were converted. Mormon emphasized that only those who were descendants of Laman and Lemuel did so. (V. 29). His editorial comment in verse 30 that relates to the hard hearts of he Amalekites and Amulonites is sobering: "And thus we can plainly discern, that after a people have been once enlightened by the Spirit of God, and have had great knowledge of things pertaining to righteousness, and then have fallen away unto sin and transgression, they become more hardened, and thus their state becomes worse than though they had never known these things". (See Commentary Reference to Mosiah 2:37).

"Before you joined this Church you stood on neutral ground," cautioned Joseph Fielding Smith, Jr. "When the Gospel was preached, good and evil were set before you. You could choose either or neither. There were two opposite masters inviting you to serve them. You left the neutral ground, and you can never get back on to it. Should you forsake the Master you enlisted to serve, it will be by the instigation of the evil one, and you will follow his dictation and be his servant". (C.E.S. Manual, p. 258).

"Now there was not one soul among all the people who ha been converted unto the Lord that would take up arms against their brethren; nay, they would not even make any preparations for war."
(Alma 24:6).

Alma
Chapter 25

In contrast to the Lamanites, who had repented of the evil they had done to the people of Anti-Nephi-Lehi, the Amalekites and Amulonites were angrier after they had slain their former brethren. "Therefore, they swore vengeance upon the Nephites". (V. 1). Instead of feeling remorseful for having committed cold-blooded murder, they focused their unabated anger on the Nephites, whom they held responsible for having created divisions along religious lines in the Lamanite nation.

Consequently, these most aggressive, militant, and hardened descendants of Nephite apostates "took their armies and went over into the borders of the land of Zarahemla, and fell upon the people who were in the land of Ammonihah and destroyed them". (V. 2, see Alma 16:9). Ironically, the wicked Nephites of Ammonihah, who had rejected Alma and Amulek, were slain by these fellow apostates living in the Land of Nephi, who had earlier rejected the Gospel message of the Sons of Mosiah. "The wicked shall slay the wicked," declared the Lord. (D&C 63:33). And so, it was.

Afterward, these "cultural Lamanites" had many battles with the Nephites during which "almost all of the seed of Amulon and his brethren, who had been the priests of Noah, were slain by the hands of the Nephites". (V. 3-4). As Abinadi had told their forefathers a generation earlier, "Thus, God executeth vengeance upon those that destroy his people". (Mosiah 17:18, see V. 9-12).

Those few Amulonites who were left fled into the east wilderness bordering the Land of Zarahemla. (V. 5). Unable to shed their murderous dispositions and blinded by their hatred, they put to death all the Lamanites who "began to be stirred up in remembrance of the words which Aaron and his brethren had preached to them in their land". (V. 6-7). It was this atrocity that finally caused the Lamanite population to reject the leadership of the Amulonites. Alma wrote: "Now this martyrdom caused that many of their brethren should be stirred up to anger; and there began to be contention in the wilderness; and the Lamanites began to hunt the seed of Amulon and his brethren and began to slay them; and they fled into the east wilderness. And behold they are hunted at this day by the Lamanites". (V. 8-9).

Many of those who had worked to overthrow the wicked rule of the Amulonites "came over to dwell in the land of Ishmael and the land of Nephi, and did join themselves to the people of God, who were the people of Anti-Nephi-Lehi. (V. 13). Binding themselves to the same covenant, and as a testament to their faith, they also "buried their weapons of war". (V. 14, see Alma 24:19 & 26:32). (Note that Mormon does not again make the textual error committed in Alma 24:19).

Just as the people of Nephi and Jacob had done hundreds of years earlier, these converts kept the Law of Moses while looking forward to the mortal ministry of Christ. (V. 15). They recognized the Law as "a type of his coming," that served to "strengthen their faith in Christ; and thus, they did retain a hope through faith, unto eternal salvation, relying upon the spirit of prophecy, which spake of those things to come". (V. 15-16). A type, then, orients our faith toward a future reality, and has symbolic significance as well as literal meaning. Therefore, by honoring the Law, these Israelites could honor Christ as well. They could keep the exacting statutes associated with the Preparatory Law, and at the same time listen to the teachings of their inspired prophets who expanded upon the principles of the Gospel of Jesus Christ.

Ammon, Aaron, Omner, and Himni and their brethren were overjoyed to witness that God had "verified his word unto them in every particular". (V. 17). For the Lord had "said unto Mosiah: Let them go up, for many shall believe on their words ... and I will deliver thy sons out of the hands of the Lamanites". (Mosiah 28:7). Mormon must have been delighted to include this account in his abridgment, for it powerfully illustrates that God always keeps His promises.

Alma
Chapter 26

This chapter recounts the message delivered by Ammon to his companions at a missionary conference in the Land of Nephi. His enthusiasm for the work is validated by the message of the Savior, that states: "If it be so that you should labor all your days in crying repentance unto this people, and bring, save it be one soul unto me, how great shall be your joy with him in the kingdom of my Father!" (D&C 18:15).

Years earlier, upon his arrival in the Land of Nephi, Ammon had declared to King Lamoni: "I desire to dwell among this people for a time; yea, and perhaps until the day I die". (Alma 17:23). He had been willing to make a lifetime commitment in order to bring salvation to a nation in tremendous need, characterizing the Lamanites as a people "in darkness, yea, even in the darkest abyss". (V. 2, see V. 15, Ether 3:14, John 8:12, Acts 26:18, 2 Corinthians 4:4-6, & 1 Peter 2:9). Contrasting the qualities of light and dark, and good and evil, he described how many had been brought from their stressful, disorganized, and disoriented existence, into "the marvelous light of God". (V. 2).

Bathed in the stunning clarity of the missionary message, those he had taught stared in wide-eyed wonder at the beautiful simplicity of the tapestry of Gospel principles that make up the Plan of Salvation. This was in sharp contrast to the slit-eyed skepticism with which the unrepentant and hard-hearted greet the truth.

Alma had compared the Lamanite converts to the forefathers of the People of Zarahemla: "He changed their hearts, and they awoke unto God. Behold, they were in the midst of darkness; nevertheless, their souls were illuminated by the light of the everlasting word". (Alma 5:7). Now Ammon used the imagery of the dramatic contrasts between life and death to illustrate the power of the Gospel to change lives. (See V. 15, Ether 3:14, John 8:12, Acts 26:18, 2 Corinthians 4:4-6, & 1 Peter 2:9).

In verses 5-7, Ammon metaphorically described the harvest to illustrate for his brethren how thousands had been gathered through their missionary efforts. "Behold, the field was ripe," he said, "and blessed are ye, for ye did thrust in the sickle, and did reap with your might, yea, all the day long did ye labor; and behold the number of your sheaves!" (V. 5). His party had come up out of the Land of Zarahemla into the highlands of Nephi to bring a message of love to their "dearly beloved brethren". (V. 9). In the absence of that message, they "would still have been racked with hatred (against the Nephites), and they would also have (remained) strangers to God". (V. 9).

So enthusiastic was Ammon as he delivered his missionary report, that his brother Aaron "rebuked him, saying: Ammon, I fear that thy joy doth carry thee away unto boasting". (V. 10). Therefore, Ammon quickly clarified his feelings to his brethren, assuring them that he recognized that by himself he could have done nothing, but that in God's strength he had worked mighty miracles. (V. 10-12).

A key to the missionary success of the Sons of Mosiah was their mastery of the scriptures. (V. 13, see Alma 17:2, & 31:5). They recognized God's word as His personal message to His children, and accepted the holy scriptures as an individually crafted blueprint for their everyday behavior, and a pattern for life's direction. Years before, God had "snatched them from (their) awful, sinful, and polluted state" and in His infinite mercy had redeemed them from the chains of hell. (V. 17). They had gained scriptural literacy as they learned the language of the voice of the Spirit.

Then, Ammon expounded upon a significant principle of missionary work: "He that repenteth and exerciseth faith," he said, "and bringeth forth good works, and prayeth continually without ceasing - unto such it is given to know the mysteries of God; yea, unto such it shall be given to reveal things which never have been revealed; yea, and it shall be given unto such to bring thousands of souls to repentance, even as it has been given us to bring these our brethren to repentance". (V. 22).

In verses 23-25 we are provided with scriptural insight into the initial reaction by the People of Zarahemla to the Sons of Mosiah when they had first expressed their desire to go on a mission to the Lamanites in the Land of Nephi. Mormon might have included this in his abridgment in order to dramatically illustrate how much faith is required to open difficult mission areas. "They laughed us to scorn," Ammon reported. "For they said unto us: Do ye suppose that ye can bring them to the knowledge of the truth? Do ye suppose that ye can convince the Lamanites of the incorrectness of the traditions of their fathers, as stiffnecked a people as they are; whose hearts delight in the shedding of blood; whose days have been spent in the grossest iniquity; whose ways have been the ways of a transgressor from the beginning?" (V. 23-24).

The Nephites living in Zarahemla had written off the Lamanites both spiritually and temporally, prematurely judging them to be beyond redemption. Rather than making the changes in their own lives necessary to fulfil their covenant of baptism concerning their missionary responsibilities, they instead said: "Let us take up arms against (the Lamanites), that we destroy them and their iniquity out of the land, lest they overrun us and destroy us". (V. 25). Their fears were legitimate, and their reaction understandable in light of their ignorance, but it was an incorrect response, nevertheless. (See Commentary Reference to Helaman 10:4).

"A favorite theme of Brigham Young was that the dominion God gives to us is designed to test us and enable us to show to ourselves, our companions, and all the heavens just how we would act if entrusted with God's power". (Hugh Nibley, "Subduing the Earth," p. 89-90). In The Book of Helaman, the Lord told Nephi that because he had been unwavering, he had passed that very test with flying colors. Thus, he was made "mighty in word and in deed, in faith and in works". (Helaman 10:5). He was given the unlimited power of God because he had demonstrated that he could be trusted to do exactly as God would do in similar circumstances.

Joseph Smith clearly taught that the exercise of priesthood power is based solely upon the principles of righteousness. If, in the capacity of the priesthood, we "undertake to cover our sins, or to gratify our pride, our vain ambition, or to exercise control or dominion or compulsion upon the souls of the children of men, in any degree of unrighteousness," the authority of our priesthood is taken from us. (D&C 121:34-37).

"You are, and always will be, independent in that stage of development to which your voluntary decisions and divine powers have led," taught Truman Madsen. "There are limits all along the way to what you can be and do. But you are not a billiard ball. No power in the universe can coerce your complete assent or dissent. This thesis on capacity translates Bergson's metaphor into breath-taking fact: 'The universe is a machine for the making of gods." ("Eternal Man," p. 18).

In the Twenty-First Century, the world continues to engage in practices that the faithful find abominable and that fills them with horror and revulsion. A natural reaction is to draw back in disgust when confronted with such depravity. Spencer W. Kimball said that in such circumstances we often become "Anti-enemy" rather than "Pro-Gospel". But what a great missionary lesson the Sons of Mosiah teach us, as we read their account! "Now, when our hearts were depressed," Ammon revealed, "and we were about to turn back, behold, the Lord comforted us, and said: Go amongst thy brethren, the Lamanites, and bear with patience thine afflictions, and I will give unto you success". (V. 27).

Ammon then described the true, underlying characteristics of those Lamanites who were subsequently converted, "their love towards their brethren," and "their hatred to sin". (V. 32, & 34). As we marvel at the sincerity of the discipleship of the People of Anti-Nephi-Lehi, we recognize that charity was critical to their commitment. As Ammon declared, "Has there been so great love in all the land? Behold, I say unto you, Nay there has not, even among the Nephites". (V. 33). Today, as we struggle to fulfil our own missionary responsibilities, perhaps we should stand back and re-examine the quality of love in our own hearts for our neighbors.

Ammon had "reason to rejoice," for when he had been born again, he had been given a second chance to fulfil his life's potential. He must have considered himself very fortunate that God had looked so favorably upon him during the rebellious years of his youth, and had been able to see into his heart. His rough exterior had been only a façade that reflected inappropriate behavior. (V. 35). His true character was only revealed when, through a spiritual rebirth, he became a new creature in Christ. (See Mosiah 27:26). In the same manner, "all mankind, yea, men and women, all nations, kindreds, tongues and people, must be born again, yea, born of God, changed from their carnal and fallen state, to a state of righteousness, being redeemed of God, becoming his sons and daughters". (Mosiah 27:25). The Sons of Mosiah, and all like them, are true "Sabra," native-born children of the Covenant. The fruit of the prickly pear cactus, the sabra, has a dry, unappealing skin. But inside it is sweet and juicy, and pleasing to the taste. When God measures us, He puts the tape around our hearts.

Joseph Smith said: "There are but a very few beings in the world who understand rightly the nature of God (and) if we do not understand the character of God, we do not comprehend ourselves". ("Teachings", p. 343). Ammon joined the ranks of the converted when he declared: God "is my life and my light, my joy and my salvation, and my redemption from everlasting wo". (V. 35). His experiences in the Land of Nephi had taught him that Heavenly Father is no respecter of persons, but he "is mindful of every people; whatsoever land they may be in; yea, he numbereth his people, and his bowels of mercy are over all the earth". (V. 37).

Alma
Chapter 27

When the war-like Lamanites, who were led by the Amalekites, realized that they could not destroy all the Nephites in the Land of Zarahemla, they returned to the Land of Nephi and renewed their hostilities against the People of Anti-Nephi-Lehi. (V. 1-2). The converted Lamanites suffered greatly because of their unyielding commitment to the covenant of non-aggression into which they had entered. (V. 3).

Ammon was moved to compassion when he witnessed "the great work of destruction" that was taking place, and he begged the king to allow him to lead the people of Anti-Nephi-Lehi "down to the land of Zarahemla". (V. 4-5). He inquired of the Lord, Who confirmed his desire, saying: "Get this people out of this land, that they perish not; for Satan has great hold on the hearts of the Amalekites, who do stir up the Lamanites to anger against their brethren to slay them". (V. 12, see Mosiah 2:37).

Thus, led by the Sons of Mosiah and their companions, all the people of Anti-Nephi-Lehi departed out of the land, and "came into the wilderness which divided the land of Nephi from the land of Zarahemla". (V. 15). When they approached the border of Zarahemla, Ammon suggested that he and his brethren go on ahead to make sure that the Nephites would not be taken by surprise and react defensively if a large body of Lamanites were to be discovered traveling toward Nephite population centers. (V. 15).

So it was that the Sons of Mosiah encountered Alma, who "did rejoice exceedingly to see his brethren; and what added more to his joy, they were still his brethren in the Lord". (Alma 17:2). That it "was a joyful meeting" is expressed no less than eight times in verses 16-18. Mormon's excellent editorial comment is enlightening: "Now was not this exceeding joy? Behold, this is joy which none receiveth save it be the truly penitent and humble seeker of happiness". (V. 18).

Alma conducted the Sons of Mosiah and their companions back to his own home in Zarahemla. After refreshment, they all visited Nephihah, and gave him a missionary report of their experiences during the previous 14 years in the Land of Nephi. (V. 20. see Alma 4:7, & 50:37). Nephihah, who all this time had righteously served as Chief Judge, "sent a proclamation throughout all the land, desiring the voice of the people concerning their brethren, who were the people of Anti-Nephi-Lehi". (V. 21). The Nephites agreed to give the refugees the Land of Jershon, and to protect them from future Lamanite aggression. "And this we do for our brethren," they declared, "on account of their fear to take up arms against their brethren lest they should commit sin; and thus, their great fear came because of their sore repentance which they had, on account of their many murders and their awful wickedness". (V. 23). Subtlety was evidently not Nephihah's strong suit. In return, the people of Anti-Nephi-Lehi were to give the Nephites a large portion of their substance. (V. 24, see Alma 43:13).

Bearing this good news, Ammon returned to the Lamanite camp with Alma. After introductions, Alma "related unto them his conversion, with Ammon and Aaron, and his brethren". (V. 25). It seems that he did this to help the Lamanites to feel more comfortable among the righteous Nephites. That the story of his own conversion had exactly that effect is attested in the record, which states: "And it came to pass that it did cause great joy among them". (V. 26).

The People of Anti-Nephi-Lehi went "down into the land of Jershon and took possession of (it); and they were called by the Nephites the people of Ammon; therefore, they were distinguished by that name ever after". (V. 26). The righteous Nephites in Zarahemla now included the People of Zarahemla, the People of Nephi, and descendants of Laman and Lemuel.

The People of Ammon represent the first mass conversion of Lamanites in The Book of Mormon chronicle. They "were distinguished for their zeal towards God, and also towards men, for they were perfectly honest and upright in all things; and they were firm in the faith of Christ, even unto the end". (V. 27). What a great testament to faith is expressed in this verse. When we are zealous, we attend to our duties and responsibilities with ardent feeling and with fervor. (See V. 30).

Their faith was so strong that they "never did look upon death with any degree of terror, (because of) their hope and views of Christ and the resurrection; therefore, death was swallowed up to them by the victory of Christ over it". (V. 28). This is one of the great blessings that follow faith. (See Commentary Reference to Alma 28:11-12). With such faith, death is a mere comma; without it, it can be an exclamation point. (Neal Maxwell).

Spencer W. Kimball wrote that the quality of peace enjoyed by the People of Ammon "comes only thru integrity. When we make a covenant with God, we must keep it at whatever cost. Let us not be like the Church member who partakes of the Sacrament in the morning, then defiles the Sabbath that afternoon. Instead, let us have integrity like Abraham (and the people of Ammon) did, observing with all soberness the solemn contracts we have made with God". ("The Example of

Abraham," "Ensign", 6/1975). The integrity exemplified by the People of Ammon would prove to be a great blessing to the Nephites in the difficult years that lay ahead.

Many years ago, Josiah Gilbert Holland expressed a hope relevant to our day: "God, give us Men and Women!" he pleaded. "A time like this demands strong minds, great hearts, true faith, and ready hands. Men and women whom the lust of office does not kill. Men and women whom the spoils of office cannot buy. Men and women who possess opinions and a will. Men and women who have honor, who will not lie, who can stand before a demagogue and damn his treacherous flatteries without winking. Tall men and women, sun-crowned, who live above the fog in public duty and in private thinking. For while the rabble, with their thumb worn creeds, their large professions, and their little deeds, mingle in selfish strife, Lo! Freedom weeps, Wrong rules the land, and Justice sleeps".

"Blessed be the name of our God; let us sing to his praise, yea, let us give thanks to his holy name, for he doth work righteousness forever."
(Alma 26:8).

Alma
Chapter 28

When hatred toward their former brethren burning even hotter, the Amalekites led a Lamanite army in pursuit of the People of Ammon through the wilderness separating the Land of Nephi from the Land of Zarahemla, resulting in "a tremendous battle (with the Nephites who had sworn to protect the people of Ammon), yea, even such an one as never had been known among all the people in the land from the time Lehi left Jerusalem". (V. 2). Tens of thousands of Lamanites were either killed or scattered abroad. (V. 3). Among the Nephites, there was also a great slaughter, followed by mourning and lamentation. (V. 3-4, see V. 10). It was a "time of solemnity, and a time of much fasting and prayer". (V. 6).

Verses 8-12 are probably direct quotations from Alma that were recorded on the Large Plates of Nephi. The account of Ammon and his brethren, as well as that of "the wars and contentions among the Nephites, and also the wars between the Nephites and the Lamanites," comprising chapters 17-28 of The Book of Alma, are summarized: "And this is the account of Ammon and his brethren, their journeyings in the land of Nephi, their sufferings in the land, their sorrows, and their afflictions, and their incomprehensible joy, and the reception and safety of the brethren in the land of Jershon ... And this is the account of the wars and contentions among the Nephites, and also the wars between the Nephites and the Lamanites". (V. 8-9).

These verses provide insightful contrasts. Both the righteous and the wicked had cause to mourn because of the great destruction in the land. Alma wrote that, on the one hand, "many thousands are mourning for the loss of their kindred, because they have reason to fear". (V. 11). On the other hand, he reported, "many thousands of others truly mourn for the loss of their kindred, yet they rejoice and exult in the hope, and even know, according to the promises of the Lord, that they are raised to dwell at the right hand of God, in a never-ending happiness". (V. 12). As the Lord explained to Joseph Smith: "Thou shalt live together in love, insomuch that thou shalt weep for the loss of them that die, and more especially for those that have not hope of a glorious resurrection. And it shall come to pass that those that die in me shall not taste of death, for it shall be sweet unto them. And they that die not in me, wo unto them, for their death is bitter". (D&C 42:45-47).

Joseph further taught: "The only difference between old and young dying is one lives longer in heaven and eternal light and glory than the other, and is freed a little sooner from this miserable, wicked world". (H.C., 4:544). The same is true of the righteous. (See Commentary Reference to Alma 40:11).

Another contrast is provided by Mormon's editorial comments that close this chapter. "And thus, we see how great the inequality of man is because of sin and transgression, and the power of the devil, which comes by the cunning plans which he hath devised to ensnare the hearts of men. And thus, we see the great call of diligence of men to labor in the vineyards of the Lord; and thus, we see the great reason of sorrow, and also of rejoicing - sorrow because of death and destruction among men, and joy because of the light of Christ unto life". (V. 13-14). He understood from a unique and terrible perspective, as he abridged the record of Alma, that only righteousness can stabilize a society and equilibrate its behavior with celestial principles.

The "tremendous slaughter among the people of Nephi" in Alma's day paled in comparison to the carnage witnessed by Mormon, who saw that "because of sin and transgression, and the power of the devil," men have great reason to sorrow. (V. 3). Nevertheless, "All are alike unto God". (2 Nephi 26:33, see 2 Nephi 30:1-2). All have the capacity to resist the power of the devil and to experience joy in the light of Christ.

John Altgeld wrote: "Two forces are operating, two voices are calling - one coming out from the swamps of selfishness and force, where success means death; and the other from the hilltops of justice and progress, where even failure brings glory. Two lights are seen on your horizon - one, the last fading marsh light of power, and the other the slowly rising sun of human brotherhood. Two ways lie open for you - one leading to an ever lower and lower plane, where are heard the cries of despair and the curses of the poor, where manhood shrivels and possessions rot down the possessor; and the other leading to the highlands of the morning, where are heard the glad shouts of humanity, and where honest effort is rewarded with immortality".

Alma
Chapter 29

Mormon's quotation from the record of Alma, begun in Alma Chapter 28:8, continues through this chapter, which is essentially a psalm of thanksgiving to God for His blessings.

Verses 1-2 recall Alma's experience recorded in Mosiah 27:11-18. If Alma could speak "with the trump of God, (and) with a voice to shake the earth," he would cry "repentance and the Plan of Redemption," instead of offering the counterfeit currency that in his day and ours has been promoted by the unenlightened and ill-informed whose great advocates still miss the mark. They ultimately fail no matter how much media attention or campaign contributions they receive.

In verse 3, Alma realized that he "ought to be content with the things which the Lord (had) allotted unto (him)". He knew that our greatest successes come from recognizing not just our God-given talents, but our limitations, as well. It requires a great deal of maturity to comprehend the scope of the Plan, its depth and breadth and height, and to realize that the continued expansion of our capabilities to our full potential can be in harmony with our provisional acceptance of who we are.

Henry D. Moyle said: "We might well be assured that we had something to do with our allotment, in our pre-existent state. This would be an additional reason for us to accept our present condition and make the best of it. It is what we agreed to do. Unquestionably, we knew before we came to this earth the conditions under which we would here exist, and live, and work. So little wonder that Alma said that we sin in the thought, or in the desire, or in the wish that we were someone other than ourselves". (C.R. 10/1952, see V. 3, & Commentary Reference to Alma 13:4).

Heavenly Father blesses his children with agency. (V. 4). "I ought not to harrow up in my desires, the firm decree of a just God," wrote Alma, "for I know that he granteth unto men according to their desire, whether it be unto death or unto life; yea, I know that he alloteth unto men, yea, decreeth unto them decrees which are unalterable, according to their wills, whether they be unto salvation or unto destruction". (V. 4). Only children and mentally incapacitated individuals are blameless before God. "He that knoweth not good from evil is blameless". (V. 5). "Seeing that I know these things," Alma reasoned, "why should I desire more than to perform the work to which I have been called?" (V. 6).

I have a conviction that we are exactly what we should be," Elder Moyle continued, "except as we may have altered that pattern by deviating from the laws of God here in mortality. I have convinced myself that we all have those peculiar attributes, characteristics, and abilities which are essential for us to progress in order that we may fulfil the full purpose of our creation here upon the earth".

The thoughts expressed in this chapter by Alma, and the corollary remarks by Elder Moyle cited above, reinforce the concept of patriarchal blessings as inspired commentaries on specific talents, capabilities, and attainable goals of each of God's mortal children. Heavenly Father knows what our potential is and remembers in detail the blessing He gave to each of us before we left His Presence for our mission on earth. Under the inspiration of His Spirit, it is the privilege of fathers and of ordained Patriarchs in the Church to reconfirm those blessing upon our heads.

Almost as an aside, Alma taught: "The Lord doth grant unto all nations, of their own nation and tongue, to teach his word, yea, in wisdom, all that he seeth fit that they should have". (V. 8). As Joseph Fielding Smith, Jr. argued: "There is no justification for the belief that all scripture is enclosed within the covers of the Holy Bible". ("Doctrines of Salvation," 1:277). "Adam's revelation did not instruct Noah to build his ark; nor did Noah's revelation tell Lot to forsake Sodom; nor did either of these speak of the Exodus. These all had revelations for themselves, and so had Isaiah, Jeremiah, Peter, Paul, John, and Joseph (Smith)". (Henry D. Moyle).

John Greenleaf Whittier wrote from the perspective of a non-member about the Restored Gospel. "In listening to these modern prophets, I discovered as I think the great secret of their success in making converts. They speak to a common feeling; they minister to a universal want. They speak a language of home and promise to weak, weary hearts, tossed and troubled, who have wandered from sect to sect, seeking in vain for the primal manifestations of the divine power".

Alma had a personal witness of that "divine power". He had been delivered from Satan's grasp, just at the moment when he was being dragged speedily down to hell. (V. 10). He also remembered the captivity of his own father and the little flock in the Land of Helam, and how "the Lord did deliver them out of bondage". (V. 11, see V. 12, & Mosiah 24:11-15).

Alma's holy priesthood calling was to "preach the word unto this people". (V. 13). The goal of his teaching was "that there might not be more sorrow upon all the face of the earth". (V. 2). So successful had he and the Sons of Mosiah been, that his joy was almost beyond description. He had seen the magnificent transformation that takes place when people accept the Gospel Plan.

In 1974, Spencer W. Kimball wrote: "I am positive that the blessings of the Lord will attend every country which opens its gates to the Gospel of Christ. Their blessings will flow in education, and culture, and faith, and love. There will come prosperity to the nations, comfort and luxuries to the people, joy and peace to all recipients, and eternal life to those who will accept and magnify it. I believe the time has come when we must change our goals and raise our sights". ("When The World Will Be Converted," "Ensign", 10/1974).

The accounts of the missionary experiences of Alma and the Sons of Mosiah were included in The Book of Mormon so that we might take courage as we face similar missionary challenges in the Last Days. In the years since President Kimball wrote the words quoted above, significant changes have taken place in the world, as the Gospel is taken to every nation, kindred, tongue, and people, and his prophetic vision is validated. The stone cut out of the mountain is rolling over the whole earth and cannot be stopped. (See Daniel 2:34). What a thrill it is for members of the Restored Church of Jesus Christ to march in the ranks of Christian soldiers who take the battle for truth directly into the camp of the willfully or ignorantly disobedient.

The message of Alma 25:17 is that Heavenly Father always keeps His promises. "And now behold, Ammon, and Aaron, and Omner, and Himni, and their brethren did rejoice exceedingly," wrote Mormon, "for the success which they had had among the Lamanites. seeing that the Lord had granted unto them according to their prayers, and that he had also verified his word unto them in every particular". A central reason for the organization of the Church is to make possible the kind of priesthood directed teaching of which Alma, the Sons of Mosiah, and their brethren are such fine examples. The goal of such teaching is to introduce the elect to the principles of the Gospel, to the covenants of God, and to the ordinances of the priesthood, and to instruct the Saints so that they may learn to keep their promises. When they do this they will be transformed into a Zion society.

In the Last Days, a unique house of learning has been established and maintained by the power of the priesthood. It is in this house that men and women make celestial covenants. Increasingly, this house is being made available to the world's population. In the temple we get our bearings on the universe. It is where we figuratively "put on the whole armor of God". (Ephesians 6:11). The key to the mysteries of the kingdom is revealed in the temple, because the key to the knowledge of God is the endowment that is bestowed there.

It is in this sense that "power in the priesthood" is vested in all those who receive their endowment in the temple. "And this greater priesthood administereth the Gospel and holdeth the key to the mysteries of the kingdom, even the key of the knowledge of God. Therefore, in the ordinances thereof, the power of godliness is manifest". (D&C 84:19-20). Because Heavenly Father desires that all his children possess this power, He has always commanded His people to build temples. (D&C 124:39).

Within 10 years of their arrival in the land of promise, the Nephites had built a temple. (See 2

Nephi 5:16, & Jacob 1:17). Nearly 500 years later, there were still references to the temple. (See Mosiah 1:18). For example, in the Land of Zarahemla, the Nephites gathered about the temple to await the appearance of the resurrected Lord. (See 3 Nephi 11:1).

It would have been natural for Alma to desire that the people receive the blessings of the temple to strengthen them against the influences of the world. "Without the ordinances thereof, and the authority of the priesthood," declared the Savior to Joseph Smith, "the power of godliness is not manifest unto men in the flesh". (D&C 84:21).

Joseph F. Smith wrote of the endowment: ", that we will not steal or bear false witness against our neighbors, or take advantage of the weak, that we will help and sustain our fellow men in the right, and take such a course as will prove most effectual in helping the weak to overcome their weaknesses and bring themselves into subjection to the requirements of heaven. We cannot neglect, slight, or depart from the spirit, meaning, intent and purpose of these covenants and agreements that we have entered into with our Father in Heaven, without shearing ourselves of our glory, strength, right and title to His blessings, and to the gifts and manifestations of His Spirit". (Improvement Era, V. 9 p. 813.)

It would be difficult to more clearly compose a statement explaining the need for establishing a covenant relationship with God. It would be equally difficult to visualize a more appropriate place in which to do so, than the House of The Lord. Therefore, the Lord commanded His people: "Organize yourselves; prepare every needful thing; and establish a house, even a house of prayer, a house of fasting, a house of faith, a house of learning, a house of glory, a house of order, a house of God". (D&C 88:119, see D&C 109:8).

Alma
Chapter 30

In our day, there are many antichrists who attempt to denigrate religion and who deny the reality of Jesus Christ. They occupy positions of leadership and exert great power in the Church of The Devil. Unfortunately, their influence is felt throughout the strata of society. (See 1 Nephi 22, & 2 Nephi 28). The account in this chapter of Korihor, a prominent antichrist in The Book of Mormon, might have been included in the abridgement by Mormon because of his similarity to the antichrists of the Last Days that Mormon saw in vision. (See Mormon 8:35).

Nephi had defined "priestcraft" as the activity of men who "preach and set themselves up for a light unto the world, that they may get gain and praise of the world; but they seek not the welfare of Zion". (2 Nephi 26:9). However, Sherem was the first Book of Mormon "anti-Christ", followed by Nehor. Anti-Christ is one who opposes Christ, the Gospel, the true Church, and sets himself up as a secular savior, or establishes any other person or system as a substitute for the Savior, and who then seeks to promote this substitute in the hearts and minds of the people. (Jacob 7:1-2-23, & Alma 1:2-16).

The People of Ammon had established themselves in their adopted Land of Jershon. (V. 1). Their humility, trust in the Lord, and commitment to their covenants were so powerful that they received many marvelous blessings. In the Last Days, a prophet of the Lord has made promises to every nation that finds itself in circumstances similar to those of the People of Ammon. (See Commentary Reference to Alma 29:13).

Beginning in 1989, the world saw the "evil empire" of communism crumble and turn to dust. Perhaps the seeds of its demise were actually sown in the humanitarian acts of its own leaders in the 1970s and 1980s, when permission was given by them to the Church of Jesus Christ of Latter-day Saints to build a temple in East Germany and to allow missionary activity behind the Iron Curtain.

Perhaps, too, the inspired counsel of the Prophet to members of the Church from Eastern Block countries facilitated the change. In 1973, for example, 700 Saints from the German Democratic Republic (East Germany) were permitted by their government to cross the Iron Curtain to attend the Munich Area Conference of the Church. Some of these Saints might have seen this trip to the West as an opportunity to escape the tyranny and repression of their native land. Some might have excitedly made elaborate plans to defect after attending the Conference. Their eager participation might have been heightened by the anticipation of personal freedom after its close.

However, in his concluding remarks at the end of the final session on Sunday afternoon, President Harold B. Lee said something like this: "And now we want to caution those Saints from certain countries whose governments have given them special permission to attend this Conference. We want to counsel the Saints to honor their word, and to be true to the trust placed in them. Think of the precedent that might be set, and the damage done to this spirit of cooperation if you were to betray this trust. Remember the 12th Article of Faith. 'We believe in being subject to kings, presidents, rulers, and magistrates, in obeying, honoring, and sustaining the law.' So, thank the Lord for the privilege of attending this Conference, and then return to your homes, and pray for change, working within the law of the land".

Many in the Church find it easy to "Follow the Prophet" on well traveled avenues dotted with conveniently located rest stops, and on brightly lighted world stages filled with the appreciative applause and laudatory comments of thousands. But placed in the setting just described, when no-one is looking, and there are no positive peer pressures to sustain correct choices, would you or I have the strength to do so?

The People of Ammon did "keep the commandments of the Lord; and they were strict in observing the ordinances of God". (V. 3). In consequence of the bloodshed resulting from war with the Lamanites, they had fasted and prayed and mourned the loss of their brethren. In their bereavement, they found comfort and solace in Gospel teachings, and their sorrow over the death of their loved was tempered by their trust in the Lord.

Benjamin Malachi Franklin (1882-1965) wrote: "My life is but a weaving between my Lord and me. I cannot choose the colors. He worketh steadily. Oftimes, He weaveth sorrow, and I in foolish pride, forget that He seeth the upper, and I the under side. Not 'til the loom is silent and the shuttles cease to fly, shall God unroll the canvas and explain the reason why. The dark threads are as needful in the Weaver's skillful hand, as the threads of gold and silver in the pattern He has planned". ("A Sourcebook of Poetry," 1968).

With the sure foundation of an eternal perspective provided by the ordinances and covenants, the Nephite nation enjoyed "continual peace" in the land. (V. 5). Then Korihor, identified by name in verse 12, made his appearance. "He was Anti-Christ, for he began to preach unto the people against the prophecies which had been spoken by the prophets, concerning the coming of Christ". (V. 6). Along with his misguided attitude of emancipation, Korihor cultivated a crusading zeal and tyrannical intolerance of opposition. He denied the reality of Jesus Christ, as do all antichrists, and actively opposed the true Church, the Gospel, and the Plan of Happiness. He promised salvation on his own terms. Thus, as noted above, both Sherem (Jacob 7:1-23) and Nehor (Alma 1:2-16) were also antichrists.

Verses 7-9 clearly establish agency as a ruling principle. In Zarahemla, "there was no law against a man's belief". (V. 7). It was only the content of Korihor's message that earned him the title of anti-Christ. (See 1 John 2:22, & 1 John 4:3). His name is interesting because of its similarity to "Kherihor," who was High Priest of Ammon and the Chief Judge who illegally seized the throne of Egypt in 1,085 B.C.

Mormon quite specifically identified Korihor as "anti-Christ," or one who actively opposes Jesus Christ and the truths of His Gospel. (V. 12). As his story unfolds, note the similarities of his persuasive arguments to those employed by Latter-day "Korihors".

Worldly scholars in our day echo the arguments advanced by Korihor. God has no place among the secular humanists in the ivory towers of academia. He would never have been granted tenure at any university. After all, He had only one major publication, it was in Hebrew, and it had no supporting references. It wasn't published in a refereed journal. Some even doubt he wrote it Himself. He may have created the world, they point out, but what has He done since? The scientific community can't even duplicate His results. He used human subjects, frequently with disastrous results. His first two pupils were expelled. When another experiment went sour, His subjects were drowned. He rarely came to class; He just told His students to read the book and listen to his graduate assistants. His office hours were irregular, and class was sometimes held on mountaintops! Some say He had His Son teach the class for Him. There is even a rumor that He is dead, or living under an assumed name in Argentina.

Korihor, too, called for a strictly scientific approach to all problems, ridiculing those who yoked themselves to "foolish things". (V. 13). His first timeworn tactic was to argue that no rational man can know of things to come. Then he declared: "Ye cannot know of things which ye do not see" (v. 15), calling the remission of sins "the effect of a frenzied mind". (V. 16). Korihor crusaded against what he characterized as the tyranny of ancient traditions and primitive superstitions, arguing that there is no need for remission of sins or atonement. (V. 16).

His next argument is used with great effect by today's antichrists. His philosophy was "every man for himself," "live for the moment," "eat, drink, and be merry, for tomorrow we die," (2 Nephi 28:7), and "when death comes, it is the end". He called for a new morality characterized by the shedding of old inhibitions. (V. 17). This is, of course, nothing but the old immorality without the feelings of guilt that comes with recognition of the transgression of God's laws. His counsel of moral relativism was good news to many of his listeners, who "lift(ed) up their heads in their wickedness," exulting in their sins, not realizing the awful consequences of their actions. (V. 18).

During the civil war that nearly tore the heart from The United States of America, President Abraham Lincoln issued the following declaration: "It is the duty of nations as well as men to own their dependence upon the over-ruling power of God, to confess their sins and transgressions in humble sorrow. Yet with assured hope that genuine repentance will lead to mercy and pardon, (we) recognize that those nations only are blessed whose God is the Lord". ("Proclamation 97 - Appointing a Day of National Humiliation, Fasting, and Prayer").

In his zeal, Korihor made a significant tactical error. He traveled from the Land of Zarahemla to the Land of Jershon, where the People of Ammon lived. These people "were once the people of the Lamanites" (V. 19), and they had experienced life from both sides of the fence. Consequently, they wouldn't tolerate Korihor's teachings. They recognized immediately that his actions necessitated a Church court, because he chose a public forum to challenge Church doctrines, and then actively sought converts to his point of view. (See V. 29). Therefore, he was bound and taken before Ammon, who was the presiding Church priesthood leader in the Land of Jershon. (V. 20).

Ammon found him guilty of the charges leveled against him, and banished him from the Land of Jershon. (V. 21). Subsequently, in the Land of Gideon, before he had the chance to do any significant damage, he was taken before Giddonah, the presiding high priest and "chief judge over the land".

The unrepentant Korihor wanted the same perverted academic freedom desired by the antichrists of the Last Days. (V. 23). But in teaching the Gospel then and now there is no license. There is only one undeviating standard of freedom of expression that is measured by fundamental orthodox doctrine and truth.

"The great objective of all our work," taught Spencer W. Kimball, "is to build character and increase faith in the lives of those whom we serve. If one cannot accept and teach the programs of the Church in an orthodox way, without reservation, he should not teach". (C.R. 4/1948).

Korihor's strategy before Giddonah was as old as the argument first expressed by Lucifer in the Grand Council in Heaven before the world was. He sought to mix truth with falsehood and with blatant distortions intended to legitimatize his radical views. First, he called for economic liberation from what he characterized as priestly exploitation. (V. 27). Then he slandered the prophets for "their traditions and their dreams and their whims and their visions and their pretended mysteries". (V. 28). "The idea that a prophet must hear or know about the thing he prophecies was well understood by Korihor, and prompted his criticism of priests whom he said had 'pretended mysteries' and who spoke of 'a being who never has been seen or known, or who never was nor ever will be.'" ("The Crime of False Prophecy Under Ancient Israelite Law," FARMS Report).

When Giddonah "saw that (Korihor) would revile even against God," he had heard enough. (V.

29). Straight away, he was sent "to the land of Zarahemla, that he might be brought before Alma, and also before the chief Judge who was governor over all the land". (V. 29). There, Alma's actions once again gave compelling evidence of his personal conviction that repentance is more effective than political power in preserving the peace. After all, he had been elected Chief Judge of the nation, the governor, and commander in chief, but he had given up these powerful positions that he might cry repentance unto dissenters. Korihor did not realize it, but Alma was at that moment his best friend and the only one who could help to calm the spiritual storm that was about to engulf him.

But standing before Alma and Nephihah, Korihor "went on to blaspheme". (V. 30). In other words, he blew his last chance for personal redemption, continuing to speak evil and to revile against God Himself. Nevertheless, Alma still sought to recover his soul by bearing down with the power of the word that had so often been effective in his missionary labors among apostates. Alma gave him a number of evidences of the truth. First among them was the joy in the hearts of the people, experienced in consequence of their strict obedience. (V. 35, see Alma 27:16). Secondly, was his reliance upon his personal testimony. (V. 41). Korihor was warned that, having "put off the Spirit of God," he had allowed himself to be put instead in the grip of Satan. (V. 42). It is not easy to explain to the uninitiated how the witness of the Holy Ghost comes. "The wind bloweth where it listeth," said the Savior, "and thou hearest the sound thereof, but canst not tell whence it cometh, and whither it goeth; so is every one that is born of the Spirit". (John 3:8).

When, in his spiritually bankrupt state, Korihor asked for a sign, Alma answered that he had been given signs enough. (V. 43). As Gordon B. Hinckley observed: "All of beauty in the Earth bears the fingerprint of the Master Creator". (C.R. 4/1978). Did not Korihor "have the testimony of all these thy brethren," asked Alma, "and also all the holy prophets? The scriptures are laid before thee," he declared, "and all things denote there is a God ... even the earth, and all things that are upon the face of it ... and (also) its motion". (V. 44).

With other inspired leaders of antiquity, Alma had a correct understanding of the order of the universe, and so declared that even "all the planets which move in their regular form do witness that there is a Supreme Creator". (V. 44). His ancestor Abraham had been a prophet. seer, and revelator, and was given the Urim and Thummim by the Lord Himself. (Abraham 3:1). The Lord told him: "It is given unto thee to know the times of reckoning, and the set time, yea, the set time of the earth upon which thou standest, and the set time of the greater light which is set to rule the day, and the set time of the lesser light which is set to rule the night ... And it is given unto thee to know the set time of all the stars that are set to give light". (Abraham 3:5, & 10).

Nephi also understood that God is the Maker and Fashioner of the universe and all things therein. He knew that "by the power of his voice doth the whole earth shake; Yea, by the power of his voice, do the foundations rock, even to the very center. Yea, and if he say unto the earth - Move - it is moved. Yea, if he say unto the earth - Thou shalt go back, that it lengthen out the day for many hours - it is done; And thus, according to his word the earth goeth back, and it appeareth unto man that the sun standeth still; yea, and behold, this is so; for surely it is the earth that moveth and not the sun". (Helaman 12:11-15).

When Joshua stood with the army of Israel in the Valley of Ajalon, he had declared "in the sight of Israel, Sun, stand thou still ... And the sun stood still, and the moon stayed, until the people had avenged themselves upon their enemies. Is not (the greater account which is perhaps more accurately detailed) written in The Book of Jasher?" (Joshua 10:12-13).

"Behold, said the Savior, "all these (manifestations of nature that may be observed with the physical senses) are kingdoms, and any man who hath seen any or the least of these hath seen God moving in his majesty and power". (D&C 88:47). "The heavens declare the glory of God, David had written, "and the firmament sheweth his handiwork". (Psalms 19:1). "And yet," continued Alma, "do ye go about, leading away the hearts of this people, testifying unto them there is no God?". Alma's question was rhetorical, for he was unable to understand how Korihor could defend such an attitude in the face of such overwhelming evidence. (V. 45). "Earth is crammed with heaven, and every common bush with fire of God. But only those who see, take off their shoes. The rest stand around picking blackberries". (Elizabeth Barrett Browning).

When Korihor persisted in his demand for a sign as the critical condition for his belief, Alma was "grieved because of the hardness of (his) heart". (V. 46). Korihor's actions dictated consequences that were unavoidable, inevitable, and unalterable. Alma agreed to grant his desire, declaring that "it is better that thy soul should be lost than that thou shouldst be the means of bringing many souls down to destruction". (V. 47). Nephi had faced a similar situation when he had encountered Laban in the dark streets of Jerusalem. (See 1 Nephi 4:13).

The sign given was not what Korihor had expected. Alma's decree was both great and terrible: "God shall smite thee," he said, "that thou shalt become dumb, that thou shalt never open thy mouth any more". (V. 47). Faced with the prospect of Alma's withering judgment, Korihor immediately tempered his words, but not quite enough to avoid the consequences of his desire to receive a sign. (V. 48). By the power of the priesthood, Korihor was struck dumb. (V. 49-50). Perhaps he was both "deaf and dumb," for when Nephihah sought to communicate with him, he asked in writing, rather than by speaking, if he was now "convinced of the power of God". (V. 51). Surprisingly, Korihor wrote back that not only did he recognize God's power, but that he "always knew that there was a God". (V. 52).

As it had slowly dawned upon Zeezrom in Ammonihah, so Korihor now began to comprehend the counterfeit nature of the power by which he was operating. He had thought of himself as Mahan, "a great destroyer," when actually he was following the dangerous path leading to Perdition, or "utter ruin". (Moses 5:31). The adversary finally betrays his followers, for he cannot deliver on the promises he has made to them. The Korihors of this world write checks that they cannot cash. Their spiritual bank accounts are overdrawn, because they have failed to make the necessary regular deposits.

Echoing the words that Sherem had used in his defense, Korihor wrote that the devil had deceived him. (See Jacob 7:16-20). Years earlier, Alma had explained to Zeezrom in Ammonihah that Satan is the adversary of the wicked, and that the disobedient are the only individuals over whom he has any power. (See Commentary Reference to Alma 12:5). His dominion over them is cruel and insensitive. Manipulating them ruthlessly, he lashes out at anything that is good. The wicked are pawns in his hands, but they are esteemed by him as nothing. His hatred is all-consuming, and so ultimately he has no use for them, because they still remind him of his Heavenly home and the associations he had there. There is something in the nature of even the most depraved soul with which the devil is extremely uncomfortable.

"The devil made me do it" is an inadequate defense, but his counterfeit doctrine had been so pleasing "to the carnal mind" of Korihor, that he had actually begun to believe it himself. Too often, we shoot the arrow blindly, and then move the target so that we can score what we mistakenly think is a bullseye. This is what Korihor had done. The discerning of spirits is a critical gift we receive from the Holy Ghost. It had withdrawn from Korihor and was no longer an influence in his life. Korihor, like so many antichrists of the Last Days, had been fanatical in his obsession with the diabolical dissemination of his distorted doctrine. He had confused the trip with the destination, and had played right into the hands of Satan, who caressed his neck with flaxen cords until he found himself bound with strong chains.

Neal Maxwell might have been writing about Korihor or one of his modern-day counterparts, when he observed that "rather than being meek and accepting, rather than pondering, we immediately want to try to fit truth into our frail, finite framework of logic or to connect it up with our limited experience. Understandably, we desire to possess the proffered truth by shaping it to fit into the contours of our existing knowledge, when what really needs to happen is that we must be overwhelmed by it, rather than to be the possessors of it. We cannot make room in our little puddle of knowledge for the sea itself. Surely that element of scale was present in Moses' realization after the panoramic vision he received, when in a great burst of both appreciation and candor, he said, 'Now, for this cause I know that man is nothing, which thing I never had supposed.' (Moses 1:10)". ("That My Family Should Partake," p. 4).

Had Korihor maintained his orthodoxy with humility, he would not have strayed into the uncharted territory of Satan's domain, where he not only lost his way, but also his eternal life, when he surrendered his agency to the adversary and became his spokesperson. For the disobedient, the day of reckoning will be a day of recognition, with the shocking realization that many of the supposed anchors of life have actually been grounded in mud and sand and on shifting shoals. It will be a day when the question will no longer need to be asked: "What is real?" Until then, many mistakenly believe they are doing the Lord's work, when they are instead on the payroll of the devil. But the celestial compass of Gospel principles founded on truth is always available to guide every disciplined traveler to safe haven before the day of reckoning. It is also there for those who have lost their way, to bring them back to the fold of the Shepherd.

In our Church experience, we are like the trees of a forest, secure in numbers. When the winds of adversity blow hard, we are unified and strengthened by our solidarity. But if we try to stand alone, no matter how great the girth of our trunk, no matter how securely planted are our roots, we risk being toppled over. We become like the "widow maker" tree, the solitary tree left over in the forest after its clearing.

As we build the home in which our spirit will live forever, we must ask ourselves, "Are we building a lean-to or a temple?" We have all the materials necessary to build our eternal lives. We are the architects of our own fate, and our blueprint should identify individual works consistent with the principles of the Gospel, and the realization that we are saved by grace after all we can do. (See 2 Nephi 25:23). We are "fellowcitizens with the saints, and of the household of God; and are built upon the foundation of the apostles and prophets, Jesus Christ himself being the chief corner stone: In whom all the building fitly framed together groweth unto an holy temple in the Lord". (Ephesians 2:18-21).

Korihor's experience with the physical manifestations of divine power prompted an immediate and profound attitude adjustment, and he "besought that Alma should pray unto God, that the curse might be taken from him". (V. 54). But from his perspective as priesthood leader, Alma confirmed and validated the terrible judgment, saying: "If this curse should be taken from thee thou wouldst again lead away the hearts of this people; therefore, it shall be unto thee even as the Lord will". (V. 55). In this case, rather than stressing the miracle of forgiveness, Alma emphasized the awfulness of sin and its inevitable consequences. God hates sin because of what it does to the sinner. Korihor had forfeited the capacity to repent, and stood condemned for his crimes, in the sense that his actions dictated consequences that were unavoidable.

He and all those who had followed his uninspired counsel ultimately understood that the Church is not on trial, nor is the Savior, but each individual is the one on trial, and each must stand alone to face the Judgment. (V. 56-57). In our day, the precedent of English common law demands a trial before one's peers, composed of a jury of 12. But God requires only 2 or 3 witnesses to validate eternal law.

The "Korihors" of this world should recognize the myriad witnesses God has provided to establish His Own word and those of His authorized representatives. "For intelligence cleaveth unto intelligence;" declared the Master, "wisdom receiveth wisdom; truth embraceth truth; virtue loveth virtue; light cleaveth unto light; mercy hath compassion on mercy and claimeth her own; justice continueth its course and claimeth its own; (and) judgment goeth before the face of him who sitteth upon the throne and governeth and executeth all things". (D&C 88:40).

Those who had been Korihor's disciples, but were not yet under the same awful condemnation, were invited to "speedily repent, lest the same judgments would come unto them". (V. 57). We are punished by our sins, and not so much for them. God doesn't apply punishment externally, the way parents do. They say: "If you don't clean up your room, you can't drive the car for a week". He says: "If you don't clean up your room, you'll have to live in it for a week". We all have to live with the consequences of our disobedience to His law. Not surprisingly, "it came to pass that (his former disciples) were all convinced of the wickedness of Korihor; therefore, they were all converted again unto the Lord". (V. 58). Do we find in this passage another example of Nephite dry humor? (See Alma 18:9, 19:5, 33:21, 46:35, & 55:32).

The disciplinary councils of the Church had acted appropriately. Korihor's punishment was just. (See v. 55). In spite of the manifestation of the sign, the Church stood ready to work with him, just as it had with his followers. But Korihor was "past repentance". "It is true," taught Spencer W. Kimball, "that the great principle of repentance is always available, but for the wicked and rebellious there are serious reservations to this statement. For instance, sin is intensely habit forming and sometimes moves men to the tragic point of no return. Without repentance there can be no forgiveness, and without forgiveness all the blessings of eternity hang in jeopardy. As the transgressor moves deeper and deeper in his sin, and the error is entrenched more deeply and the will to change is weakened, it becomes increasingly near hopeless, and he skids down and down until either he does not want to climb back, or he has lost the power to do so". ("The Miracle of Forgiveness," p. 117).

Korihor was a broken man, going "about from house to house, begging food for his support". (V. 58). In his spiritual blindness, he went to those who could least help him out of his difficulty, "among a people who had separated themselves from the Nephites and called themselves Zoramites". (V. 59).

Near the close of his ministry, Mormon wrote: "The judgments of God will overtake the wicked". (Mormon 4:5). When he closed his abridgment of the account of Korihor, he observed that in the land "called Antionum, which was east of the land of Zarahemla," the antichrist was "run upon and trodden down, even until he was dead". (V. 59, & Alma Chapter 31:3).

Mormon's editorial comment closing this chapter is most perceptive and is universally applicable: "And thus, we see the end of him who perverteth the ways of the Lord; and thus, we see that the devil will not support his children at the last day, but doth speedily drag them down to hell". (V. 60). The adversary finally betrays his followers, because he cannot deliver on his promises. His enticements lead Father's children into conceptual cul de sacs and doctrinal dilemmas from which there is no exit except retreat. His cunning caresses entice the weak to plunge into a perceived freedom that is really a bottomless pit of misery. In a perverted, twisted way, "the devil seeks that all men might be miserable like himself". (2 Nephi 2:27).

We never do evil so cheerfully as when we think we are doing good. We must be especially vigilant, lest we be snared, as was Korihor. We must avoid embracing "idea-gods" that rivet our attention, consume our energies, and demand our devotion. (Neal A. Maxwell). Sitting with our engines idling while wasting time in telestial traffic jams can damage our desire and capacity to move forward. We must not look beyond the mark, for our destination is well-defined. One of the problems with antichrists is that they confuse knowledge for intelligence, and think that when they are learned they are wise. They fail to understand that to be learned is good, but only if they will hearken unto the counsels of God. (See 2 Nephi 9:28-29). There is a great lesson to be learned in Alma Chapter 30. If it is taken to heart, it could protect our testimonies and even save our souls.

Alma
Chapter 31

Chapters 31-35 chronicle the mission to the Zoramites by "Alma, and Ammon, and their brethren, and also the two sons of Alma". (V. 5, & Alma Chapter 35:14). They also deal with one of the great perversions of Christianity that immediately followed the account of the antichrist Korihor. Alma's heart was sickened by the apostasy of these people (v. 1) whose counterparts in the Last Days "seek not the Lord to establish his righteousness, but every man walketh in his own way, and after the image of his own god, whose image is in the likeness of the world, and whose substance is that of an idol, which waxeth old and shall perish in Babylon, even Babylon the great, which shall fall". (D&C 1:16).

"It was a cause of great sorrow to Alma" to realize that the Zoramites had become cultural Lamanites. (V. 2, see Alma 43:4). The Zoramites lived in the buffer state of Jershon, that was adjacent to the wilderness "which was full of the Lamanites" who were always anxious to weaken the moral, spiritual, and physical fiber of their Nephite neighbors. (V. 3). Deep in the shadows of the nearby jungle, away from prying eyes, the Zoramites had probably initiated an active correspondence with the Lamanites. In doing so, they had forgotten that "vice is a monster of so frightful mien, as to be hated needs but to be seen. Yet. In too oft, familiar with her face, we first endure, then pity, then embrace". (Alexander Pope). We all live in the midst of spiritual Babylon, adjacent to the jungle of worldliness, but we must never relax our standards, surrender to the rising tide of mediocrity swirling beneath us and threatening to undermine our footings, submit to lascivious lifestyles that cater to increasingly decadent, debauched, dissolute, and depraved deviations, make even small concessions to the trendy demands of the devil's devotees that insidiously encroach upon our principles, allow the gradual erosion of our ethics by the relentless pounding and persistent pressures of popular perversions that are so prevalent, pervasive, and powerful, or be lulled into complacency by the siren song of Satan's sentinels, who have always had a death-wish and whose behavior leads them to inevitable cultural suicide. Time and again, spiritual Babylon reminds us of the wretched souls whose mental and emotional instability and twisted logic justify a "Death by Cop" scenario. Self-destructive behavior is an easy lifestyle choice for those who are so miserable that they just want to be put out of their misery. Spiritual Babylon has never been able to understand the focus, determination, and undeviating standard that is embraced by celestial bound individuals.

Neal Maxwell wrote: "Whenever individuals believe that there are no absolute values, there are, ultimately, no sin and no crime. If there is no cosmic yardstick by which we can really measure things, how can we punish people for falling short by feet or inches? Dostoevsky predicted that the sages of our time would say, in fact, there is no crime, there is no sin, there is only hunger". ("Freedom: A Hard Doctrine").

However, in our day of enlightenment and restoration of truth, the Spirit confirms that we are the offspring of God our Father, sons and daughters of the King of Heaven, heirs of the Covenant He made with Abraham. In France during the Middle Ages, the successor to the throne was known as the Dauphin. During the reign of his father, unscrupulous and crafty counselors tried every means to corrupt the Dauphin and to thereby render him ineligible to inherit the throne. In all of their attempts, however, they were unsuccessful. Finally, in resignation, they asked him, "How is it that with all our enticements we have been unable to corrupt your standards?" His reply was simple: "I am a King's son".

"Who are these children coming down like gentle rain through darkened skies, with glory trailing from their feet as they go, and endless promise in their eyes? Who are these young ones growing tall, growing strong, like silver trees against the storm; who will not bend with the wind or the change, but stand to fight the world alone? These are the few, the warriors saved for Saturday, to come the last day of the world. These are they, on Saturday. These are the strong, the warriors rising in their might to win the battle raging in the hearts of men, on Saturday. Strangers from a realm of light, who have forgotten all, the memory of their former life, the purpose of their call. And so, they must learn why they're here, and who they really are". (Doug Stewart, "Saturday's Warrior").

When they arrive on the world stage, Saturday's Warriors face a gauntlet of intimidation, every form of murder, harassment, ridicule, twisted logic, fake news, doublespeak, depraved reason, counterfeit and competing lifestyles, and unenlightened science. "The natural man is an enemy to God, and has been from the fall of Adam, and will be, forever and ever," explained King Benjamin, "unless he yields to the enticicings of the Holy Spirit, and putteth off the natural man and becometh a saint through the atonement of Christ the Lord, and becometh as a child, submissive, meek, humble, patient, full of love, willing to submit to all things which the Lord seeth fit to inflict upon him, even as a child doth submit to his father". (Mosiah 3:19).

The Nephites were fearful that the Zoramites, who had knowledge of neither their noble heritage nor their divine potential, might enter into a conspiratorial dialogue with the Lamanites that "would be the means of great loss on the part of the Nephites". (V. 4). In fact, this is just what shortly thereafter happened. (See Alma 35: 10- 11, 43:6-10, 46:7 & 30, & 47:1).

In his years of missionary work, Alma had learned to be guided by the Spirit. It did not fail him now, for it whispered to him that he "should try the virtue of the word of God" with the Zoramites. (V. 5). How powerful was the preaching of the word? It "had a great tendency to lead the people to do that which was just, yea, it had had more powerful effect upon the minds of the people than the sword, or anything else". (V. 5, see Alma 5:61, & Helaman 6:37).

In a variety of ways, Heavenly Father has always provided direction for His children. The Nephites were given the Rod of Iron, or the word of God, that would lead them along a strait and narrow path directly to the tree of life. (1 Nephi 19-20, & 30). Soon thereafter, they received the "Liahona," that is an old word from the language of the fathers, needing to be interpreted by Alma as "a compass". (Alma 37:38). Speaking to our day, he taught that "it is as easy to give heed to the word of Christ (our compass) which will point you to a straight course to eternal bliss, as it was for our fathers to give heed to this compass, which would point unto them a straight course to the promised land. Do not let us be slothful (or move slowly) because of the easiness of the way". Instead, "Look to God, and live". (Alma 37:38-47).

In all ages of the world, God has raised up prophets to testify of His existence, of His Plan of Happiness, and of the Redeemer of the World. "Surely the Lord God will do nothing, but he revealeth his secret unto his servants the prophets". (Amos 3:7). Yes, "there is a God in heaven that revealeth secrets, and maketh known ... what shall be in the latter days". (Daniel 2:28). As the Lord said of Joseph Smith and Sidney Rigdon: "For by my Spirit will I enlighten them, and by my power will I make known unto them the secrets of my will - yea, even those things which eye has not seen, nor ear heard, nor yet entered into the heart of man". (D&C 76:10). The Latter-day Saints believe "all that God has revealed, all that He does now reveal, and (they) believe that He will yet reveal many great and important things pertaining to the Kingdom". (8th Article of Faith).

Is the way easy, or is it difficult? For the Israelites in the Wilderness of Sinai, it was only necessary that they look upon the Brazen Serpent, the staff of Moses, typifying Christ. "And as many as should look upon that serpent should live, even so as many as should look upon the Son of God, with faith, having a contrite spirit, might live, even unto that life which is eternal. (Helaman 8:13-16)

Our trials are not really so sophisticated. Noah preached of the flood. Ezra Taft Benson warned of a flood of pornography that is inundating the world. Moses wrote of the bondage of Israel in Egypt, and President Benson of the temporal bondage of financial indebtedness and of the spiritual bondage that comes from sacrificing agency to the popular idols of the day. Elijah rebuked those who worshiped Baal. President Benson cautioned us against spiritual death that comes from the worship of contemporary gods of wood and of stone. Joseph endured seven years of famine in Egypt. Our leaders have counseled us since 1937 to have our year's supply, reminding us that Noah preached for 100 years before the floods came. The Nephites wrote about the depravations of the Band of Gadianton. Through Joseph Smith, the Lord cautioned us against "the evils and designs which do and will exist in the hearts of conspiring men in the last days". (D&C 89:4). The Old Testament condemned murder; our priesthood leaders today expose the deception and damnable heresy of "pro-choice". The dietary code of the Law of Moses set the Israelites apart from their neighbors, as does our Word of Wisdom. The Apostles warned of unnatural affection, while our prophets condemn "alternative lifestyles" as deviant behavior of the most abominable nature.

The message is the same. "We talk of Christ, we rejoice in Christ, we preach of Christ, we prophesy of Christ, and we write according to our prophecies, that our children may know to what source they may look for a remission of their sins". (2 Nephi 25:26). Christ was, is, and shall ever be the light and life of the world. Meanwhile, the Earth is plunging wildly, blindly, and ignorantly toward the falls. The rapids already appear, and we are being engulfed in them. The cataract looms ominously on the horizon:

"They were singing, shouting, laughing, and talking about their personal victories and adventures, as the boat carried them peacefully along the slowly moving river. In their merriment, they did not notice a quiet quickening of the current. Their preoccupation with each other kept them from paying much attention to one who appeared on the nearby shore, waving excitedly for them to make their way to safety. A few waved back with curious smiles, but continued on with their immediate interests.

'Rapids! Falls! Change your direction! Come to shore quickly!' was the man's urgent call that was repeated over and over; but they were unconcerned until they happened to observe the faster current, and looked ahead to see a short stretch of white-capped waves dashing around and over jagged rocks. An increasing roar indicated that suddenly, the river would drop from sight, spilling into a roaring chasm of churning, foamy water.

With screams of horror, they lunged for the oars and began to row frantically for shore. But it was too late - they had waited too long. The power of the current was too strong, and into the rapids they plunged - tossing, turning, shrieking, and cursing. Finally, over the falls they went to a watery grave.

Knowing that the world is largely preoccupied with material and physical pleasures as it drifts faster and closer toward the coming calamities, a loving Lord has called special servants to raise a resounding voice of warning. Repent! Change the patterns of living before it is too late! Row diligently toward the shore of the loving grace of Jesus Christ, follow the counsel of His prophet, and avoid the rocks and shoals of calamity and judgment that are just ahead". (Marvin J. Ashton, Ensign, 11/1989, p. 36).

As Ezra Taft Benson declared: "We have The Book of Mormon, we have the members, we have the missionaries, we have the resources, and the world has the need. The time is now". (C.R. 10/1988).

By 1990, the 50 millionth copy had been printed for distribution by members and missionaries. That number doubled by 2000, with the Church printing an average of one copy every seven seconds over the next decade—a rate the Church has sustained to reach the projected 150 million by 2011. As of October 2020, the Church has published 192 million copies of the Book of Mormon in 112 languages.

"Come, listen to a prophet's voice, and hear the word of God!. And in the way of truth rejoice!. And sing for joy aloud. Thru erring schemes in days now past, the world has gone astray. Yet Saints of God have found at last the strait and narrow way. Then heed the words of truth and light that flow from mountains pure. Yea, keep his law with all thy might, 'til thine election's sure". ("Come Listen to a Prophet's Voice" Hymn #22).

Alma recognized the virtue of the word, or its incredible power to touch the hearts of the people. An example from the life of the Savior teaches this principle. During His earthly ministry, Jesus was filled with the Spirit of God, and so it was natural that the spiritually hungry were drawn to Him. In Him they satisfied their yearnings.

Jesus, in turn, being a wellspring of the Spirit, sensed each moment when need drew upon that source: "And a certain woman, which had an issue of blood twelve years, and had suffered many things of many physicians, and had spent all that she had, and was nothing bettered, but rather grew worse, when she had heard of Jesus, came in the press behind, and touched his garment. For she said, If I may touch but his clothes, I shall be whole. And straightway the fountain of her blood was dried up; and she felt in her body that she was healed of that plague. And Jesus, immediately knowing in himself that virtue had gone out of him, turned him about in the press, and said, Who touched my clothes?" (Mark 5:25-30).

The spiritually hungry came to the Mortal Messiah to satisfy their yearnings. Jesus, in turn, being a wellspring of the Spirit, sensed every moment when a need drew upon that source. This story in Mark gives us assurance that God is sensitive to our needs, and does hear our prayers. In conformity to spiritual law, we can tap into and draw upon the life force that is the Spirit of God. When we do so, we are, in effect, touching His garment.

One of David O. McKay's favorite poems reads: "The builder who first bridged Niagara's gorge, before he swung his cable, shore to shore, sent out across the gulf his venturing kite, bearing a slender cord for unseen hands to grasp upon the further cliff and draw a greater cord, and then a greater yet; 'til at last across the chasm swung the cable - then the mighty bridge in air! So may we send our little timid thoughts, across the void, out to God's reaching hands. Send our love, and faith, to thread the deep, thought after thought, until the little cord, and we, are anchored to the Infinite!" Edward Markham).

This is the process of sanctification by which we are cleansed from the effects of sin. It happens when the Gospel has driven the law into our inward parts (Jeremiah 31:33) and we become "firmer and firmer in the faith of Christ". (Helaman 3:35). "Sanctify yourselves," He commands us, "that your minds become single to God, and the days will come that you shall see him; for he will unveil his face unto you". (D&C 88:68). Thus, spiritually renewed, we stand prepared to enter His presence.

The word of God is the only solution to the problems we face. "Proposed remedies to the world's present predicament will prove futile," predicted Marion G. Romney. "There are no armaments, no governmental schemes, no international organizations, and no mechanisms for the control of weapons which can preserve an unrighteous people". (C.R. 4/1953, see Alma 41:10 & Helaman 13:38).

When Alma embarked on his mission to the Zoramites, he had three sons. The eldest, whose name was Helaman, remained behind in Zarahemla. The other two, Shiblon, and Corianton, he took with him. (V. 7). About all we know of the Zoramites is that they were Nephite "dissenters" or apostates who had fallen into great errors. (V. 9-11, see Alma 24:30, & Commentary Reference to Mosiah 2:37). The missionaries were surprised to find that the Zoramites had built synagogues in their land in which they worshiped one day each week. Their religious experience was basically restricted to the time spent while they were in Church. (V. 11).

They had a perverted way of expressing their faith, that reflected their misconception of the nature of God. "For they had a place built up in the center of their synagogue, a place for standing, which was high above the head; and the top thereof would only admit one person. Therefore, whosoever desired to worship must go forth and stand upon the top thereof, and stretch forth his hands towards heaven, and cry with a loud voice". (V. 13-14). This structure is reminiscent of the ziggurat of Babel that the people constructed in the false hope that the top thereof would reach all the way to heaven. (See Genesis 11:4).

But we do not draw nearer to God by constructing elaborate edifices (some of our latter-day temples notwithstanding). The wicked Zoramites were not teachable, for they could not see the need to draw near to God Himself in order to perfect their lives. They lacked humility, the key therapy that is necessary if we are to unclog our spiritual circulation as a precursor to changing hearts. Ultimately, Alma was successful only among the poor members of their society. (See Alma Chapter 32).

The expressions of the false doctrine of the Zoramites in their set prayers were riddled with the elements of apostasy. "We believe ... that thou wilt be a spirit forever," they declared. "There shall be no Christ ... Thou hast elected us that we shall be saved". (V. 15-17). They believed God is a spirit only, and denied the divinity of Christ and the inspiration of their Nephite forefathers. They also made worship a formality that was reserved for the Sabbath.

They embraced the distorted doctrine of predestination. Denying the ruling supremacy of agency, they felt that they were "a chosen and a holy people". (V. 18). In a weekly statement reflecting their own pride, "every man did go forth (unto the Rameumptum, as it was called) and offer up these same prayers". (V. 20). This astonished Alma and his brethren, and his sons "beyond all measure," for they were accustomed to more intimate conversations with God. (V. 19).

"At one level, we all indulge the daily clichés and more or less mean them: 'Forgive us,' or 'Help us to overcome our weaknesses.'. At a deeper level, we voice actual present feelings, even when they are raw, ugly, miserable ones: 'Father, I feel awful,' or 'I am racked with anxiety.' But there is a deeper level, the inmost of which often defies words, even feeling words. This level may be likened to what the scriptures call 'groanings which cannot be uttered.' (Romans 8:26). Turned upward, they become the most powerful prayer-thrusts of all. There is a wordless center in each of us". (Truman Madsen, "Christ & The Inner Life", p. 17-18).

The distorted understanding of the spiritually illiterate has similarly shocked missionaries in all ages. B.H. Roberts related has experience as a young Elder while serving in the Southern States Mission: "As Brother Palmer and I stepped into the Church, we found the pastor engaged in prayer, and what was my surprise to hear him say: 'O Lord, help us to understand that we have enough of Thy word; that the canon of scripture is full. Help us to believe, O Lord, that the awful voice of prophecy will no more be heard; help us to believe that revelation has ceased, that Thou wilt no more speak to man.' Well, thought I, there is a wide difference between the ideas contained in that person's prayer and what we are going to preach!" ("Defender of The Faith," p. 108).

The place where the established prayers of the Zoramites were offered was called "Rameumptom, which, being interpreted, is the holy stand". (V. 21). That the name had to be translated into Nephite indicates that the Zoramites had their own strange dialect. A possible root of this word, however, is "Ram", which in Hebrew means "a high place", as in the Hill "Ramah", or in the names of the towns "Ramallah", and "Rameem", in Israel.

Each week, after "the selfsame prayer" had been offered, the people "returned to their homes, never speaking of their God again until" the following Sabbath day. (V. 22-23). Their weekday activities were uninfluenced by belief in God, for whatever faith they still possessed was dormant. Religious expressions were confined to the Sabbath, and were sterile, devoid of vitality, impotent, and without power. With this in mind, James taught: "Faith without works is dead, being alone". (James 2:14).

Alma was grieved, for he saw that saving faith in the Lord was missing, and it its place were pride and materialism. (V. 24). The last 20 verses of this chapter contrast the Zoramite prayer (v. 15-18) with that of Alma on behalf of his missionary brethren and these lost sheep. (V. 26-35).

Alma asked God: "How long wilt thou suffer that such wickedness and infidelity shall be among this people?" (V. 30). Latter-day prophets have called attention to the same dangers within the

Restored Church. J. Reuben Clark, Jr. cautioned: "The ravening wolves are amongst us, from our own membership, and they more than any others, are ... in sheep's clothing, because they wear the habiliments of the priesthood. We should be careful of them". (C.R. 4/1949). When members of the Church are unfaithful to their covenants, they are guilty of the most serious infidelity, being untrue to the King of Heaven.

In our day, the cleansing of the earth will start with the members of The Church of Jesus Christ of Latter-day Saints. "Behold, vengeance cometh speedily upon the inhabitants of the earth, a day of wrath, a day of burning, a day of desolation, of weeping, of mourning, and of lamentation; and as a whirlwind it shall come upon all the face of the earth, saith the Lord. And upon my house shall it begin, and from my house shall it go forth, saith the Lord; First among those among you, saith the Lord, who have professed to know my name and have not known me, and have blasphemed against me in the midst of my house, saith the Lord". (D&C 112:24-26).

To his great credit, Alma never lost sight of his desire to bring the Zoramites back into the fold of God. He prayed: "O Lord, wilt thou grant unto us that we may have success in bringing them again unto thee in Christ. Behold, O Lord, their souls are precious, and many of them are our brethren; therefore, give unto us, O Lord, power and wisdom that we may bring these, our brethren, again unto thee". (V. 34-35). He recognized how important it was that his missionary companions be "filled with the Holy Spirit," and to this end he laid his hands on their heads and gave them priesthood blessings. (V. 36, see 3 Nephi 18:36). Consequently, their love of the Savior and zeal for the ministry so completely overshadowed their trials that the work continued unimpeded and without distraction.

This chapter deals with the Zoramites, a people who were mired in apostasy largely because they had become preoccupied with the mechanics of the Gospel. They did not know God. They did not know how to pray to Him. Their worship services were a caricature of the true order. "We must not be caught in the bind of building a Church and killing the articles of its faith," warned Alvin R. Dyer, "or permitting form to triumph over spirit. The Church and kingdom of God is built by the ardor and conviction of its members. We must be alert to the expansion of its assets at the cost of lost conviction. When buildings or institutions grow bigger and bigger, let us be fearful lest the Spirit thin out". ("A Foundation for Education").

The Zoramites were spiritually sick, and Alma sought to heal them by applying the balm of Gilead. He was eminently prepared to do this, and through preaching the word of God to this people, his purpose was accomplished. "Now this was according to the prayer of Alma; and this because he prayed in faith". (V. 38).

Alma
Chapter 32

Those who read this chapter on faith must remember that Alma was not speaking to members of the Church who had a sound understanding of basic Gospel principles, but to the poor Zoramites who had been living in a state of apostasy and had been taught only false doctrine. Therefore, his spiritually immature listeners were capable of processing the details of only the initial steps that must be taken to develop faith. Alma explained only the first part of the process, and not all there is to understand about faith. It is important for members of the Church who have a firm foundation in Gospel principles to keep this in mind when reading his oft-quoted discourse on faith. (See Commentary References in Ether Chapter 12).

Alma was on solid ground when he invited the Zoramites to test the truths of the Gospel. The Apostle James also challenged: "If any of you lack wisdom, let him ask of God, that giveth to all men liberally, and upbraideth not; and it shall be given him". (James 1:5). Joseph Smith put this promise to the test with spectacular results. (See J.S.H. 1:17). So have countless others who have prayed with the desire to know of the divine authenticity of the Latter-day Restoration.

Alma first taught the people in their synagogues. (V. 1-2). Evidence of the depth of apostasy of the Zoramites is revealed by the designation of their places of assembly as "synagogues" and not as "Churches". The Book of Mormon invariably uses "synagogue," that is a Greek word, to designate early Jewish assemblies, and "Church," from the Greek "ecclesia," to designate such assemblies after they had become Christian. It is hard to think of more appropriate terms, bearing in mind that this is a translation, and the purpose of the words is not to convey what the Nephites called their communities, but only how we are to picture them in our own minds. (See D&C 66:7, Mosiah 25:13, Alma 19:34, 21:16, 23:4, & 32:1-4).

The wealthy Zoramites, who likely wore "fine twined linen," scorned their poorer brethren "because of the coarseness of their apparel". (V. 2, see 1 Nephi 13:7-8, Mosiah 10:5, Alma 1:29 & 4:6). The temporally disadvantaged Zoramites were "poor as to the things of the world, (but) also they were poor in heart". (V. 3). In other words, their straitened circumstances fostered humility, and in turn, teachability. (See V. 6, 8, & 12). They came to Alma expressing a common concern of those who seek the truth but do not know where or how to find it: "We have no place to worship our God," they lamented, "and behold, what shall we do?" (V. 5). They did not understand their true relationship to God and His Son, and thought that they could only worship within the structured setting within their synagogues. (See Alma 33:2).

Alma was overjoyed that the poor Zoramites had come to him, for he "beheld that their afflictions had truly humbled them, and that they were in a preparation to hear the word". (V. 6). Immediately, he clarified two basic principles that they had grossly misunderstood. First, he explained that God can be worshipped wherever one may be, and secondly, that every day is a day of worship. (V. 10-11).

Alma realized that the Zoramites had been blessed because circumstances had compelled them to be humble. He knew that with proper Gospel instruction, their humility would lead them through faith and repentance, to mercy and forgiveness via the ordinances of the Gospel, and finally to salvation through the grace of God. (V. 13). The guiding lights of correct principles would lead them to even greater humility and meekness "because of the word". (V. 14). Alma understood that when seeds are planted in fertile soil, modesty, courtesy, and mildness are nurtured. (V. 15).

Alma wanted the Zoramites to enjoy the blessings related to enduring to the end in the light of the Gospel. Although endurance is often cast in a negative light, as in "enduring pain" or "enduring persecution," it can ultimately be positive and pleasant. However, to be so, it carries a performance cost.

If we wish to have physical endurance, for example, we must pay the price. Good diet and the mental and physical discipline of exercise is an essential ingredient. But when we have developed physical endurance, new heights may be achieved that would otherwise have been beyond our reach. With a sound body, we can choose from a wider variety of options, and agency to do so seems to have no bounds. Walk all day without fatigue? Participate in consecutive endowment sessions? Ski in the mountains? Hike to a lake for a day of fishing? Play three sets of tennis, or a round of golf? Given the natural limitations of age and individual temporal circumstances, when we possess physical endurance there are many worthwhile and uplifting activities from which to choose.

Nor does spiritual fitness, or endurance, come without effort. A testimony of the Gospel and its exalting principles is not an unearned gift. Rather, we read such things as: "Behold, you have not understood; you have supposed that I would give it unto you, when you took no thought save it was to ask me. But behold, I say unto you, that you must study it out in your mind". (D&C 9:7-8). Lorenzo Snow declared: "It is impossible to advance in the principles of truth, to increase in heavenly knowledge, except we exercise our reasoning faculties and exert ourselves". Agency is not free. It is purchased at a substantial price.

If we desire a testimony of family home evening, we must understand and obey the laws of the Gospel associated with that principle. "For all who will have a blessing at my hands shall abide the law which was appointed for that blessing, and the conditions thereof". (D&C 132:5, see D&C 130:20-21). If we want to know that The Book of Mormon is the word of God, we must read with a desire to receive a witness. (See Moroni 10:4). If we want to know that obedience to the Gospel Plan is the path to happiness, we need to try the virtue of the word of God.

God has promised us "knowledge by (the) Holy Ghost, yea, by the unspeakable gift of the Holy Ghost". (D&C 121:26, see D&C 1:38). When this happens, and we become the lucky recipients of testimony, we can receive the intrinsic knowledge that a principle is true. No one can rob us of that testimony, but we can forfeit it by embracing a lifestyle that alienates the confirming Spirit.

The scriptures teach with clarity and finality: "All saints who remember to keep and do these sayings, walking in obedience to the commandments, shall receive health in their navel and marrow to their bones; and shall find wisdom and great treasures of knowledge, even hidden treasures; and shall run and not be weary, and shall walk and not faint. And I, the Lord, give unto them a promise, that the destroying angel shall pass them by, as the children of Israel, and not slay them". (D&C 89:18-21). With testimony leading to conversion, the angels in heaven will wrap us in their encircling arms.

During his ministry among the Zoramites, Alma's exhausting confrontation with Korihor must have been fresh in his mind. (Alma 30). Perhaps he was thinking of that antichrist when he told the Zoramites: "There are many who do say: If thou wilt show unto us a sign from heaven, then we shall know of a surety; then we shall believe". (V. 17). He wanted to teach the Zoramites about saving faith without being reduced to giving them a sign in order to satisfy the need for theological titillation required by faithless apostates, and so he was meticulous to carefully establish a foundation for the lesson to follow.

Every discussion of faith must distinguish it from its caricatures. It is not naiveté or gullibility, nor is it wishful thinking. It is more than confidence and greater than optimism. Faith and positive thinking go hand in hand, but faith is more than an attitude. Within the Zoramite framework, Alma sought to teach that receiving heavenly signs cannot generate faith. In fact, he told the Zoramites that they should not desire a sign, because faith precedes the miracle. He explained that during the genesis of faith, it is necessary to take a few steps into the darkness, and then the spiritual strong searchlight will illuminate the way. Only after the trial of our faith will it be confirmed by direct experience, and will the Spirit validate God as its Author and Finisher.

This is why Alma carefully taught the Zoramites: "If a man knoweth a thing he hath no cause to believe (or exercise faith), for he knoweth it". (V. 18). That is to say, in its initial stages of development, faith is not knowledge. If a sign were to be given before our transformation through faith, we might have a sure knowledge of the principle, but it would have come to our undisciplined mind without the necessary expenditure of faith. This was Korihor's fatal flaw. He demanded a sign from heaven without the appropriate and necessary exercise of faith.

Under proper circumstances, though, as we gain spiritual maturity "by doing our duty, faith increases until it becomes perfect knowledge". (Heber J. Grant, C.R. 4/1934). Certainly, God Himself is full of faith, and yet He is omniscient. There is nothing that He does not know. For our part, as imperfect mortals struggling to believe what we do not see, the reward of our maturing faith is to see what we believe. Some things just have to be believed to be seen.

But Heavenly Father has not left us destitute, and He has not abandoned us to blindly tap our way through the lone and dreary world. "Faith in Christ is not a leap in the dark. It is, instead, trust in what the spirit learned eons ago; and religious recognition is just that, a re-cognition, a re-knowing, the sum of existence. If we thwart or suppress that instinctive response, we are accountable, and to a degree, we condemn ourselves. We knew Christ before this life, we know Him here, and we will know Him hereafter. His sheep do indeed know His voice. And thus, the impact of truth on man is a test of man"; it is a test of our faith. (Truman Madsen, Commentary on "B.H. Roberts, The Way, The Truth and The Life").

Thus, Alma taught: "How much more cursed is he that knoweth the will of God and doeth it not, than he that only believeth, or only hath cause to believe, and falleth into transgression?" (V. 18). Belief is a mental assent to the truth or actuality of a concept without the moral element of responsibility that we call faith. (V. 21). To those to whom much is given, however, much is expected. The gift of faith demands action. Therefore, when we exercise our moral agency, "without works (it) is dead, being alone". (James 2:17). Faith is an action verb.

"Without faith, one is free, and that is a pleasant feeling at first. There are no questions of conscience, no constraints, except the constraints of custom, convention, and the law, and these are flexible enough, for most purposes. It is only later that the terror comes. We are free in chaos, in an unexplained and unexplainable world, in a desert from which there is no retreat but inward toward our hollow core". (Morris West, "The Devil's Advocate"). Agency is meaningful when faith drives us to purposeful performance.

Therefore, Alma told the Zoramites: "Now of this thing ye must judge. Behold, I say unto you, that it is on the one hand even as it is on the other; and it shall be unto every man according to his work". (V. 20). He was asking the Zoramites, posed to make life's most important decisions, to cast aside their fears and take a tremendous step as they stood at the crossroads. (See Joshua 24:15). As Robert Frost wrote: "I shall be telling this with a sigh somewhere ages and ages hence: Two roads diverged in a wood, and I, I took the one less traveled by, and that has made all the difference". ("The Road Less Traveled").

Alma hoped the Zoramites would develop faith unto salvation, knowing full well that Heavenly Father does not expect us to exercise faith in things for which there is insufficient evidence. As this sermon unfolded, Alma would give the Zoramites a formula for the development of fledgling faith that would be the key to their liberation from enslavement to apostate religious dogma. The next move would be theirs to make.

In matters of faith, it is we, and not the Lord, who are on trial. At the Bar of Justice, the evidence will be presented, and our previous conformity with or rejection of eternal law will determine our reward or punishment. The trial we call mortality is eminently fair because of our capacity, even our innate tendency, to develop saving faith.

Because they had neither a doctrinal nor an experiential foundation in faith, the Zoramites were told: "Faith is not to have a perfect knowledge of things; therefore, if ye have faith ye hope for things which are not seen, which are true". (V. 21, see Hebrews 11:1). This is correct, but only in the ultimate sense. The important point that Alma was trying to make was that faith is unnecessary if the object of our faith is demonstrable to the physical senses. In Alma's usage, verse 21 might more clearly read: "Faith is not to have a perfect knowledge of things gained through our own experiences". Remember that Korihor's demand for a sign had been the condition for his faith, since he trusted only his physical senses. This rational approach is the enemy of faith. Thus, secular humanism and other similar ideologies destroy faith and are devilish doctrines, subtle though they may be. They are abominable to God because they thwart the development of faith.

Truth, on the other hand, is at the very foundation of faith. Heavenly Father will not lead us to have faith in that which is false, for example, in professional faith healers. In these cases, Satan is responsible for the healing, for he has limited power over life and death. (See Job 2:6). Nevertheless, God sanctions those evincing pure and simple faith. Hence, there are numerous examples of healing by those without the priesthood.

Faith may lead us to believe the truth "in the first place," to obtain mercy. (V. 23). It is a motivating catalyst, for the horizon of our faith extends only as far as our deeds. This is why works are an important companion to vital, active faith. (See James 2:17, & Matthew 5:16). Faith without action, without good works, has no life generating or sustaining power, because alone it is impotent. It is the sizzle without the steak. It does not lead to enduring purposeful performance.

Even Martin Luther understood faith to be more than intellectual assent. It is "vital, personal self-committal to a practical belief. He heartily approved of good works; what he denied was their efficacy for salvation. 'Good works,' he said, 'do not make a good man, but a good man does good works'. And what makes a man good? Faith in God, and Christ". (Will Durant, "The Lessons of History: The Reformation," 374-375).

After the aside in verses 22-25, Alma returned to his subject in verse 26: "Now, as I said concerning faith - that it was not a perfect knowledge - even so it is with my words. Ye cannot know of their surety at first, unto perfection, any more than faith is," at first, "a perfect knowledge". (V. 26). Therefore, in verses 27-43, Alma proposed an experiment to generate incipient faith. He asked the Zoramites to "awake and arouse (their) faculties, even to an experiment upon (his) words". (V. 27). The experiment involved desire (v. 27), planting a seed (v. 28), nourishing it (V. 37-41), and harvesting fruit. (V. 42-43).

They were to "exercise a particle of faith" even if it was no more than the "desire to believe". (V. 27). The principle that the Zoramites were asked to believe was that the Son of God would come and atone for the sins of the world. (See Alma 33-35). Alma was counting on the fact that "truth as well as untruth may be recognized by its effects. Rendering obedience to its principles of action may test the claims of the Gospel. Practicing our religion is the most direct method of gaining a testimony of the truth". (John Widtsoe).

Comparing the word to a seed, Alma asked the Zoramites to "give place," or to study, pray and commit themselves to a specific plan of action. Consequently, they would feel the word enlarge their souls and enlighten their understanding. (V. 28, see V. 29-33). As Brigham Young said: "Every Gospel principle carries within it a witness that it is true". Within the economy of the Gospel, "we often catch a spark from the awakened memories of the immortal soul, which lights up our whole being as with the glory of our former home". (Joseph F. Smith, "Gospel Doctrine," p. 14).

In the Last Days, the missionaries often ask those who are introduced to the Church to engage in the experiment suggested by Alma, to determine for themselves the validity of the message of The Restoration and of The Book of Mormon itself. As Hugh Nibley has said: "We are not laying down ground rules for taste, or saying that The Book of Mormon is good because some people like it, or bad because others do not. What we are saying is that The Book of Mormon, whatever one may think, is one of the great realities of our time, and that what makes it so, is that certain people believe it. Its literary or artistic qualities do not enter into the discussion. It was written to be believed. Its one and only merit is truth. Without that merit, it is all that nonbelievers say it is. With it, it is all that believers say it is". ("Of All Things," p. 93).

It is important to emphasize the very narrow sense in which Alma proposed the experiment to the Zoramites. After its completion, their knowledge of that one specific principle would be perfect, and the faith required to accept it would have been profitably expended, and so would become "dormant". (V. 34).

Thus, the successful completion of the experiment would result in a budding testimony of that Gospel principle. Testimony is composed of three essential ingredients. First is the recognition, or acknowledgement, of an eternal principle. Second is an understanding of the Lord's counsel concerning the principle, and third is direct experience with the principle, which is the fruits of faith. The Zoramites had been asked to experiment only on the words of Alma, whose objective was to introduce them to direct experience with a specific principle of the Gospel. He recognized that they would first have to build on a desire to believe, and then establish the groundwork of knowledge that would only then provide a solid foundation for their newfound faith.

As Alma explained: "Neither must ye lay aside your faith, for ye have only exercised your faith to plant the seed that ye might try the experiment to know if the seed was good". (V. 36). As the seed was nurtured, it would "grow up, and bring forth fruit". (V. 37). In other words, additional knowledge would be added to the expanding foundation of faith.

But if the seed were neglected, Alma cautioned: "Behold, it will not get any root; and when the heat of the sun cometh and scorcheth it, because it hath no root it withers away". (V. 38). This, he explained, is "because your ground is barren, and ye will not nourish the tree". (V. 39). There is no revelation where there is no student. In addition, as long as people ask the wrong questions, they will be at odds with biblical faith. The rational mind will never bridge the gap between the secular and the divine. "As humanity continues to struggle with death, despair, hopelessness, fear, and anxiety, the scriptures speak a far more relevant message to society than any rational explanation". ("Newsweek," 11/1980).

"If you will not nourish the word," cautioned Alma, you must not think that the experiment failed. You "can never pluck of the fruit of the tree of life" if you have not accepted the fact that perspiration must precede inspiration. (V. 40). If we choose mediocrity, rationalization, selfish pleasures, things of the world, the honors of men, or willful disobedience over soul-sweat, our priorities are out of order, and we will fail the experiment. As long as we remain in this state, we can never partake of the fruit of the tree of life. The world before us will appear as a barren desert, devoid of refreshing oases, the welcome shade of trees, and the abundance of well-watered and fruited gardens.

"But if ye will nourish the word," explained Alma, "it shall take root; and behold it shall be a tree springing up unto everlasting life," reminiscent of the tree in Lehi's dream that represented the love of God and its ultimate expression of eternal life. (V. 41, see 1 Nephi 8:10-12). Alma cautioned the Zoramites that it would take diligence and patience to "reap (the) rewards of (their) faith". (V. 42-43). We call these efforts "enduring to the end in righteousness," in a process wherein faith is multiplied unto us.

This message from Alma to the poor Zoramites is as relevant today as it was two thousand years ago, because the world now faces the same temporal problems and is in the same spiritual predicament. In materialistic western societies that reflect the conditions found so long ago among the more affluent Zoramites, the challenges are even greater.

We seem to be in a quandary from which there is no escape. Latter-day Zoramites "tend to fill space, as if what they have, what they are, is not enough. Being affluent, they strangle themselves with what they can buy, things whose opacity obstructs their ability to see what is really there". (Gretel Erlich, "Under Wyoming's Skies," The Atlantic Magazine).

We can learn from the account of Alma's missionary efforts among the Zoramites that we should take specific measures to avoid the pitfalls associated with seeking "for things (we cannot) understand". (Jacob 4:14). In their spiritual immaturity, the Zoramites required milk, and not meat, to nourish the quality of their belief. (See 1 Corinthians 3:2, & Hebrews 5:12). The tender shoots that would spring from their young testimonies would be carefully nurtured in accordance with Alma's wise formula, without the ecclesiastical embroidery that often needlessly complicates the simple message of the Gospel.

Alma
Chapter 33

Chapter 33 reinforces the introductory concepts on faiths that the spiritually immature Zoramites had received, and that are recorded in chapter 32. (V. 1).

Alma focused on one of the Zoramites' incorrect beliefs in order to teach a great principle: "If ye suppose that ye cannot worship God, ye do greatly err," he explained, "and ye ought to search the scriptures; if ye suppose that they have taught you this, ye do not understand them". (V. 2). Alma knew that scripture mastery is essential to the development of an eternal perspective that is, in turn, critical to the fulfilment of our destiny. If we don't know where we're going, if any direction or destination will do, that's where we'll end up, and we won't even care if we made the trip. (See Commentary Reference to V. 16).

Verse 5 articulates the Zoramites' great concern: "We have no place to worship our God; and behold, what shall we do?" Mormon recorded in the next 37 verses Alma's response, wherein he taught the fundamentals of faith, knowledge, and testimony. Alma did not expound on the scriptures that deal with these principles, but only introduced the concepts by employing easily understood analogies.

Their petition gave him the opportunity to bear down on the Zoramites with the power of pure testimony or independent witnesses, in the scriptures. He recalled the testimonies of Zenos, Zenock, and Moses to ratify the principle that we must plant the seed before we can hope to reap the blessing. In this case, the seed Alma had in mind was belief in the coming life and mission of the Son of God. Mormon used all these witnesses, including Alma, to testify of these truths to the readers of The Book of Mormon. (See Mosiah 18:10, 2414, Alma 10:12, 30:45, 34:33, & 3 Nephi 7:15)

Verses 4-11 concern scriptures from the Plates of Brass that today are no longer found in any existing Old Testament manuscripts. (See Commentary Reference to l Nephi 19:10-17, & Jacob 5:1). Because the references are found in The Book of Mormon, their witness also carries the weight of divine approval. After all, "we believe The Book of Mormon to be the word of God". (8th Article of Faith).

Zenos had taught that Heavenly Father's children must pray when in the wilderness, in their fields, houses and closets, in their congregations, and even when they are cast out of their assemblies. (V. 4-10). This scripture would have particularly touched the poorer Zoramites, inasmuch as they could relate so intimately to the persecution Zenos had experienced.

Focusing on their empathy with Zenos, Alma asked them: "Do ye believe those scriptures which have been written by them of old?" (V. 12). If so, it would naturally follow that the Zoramites would also believe in the Son of God. (V. 14)

To reinforce the witness of Zenos, Alma invoked the name of the prophet Zenock, who had suffered a martyr's death in defense of his testimony of the Son of God. (V. 15-17). Finally, Alma called upon the example of the revered prophet Moses, who had raised up a type "in the wilderness, that whosoever would look upon it might live. And many did look and live". (V. 19, see Commentary Reference to Alma 37:45). This type is a reference to the brass serpent that was understood by the Israelites to be a representation of the Messiah, who would save all those who would look to Him. "And as many as should look upon that serpent should live, even so as many as should look upon the Son of God with faith, having a contrite spirit, might live, even unto that life which is eternal. And now behold, Moses did not only testify of these things, but also all the holy prophets, from his days even (backward) to the days of Abraham". (Helaman 8:15).

Verse 20 is particularly significant in our day. "But few understood the meaning of those things, and this because of the hardness of their hearts. But there were many who were so hardened that they would not look, therefore they perished. Now the reason they would not look is because they did not believe that it would heal them". (V. 20). Today, the Lord Himself is often given metaphysical compliments that turn out to be insults. Either the Lamb of God is mighty to save, and had the power to cleanse us of unrighteousness, or He had no power beyond the persuasive effects of His own teachings. (See Alma 7:14). Either He was the Son of God come to earth to work out the Atonement, or He was a fraud of monumental proportions. But let us not confuse the issue by suggesting that He was only a gifted teacher, or merely a great Rabbi. Rallying around noble principles cannot save us. We can be redeemed only in the precious blood of the Holy One of Israel.

Christ said of the Last Days: "False prophets shall rise, and shall deceive many". (Matthew 24:11). He did not say that there would be no prophets, but only that there would be confusion because of false prophets, whose messages are often accompanied by the kind of gaudy paraphernalia that attracts the curious, but demands no commitment. Moths are drawn to the fire, but they flirt with death in a deadly dance with the flickering flame.

President Kimball once observed: "Looking for the spectacular, we often miss the constant flow of revealed communication that comes". Because this is true of society as well as of Saints, the Lord's authorized servants, who have been commissioned to preach the saving principles of the Gospel, frequently have a difficult time finding the listening ear of an audience. In contrast to the messages of Madison Avenue that are pleasing to those with itching ears and carnal natures, theirs strike more sensitive and selective chords.

Evidence that society focuses on worldly matters comes from the Spokane Area Conference of the Church, held May 10-11, 1986. Headlines in the local newspapers that weekend should have declared to a spellbound city: "Largest Priesthood Gathering Ever Held in Northwest," "Apostles of the Lord Visit Spokane," and "Ten Thousand Saints of The Highest Assemble". In fact, there was no reference whatsoever to the Conference in the media. Instead, it reported on the state of the economy, the political fortunes of prominent politicians, the outcome of baseball games, and other telestial trivia.

Satan's efforts are concentrated on attempts to weaken the intrinsic yearning in each of us to live in harmony with the majestic clockwork. For example, since the destroyer is familiar with the purpose of the temple, he has made a direct frontal assault on the family, that indirectly frustrates the work that goes on in the House of the Lord. This hinders the stated mission of the Church, which is to bring people to Christ through participation in the ordinances of the priesthood.

If the subject were not so serious, and did not have such significant eternal consequences for those living in the Last Days, we might almost detect a bit of dry humor in Alma's next remark: "O my brethren, if ye could be healed by merely casting about your eyes ... would ye not behold quickly, or would ye rather harden your hearts in unbelief, and be slothful, that ye would not cast about your eyes, that ye might perish?" (V. 21, see Alma 18:9, 19:5, 30:58, 33:21, 46:35, & 55:32).

So, as we read about the Zoramites, we see that they were given solid doctrine that was built upon the delicate foundation of faith that had been established by Alma in his discourse recorded in chapter 32. (V. 22). As Alma said: "I desire that ye shall plant this word in your hearts, and as it beginneth to swell even so nourish it by your faith. And behold, it will become a tree, springing up in you unto everlasting life". (V. 23).

He promised them that if they would do this, the burdens that felt crushing to them would "be light, through the joy of his Son". Perhaps Alma had heard his own father bear testimony that the Lord lightens the burdens of His people, according to their faith. "And I will also ease the burdens which are put upon your shoulders," the Lord had promised Alma, "that even you cannot feel them upon your backs, even while you are in bondage; and this will I do that ye may stand as witnesses for me hereafter, and that ye may know of a surety that I, the Lord God, do visit my people in their afflictions". (Mosiah 24:14).

In reassuring words, Alma the Younger spoke comfort to the souls of the Zoramites: "And even all this can ye do, if ye will". (V. 23, see Commentary Reference to Mosiah 24:14). So it is today.

"A type was
raised up in the wilderness,
that whosoever would look upon
it might live. And many did
look upon it and live."
(Alma 33:19).

Alma
Chapter 34

"In the mouths of two or three witnesses shall every word be established". (Deuteronomy 17:6, see 2 Corinthians 13:1). Therefore, "Amulek (now) arose and began to teach" the Zoramites. He understood that the principles upon which Alma had expounded had been previously taught to the Zoramites. (V. 2). But their dissention had clouded their understanding; what light and knowledge they had accumulated had been lost because of apostasy. Now it was necessary that their minds be prepared and cultivated anew, that with patience and in faith the word might be planted in their hearts, that they might "try the experiment" that had been proposed by Alma. (V. 3-4).

Amulek first reiterated the testimony of the prophets. (V. 6-7, see Helaman 8:19-21). Then he added his own witness to the already impressive list. "I will testify unto you of myself that these things are true," he declared.

Amulek's intention was to teach the Zoramites principles of the Gospel from the basis of their own level of understanding, which was the Law of Moses. (V. 8-17, see Mosiah 3:15-27). Therefore, he spoke of the Atonement, describing it as "a great and last" or "an infinite and eternal sacrifice". (V. 10, see D&C 20:17). It was immeasurably and inconceivably great, and ended the Mosaic Law of Carnal Commandments and the practice of blood sacrifice for sin with which the Israelites were familiar. "Then shall the law of Moses be fulfilled;" he said, "yea, it shall all be fulfilled, every jot and tittle, and none shall have passed away". (V. 13)

"This is the whole meaning of the law, every whit pointing to that great and last sacrifice; (that) will be the Son of God". (V. 14). The Zoramites, who were familiar with the sacrificial ordinances of the Law of Moses, were guided by Amulek via that Law to the Savior, who would "bring salvation to all those who (should) believe on his name; this being the intent of this last sacrifice". The blood of the Savior would redeem all who would exercise "faith unto repentance". (V. 15). The Law of Moses would be a schoolmaster to bring them unto Christ. (See Galatians 3:24, 2 Nephi 25:24-30, Mosiah 12:27-13:32, 3 Nephi 9:17, 15:1-10, D&C 84;23-27).

"Thus, mercy can satisfy the demands of justice, and encircles them in the arms of safety, while he that exercises no faith unto repentance is exposed to the whole law of the demands of justice; therefore, only unto him that has faith unto repentance is brought about the great and eternal Plan of redemption". (V. 16, see Alma Chapter 42). Of course, baptism for the remission of sins and the other priesthood-administered ordinances are also necessary. (See Alma 9:27).

Next, Amulek taught the Zoramites about the relationship of prayer to true worship and faith. (V. 17, see Alma 32:3-11). Prayer is a way to exercise faith and is a powerful weapon against the devil. Joseph Fielding Smith, Jr. taught: "No man can retain the spirit of the Lord unless he prays". In the next few verses, Amulek got very specific, partly because the Zoramites had been incorrectly taught to pray only in a very stylized and ineffective way. (V. 18-27).

Paul wrote: "Pray without ceasing". (1 Thessalonians 5:17). But Amulek cautioned: "After ye have done all these things, if ye turn away the needy, and the naked, and visit not the sick and afflicted, and impart of your substance, if ye have, to those who stand in need, behold your prayer is vain and availeth you nothing, and ye are as hypocrites who do deny the faith. (V. 28, see Mosiah 4:16-17, & 18:28). In His teachings, the Savior warned against vain repetitions in prayer and helped His disciples to understand how to avoid such a practice: "But when ye pray," he cautioned, "use not vain repetitions, as the heathen do: for they think that they shall be heard for their much speaking". (Matthew 6:7). Amulek likewise taught the Zoramites how to keep their prayers free of vanity and hypocrisy.

Something is done "in vain" when it is without effect, or without the desired or intended result. For example, to "try in vain" is to try without success. The reason taking the name of the Lord in vain is blasphemous is because it is using His name inappropriately and without authority. Those who do so are imposters, invoking the name of Deity in a false, misleading, and counterfeit way. This is Satan's approach, in contrast to the righteous use of the name of God by those who bear His priesthood authority.

Instead, Amulek encouraged the Zoramites to "fulfil the royal law according to the scripture: Thou shalt love thy neighbor as thyself". (James 2:8, see V. 29). There is no vanity in those whose hearts have charity. We do not show our love for the Savior by honking our horns.

Echoing the words of Alma, Amulek exhorted the Zoramites to heed the witnesses they had cited, and "come forth and bring fruit unto repentance". (V. 30). He promised them that the Plan of Redemption would then "immediately" be energized in their lives. (V. 31). His audience was the poorer class of Zoramites who were humble and teachable, but who were apostate, nevertheless. The Merciful Plan of the Creator and the effect of the Atonement could be applied immediately in their behalf, if they would only exercise faith unto repentance.

Verses 32-35 clearly teach that now is the time to repent. (See Mormon 9:3-4, & D&C 138:50).

Nevertheless, repentance after death is not impossible. (See 1 Peter 3:19-20). But it is a lot easier in mortality. This is the time when we are more susceptible to change. We are more pliable. When clay is soft it is much easier to mold. The last group in the spirit prison of the unjust will be resurrected 1,000 years after the Savior comes, perhaps because it will be so much more difficult for them to repent after this life is over. (See Commentary Reference to 2 Nephi 4:32, & D&C 76:73, 138:8 & 28, Isaiah 61:1, 1 Peter 3:19 & Moses 7:57).

"Behold, this life is the time for men to prepare to meet God; yea, behold the day of this life is the day for men to perform their labors. (V. 32). If we "procrastinate the day of (our) repentance until the end," we unwittingly yield ourselves to the adversary. (V. 33). Perhaps this is one of the reasons why Alma later counseled his son Corianton that wickedness never was happiness, and that it was, in fact, contrary to the nature of happiness. (Alma 41:10-11).

When Amulek characterized life in the spirit prison as "the night of darkness wherein there can be no labor performed," he was not saying that repentance is impossible there, but only that in the Spirit Prison, Justice demands direct payment in cash, rather than vicarious payment through repentance and the Atonement. (V. 34).

Spencer W. Kimball taught: "It is true that the great principle of repentance is always available, but for the wicked and rebellious there are serious reservations to this statement. As transgressors moves deeper and deeper in their sins, and their errors are entrenched more deeply and the will to change is weakened, it becomes increasingly near hopeless, and they skid down and down until either they do not want to climb back, or they have lost the power to do so". ("The Miracle of Forgiveness," p. 117, see V. 35).

Unless we repent, the Spirit of the Lord is withdrawn and we remain spiritually dead, just as if there had been no redemption made. (V. 35, see Mosiah 16:5, Alma 11:41, 12:18, Helaman 14:18, & Moroni 7:48). But forgiveness through repentance can be so total and complete that Amulek utilized the vivid imagery of a garment soaked in the redeeming blood of the Savior when describing the process to the Zoramites, telling them "their garments should be made white through the blood of the Lamb". (V. 36).

Summarizing the principles he had taught, Amulek said: "I desire that ye should remember these things". (V. 37). First, "contend no more against the Holy Ghost". Second, "receive it". Third, "take upon you the name of Christ". Fourth, "humble yourselves". Fifth, "worship God". Sixth, "live in thanksgiving daily". Seventh, "be watchful unto prayer continually". Eighth, "have patience". (V. 38-40). His was a simple and pragmatic approach, adapted to the capacity of those with the weakest faith. But it was and continues to be an easily understood blueprint for those striving to live their lives as Saints.

"This life is the time for men to prepare to meet God; yea, behold, the day of this life is the day for men to perform their labors."
(Alma 34:32).

Alma
Chapter 35

With the exception of Alma 36-42, the next 44 consecutive chapters in The Book of Mormon deal with wars and their consequences. Alma Chapter 35 took place about 74 years before the coming of Christ. Then, Chapter 1 of Helaman identifies the signs of the Savior's birth. Significantly, Mormon inserted Alma Chapters 36-42 to identify the concerns of Alma for his loved ones as they were about to face long and drawn-out conflicts.

There are 68 chapters in The Book of Mormon that are devoted to warfare between the Nephites and Lamanites. This is nearly one third of the entire record. Mormon knew that we would live in a time of "wars and rumors of wars", and he evidently wanted us to be prepared for the experience.

Joseph Smith's Revelation and Prophecy on War sounds like it comes from the pages of The Book of Mormon, but it deals with our day: "The time will come that war will be poured out upon all nations ... And thus, with the sword and by bloodshed the inhabitants of the earth shall mourn; and with famine and plague, and earthquake, and the thunder of heaven, and the fierce and vivid lightning also, shall the inhabitants of the earth be made to feel the wrath, and indignation, and chastening hand of an Almighty God, until the consumption decreed hath made a full end of all nations ... Wherefore, stand ye in holy places, and be not moved, until the day of the Lord come; for behold, it cometh quickly, saith the Lord." (D&C 89:2, 6, & 8),

Chapter 35 deals with two contrasting results of Gospel preaching. Its opening verses inform us that the missionaries all left Antionum, that was east of Zarahemla, and went into the Land of Jershon, where the converted Lamanites known as the People of Ammon lived. (V. 1-2, see Alma 31:3).

The wicked Zoramites back in Antionum were angry because of the success of the missionaries among their poor brethren. When the representatives of the Lord Jesus Christ carry the Gospel message to an apostate people, enlightening their minds and correctly orienting them toward eternal truths, the livelihood of those who engage in priestcraft is threatened, and conflict almost inevitably results. (V. 3, see 1 Nephi 8:33, 2 Peter 2:21, & Hebrews 6:4-6).

The apostasy of the Zoramites was not unlike that of the Christians during the time their Church was sanctioned by Rome. The third century Christian Father Eusebius reflected: "But with our greater freedom a change came over us. We yielded to pride and sloth. We yielded to mutual envy and abuse. We warred upon ourselves as occasion offered, and we used the weapons and the spears of words. Leaders fought with leaders and laity formed factions against laity. Unspeakable hypocrisy and dissimulation traveled to the farthest limits of evil". ("The Essential Eusebius", "Church History" Book 8, Chapter 1).

In Antionum, the consequence of hard-core Zoramite apostasy was that "those who were in favor of the words which had been spoken by Alma and his brethren were cast out of the land". (V. 6). These refugees from persecution came into Jershon, where the People of Ammon, true to their baptismal covenants, "did nourish them, and did clothe them, and did give unto them lands for their inheritance". (V. 9). This only angered the wicked Zoramites further, who began to breathe out threats "against the people of Ammon, and also against" their Nephite guardians, as well. (V. 10). Alma's worst fears about an alliance of the Zoramites with the Lamanites were about to be realized. (V. 11, see Commentary Reference to Alma 31:4, Alma 43:4, & 13, 47:35, & Helaman 3:16).

Consequently, the People of Ammon, who had sworn a covenant of non-aggression, were evacuated by the Nephites from the Land of Jershon, that bordered the wilderness toward the Land of Nephi and that was vulnerable to Lamanite attack. (V. 13, see Alma 27:22-23).

The missionaries were also withdrawn to Zarahemla, secure in the knowledge that those whom they had converted were also in relative safety, with the armies of the Nephites occupying defensive positions in their former home in the Land of Jershon. (V. 14). Upon his return to Zarahemla, however, Alma was pained to find that "the hearts of the people (there) began to wax hard, and that they began to be offended because of the strictness of the word". (V. 15). In these circumstances, with the spectre of both internal and external threats to the temporal and spiritual security of his family members, Alma "caused that his sons should be gathered together, that he might give unto them every one his charge, separately, concerning the things pertaining unto righteousness". (V. 16).

Conditions in our day reflect those found in Zarahemla in 73 B.C., and so it is equally important for today's parents to provide coherent guidelines of behavior for their children. They will teach them how to correctly deal with the events that affect them, enabling them to build a firewall of protection from the worldly influences that encroach upon the fortress of their spiritual security. By internalizing Gospel principles, their youth will create impenetrable shields of faith, and with eternal perspective, they will learn to personalize the Plan of Happiness even when the simplicity of the message is clouded by the sophistry of Satan. With the aid of the Holy Ghost, his fingerprints will be more easily distinguished.

The sturdiest plants that bear the best fruit are those that have deep roots in good, rich soil. So should it be with our children. They must be provided with the best that we are able to offer in music and art, conversation, example, decency, virtue, honor, and spirit. Our children should be allowed to grow freely, but we must be sure to provide rich Gospel soil in order to create an environment for growth. The spirit of the 13th Article of Faith should permeate our homes. "If there is anything virtuous, lovely, or of good report or praiseworthy, we seek after these things". To the extent that we do this, we may expect to see our children blossom as champions for righteousness. "Train up a child in the way he should go, and when he is old, he will not depart from it". (Proverbs 22:6). "Happiness" after all, "is the object and design of our existence, and will be the end thereof, if we pursue the path that leads to it, and this path is virtue, uprightness, faithfulness, holiness, and keeping all the commandments of God". (Joseph Smith, "Teachings," p. 255).

That Alma wanted these same opportunities for his own children is evident by the sensitive counsel he gave to each of them, that Mormon recorded in the following chapters. As we read these, we appreciate Alma's humanity and recognize once again that he is not so very different from concerned parents in our ages who struggle to raise their children in the midst of difficult circumstances.

"And it came to pass that after the more popular part of the Zoramites had consulted together concerning the words which had been preached unto them, they were angry because of the word, because it did destroy their craft."
(Alma 35:3).

Alma
Chapter 36

Chapter 36 is a chiasm in 14 parts that attests to the concentration of The Book of Mormon, as well as to the Hebraic style that permeates this record of Alma's advice to Helaman. Together with the next 6 chapters in the text, it records Alma's counsel to all three of his sons. First, it was Alma's devout wish that Helaman would hear his words and learn of him. (V. 3). He went about this by recounting the elements of his own conversion. He had a clear and unapologetic realization of his sins and iniquities (V. 13), and consequently a deep godly sorrow for his sins. (V. 12-16). Then, when he appealed to the Savior (V. 17-18), he had received spiritual enlightenment and great joy. (V. 19-28). Finally, for his faithfulness and obedience, he had been rewarded with the opportunity to enjoy a life of righteousness and service. (V. 24-26).

In verse 10, Alma recalled how his afflictions had lasted for "the space of three days and three nights". Since it is clear from Mosiah 27:22-23 that the priests who had attended him had fasted for only two days and two nights, the logical explanation is that they waited a day before beginning to do so. In any event, during that time, Alma was brought to a vivid remembrance of his sins. He was thus "racked with eternal torment," (V. 12), "tormented with the pains of hell," (V. 13), and suffered "inexpressible horror" at the thought of coming into the presence of God. (V. 14).

The scriptures record Alma's confession that he "had murdered many of (Heavenly Father's spirit) children," but clarify that he had "rather, led them away unto destruction", which is just as harmful. (V. 14, see Commentary Reference to Alma 24:19). That he had contributed to their spiritual demise caused him to be "racked, even with the pains of a damned soul". (V. 15).

In the midst of this almost indescribable torment, Alma recalled the things that his father had taught, and that made all the difference. (V. 17). After begging his Savior for mercy, he "was harrowed up by the memory of (his) sins no more". (V. 19). The contrast in his feelings was complete. As he expressed to Helaman: "My soul was filled with joy as exceeding as was my pain!" (V. 20).

The unique source of that peace was Alma's complete and all-encompassing repentance for his sins, the overarching power of the Savior's Atonement, and Heavenly Father's complete forgiveness. Such was his cleansing, that he was able to stand on his feet, and "manifest unto the people that (he) had been born of God". (V. 23). As Parley P. Pratt declared: "I have received the holy anointing, and I can never rest until the last enemy is conquered, death destroyed, and truth reigns triumphant". (1853 sermon entitled "Spiritual Communication" p. 172-183, published in J.D., 1:6-15).

Alma declared to his son: "From that time even until now, I have labored without ceasing, that I might bring souls unto repentance, that I might bring them to taste of the exceeding joy of which I did taste; that they might also be born of God, and be filled with the Holy Ghost". (V. 24). The repentance process might be difficult, but it is the path we must follow in order to taste the fruit of the Tree of Life. This is eternal life, that is the highest expression of the love of God.

Marion G. Romney taught: "No person whose soul is illuminated by the burning Spirit of God can in this world of sin and dense darkness remain passive". Alma is a good example of how we may progress spiritually, and then begin to influence others in the same manner. We cannot lift others unless we stand on higher ground.

As Alma told his son: "Because of the word, many have been born of God, and have tasted as I have tasted". (V. 26). Being "born again" was a recurring theme for Alma. In The Book of Alma the expression "born again" is used four times, in Alma 5:49, 19:13, 36:23, and here in 36:23. The expression "born of God" is used nine times, in Alma 5:14, 7:10, 7:14, 22:15, 36:5, 36:23, 36:24, 36:26, and 38:6. With this in mind, Alma set the stage for Helaman to see the need to listen to his words, and so he dwelt at length upon just what it was he wished Helaman to do, and how he was to accomplish it. This is the subject of Chapter 37.

Alma
Chapter 37

Alma counseled his son on many different subjects in this chapter, probably because of the great responsibility that was being given to him. Initially, Helaman was commanded to "take the records" into his possession, that had been entrusted to Alma 19 years earlier by King Mosiah. (V. 1, see Commentary Reference to Mosiah 28:20).

Prominent among these were The Plates of Nephi. Helaman was to continue the record upon the Large Plates of Nephi. (V. 2). All the plates, Alma explained to Helaman, had been kept for a wise purpose. (V. 2). The Plates of Brass had "the records of the holy scriptures upon them," including "the genealogy of (their) forefathers". (V. 3). These plates would yet fulfil prophecy, for they were to be "kept and preserved by the hand of the Lord until they should go forth unto every nation, kindred, tongue, and people, that they shall know of the mysteries contained thereon". (V. 4, see Mosiah 2:9). By these mysteries was meant history and doctrine discerned and understood only by the power of the Spirit.

The verse that follows is interesting because it may tell us something about the physical characteristics of the plates themselves. "And now behold, if they are kept, they must retain their brightness; yea, and they will retain their brightness; yea, and also shall all the plates which do contain that which is holy writ". (V. 5, see 1 Nephi 5:19). This suggests that the quality of "brightness" refers to the substance of the messages inscribed on the various plates.

The Three Witnesses to The Book of Mormon wrote only that they had "seen the plates which contain this record" without reference to the specific composition of the metal, although they went into great detail to describe the engravings themselves and their purpose to benefit humanity. Various record-keepers referred to "plates of ore". (See 1 Nephi 19:1, Mosiah 21:27, and Mormon 8:5). When the prophets referred to a specific material, it was generally to "brass". (See 1 Nephi 3:3, 3:12, 3:24, 4:16, 4:24, 4:28, 5:10, 5:14, 5:18-19, 13:23, 19:21-22, 22:1, 22:30, 2 Nephi 4:2, 4:5, 5:12, Omni 1:14, Mosiah 1:3, 1:16, 10:16, 28:11, 28:20, Alma 37:3, 3 Nephi 1:2, & 10:17). "Plates of gold" are mentioned only in Mosiah 8:9 and 28:11, where they specifically refer to the

24 Gold Plates of Ether. Mormon, who had access to all the records and who abridged many of them, never referred to plates of gold.

His son Moroni twice referred to the plates, but only in reference to hiding them in the earth. (See Ether 15:11, & Mormon 8:4). Likewise, "Ammaron, being constrained by the Holy Ghost, did hide up the records which were sacred, yea, even all the sacred records which had been handed down from generation to generation, which were sacred". (4 Nephi 1:48-49). It may simply be that the custodians of the record were more focused on the message than on the material.

Because gold itself was much more plentiful in the Lands of The Book of Mormon, it many have not mattered to them of what material the plates were crafted. Jacob reported that his people, who still had an "Old World" mindset, had "begun to search for gold, and for silver, and for all manner of precious ores". Note that Jacob qualified as "precious" the ore his people sought. "In the which," or in these precious materials, he continued, "this land...doth abound most plentifully". (Jacob 2:12). In the same vein, Mormon reported: "Both the Lamanites and the Nephites ... did have an exceeding plenty of gold, and of silver, and of all manner of precious metals". (Helaman 6:9). As had Jacob before him, Mormon characterized the hoarded materials as "precious metals".

We do know that the Eight Witnesses to The Book of Mormon testified that the plates they were shown and "hefted" had "the appearance of gold" and that Joseph Smith wrote in his History that Moroni told him that the book that was hidden in the Hill Cumorah was "written upon gold plates". (J.S.H. 1:34). But The Book of Mormon record itself does not corroborate Moroni's characterization of the gold composition of the plates. In the Church, however, it is commonly accepted that the records, other than the Plates of Brass, were "gold plates". Gold has always denoted value, and at the very least, the precious gift of The Book of Mormon is equivalent to the gifts of gold, frankincense, and myrrh, bestowed by the Wise Men of the East upon the Christ child in Bethlehem.

Interestingly, however, none of The Book of Mormon authors describe their records as "gold plates," with the prominent exception of the Plates of Ether, that are specifically characterized as being of "pure gold". (Mosiah 8:9). Nephi's record was engraven upon "plates of ore". (1 Nephi 19:1). It was the record upon these plates that was pleasing to Mormon and not the plates themselves. (The Words of Mormon, 1:4). As a matter of fact, when occasion arose, the various record keepers in The Book of Mormon almost pointedly described only the intrinsic quality of the plates entrusted to their care, while pointedly and characteristically ignoring the temporal value of the metal upon which the records were engraven.

In any case, Alma told Helaman that the records would "retain their brightness". (V. 4). Perhaps there is an intended dual meaning here. On the one hand, if the plates were to be easily inscribed upon, they might be less tarnish resistant. In the Old Testament, "the word 'nechosheth' is sometimes improperly translated (as) 'brass.' In most places, the correct translation would be 'copper,' although it may sometimes possibly mean 'bronze,' a compound of copper and tin". ("Smith's Bible Dictionary," p. 97). Oxidation easily clouds the luster of these metals. On the other hand, the clearly understood messages of the records would be preserved for future generations, who would be dazzled by the brightness of their simplicity.

In verse 6, Alma apologized in advance for quoting a Hokmah, or aphorism, to his son: "Now ye may suppose that this is foolishness in me". Alma might have thought it trite, but these Hebrew "folk sayings" conveyed a depth of meaning far beyond their few and simple words: "By small and simple things are great things brought to pass; and small means in many instances doth confound the wise". (V. 6, see V. 7).

Alma elaborated on this theme by reminding his son that the records had enlarged the memory of the people (V. 8), brought men to a knowledge of God (V. 8-9), convinced many Lamanites of the errors of their ways and of the false traditions of their fathers (V. 9-10), and would yet show the power of God to future generations. (V. 14). Alma was truly in awe of the power of the word of God, represented by the Nephite records that had been kept for nearly 600 years, by the Plates of Brass, that were even older, and by the other relics and emblems of power and authority kept by the Nephite prophets.

He was always ready to acknowledge that there were certain points of doctrine that were not clear to him. To his son, he declared: "Now these mysteries are not yet fully made known unto me; therefore, I shall forbear". (V. 11). He felt that it was always better to keep his opinion to himself, rather than to speculate without the foundation of fact or specific revelation. Sometimes it is better to remain silent and be thought a fool, than to speak and remove all doubt.

When counseling his son Corianton, Alma would emphasize: "There are many mysteries which are kept, that no one knoweth them save God himself". (Alma 40:3, see D&C 25:4, 121:26, & 124:41). But here Alma reassured his son Helaman that when God withholds understanding from His children, it is "for a wise purpose," and that there is no intent to mislead or deceive. We can always be confident that "his paths are straight". (V. 12).

Alma then gave Helaman counsel that would be critical to the continuing security of the records: "But if ye keep the commandments of God, and do with these things which are sacred according to that which the Lord doth command you, (for you must appeal unto the Lord for all things whatsoever ye must do with them) behold, no power of earth or hell can take them from you". (V. 16). This counsel must have been comforting to Joseph Smith as well, and it is obvious from an appraisal of his experiences with the records between 1823 and 1829 that he followed it well.

Next, Helaman was given advice concerning the Gold Plates of Ether. (V. 21-27). Alma spoke in these verses of a different kind of mystery, urging Helaman to keep those plates to himself. (V. 21). He said: "My son, I command you that ye retain all the oaths (of the Jaredites), and their covenants, and their agreements in their secret abominations; yea, and all their signs and their wonders ye shall keep from this people, that they know them not, lest peradventure they should fall into darkness also, and be destroyed". (V. 27, see Helaman 6:21, & Ether 8:16).

Moroni abridged The Book of Ether from the 24 Gold Plates found by the People of Limhi, and explained why he did so. (See Mosiah 8:9). "And this cometh unto you, O ye Gentiles, that ye may know the decrees of God - that ye may repent, and not continue in your iniquities until the fulness come, that ye may not bring down the fulness of the wrath of God upon you as the inhabitants of the land (the Jaredites) have hitherto done". (Ether 2:11, & Alma 37:22). This theme is consistent with that introduced by Alma at the beginnings of the chapters currently under study, that are devoted to the counsel of Alma to his sons.

The "interpreters" spoken of by Alma in verse 21 refer to the Urim and Thummim, that evidently were found at the same time the 24 Gold Plates of Ether were discovered. Alma quoted the Lord, who said: "I will prepare unto my servant Gazelem, a stone, which shall shine forth in darkness unto light". (V. 23). "Gazelem" is rendered "seer" in D&C 104:26, and might have reference to Joseph Smith, or it might identify a seer stone, or the Urim and Thummim, that is translated "lights and perfections".

Through the use of the Urim and Thummim, Mosiah has been able to translate the 24 Gold Plates of Ether, and to "bring forth out of darkness unto light all (the) secret works and abominations" of the Jaredites. (V. 25). Because of that translation, it was plain to the Nephites that "thus far, the word of God has been fulfilled". (V. 26). That is to say, all those who possess the land of promise and do not repent "should be destroyed from off the face of the earth". (V. 22).

Helaman was specifically commanded by Alma to teach the people to "abhor such wickedness and abominations and murders" as were found among the Jaredites," and also to "teach them that these people were destroyed on account of their wickedness and abominations and their murders". (V. 29-30).

Alma reiterated his injunction to Helaman to "trust not those secret plans unto this people, but teach them an everlasting hatred against sin and iniquity". (V. 32). The rest of this chapter contains the kind of counsel that children should expect to receive from caring parents. It is not sugar-coated, but is, nevertheless, tempered with love.

First, Alma exhorted Helaman to teach the people the basic principles and ordinances of the Gospel. (V. 33). Then he counseled his son to always seek in earnest the Kingdom of God. (V. 34). Next, he implored Helaman to develop the capacity to wisely apply the knowledge he had gained in his youth. (V. 35, see Proverbs 22:6). He was counseled to involve the Lord in all his actions. (V. 36). "Counsel with the Lord in all thy doings," was Alma's advice, "and he will direct thee for good". (V. 37). What naturally followed was an aside from Alma dealing with a unique device from the

Lord, which the Nephites had employed to guide them. It was what the fathers had called "a ball, or director - or our fathers called it Liahona, which is, being interpreted, a compass". (V. 38).

This is the first reference to the Liahona by name in the scriptures. "Liahona" is clearly an "Old World" word from the forgotten language of the fathers, that had to be interpreted as "compass" for present readers. "Compass" refers to a pair of things in motion, the nature of that motion being a circle. This fits the description given by Nephi of the Liahona as "a round ball of curious workmanship; and it was of fine brass. And within the ball were two spindles; and the one pointed the way whither we should go into the wilderness". (1 Nephi 16:10).

That the Liahona is an object lesson is evident by Alma's explanation to his son: "These things are not without a shadow, for as our fathers were slothful to give heed to the compass (now these things were temporal) they did not prosper; even so it is with things which are spiritual". (V. 43, see V. 44-45).

The Liahona worked "according to their faith in God". (V. 40). Alma characterized its operation as "a miracle," but he went to great lengths to explain to Helaman the principles by which it functioned. Religion becomes magical when, in our efforts to rationally explain miracles, the power by which events occur is transferred from God to the objects themselves. Alma wanted to avoid his son's misinterpretation of the power by which the Liahona operated.

We have seen that the Bible itself became a magic book in men's eyes, conveying power and knowledge without the aid of revelation. Over the centuries, priesthood acquired the status of an office that automatically bestowed power and grace, regardless of the spiritual or moral qualifications of its possessor. The stories from The Book of Mormon help to bring our understanding of the eternal principles of the Plan of Salvation into perspective. Thus, we should neither be incredulous when reading them, nor should we fall into the trap of accepting them on blind faith. (See V. 35). The Spirit is always a steadying influence that tempers our interpretation of eternal principles.

Alma warned Helaman that because the great miracle of showing the family of Lehi the way through the wilderness was wrought "by small means, they were slothful, and forgot to exercise their faith". (V. 41). He did not want Helaman to trivialize the simplicity of the Liahona, nor did he want him to miss the point that it is important to heed the quiet messages of the Gospel Plan when they come in an unassuming manner.

"For behold, it is as easy to give heed to the word of Christ, which will point to you a straight course to eternal bliss, as it was for our fathers to give heed to this compass, which would point unto them a straight course to the promised land". (V. 44). As it was for Alma and his people, so it is for us. The Word of Christ is our Liahona. If we follow this "compass," we will find that no wind can blow except it fills our sails.

A good mariner can read the weather like a book, can focus his nautical skills, and use his available equipment to trim his sails and set a course that will lead him unerringly to safe harbor. The same wind that might cause a less seaworthy vessel to founder, fills the sails of the vessel whose helmsman is a skilled seafarer. A sailor does not necessarily see the port that is his final destination. Sometimes, it is over the horizon, and sometimes the tack of the vessel appears to be taking the ship away from its objective. But if correct principles are followed, the landfall is always sure.

The best Mariner of all, and the One in control of the elements around Him, was the Savior. The scriptures tell us: "When he was entered into a ship, his disciples followed him. And behold, there arose a great tempest in the sea, insomuch that the ship was covered with the waves; but he was asleep. And his disciples came to him, and awoke him, saying, Lord, save us; we perish. And he saith unto them, Why are ye fearful, O ye of little faith? Then he arose and rebuked the winds and the sea; and there was a great calm. But the men marveled, saying, What manner of man is this, that even the winds and the sea obey him!" (Matthew 8:23-27).

The voice of the Son of God came to Nephi and commanded him: "Follow me, and do the things which ye have seen me do". (2 Nephi 31:12). In the Doctrine and Covenants, we are admonished: "Stand, therefore, having your loins girt about with truth, having on the breastplate of righteousness and your feet shod with the preparation of the Gospel of peace; taking the shield of faith wherewith ye shall be able to quench all the fiery darts of the wicked. And take the helmet of salvation, and the sword of my Spirit and be faithful until I come, and ye shall be caught up, that where I am ye shall be also. Amen. (D&C 27:16-18).

Alma continued, asking Helaman: "Is there not a type in this thing? For just as surely as this director did bring our fathers, by following its course, to the promised land, shall the words of Christ, if we follow their course, carry us beyond this vale of sorrow into a far better land of promise". (V. 45). An outward observance without any real inward meaning is only a ceremony. But a rite that has a present spiritual meaning is a symbol; and if, besides, it also points to a future reality, conveying at the same time, by anticipation, the blessing that is yet to appear, it is a type.

This chapter plumbs the depths of our mortal experience and suggests a vital link between the secular and the divine, and between the earth and heaven. A grasp of the symbolism of the Gospel and the application of the principles taught to Helaman by Alma constitutes a stairway to the stars. (See Alma 25:15, 33:19-22, & Helaman 8:14-15).

Alma concluded his farewell messages to each of his sons in the same way. (See Alma 38:15, & 42:31). It is possible that Helaman received more counsel and instruction than Shiblon or Corianton because he had the greater responsibility, having been entrusted with the records.

Alma exhorted Helaman to "look to God and live". (V. 47). Joseph Smith learned: "Sanctification through the grace of our Lord and Savior Jesus Christ is just and true, to all those who love and serve God with all their mights, minds, and strength". (D&C 20:31). The only motive strong enough to encourage men and women to exercise the self-control required by the Gospel of Jesus Christ is love of God. Alma hoped that this quality might find expression in his son Helaman, and he was not to be disappointed.

"I was racked with eternal
torment, for my soul was harrowed
up to the greatest degree and racked with
all my sins. Yea, I did remember all my sins
and iniquities, for which I was tormented with the
pains of hell; yea, I saw that I had rebelled against my
God, and that I had not kept his holy commandments.
Yea, I had murdered many of his children, or rather, led
them away unto destruction; yea, and in fine so great
had been my iniquities, that the very thought of
coming into the presence of my God did rack
my soul with inexpressible horror."
(Alma 36:12-14).

Alma
Chapter 38

Although this chapter recounts the commandments of Alma to his son Shiblon, it is filled with advice for young people of all times. While yet in his youth, Shiblon had already been subjected in the mission field to all manner of afflictions and had even been "stoned for the word's sake". (V. 4-5). Through it all, he had suffered "with patience, because the Lord was with (him)". (V. 4).

Alma shared his conversion story with his son, because he wanted Shiblon to gain wisdom, that he might learn "that there is no other way or means whereby man can be saved, only in and through Christ". (V. 9). Alma's own early experiences dramatically illustrated this point of doctrine.

Alma was proud that his son had been called to serve, and he wanted him to be an effective missionary. Therefore, Shiblon was counseled to "use boldness, but not overbearance". (V. 12). He was further admonished to bridle all his passions, including the craving for sexual gratification, as well as an unreasonable desire for food, shelter, or clothing. The sin is in the unbridled passion for these things.

After giving additional counsel, Alma invoked his blessing on Shiblon, and sent him out with his brothers to "teach the word". (V. 15, see Alma 37:47, & 42:31).

"Now, my son, I would not that
ye should think that I know these
things of myself, but it is the Spirit
of God which is in me which maketh
these things known unto me; for if
I had not been born of God I should
not have known these things."
(Alma 38:6).

Alma
Chapter 39

Chapter 39 is the first of four chapters devoted to counsel given to Corianton by his father Alma. His instruction is extensive, because Corianton had gotten off to a shaky start on his mission, had not observed the steadiness of his elder brothers, had not been faithful and diligent in keeping the commandments, and had gone astray. (V. 1, see v. 10). Nor had he listened attentively to the counsel of his father, but rather had boasted in his own strength and wisdom. (V. 2). As Mark Twain observed: "When I was a boy of fourteen, my father was so ignorant I could hardly stand to have the old man around. But when I got to be twenty-one, I was astonished at how much he had learned in seven years".

Even worse, Shiblon had forsaken the ministry, leaving the mission field to "go over into the land of Sidon among the borders of the Lamanites, after the harlot Isabel". (V. 3). This is one of only three women mentioned by name in the entire Book of Mormon. The others are Sariah (1 Nephi 2:5) and Abish (Alma 19:16). How nice it would have been if, instead, the Nephites could have held Isabel's name in fond remembrance. She had seduced many young men, but her enticements could not excuse the behavior of Corianton. (V. 4). His sin was "an abomination in the sight of the Lord," because unchastity always threatens to upset the order of the Plan of Salvation. (V. 5). Every soul has the right to come into the world in a legitimate way, and Corianton had flirted inappropriately with the powers of procreation.

"The power of creation is not an incidental part of the Plan of Salvation," said Boyd K. Packer. "It is essential to its operation. It is a sacred and significant power, and it is good when properly exercised. Much of the happiness in this life depends on how the power is used; with it one can establish a home, a dominion of influence and opportunity". (C.R. 4/1972). Unchastity is the misuse of that sacred power whose operation is essential to the eternal Plan of Happiness. Immorality lays the foundation for discontent, despondency, depression, despair, disagreement, and discord in the home, and it robs the soul of resistance to, and recuperative ability from, other evils.

The only sin Corianton could have committed that would have been worse than his fornication with Isabel would have been "the shedding of innocent blood or denying the Holy Ghost". (V. 5, see D.H.C., V. 6:314-315). Alma said that denying the Holy Ghost "is a sin which is unpardonable," and that it would not be easy "to obtain forgiveness" after committing such an act, because it lies beyond the redemptive power of Christ to atone for that particular sin. (V. 6).

Alma was constrained to dwell upon Corianton's sin for his own good. (V. 7). This wayward son was told: "Ye cannot hide your crimes from God; and except ye repent, they will stand as a testimony against you at the last day". (V. 8, see D&C 88:109). Joseph F. Smith once declared: "Let God Almighty touch the mainspring of the memory, and you will find that you have not even forgotten a single idle word that you have spoken". ("Improvement Era", (5/1903, p. 503-4)

Corianton was told to "cross" himself in all the things in which he had been counseled. (V. 9). The Savior said: "For a man to take up his cross is to deny himself all ungodliness, and every worldly lust and keep my commandments". (J.S.T. Matthew 16:26, see Matthew 16:24, 3 Nephi 12:30, & Commentary Reference to Jacob 1:8).

Alma further instructed Corianton to give heed to the counsel of his elder brothers and to be on his guard against the vain and foolish temptations of youth. (V. 10-11). Alma pointed out to Corianton that Satan had capitalized on his weaknesses to thwart his father's own missionary efforts, "for when (the Zoramites) saw your conduct," Alma said, "they would not believe in my words". (V. 11, see Matthew 18:6-7). The devil had scored a major victory among the Zoramites when Corianton succumbed to his temptations, for "the destruction of the soul is the destruction of the greatest thing that has ever been created". (Joseph Fielding Smith, Jr., "Doctrines of Salvation," 1:314).

The Lord counseled Joseph Smith: "If thy brother or sister offend thee, thou shalt take him or her between him or her and thee alone; and if he or she confess thou shalt be reconciled". (D&C 42:88). It was just such a reconciliation that Alma desired. He exhorted Corianton not only to refrain from his iniquities, but also to turn to the Lord with all his might, mind, and strength. (V. 12-13). Further, he was counseled to return to the mission field among the Zoramites, and confess his sins to the appropriate priesthood authorities. (V. 13). Perhaps some good could be salvaged from this most unfortunate experience.

As a perceptive father, Alma could see that much of Corianton's troubles stemmed from his shallow understanding of even the most basic principles of the Gospel. Unfortunately, when he had received his call, he was not well prepared to enter the mission field. Consequently, the devil had seized upon his doctrinal weaknesses. Satan knows who the Lord's servants are; they are all marked men and women. Therefore, they require the special protection of the Melchizedek Priesthood, the endowment of spiritual power received only in the Lord's House, a blessing and setting apart by file leaders, the continual prayers of the faithful, a solid foundation of doctrinal understanding, and a firm and abiding testimony of the Savior, and the Plan of Salvation itself. In the following verses and chapters, Alma would teach Corianton the basic doctrines concerning the Coming of Christ (Alma 39:15-19), the resurrection of the dead (Alma 40:1), restoration (Alma 41:1), and Justice and Mercy. (Alma 42:1).

Interestingly, Corianton wondered: "Why these things should be known so long beforehand?" (V. 17). The Coming of the Lord seemed so remotely distant that he did not think it relevant to his day. In fact, the birth of the Savior was only 73 years in the future. If the Second Coming of the Lord is as close for us, should not the messages of the Restoration be as relevant to our present circumstances?

The world, though, would rather focus its attention and energy on "more pressing matters". And so, we spend our time building, and obtaining, and accumulating, and securing our temporal well-being, while the eternal welfare of our souls hangs in the balance. The Sword of Damocles hangs over us. We waste the precious time allotted to us; most of us spend our time far less wisely than we spend our money.

One measure of a successful person is the thought with which they spend their time, the care with which they make time, the diligence with which they find time, and the discipline with which they take time. This creative process, if you will, actually gives such individuals more time to accomplish their worthy goals in their busy lives.

Ultimately, though, we will all find that time is an artificial dimension, and that we come from a better realm where success is measured, instead, by accomplishment, by the building of character, and by giving service. As Carol Lynn Pearson wrote: "Oh this world has more of coming and of going than I can bear. I guess it's eternity I want, where all things are, and always will be; where I can hold my loves a little looser; where, finally, we realize that Time is the only thing that really dies". (From "Optical Illusion"). We will probably never be able to come to grips with time, for now we see through a glass darkly. One day, however, we will be able to "go forth from our dwelling place and discarding the poor lenses of the body, peer through the telescope of truth into the infinite reaches of immortality". (Helen Keller).

Alma answered his son's question ("Why these things should be known so long beforehand?") by asking his own: "Is it not as necessary that the Plan of redemption should be made known unto this people as well as unto their children?" (V. 18). "Is it not as easy at this time for the Lord to send his angel to declare these glad tidings unto us as unto our children, or as after the time of his coming?" (V. 19).

As Joseph Smith declared: "Does it remain for a people who never had faith enough to call down one scrap of revelation from heaven, and for all they have now are indebted to the faith of another people who lived hundreds and thousands of years before them, does it remain for them to say how much God has spoken and how much he has not spoken?" (H.C., 2:17-18).

"Turn to the Lord
with all you mind,
might, and strength."
(Alma 39:13).

Alma
Chapter 40

Even though Corianton had been called to serve as a missionary, there were serious deficiencies in his knowledge of basic Gospel principles. This can be traced back to his superficial familiarity with the scriptures. The lack of understanding that likely contributed to his transgression while he was serving as a missionary underscores the need for sustained and meaningful Gospel scholarship. Perspiration, or "brain sweat," as B.H. Roberts called it, precedes inspiration.

As Alma counseled Corianton, he perceived that he was having trouble understanding the principle of the resurrection of the dead. (V. 1). In Alma's Day, no one had yet been resurrected. Mortality would "not put on immortality until after the coming of Christ. (For) behold, he bringeth to pass the resurrection of the dead". Therefore, Alma taught: "The resurrection is not yet". (V. 2-3). The First Fruits of the Resurrection would not take place for over a hundred years. Alma knew that the Holy Ghost could prepare Corianton to understand the Gospel principle of resurrection, for it is a mystery kept from the world because it can only be spiritually discerned. (V. 3, see Commentary Reference to Mosiah 1:5).

As we read Alma's counsel to his son, we are taught: "There are many mysteries which are kept, that no one knoweth them save God himself". (V. 3, see Alma 37:11). Therefore, we should not be impatient to gain an intellectual or even a spiritual mastery of that which is apparently beyond our comprehension, or that is unnecessary for us to have at this stage of our development. Perhaps Alma was referring to the fact that the mystery of resurrection was particularly difficult for even the spiritually mature and scripturally literate of his day to understand. Certainly, it was a difficult doctrine even for the Savior's own apostles to master, both during and immediately after His mortal ministry drew to a close. It remains so today.

It was Alma's faith, nevertheless, that "there is a time appointed that all shall come forth from the dead". (V. 4). It was not important to him to know specifically when that time was. (V. 5). He had developed an eternal perspective, and knew that "time only is measured unto men". (V. 8). He knew that "there's no time like the present, and no present like time. And life can be over in the space of a rhyme." (Georgia Bynge). For God resides "on a globe like a sea of glass and fire, where all things are manifest, past, present, and future, and are continually before the Lord". (D&C 130:7, see "Teachings," p. 220, & Commentary Reference to Helaman 12:5). "The past, the present, and the future exist as one. They breathe together." (Harriet Beecher Stowe).

The scriptures make a valiant effort to describe God's perspective. But it remains that men and women, trapped in time, can only indirectly appreciate the eternities. "Even now, time is clearly not our natural dimension," said Neal A. Maxwell. "Thus it is, that we are never really at home in time. Alternately, we find ourselves impatiently wishing to hasten the passage of time, or to hold back the dawn. We can do neither, of course. Whereas the bird is at home in the air, we are clearly not at home in time, because we belong to eternity. Time, as much as any one thing, whispers to us that we are strangers here. If time were natural to us, why is it that we have so many clocks and wristwatches?" (B.Y.U. Speeches of The Year, 1979).

Alma had a clear vision "concerning the state of the soul between death and the resurrection", teaching "that the spirits of all men, as soon as they are departed from this mortal body, yea, the spirits of all men, whether they be good or evil, are taken home to that God who gave them life". (V. 11). Nevertheless, they are not immediately brought into the actual presence of God. (See Brigham Young, J.D., 3:368). Rather, "the spirits of those who are righteous are received into a state of happiness, which is called paradise, a state of rest, a state of peace, where they shall rest from all their troubles and from all care, and sorrow". (V. 12). Paradise is not a state of perfect happiness, for that is possible only in the resurrection. As the Lord said: "The elements are eternal, and (only) spirit and element inseparably connected, receive a fulness of joy, and when separated, man cannot receive a fulness of joy". (D&C 93:23-24).

Verse 13 teaches that the spirit world has a second major division called outer darkness. (See V. 21). The wicked, who are evil and "have no part nor portion of the Spirit of the Lord," are cast into outer darkness, that is "a state of awful, fearful looking for the fiery indignation of the wrath of God". (V. 13-14, see Mosiah 15:22-26, & D&C 19:11-17). Alma indicated that the wicked would remain in this state "until the time of their resurrection". (V. 14). In other words, as James E. Talmage taught: "The Spirit Prison of The Unjust (See D&C 76:73, 138:8 & 28, Isaiah 61:1, 1 Peter 3:19 & Moses 7:57 is a place of correction for those who have committed all but the unpardonable sin. When the penalty has been paid and Justice has been satisfied, the sinner will be released from hell, prepared to be resurrected to a kingdom of glory. True, the scriptures speak of endless punishment, and depict everlasting burnings, eternal damnation, and the sufferings incident to unquenchable fire, as features of the judgment reserved for the wicked. But none of these awful possibilities are anywhere in scripture declared to be the unending fate of the individual sinner. Blessing or punishment ordained of God is eternal, for He is eternal, and eternal are all His ways. His is a system of endless and eternal punishment, for it will always exist as the place or condition provided for the rebellious and disobedient, but the penalty as visited upon the individual will terminate when through repentance the necessary reform has been effected and the uttermost farthing paid. Even to hell there is an exit as well as an entrance, and when sentence has been served, commuted perhaps by repentance and its attendant works, the prison doors shall open and the penitent captive be afforded opportunity to comply with the law, which he aforetime violated. But the prison remains, and the eternal decree prescribing punishment for the offender stands unrepealed. So it is, even with the penal institutions established by man". (James E. Talmage, "The Vitality of Mormonism", p. 264-265).

Alma clarified for Corianton that the consignment of departed souls to the world of spirits is not akin to resurrection. (V. 15-17). "Nay," he said. The first resurrection "meaneth the reuniting of the soul with the body, of those from the days of Adam down to the resurrection of Christ". (V. 18).

It was Alma's correct opinion that "the souls and the bodies (of the righteous) are reunited at the resurrection of Christ, and his ascension into heaven". (V. 20, see Mosiah 15:22-26, & "Doctrines of Salvation," 2:300). We learn from other scriptures that the wicked, though, will be resurrected only at the end of the Millennium. (See D&C 76:81-85, & 88:100-101).

A wonderful truth was taught when Alma declared: "The soul shall be restored to the body, and the body to the soul; yea, and every limb and joint shall be restored to its body; yea, even a hair of the head shall not be lost; but all things shall be restored to their proper and perfect frame". (V. 23, see Alma 41:3, H.C., 4:555-556). Joseph Fielding Smith, Jr. shed more light on this doctrine, when he explained: "All deformities and imperfections will be removed, and the body will conform to the likeness of the spirit". ("Doctrines of Salvation," 2:289, see D&C 77:2). Joseph F. Smith put it this way: "From the day of the resurrection, the body will develop until it reaches the full measure of the stature of its spirit". ("Gospel Doctrine," p. 23).

Perhaps, when they come into the world, every man and every woman have a full measure of light that represents the purity of the Spirit. Living might be a process of detraction, in the sense that we lose intrinsic light as we succumb to worldly cares. The judgment may be a measurement of the numbers of foot-candles of light remaining that we bring to the judgment seat. "Our birth," after all, "is asleep and a forgetting. The soul that rises with us, our life's star, hath had elsewhere its setting, and cometh from afar. Not in entire forgetfulness, and not in utter nakedness, but trailing clouds of glory do we come, from God, who is our Home". (William Wordsworth, "Ode on Intimations of Immortality").

As we continue to progress, we slowly regain the glory of our former home. "I have warmed both hands before the fire of life," wrote Sir William Mulock. "The rich spoils of memory are mine. Mine, too, are the precious things of today. The best of life is always further on. Its real lure is hidden from our eyes somewhere behind the hills of time". ("Light My Lamp").

"And then shall the righteous shine forth in the Kingdom of God". (V. 25). In contrast, those who have lost the capacity to repent, who have died "as to things pertaining to things of righteousness," whose countenances no longer reflect the Light of Christ, will "drink the dregs of a bitter cup". (V. 26).

"The soul shall be restored to the body, and the body to the soul; yea, and every limb and joint shall be restored to its body; yea, even a hair of the head shall not be lost; but all things shall be restored to their proper and perfect frame. And now, my son, this is the restoration of which has been spoken by the mouths of the prophets."
(Alma 40:23-24).

Alma
Chapter 41

Even those who have been called to preach the Gospel risk falling into transgression in consequence of a shallow understanding of principles and doctrines. As Alma had declared to the inhabitants of Ammonihah: "Behold, the scriptures are before you; if ye will wrest them it shall be to your own destruction". (Alma 13:20). Picking apart the scriptures can distort the doctrines into meaningless fragments without any coherent connection.

Until Corianton understood and was committed to the Gospel Plan, he could not rebuild his troubled life and could not perform the labor to which he had been called. Therefore, his father first sought to explain the doctrine of Justice that had been troubling him. (V. 1-2). The two contrasting states of the inhabitants of the Spirit World are typified by the characteristics of happiness and misery. Justice demands: "All things shall be restored to their proper order, everything to its natural frame, raised to endless happiness to inherit the kingdom of God, or to endless misery to inherit the kingdom of the devil". (V. 4).

The mortal mission of the Savior was to "redeem those who will be baptized unto repentance, through faith on his name. (Alma 9:27, see V. 6-7). The Atonement is of effect for those who enter into the covenants and repent. (See Mosiah 26:22). This is the Gospel Plan, that all might have the opportunity to benefit from the Law of Mercy, that the Savior of the world might satisfy the demands of the Law of Justice through His Atonement for sin.

""Happiness is the object and design of our existence and will be the end thereof, if we follow the path that leads to it. And this path is virtue, uprightness, faithfulness, holiness, and keeping all the commandments of God. In obedience there is joy and peace . . . and as God has designed our happiness ... He never has, He never will, give a commandment to His people that is not calculated in its nature to promote that happiness which He has designed." (History of the Church, 5:134-135, see Commentary Reference to 2 Nephi 2:13). But God will always grant to His children agency to choose their own path, "for behold, they are their own judges, whether to do good or do evil". (V. 7). We can choose our own actions, but we cannot choose to escape their consequences.

"The decrees of God are unalterable; therefore, the way is prepared that whosoever will, may walk therein and be saved". (V. 8). But we cannot "be restored from sin to happiness". (V. 10).

For emphasis, Alma quoted a Hebrew Hokmah: "Wickedness never was happiness". (V. 10, see 2 Nephi 2:13, Alma 40:12, and Essay: "Happiness"). In the words of Samuel, the Lamanite: "Ye have sought all the days of your lives for that which ye could not obtain; and ye have sought for happiness in doing iniquity, which thing is contrary to the nature of that righteousness which is in our great and Eternal Head". (Helaman 13:38). Every law has both a blessing and a punishment affixed to it. When the law is obeyed, a blessing is given that results in happiness or joy. When the law is disobeyed, punishment is inflicted that results in unhappiness, misery, or despair, which is the feeling of hopelessness that accompanies disobedience.

As Alma explained: "All men that are in a state of nature, or I would say, in a carnal state, are in the gall of bitterness and in the bonds of iniquity; they are without God in the world, and they have gone contrary to the nature of God; therefore, they are in a state contrary to the nature of happiness". (V. 11). The Savior taught: If men lack vision, and build "upon the works of men, or upon the works of the devil, verily I say unto you they have joy in their works for a season, and by and by the end cometh, and they are hewn down and cast into the fire, from whence there is no return". (3 Nephi 27:11, see Mormon 2:13).

As Corianton listened to his father, he began to understand that "the meaning of the word restoration is to bring back again evil for evil, or carnal for carnal, or devilish for devilish, good for that which is good; righteous for that which is righteous; just for that which is just; (and) merciful for that which is merciful". (V. 13). So important was this principle, that Alma constructed his counsel in the form of a chiasm that is preserved in verses 13-15.

Sometimes, it is very difficult to tell just what brings us happiness. Both poverty and wealth have failed miserably. Neither fame nor anonymity holds the key. Neither sickness nor health has the ability. Both principalities and the absence of worldly influence are inadequate. Neither beauty nor the beast has the advantage. We often forget that when we pray for rain, and our prayers are answered, we are going to also have to deal with some mud. "The dark threads are as needful in the weaver's skillful hand as the threads of gold and silver, in the pattern he has Planned". (Benjamin M. Franklin). We can never hope to understand the answers we receive, if we continue to ask the wrong questions. Life has no coherence, and is in fact, a cruel joke, without the spiritual symmetry, balance, and inherent happiness of the Lord's fitness program. That is why Moroni taught: "Despair cometh because of iniquity".

Alma closed this portion of his exhortation to Corianton by applying the principle of restoration directly to his son: "Therefore, my son, that you are merciful unto your brethren; deal justly, judge righteously, and do good continually; and if ye do all these things then shall ye receive your reward; yea, ye shall have mercy restored unto you again; ye shall have justice restored unto you again; ye shall have a righteous judgment restored unto you again; and ye shall have good rewarded unto you again". (V. 14). He would find happiness. The fundamental truth he wanted to emphasize was that restoration is intensely personal and of profound relevance to every individual who yearns to be happy, for "that which ye do send out shall return unto you again". (V. 15).

"According to justice, the plan of redemption could not be brought about, only on conditions of repentance of men in this probationary state, yea, this preparatory state, for except it were on these conditions, mercy could not take effect except it would destroy the work of justice … and the plan of mercy could not be brought about except an atonement should be made. Therefore, God himself atoneth for the sins of the world, to bring about the plan of mercy, to appease the demands of justice, that God might be a perfect, just God, and a merciful God also". (Alma 42:13-15).

Alma
Chapter 42

Arguably, Alma Chapters 12 and 42 comprise the best explanations in all scripture regarding the justice and mercy of God, and they should be studied together. Mormon recognized that this was powerful doctrine, and when he abridged the records, he was inspired to transcribe the account of Alma's ministry in the first-person tense on the Plates of Mormon. Thus, when we study these discourses verbatim, we get the feeling that Alma is speaking directly to us. Alma taught his son these principles because Corianton had been excusing wrong behavior, claiming that it was unjust to punish sinners. (V. 1, see V. 30).

In Alma Chapter 11, we learned about the defection of a lawyer named Zeezrom who had been converted in Ammonihah to the Gospel, and we were introduced to Antionah, a chief ruler in that city who had then taken up the gauntlet to confront Alma and Amulek. He was a child of the devil who used a misrepresentation of the scriptures as ammunition to attack the missionaries. This is a standard battle plan of Satan that his disciples frequently employ. Alma's encounter with Antionah illustrates that even the wicked can be familiar with the scriptures, but because their understanding is skewed, they wrest them in a twisted and perverted way, distorting their true meaning into a caricature of truth.

In Alma Chapter 12, Alma had answered the question that had been posed by Antionah: "What does the scripture mean, which saith that God placed cherubim and a flaming sword on the east of the garden of Eden, lest our first parents should enter and partake of the fruit of the tree of life, and live forever?" (Alma 12:21, & Genesis 3:24). Now, in Alma Chapter 42, he taught his son about these same principles because Corianton had been excusing his own behavior with the same weak argument, claiming that it was unjust to punish sinners. Alma addressed the concerns of both Antionah and Corianton, basing his remarks on the reality that justice is the unalterable decree of God that declares that both righteousness and sin dictate their own consequences.

Fortunately, Alma was more familiar with the scriptures and with the doctrines of the Kingdom than were either Antionah or Corianton. He was able to explain to both that there is another dimension to Genesis 3:24 that takes into consideration the pitfall that would have been created had Adam been permitted to stretch forth his hand and partake of the fruit of the tree of life. In Ammonihah, Antionah's shallow Gospel scholarship led him to the erroneous conclusion that the only way to live forever was to "partake of the fruit of the tree of life". (Alma 12:21). Antionah reasoned that mankind had a justification for sinning because God had placed cherubim and a flaming sword on the east of the Garden of Eden to guard the way to the tree. He mistakenly thought that the key to eternal life was simply partaking of the fruit. It was his belief that with cherubim and a flaming sword blocking the way to immortality, there would be "no possible chance that they should live forever". (Alma 12:21).

Antionah was too literal in his private interpretation of scripture. He did not take into consideration the ramifications of what would happen within the matrix of the Plan of Salvation were Adam, in his fallen state, to have stretched forth his hand and partaken of the fruit of the tree of life. He did not consider that, were he to do so, Adam would have lived forever, but would have been alienated from God's presence. Thus, Antionah's question provided Alma with a perfect teaching moment to explain to the wicked people of Ammonihah that, rather than justifying wicked behavior, the referenced scripture should instead have afforded them a strong incentive to propel them to seek and embrace another way whereby they might live forever, not in sin, but in purity and glory. Antionah's ignorance gave Alma the opportunity to teach the people of Ammonihah about agency, justice, atonement, mercy, repentance, forgiveness, and redemption. It allowed Alma to reveal to Antionah and his brethren how to proactively deal with the unalterable decrees of God that relate to the wicked.

Alma correctly taught that, subtle though the symbolism might be, working out our salvation has less to do with cherubim and more to do with redemption. In the absence of repentance for our sins and without the benefit of the Gospel Plan, we would ultimately be miserable, living forever in our sins. He told Antionah: "And now behold, if it were possible that our first parents could have gone forth and partaken of the tree of life they would have been forever miserable, having no preparatory state; and thus, the Plan of Redemption would have been frustrated, and the word of God would have been void, taking none effect". (Alma 12:26). Without the option of redemption from sin, if Adam and Eve had partaken of the fruit of the tree of life, which is eternal life, or the highest expression of the love of God, it would not have been possible thereafter for them to sustain a celestial existence. They would have had to do it on their own, and frankly, they lacked the spiritual horsepower. They would have forever remained in their filthy condition, stained by sin, and would have been incapable of observing celestial principles. Thus, the Plan of Salvation would have been frustrated, and God's mission statement, to bring about our immortality and eternal life, would have been nullified.

The scenario Alma outlined to the people of Ammonihah and later to his son Corianton (in the present Chapter Alma 42) demonstrated that this was not to be the case. The transgression of Adam and Eve resulted in alienation from His presence, that is spiritual death, and their expulsion from the Garden resulted in mortality, making eventual temporal death inevitable.

But Adam and Eve and their posterity had not been created to live forever in the morally static vacuum of the Garden. Mortality is really our only opportunity to become acquainted with evil as well as with good, with darkness as well as with light, with error as well as with truth, and with punishment for the infraction of eternal laws as well as with the blessings that follow obedience. Ralph Waldo Emerson once asked: "What is the use of immortality to one who cannot wisely use half an hour?" This is why Alma and so many other parents have invested so much time and energy teaching their children correct principles and training them in their proper execution.

Alma told Antionah: "This is the thing which I was about to explain". (Alma 12:22). Alma then taught that we came into this world to die. This creates a host of problems, but the Plan addresses each one and offers elegant solutions. For "we see that Adam did fall by the partaking of the forbidden fruit, according to the word of God; and thus, we see that by his fall, all mankind became a lost and fallen people. And now behold, I say unto you that if it had been possible for Adam to have partaken of the fruit of the tree of life at that time, there would have been no death, and the word would have been void, making God a liar, for he said: If thou eat thou shalt surely die". (Alma 12:23).

This would have voided the Plan of Salvation. Death is our only exit from mortality, and it is an integral and essential component of the Merciful Plan of our Father that caused us to shout for joy when it was explained to us during our pre-mortal curriculum. When Adam and Eve were placed in the Garden of Eden, it was with the understanding that they would transgress God's law in order to trigger their mortality. When they were later expelled from the Garden in consequence of that transgression, the cherubim and a flaming sword insured that they would not jeopardize the mission they had accepted at the Council in Heaven before the world was. Because a Savior had been provided for them, both Justice and Mercy could be served.

Alma taught Antionah that the Fall was a key component of the Plan, inasmuch as it gave Adam and Eve and their posterity the opportunity to sojourn on the Earth to prepare for their resurrection. "And we see that death comes upon mankind, yea, the death which has been spoken of by Amulek, which is the temporal death; nevertheless there was a space granted unto man in which he might repent; therefore this life became a probationary state; a time to prepare to meet God; a time to prepare for that endless state which has been spoken of by us, which is after the resurrection of the dead". (Alma 12:24).

The death of our physical bodies is an awe-inspiring element of the Gospel Plan. In fact, "it was appointed unto men that they must die; and after death, they must come to judgment, even that same judgment of which we have spoken, which is the end". (Alma 12:27). In The Book of Mormon, with broad strokes the prophets paint a wonderfully vibrant portrait of the Plan, and after carefully studying their teachings that relate to it, the ultimate purpose of the Fall snaps into sharp focus. We can almost hear Father in Heaven explaining how Adam and Eve would transgress His law in order to become mortal so they and all of their posterity could die. We can clearly see how the Fall allows us to prepare for our glorious resurrection. The Spirit teaches us that through the Atonement, we may receive the kinds of immortal bodies that we will need in order to be able to endure celestial fire. The beauty of it is that our judgment will not come until we have had the opportunity during mortality to conform our lives with exactness to the principles of the Plan of Redemption.

"And after God had appointed that these things should come unto man, behold, then he saw that it was expedient that man should know concerning the things whereof he had appointed unto them; Therefore, he sent angels to converse with them, who caused men to behold of his glory. And they began from that time forth to call on his name; therefore, God conversed with men, and made known unto them the Plan of Redemption, which had been prepared from the foundation of the world; and this he made known unto them according to their faith and repentance and their holy works". (Alma 12:28-30). Alma hoped that as he taught the people of Ammonihah these truths, and later when he taught Corianton, as well, they would receive a spiritual confirmation.

Men and women were to be instructed sufficiently, and then to have the opportunity to act for themselves. Satan's way is coercive, but the "perfect law of liberty" presupposes our exercise of free will. However, unless our behavior is in harmony with the laws of the Gospel, our unbridled freedom will lead to tyranny. We are free to choose, but we cannot choose to escape the consequences of our poor choices. If we violate the commandments, we must repent, for we have the power within us to be "as Gods, knowing good from evil," and we are "in a state to act according to (our) wills and pleasures, whether to do evil or to do good". (Alma 12:31).

Adam and Eve were unequivocally taught about the penalty that would follow their violation of the commandments. "God gave unto them commandments, after having made known unto them the Plan of Redemption, that they should not do evil, the penalty thereof being a second death, which was an everlasting death as to things pertaining unto righteousness; for on such the Plan of Redemption could have no power, for the works of Justice could not be destroyed, according to the supreme goodness of God". (Alma 12:32). Because God respects agency, He couldn't nullify the demands of Justice as they bore down on Adam and Eve and their posterity, following the Fall. Nor would He desire to do so, because there was an elegant solution to Adam's quandary, that had been built into the Plan.

God provided another way for us to partake of the fruit of the tree of life. He called "on men, in the name of his Son, (this being the Plan of Redemption which was laid) saying: If ye will repent, and harden not your hearts, then will I have mercy on you, through mine Only Begotten Son. Therefore, whosoever repenteth, and hardeneth not his heart, he shall have claim on Mercy through mine Only Begotten Son, unto a remission of his sins; and these shall enter into my rest". (Alma 12:33-34). Whoever would have faith in Christ and repent would gain a remission of their sins, because of their claim on Mercy through His Atonement. Those who refused to repent because of the hardness of their hearts would not be able to enter into the Rest of God or the Fulness of His Glory, for obvious reasons.

"And now, my brethren," Alma had urged the people of Ammonihah, "behold I say unto you, that if ye will harden your hearts ye shall not enter into the rest of the Lord; therefore your iniquity provoketh him that he sendeth down his wrath upon you as in the first provocation, (when Adam and Eve suffered physical death) yea, according to his word in the last provocation as well as the first, (when, without repentance, we will die spiritually) to the everlasting destruction of your souls; therefore, according to his word, unto the last death, as well as the first". (Alma 12:36). Thus, Alma had extended an olive branch to the wicked people of Ammonihah. He was offering them one last opportunity to avoid complete physical and spiritual destruction.

Years after he had clarified the principles of agency, justice, atonement, mercy, repentance, forgiveness, and redemption to the people of Ammonihah, Alma sat down with his son, Corianton, asking: "I perceive there is somewhat more which doth worry your mind, which ye cannot understand - which is concerning the justice of God in the punishment of the sinner; for ye do try to suppose that it is injustice that the sinner should be consigned to a state of misery. Now, behold, my son, I will explain this thing unto thee". Then, just as he had for Antionah, Alma refreshed the memory of Corianton, reminding him that at the time of Adam and Eve's transgression, when they were driven into the lone and dreary world, God "placed at the east end of the Garden of Eden, cherubim and a flaming sword which turned every way, to keep the tree of life". (V. 1-2). Our very concerned Father did this because "the man (Adam) had become as God, knowing good and evil," and now the very real possibility existed that he would "put forth his hand, and take also of the tree of life, and eat and live forever" in his sins, not have had the opportunity to repent. (Alma 42:3, & Genesis 3:22).

As we have learned from our study of Alma's ministry in Ammonihah, if he were to have done this without regard to the Plan of Salvation that was designed for just such a scenario, the Plan itself would have been frustrated because the Law of Mercy would have been powerless to satisfy the demands of the Law of Justice. In order to demonstrate for Adam and Eve the necessity of obedience to both these laws and to impress upon them the importance of the infinite and eternal Atonement that would reconcile the two, "the Lord God placed cherubim and the flaming sword, that he should not partake of the fruit". (V. 2-3). He used this notable symbolism to impress upon the mind of Adam the necessity of Atonement to reconcile the opposing laws of Justice and Mercy.

Alma had very effectively used the same illustration ten years earlier in Ammonihah, explaining that it is imperative that the symbolism employed should focus our attention on the doctrine that eternal life is gained by redemption and not by the overpowering of cherubim with weapons superior to flaming swords. He had shown that by placing these to guard the tree of life, Heavenly Father had prevented Adam and Eve and their posterity from inappropriately partaking of the fruit of the tree of life, and thus from living forever in their sins. With this explanation, both the people of Ammonihah and Corianton were prevented from having any basis for justifying sinful behavior.

Satan, who was a liar from the beginning, had attempted to foil the Plan of Salvation by substituting his own counterfeit, unworkable alternative that would not have required at Atonement. He must have thought his idea was brilliant, inasmuch as it would conveniently sidestep the laws of Justice and Mercy. His promotional efforts had been thwarted, but at a great cost in lives. Instead, with the implementation of the Plan, mankind would be provided with "a probationary time," a time of testing, or of putting to the proof questions that in this case would be: "Will men and women serve God, if given the opportunity? (V. 4). Will they recognize Christ as their Savior, and exercise faith unto repentance?" The flaming sword would prevent Adam from ignorantly nullifying his opportunity to participate in this learning laboratory, and the cherubim would guarantee that, though imperfect in his obedience, he could learn to be perfect in his repentance and in his service to God. (V. 4). Both the cherubim and a flaming sword were central to the successful operation of a Plan that hinged on Atonement.

"For behold, if Adam had put forth his hand immediately, and partaken of the tree of life, he would have lived forever, according to the word of God, having no space for repentance; yea, and also the word of God would have been void, and the great Plan of Salvation would have been frustrated". (V. 5). The Plan of Salvation is variously called the Merciful Plan of the Great Creator (2 Nephi 9:6), the Plan of our God (2 Nephi 9:13), the Great and Eternal Plan of Deliverance from Death (2 Nephi 11:5), the Plan of Redemption (Alma 29:2), the Great Plan of the Eternal God (Alma 34:9), the Great and Eternal Plan of Redemption (Alma 34:16), the Great Plan of Redemption (Alma 34:31), the Plan of Restoration (Alma 41:2), the Great Plan of Salvation (V. 5), the Great Plan of Happiness (Alma 42:8), the Plan of Mercy (V. 15), the Plan of Happiness (V. 16), and the Great Plan of Mercy (V. 31), because it makes possible the resurrection of otherwise imperfect mortals to eternal lives of glory by harmonizing justice with mercy. (See Essay: "Plan of Salvation"). "Now, if it had not been for the Plan of Redemption," Alma had told the people of Ammonihah, "which was laid from the foundation of the world, there could have been no resurrection of the dead; but there was a Plan of Redemption laid, which shall bring to pass the resurrection of the dead". (Alma 12:25).

The cherubim became involved in order to guarantee that the Plan would not be frustrated in the sense that Justice would trump Mercy. Meanwhile, the issue of Adam's transgression in the Garden needed to be addressed, for "as they were cut off from the tree of life they should be cut off from the face of the earth". (V. 6). Justice now demanded that "man became lost forever, yea, they became fallen man. And now, ye see by this that our first parents were cut off both temporally and spiritually from the presence of the Lord". (V. 6-7). So it was, that "they became subject to follow after their own will". (V. 7). The supernal principle of agency was honored, even if it meant that Justice must be served. Thus, "it was appointed unto man to die" rather than to reclaim him without redemption "from this temporal death, for that would (have) destroy(ed) the great Plan of

Happiness. Therefore, as the soul could never die, and the Fall had brought upon all mankind a spiritual death as well as a temporal, that is, they were cut off from the presence of the Lord, it was expedient that mankind should be reclaimed from this spiritual death". (V. 6-9).

In our fallen state, we are subjected to the influences of Satan. When we have no experience with the Divine for reference, and we are alienated from God by spiritual death, we become carnal, sensual, and devilish, by nature. Alma explained: "This probationary state became a state for them to prepare; it became a preparatory state. And now remember, my son, if it were not for the Plan of redemption, as soon as they were dead their souls were miserable, being cut off from the presence of the Lord". (Alma 42:11). Justice would demand that they eternally suffer the consequences of their own actions. (Alma 42:12). They would be "in the grasp of justice; yea, the justice of God, which (would consign) them forever to be cut off from his presence". (V. 14).

This is why, from the Fall of Adam, God has provided us with the Plan of Salvation, that mortality might be a preparatory state, where we might develop the qualities required for redemption from spiritual death. As Alma clarified: "And now, there was no means to reclaim men from this fallen state, which man had brought upon himself because of his own disobedience; Therefore, according to justice, the Plan of Redemption could not be brought about, only on conditions of repentance of men in this probationary state, yea, this preparatory state; for except it were for these conditions, mercy could not take effect except it should destroy the work of justice". (V. 12-13). The beauty of the Plan of Redemption, then, is that it meets the demands of perfect Justice through the infinite mercy of a loving Heavenly Father. The Plan allows God to be both just and merciful at the same time, because of the Atonement.

As Alma explained: "Now the work of Justice could not be destroyed; if so, God would cease to be God. And thus, we see that all mankind were fallen, and they were in the grasp of justice; yea, the justice of God, which consigned them forever to be cut off from his presence. And now, the Plan of Mercy could not be brought about except an Atonement should be made; therefore, God Himself atoneth for the sins of the world, to bring about the Plan of Mercy, to appease the demands of Justice, that God might be a perfect, just God, and a merciful God also". (V. 13-15). The Atonement allowed God to satisfy Justice and still mercifully reclaim His children from physical and spiritual death in one brilliant stroke. The Savior became the Master of the situation. In His sacrifice, the debt would be paid, the redemption made, the covenant fulfilled, Justice satisfied, the will of God done, and all power given to the Son by divine investiture of authority.

"Now, repentance could not come unto men except there were a punishment, which also was eternal as the life of the soul should be, affixed opposite to the Plan of Happiness, which was as eternal also as the life of the soul. Now, how could a man repent except he should sin? How could he sin if there was no law? How could there be a law save there was a punishment? Now, there was a punishment affixed, and a just law given, which brought remorse of conscience unto man. Now, if there was no law given - if a man murdered he should die - would he be afraid he would die if he should murder? And also, if there were no law given against sin men would not be afraid to sin. And if there was no law given, if men sinned what could justice do, or mercy either, for they would have no claim upon the creature?" (V. 16-21).

Alma had certainly studied the counsel of Father Lehi, recorded on The Plates of Lehi that were in his possession, and on the doctrine they contained, he based the next section of his remarks to Corianton. He affirmed: "There is a law given, and a punishment affixed, and a repentance granted, which repentance, mercy claimeth. Otherwise, Justice claimeth the creature and executeth the law, and the law inflicteth the punishment; if not so, the works of justice would be destroyed, and God would cease to be God. But God ceaseth not to be God, and mercy claimeth the penitent, and mercy cometh because of the atonement; and the atonement bringeth to pass the resurrection of the dead; and the resurrection of the dead bringeth back men into the presence of God; and thus, they are restored into his presence, to be judged according to their works, according to the law and justice". (V. 22-23).

"Is justice dishonored?" asked John Taylor. "No, it is satisfied; the debt is paid. Is righteousness forsaken? No, this is a righteous act. All requirements are met. Is judgment violated? No, its demands are fulfilled. Is mercy triumphant? No, she simply claims her own. Justice, judgment, mercy, and truth all harmonize as the attributes of Deity". ("Mediation and Atonement," p. 171-172). President Taylor echoed Alma, who said: "Mercy claimeth the penitent, and mercy cometh because of the Atonement; and the Atonement bringeth to pass the resurrection of the dead; and the resurrection of the dead bringeth back men into the presence of God. For behold, Justice exerciseth all his demands, and also mercy claimeth all which is her own; and thus, none but the truly penitent are saved". (V. 23-24, note the gender pronouns). Our innate desire to be clean is a celestial spark that God has put into each of us for the purpose of saving our souls.

These "great and eternal purposes ... were prepared from the foundation of the world. And thus, cometh about the salvation and the redemption of men, and also their destruction and misery". (V. 26). President Taylor further taught: "To the Son is given the power of the resurrection, the power of the redemption, the power of salvation, the power to enact laws for the carrying out and accomplishment of the design. Hence, life and immortality are brought to light, the Gospel is introduced, and He becomes the Author of eternal life and exaltation". ("Mediation and Atonement," p. 171-172).

As Amulek had explained to the Zoramites: "Mercy can satisfy the demands of Justice, and encircles (repentant souls) in the arms of safety, while he that exercises no faith unto repentance is exposed to the whole law of the demands of Justice; therefore, only unto him that has faith unto repentance is brought about the great and eternal Plan of Redemption". (Alma 34:16). Faith, without works of repentance made possible because of the Atonement, is dead, because alone it has insufficient power to save. Anciently, the psalmist had explored this relationship between Justice and Mercy. "Justice and judgment are the habitation of thy throne: Mercy and truth shall go before thy face". (Psalms 89:14). Latter-day revelation sheds additional light on these foundation principles: "Mercy hath compassion on mercy and claimeth her own; Justice continueth its course and claimeth its own; judgment goeth before the face of him who sitteth upon the throne and governeth and executeth all things". (D&C 88:40, note the interesting use of gender specific pronouns in this verse).

"What, do ye suppose that mercy can rob justice?" Alma asked Corianton. "I say unto you, Nay; not one whit. If so, God would cease to be God". (V. 25). The Savior's mission on Earth was principally to "redeem those who (would agree to) be baptized unto repentance, through faith on his name". (Alma 9:27). For his part, at the end of his counsel to Corianton relating to Justice and Mercy, Alma reminded him that the only payment required for the gift of salvation is "the heart and a willing mind". (D&C 64:34). The only things that we must give up are our sins. (See Alma 22:18). Therefore, Alma counseled his son to "only let your sins trouble you, with that trouble which shall bring you down unto repentance". (V. 29).

The turning point for Corianton was the conscious recognition of his sins. (See Jeremiah 6:15). When he had cleared this hurdle, and with a greater understanding of the operation of both Justice and Mercy and of the relationship and harmony between the two that was made possible by the Plan of Redemption, his father warned him to cease excusing himself in sin:. "O my son, I desire that ye should deny the justice of God no more. Do not endeavor to excuse yourself in the least point because of your sins, by denying the justice of God; but do let the justice of God, and his mercy, and his long-suffering have full sway in your heart; and let it bring you down to the dust in humility". (V. 30).

Lehi had also weighed in on the relationship between Justice and Mercy, in his discourse on opposition. "For it must needs be that there is an opposition in all things," he had said. (2 Nephi 2:11). Opposition can lead to both desirable and undesirable consequences. Without it, "righteousness could not be brought to pass, neither wickedness, neither holiness nor misery, neither good nor bad". Without it, there could be "no life neither death, nor corruption nor incorruption, happiness nor misery, neither sense nor insensibility". (2 Nephi 2:11). Without opposition, the Law and the Savior's intercession for men and women "must needs have been created for a thing of naught; wherefore there would have been no purpose in the end of its creation". The very "wisdom of God and his eternal purposes, and also the power, and the mercy, and the justice of God" would have been destroyed. (2 Nephi 2:12).

Without law, there could be no sin, reasoned Lehi, and without sin, there could be no righteousness. "And if there be no righteousness there be no happiness. And if there be no righteousness nor happiness there be no punishment nor misery. And if these things are not there is no God. And if there is no God we are not, neither the Earth; for there could have been no creation of things, neither to act nor to be acted upon; wherefore, all things must have vanished away". (2 Nephi 2:13).

Lehi's view of the Fall of Adam provides an interesting perspective on the basic claims of Christianity and 2 Nephi 2:14-17 offers a wealth of information on this subject. In the beginning, "to bring about his eternal purposes in the end of man, after he had created our first parents, and the beasts of the field and the fowls of the air, and in fine, all things which are created," God presented Adam and Eve with "the forbidden fruit in opposition to the tree of life; the one being sweet and the other bitter". (2 Nephi 2:15).

"Wherefore, the Lord God gave unto man that he should act for himself. (But) man could not act for himself save it should be that he was enticed by the one or the other". (2 Nephi 2:16). Thus, in the Garden of Eden, God honored the principle of opposition in all things, and permitted the devil to "tempt the children of men, or they could not be agents unto themselves; for if they never should have bitter they could not know the sweet. Wherefore, it came to pass that the devil tempted Adam, and he partook of the forbidden fruit and transgressed the commandment, wherein he became subject to the will of the devil, because he yielded unto temptation". (D&C 29:39-40). But Lehi correctly understood that Adam had not been deceived. His was an intelligent, conscious decision, the result of an understanding of the requirements of the Gospel Plan.

The Fall resulted, and Adam and Eve "were driven out of the garden of Eden, to till the Earth". (2 Nephi 2:19). The scriptures clearly teach that Adam and Eve were the first of Heavenly Father's children to live on this earth. "Father Adam (was) the Ancient of Days, and father of all, and (husband to) our glorious Mother Eve". (D&C 138:38-39). So began "the family of all the earth". (2 Nephi 2:20).

Lehi next taught that the first generations of mankind following the expulsion of Adam and Eve from the Garden lived to great age so that they might have time to repent. "And the days of the children of men were prolonged, according to the will of God, that they might repent while in the flesh; wherefore, their state became a state of probation, and their time was lengthened, according to the commandments which the Lord God gave unto the children of men: For he gave commandment that all men must repent, for he showed unto all men that they were lost, because of the transgression of their parents". (2 Nephi 2:21).

Lehi was emphatic that had Adam not transgressed the Law in the Garden, he would have vegetated there forever in a morally static state of limbo. "And now, behold, if Adam had not transgressed he would not have fallen, but he would have remained in the Garden of Eden, and all things which were created must have remained in the same state in which they were after they were created; and they must have remained forever, and had no end. And they would have had no children; wherefore they would have remained in a state of innocence, having no joy, for they knew no misery; doing no good, for they knew no sin". (2 Nephi 9:22-23). Life in Eden may have been idyllic, but it was not ideal. Our Father knew that Adam and Eve must fall as a critically operative part of the Plan of Salvation, for "all things have been done in the wisdom of him who knoweth all things". (2 Nephi 9:24).

Thus, "Adam fell that men might be, and men are that they might have joy". (2 Nephi 9:25). In a grand summary of his discourse on opposition and the Fall of Adam, Lehi's simple aphorism speaks volumes and is one of the basic messages of the Restoration. When the Fall of Adam is considered in conjunction with the Atonement of Christ, it is clear that both are part of God's Plan of Eternal Progression for His children, who could only attain a fulness of joy in a personal, tangible, resurrection. "For man is spirit, the elements are eternal, and spirit and element, inseparably connected, receive a fulness of joy". (D&C 93:33).

When Lehi returned to his original discussion after this parenthetical aside, he explained: "The Messiah cometh in the fulness of time, that he may redeem the children of men from the fall. And because that they are redeemed from the fall they have become free forever, knowing good from evil; to act for themselves and not to be acted upon, save it be by the punishment of the law at the great and last day, according to the commandments which God hath given". (2 Nephi 2:26). Thus, a way was provided for the family of man to triumph in spite of the transgression of Adam and Eve that brought about temporal and spiritual death; temporal death because of the separation of the body from the spirit at the close of our mortal existence, and spiritual death because of our alienation from the Spirit of God in the absence of an Atonement, at the time of our judgment.

"Wherefore, men are free according to the flesh; and all things are given them which are expedient unto man. And they are free to choose liberty and eternal life, through the great Mediator of all men". (2 Nephi 2:27). Heavenly Father always honors the eternal principle of agency. It is riskier, but it is the only way. Rather than enslaving us in good habits, He repeatedly gives us the opportunity to recommit ourselves to our covenants of obedience to true and eternal principles.

On the other hand, we "may choose captivity and death, according to the captivity and power of the devil; for he seeketh that all men might be miserable like unto himself". (2 Nephi 2:27). "The Spirit is pure," taught Brigham Young, and is "under the special control and influence of the Lord, but the body is of the Earth, and is subject to the power of the devil, and is under the mighty influence of that fallen nature that is of the Earth. If the Spirit yields to the body, the devil then has power to overcome the body and spirit of that man, and he loses both."

Jacob also had something to say about the same principles taught by his father Lehi and his descendant Alma. He urged his people to avoid spiritual sclerosis by repenting "with full purpose of heart". (Jacob 6:5). He knew that hardening of the spiritual arteries is a sign of a self-defeating illness that, left untreated, will effectively kill the Spirit. He posed questions loaded with powerful action verbs that were intended to rivet the attention of his listeners upon the mysteries of the kingdom and the solemnities of eternity. "Will ye reject Christ," he asked, "and deny (His words), and the power of God, and the gift of the Holy Ghost, and quench the Holy Spirit, and make a mock of the great Plan of Redemption?" (Jacob 6:8).

His message, like Lehi's before him and Alma's after him, was a call to repentance. If we do not repent, the Holy Spirit that burns like a fire will be quenched, and the Atonement of Christ will be neutralized and powerless to save us. Without repentance and forgiveness, we will stand before the Bar of God with "shame and awful guilt" because, as we have learned, without the Atonement, the Law of Mercy is required to yield to the exacting demands of the Law of Justice. (Jacob 6:9).

Jacob put it bluntly: "According to the power of justice, ye must go away into that lake of fire and brimstone, whose flames are unquenchable, and whose smoke ascendeth up forever and ever, which … is endless torment". (Jacob 6:10). So, the logical path to follow is to "repent and enter in at the strait gate, and continue in the way which is narrow, until ye shall obtain eternal life". (Jacob 6:11). This verse recapitulates the line of thought begun earlier, when Jacob asked: "I beseech of you in words of soberness that ye would repent, and come with full purpose of heart, and cleave unto God as he cleaveth unto you". (Jacob 6:5).

Faith and repentance lead us to the strait gate of baptism. When we pass through this gate, we obtain a remission of sins, gain membership in the Church, and the door swings open revealing a path that leads to our personal sanctification through repentance and receipt of the Holy Ghost. The way is strait and narrow, and the Gospel standard is undeviating, with no room for rationalization or compromise. There is no latitude in God's declaration that he "cannot look upon sin with the least degree of allowance". (D&C 1:31). But it is a workable program, none-the-less.

After explaining the great Plan of Redemption to his people, that solved the dilemma created by God's demand for perfection coupled with our inability to live sinless lives, Jacob simply stated: "O be wise; what can I say more?" He had exhaustively explored the ramifications of the Plan, that solved the dilemma created by God's demand for perfection coupled with our inability to lead sinless lives. At the conclusion of his address, Jacob simply said: "O be wise. What can I say more?" (Jacob 6:12).

Back in Zarahemla, (see Alma 35:14). Alma called his son Corianton to return to his missionary labors. "And now, O my son, ye are called of God to preach the word unto this people. And now, my son, go thy way, declare the word with truth and soberness, that thou mayest bring souls unto repentance, that the great Plan of mercy may have claim upon them". (V. 31).

That Corianton was faithful to his father's counsel is evident from a reference to him in the abridged record of Shiblon. Seventeen years later, Mormon recorded that Shiblon "was a just man, and he did walk uprightly before God; and he did observe to do good continually, to keep the commandments of the Lord his God; and also did his brother" Corianton. (Alma 63:2, see Alma 49:18-19).

Alma
Chapter 43

Chapters 43-62 record the Nephite-Lamanite Wars of 74-61 B.C. In fact, The Book of Mormon now commences a chronicle of 43 consecutive chapters on war and the perceptive reader will gain an understanding of the underlying ideological conflicts behind the great struggles. As Mormon wrote: "Behold, I speak unto you as if ye were present, and yet ye are not. But behold, Jesus Christ hath shown you unto me, and I know your doings. (Mormon 8:35).

"The past is prologue," wrote Shakespeare. ("The Tempest," Act 2, scene 1, 245-254). The phrase, penned for "The Tempest," was intended to imply that our past is merely a prologue, or an introduction to the great adventure upon which we will embark if we follow through on our plans. This interpretation teaches that what has come before on our journey through life doesn't matter in the grand scheme of things, because a new future lies before us, subject to the choices we will yet make.

However, the way the phrase is generally used today, it means the exact opposite of its original meaning. Today, one would turn the phrase and say that because the past defines the present, it determines the future. This interpretation is not necessarily incorrect, because, in this context, we might say that "those who fail to learn the lessons of history are doomed to repeat their mistakes."

When Victor Hugo sensed that the end was near, he implied that he understood the former application of the phrase. He wrote: "I feel in myself future life. I am like a forest that has been more than once cut down. The new shoots are stronger and livelier than ever. I am rising, I know, toward the sky. The sunshine is over my head. The Earth gives me its generous sap, but the heavens enlighten me with the reflection of unknown worlds. Winter may be approaching, but eternal spring is in my heart, I breathe the fragrance of the lilacs, the violets, and the roses, as at twenty years. The nearer I approach the end, the clearer I hear around me the immortal symphonies from a world that invites me to partake of its energy. It is a marvelous, yet simple truth that the tomb is not a blind alley, but an open thoroughfare. It closes in the twilight to open on the dawn. My work is only a beginning, and it is hardly above its foundation. I would gladly see it mounting forever."

Mormon must have included these chapters on war because he wanted us to learn from the mistakes of his people and not suffer ourselves the same consequences of disobedience, because the circumstances of our lives are really very similar. As Nephi said, "I did liken all scripture unto us, that it might be for our profit and learning". (1 Nephi 19:23).

In Chapter 43, we return to Mormon's abridgement of the Large Plates of Nephi. These plates continued to the chronicle the missionary labors of Alma and his sons, but Mormon chose to write only that "they preached the word, and the truth, according to the spirit of prophecy and revelation; and they preached after the holy order of God by which they were called". (V. 2). The record of Alma then officially ends with Alma chapter 44, although there is a post-script by his son Helaman in the first 19 verses of Alma chapter 45.

Mormon turned his attention once again to the struggles between Zerahemnah, the Lamanite leader of that day, and Moroni and Lehi, two of the principal Nephite leaders. (See Alma 35:13). To Alma's great consternation, the Zoramites had become Lamanites. (V. 4, see Alma 31:2). These apostates formed a great army who, with their Lamanite brethren, waged war against the Nephites. (V. 4-5).

The Amalekites were Nephite apostates who "were of a more wicked and murderous disposition than the Lamanites," and so they were "appointed chief captains over the Lamanites" (V. 6), "they being the most acquainted with the strength of the Nephites, and their places of resort, and the weakest parts of their cities". (Alma 48:5, see Commentary Reference to Alma 21:2).

The effectiveness of a smear campaign as a means to personal power is attested in verse 7, where we learn that Zerahemnah manipulated the Amalekites because of "their hatred towards the Nephites, that he might bring them into subjection to the accomplishments of his designs". (See V. 43-44).

Satan's efforts are always directed at the destruction of free will. Zerahemnah was himself an angel of death who sought "to stir up the Lamanites to anger against the Nephites; this he did that he might usurp great power over them, and also that he might gain power over the Nephites by bringing them into bondage". (V. 8, see V. 29, & Commentary Reference to Alma 10:23).

The war between the forces of good and evil that had begun in heaven continues on earth to the present day with the same stratagems. Only the field of battle has changed. The Nephites' desire "was to support their lands, and their houses, and their wives, and their children, that they might preserve them from the hands of their enemies; and also, that they might preserve their rights and their privileges, yea, and also their liberty, that they might worship God according to their desires". (V. 9, see V. 47).

The Nephites knew that if they should fall under the domination of the Lamanites, "whosoever should worship God in spirit and in truth, the true and the living God, the Lamanites would destroy". (V. 10). Even in our day, in societies protected by legislative guarantees of personal freedom, an Apostle of The Lord has warned: "Martyrdom is not a thing of the past only, but of the present and of the future, for Satan has not yet been bound, and the servants of the Lord will not be silenced in the final age of warning and judgment. There are forces and powers in the world today, which would silence the tongue and shed the blood of every true witness of Christ in the world, if they had the power and the means to do it". (Bruce R. McConkie, "Mormon Doctrine," p. 469, see Commentary Reference to Mosiah 17:20).

In Book of Mormon times, those forces and powers were composed of "Lamanites, who were a compound of Laman and Lemuel, and the sons of Ishmael, and all those who had dissented from the Nephites, who were Amalekites and Zoramites, and the descendants of the priests of Noah". (V. 13, see Mosiah 23:31-32). This group was "as numerous, nearly, as were the Nephites". (V. 14). The fact that the army mounted by the Lamanites was "more numerous, yea, by more than double the number of the Nephites" indicates that the Lamanites were oriented toward warfare much more so than were the Nephites. (V. 51).

At this point in the record, we are introduced to a man who would have a profound effect upon the fortunes of the Nephite people for hundreds of years, and one who impressed Mormon greatly. "His name was Moroni". (V. 16). He was a man who understood that "the task ahead of us is never as great as the power behind us". (J. Reuben Clark, Jr.). Moroni had a burning zeal to see the Nephite nation triumph in righteousness over their Lamanite adversaries. He personified one envisioned by Sir Walter Scott, who wrote: "Breathed there a man with soul so dead, who never to himself has said 'This is my own, my native land!' Whose heart hath ne'er within him burned, as home his footsteps he hath turned from wandering on a foreign strand?" ("The Lay of The Last Minstrel").

Moroni was only 25 years old when he took command of the armies of the Nephites, but he had new and innovative ideas regarding warfare that proved to be very effective when the Nephite armies confronted the Lamanites. (See V. 17-21). He may have been introduced to these strategies in Mosiah's translation of the 24 Gold Plates of Ether that contained an account of the wars of the Jaredites. (See Alma 37:23-28 & Alma 50:14 for a description of new methods of fortification). If so, this may have given him a tactical advantage over the Lamanites, who did not have access to this record. (See Mosiah 28:12). In fact, it would take the Lamanites about two years before they would also adopt these new techniques of warfare. (See Alma 49:6).

After successful introductory skirmishes with the Lamanites, and in conformity with ancient Israelite custom, Moroni sent representatives to the prophet Alma, "desiring him that he should inquire of the Lord whither the armies of the Nephites should go to defend themselves against the Lamanites". (V. 23). "And it came to pass that the word of the Lord came unto Alma". (V. 24).

Once again, the successful secret weapons of the Nephite armies were individual and collective obedience, and guidance from the Holy Ghost.

Moroni also sent "spies round about, that he might know when the camp of the Lamanites should come". (V. 28). Mormon was a real sticker for fair play, and in the record he apologized for Moroni's use of espionage: "Knowing that it was the only desire of the Nephites to preserve their lands, and their liberty, and their Church, therefore he thought it no sin that he should defend them by stratagem; therefore, he found by his spies which course the Lamanites were to take". (V. 30).

Thus, commenced what Mormon called "the work of death". (V. 37, see V. 38, Alma 44:20, & Commentary Reference to 2 Nephi 26:2). The Lamanites fought "like dragons". (V. 44). "Nevertheless, the Nephites were inspired by a better cause, for they were not fighting for monarchy nor power, but ... for their homes and their liberties, their wives and their children, and their all, yea, for their rites of worship and their Church". (V. 46, see V. 47).

Robert L. Simpson counseled young men of the Church: "To whatever country your citizenship commitment might be, you honor it, you obey it, and you sustain it. To do otherwise would be contrary to law and order, which is the basis of the priesthood wherever it is established". (C.R. 10/1970). There are two conditions that may justify a truly Christian man to enter a war, taught David O. McKay in April 1942, just four months after the United States entered World War II: "An attempt by others to dominate and deprive him of his agency, and loyalty to his country. Possibly there is a third, that is defense of a weak nation that is being unjustly crushed by a strong and ruthless one". (C.R. 4/1942).

Moroni was a passionate leader who inspired his troops such that "they began to stand against (the numerically superior forces of) the Lamanites with power; and in that selfsame hour that they cried unto the Lord for their freedom, the Lamanites began to flee before them". (V. 50).

Another of Moroni's excellent qualities was compassion. Although his army had encircled that of the Lamanites, and was in a position to destroy it, "now Moroni, when he saw their terror, commanded his men that they should stop shedding their blood". (V. 54).

Alma
Chapter 44

Moroni attempted to reason with Zerahemnah, the Lamanite leader, arguing that the Nephites sought neither power nor to bring the Lamanites into bondage. (V. 1). He pointed out that the Nephites had prevailed over the Lamanites only because of their religion and their faith. (V. 2).

He offered to release the encircled Lamanite army under the following condition: "We will spare your lives," he said, "if ye will go your way and come not again to war against us". (V. 6). Verses 5-6 help us to understand why he was so secure in making this proposition. The Nephites had tremendous support from all that was most dear to them: their faith and religion, their rites of worship and Church; and their wives and children. The enjoyment of their liberty and their agency bound them to their land and country. These things, and "the maintenance of the sacred word of God" were responsible for their confidence and their happiness. (V. 5).

"And now, Zerahemnah," declared the young captain, "I command you, in the name of that all-powerful God, who has strengthened our arms that we have gained power over you, by our faith, by our religion, and by our rites of worship, and by our Church, and by the sacred support which we owe to our wives and our children, by that liberty which binds us to our lands and our country; yea, and also by the maintenance of the sacred word of God, to which we owe all our happiness; and by all that is most dear unto us. Yea, and this is not all; I command you by all the desires which ye have for life". (V. 5).

To Zerahemnah, Moroni's words that followed must have been sobering, for he said: "And now, if ye do not this, behold, ye are in our hands ... and then we shall see who shall have power over this people; yea, we will see who shall be brought into bondage". (V. 7). As David had said to the Philistine: Thou comest to me with a sword, and with a spear, and with a shield: but I come to thee in the name of the Lord of hosts, the God of the armies of Israel, whom thou hast defied. This day will the Lord deliver thee into mine hand." (1 Samuel 17:45-46).

Zerahemnah was duly impressed, and promptly handed over his weapons, but he would not take the required oath, because he knew he could not keep it. (V. 8-9). As wicked as he was, Zerahemnah was not an oath breaker. At this, "Moroni returned the sword and the weapons of war, which he had received, unto Zerahemnah, saying: Behold, we will end the conflict". (V. 10).

Zerahemnah rushed forward to kill Moroni, but instead had his scalp removed by an alert Nephite soldier. (V. 12-14). This is an interesting episode, but really establishes no historical precedent to the practice among Native Americans of scalping their enemies. This custom did not come into general use until the 17th century, and then it was at the instigation of Europeans.

Zerahemnah's scalp wound caused many of the Lamanites to reconsider the Nephite peace terms, and so "many came forth and threw down their weapons of war at the feet of Moroni, and entered into a covenant of peace". (V. 15). This caused other Lamanites to become even angrier, however, and hostilities with them reached a feverish pitch. (V. 16-18).

Finally, when Zerahemnah saw that his army was about to be destroyed, he "cried mightily unto Moroni, promising that he would covenant and also his people with them, if they would spare the remainder of their lives, that they never would come to war against them". (V. 19). So, the work of death ceased, the Lamanite army gave up its weapons, and it was allowed to depart into the wilderness toward the Land of Nephi. (V. 20).

In view of Zerahemnah's threats, Moroni would have been justified in finishing off the Lamanite army as a preventive measure, but he would not condemn them for a crime they had not yet committed, and in offering them a chance to repent, he was giving them an opportunity to become his friends, which, as we shall see, many of them did.

In this on-going account of war between the Nephites and Lamanites, everything is strictly authentic, with the proper emphasis correctly placed. "Strategy and tactics are treated with the knowledge of an expert; logistics and supply, armaments and fortifications, recruiting and training, problems of morale and support from the home front, military intelligence from cloak and dagger to scouting and patrolling; interrogation, guarding, feeding, and exchange of prisoners, propaganda and psychological warfare, rehabilitation and resettlement, feelers for peace and negotiation; treason, profiteering and exploitation of the war economy - it is all there". (Hugh Nibley, "Since Cumorah," p. 329).

Even these chapters where war commands center stage can serve to teach us valuable lessons and can strengthen our testimonies of The Book of Mormon. They can also illustrate how to live when we find ourselves in circumstances similar to the Nephites.

Alma
Chapter 45

To their credit, the Nephites celebrated their great military victory by engaging in fasting and prayer. (V. 1). Nevertheless, with solemnity, Alma prophesied to Helaman that after 400 years had passed away the Nephites would dwindle in unbelief because of iniquity, and that as a nation they would be destroyed. (V. 10 & 14).

We understand from Alma's prophecy that in the last great battles, every faithful Nephite would be hunted down and killed. Others who would renounce their religion would "be numbered among the Lamanites, and (would) become like unto them". (V. 14). The land itself would suffer a curse and enjoy a blessing simultaneously. It would be cursed "unto every nation, kindred, tongue, and people, unto destruction, which do wickedly" and blessed unto "all those who should stand fast in the faith from that time henceforth". (V. 16-17).

After 18 years of service as the prophet of God ministering among the people, "Alma departed out of the land of Zarahemla, as if to go into the land of Melek. And it came to pass that he was never heard of more; as to his death or burial we know not of". (V. 18, see 3 Nephi 1:2-3). Alma was likely translated, for "the saying went abroad in the Church that he was taken up by the Spirit, or buried by the hand of the Lord, even as Moses". (V. 19, see D&C 84:25, & "Doctrines of Salvation," 2:107 & 110).

Translation is a doctrine that is peculiar to the Church of Jesus Christ of Latter-day Saints. (See Essay: "A Whirlwind into Heaven"). Only with the perspective of companion scriptures to the Bible, latter-day revelation, the teachings of modern prophets, and the understanding that comes from the Holy Ghost, are members of the Church in a position to understand its importance and relevance to personal participation in the Plan of Salvation. Christ told the three Nephite disciples: "Ye shall never taste of death". (3 Nephi 28:7). They would continue to live as mortal beings, and would eventually die, but would "never endure the pains of death," but when Christ would come in His glory, they would "be changed in the twinkling of an eye from mortality to immortality". (3 Nephi 28:8).

Perhaps because Alma had already suffered so acutely for his own sins, but had then been born again, and so looked forward with such great faith to the promise of God's Rest through obedience to the Plan of Salvation, Redemption, and Happiness, he was allowed to avoid the unpleasant side effects that sometimes accompany the transition from mortality to immortality.

"Translated beings are still mortal, and will have to pass through the experience of death, although this will be instantaneous. Translated beings have not passed through death, that is, they have not had the separation of the spirit and the body". (Joseph Fielding Smith, Jr., "Answers to Gospel Questions," 1:165, 2:46). The Doctrine and Covenants teaches that all those who were translated before the resurrection of Christ were likely resurrected themselves at that time. (See D&C 133:54-55).

The Savior said that translated beings would enjoy other gifts as well. "And again, ye shall not have pain while ye shall dwell in the flesh, neither sorrow save it be for the sins of the world". (3 Nephi 28:9). The accounts of Alma's ministry in The Book of Mormon affirm that the Gospel Plan caused his heart to swell, and it was only when he contemplated the fallen state of the unrighteous that he was sad.

A fulness of joy comes in the resurrection but missionary work can point us toward the same quality of happiness. (See D&C 93:20-2, § 33). The Savior told the Three Nephite disciples: "And for this cause ye shall have fulness of joy; and ye shall sit down in the kingdom of my Father; yea, your joy shall be full". (3 Nephi 28:10). The continuing focus of attention on their less fortunate brethren by those enlisted in the missionary army of Jesus Christ will eventually bring them into complete harmony with the attributes of their Father in Heaven, whose concern is for the eternal welfare of all of His children. "And ye shall be even as I am, and I am even as the Father, and the Father and I are one," said the Savior to the Three Nephites. (3 Nephi 28:10). There is no mistaking here the importance of missionary work in the eyes of Jesus Christ.

When Mormon wrote about the Three Nephites, he described their change "into an immortal state, that they could behold the things of God". (3 Nephi 28:15). "And now, whether they were mortal or immortal, from the day of their transfiguration, I know not". (3 Nephi 28:17). He only knew "that there must needs be a change wrought upon their bodies, or else it needs be that they must taste of death". (3 Nephi 28:37).

"Therefore, that they might not taste of death there was a change wrought upon their bodies, that they might not suffer pain nor sorrow save it were for the sins of the world". (3 Nephi 28:38). Not only would they not grow older, but also while tarrying in this special state they would not experience the challenges of adversity normally associated with mortality.

"Now this change," wrote Mormon, "was not equal to that which shall take place at the last day; but there was a change wrought upon them, insomuch that Satan could have no power over them, that he could not tempt them; and they were sanctified in the flesh, that they were holy, and that the powers of the earth could not hold them". (3 Nephi 28:39). Indeed, to say that they were merely mortal would be a gross understatement.

To this day, they remain in their sanctified state, endowed with the power of God and completely dominant over Satan. However, they will not interfere in the course of human events to change history, but will always allow agency to rule in our affairs. Their mission is to bring souls unto Christ. They will not allow Satan to thwart that mission as long as those to whom they minister do not willfully rebel and reject their invitation.

The Three Nephites are to remain on the earth as translated beings "until the judgment day of Christ; and at that day they (are) to receive a greater change," to be resurrected "into the kingdom of the Father to go no more out, but to dwell with God eternally in the heavens". (3 Nephi 28:40).

Mormon's experience with the Three Nephites was more than anecdotal. It was direct and personal, for he wrote: "I have seen them, and they have ministered unto me". (3 Nephi 28:26, see Mormon 8:11). Perhaps the Spirit witnessed to him, or perhaps it was revealed by the Three Nephites to Mormon that they would minister to the Gentiles, and among them "a great and marvelous work (would be) wrought by them, before that judgment day". (3 Nephi 28:27 & 32).

Mormon did not disclose if he ever had personal experiences with Alma. He only wrote: "Has the day of miracles ceased? Or have angels ceased to appear unto the children of men? Or has he withheld the power of the Holy Ghost from them? Or will he, so long as time shall last, or the Earth shall stand, or there shall be one man upon the face thereof to be saved? Behold I say unto you, Nay; for it is by faith that miracles are wrought, and it is by faith that angels appear and minister unto men; wherefore, if these things have ceased wo be unto the children of men, for it is because of unbelief, and all is vain". (Moroni 7:36-37).

Joseph Smith certainly enjoyed such associations. The Prophet spoke to John Wentworth of "many visits from the angels of God unfolding the majesty and glory of the events that should transpire in the Last Days". (H.C., 4:537). John Taylor said that Joseph "not only had the principles of the Gospel developed but was conversant with the parties who officiated as the leading men" in former ages. (J.D., 20:174-5). He also declared that Joseph had "communication not only with the Lord, but with the ancient apostles and prophets; such men, for instance as the apostles that lived on this continent". (J.D., 21:94, see J.D., 17:374).

Joseph's mother said: "He would describe the ancient inhabitants of this continent, their dress, mode of traveling (evidently on foot, since the wheel is mentioned only once, in 2 Nephi 15:28, and that in a quotation from Isaiah), and the animals upon which they rode (although Book of Mormon references to beasts of burden are scant). (See 1 Nephi 18:25, 2 Nephi 12:7, 15:28, Enos 1:21, Alma 18:9-10 & 12, 20:6, 3 Nephi 3:22, 4:4, 6:1, 21:4, & Ether 9:19); their cities, their buildings, with every particular; their mode of warfare; and also, their religious worship. This he would do with as much ease, as if he had spent his whole life among them". (Lucy Mack Smith, "History of Joseph Smith," p. 83).

"Joseph received instructions from the Lord by inspiration and by visitation from heavenly personages. The angel Moroni communicated with him often. Each year in September, Joseph visited the hill, and the angel enlightened him concerning his labors with the ancient record. Many ancient prophets and apostles appeared to Joseph during his formative years, imparting knowledge and furnishing him direction. Personalities who had once lived on the Western Hemisphere and had contributed to the record Joseph was to receive, appeared and acquainted him with particulars about the people mentioned in the golden book. Nephi, Alma, Mormon, and the disciples chosen by the Savior when He appeared to the ancient Americans were among those who revealed themselves to him. These heavenly personages made their appearances to him before he received the Nephite record in September 1827". (Ivan Barrett, "Joseph Smith and The Restoration," p. 68).

Mormon prophesied that the Three Nephites would visit "all nations, kindreds, tongues and people, and (would) bring out of them unto Jesus many souls, that their desire (might) be fulfilled, and also because of the convincing power of God which (would be) in them". (3 Nephi 28:28-29). Their ministry, it would seem, has known no bounds, as it has ranged over the earth through sixteen centuries.

"And they are as the angels of God, and if they shall pray unto the Father in the name of Jesus they can show themselves unto whatsoever man it seemeth them good. Therefore, great and marvelous works shall be wrought by them". (3 Nephi 28:30-31).

After the disruptions caused by the recent war, and following the translation of Alma, "Helaman and his brethren went forth to establish the Church again in all the land". (V. 22). To assist them, "they did appoint priests and teachers throughout all the land, over all the Churches". (V. 22, see 2 Nephi 5:26, Jacob 1:8, Mosiah 6:3, and especially Alma 49:30).

That these reform efforts were necessary is obvious, as we read Mormon's report that the Nephite people would not listen to the counsel of Helaman and his brethren, nor would they "walk uprightly before God". (V. 23-24). Once again, pride, that was the recurring cause of Nephite wickedness, reared its ugly head.

Alma
Chapter 46

This chapter is a carefully constructed blend of abridgement and direct quotes. It contains quite a bit of symbolism relevant to our day. The story is filled with types, shadows, and idiomatic expressions foreign to most of us in the Western world, but that were no stranger to the Eastern mind.

In this chapter, a new leader of dissenters by the name of Amalickiah arose in Zarahemla. (V. 2). We have already become acquainted with Laman, Lemuel, Sherem, Amulon, Nehor, Amlici, Zeezrom, Korihor, and Zerahemnah. All were personally ambitious and unscrupulous, aspiring to be king or religious head of the people. All were clever speakers and propagandists, skilled in the use of flattering words, and all sought to undermine or seize the highest authority of both the Church and state, being particularly opposed to popular government and drawing support from those who sought to overthrow it.

Amalickiah fit the pattern perfectly, and "was desirous to be king". (V. 4). Ambitious local officials who were also seeking personal power saw in him an avenue for their own self-aggrandizement. (See V. 5). They were professional career politicians who had no concern for the welfare of the nation, but were blinded by their own ambitions and selfish goals. They should have heeded the words of Amulek, who had declared: "And now behold, I say unto you, that the foundation of the destruction of this people is beginning to be laid by the unrighteousness of your lawyers and your judges". (Alma 10:27). Mormon's editorial comment is particularly significant. "And thus were the affairs of the people of Nephi exceedingly precarious and dangerous". (V. 7). Royalists (v. 4), lawyers (v. 4), and many apostate Church members (v. 7), formed a dangerously powerful coalition that threatened a government that had just negotiated a tentative peace settlement with an enemy of vastly superior numbers.

Mormon continued: "Thus, we see how quick the children of men do forget the Lord their God; yea, how quick to do iniquity, and to be led away by the evil one". (V. 8). Satan, that insufferable insomniac, is always at work, capitalizing on our pride and our vanity. As Mormon studied the record of Helaman, he could clearly see "the great wickedness one very wicked man can cause to take place among the children of men". (V. 9). In fact, this is the point of the entire narrative through Alma Chapter 62.

"Stirring people up to anger is the specialty of the great troublemakers in The Book of Mormon, who find it the surest road to personal prominence and power". (Hugh Nibley, "Since Cumorah," p. 340). In doing so, Amalickiah sought "to destroy the foundation of liberty" of the Nephite people. (V. 10). As Ezra Taft Benson taught: "The one great revolution in the world is the struggle for human liberty". (C.R. 10/1962).

When Moroni "heard of these dissensions, he was angry with Amalickiah". (V. 11). No one saw more clearly than he where this was leading. All that he had achieved at such great cost was quickly unraveling, and was going to be lost if he did not act quickly.

"And it came to pass that he rent his coat; and he took a piece thereof, and wrote upon it - In memory of our God, our religion, and freedom, and our peace, our wives, and our children - and he fastened it upon the end of a pole. And he fastened on his headplate, and his breastplate, and his shields, and girded on his armor about his loins; and he took the pole, which had on the end thereof his rent coat, (and he called it the title of liberty) and he bowed himself to the earth, and he prayed mightily unto his God for the blessings of liberty to rest upon his brethren, so long as there should a band of Christians remain to possess the land". (V. 12-13).

This resembles the Battle Scroll of The Children of Light, in the Qumran Community. (See "Approach to The Book of Mormon," p. 178-189, & "Since Cumorah," p. 273-275). Moroni's action represented true patriotism, which is the application of Christian principles on behalf of the national family. Patriots, or true Christians, love right above consensus, but often fight lonely battles. "For thus, were all the true believers of Christ, who belonged to the Church of God, called by those who did not belong to the Church". (V. 14). "Remember that this is a translation. What the old Nephite word for 'Christian' was, we cannot even guess". (Hugh Nibley, "Approach to The Book of Mormon," p. 147-148). In fact, the term "Christian" occurs just four times in The Book of Mormon, three times in this chapter (verses 13, 15, 16), and in Alma 48:10.

Moroni's next action was to bless the land as "a chosen land, and the land of liberty". (V. 17). It was Zion. This is similar to the practice described in the Battle Scroll that was to formally bless the hosts of Israel and to curse the land of their enemies before the battle. (See "Since Cumorah," P. 275). "And he said, Surely God shall not suffer that we, who are despised because we take upon us the name of Christ, shall be trodden down and destroyed". (V. 18). Again, the Battle Scroll from Qumran described the Children of Light as the poor and outcast of the earth, despised and threatened with extinction by the Gentiles. (Hugh Nibley, "Since Cumorah," p. 274).

The patriotic fervor with which Moroni displayed the title of liberty caused the people to come "running together with their armor girded about their loins, rending their garments in token, or as a covenant that they would not forsake the Lord their God". (V. 21). This was their first covenant.

Then "they cast their garments at the feet of Moroni, saying: We covenant with our God, that we shall be destroyed if we shall fall into transgression; yea, he may cast us at the feet of our enemies, even as we have cast our garments at thy feet to be trodden under foot, if we shall fall into transgression". (V. 22). This was their second promise, in a gesture of covenant and submission. This practice agrees with the Old-World ritual of trampling one's garments in token of having cast away an old way of life and as a symbol of trampling one's old sins under foot. (Hugh Nibley, "Since Cumorah," p. 276).

The explanation of the symbolism of the rent garment given by Moroni in the following verses has particular reference to his descendants among Book of Mormon peoples. It is a part of the story of Joseph found on the Plates of Brass, but not in the Book of Genesis. "Moroni said unto them: Behold, we are a remnant of the seed of Jacob (or Israel), yea, we are a remnant of the seed of Joseph, whose coat was rent by his brethren into many pieces; yea, and now behold, let us remember to keep the commandments of God, or our garments shall be rent by our brethren, and we be cast into prison, or be sold, or be slain. Yea, let us preserve our liberty as a remnant of Joseph; yea, let us remember the words of Jacob (or Israel), before his death, for behold, he saw that a part of the remnant of the coat of Joseph was preserved and had not decayed. And he said - Even as this remnant of garment of my son hath been preserved, so shall a remnant of the seed of my son be preserved by the hand of God, and be taken unto himself, while the remainder of the seed of Joseph shall perish, even as the remnant of his garment ... And now who knoweth but what the remnant of the seed of Joseph, which shall perish as his garment, are those who have descended from us? Yea, and even it shall be ourselves if we do not stand fast in the faith of Christ". (V. 23-27).

The symbol of the title of liberty had the desired effect, and the Nephites rallied behind it. (V. 28-29). As a matter of fact, even some of those who had initially supported Amalickiah began to doubt him. (V. 29).

Expediency prevailed for Amalickiah, discretion being the better part of valor, and he fled the Land of Zarahemla with the intention of joining the Lamanites in the Land of Nephi. (V. 29). Moroni knew that Amalickiah would stir them up to anger against the (Nephites). "Therefore, he led his army into the wilderness to prevent the escape of the Amalickiahites". Although their leader and a small number of his men eluded capture, the rest were "taken back into the land of Zarahemla". (V. 31-33).

Moroni had been given special military powers "by the chief judges and the voice of the people". (V. 34). "And it came to pass that whomsoever of the (apostate Nephite) Amalickiahites that would not enter into a covenant (or an oath) to support the cause of freedom, that they might maintain a free government, he caused to be put to death". (V. 35). Understandably, "there were but few who denied the covenant of freedom". (V. 35, see "B.Y.U. Studies," 20:2). Here we encounter another rare example of dry humor in The Book of Mormon. (V. 21, see Alma 18:9, 19:5, 30:32, 30:58, 33:21, & 55:32).).

"And it came to pass also, that he caused the title of liberty to be hoisted upon every tower which was in the land". (V. 36). Truly, there is but one Gospel Standard. In contrast, the world's standards have morphed into unrecognizable forms amidst the shifting sands of expediency and situational ethics. No longer is our morality founded upon unchanging principles of righteous living, but we instead trumpet the rationalization that the end justifies the means. We see forces at work in our own country that would validate the suspension of individual constitutional guarantees in the name of collective freedom and state security. But, as Ezra Taft Benson declared: "Constitutional principles are akin to the revelations of God. To turn from true and correct principles is to risk loss of personal freedom and lose of our eternal life".

We should be proud of our honesty with ourselves and with others, true to proven principles, faithful to our covenants, and diligent in doing good to all, in whatever circumstances we might find ourselves. The Golden Rule should be committed not just to memory, but also to life itself, for we believe in every principle that uplifts, motivates, and inspires us to be better. Our hope for the future is bright, as the Light of the world beckons us to follow His Shining Example, and we are comforted in our trials as we endure adversity. Truly, if there is anything at all that is virtuous, lovely, or of good report or praiseworthy, we seek after these things, because light cleaves unto light, and intelligence to intelligence.

Because of Moroni's appeal to patriotism, and because "Helaman and the high priests did also maintain order in the Church," there was peace and rejoicing among the members for four years. (V. 38). Those who died firm in the faith "went out of the world rejoicing". (V. 39). Others died "with fevers, which at some seasons of the year were very frequent in the land" because of "the nature of the climate". (V. 40). This is the only reference in The Book of Mormon where disease is related to the climate, and is an indication that the Land of Zarahemla might have been situated in a tropical or subtropical zone. This is also the only reference to "climate" itself and to "fever" (with the exception of Zeezrom's fever, that had been "caused by the great tribulations of his mind on account of his wickedness". (Alma 15:3, see Commentary Reference to Alma 22:27).

From time to time, Mormon came tantalizingly close to revealing more detailed descriptions of the climate, for example, when he related the story of Teancum and his servant, who had crept "into the camp of Amalickiah; and behold, sleep had overpowered them because of their much fatigue, which was caused by the labors and heat of the day". (Alma 51:33). We also know that travel in the wilderness, (or jungle?), must have been difficult, for Mormon reported of the Sons of Mosiah that "they did suffer much, both in body and in mind, such as hunger, thirst, and fatigue". (Alma 17:5).

Alma
Chapter 47

The examples of Moroni and Amalickiah provide excellent contrasts between the Lord's and the devil's leaders. In this chapter, we shall learn how Amalickiah, who, having eluded Moroni's army in the wilderness between Zarahemla and the Land of Nephi, was finally able to rise to power by fraud and deceit". (Alma 48:7). With a small band of followers, he had climbed toward the Land of Nephi, as he pushed southward through the wilderness, finally reaching the sanctuary of that Lamanite stronghold. (V. 1). There, he was warmly received by the Lamanite king, who "sent a proclamation throughout all his land, among all his people, that they should gather themselves together again to go to battle against the Nephites". This is what Moroni had feared would happen. (V. 2, see Alma 46:30). However, the Lamanites had just experienced the horrors of war, and so the order was coolly received by many of them. (V. 2).

In fact, a number of the Lamanites who had embraced pacifism fled to "the place which was called Onidah". (V. 5). Amalickiah had been given command of that part of the Lamanite army that was still loyal to the king, and he took that army to Onidah. (V. 3, & 9). Always plotting, his objective this time was to "gain favor with the armies of the Lamanites, that he might place himself at their head and dethrone the king and take possession of the kingdom". (V. 8).

Amalickiah's reputation as an untrustworthy Nephite turncoat must have preceded him, because the leader of the Lamanites at Onidah, an individual by the name of Lehonti, would not meet with him, despite repeated invitations. Finally, the two men got together and formed a conspiracy whereby the two opposing Lamanite armies might unite under Lehonti's command. (V. 13-16). Lehonti should have given heed to his intuition, because as soon as the opportunity presented itself, the treacherous Nephite apostate murdered him. (V. 17-18). Amalickiah was appointed commander of the united armies, and he wasted no time in marching to the City of Nephi to confront the king of the Lamanites and quickly carry out the next phase of his conspiracy. (V. 19-20).

The king misunderstood the intentions of the army that appeared at his city gates, thinking that Amalickiah had been successful in compelling the pacifistic Lamanites to take up arms against the Nephites. (V. 21, see V. 3). This mistake cost him his life, because with his defenses down, the servants of Amalickiah were able to enter the city without resistance and summarily execute him without hesitation or remorse. (V. 22-24). The king's servants, who were the only ones who had witnessed the assassination, fled for their lives into the wilderness, "came over into the land of Zarahemla and joined the people of Ammon". (V. 29). Meanwhile, back in the City of Nephi, not only its inhabitants but also the widow of the king embraced Amalickiah; all were totally unaware of his deception and the conspiracy being carried out in their midst. (V. 30-35).

"Thus, by his fraud, and by the assistance of his cunning servants, he obtained the kingdom; yea, he was acknowledged king throughout all the land, among all the people of the Lamanites, who were composed of the Lamanites and the Lemuelites and the Ishmaelites, and all the dissenters of the Nephites, from the reign of Nephi down to the present time". (V. 35, see Alma 35:10 & 43:13, & Helaman 3:16). Mormon ended his commentary on this episode by recording: "It is strange to relate, not long after their dissensions, they became more hardened and impenitent, and more wild, wicked and ferocious than the Lamanites". (V. 36, see Commentary Reference to Alma 24:30). These apostates were past repentance, having sunk so low that they had neither the inclination nor the capacity to repent. The Spirit had ceased striving with them, and they were left alone to deal with the raw and ugly natural inclination to be carnal, the revolting proclivity to be sensual, and the repulsive tendency to be devilish. They knew neither the Lord nor His ways, nor would they follow His counsel. Latter-day examples of these Nephite dissenters provide dramatic negative counterpoint to all who have embraced the Gospel but continue to struggle with temptation.

*Alma
Chapter 48*

Mormon's desire in this chapter was to teach us that one righteous man can truly make a difference regarding the outcome of the battle that rages in our hearts. (See V. 17). Captain Moroni had sought the guidance of the Lord through the living prophet (Alma 43:23-26), was concerned for those who served under him (Alma 43:18-21), used strategy (Alma 43:27-35), was magnanimous in forgiveness, but firm in the right. (Alma 44:20). He was patriotic, prayerful, and provided a standard for the righteous to follow (Alma 46:11-20), and had set an example of nobility for all to emulate. (See Alma 48:11-18).

At the other end of the spectrum, Amalickiah sought the favor of the devil in his blind quest for power and domination. (V. 2-3). In a dance of death, he courted Satan, "who has power over his own dominion". (D&C 1:35). "His is the power of delusion, confusion, strife, bitterness, and class distinction, and not one of peace and righteousness". (Joseph Fielding Smith, Jr. "Doctrines of Salvation," 3:315). In their bewilderment, the uncertainty of the apostate Nephites led to acrimony. Because they were prone to contention and conflict, they easily became overtly hostile, subject to outbursts of anger, and their animosity sewed the seeds of discord. Truly, Amalickiah, the minister of Satan, "had accomplished his design, for he had hardened the hearts of the Lamanites and blinded their minds, and stirred them up to anger". (V. 3).

In contrast, Moroni had been readying the Nephites for war by preparing the minds of the people to be faithful unto the Lord their God". (V. 7). He "was a strong and a mighty man; he was a man of perfect understanding, a man whose heart did swell with thanksgiving to his God, a man who did labor exceedingly for the welfare of his people, a man who was firm in the faith of Christ". (V. 11-13). As we have seen, he was always quick to deal mercifully with a repentant enemy. Even the Lamanites would finally be convinced that his policies were superior to their campaign of hatred and warfare. (See Alma 62:15-17 & 27-29).

Moroni had a higher purpose, for he "had sworn with an oath to defend his people, his rights, and his country, and his religion, even to the loss of his blood". (V. 13). "Our stand for freedom is a most basic part of our religion. It helped us get to this Earth, and our reaction to freedom in this life will have eternal consequence. We have many duties, but we have no excuse that can compensate for our loss of liberty". (Ezra Taft Benson, C.R. 10/1966).

Combatants on both sides fought during the War in Heaven with intensity and single-minded purpose. The battles were not waged with guns and bombs, but rather with two contrasting and diametrically opposed, utterly irreconcilable ideologies. One would give the spirit children of our Heavenly Father the opportunity to exercise moral agency, or free choice within the matrix of an understanding of the Plan of Salvation, during a mortal probation. The other would compel, or require, obedience. One ideology personified the Author of the Plan, Who was our Father in Heaven. The other ideology was a fraud, a counterfeit, bogus, and inoperable fake, conjured up by the "liar from the beginning," he who has been labeled the very "father of lies". (See 2 Nephi 2:18, & Moses 4:4). Obedience to one of the ideologies promised life and light, the stark reality and cold calculation of the other could delver only death and darkness. The conflict in the pre-mortal existence was a life-or-death struggle, and unfortunately there were eternal casualties.

That we fought on the side of the Firstborn is attested by our presence here in mortality. We have kept our first estate, have been "added upon," and now on the Earth we will be tested further, to see if we will do all things whatsoever the Lord God will command us. And we who keep our second estate shall have glory added upon our heads forever and ever. (See Abraham 3:25-26)

Central, then, to Satan's battle Plan in the pre-mortal existence was the clever utilization of ideology intended to conflict with the harmony of the Plan of Salvation proposed by Heavenly Father. His objective has always been to disrupt lines of clear communication, distort doctrine, and wrest scriptures into twisted caricatures of inspired instructions that should be easily understood and pleasantly performed. After 4,000 years of temporal existence, the war still raged on the Earth among the Nephites and Lamanites, as Satan turned once again to his favored the tactic of false ideology.

In our own day, as we witness the spiritual darkness in which much of the world finds itself, we begrudgingly acknowledge the success of his program. We read in the newspapers an account by the Central Intelligence Agency, assessing as good the likelihood that a major drug lord will be elected to the leadership of at least one Latin American country during the next ten years. It is revealed that the Colombian Drug Cartel has offered to pay off that country's national debt, a sum of several billions of dollars, if it is given a guarantee that it can operate unrestrained and without government interference. The U.S. Department of Agriculture reports that in several states, marijuana is the largest cash crop. LGBTQ activists in our cities march in support of their deviant lifestyle.

Ward leaders ponder the significance of Activity Reports that show Sacrament meeting attendance to be just 55% of our membership. We learn that only 60% of those endowed in the temple currently hold recommends, and that only 75% of those who hold them actually attend the temple regularly.

Satan's Plan has always been to thwart our progression. He will ever "rage in the hearts of the children of men, and stir them up to anger against that which is good. And others will he pacify, and lull them away into carnal security, and thus, the devil cheateth their souls, and leadeth them away carefully down to hell. And behold, others he flattereth away, and telleth them there is no hell, and thus, he whispereth in their ears until he grasps them with his awful chains from whence there is no deliverance". (2 Nephi 28:20-22). He is the master of disguise whereby he might lead them "by the neck with a flaxen cord, until he bindeth them with his strong cords forever". (2 Nephi 26:22)

The Book of Mormon, that has been called "a blueprint for survival in the Last Days," chronicles the Nephites' responses over a thousand years to both internal and external threats to their temporal and spiritual security, that are representative of those we face today. The great prophet Mormon wrote: "Behold, I speak unto you as if ye were present, and yet ye are not. But behold, Jesus Christ hath shown you unto me, and I know your doing". (See Mormon 8:35). Inasmuch as Mormon abridged into our record just one percent of the information available to him, it follows that what we do have in the Holy Scripture known as The Book of Mormon must have been considered by him to be invaluable. (See 3 Nephi 5:8).

What did a Nephite prophet say about the internal threats to the security of his nation? When Alma The Younger initiated his mission to the apostate Zoramites, Mormon observed: "And now, as the preaching of the word had a great tendency to lead the people to do that which was just - yea, it had had more powerful effect upon the minds of the people than the sword, or anything else, which had happened unto them - therefore Alma thought it was expedient that they should try the virtue of the word of God". (Alma 31:5).

Marion G. Romney declared in General Conference: "Proposed remedies to the world's present predicament will prove futile. There are no armaments, no governmental schemes, no international organizations, and no mechanisms for the control of weapons which can preserve an unrighteous people". (C.R., 4/1953). This observation is even more relevant now than when it was made many years ago.

Ancient and modern prophets have counseled us to incorporate into our lives the formidable and fearsome weapons of the Doctrine of Christ contained in The Book of Mormon. Ezra Taft Benson has declared: "We commend that vast number of faithful Saints who individually and as families are changing their lives and cleaning the inner vessel, through the daily reading of The Book of Mormon". (C.R., 10/1988).

What, then, did a Nephite prophet say about internal threats to the security of his nation?. Around

25 years before the birth of the Savior, in the Land of Zarahemla, a group called "Gadianton's robbers and murderers" wreaked havoc on the righteous Lamanites who had been converted to the Gospel. (See Helaman 6:18). Satan had stirred up the hearts of the Nephites to such a degree that a majority of them had apostatized and united with Gadianton, entering into secret oaths and covenants. These were circumstances that clearly posed a moral threat and mortal danger to the integrity of the nation. Mormon's editorial comments in the record are particularly insightful: "And thus, we see that the Nephites did begin to dwindle in unbelief, and grow in wickedness and abominations, while the Lamanites began to grow exceedingly in the knowledge of their God; yea, they did begin to keep his statutes and commandments, and to walk in truth and uprightness before him. And thus, we see that the Spirit of the Lord began to withdraw from the Nephites, because of the wickedness and the hardness of their hearts. And thus, we see that the Lord began to pour out his Spirit upon the Lamanites, because of their easiness and willingness to believe in his words". (Helaman 6:34-36). Lamanites would yet become nursing mothers to their Nephite brethren.

Here we have a situation where it was the Nephites who turned from the scriptures and the living oracles, and thereby dwindled in unbelief "in the space of not many years" and where it was the Lamanites who were filled with the Spirit because they were humble, teachable, and willing to believe and incorporate the doctrine of Christ into their lives. (See Helaman 6:32).

But what of the threat to their security posed by the Gadianton Band? These Lamanites, these humble followers of Christ, put off the natural man, who is an enemy of God, and took the nobler path. (See Mosiah 3:19). "And it came to pass that the Lamanites did hunt the band of robbers of Gadianton; and they did preach the word of God among the more wicked part of them, insomuch that this band of robbers was utterly destroyed from among the Lamanites". (Helaman 6:37). The Lamanites went out and defeated the Gadianton Band with the most powerful weapon at their disposal. In our day, Ezra Taft Benson has declared: "We have The Book of Mormon, we have the members, we have the missionaries, we have the resources, and the world has the need. The time is now". (C.R. 10/1988). Edwin Markham may have been thinking of the "Gadianton Robbers" in our midst when he penned the following lines that illustrate with simplicity the theme of the missionaries' message to the Lamanites: "He drew a circle that shut me out, Heretic, rebel, a thing to flout. But Love and I had the wit to win. We drew a circle that took him in". "Press forward with a steadfastness in Christ," Nephi had counseled, "having a perfect brightness of hope, and a love of God and of all men," including Gadianton Robbers. "Wherefore, if ye shall press forward, feasting upon the word of Christ, and endure to the end, behold, thus saith the Father: Ye shall have eternal life". (2 Nephi 31:20)

Surely one of Mormon's purposes for including the account of Moroni and of the righteous Lamanites in his abridged record was his hope that we might learn to use Nephite teaching techniques to overcome the evil influences of our day that threaten our physical and spiritual security. He hoped we might use the power of the Word to convert a world that is rushing blindly toward the precipice of spiritual oblivion and the pit of despair.

It was Moroni's hope that God Himself would provide the Nephites with an Early Warning System, if only the people would remain faithful. The keystone of their national defense was unity at home. (V. 14-15). Note how Helaman and his brethren also contributed to Nephite preparedness by preaching the Gospel: They "were no less serviceable unto the people than was Moroni," observed Mormon, "for they did preach the word of God". (V. 20).

Mormon was obviously impressed with his ancestor Moroni as he studied the records, for he inserted this editorial comment in his abridgement: "Yea, verily, verily I say unto you, if all men had been, and were, and ever would be, like unto Moroni, behold, the very powers of hell would have been shaken forever; yea, the devil would never have power over the hearts of the children of men". (V. 17, see Alma 50:23). Mormon gave his own son the name Moroni, perhaps in the hope that in his own trials he would be able to stand as firmly as had his namesake.

Moroni only reluctantly led his people to battle against the Lamanites. (V. 21). The Nephites "were sorry to take up arms against the Lamanites, because they did not delight in the shedding of blood; yea, and this was not all - they were sorry to be the means of sending so many of their brethren out of this world into an eternal world, unprepared to meet their God". (V. 23). Certainty these Nephites lost neither their eternal perspective nor their concern for the welfare of the Lamanites, "who were once their brethren". (V. 24)

"Helaman and his brethren
were no less serviceable unto the people
than was Moroni; for they did preach the
word of God, and they did baptize unto
repentance all men whosoever would
hearken unto their words."
(Alma 48:19).

Alma
Chapter 49

The long-awaited confrontation finally arrived, as the army of the Lamanites came down out of the Land of Nephi. (V. 10). They determined to attack the rebuilt City of Ammonihah, inasmuch as they had so easily destroyed it six years earlier. (V. 1-3, see Alma Chapter 16).

The Lamanites had learned a thing or two since their last battle with the Nephites, and they were prepared "with shields, and with breastplates; and with garments of skins to cover their nakedness". (V. 6, see Alma 43:21). This is a good indication that the arms race was alive and well even in ancient times. The Nephites had also "prepared for (the Lamanites) in a manner which never had been known among the children of Lehi". (V. 7). Therefore, the Lamanites were astonished, and their straightforward offensive strategy was thwarted. The military's ingrained habit is to prepare for the next war in terms of the last one. This was not good enough for the Lamanites, in light of Moroni's inspired preparation.

King Amalickiah did not lead this Lamanite army, which was a good thing for them, for if he had, "he would have caused the Lamanites to have attacked the Nephites at the City of Ammonihah; for behold, he did not care for the blood of his people". (V. 10). Even Moroni cared more for them than did their own leader. (See Alma 48:23. see Alma 52:32, & 37).

By a complete organizational shakeup at home, Moroni had denied the Lamanites the use of certain facilities they had thought would easily fall into their hands, possibly through Nephite incompetence or corruption. Therefore, the "chief captains durst not attack the Nephites at the City of Ammonihah". (V. 11). Instead, they retreated into the wilderness, and turned their attention to the Land of Noah. (V. 12). This was just what Moroni wanted them to do, "for he had supposed that they would be frightened at the city (of) Ammonihah; and as the City of Noah had hitherto been the weakest part of the land, therefore, they would march thither to battle". (V. 15). The Lamanites knew that the Land of Noah had been poorly defended in the past and had a reputation as the weakest region in the Land of Zarahemla. But they were unaware of significant defensive improvements that had recently taken place there. (V. 12-15).

The supreme test of effective military leadership is to have the enemy play your game, making just the moves you want him to make. The Lamanite "chief captains had sworn an oath that they would destroy the people of (the City of Noah)". (V. 13). But they "could not get into their forts of security by any other way save by the entrance, because of the highness of the bank which had been thrown up, and the depth of the ditch which had been dug round about". (V. 18). Furthermore, "that same Lehi who fought (against) the Lamanites in the valley on the east of the river Sidon" was in command of the Nephite forces. (V. 16, see Alma 43:35). The Lamanites had good cause to fear his formidable military leadership skills. (See Alma 52:31).

Because of their oath and their fanatical desire to destroy the Nephites, the Lamanites blindly attacked the Nephite stronghold with disastrous results. "Instead of filling up their ditches by pulling down the banks of earth, they were filled up in a measure with their dead and wounded bodies". (V. 22, see V. 19-21, & Commentary Reference to Alma 53:33). There is interesting archaeological evidence that supports Mormon's description of these defensive fortifications at Nephi. At Becan, in the Yucatan, (A.D. 150-450), the center of the site is surrounded by a ditch almost two kilometers long, and averaging 16 meters across. The makers had piled up the earth to form a ridge on the inner side of the ditch, making it almost impossible to carry weapons uphill from outside the fortification.

Because Moroni's soldiers had prepared so effectively, at the battle at the City of Noah "more than a thousand of the Lamanites were slain; while, on the other hand, there was not a single soul of the Nephites which were slain". (V. 23). The Lamanite dead included every one of the Zoramite chief captains who had sworn an oath to destroy the Nephites. (See Alma 48:5, & V. 13).

When the Lamanite army straggled back to the Land of Nephi and recounted to Amalickiah what had happened, he, "who was a Nephite by birth was exceedingly wroth, and he did curse God, and also Moroni; swearing with an oath that he would drink his blood". (V. 25, & 27). At every step, Moroni had barred the way for Amalickiah to succeed. It is no wonder that the elimination of this troublesome Nephite became an obsession for Amalickiah.

"On the other hand, the people of Nephi did thank the Lord their God, because of his matchless power in delivering them from the hands of their enemies". (V. 28). "Helaman, and Shiblon, and Corianton, and Ammon and his brethren" continued to minister to the people by the authority of the Melchizedek Priesthood, Satan was held in check, and "there was continual peace" among the people of Nephi. (V. 30, see Alma 48:10).

Alma
Chapter 50

In spite of the peace enjoyed by the Nephites in the Land of Zarahemla, "Moroni did not stop making preparations for war". (V. 1). "God could doubtless avert war, prevent crime, destroy poverty, chase away darkness, overcome error, and make all things bright, beautiful, and joyful," wrote Spencer W. Kimball. "But this would involve the destruction of a vital and fundamental attribute in man - the right of agency. It is for the benefit of His sons and daughters that they become acquainted with evil, as well as with good, with darkness as well as with light, with error as well as truth, and with the results of the infraction of eternal laws" as well as with the blessings that follow obedience. ("Messages of The First Presidency," 4:325). Mortality is our only opportunity to experience these evils and to learn obedience, even as we endure adversity.

Sometimes the challenge comes from an external source, and sometimes we must conquer ourselves. A member of a successful Mount Everest expedition was asked how those who would make the summit attempt were chosen from among the members of the climbing party. He replied that at 25,000 feet there were three factors bearing down on every climber. First, was the unrelenting cold. It penetrated to the very core to such an extent that the climber had to fight an almost overwhelming urge to stop climbing. Second was the sickness that accompanies strong exertion at high altitude. When a climber felt sick, he wanted to stop climbing. Third was fatigue, when distance is not measured in miles, or yards, or feet, but in the mental and physical discipline required to put one foot in front of the other. Every muscle screamed out the message to stop climbing. In reality, then, no one else chose who would be on the team to reach the top; rather, each individual climber chose for himself.

In Zarahemla, the Nephites were driven by a sense of urgency to complete their line of fortification facing the Land of Nephi to the southward. (V. 2-16). They fulfilled the words of the Lord, who had said to Lehi: "Blessed art thou and thy children; and they shall be blessed, inasmuch as they shall keep my commandments they shall prosper in the land". (V. 20, see 2 Nephi 1:20, Mosiah 1:7, Alma 9:13, Alma 37:13, & 3 Nephi 5:22).

Ezra Taft Benson echoed these words, when he made the bold statement that "no nation has ever perished that has kept the commandments of God". (C.R. 10/1979). Mormon said of these Nephites: "Those who were faithful in keeping the commandments of the Lord were delivered at all times". (V. 21). From his perspective at the tail end of the thousand-year history of the Nephite people, he was moved to observe of these times: "There never was a happier time among the people of Nephi, since the days of Nephi, than in the days of Moroni". (V. 23).

On the other hand, he wrote of the Nephites, in general: "It has been their quarrelings and their contentions, yea, their murderings, and their plundering, their idolatry, their whoredoms, and their abominations, which were among themselves, which brought upon them their wars and their destructions". (V. 21). Exactly the same conditions prevail today in Western societies, and yet they ignorantly press on with their uninspired social, economic, political, and military agendas, thinking all the time that their gods of wood and stone will protect them.

In Zarahemla, after only three years of peace and prosperity, there began to be a warm contention between the Nephites in "the land of Morianton and the land of Lehi". (V. 25-26). The situation deteriorated quickly until bloodshed among the Nephites seemed inevitable. As the fabric of their society disintegrated, escalating civil disturbances threatened to overthrow of their liberty and exposed them to the scourge of Lamanite aggression, who hated everything about Nephite culture. (V. 32).

Only Moroni's quick action averted disaster, but more importantly, his humane policy toward the combatants, forgoing all reprisals and reparations, insured a happy ending to the episode, with the original antagonists once again joined in friendship. The dissenters made a covenant "to keep the peace," and so "they were restored to the land of Morianton, and a union took place between them and the people of Lehi; and they were also restored to their lands". (V. 36).

With this threat to Nephite temporal and spiritual security so fresh in the minds of the people, "Nephihah, the second chief judge, died, (Alma was the first) having filled the judgment seat with perfect uprightness before God". (V. 37). It was critical that the Nephites find another political leader who would also covenant "to judge righteously, and to keep the peace and the freedom of the people, and to grant unto them their sacred privileges to worship the Lord their God, yea, to support and maintain the cause of God all his days, and to bring the wicked to justice according to their crime". (V. 39).

The examples of righteous judges in Zarahemla dramatically illustrate the power of even a handful of inspired government leaders to positively influence an entire culture and hold evil in check. We read that Pahoran, the son of Nephihah, "was appointed chief judge and governor over the people, with an oath and sacred ordinance". (V. 39). He began his reign in 67 B.C., twenty-four years after the death of King Mosiah, and for fifteen years guided the Nephites through perilous times. The history of their nation, with Pahoran at the helm, is interesting to latter-day readers for its relevance to our times.

Characteristically, when a financial crisis or terrorism threat occurs, there is a strident call for strong leadership and instant response. Think of the knee-jerk reaction in the immediate aftermath of 9/11: The Patriot Act, and the subsequent erosion of civil liberties and constitutional guarantees. Recall the banking and market "reforms," and the bailouts and stimulus packages that were rushed through Congress in the aftermath of the worldwide economic meltdown in 2009. N-one need remind us of the erosion of constitutional liberties during and after the Covid-19 epidemic, that continues unabated to this day. The more grave the circumstances, the more the people look for security from leaders who typically respond with draconian measures in an uncomfortably dictatorial fashion, usurping powers not specifically vested in them by the law of the land. Nevertheless, the people have historically applauded their actions even as they have conceded the loss of their own civil liberties.

The typical unfolding of events, then, is from democracy to fascism that destroys the earlier republican institutions. Citizens endure a political movement or regime that exalts nation above the individual, and that stands for a centralized autocratic government headed by a dictatorial leader, severe economic and social regimentation, and forcible suppression of opposition.

Among the populace, inequality is first rationalized, then validated, and finally accepted as a given. Liberty suffers as society becomes less egalitarian, even as Conventional Wisdom justifies attitude adjustments. What is often misunderstood about fascism is that it is not a blatant dictatorship, nor is it a covert action. It is done with the tacit approval of Congressional oversight. In fact, the people demand it! They embrace Caesar, and he is welcomed for dinner and a fireside chat. Caesarism is the result of a natural progression by a free people who no longer desire to carry the burdens of responsibility or personal accountability, and who enthusiastically turn their rights and privileges over to one branch of government, or even to one individual within that branch, with a big sigh of relief. The road to Caesarism is practical and pragmatic and the abuse of checks and balances is barely noticed and soon forgotten. But concentrated power and centralized authority are escapes from freedom, nevertheless. This was the situation in Zarahemla in 67 B.C., which is a chilling reminder that history does tend to repeat itself. The question always boils down to this: "Can our collective consciousness be so traumatized that we eagerly sacrifice our individual liberties in exchange for an authoritarian central government that guarantees security?"

Today we have charismatic leaders whose specialty is to capitalize on our distress and bang the drums of war in order to whip us into a nationalistic fervor. We allow their rhetoric to reach a fever pitch, causing our blood to boil with prejudice, suspicion, doubt, misgivings, mistrust, and even hatred of those whom we have not taken the time to understand. We face the spectre of voluntarily surrendering our rights and responsibilities to leaders who realize they do not need to work very hard to usurp our privileges, concentrate their power, and centralize and consolidate their authority. Infused with fear, and in a frenzy when rational approaches to problem-solving are castigated by the media as out-moded, out-dated, and out of touch, we give up our rights not to the highest bidder, but to the loudest and most persistent jingoist.

"And thus we see how merciful and just are all the dealings of the Lord, to the fulfilling of all his words unto the children of men; yea, we can behold that his words are verified." (Alma 50:19).

Alma
Chapter 51

In a knee-jerk reaction to the Lamanite threat, the spectre of a dictatorial government reared its ugly head in the Land of Zarahemla. The members of a faction called the king-men "were desirous that the law should be altered in a manner to overthrow the free government and to establish a king over the land". (V. 5). Those who opposed this action were called freemen. (V. 6). Righteous kings who bear the priesthood are the ideal (See Mosiah 29:13), but when the people desire worldly kings, "like all the nations" (1 Samuel 8:5), they invite tyranny in their midst. (See Commentary Reference to Alma 50:39).

Freedom is not compatible with the security afforded by a prison cell, where armed guards are at the ready to quell every disturbance to the status quo, or within the sanctuary of an intensive care unit, where life-support devices are always available to countermand a DNR order. Life entails the assumption of risk. Our tendency to look to the government for job security, financial security, and social security speaks for itself. It is the evidence of our desire to avoid risk. Caesar provides our security and assumes the risk, but at a hefty price. Ultimately, we will be asked to pay in spades, with a pound of flesh. Because the freemen understood this, they responded quickly and decisively.

They would have agreed with the American Declaration of Independence, that unequivocally formalized the principle: "Governments are instituted among men, deriving their just powers from the consent of the governed". Among the Nephites, it came to pass that "this matter of their contention was settled" in a similar fashion, "by the voice of the people in favor of" the chief judge Pahoran, and "the freemen". (V. 7). The Lord has similarly instructed the Latter-day Saints: The "law of the land which is constitutional, supporting that principle of freedom in maintaining rights and privileges, belongs to all mankind, and is justifiable before me. Therefore, I, the Lord, justify you, and your brethren of my Church, in befriending that law which is the constitutional law of the land; and as pertaining to law of man, whatsoever is more or less than this, cometh of evil". (D&C 98:5-7).

Alistair Cooke observed: "We can make one fairly certain generalization about the cause of revolutions. When the people in power can neither keep the consent of the governed, nor keep down the dissent of the governed, then there will be a blowup". ("America," p. 122). Indeed, in Zarahemla "this was a critical time for such contentions to be among the people of Nephi; for behold, Amalickiah (note the similarity of his name to "Al Qaeda") had again stirred up the hearts of the people of the Lamanites against the people of the Nephites, and he was gathering together soldiers from all parts of his land, and arming them, and preparing for war with (coldly methodical) diligence". (V. 9). He intuitively knew that time was his ally, and that if he allowed the Nephite nation more time to weaken its moral fiber, his adversaries could be more easily defeated.

Even though the desires of the king-men had been nullified by the voice of the people, they still "were supported by those who sought power and authority over the people". (51:8). The hidden agenda of the king-men was to wrest control of the government in Zarahemla, so that they could exercise unrighteous dominion over the People of Nephi. Furthermore, their foreign policy was one of appeasement, for "they would not take up arms to defend their country" against the external threat of the Lamanites. (V. 13).

When Moroni learned of these seditious acts, he immediately sent a petition to the governor, requesting authorization to institute special military powers to "compel those dissenters to defend their country, or to put them to death". (V. 15). Under the circumstances, his request "was granted according to the voice of the people". (V. 16). This was no small group of rabble-rousers. In the ensuing confrontation, four thousand of the dissenters were killed, and "those of their leaders who were not slain in battle were taken and cast into prison, for there was no time for their trials at this period". (V. 19). The emergency was so acute that they were sent to the Nephite equivalent of Guantanamo Bay to be interred. The rest "yielded to the standard of liberty … and thus, Moroni put an end to those king-men". (V. 20-21).

President Abraham Lincoln, in his first Inaugural Address (March 1861), envisioned the preservation of latter-day Zarahemla with these stirring words, relevant to the Twenty-First Century: "The mystic chords of memory, stretching from every battlefield and patriot grave to every living heart and hearthstone all over this broad land, will yet swell the chorus of the Union when again touched, as surely they will be, by the better angels of our nature". President Lincoln was urging us to look beyond the animal instincts that so often blur the vision of "the better angels of our nature."

That vision requires our domestic and foreign policies to be indistinguishable from our ecclesiastical example. A hundred and fifty years ago, Daniel Webster declared: "If we and our posterity shall be true to the Christian religion, and if we and they shall live always in the fear of God and shall respect his commandments, we may have the highest hopes for the future fortunes of our country. It will have no decline and fall, but it will go on prospering. But, if we or our posterity shall reject religious instructions and authority, violate the rules of morality, and recklessly destroy the political constitution which holds us together, no man can tell how sudden a catastrophe may overwhelm us, that shall bury all of our glory in profound obscurity". (Daniel Webster, "The Dignity and Importance of History – A Prophetic Warning" An address delivered before the New York Historical Society, 2/23/1852).

At close hand, we must recognize that the looming tragedy is not what may happen to our society, but what we may have already done to ourselves. The Savior admonished us to stand our ground. "Stand in the office which I have appointed unto you," He said. "Succor the weak, lift up the hands which hang down, and strengthen the feeble knees". (D&C 81:5). There is in the world today a flight from that level of responsibility. Ours is the age of passing the buck, the half-done job, of undeserved entitlement, and of mediocre effort. Our citizenship requires a higher standard and correspondingly greater effort. The damage may already be done, but it is not yet irreversible.

We must remain steady, even when the world heads toward chaos, teetering on the precipice of destruction. As Josiah Gilbert Holland wrote: "God, give us Men! A time like this demands strong minds, great hearts, true faith, and ready hands. Men whom the lust of office does not kill. Men whom the spoils of office cannot buy. Men who possess opinions and a will. Men who have honor; men who will not lie. Men who can stand before a demagogue and damn his treacherous flatteries without winking. Tall men, sun-crowned, who live above the fog in public duty and in private thinking. For while the rabble, with their thumb worn creeds, their large professions, and their little deeds, mingle in selfish strife, Lo! Freedom weeps, Wrong rules the land, and Justice sleeps".

Mormon recorded that the City of Nephihah did not, at this time, fall to the Lamanites, for "Amalickiah would not suffer the Lamanites to go against the City of Nephihah to battle". (V. 25). But in the next verse, this city is listed among those that the Lamanites did possess, "all of which were on the east borders by the seashore". (V. 26). Whether Mormon intended to include Nephihah on the list or it was done so in error, the city was, in fact, eventually lost to the enemy about five years later. (See Alma 59:7-11).

This small ambiguity in the record is another good illustration of the difficulty encountered by the prophets when engraving upon metal plates. Since there was no way to go back and edit the record, either the record had to be left to stand as it had been written, or clarifications had to be made in subsequent sentences and verses. (See Commentary Reference to Alma 24:19, & Essay: "Writing on Metal Plates Was a Pain").

The emergency had been real, for the Lamanites were once again on the move in Zarahemla, taking possession of many cities. (V. 22-28). Their success could, in part, be attributed to the internal contention among the Nephites, that not only threw them into turmoil, but also put them at risk because they could no longer rely upon the Lord's continuing protection.

Nephite and Lamanite confrontation then reached a climax when a Nephite general by the name of Teancum stole into the Lamanite camp and slew Amalickiah. (V. 29-37). For the time being, this alleviated the threat by the Lamanites, for it had been Amalickiah who had stirred up the Lamanites to anger against the Nephites, in the first place. (See Alma 46:31).

Alma
Chapter 52

Perhaps Teancum had been successful in penetrating the Lamanite camp because it was "New Year's Eve" and the Lamanites had been out partying. For it was "on the first morning of the first month of the twenty and sixth year of the reign of the Judges over the people of Nephi," that they awoke to find Amalickiah dead in his tent. (V. 1). This so unnerved them that "they abandoned their design in marching into the land northward, and retreated with all their army into the city of Mulek". (V. 2). Teancum used this lull in the fighting to strengthen his positions. (V. 5-7). "And Moroni also sent orders unto him that he should retain all the prisoners who fell into his hands; for as the Lamanites had taken many prisoners, that he should retain all the prisoners of the Lamanites as a ransom for those whom the Lamanites had taken". (V. 8). Inasmuch as the Nephites were outnumbered, every soldier obtained through prisoner exchange would mean more to them that it would to the Lamanites. (See Alma 54:1-2).

Moroni was also desirous that the army of Teancum scourge, or harass, the Lamanites at every turn, and be alert to seize any opportunity to "take again by stratagem or some other way those cities which had been taken out of their hands". (V. 10). He would have helped Teancum do this, but at the moment he was pinned down by the Lamanites "in the borders of the land by the west sea". (V. 11 see V. 12-13).

Thus, the Nephites were in the dangerous position of fighting an enemy of superior numbers on two different fronts. (V. 14). The Nephites tried unsuccessfully for almost a year to gain an advantage, that they might strike at the City of Mulek, and retake it. (V. 17). Finally, "it came to pass that Moroni did arrive with his army at the land of Bountiful," and his army was joined with that of Teancum. (V. 18).

Moroni and Teancum and many of the chief captains held a council of war to decide "what they should do to cause the Lamanites to come out against them to battle". (V. 19). To a Zoramite named Jacob, who was the leader of the Lamanites within the fortified City of Mulek, they issued a challenge to meet them on the field and fight it out. (V. 20). The Nephite commanders hardly expected the comfortably situated Lamanites to comply with a request so disadvantageous to themselves, but it was worth a try, and anyway, it was the conventional thing to do. It didn't work, of course, and so Moroni no longer held any hope "of meeting them upon fair ground". (V. 21). He realized that if the Lamanites could be coaxed out of Mulek to engage the Nephites on the open plain, the ensuing battle might be a fair contest of strength. "Therefore, he resolved upon a plan that he might decoy the Lamanites out of their strongholds". (V. 22).

Moroni withdrew into the wilderness, leaving Teancum and his smaller force outside the walls of Mulek. (V. 22). The Lamanites were quick to take advantage of this apparent Nephite tactical error, and came out to destroy their adversaries. (V. 23). Teancum initiated a measured retreat, and soon both armies were far enough away from Mulek to allow Moroni's concealed army to march into the relatively undefended city. (V. 24). Once within the city walls, they "slew all those who had been left to protect the city, yea, all those who would not yield up their weapons of war". (V. 25). Moroni's policy of compassion and forbearance, wherein he would spare all those who would renounce war, was still in effect.

What followed was a classical military exercise. The Lamanite army pursuing Teancum was led "near the city Bountiful, and then they were met by Lehi and a small army, which had been left to protect the city Bountiful". (V. 27). These seasoned Nephites were well-rested and prepared for battle, and took over for Teancum's army that had been in the field for some time. Because the Lamanites were tired from their push through the wilderness, rather than engaging Lehi in battle, they retreated toward what they supposed would be sanctuary within the fortified city of Mulek. (V. 28).

As they approached the city, though, they found themselves "surrounded by the Nephites, by the men of Moroni on one hand, and the men of Lehi on the other, all of whom were fresh and full of strength; but the Lamanites were wearied because of their long march". (V. 31). "And Moroni commanded his men that they should fall upon them until they had given up their weapons of war". (V. 32).

Because Jacob was a Zoramite, he had "an unconquerable spirit," and so he "led the Lamanites forth to battle with exceeding fury against Moroni". (V. 33). As Mormon had observed, "not long after their dissensions (the Zoramites) became more hardened and impenitent, and more wild, wicked and ferocious than the Lamanites". (Alma 47:36). Jacob's course was suicidal, but he was blinded to its consequences, and so, as he marched into the breech, he dragged many of his companions with him down to hell.

This class of Zoramite dissenters, of whom Jacob was representative, were like those who suffer from compulsions and have arrived at that condition because of repeated and successive reactions, until a point is reached where, as William James explained, "unlimited freedom leads to unlimited tyranny". Jacob had incorrectly believed that he could safely disregard the principles of conduct that are consistent with civilized behavior.

On the contrary, the choices he had made ultimately required his forfeiture of agency. His obsession to destroy the Nephites at whatever cost sealed his fate. He believed his private immorality would not damage those about him. This could not be so, "any more than there can be a private smallpox, or a cloistered cholera. The unloved, undisciplined soul set forth in the stream of humanity can be more dangerous than raw sewage". (Neal Maxwell).

"And it came to pass that they fought on both hands with exceeding fury; and there were many slain on both sides; yea, and Moroni was wounded, and Jacob was killed". (V. 35). Although Moroni was a great warrior, he was always magnanimous in victory, and quick to lower his weapons. In the Lamanite army's rout that followed, Moroni "said unto them: If ye will bring forth your weapons of war and deliver them up, behold we will forbear shedding your blood". (V. 37). "And it came to pass that when the Lamanites had heard these words, their chief captains, all those who were not slain, came forth and threw down their weapons of war at the feet of Moroni, and also commanded their men that they should do the same". (V. 38). Those who would not do so were taken prisoner". (V. 39).

"And thus were the Nephites in those dangerous circumstances in the ending of the twenty and sixth year of the reign of the judges over the people of Nephi." (Alma 52:14).

Alma
Chapter 53

The logistics of handling increasing numbers of prisoners of war was becoming a problem for the Nephites, who were already short on both manpower and supplies. (See Alma 54:2). The best solution was to put them to work, and so the Lamanites were made "to go forth and bury their dead, yea, and also the dead of the Nephites who were slain". (V. 1). Then they were compelled to establish Nephite fortifications by "laboring in digging a ditch round about the land, or the city, Bountiful". (V. 3-5, see Commentary Reference to Alma 24:19).

Mormon recorded: "It came to pass that Moroni had thus gained a victory over one of the greatest of the armies of the Lamanites, and had obtained possession of the city of Mulek, which was one of the strongest holds of the Lamanites in the land of Nephi". (V. 6). As he abridged the records, Mormon was obviously impressed that they had achieved this substantial accomplishment.

Earlier, Mormon had indicated that Mulek was located in the greater Land of Zarahemla, and not in the Land of Nephi, for the city was "on the east borders by the seashore". (Alma 5:26). Perhaps Mormon now characterized Mulek as being situated in the Land of Nephi because the Lamanites now possessed it, as they did the land to the south, or this could be the one reference in The Book of Mormon to a Land of Nephi in the north. Mormon's identification of the City of Mulek as being in the Land of Nephi could also have been an error, one of the "faults of men" in the record. (See Mormon 8:17, 8:12, & 9:31).

Another interesting geographical reference is found in verse 8, that concerns "the armies of the Lamanites, on the west sea, south". Inasmuch as the Nephites had left the land of their inheritance and moved northward to the Land of Nephi, and then later still further north to the Land of Zarahemla, the sea originally identified as "the west sea," is now identified in the record as "the west sea far to the south," (see V. 22), or simply, as "the west sea, south".

The Nephites had spent most of the twenty seventh and twenty eighth years of the reign of the judges regrouping and "preparing for war, yea, and in making fortifications to guard against the Lamanites, yea, and also delivering their women and their children from famine and affliction, and providing food for their armies". (V. 7). The war had caused a major lifestyle disruption in the Land of Zarahemla, and it was all the Nephites could do to maintain the integrity of their economic and social infrastructure. There had been a political shake-up as well, manifest by "dissensions and intrigue" such that the Nephite nation was "placed in the most dangerous circumstances". (V. 9).

At this point in his abridgment, Mormon inserted an account of "the people of Ammon, who, in the beginning, were Lamanites; but by Ammon and his brethren, or rather by the power and word of God, they had been converted unto the Lord". (V. 10, see Commentary Reference to Alma 24:19, & Alma 27:26).

For the past twelve years, because of their covenant of non-aggression, the Nephites had protected these people who were now "moved with compassion and were desirous to take up arms in the defence of their country". (V. 13, see Alma 24:27). They were not immune to the effects of Moroni's emotional and patriotic call to respond to the title of liberty. (See Alma 46:12-22).

"But behold, as they were about to take their weapons of war, they were overpowered by the persuasions of Helaman and his brethren, for they were about to break the oath which they had made". (V. 14). In yet another way, the influence of Alma the Younger was felt among his people. (We see The Butterfly Effect, once again). He had taught his sons well, and their righteous influence on the People of Ammon protected them from breaking their covenants with God. Just so should we honor our own baptismal covenants, the oath and covenant of the priesthood, our temple covenants, and the exhortations of our religious leaders to be faithful and to stand fast in obedience, nothing wavering.

The honor and integrity of the People of Ammon was preserved, and their self-esteem maintained, for "they had many sons, who had not entered into (the) covenant that they would not take their weapons of war to defend themselves against their enemies; therefore, they did assemble themselves together at this time, as many as were able to take up arms, and they called themselves "Nephites". (V. 16). Here we have another example of the blurring of the classical lines of distinction between "Nephites" and "Lamanites".

These young men had witnessed the tremendous power inherent in sacred promises made to God, and "they entered into (an equally powerful) covenant to fight for the liberty of the Nephites, yea, to protect the land unto the laying down of their lives; yea, even they covenanted that they never would give up their liberty, but they would fight in all cases to protect the Nephites and themselves from bondage". (V. 17). Mormon was obviously impressed with these young men, and felt that latter-day readers might benefit from their example.

It had been vexing to Moroni that a substantial portion of Nephite resources had been allocated to the defense of the People of Ammon, but there is never a hint in the record that they begrudged those people their pacifism. As a matter of fact, "they never had hitherto been a disadvantage to the Nephites". (V. 18).

Nevertheless, at the end of two years of preparation for war, and at a time when there was internal instability within the Nephite nation, it must have come as a wonderful surprise to Moroni to suddenly have an additional 2,000 able-bodied volunteers at his disposal. (V. 19). "And they were all young men, and they were exceedingly valiant for courage, and also for strength and activity" in the Church, "but behold, this was not all - they were men who were true at all times in whatsoever thing they were entrusted. Yea, they were men of truth and soberness, for they had been taught to keep the commandments of God and to walk uprightly before him". (V. 20-21, see Alma 17:2, & 56:47).

Together with his brethren, Helaman had exhorted their parents to keep their covenant, and now he marched "at the head of his two thousand stripling soldiers, to the support of the people in the borders of the land on the south by the west sea". (V. 22, see Commentary Reference to V. 8). "And thus ended on a happy note the twenty and eighth year of the reign of the judges over the people of Nephi". (V. 23)

"And they were all young men,
and they were exceedingly valiant for
courage, and also for strength and activity;
but behold, this was not all – they were men who
were true at all times in whatsoever thing they were
entrusted. Yea, they were men of truth and soberness,
for they had been taught to keep the commandments
of God and to walk uprightly before him."
(Alma 53:20-21).

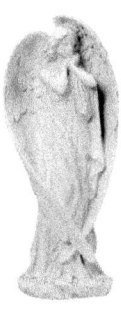

Alma
Chapter 54

Moroni was anxious to negotiate a prisoner exchange with the Lamanites, because "he desired the provisions which were imparted for the support of the Lamanite prisoners for the support of his own people; and he also desired his own people for the strengthening of his army". (V. 2). In addition, "the Lamanites had taken many women and children" prisoners, and Moroni understandably was anxious to liberate them. (V. 3, & 11). Therefore, he sent an epistle to his Lamanite counterpart. (V. 5-14). Its content helps us to better understand Moroni's personality. His message was a clear and unmistakable warning, even a clarion call, to repent or face the consequences. He recognized that it was still his responsibility to teach Ammoron and his Lamanite army the Gospel, insofar as it was possible to do so.

A purpose of teaching is to assist first in the development of internal attitude control, which is the ability to thoughtfully respond with fresh ideas and bold new concepts, rather than to react mechanically and primitively to challenging situations. Throughout their history, their failure to act independently had been the Lamanites' big problem. They typically were bound by a belief system that narrowed their focus of attention to "the tradition of their fathers". Thus, they reacted predictably, short-sightedly, and negatively to the continual entreaties of their Nephite brothers and sisters. (See Mosiah 10:12-17). True learning is the catalyst that changes behavior. When inspired teachers help us to deepen our insights, we are led to personal attitude adjustments and course corrections relating to our life's direction that get us back on track so we can more easily reach our righteous objectives.

Unfortunately, Moroni was only being realistic in his pessimism about how his exhortation to the Lamanites would be received. He wrote: "But as ye have once rejected these things, and have fought against the people of the Lord, even so I may expect you will do it again". (V. 8). Nevertheless, he wrote: "And now behold, we are prepared to receive you". (V. 9). Moroni's love of God and love of people could have been the most influential and determining positive factors acting upon the Lamanites, for his epistle had as its foundation the faith that at the head of the Church stands the greatest Teacher of us all, Who has the power to change lives. The Spirit could have softened the hearts of the Lamanites to accept Jesus Christ as their Savior, had they been teachable. Moroni knew that his cause was just, and so with confidence, he swore an oath, declaring: "As the Lord liveth, our armies shall come upon you except ye withdraw, and ye shall soon be visited with death, for we will retain our cities and our lands; yea, and we will maintain our religion". (V. 10). It was now up to the Lamanites to act upon Moroni's epistle.

Perhaps Moroni was familiar with David's encounter with the Philistines, likely recorded on the Plates of Brass, wherein he said: "Thou comest to me with a sword, and a spear, and with the shield: but I come to thee in the name of the Lord of hosts, the God of the armies of Israel, whom thou hast defiled. This day will the Lord deliver thee into mine hand ... and all this assembly shall know that the Lord saveth not with the sword and spear: for the battle is the Lord's, and he will give you into our hands". (1 Samuel 17:45-47).

In this case, Ammoron wrote a reply to Moroni that rehearsed once again the time-worn complaints of the Lamanite nation: "Behold, your fathers did wrong their brethren, insomuch that they did rob them of their right to the government when it rightly belonged unto them". (V. 17). Not only did he reject Moroni's counsel, but he also breathed the threat that he would "wage a war which (should) be eternal, either to the subjecting the Nephites to (the Lamanites') authority, or to their eternal extinction". (V. 20).

He declared: "Concerning that God whom ye say we have rejected, behold, we know not such a being". (V. 21). Therein lay the root of the problem. Ammoron identified himself as "a descendant of Zoram," an apostate Nephite and stranger to God who was entrenched in his wicked ways, and who was particularly unreceptive to the softening influence of the Spirit. (V. 23).

Alma
Chapter 55

Following Ammoron's response to his epistle, Moroni declared: "I will give unto him according to my words; yea, I will seek death among them until they shall sue for peace". (V. 3). He had also devised a stratagem to obtain the release of the Nephite prisoners, and he determined to carry it out. (V. 16, see Alma 54:3). Among his men, he found a Lamanite who had been one of the servants of the king who was murdered by Amalickiah. (V. 5, see Alma 47:29). This man was sent with a large quantity of wine to the Lamanite City of Gid, where the prisoners were being held. (V. 4-8). When he encountered Lamanite sentries, he explained that he had escaped from the Nephites. Then, he shared his wine with those who were guarding the prisoners, and they were soon completely inebriated. (V. 9-14).

For some reason, the Lamanites seem to have been particularly susceptible to the influences of alcohol. This fact was not lost on the Nephites, who several times in Book of Mormon history used wine to render the Lamanites physically incapable of responding to Nephite initiatives. In this instance, Moroni was notified that the Lamanite guards had been neutralized, and with his men he entered the city carrying many weapons that were quickly distributed to every prisoner who could fight, "even to their women, and all those of their children, as many as were able to use a weapon of war". (V. 17). Desperate circumstances call for drastic measures.

In his abridgement, Mormon does not reveal whether a pig was involved in this plot. He didn't record the following, although it does have relevance. "Twas an evening in October, I'll confess I wasn't sober, I was carting home a load with manly pride. When my feet began to stutter, and I fell into the gutter, and a pig came up and lay down by my side. Then, I lay there in the gutter, and my heart was all a-flutter, til a lady, passing by, did chance to say: 'You can tell a Lamanite that boozes by the company he chooses'. Then the pig got up and slowly walked away." (Benjamin Burt).

"The Nephites could have (easily) slain" the Lamanites. (V. 18). "But behold, this was not the desire of Moroni; he did not delight in murder or bloodshed, but he delighted in the saving of his people from destruction; and for this cause he might not bring upon him injustice, he would not fall upon the Lamanites and destroy them in their drunkenness". (V. 19).

It is our natural reaction to become "anti-enemy" when we are threatened, rather than "pro-Gospel". Moroni's policies toward the Lamanites repeatedly illustrated his benevolence and equanimity toward mortal enemies. These qualities reinforce Mormon's assessment of the man's character: "If all men had been, and were, and ever would be, like unto Moroni, behold, the very powers of hell would have been shaken forever; yea, the devil would never have power over the hearts of the children of men". (Alma 48:17). "And thus (the Lamanites) saw that the Nephites had power over them; and in these circumstances they found that it was not expedient that they should fight with the Nephites; therefore, their chief captains demanded their weapons of war, and they brought them forth and cast them at the feet of the Nephites, pleading for mercy". (V. 23 see Commentary Reference to Alma 30:58, Alma 46:35, & V. 32).

This was exactly what Moroni had hoped for, and he took many prisoners who were immediately put to work "strengthening the fortifications round about the City of Gid". (V. 24-25). "And it came to pass that the Nephites began again to be victorious, and to reclaim their rights and their privileges". (V. 28).

The Lamanites tried every trick to gain the advantage over the Nephites, "but in these attempts they did lose many prisoners". (V. 29). They even pulled the time-worn "poisoned wine trick," but the Nephites were on to them: "And many times did they attempt to administer of their wine to the Nephites, that they might destroy them with poison or with drunkenness. But behold, the Nephites were not slow to remember the Lord their God in this their time of affliction. They could not be taken in their snares; yea, they would not partake of their wine, save they had first given to some of the Lamanite prisoners". (V. 30-31). "And they were thus cautioned that no poison should be administered among them; for if their wine would poison a Lamanite, it would also poison a Nephite, and thus, they did (compel the Lamanite prisoners to first) try all their liquors". (V. 32). Do we detect another example of dry humor here? (See Alma 18:9, 19:5, 30:58, 33:21, & 46:36).

Moroni next concentrated his efforts on strengthening the fortifications of Gid, Bountiful, and especially Morianton, until the whole region "had become an exceeding stronghold". (V. 33).

Alma
Chapter 56

At this point in his abridgement, Mormon inserted an epistle from Helaman to give the reader a more comprehensive historical perspective. This comprises chapters 56-58 in The Book of Alma, and is one of the greatest and most faith promoting war stories in The Book of Mormon.

Helaman first rehearsed for Moroni the circumstances that found him at the head of "two thousand of the sons of those men whom Ammon brought down out of the land of Nephi". (V. 2-8). Then he recounted how he marched with those young men to the city of Judea, to assist Antipus". (V. 9). He called these young men "his sons," because of their worthiness. (V. 10). They were welcomed in Judea because the Lamanites had killed a vast number of Nephite soldiers there. (See V. 17). Helaman mourned their loss, but consoled himself on this point: "That they (had) died in the cause of their country and their God, yea, and they (were) happy". (V. 11). After all, "if, in this life only, we have hope in Christ, we are of all men most miserable". (1 Corinthians 15:19).

"If, in the pre-mortal existence, we looked forward to birth, which was the leaving of our Father and our eternal family, how much more we must have looked forward to death, which would be a later and essential step in coming home. Mortality is the prerequisite to immortality. It is by passing the tests and gaining the progress of this world that we obtain eternal life. Thus, death is as important as birth, and both are among the essential transitions in the Father's Plan for our salvation". (Richard Eyre, "The Birth That We Call Death," p. 37). "Death hath passed upon all men, to fulfil the merciful Plan of the great Creator". (2 Nephi 9:6).

In fact, the anniversary of our death will be the birth date of our immortal soul. It was this philosophical viewpoint that motivated Socrates to declare: "Look death in the face with joyful hope, and consider this a lasting truth: The righteous man has nothing to fear, neither in life, nor in death, and the gods will not forsake him".

Since we are spiritual beings having a mortal experience, it could be argued: "Life actually has no significance except as a preparation for the ultimate goal of death". (Carl Jung). If that is true, then "we ought not to measure life by the hopes and enjoyments of this world, but by the preparation it makes for another - looking forward to what we shall be, rather than backward to what we have been". (Charlie Munger).

Death is not extinguishing the light; it is putting out the lamp because the dawn has come. (Rabindraneth Tagore). "Our birth is but a sleep and a forgetting," (Wordsworth), while death is an awakening and a remembering. In a sense, our mortal lives are but pre-natal experiences.

The war in the Land of Zarahemla had taken a particularly ominous turn in the theater of operations in which Helaman fought, because the Lamanites had adopted a "cry havoc" position. In the ancient world, only the ruler could "cry havoc," for that awful decree meant "Kill everyone - take no prisoners". In fact, the Lamanites had retained only Nephite chief captains as prisoners, "for none other have they spared alive," reported Helaman. (V. 12).

The two thousand stripling warriors had marched through "the land of Manti, or the City of Manti, and the City of Zeezrom, and the City of Cumeni, and the City of Antiparah". (V. 14, see Commentary Reference to Alma 24:19). Understandably, the Nephites "were depressed in body as well as in spirit, for they had fought valiantly by day and toiled by night to maintain their cities; and thus they had suffered great afflictions of every kind". (V. 16).

By the means of chastisement, they were learning to endure to the end in righteousness. The runner James Fixx wrote about how he developed his own capacity for endurance. "When we race," he said, "strange things happen to our minds. The stress of fatigue sometimes makes us forget why we wanted to race in the first place. In one of my early marathons, I found myself unable to think of a single reason for continuing. Physically and mentally exhausted, I dropped out of the race. Now, I won't enter a marathon unless I truly want to finish it. If, during the race, I can't remember why I wanted to run in it, I tell myself, 'Maybe I can't remember now, but I know I had a good reason when I started.' I've finally learned how to fight back when my brain starts using tricky arguments". ("The Complete Book of Running," p. 92).

The twenty-sixth year of the reign of the judges ended in a relative stalemate between the Nephites and Lamanites. (V. 18-26). Each group spied on the other, waiting for an advantage to take the initiative. (V. 22, & 35). After some time, the Sons of Helaman received care packages from home that must have boosted their spirits as well as their storehouses. (V. 27).

Finally, the Nephites once again carried out their old "divide the army and lead the Lamanites into the open" trick. (V. 30-41). The untested Sons of Helaman "had never fought yet they did not fear death; and they did think more upon the liberty of their fathers than they did upon their (own) lives; yea, they had been taught by their mothers, that if they did not doubt, God would deliver them". (V. 47). This verse is one of the greatest tributes in the scriptures to mothers. These women had obviously accepted their special calling with profound sobriety and had probably sacrificed other opportunities for self-fulfillment to instead nurture their sons. As a writer once asked: "Are women who enjoy motherhood intellectual dropouts? What would have become of the human race had Eve rejected motherhood in favor of pursuing a more gratifying career in the already promising apple industry?" ("Time Magazine", 9/30/1974).

This reference to the influence of mothers is all the more remarkable, because these women were Lamanite converts to the Church. Perhaps because they had seen life from both sides of the fence, they were particularly attentive to the spiritual maturation of their sons.

As they have watched them grow, Latter-day mothers have probably had the same thoughts and prayers for their own sons: "My son starts school tomorrow," wrote one. "It's going to be strange and new to him for a while. I hope he is treated gently. Up to now, he's been king of the roost, and boss of the backyard. I have always been around to repair his wounds and to soothe his feelings. But now, things are going to be different. He's going to walk down the front steps, wave his hand, and start on a great adventure that will probably include conflict, tragedy, and sorrow. To live his life in the world will require faith, love, and courage. So, I pray that the world will take him by his young hand and teach him the things he will need to know. He will have to learn that not all men are just and true. But I hope he also learns that for every scoundrel there is a hero, for every crooked politician there is a dedicated leader, and that for every enemy there is a friend. I hope he learns early in his life that the bullies are the easiest people to lick. May he learn of the wonders of books. May he have quiet time to ponder the eternal mystery of birds in the sky, bees in the air, and flowers on the hill. May he be taught that it is far more honorable to fall than it is to cheat. I pray that he might have faith in his own ideas, even if everyone else tells him they are wrong. He will need the strength to avoid following the crowd when everyone else is jumping on the bandwagon. So, I hope he might learn to filter all he hears on a screen of truth and to take only the good that comes through. It will be okay for him to sell his brawn and his brains to the highest bidder, but he must never put a price on his heart or his soul. He must close his ears to the howling mob, and stand to fight, if he thinks he is right. I hope he is taught gently, but without being coddled, because only the test of fire makes fine steel. I know this is a lot to ask, but it is my constant hope and prayer. After all, he's such a nice little fellow!" (Dan Valentine, "Ideals Scrapbook").

Helaman led his "stripling Ammonites" into a battle that raged fiercely. (V. 49-54, see v. 57). When the Lamanites finally surrendered, Helaman "numbered those young men who had fought with (him), fearing lest there were many of them slain". (V. 55). Making an accounting of one's troops is always a gut-wrenching experience for a leader after a battle, but for a man like Helaman who counted his soldiers as his own sons, it would have been particularly traumatic.

Imagine the satisfaction with which Helaman must have continued his war report to Moroni, when he recorded: "But behold, to my great joy, there had not one soul of them fallen to the earth;

yea, and they had fought as if with the strength of God; yea, never were men known to have fought with such miraculous strength; and with such mighty power did they fall upon the Lamanites, that they did frighten them; and for this cause did the Lamanites deliver themselves up as prisoners of war". (V. 56).

Alma
Chapter 57

Back in the Lamanite camp, Ammoron suggested that the Nephites release prisoners in exchange for the City of Antiparah. (V. 1-3). When this offer was declined, the Lamanites abandoned that city as indefensible. (V. 4). Then, early in the twenty-ninth year of the reign of the judges, the Nephites welcomed reinforcements from the Land of Zarahemla, that included sixty more of "the sons of the Ammonites". (V. 6).

With their numbers bolstered, the Nephites laid siege to the City of Cumeni. (V. 7-9). A Lamanite supply train attempted to get through the Nephite lines, but was intercepted. Perhaps thinking of his dark-skinned young protégés, Helaman wrote: "And we, instead of being Lamanites, were Nephites; therefore, we did take them and their provisions". (V. 10, see Commentary Reference to Alma 30:58). The siege accomplished its purpose, and the Lamanites "yielded up the city" of Cumeni to the Nephites. (V. 12).

As a result, so many prisoners were taken that it was all the Nephite army could do to keep them under control, so a detachment was dispatched to take them to the Land of Zarahemla. (V. 13-16). Unfortunately, on the way, these prisoners rose up in rebellion, and "the greater number of them were slain, and the remainder of them broke through and fled". (V. 33).

Back at the City of Cumeni, things were getting out of hand, as well. As soon as Ammoron had resupplied his army with fresh troops and provisions, an attack was launched against the Nephites. (V. 16). Helaman reported: "My little band of two thousand and sixty fought most desperately; yea, they were firm before the Lamanites, and did administer death unto all those who opposed them. And as the remainder of our army were about to give way before the Lamanites, behold, those two thousand and sixty were firm and undaunted. Yea, and they did obey and observe to perform every word of command with exactness; yea, and even according to their faith it was done unto them; and I did remember the words which they said unto me that their mothers had taught them. And now behold, it was these my sons to whom we owe this great victory". (V. 19-22).

Miraculously, although a thousand of their brethren were slain, "there was not one soul of (the Sons of Helaman) who did perish," even though every single one "had received many wounds". (V. 25). "And we do justly ascribe (their deliverance) to the miraculous power of God," wrote Helaman, "because of their exceeding faith in that which they had been taught to believe - that there was a just God, and whosoever did not doubt, that they should be preserved by his marvelous power. Now this was the faith of these of whom I have spoken; they are young, and their minds are firm, and they do put their trust in God continually". (V. 26-27).

Echoing the faith of his father Alma, Helaman wrote of other Nephite warriors who died in battle: "I trust that the souls of them who have been slain have entered into the rest of their God". (V. 36. see Alma 16:17).

Alma
Chapter 58

Helaman continued his epistle to Moroni, describing how they once again tried the "divide their army and lead the enemy into the open" trick, (See Alma 56:30-31), but this time the Lamanites "remembered that which we had hitherto done; therefore, we could not decoy them away from their strongholds". (V. 1).

Again, there was a stalemate, with each side jockeying for strategic position. (V. 2-7). As the Nephite provisions dwindled, the situation became more desperate. Finally, a supply train arrived accompanied by two thousand warriors. Helaman made a point to emphasize that "this is all the assistance which we did receive, to defend ourselves and our country from falling into the hands of our enemies; yea, to contend with an enemy which was innumerable". (V. 8).

In an age of poor communications, Helaman was at a loss to understand why the government in Zarahemla did not provide his army with more assistance. "And now the cause of these our embarrassments, or the cause why they did not send us more strength unto us, we knew not". (V. 9, see V. 34).

His army did the only reasonable thing left to do under the circumstances. "We did pour out our souls in prayer to God, that he would strengthen us and deliver us out of the hands of our enemies". (V. 10). "Yea, and it came to pass that the Lord our God did visit us with assurances that he would deliver us; yea, insomuch that he did speak peace to our souls, and did grant unto us great faith, and did cause us that we should hope for our deliverance in him". (V. 11).

In the wilderness adjacent to the City of Manti, the stage was finally set for a confrontation with the superior Lamanite force. Helaman stated that the enemy "saw that we were not strong, according to our numbers". (V. 15). But the power of God was with them. In the end, after the clash of titans, "the Lamanites did flee out of all this quarter of the land". (V. 30). Helaman again asked Moroni why they had not been given more support. He recorded his concern that perhaps some political intrigue in Zarahemla had prevented the authorities from assisting the army in the field. (V. 36). But he assured Moroni that in spite of his apprehension about the stability of the government, his sons were stalwart. They "stand fast" he said, "in that liberty wherewith God has made them free; and they are strict to remember the Lord their God from day to day; yea, they do observe to keep his statutes, and his judgments, and his commandments continually; and their faith is strong in the prophecies concerning that which is to come". (V. 40).

Alma
Chapter 59

As soon as Moroni had the opportunity to process the epistle from Helaman, he wrote to Pahoran, who was the chief judge in the Land of Zarahemla, "desiring that he should cause men to be gathered together to strengthen Helaman". (V. 3). Then he set about the task of formulating plans to "obtain the remainder of those possessions and cities which the Lamanites had taken from them". (V. 4).

Even as he did so, the Lamanites attacked the City of Nephihah and overpowered its defenders. (V. 5-8). Moroni had underestimated the strength of the Lamanites and supposed that the Nephite government on its own initiative would have dispatched sufficient provisions and personnel to protect the city. (V. 9). Consequently, he "was angry with the government, because of their (apparent) indifference concerning the freedom of their country". (V. 13).

When the City of Nephihah fell, Moroni and his military strategists "doubted and marveled also because of the (supposed) wickedness of the people, and this because of the success of the Lamanites over them". (V. 12). "True Latter-day Saints are law abiding and God fearing. Their allegiance is to good government, the kind in which God is given a central place. It was the assumed lack of these essentials that angered Moroni, and caused him to write sharply to Pahoran". (C.E.S. "Book of Mormon Study Manual," p. 345, see Alma Chapters 60 & 61).

"And it came to pass that Moroni was angry with the government, because of their indifference concerning the freedom of their country."
(Alma 59:13).

Alma
Chapter 60

The lesson in patriotism contained in chapters 60 and 61 is one of the finest in scripture, and shows what a united people can accomplish when freedom is their goal, and the Lord is their God. The message is most timely in an age when many are seeking to overthrow established governments in which God given liberties are still protected rights. This chapter comprises yet another epistle that Mormon inserted into the record. It is not the most tactful letter, but it identifies Moroni's righteous indignation at what he perceived as the government's ignorance of its obligations and responsibilities.

Moroni asked: "And now behold, we desire to know the cause of this exceeding great neglect; yea, we desire to know the cause of your thoughtless state. Can you think to sit upon your thrones in a state of thoughtless stupor, while your enemies are spreading the work of death around you?" (V. 6-7). "Sin is waste. It is doing one thing when you should be doing other and better things for which you have the capacity. Those officials whom Moroni chided because they 'sit upon (their) thrones in a state of thoughtless stupor' were not deliberately or maliciously harming anyone - but they were committing a grave sin.

(For example), why do people feel guilty about T.V. (or cell phones, or social media)? What is wrong with it? Just this: It shuts out all the wonderful things of which the mind is capable, leaving it drugged in a state of thoughtless stupor. Nor is God is pleased with us for merely sitting in meetings. "How vain and trifling have been our spirits, our conferences, our councils, our meetings, our private as well as public conversations," wrote the Prophet Joseph Smith from Liberty Jail. 'Too low, too mean, too vulgar, too condescending for the dignified characters called and chosen of God.'" (Hugh Nibley, "Zeal Without Knowledge," p. 264-265).

Moroni was outraged that thousands of Nephites had needlessly died while the government supposedly withheld reinforcements and provisions. He charged the authorities with mismanagement and a dereliction of their duties and responsibilities, and felt that the pain and suffering he had both witnessed and experienced was, in itself, a condemnation of Nephite leadership. (V. 8-12).

But, as Mormon pointed out, "the Lord suffereth the righteous to be slain that his justice and judgment may come upon the wicked; therefore, ye need not suppose that the righteous are lost because they are slain; but behold, they do enter into the rest of the Lord their God". (V. 13, see Alma 13:5, & 14:11). These fallen Nephites would become a potent missionary force in the Spirit World, where they would have the opportunity to carry the message of the Gospel to their former enemies on earth. "Many of our boys who bear the priesthood and are worthy to do so will be called to that missionary service after they have departed this life," said Harold B. Lee in a sobering statement during the opening months of the involvement of the United States in World War II. (C.R. 10/1942).

Moroni had made serious accusations thus far in his epistle, but the worst was yet to come. "And now behold, I say unto you, I fear exceedingly that the judgments of God will come upon this people, because of their exceeding slothfulness, yea, even the slothfulness of our government, and their exceedingly great neglect towards their brethren". (V. 14). "Those who sit in their places of power in a state of thoughtless stupor are those rulers in the world who, in a frenzy of hate and lust for unrighteous power and dominion over their fellow men, have put into motion eternal forces they do not comprehend and cannot control". (President Heber J. Grant, C.R. 10/1942).

Moroni lamented the dissension that had erupted within the Nephite nation when the king-men had not been true to the cause of freedom. (V. 16). He recounted the atrocities that had been perpetrated upon the Nephites, all "because of the great wickedness of those who are seeking for power and authority, yea, even those king-men". (V. 17).

As an editorial in the New York Times, in the summer of 1972, put it so succinctly: "War is an ugly thing, but not the ugliest of things. The decayed and degraded state of moral and patriotic feeling that thinks nothing is worse than a war is itself worse. A man who has nothing which he cares about more than his personal safety is a miserable creature who has no chance of being free unless made and kept so by the exertion of better men than himself".

Getting carried away, Moroni forgot his decorum and asked bitterly: "But why should I say much concerning this matter? For we know not but what ye yourselves are seeking for authority. We know not but what ye are also traitors to your country". (V. 18). He wondered if Pahoran felt that he had a blanket of security about him, situated as he was "in the heart of (the) country," far from the battlefield, if he had "forgotten the commandments of the Lord," if he supposed that the Lord would deliver the Nephites while their leaders put forth no effort on their own behalf, or if he would sit idly by, while thousands of his countrymen were dying. (V. 19-22).

It is obvious that the more Moroni wrote, the more agitated he became. In his fervor, he threatened open rebellion against the Nephite government if they would not show a true spirit of freedom manifest by their immediate support of the Nephite armies. (V. 23-30).

The same Moroni who began his letter with a profession of ignorance and a request for more information, now brought a flat accusation to the chief judge, and flung a challenge at the government itself. (V. 29-30). "Ye know that ye do transgress the laws of God, and ye do know that ye do trample them under your feet". (V. 33). Moroni was right about every point except for one - he had accused the wrong man.

It is strange that this man who had deplored more than anything else the contentions among the Nephites as the principal cause of their misfortunes in war, should now propose to add to the turmoil by stirring up insurrection. (V. 27). But he was bursting with the pent-up emotions and accumulated memories of reverses that should have been avoided, misery that might have been spared, lives that could have been saved, and operations that may well have ended the war had the necessary support been forthcoming from home. His anger was solely in the interest of liberty. "Behold, I am Moroni, your chief captain. I seek not for power, but to pull it down. I seek not for honor of the world, but for the glory of my God, and the freedom and welfare of my country". (V. 36).

"We did pour out our souls in
prayer to God, that he would strengthen
us and deliver us out of the hands of our enemies,
yea, and also give us strength that we might retain our
cities, and our lands, and our possessions, for the support
of our people. Yea, and it came to pass that the Lord our God
did visit us with assurances that he would deliver us; yea,
insomuch that he did speak peace to our souls, and
did grant unto us great faith, and did cause
that we should hope for our deliverance
in him." (Alma 58:10-11).

Alma
Chapter 61

Perhaps, in Chapters 61 & 62, Mormon wanted latter-day readers to see the greatness of Moroni's love of liberty, as well as Pahoran's forgiving and gentle spirit. This chapter, then, comprises Pahoran's response to Moroni's burning accusations and threats. Fortunately, the man wrongly accused was worthy of his high office, as revealed by his wise, temperate, and constructive reply.

Pahoran had been "appointed chief judge and governor over the people, with an oath and sacred ordinance to judge righteously, and to keep the peace and the freedom of the people, and to grant unto them their sacred privileges to worship the Lord their God, yea, to support and maintain the cause of God all his days, and to bring the wicked to justice according to their crime. And Pahoran did fill the seat of his father". (See Commentary Reference to Alma 50:39-40.

About five years later, came the real challenge to his leadership skills. He related to Moroni how sorry he was to hear how his army in the field had been under straitened circumstances. (V. 2). Then, darkly, he painted a picture of political intrigue and conspiracy in Zarahemla, with the king-men again rising up in rebellion against the chief judge and the freemen supporting his legitimate government. (V. 3-4).

Things had gotten so bad that Pahoran was in exile, having been "driven from the City of Zarahemla to the land of Gideon, with as many men as it were possible" to accompany him. (V. 5). Those who would sustain Pahoran immediately responded to his proclamation appealing for support, "flocking daily (to Gideon), to their arms, in the defence of their country and their freedom, and to avenge (their) wrongs". (V. 6).

"What is meant by sustaining a person?" asked John Taylor. "Do we understand it? If I vote that I will sustain (a man) in his capacity, I will welcome him and treat him with consideration, kindness, and respect, and if I need counsel I will ask it at his hand. I would not say anything derogatory to his character. If anybody in my presence were to whisper something about him disparaging to his reputation, I would say, 'Look here! Did you not hold up your hand to sustain him? Then why do you not do it?' If any man make an attack upon his reputation, I would defend him in some such way". (J.D., 21:207-208).

The same critical situation that had existed in Zarahemla at the outset of Pahoran's rule was repeating itself, with the Nephite government and way of life hanging in the balance. The shift in focus in Mormon's abridgement is startling for its irony, because after so many chapters dealing with their responses to the external threat of the Lamanite armies, we come full circle to address the real problem facing the Nephites. The old royalist crowd that Moroni knew so well had gotten "possession of the land, or the city, of Zarahemla," and had actually reopened correspondence with the Lamanites. (V. 8, see Commentary Reference to Alma 24:19, & Alma 51).

Pahoran's magnanimity is obvious in his letter to Moroni: "And now, in your epistle you have censured me, but it mattereth not; I am not angry, but do rejoice in the greatness of your heart. I, Pahoran, do not seek for power, save only to retain my judgment-seat that I may preserve the rights and the liberty of my people. My soul standeth fast in that liberty in the which God hath made us free". (V. 9).

There was "abroad in the land a kind of distorted fascination with freedom which obscured the limitations of freedom, when freedom was pursued blindly and for its own sake". (Neal Maxwell, "Freedom-A Hard Doctrine," B.Y.U. Devotional, April 27, 1972). Freedom of individual action is an eternal right, and a principle that we see in evidence from the dawn of pre-mortal existence. The problem with the king-men was that they sought to deny others that basic freedom of self-determination. Heavenly Father so loved His spirit children that He allowed them to follow their own inclinations during the ideological war in heaven. The result, of course, was that a third part of the host was cast out of the presence of God as the result of open rebellion.

Likewise, during Christ's mortal ministry, the Gospel message was presented to all who would listen, without force being applied to compel the disobedient to obey the commandments whereby they might be saved. Their freedom of choice was never withheld. The simple message was: "Follow this counsel and see if this doctrine is mine, or His who sent me". The same quality of love was extended to all, and was unconditional in its bestowal.

When we read of the conspiracy of the king-men, however, we can easily identify Satan's fingerprints all over its blueprints. Those who are disciples of that master deceiver will never be able to grasp the principle that change for the good must come from within and cannot be manipulated from without. The king-men were blinded to this concept, and so the poor excuse for "peace" they attempted to secure by an alliance with the Lamanites was short-sighted, ill-conceived, and doomed to failure. (See V. 8). As David O. McKay declared: "Men may yearn for peace, cry for peace, and work for peace, but there will be no peace until they follow the path pointed out by the living Christ". ("Improvement Era," 10/1960).

Pahoran was determined to preserve the government even if it required shedding the blood of the king-men. (V. 11). "Therefore, my beloved brother, Moroni, let us resist evil, and whatsoever evil we cannot resist with our words, yea, such as rebellions and dissensions, let us resist them with our swords, that we may retain our freedom, that we may rejoice in the great privilege of our Church, and in the cause of our Redeemer and our God". (V. 14).

The chief judge was also the commander-in-chief of the Nephite armies in the field, and in that capacity he gave direct orders to Moroni to return to the Land of Gideon, and put an end to this "great iniquity". (V. 15-18). Even in the face of this dire emergency, Pahoran was hesitant to use force against his countrymen. But after reading Moroni's epistle, he recognized its wisdom and received inspired counsel that he should go against them, "except they repent". (V. 19-20).

Perhaps, in Alma Chapters 61 &
62, Mormon, who abridged the records,
wanted latter-day readers to appreciate the
greatness of Moroni's love of liberty, as well as
Pahoran's gentle and forgiving spirit. This
chapter consists of Pahoran's response to
Captain Moroni's burning accusations
and threats. Fortunately, the man
wrongly accused was worthy of
his high office, as revealed
by his wise, temperate,
and constructive
reply.

Alma
Chapter 62

Moroni's shattered confidence in Pahoran was immediately restored when he received his epistle. In fact, "his heart did take courage, and was filled with exceeding great joy". (V. 1). Following orders, he took a small detachment and marched towards the Land of Gideon, raising "the standard of liberty in whatsoever place he did enter, and gained whatsoever force he could in all his march". (V. 2-3).

Thousands of Nephites rallied to his call, so that when he finally entered Gideon, his army was stronger than that of "Pachus, who was the king of those dissenters who had driven the freemen out of the land of Zarahemla and had taken possession of the land". (V. 5-6). Pachus was slain in battle, his soldiers taken prisoner, "and Pahoran was restored to his judgment-seat". (V. 8).

Pachus and his men had been committed to the violent overthrow of the legitimate government, which would have resulted in the loss of Nephite freedom. (See Alma 61:8). Therefore, "those king-men (who) would not take up arms in the defence of their country, but would fight against it, were put to death". (V. 9, see Helaman 1:8). "And whosoever was found denying their freedom was speedily executed according to the law". (V. 10, see Alma 51:15). The choice was not only between physical life and death, but also between eternal life and spiritual death.

With unity restored in Zarahemla, Pahoran was able to muster twelve thousand soldiers to reinforce Helaman, Teancum, and Lehi. (V. 12-13). Then he marched with Moroni toward the City of Nephihah, overpowered a body of Lamanites on the way, and "caused them to enter into a covenant that they would no more take up their weapons of war against the Nephites". (V. 14-16).

Remarkably, "when (the Lamanites) had entered into this covenant (the Nephites) sent them to dwell with the people of Ammon, and they were in number about four thousand who had not been slain". (V. 17). There was a new spirit in the air. Moroni's patience and humanity in dealing with the defeated Lamanites was beginning to bear fruit. (See V. 27-28). Plainly, everyone was getting rather tired of war, when thousands of Lamanite warriors began to see that the People of

Ammon were the only really sensible ones after all. (See Alma 23). In the end, no-one wins at war. (See Mormon 8:8).

Once at the City of Nephihah, Moroni's army was thwarted by the very fortifications it had earlier raised round about all the cities in the Land of Zarahemla. It was the Nephites' usual strategy to lure the Lamanites from their strongholds, but this time they would not be led into that particular trap. (V. 19). Instead, Moroni's army crept into the city without detection, and "obtained possession of the City of Nephihah without the loss of one soul; and there were many of the Lamanites who were slain". (V. 20-26). Understandably, "many of the Lamanites that were prisoners were desirous to join the people of Ammon and become a free people. And it came to pass that as many as were desirous, unto them it was granted according to their desires. Therefore, all the prisoners of the Lamanites did join the people of Ammon, and did begin to labor exceedingly, tilling the ground, raising all manner of grain, and flocks and herds of every kind". (V. 27-29). We can change our nature, after all.

And so, the wicked Lamanites, who had made life a hell for the Nephites for as long as anyone could remember, whose territories and resources in the Land of Nephi still remained intact and unravaged by war, and who outnumbered the Nephites by a wide margin, were dismissed without even a reprimand, and in short order became model citizens of Nephite society.

Now focusing their strength on the Land of Lehi, and then the Land of Moroni, the Nephites drove the remaining armies of the Lamanites to the "borders by the wilderness on the south, and in the borders by the wilderness on the east". (V. 30-34).

Teancum, who had fought so valiantly in so many Nephite campaigns, "was exceedingly angry with Ammoron," who had been responsible for "this great and lasting war which had been the cause of so much bloodshed, yea, and so much famine". (V. 35). In his anger, he thought to repeat his bold penetration of the Lamanite camp, thinking to slay Ammoron as he lay in his tent, as he had his brother Amalickiah. (See Alma 51:34).

"And he went forth with a cord, from place to place, insomuch that he did find the king; and he did cast a javelin at him, which did pierce him near the heart. But behold, the king did awaken his servants before he died, insomuch that they did pursue Teancum, and slew him". (V. 36). Teancum "had been a man who had fought valiantly for his country, yea, a true friend to liberty; and he had suffered very many sore afflictions". (V. 37). But he did not live to see the defeat of the Lamanite army, or its expulsion from the Land of Zarahemla. He had seen the evil attendants to prolonged warfare. "For the space of many years ... there had been murders, and contentions, and dissensions, and all manner of iniquity among the people of Nephi". (V. 39-40). Only "for the righteous sake, yea, because of the prayers of the righteous" had the Nephites been spared. (V. 40). "And there was once more peace established among the people of Nephi". V. 42).

Sadly, as a result of this prolonged fratricidal conflict, many Lamanites had become more hardened in their hearts, but at the same time "many were softened because of their afflictions, insomuch that they did humble themselves before God, even in the depth of humility. (V. 41). Those who had covenanted to renounce war mingled with the society of the People of Ammon, and were taught the Gospel. Helaman put away his weapons of war, and armed with the scriptures, took it upon himself to again "preach unto the people the word of God". (V. 44-45). "And it came to pass that they did establish again the Church of God, throughout all the land". (V. 46).

As for Moroni, he "yielded up the command of his armies into the hands of his son, whose name was Moronihah; and he retired to his own house that he might spend the remainder of his days in peace". (V. 43). Less than one year later, he died. (See Alma 63:3). He was only about 43 years of age. All around him, the world had gone mad. But Moroni had been an island in the storm, and his example and leadership a refuge from the uncertainties of life in Zarahemla. "The stars fade away, the sun himself grow dim with age, and nature sink in years; But (Moroni) shalt flourish in immortal youth, unhurt amidst the war of elements, the wreck of matter, and the crash of worlds". (Joseph Addison, "Cato," Act 5, Scene 1).

"Old soldiers never die; they just fade away." Perhaps he had finally been worn down by the privations endured through so many military campaigns. Longfellow had men like Moroni in mind, when he wrote: "Tell me not, in mournful numbers, life is but an empty dream! For the soul is dead that slumbers, and things are not what they seem. Life is real. Life is earnest!. And the grave is not the goal. Dust thou art, to dust thou returnest was not spoken of the soul. Not enjoyment, and not sorrow, is our destined end or way; but to act, that each tomorrow finds us farther than today. Lives of great men all remind us we can make our lives sublime, and departing, leave behind us footprints on the sands of time. Let us then be up and doing, with a heart for any fate; still achieving, still pursuing. Learn to labor, and to wait".

Even though Mormon greatly admired Moroni, he chose not to include any details about his personal life in the religious record of the Nephites during these fateful years. Nevertheless, we can be sure that Moroni's personal and public lives were harmoniously governed and intertwined by the same noble principles. He gave so much of himself to the welfare of his country; surely he had a family that was willing to subjugate its own happiness to the common welfare and understood that its husband and father was a man of the people, and a man of destiny, who was willing to lay down his life on the altar of sacrifice, and "willing to give up his todays, so that others might enjoy their tomorrows." (The Cemetery of The Pacific, Honolulu, Hawaii).

As Moroni completed his final acts of duty and responsibility, of faithful service and Christ-like compassion, and breathed his last contented sigh, the following could have been observed of him: "Here you are, home from your mission. It seems like it was such a short time. Think of the people you met, the people you helped. Think how you have grown, physically and spiritually. It seems like you were a child, so immature, when you left home such a short time ago. There is mother, waiting to embrace you, standing just a bit behind father, who is bursting with pride. Are those tears of happiness on mother's cheeks? Father first strikes hands with you, and then embraces you warmly. You are shown to your room; it is ready for your homecoming. It seems like such a short time ago that you left it, just as you see it now. The feelings are resonant, and you know this is where you belong. This is a real homecoming - home to Heavenly Father and Mother". (Anonymous)

With peace restored in the land, "Helaman and his brethren went forth, and did declare the word of God with much power unto the convincing of many people of their wickedness, which did cause them to repent of their sins and to be baptized unto the Lord their God. And it came to pass that they did establish again the Church of God, throughout all the land. Yea, and regulations were made concerning the law" so that the abuses of the past might not be repeated. "And their judges, and their chief judges were chosen," with Pahoran returning to the judgment-seat. And "they did humble themselves exceedingly ... And they did pray unto the Lord their God continually". (V. 44-51).

Mormon chronicled how peace was maintained, in verses 45-51. Helaman had been instrumental in establishing Nephite prosperity during sixteen years as warrior, prophet, and record-keeper. Finally, "in the thirty and fifth year of the reign of the judges over the people of Nephi," Helaman died, one of the last of the principal players to make his exit from the great drama that had unfolded in the Land of Zarahemla. (V. 52).

In another 57 years, the Mortal Messiah would be born in Bethlehem. These times would be pivotal in Zarahemla, and in the commotion, many would lose their way. But for Helaman, the battle was over. Crossing the bar, he would enjoy God's Rest that his father Alma had so often described to him. Now, he would "think of stepping on shore, and finding it heaven; of taking hold of a hand, and finding it God's hand; of breathing a new air, and finding it celestial air; of feeling invigorated, and finding it immortality; of passing from storm and tempest to an unbroken calm, and of waking up, and finding it Home!" (Anonymous).

Alma
Chapter 63

This chapter is Mormon's abridgement of the record of Shiblon, who "took possession of those sacred things which had been delivered unto Helaman by Alma". (V. 1, see V. 10-12). Both he and Corianton would prove to be as faithful as had been their brother Helaman. (V. 2).

A tantalizing reference is made to a group "of five thousand and four hundred men, with their wives and their children, (who) departed out of the land of Zarahemla into the land which was northward". (V. 4). They evidently traveled by land, and when time passed and no word had been received concerning them, "it came to pass that (a man named) Hagoth, he being an exceedingly curious man, therefore he went forth and built him an exceedingly large ship, on the borders of the land Bountiful, by the land Desolation, and launched it forth into the west sea, by the narrow neck which led into the land northward". (V. 5). Many Nephites boarded this ship and "took their course northward". (V. 6). Other ships were built, and when the first returned, they were all provisioned "and set out again to the land northward". (V. 7). In the intervening 400 years between that event and Mormon's abridgement of the record, nothing was ever again heard of these settlers. Mormon wrote only that he supposed "they were drowned in the depths of the sea". V. 8). In only 100 years (5 generations), if that group of 5,000 survived and prospered, it could easily have mushroomed to a population of 80,000 or more.

Other adventurous Nephites constructed yet another ship, and as Mormon recorded "wither she did go we know not". (V. 9). In addition, "there were many people who went forth into the land northward". (V. 10). Perhaps one or more of these groups mingled with indigenous peoples of North America, who had previously migrated from other lands, as well.

It is pure speculation to attempt to determine where these Nephite emigrants might have settled, but it is a common belief in the Church that they spread over the Pacific islands, and even reached New Zealand. David O. McKay, when dedicating the New Zealand Temple, prayed: "We express gratitude that to these fertile islands Thou didst guide descendants of Father Lehi, and hast enabled them to prosper". ("Church News," 5/10/1958). When Shiblon died, his younger brother

Corianton had already "gone forth to the land northward in a ship". (V. 10). We never again encounter Corianton in The Book of Mormon. It would be nice if we knew that this righteous son of Alma the Younger, and grandson of Alma, had carried on the tradition of his family, providing spiritual guidance to an even more isolated branch of Israel, and became "a fruitful bough, even a fruitful bough by a well, whose branches run over the wall". (Genesis 49:22).

Centuries earlier, Lehi's son Jacob had written: "The time passed away with us, and also our lives passed away like as it were unto us a dream, we being a lonesome and a solemn people, wanderers, cast out from Jerusalem, born in tribulation, in a wilderness, and hated of our brethren". (Jacob 7:26). Perhaps the past is prologue, after all. (See Commentary Reference to Alma 43:1).

The eldest son of Alma had been Helaman, whose own son was named Helaman as well, and it was he upon whom the sacred records and emblems of authority were now conferred. (V. 11). In addition, "all those engravings which were in the possession of Helaman were written and sent forth among the children of men throughout all the land, save it were those parts which had been commanded by Alma should not go forth". (V. 12, see Alma 37:27-32). In other words, Helaman thought it expedient that the Nephites have their own personal copies of the scriptures. It would be fascinating if some fragmentary evidence of these scriptures had survived in a Meso-American Codex. In the mid-Sixteenth Century, Franciscan missionaries burned nearly all of the Maya's written records in an effort to eradicate their religion. Today, only a handful of codices survive.

The Book of Alma ends on a note of uncertainty, with Nephite dissenters again crossing over to the Lamanites after only four years of peace. These apostates were likely responsible for stirring up to anger the Lamanites in the Land of Nephi, for an army emerged from the wilderness that was repulsed in the Land of Zarahemla by the army of Moronihah, the warrior son of Moroni. (V. 14-15).

Observations

The Book of
Mormon was designed to
nudge us off our complacency
plateaus, as we steer away from
the trendy cafés situated along
the broad avenues of Idumea.
It transports us as upon the
wings of eagles beyond the
boundaries of our self-
imposed limitations
along a highway
that leads all
the way to
heaven.

As
we discover
more about The
Book of Mormon
and our circles of
wisdom expand, so
also do the borders of
darkness. The more we
know, the more we need
to learn. It should do no
violence to our faith if we
realize that, with a greater
understanding of doctrinal
truths, there might still be
additional questions that
relate to the mysteries of
the kingdom, to which
we could turn our
attention.

In moments
of weakness, we may
allow ourselves to act as do
adults. We may be distracted
from the principles of The Book
of Mormon, thinking that we are
putting away childish things. But
we'll sacrifice to a degree our ability
to express ourselves naturally, and
with an unrestrained spontaneity.
Similarly, when we stop seeing
the world through the eye
of faith, we can lose
our joie de
vivre.

Those who have
learned to swim with
sharks are characterized
as "seasoned veterans," and
yet, the process fails to tenderize
them. Instead, it curses them with a
thick skin containing few sensory
nerve endings, leaving them with
dangerously little room for the
nurturing influence that The
Book of Mormon could
have provided.

The shield of faith
that is provided by our
familiarity with Book of
Mormon guiding principles
safeguards us from the worldly
contaminants and the cankering
influences of material prosperity,
as well as from the temptation
to fill space with the telestial
trinkets that can so easily
corrupt our souls if they
are not handled with
prayer, care, and
discretion.

The doctrines
that are emphasized
within The Book of Mormon
can serve to disinfect us from
the caustic influence of Idumea,
while decontaminating us from
the toxicity that is so prevalent
in the world. They neutralize
the homogenization process
that occurs when we are
tossed to and fro by
both the vagaries
of men and the
vicissitudes
of life.

When we think of the
multitude of angels who
are thinly disguised as our
families and friends, who have
helped us in our efforts to embrace
The Book of Mormon, we recall the
counsel of Sir Isaac Newton, who,
when pressed to reveal the secret
behind his accomplishments,
simply replied: "I stood
on the shoulders of
giants."

The
Book
of Mormon
reaffirms the
Lord Jesus Christ
as the Father of our
spiritual regeneration,
and like the parent we all
aspire to be, He will be there
to bind our wounds and heal
our infirmities every time we
stumble and whenever we fall
because of the weight we have
been trying to carry all by
ourselves. Even though we
may not remember Him,
the Savior will never
forget about
us.

Divine tutorial training is essential to Book of Mormon scholarship, and embraces the trials we all face. It views them as nothing but pop quizzes in the learning laboratory of life. It prepares us for the final exam that will come after the conclusion of our mortal curriculum. The word "Atonement" begins with the letter A which is the grade that we should all receive for our efforts. The paper that we submit to our Mentor, and that has been entitled "Our Dissertation on Life" will be marked by Him in red pencil, to symbolize His blood that has been shed for the sins of all of our Heavenly Father's children. If a golden star were ever to be awarded in recognition of achievement, it would most deservedly be given to Him.

Who would
consciously choose to
lead a marginalized life, or
to become spiritually depleted
on a personal or an institutional
level? We perish because our faith has
failed us. But how many of us have the
courage to realize that it is the other way
around; that it is we who have failed our
faith in The Book of Mormon? Luckily,
if we are blessed with the gift of time,
we can change all that, starting
right now. Carpe diem!

The Nephites quickly learned that when we sling mud, we lose ground. If we hope to successfully deal with the inequalities of life and escape the quicksand of self-pity, we must change our nature and become new creatures in Christ who are light on their feet and quick to respond to His counsel.

Personal revelation lies at the foundation of the living, vital, quickened Gospel of Jesus Christ, and it is a cornerstone of a deep and abiding faith in The Book of Mormon. And so it is, that with our preparation of faith and His quiet sensitivity, the Holy Ghost whispers that it is time for action, for many are called, but few there be that are chosen to testify of the divinity of the work.

As we
embrace The Book
of Mormon, precious
emanations of familiar
and soothing oscillations
of energy that resonate from
within the limitless reserves of
the Spirit will be selflessly shared
by the Holy Ghost, Who will carry us
along on rolling waves of revelation
toward a shoreline of stability that
nurtures a more sure and abiding
witness of the divinity of the
Savior of the world.

If we could embrace the spiritual equivalent of the Weight Watchers program, we would have less trouble sleeping, less difficulty focusing, and less of a problem concentrating on the principles of the Gospel that are clearly defined in The Book of Mormon.

Engaging in conduct that was sinful might have seemed to be fashionable to the wicked Lamanites, but unlike the principles and doctrine of The Book of Mormon, styles are ephemeral and can turn on a dime. Even the Nephites should have listened to the warning: "There's no time like the present, and no present like time, and life can be over in the space of a rhyme." (Georgia Byng).

The
Plan of
God provided
both the Nephites
and Lamanites with
the means to reset their
spiritual appestat whenever
they noticed that it was out
of whack and they found
themselves indulging,
and even binge
eating, in
sin.

We know from the scriptural
casualty count that the ideological
warfare following Lucifer's disruption of a
heavenly council resulted in a rebellious third
part of Father's children losing their privilege
to be clothed in bodies. (See 2 Nephi 24:12).
For those who remained faithful during
the pre-earth existence, however, came
humbling liabilities, and so the
Plan required our Creator to
die for our sins, only
conditional upon
repentance.

It was thru the Atonement,
Jacob taught, that the Nephites
could receive the kinds of immortal
bodies that they would need in the
resurrection, if they were to hope
to thrive in celestial fire.
(See Jacob 4:11).

Repentance provided a
way for the Nephites to increase
their metaphysical metabolism, that
they might burn off as much of the
fat of faithlessness as they could,
when their hearts were broken
in the fiery hot crucible
of contrition.

Without the
shield of protection
that is provided by our
obedience to the principles of
The Book of Mormon, we are at a
greater risk of strangling ourselves
with material temptations whose opacity
obstructs our ability to see how God has
so thoughtfully laid out before us the
smorgasbord of life, inviting us to
freely partake of its delights
with only a few words of
dietary caution.

The
Nephites'
innate desire
to be clean found
expression in celestial
sparks that ignited their
sense of urgency to repent.

As Edmund Dantès
observed on the concluding
pages of Alexandere Dumas' "The
Count of Monte Cristo," "only a man
who has felt ultimate despair is capable
of feeling ultimate bliss. It is necessary to
have wished for death, in order to know how
good it is to live. Live then, and be happy, and
never forget that, until the day God deigns to
reveal the future, the sum of human wisdom
will be contained in these words: wait and
hope." We wait and hope, with faith in The
Book of Mormon, and in its legal tender
that is all the currency we will need to
purchase the golden tickets for our
passage on a train that is bound
for the glory of our celestial
home, with our Father
in Heaven.

A pulsing
arpeggio ignites our
souls with passion, and
quickens our testimonies of
The Book of Mormon. It is this
catalyzing inspiration that was
conspicuously missing from the
pedantic charade of righteous
behavior that was embraced
by the Pharisees of old,
and that is present in
so many circles
even today.

The
Book of Mormon
generates repetitive
opportunities to smell
the delicious aroma of
the bread of life that is
baking in a heavenly
oven, as we steadily
move along on the
path that leads to
the threshold of
our celestial
home.

At its core, the doctrine of Christ (2 Nephi 32:6) becomes a perfectly liberating law that allows us to reach our potential in a mutually supportive atmosphere of interdependency with the Savior.

When we pray about
The Book of Mormon, there
are alarm bells in heaven that are
triggered to harness the immediate
and undivided attention of our
Father, Jesus Christ, and
the Holy Ghost.

The Book of
Mormon envisions a
Utopian society, but it
also provides repentance
as a practical solution for
for those whose agency
has led them away
from the Rod
of Iron.

450

People think
that they can be
happy if they wander
and play, forgetting that
a key feature of The Plan
is to ponder and pray, which
thing leads them to appreciate
The Book of Mormon. Only then
will they find the happiness
that has been prepared
for the Saints.

Today, the
electronic media
gets in the way of
our relationship with
the Holy Ghost that has
always been fundamental
to the successful execution
of Moroni's promise to those
who are prayerfully and
carefully reading The
Book of Mormon.

The Book
of Mormon is like a
chiropractic adjustment
to treat spiritual scoliosis.
It heals us and strengthens
our backs, that we might be
strong and healthy enough
to bear the crosses of the
world without a single
word of complaint.

The Book of Mormon's power is that it has the depth, breadth, height, and capacity, in short, the might and majesty, within which all of God's children may be enveloped within His tender embrace.

Over the years, our Father
in Heaven has gotten to know
us quite well, and has taken care to
provide for our welfare, as we shoot the
rapids of life. The protective vest that we
call The Book of Mormon can help us
to keep our heads above water as
we struggle to breathe in the
turbulence of telestial
torrents.

Obedience to the principles that are espoused by Book of Mormon prophets gives us the capacity to stretch our spiritual muscles to their divine potential, uninhibited by the restraints and limitations that accompany poor choices.

As long as the
life vest of The Book of
Mormon remains securely
in position and tight against
our chest, we will be prepared to
deal with whatever challenges the
rapids of life might choose to throw
our way. As a necessary contrary,
high water can even be our friend,
as it propels us down the river of
life, swiftly carrying us over
rocks and in the direction
direction of our
dreams.

Even when
we feel that we are fully
engaged, our recommitment to
the regular study of The Book of
Mormon can bless us with repetitive
moments of confirmation when we can
say, as did members of the Church in
Zarahemla, that through the miracle
of forgiveness our hearts have once
again been changed through
faith on the name of
Christ.

If we allow ourselves
to become isolated from the
sensitivity to our surroundings
that is nurtured by repentance, we
may become inured to our condition
in the sense that we are past feeling.
(See 1 Nephi 19:9). If that is so, the
power of the Atonement is of no
effect and the Savior suffered
in the Garden of Gethsemane
and died on the Cross at
Calvary, for naught.

The influence of the Light of Christ encourages us to fix our sights on true north and on the one book that has been calculated to lift us to higher plateaus of personal progress. Work we must, but book-group is free. The one that we're studying now is focused on the Savior of the world.

As we follow
the path that leads
to happiness, we make
frequent stops at sites that
are prominently marked by
signs inviting us to pause for
repentance and refreshment, as
we recommit ourselves to proven
principles. These travelers' aids
have been clearly identified
throughout The Book
of Mormon.

Satan
uses telestial
trivia relying on the
treasures of the earth as
counterfeit pleasures for the
prescription of God's Plan that is
found within The Book of Mormon,
and that identifies the steps we must
take if we wish to follow the one true
pathway that leads to lasting
happiness.

When we determine to make our study of The Book of Mormon a regular habit, the Holy Spirit gives us fire for the deed.

The
vision of
our potential is
unclouded by the
myopia of manner,
the cloudy cataracts
of convention, or by the
presbyopia of procedure.
When we are at our very
best, and in particular
if we have determined
to follow the counsel
found in The Book
of Mormon, we can
appreciate the all-
seeing eye of
Jehovah.

Author's Note

The Book of Mormon is a blueprint for our survival in The Last Days. It helps us to become the architects of our own fate and the masters of our destiny; to be as "children coming down like gentle rain through darkened skies, with glory trailing from our feet as we go, and endless promise in our eyes. We are strangers from a realm of light, who have forgotten all - the memory of our former life and the purpose of our call." But with the help of The Book of Mormon, we may learn why we're here, and who we really are. (Doug Stewart, "Saturday's Warrior," adapted).

The Book of Mormon allowed the Restoration to move forward and the Church to be organized. It gave us the gift of a fifth gospel (3 Nephi) that summarizes Christ's ministry in the New World. It fulfilled the prophecies of Isaiah and Ezekiel. (See Isaiah 29:14 & Ezekiel 37:16-17). It has empowered Church members to stand out prominently among their Christian neighbors, and it has endowed them with an element of singularity that distinguishes them from other Christian denominations, allowing the line in the sand separating the faithful from the world to be more clearly defined.

Because of The Book of Mormon, those who make their home in Idumea are differentiated from those who embrace the gospel. It gives its believers symmetry, balance, harmony, clarity, focus, and purpose. It illustrates stories of inspiration that touch them personally and individually, and it blesses them with truth in untarnished majesty that may be proclaimed without qualification or apology to the world. Those who read it unleash the unrestrained power of the Holy Ghost. Their lives are touched by invention, investigation, innovation, insight, intuition, and inspiration, whose catalyst is the Spirit.

Because of The Book of Mormon, we have another witness of Christ, and we learn to rely on Him not only as our protector but also as the generator of life itself. It provides a standard by which we may judge the Bible, and it describes a weapon that is more powerful than military might. Within its pages, the essential ordinance of baptism is re-defined, and the army of God is equipped with superior firepower as it teaches the nations with the word of God. Those who read it draw upon the life experiences of heroes from the past, and learn life-lessons from their own similar challenges.

Because of mentors in The Book of Mormon, we can better understand the saving principles and ordinances of the Gospel. With their profound spiritual insight, we discover who our Savior is, and we learn more about ourselves. With a correct understanding of the Fall, of repentance, and of the Atonement, we are no longer held hostage by guilt, but instead feel the sweet miracle of forgiveness. The Book of Mormon guides us to horns of sanctuary that are our refuge from a violent world, and it shows us how to be born again. It gives us the confidence to feel the tender mercies of God, experience His magnificent grace, find our way home, and obtain His Rest.

Without The Book of Mormon, the Church could not have been organized. So important is The Book of Mormon, that The Church of Jesus Christ of Latter-day Saints was only organized immediately following its publication. Fully ten years earlier, Joseph Smith had communed with The Father and The Son in the Sacred Grove. Three years later, he received several visits from the Angel Moroni. Between 1823 and 1830, he became personally acquainted with all of the important characters in The Book of Mormon and enjoyed additional visits from Moroni. Still, so important was The Book of Mormon to the Restoration of the Gospel, that the Church was not organized until it was hot off the press.

Without The Book of Mormon record, we would have no corroborating evidence that Christ fulfilled His promise to feed His other sheep. "Other sheep I have, which are not of this fold," He had said. "Them also I must bring, and they shall hear my voice; and there shall be one fold, and one shepherd." (John 10:16).

"And if ye shall believe in Christ ye will believe in these words, for they are the words of Christ, and he hath given them unto me; and they teach all men that they should do good. And if they are not the words of Christ, judge ye - for Christ will show unto you, with power and great glory, that they are his words, at the last day; and you and I shall stand face to face before his bar; and ye shall know that I have been commanded of him to write these things." (2 Nephi 33:10-11).

Without The Book of Mormon, prophecy would not have been fulfilled. The words of Christ are made known in The Book of Mormon, as well as in the Bible," and they have been "established in one." (1 Nephi 13:41). As Ezekiel wrote: "Take thee one stick, and write upon it, For Judah, and for the children of Israel his companions: then take another stick, and write upon it, For Joseph, the stick of Ephraim, and for all the house of Israel his companions. And join them one to another into one stick; and they shall become one in thine hand." (Ezekiel 37:16-17).

2,500 years before the visit by Moroni to Joseph Smith, Isaiah prophesied of the Lord's ministry: "I will proceed to do a marvellous work among this people, even a marvellous work and a wonder." (Isaiah 29:14). God did so with the translation, publication, and distribution of The Book of Mormon.

Without The Book of Mormon, Church members would stand out far less prominently as Christians. The great Book of Mormon prophet Benjamin exhorted: "I would that ye should take upon you the name of Christ, all you that have entered into the covenant with God that ye should be obedient unto the end of your lives. And it shall come to pass that whosoever doeth this shall be found at the right hand of God, for he shall know the name by which he is called; for he shall be called by the name of Christ." (Mosiah 5:8-10).

Without The Book of Mormon, the Church would lose much of its prominent singularity. "Take away the Book of Mormon and the revelations, and where is our religion? We have none." (Joseph Smith, Teachings, p. 71). The Book of Mormon sets Latter-day Saints apart as a peculiar people. To be peculiar in a biblical sense is to be "one's very own, exclusive, or special." (Bible Dictionary). Moroni told Joseph Smith: "Wherever the sound (of the Restoration) shall go it shall cause the ears of men to tingle, and wherever it shall be proclaimed, the pure in heart shall rejoice." ("Latter Day Saints' Messenger and Advocate", 2/ 1835, p. 79-80).

Without The Book of Mormon, Joshua's line in the sand would be far less clearly defined. Mormon observed "that after a people have been once enlightened by the Spirit of God, and have had great knowledge of things pertaining to righteousness, and then have fallen away into sin and transgression, they become more hardened, and thus their state becomes worse than though they had never known these things." (Alma 24:30).

Joseph Fielding Smith, Jr. cautioned the Saints: "When you joined the Church you enlisted to serve God. When you did that, you left the neutral ground, and you can never get back on to it. Should you forsake the Master you enlisted to serve, it will be by the instigation of the evil one, and you will follow his dictation and be his servant." (C.E.S. Manual, p. 258).

Without The Book of Mormon, we would have fewer negative examples of those who embrace darkness rather than the Gospel. Mormon said of those who did not belong to the Church, that they "did indulge themselves in sorceries, and in idolatry or idleness, and in babblings, and in envyings and strife, wearing costly apparel, being lifted up in the pride of their own eyes; persecuting, lying, thieving, robbing, committing whoredoms, and murdering, and all manner of wickedness." (Alma 1:32).

Without The Book of Mormon, we would have less symmetry, balance, harmony, clarity, focus, and purpose in our lives. President Ezra Taft Benson told the Saints that a Church member who does not study The Book of Mormon, "is placing their soul in jeopardy and neglecting that which could give spiritual and intellectual unity to their whole life". (C.R., 4/1975).

Without The Book of Mormon, we would have fewer stories of inspiration that touch us personally and individually. From within its pages, we can almost hear Moroni's voice: "Behold, I speak unto you as if ye were present, and yet ye are not. But behold, Jesus Christ hath shown you unto me, and I know your doing." (Mormon 8:35).

Without The Book of Mormon, there would be less truth in the world. The Book of Mormon "was written to be believed. Its one and only merit is truth. Without that merit, it is all that nonbelievers say it is. With it, it is all that believers say it is." (Hugh Nibley. "Of All Things," p. 93). Although it is the rule, as Washington Irving observed, that "history fades into fable; fact becomes clouded with doubt and controversy; the inscription moulders from the tablet; the statue falls from the pedestal," and that "columns, arches, pyramids are but heaps of sand, and their epitaphs, nothing but characters written in the dust," yet The Book of Mormon stands as a shining example of the divine model.

Without The Book of Mormon, we would miss, terribly, its witness of truth. The Book of Mormon "illumines reality, vitalizes memory, provides guidance in daily life, and brings us tidings of antiquity." It is "the evidence of time, the light of truth, the life of memory, the directress of life, the herald of antiquity, committed to immortality." (Cicero, "De Oratore," ii, 36). On its pages, "the centuries roll back to the ancient age of gold." (Horace, "Odes," IV, ii, 39).

Without The Book of Mormon, we would lack a sure witness of Jesus Christ. "For behold, (The Book of Mormon) is written for the intent that ye may believe (the Bible); and if ye believe (the Bible) ye will believe (The Book of Mormon) also; and if ye believe (The Book of Mormon) ye will know concerning your fathers, and also the marvelous works which were wrought by the power of God among them." (Mormon 7:9).

Without The Book of Mormon, we would have fewer opportunities to learn how to rely on the Savior. "No one can lift themselves to celestial glory. Our growth depends on the light of Christ, guidance of the Holy Ghost, and the power of the priesthood that is given us by God and his Son. The religion of Jesus Christ is not just a philosophy of life; it is the generator of life. If you go it alone, you cannot succeed. If you receive His power, you will increase and make it. There is no other way." (Sunday School Course Manual).

Without The Book of Mormon, we would lose an excellent standard by which to judge the Bible and other scriptures. For example, we would not have the Lord's teachings to the Nephites that are similar to His Sermon on The Mount, and we would lack the powerful recitations of Isaiah and of Malachi that are reiterated in its pages. In fact, "The Book of Mormon is the keystone of our religion and the most correct book ever written, and (we) can draw nearer to God by abiding by its precepts than any other book." (Joseph Smith)

Without The Book of Mormon, to what other body of scripture would we turn to emphasize the powerful premise that the pen is mightier than the sword? President Benson urged us to recommit ourselves to a study of The Book of Mormon. "If you do so," he promised, "you will find, as Alma did, that 'the word (has) a great tendency to lead the people to do that which is just - yea, it (has) more powerful effect upon the minds of the people than the sword, or anything else which (has) happened to them.' (Alma 31:5)." (C.R., 4/1986).

Without The Book of Mormon, where would we go to learn so clearly that one must have authority to administer the ordinances of the Gospel? Alma and his sons "preached the word, and the truth, according to the spirit of prophecy and revelation; and they preached after the holy order of God by which they were called." (Alma 43:2). If all churches were equal, then the true Church would not exist anywhere. If, in education, any program were the equal of any other, then receiving any degree would be based upon an indiscriminate course of study that would qualify the recipient in all fields of study. But this is contrary to the order of God.

Without The Book of Mormon there would be confusion regarding the ordinance of baptism. "The first fruits of repentance is baptism; and baptism cometh by faith unto the fulfilling the commandments; and the fulfilling the commandments bringeth remission of sins; and the remission of sins bringeth meekness, and lowliness of heart; and because of meekness and lowliness of heart cometh the visitation of the Holy Ghost, which Comforter filleth with hope and perfect love, which love endureth by diligence unto prayer, until the end shall come, when all the saints shall dwell with God." (Moroni 8:25-26).

Without The Book of Mormon, the soldiers in the army of Christ could not so easily preach, teach, expound, and exhort, as they bear witness of Christ. Mormon explained that The Sons of Mosiah "had given themselves to much prayer, and fasting; therefore, they had the spirit of prophecy, and the spirit of revelation, and when they taught, they taught with the power and authority of God." (Alma 17:3). "God help all honest men," said Marion G. Romney, "to be born again and come to be of sound understanding and to know the word of God and maintain the spirit thereof by study, fasting, prayer, and work, that we may be blessed with His power and authority!" (C.R., 10/1941).

Without The Book of Mormon, we might well lack the confidence to proclaim the Gospel. Through Isaiah, the Lord said: "Then shall ye, who are a remnant of the house of Jacob, go forth among (the nations); and ye shall be in the midst of them who shall be many; and ye shall be among them as a lion among the beasts of the forest, and as a young lion among the flocks of sheep, who, if he goeth through both treadeth down and teareth in pieces, and none can deliver." (3 Nephi 20:16).

Armed with The Book of Mormon, the mighty missionary army of the Lord's Church is "clear as the moon, and fair as the sun, and terrible as an army with banners." (D&C 5:14). "The nations of the earth shall tremble because of her, and shall fear because of her terrible ones." (D&C 64:43). "And it shall be said among the wicked: Let us not go up to battle against Zion, for the inhabitants of Zion are terrible; wherefore we cannot stand." (D&C 45:70). "Fear may seize upon them, and they shall stand afar off and tremble. And all nations shall be afraid because of the terror of the Lord, and the power of his might." (D&C 45:74-75).

Without The Book of Mormon, we would know nothing of the life experiences of so many others of God's children, who are so much like ourselves. "Behold, this is a choice land, and whatsoever nation shall possess it shall be free from bondage, and from captivity, and from all other nations under heaven if they will but serve the God of the land, who is Jesus Christ." (Ether 2:12). Without The Book of Mormon, it would be more difficult to understand that "happiness is the object and design of our existence, and will be the end thereof, if we follow the path that leads to it, and this consists of faith, virtue, uprightness, and keeping all the commandments of God." (Joseph Smith).

Without The Book of Mormon, to whom would we turn for mentors such as Captain Moroni? "Yea, verily, verily I say unto you, if all men had been, and were, and ever would be, like unto Moroni, behold, the very powers of hell would have been shaken forever; yea, the devil would never have power over the hearts of the children of men." (Alma 48:17). We would never have known men like Nephi, Jacob, Benjamin, Alma, The Sons of Mosiah, Abinadi, Helaman, and Samuel The Lamanite. We would miss the anticipation of striking hands with them when we meet at the pleasing bar of Christ. (See Jacob 6:13, 2 Nephi 33:15 & Moroni 10:27).

Without The Book of Mormon, there would be a conspicuously empty space on the bookshelf of time, instead of a prominently displayed chronicle written especially for our age. Hugh Nibley observed: "It is an exciting thing to discover that the man Lehi was a real historical character ... but it is far more important and significant to find oneself in this Twentieth Century standing as it were in his very shoes." ("The World and The Prophets," p. 196).

Without The Book of Mormon, we would less effectively cope with the mysteries of God, which are the saving principles and ordinances of the Gospel, received by the faithful through personal revelation. They are sacred. It is given unto many to know these mysteries, "nevertheless they are laid under a strict command that they shall not impart only according to the portion of his word which he doth grant unto the children of men, according to the need and diligence which they give unto him." (Alma 12:9). In other words, by judiciously exercising their knowledge of gospel principles that are explained in The Book of Mormon, the faithful can benefit from spiritual insight while at the same time guarding pearls that might otherwise be cast before swine, or trampled underfoot. (Matthew 7:6).

King Benjamin's discourse in The Book of Mosiah is a classic example of a General Conference type of address wherein the saving principles were unfolded to the membership of the Church. When we read his words, faithfully recorded verbatim by the prophet-historian Mormon, it is clear that he was concerned that his people might trifle with the words that he should speak. He recognized the serious nature of his topic, and wanted them to hearken to him, or pay strict attention, and to open their ears to listen carefully, and their hearts to feel the Spirit of his message, and their minds to understand. (Mosiah 2:9). This episode is one of many in The Book of Mormon that illustrate how the mysteries of God may be unfolded to our view. We have the testimony of Christ Himself that The Book of Mormon contains a comprehensive body of doctrine, "even the fullness of (His) everlasting gospel." (D&C 27:5).

Armed with The Book of Mormon, the Lord told Joseph Smith and Sydney Rigdon: "The time has verily come (December 1, 1831) that it is necessary and expedient in me that you should open your mouths in proclaiming my gospel, the things of the kingdom, expounding the mysteries thereof out of the scriptures according to that portion of the Spirit and power which shall be given unto you." (D&C 71:1). Joseph described his subsequent experience in these words: "Our minds being now enlightened, we began to have the scriptures laid open to our understandings, and the true meaning and intention of their more mysterious passages revealed unto us in a manner which we never could attain to previously, nor ever before had thought of." (J.S.H. 1:74).

To the faithful, the Lord promised: "I will reveal all mysteries, yea, all the hidden mysteries of my kingdom from days of old, and for ages to come." (D&C 76:7). Nevertheless, there were certain points of doctrine that were not yet clear. To his son, Alma declared: "Now these mysteries are not yet fully made known unto me; therefore, I shall forbear." (Alma 37:11). He felt that it was always better to keep one's opinion to oneself, rather than to speculate without the foundation of fact or specific revelation. Sometimes it is better to remain silent and be thought a fool, rather than to speak and remove all doubt.

Without The Book of Mormon, we would know far less about the purpose of life. "And now, I would commend you to seek this Jesus of whom the prophets and apostles have written, that the grace of God the Father, and also the Lord Jesus Christ, and the Holy Ghost, which beareth record of them, may be and abide in you forever." (Moroni, in Ether 12:41). Because of this book, we know that "Adam fell that men might be, and men are, that they might have joy," (2 Nephi 2:25), that "wickedness never was happiness," (Alma 41:10), and that we must hold "fast to the rod of iron". (1 Nephi 8:30). We are counseled: "Watch yourselves, and your thoughts, and your words, and your deeds". (Mosiah 4:30). But we also know: "By the power of the Holy Ghost, (we) may know the truth of all things," (Moroni 10:5), and that "when (we) are in the service of (our) fellow beings, (we) are only in the service of (our) God." (Mosiah 2:17).

Without The Book of Mormon, personal accountability would receive far less emphasis. It teaches that we "are free according to the flesh, and all things are given (to us) which are expedient unto men. And (we) are free to choose liberty and eternal life, through the great Mediator of all men, or to choose captivity and death, according to the captivity and power of the devil." (2 Nephi 2:27)

Without the unequivocal teachings in The Book of Mormon that are related to the Atonement of Jesus Christ, guilt might hold our future hostage. "Do ye suppose that ye shall dwell with (Heavenly Father) under a consciousness of your guilt?" asked Moroni. "Do ye suppose that ye could be happy to dwell with that holy Being, when your souls are racked with a consciousness of guilt that ye have ever abused his laws?" (Mormon 9:3).

Without The Book of Mormon, the tender mercies of the Savior, and the sweet miracle of forgiveness might be less lovingly treated. (See 1 Nephi 1:20, 8:8 & Ether 6:12). Fortified by Mormon's discourse on faith, hope, and charity, The Book of Mormon reports that "as oft as (the disciples of Christ) repented and sought forgiveness, with real intent, they were forgiven." (Moroni 6:8)

Without The Book of Mormon, we might be less likely to find peace in a violent world. Its gift is the peace of the Savior of the world, "not the peace of ease, of luxury, idleness, absence of turmoil, and strife, but the peace born of the righteous life, the peace that lifts the soul, that day by day brings us closer to the home of Eternal Peace, the dwelling place of our Father." (J. Reuben Clark, Jr.)

Without The Book of Mormon, we might not clearly understand that we have been born again. Those who enter into the Covenant "are born of him." (Mosiah 5:7). "All mankind ... must be born again, yea, born of God, changed from their carnal and fallen state, to a state of righteousness, being redeemed of God, becoming his sons and daughters." (Mosiah 27:25). A "Born Again Christian" is one who is in a covenant relationship with the Lord, and since only members of Christ's true Church can accomplish that by revelation and through the authority of the priesthood, if follows that the only real Born Again Christians are those who have a testimony of the divine authenticity of The Book of Mormon and follow its revelatory teachings that lead to faith, repentance, baptism, and the receipt of the Holy Ghost.

Without The Book of Mormon, we might not recognize the signs that confirm we have been born again. "And now behold, I ask of you, my brethren of the church, have ye spiritually been born of God? Have ye received his image in your countenances? Have ye experienced this mighty change in your hearts?" (Alma 5:14).

Without The Book of Mormon, finding our way home would be much more difficult. "Think of stepping on shore and finding it heaven. Of taking hold of a hand and finding it God's hand. Of breathing a new air and finding it celestial air. Of feeling invigorated and finding it immortality. Of passing from storm and tempest to the unbroken calm of God's Rest. Of waking up, and finding it Home." (Anonymous).

Without following the teachings and admonitions that are found within the pages of The Book of Mormon, we could not attain God's Rest. "We live in a day and in a world full of doubts and confusion, where people do not know what to believe, where tensions are high, where the pace is frantic and progress in terms of righteousness is not a popular goal. Violence and crudity are everyday patterns all around us. What a blessing it is to know there is a haven, a place of rest from the turmoil of the world. The prophets and the Savior have called upon us to enter into the rest of the Lord, where life has purpose and direction, and where priesthood power is possible." ("Gospel Doctrine Manual," p. 79)

Without The Book of Mormon, we might never know the truth of all things. (See Moroni 10:5). "He that will not harden his heart," taught Alma, "to him is given the greater portion of the word, until it is given unto him to know the mysteries of God, until he know them in full." (Alma 12:10).

The Book of Mormon contains a unique promise, found nowhere else in scripture. Moroni's formula is simple: "And when ye shall receive these things, I would exhort you that ye would ask God, the Eternal Father, in the name of Christ, if these things are not true; and if ye shall ask with a sincere heart, with real intent, having faith in Christ, he will manifest the truth of it unto you, by the power of the Holy Ghost. And by the power of the Holy Ghost ye may know the truth of all things." (Moroni 10:4-5).

Moroni firmly believed that it is the power of God that works miracles in our lives. He knew that the Light of Christ, sometimes called the Spirit of God or the Holy Spirit, and the Holy Ghost have been provided to nurture religious recognition leading to conversion. Therefore, he urged those who would read and study The Book of Mormon to "deny not the gifts of God, for they are many." (Moroni 10:8). All these gifts, he said, "are given by the manifestations of the Spirit of God unto men (and women), to profit them." (Moroni 10:8).

Without The Book of Mormon, there would be less joy in the world. Mormon said of those living after the ministry of the Savior among the Nephites: "Behold, there never was a happier time among the people of Nephi, since the days of Nephi, than in the days of Moroni." (Alma 50:23). Our day is also a wonderful time to be alive. A millennial era approaches. "How do you prepare for the Second Coming?" asked President Gordon B. Hinckley. "Well, you just do not worry about it. You just live the kind of life that, if the Second Coming were to happen tomorrow, you would be ready. Nobody knows what is going to happen. Our responsibility is to prepare ourselves, to live worthy of the association of the Savior, to deport ourselves in such a way that we would not be embarrassed if He were to come among us." ("Church News", 1/2/1999, p. 2).

Without The Book of Mormon, there would be less hope in the world. "Teenagers sometimes ask: "What's the use?" said Boyd K. Packer. "The world will soon be blown all apart and come to an end." That feeling comes from fear, not from faith. No one knows the hour or the day, but the end cannot come until all of the purposes of the Lord are fulfilled. Everything that I have learned from the revelations and from life convinces me that there is time and to spare for you to carefully prepare for a long life. One day you will cope with teenage children of your own. That will serve you right. Later, you will spoil your grandchildren, and they, in turn, will spoil theirs." (C.R., 4/89).

The scripture may yet be written that there never was a happier time among the children of men, than among those who had developed the habit of carefully and prayerfully studying The Book of Mormon, and using the principles taught therein, to guide them with safe passage through perilous times.

It is
heartbreaking when
children of God who have
matriculate in the curriculum
of the Gospel and have embraced
The Book of Mormon cannot sustain
their saving faith. They set their sights
too low, too easily reaching watered-down
objectives. They no longer stretch themselves,
and rarely venture out of the supposed comfort
zones to which they have retreated. They have
precious little to show for their consistently
timid efforts that deny the faith and
have become the 'face' of their
habitual expressions.

Addendum
A Sampling of Scriptures
(Mosiah - Alma)

"It came to pass that after
Mosiah had done as his father
had commanded him, and had made
a proclamation throughout all the land,
that the people gathered themselves together
throughout all the land, that they might
go up to the temple to hear the words
which king Benjamin should
speak unto them."
(Mosiah 2:1).

"And now I ask, can ye
say aught of yourselves? I answer
you, Nay. Ye cannot say that ye are
even as much as the dust of the earth;
yet ye were created of the dust of the
earth; but behold, it belongeth
to him who created you."
(Mosiah 2:25).

"Salvation cometh to none such
except it be through repentance and faith
on the Lord Jesus Christ. And the Lord God hath
sent his holy prophets among all the children of men, to
declare these things to every kindred, nation, and tongue,
that thereby whosoever should believe that Christ should come,
the same might receive remission of their sins, and rejoice
with exceedingly great joy." (Mosiah 3:12-13).

"Many signs, and wonders, and types, and shadows showed he unto them, concerning his coming, and also holy prophets spake unto them concerning his coming."
(Mosiah 3:15).

"The natural man is
an enemy to God, and has
been from the fall of Adam, and
will be forever and ever, until he yields
to the enticings of the Holy Spirit, and
putteth off the natural man and becometh
a saint through the atonement of Christ, the
Lord, and becometh as a child, submissive,
meek, humble, patient, full of love, willing
to submit to all things which the Lord
seeth fit to inflict upon him, even as
a child doth submit to his
father". (Mosiah 3:19).

"Believe in God; believe that he is, and that he created all things, both in heaven and in earth." (Mosiah 4:9).

"Are we
not all beggars? Do
we not all depend upon
the same Being, even God,
for all the substance which we
have, both food and raiment,
and for gold, and for silver,
and for all the riches which
we have of every kind?"
(Mosiah 4:19).

"He has poured out his Spirit upon you, and has caused that your hearts should be filled with joy, and has caused that your mouths should be stopped that ye could not find utterance, so exceedingly great was your joy. And ... God, who has created you, on whom you are dependent for your lives and for all that ye have and are, doth grant unto you whatsoever ye ask that is right, in faith, believing that ye shall receive." (Mosiah 4:20-21).

"See that all … things
are done in wisdom and order;
for it is not requisite that a man should
run faster than he has strength And again,
it is expedient that he should be diligent, that
thereby he might win the prize; therefore,
all things must be done in order."
(Mosiah 4:27).

Even when life was good,
the Nephites remained unclean in
the sight of God because they were unable,
of themselves, to remove the stain of sin from
their holy garments as long as they refused to
maintain undeviating obedience to the
celestial principle of repentance.
(See Mosiah 5:5).

"The covenant which
ye have made is a righteous
covenant. And now, because of the
covenant which ye have made, ye shall
be called the children of Christ, his sons,
and his daughters; for behold, this day he
hath spiritually begotten you; for ye say
that your hearts are changed through
faith on his name; therefore, ye are
born of him and have become his
sons and his daughters".
(Mosiah 5:6-7).

"I would that ye should
take upon you the name of Christ,
all you that have entered into the covenant
with God, that ye should be obedient unto the end
of your lives. And it shall come to pass that whosoever
doeth this shall be found at the right hand of God, for he
shall know the name by which he is called; for he shall be
called by the name of Christ. And … whosoever shall not
take upon him the name of Christ must be called by
some other name; therefore, he findeth himself
on the left hand of God." (Mosiah 5:8-10).

"Lift up your heads and rejoice, and put your trust in God, in that God who was the God of Abraham, and Isaac, and Jacob; and also, that God who brought the children of Israel out of the land of Egypt, and caused that they should walk through the Red Sea on dry ground, and fed them with manna, that they might not perish in the wilderness; and many more things did he do for them." (Mosiah 7:19).

"Now Ammon said unto him: I can assuredly tell thee, O king, of a man that can translate the records; for he has wherewith that he can look, and translate all records that are of ancient date; and it is a gift from God … And Ammon said that a seer is a revelator and a prophet also; and a gift which is greater can no man have … But a seer can know of things which are past, and also, of things which are to come, and by them shall all things be revealed, or rather, shall secret things be made manifest, and hidden things shall come to light, and things which are not known shall be made known by them, and also, things shall be made known by them which otherwise could not be known." (Mosiah 8:13 & 16-17).

"They were supported in their laziness, and in their idolatry, and in their whoredoms, by the taxes which king Noah had put upon his people; thus did the people labor exceedingly to support iniquity."
(Mosiah 11:6).

"These are they who have
published peace, who have brought
good tidings of good, who have published
salvation; and said unto Zion: Thy God reigneth!
And O how beautiful upon the mountains were their
feet! And again, how beautiful upon the mountains are
the feet of those that are still publishing peace! And again,
how beautiful upon the mountains are the feet of those who
shall hereafter publish peace, yea, from this time henceforth
and forever! And behold, I say unto you, this is not all. For
O how beautiful upon the mountains are the feet of him
that bringeth good tidings, that is the founder of
peace, yea, even the Lord, who has redeemed
his people; yea, him who has granted
salvation unto his people."
(Mosiah 15:14-18).

"He commanded them
that they should preach nothing
save it were repentance and faith on
the Lord, who had redeemed his people."
(Mosiah 18:20).

"Look forward with one eye,
having one faith and one baptism,
having (your) hearts knit together in
unity and in love, one towards another."
(Mosiah 18:21).

"And now, Alma was their high priest,
he being the founder of their church. And it
came to pass that none received authority to preach
or to teach except it were by him from God. Therefore,
he consecrated all their priests and all their teachers; and
none were consecrated except they were just men ... and it
came to pass that king Mosiah granted unto Alma that
he might establish churches throughout all the land of
Zarahemla; and gave him power to ordain priests
and teachers over every church." (Mosiah
23:16-17 & 25:19).

"The voice of the
Lord came to (Alma) saying ... This
is my church; whosoever is baptized shall be
baptized unto repentance. And whomsoever
ye receive shall believe in my name;
and him will I freely forgive."
(Mosiah 26:14 & 22).

"The Sons of Mosiah were numbered among the unbelievers; and also, one of the sons of Alma ... And he was a man of many words, and did speak much flattery to the people; therefore, he led many of the people to do after the manner of his iniquities. And hoe became a great hinderment to the prosperity of the church of God; stealing away the hearts of the people; causing much dissention among the people; giving a chance for the enemy of God to exercise his power over them."
(Mosiah 27:8-9).

"The angel of the Lord
appeared unto them; and he
descended as it were in a cloud;
and he spake as it were with a voice
of thunder, which caused the earth
to shake upon which they stood."
(Mosiah 27:11).

The Lord told Alma that he should "marvel not that all mankind, yea, men and women, all nations, kindreds, tongues, and people, must be born again; yea, born of God, changed from their carnal and fallen state to a state of righteousness, being redeemed of God, becoming his sons and daughters; and thus," Alma was taught, "they become new creatures; and unless they do this, they can in nowise inherit the kingdom of God". (Mosiah 27:25-26).

"They were desirous that salvation should be declared to every creature, for they could not bear that any human soul should perish … even the very thought that any soul should endure endless torment did cause them to quake and tremble."
(Mosiah 28:3).

"It is better that a man should be judged of God than of man, for the judgments of God are always just, but the judgments of man are not always just. Therefore, if it were possible that you could have just men to be your kings, who would establish the laws of God, and judge this people according to his commandments ... then it would be expedient that you should always have kings to rule over you".
(Mosiah 29:12-13).

"He changed their hearts; yea, he awakened them out of a deep sleep, and they awoke unto God. Behold, they were in the midst of darkness; nevertheless, their souls were illuminated by the light of the everlasting word."
(Alma 5:7).

"I ask of you, my brethren of the church, have ye spiritually been born of God? Have ye received His image in your countenances? Have ye experienced this mighty change in your hearts?" (Alma 5:14).

In all cases, be we Nephites or Lamanites, Jews or Gentiles, Latter-day Saints or Evangelical Christians, spiritual neglect requires drastic action. The plastic surgery of repentance is indicated if we hope to experience a reversal of our fortunes, and if the likeness and image of God is to be reflected in our countenances.
(See Alma 5:14).

"If ye have felt to sing the song of redeeming love, I would ask, can ye feel so now?" (Alma 5:26).

"The things which are to come … are made known unto me by the Holy Spirit of God…. I have fasted and prayed many days that I might know these things of myself. And now I do know of myself that they are true; for the Lord God hath made them manifest unto me by His Holy Spirit; and this is the spirit of revelation which is in me."
(Alma 5:44 & 46).

God "cannot walk
in crooked paths; neither doth
he vary from that which he hath said;
neither hath he a shadow of turning from
the right to the left, or from that which is
right to that which is wrong; therefore,
his course is one eternal round."
(Alma 7:20).

"Satan had gotten great hold upon the hearts of the people of the city of Ammonihah; therefore, they would not hearken unto the words of Alma. Nevertheless, Alma labored much in the spirit, wrestling with God in mighty prayer, that he would pour out his Spirit upon the people who were in the city, that he would also grant that he might baptize them unto repentance." (Alma 8:9-10).

God "would rather
suffer that the Lamanites
might destroy his people who are
called the people of Nephi. (For) after
having had so much light and so much
knowledge given unto them from the Lord
their God; yea, after having been such a highly
favored people of the Lord ... having been visited by
the Spirit if God; having conversed with angels, and
having been spoken unto by the voice of the Lord; and
having the spirit of prophecy and the spirit of revelation,
and also, many gifts ... if this people who have received so
many blessings from the hand of the Lord, should transgress
contrary to the light and knowledge which they do have ... if
they should fall into transgression, it would be far more
tolerable for the Lamanites than for them."
(Alma 9:19-23).

"The spirit and the body shall be reunited again in its perfect form, both limb and joint shall be restored to its proper frame."
(Alma 11:43).

"It was appointed unto men
that they must die; and after death,
they must come to judgment."
(Alma 12:37).

"And this is the manner after which they were ordained – being called and prepared from the foundation of the world according to the foreknowledge of God, on account of their exceeding faith and good works; in the first place being left to choose good or evil."
(Alma 13:3).

"And there was no
inequality among them; the Lord did
pour out his Spirit on the face of the land
to prepare the minds of the children of men,
or to prepare their hearts to receive the word
which should be taught among them
at the time f his coming."
(Alma 16:16).

"Now these sons of Mosiah
were with Alma at the time the angel
first appeared unto him; therefore, Alma did rejoice
exceedingly to see his brethren; and what added more
to his joy, they were still his brethren in the Lord; yea, and
they had waxed strong in the knowledge of the truth; for they
were men of a sound understanding and they had searched
the scriptures diligently, that they might know the word
of God. But this is not all; they had given themselves
to much prayer, and fasting; therefore, they had
the spirit of prophecy and … of revelation, and
when they taught, they taught with the
power and authority of God."
(Alma 17:2-3).

The Sons of Mosiah had been teaching the word of God for fourteen long "years among the Lamanites, having had much success in bringing many to the knowledge of the truth; yea, by the power of their words many were brought before the altar of God, to call on his name and confess their sins before him."
(Alma 17:4).

Ammon "stood by the waters of Sebus ... and began to cast stones at (the Lamanite ruffians) with his sling; yea, with mighty power he did sling stones amongst them; and thus, he slew a certain number of them, insomuch that they began to be astonished at his power". (Alma 17:34 & 36).

"Blessed art thou because of thy exceeding faith; I say unto thee, woman, there has not been such great faith among all the people of the Nephites." (Alma 19:10).

"I will give away all my sins
to know thee, and that I may be raised
from the dead, and be saved at the last day."
(Alma 22:18).

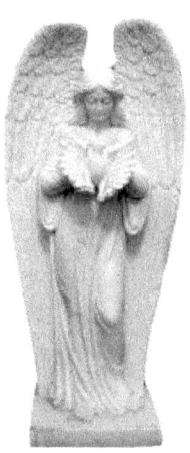

"Now there was not one soul among all the people who had been converted unto the Lord that would take up arms against their brethren; nay, they would not even make any preparations for war."
(Alma 24:6).

"Blessed be the name of our God; let us sing to his praise, yea, let us give thanks to his holy name, for he doth work righteousness forever." (Alma 26:8).

"Do ye remember, my brethren, that we
said unto our brethren in the land of Zarahemla,
we go up to the land of Nephi, to preach unto our brethren,
the Lamanites, and they laughed us to scorn? For they said
unto us: Do ye suppose that ye can convince the Lamanites of the
incorrectness of the traditions of their fathers, as stiffnecked a
people as they are; whose hearts delight in the shedding
of blood; whose days have been spent in the grossest
iniquity; whose ways have been the ways of a
transgressor from the beginning?"
(Alma 26:23-24).

Thru the miracle of the infinite, continuing, uninterrupted, unspoiled, uncorrupted, enduring, unfathomable and immeasurable grace of God, we are "swallowed up" in joy, to the exhausting of our strength.
(Alma 27:17).

The People of
Ammon "were among the people
of Nephi, and (were) also numbered
among the people who were of the church of
God. And they were also distinguished for
their zeal towards God, and also towards
men; for they were perfectly honest and
upright in all things; and they were
firm in the faith of Christ."
(Alma 27:27).

"O, that I were an angel, and could have the wish of mine heart, that I might go forth and speak with the trump of God, with a voice to shake the earth, and cry repentance unto every people! Yea, I would declare unto every soul, as with the voice of thunder, repentance and the plan of redemption that they should repent and come unto our God, that there might not be more sorrow upon all the face of the earth."
(Alma 29:1-2).

God "granteth unto men according to their desire, whether it be unto death or unto life; yea, I know that he allotteth unto men, yea, decreeth unto them decrees which are unalterable, according to their wills, whether they be unto salvation or unto destruction".
(Alma 29:4)

"Now there was no law against a man's belief;
for it was strictly contrary to the commands of God
that there should be a law which should bring men on to
unequal grounds. For thus saith the scripture: Choose ye
this day, whom y will serve. Now if a man desired
to serve God, it was his privilege; or rather, if he
believed in God it was his privilege to serve
him; but if he did not believe in him,
there was no law to punish him".
(Alma 30:7-9).

"Behold, I have all things
as a testimony that these things
are true; and ye also have all things
as a testimony unto you that they are
true; and will ye deny them? Believest
thou that these things are true?"
(Alma 30:41).

"The scriptures are laid before thee, yea, and all things denote there is a God; yea even the earth, and all things that are upon the face of it, yea, and its motion, yea, and also, all the planets which move in their regular form do witness that there is a Supreme Creator."
(Alma 30:44).

"And now, as the preaching
of the word had a great tendency
to lead the people to do that which was
just – yea, it had had a more powerful effect
upon the minds of the people than the sword, or
anything else, which had happened unto them –
therefore, Alma thought it was expedient that
they should try the virtue of the word of
God." (Alma 31:5).

"They have cast us out of our synagogues which we have labored abundantly to build with our own hands; and they have cast us out because of our exceeding poverty; and we have no place to worship our God; and behold, what shall we do?"
(Alma 32:5).

"If ye will awake and arouse your faculties, even to an experiment upon my words, and exercise a particle of faith, yea, even if ye can no more than desire to believe, let this desire work in you, even until ye believe in a manner that ye can give place for a portion of my words." (Alma 32:27).

"Now, we will compare
the word unto a seed. Now, if ye give place,
the seed may be planted in your heart, behold,
if it be a true seed, or a good seed, if ye do not cast it
out by your unbelief, that ye will resist the Spirit of the
Lord, behold, it will begin to swell within your breasts, and
when you feel these swelling motions, ye will begin to say
within yourselves – It must be a good seed, or that the
word is good, for it beginneth to enlarge my
soul, yea, it beginneth to enlighten my
understanding, yea, it beginneth
to be delicious to me."
(Alma 32:28).

"Whatsoever
is light, is good."
(Alma 32:35).

"Because of your
diligence and your faith and your
patience with the word in nourishing it,
that it may take root in you, behold, by and
by ye shall pluck the fruit thereof, which is most
precious, which is sweet above all that is sweet, and
which is white above all that is white, yea, and pure
above all that is pure; and ye shall feast upon this
fruit even until ye are filled, that ye hunger not,
neither shall ye thirst. Then, my brethren, ye
shall reap the rewards of your faith, and
your diligence, and patience, and
(your) long-suffering."
(Alma 32:42-43).

Our repentance paves the way for our Father in Heaven to be both just and merciful at the same time; and all is made possible because of the Savior's Atonement. (See Alma 34:16).

Those of
weak character
might think they
can somehow sashay
past the requirements of
repentance, but that is only
because they've never enjoyed
the promenade of those living
on the strait and narrow path
thanks to the therapeutic and
liberating influence of the
Atonement of the Savior.
(See Alma 34:31).

"I was racked with eternal
torment, for my soul was harrowed
up to the greatest degree and racked with
all my sins. Yea, I did remember all my sins
and iniquities, for which I was tormented with the
pains of hell; yea, I saw that I had rebelled against my
God, and that I had not kept his holy commandments.
Yea, I had murdered many of his children, or rather, led
them away unto destruction; yea, and in fine so great
had been my iniquities, that the very thought of
coming into the presence of my God did rack
my soul with inexpressible horror."
(Alma 36:12-14).

"I could remember my pains no more; yea, I was harrowed up by the memory of my sins no more."
(Alma 36:19).

Thru our
faith in His Plan,
God has ingeniously
cultivated our capacity to
recapture the innocence and
the wide-eyed wonder of youth.
Its enlightening provisions that
are described by Alma to Corianton
have the power to reintroduce us to our
primeval childhood, giving each of us
another chance to get it right. We can
all live happily ever after, because
fairytales still come true.
(See Alma 39-42).

"I give it as my opinion..."
(Alma 40:20).

Satan, who was a liar from the beginning, even now continues his efforts to foil the Plan of Salvation with the substitution of his own counterfeit, unworkable alternative that would not require repentance or the Atonement. Fortunately, in the setting of the Council in Heaven, most of our Heavenly Father's children were able to see though his deception. So were the Nephites, in general, able to do so. (See Alma 41:1). And we still can, even today.

Without
our purposeful
repentance, we cannot
reasonably expect to inherit
the glory of heavenly realms;
especially if we have aforetime
been agreeable to abide by only
telestial or terrestrial principles
that put fewer demands upon
our discipleship than would
celestial laws. (See Alma
41:2-7)

"Do not suppose, because it has been spoken concerning restoration, that ye shall be restored from sin to happiness. Behold, I say unto you, wickedness never was happiness."
(Alma 41:10).

As Corianton
listened to Alma, he began
to understand that restoration
means "to bring back again evil for
evil, or carnal for carnal, or devilish
for devilish, good for that which is
good; righteous for that which is
righteous; just for that which
is just; merciful for that
which is merciful".
(Alma 41:13).

Our salvation
has less to do with
cherubim and a flaming
sword, (see Alma 42:3), and
more to do with Mercy and
our redemption from the
inexorable demands
of Justice.

"According to justice, the plan of redemption could not be brought about, only on conditions of repentance of men in this probationary state, yea, this preparatory state, for except it were on these conditions, mercy could not take effect except it would destroy the work of justice … and the plan of mercy could not be brought about except an atonement should be made. Therefore, God himself atoneth for the sins of the world, to bring about the plan of mercy, to appease the demands of justice, that God might be a perfect, just God, and a merciful God also". (Alma 42:13-15).

"And thus God bringeth about his great and eternal purposes, which were prepared from the foundation of the world." (Alma 42:26).

"And it came to pass that he rent his coat; and he took a piece thereof, and wrote upon it – In memory of our God, our religion, and freedom, and our peace, our wives, and our children – and he fastened it upon the end of a pole." (Alma 46:12).

"Those who did
belong to the church were faithful;
yea, all those who were true believers in
Christ took upon them, gladly, the name
of Christ, or Christians as they were
called, because of their belief in
Christ who should come."
(Alma 46:15).

"Behold, whosoever will
maintain this title (of liberty)
upon the land, let them come forth
in the strength of the Lord, and enter
into a covenant that they will maintain
their rights, and their religion, that
the Lord God may bless them."
(Alma 46:20).

"If all men had been,
and were, and ever would be
like unto Moroni, behold, the very
powers of hell would have been shaken
forever; yea, the devil would have
no power over the hearts of
the children of men".
(Alma 48:7).

"Now they never had fought, yet they did not fear death; and they did think more upon the liberty of their fathers than they did upon their lives; yea, they had been taught by their mothers, that if they did not doubt, God would deliver them. And they rehearsed unto me the words of their mothers, saying: We do not doubt our mothers knew it." (Alma 56:47-48).

"We did pour out our souls in prayer to God, that he would strengthen us and deliver us out of the hands of our enemies, yea, and also give us strength that we might retain our cities, and our lands, and our possessions, for the support of our people. Yea, and it came to pass that the Lord our God did visit us with assurances that he would deliver us; yea, insomuch that he did speak peace to our souls, and did grant unto us great faith, and did cause that we should hope for our deliverance in him." (Alma 58:10-11).

"They stand fast in that liberty wherewith God has made them free; and they are strict to remember the Lord their God from day to day; yea, they do observe to keep his statutes, and his judgments, and his commandments continually; and their faith is strong in the prophecies concerning that which is to come."
(Alma 58:40).

"I told the brethren that the Book of Mormon was the most correct of any book on earth, and the keystone of our religion, and (we) would get nearer to God by abiding by its precepts, than by any other book."
(Joseph Smith).

Commentary and Compendium Index

Commentary Volume One
Born in The Wilderness

- 1 Nephi
- 2 Nephi
- Jacob
- Enos
- Jarom
- Omni
- Words of Mormon
- Observations
- Author's Note
- Addendum – A Sampling of Scriptures

Commentary Volume Two
Voices From The Dust

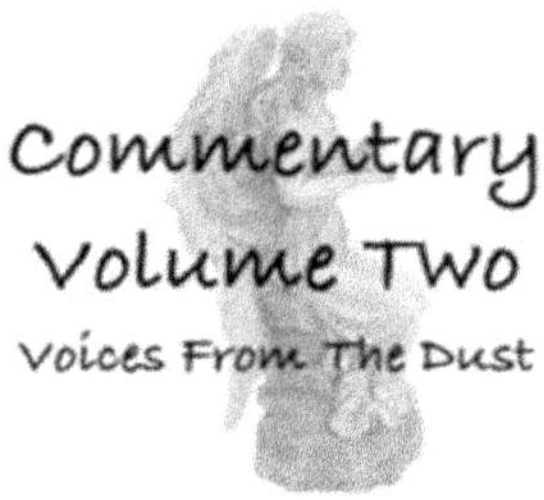

- Mosiah
- Alma
- Observations
- Author's Note
- Addendum – A Sampling of Scriptures

Commentary Volume Three
Journey to Cumorah

- Helaman
- 3 Nephi
- 4 Nephi
- Mormon
- Ether
- Moroni
- Observations
- Author's Note
- Addendum – A Sampling of Scriptures

Compendium
Volume One

- Questions Answered by The Book of Mormon
- Observations
- Familiar Scriptures

Compendium
Volume Two

- Questions Answered by The Book of Mormon
- Without The Book of Mormon
- Observations
- A Few of My Favorite Things
- Familiar Scriptures

Compendium
Volume Three

- Observations
- Essays That Relate to Teachings in The Book of Mormon

Compendium
Volume Four

- Observations
- Essays That Relate to Teachings in The Book of Mormon

Compendium
Volume Five

- Observations
- Essays That Relate to Teachings in The Book of Mormon

Compendium
Volume Six

- Observations
- Essays That Relate to Teachings in The Book of Mormon

Compendium
Volume Seven

- Hebrew Poetry in The Book of Mormon
- Synonymous Parallelism
- Antithetical Parallelism
- Synthetic Parallelism
- Climactic Parallelism
- Chiasmus
- List of Book of Mormon Scriptures That Illustrate Hebrew Poetry
- Observations
- Introduction to The Isaiah Chapters
- "And it came to pass" in The Book of Mormon
- "And thus we see" in The Book of Mormon
- "Behold" in The Book of Mormon

A Book of Mormon Commentary

Born in The Wilderness
Volume One
First Nephi thru Words of Mormon

Voices From the Dust
Volume Two
Mosiah thru Alma

Journey to Cumorah
Volume Three
Helaman thru Moroni

Compendium
Volumes One – Seven

www.ingramcontent.com/pod-product-compliance
Lightning Source LLC
Chambersburg PA
CBHW061400010526
44107CB00012B/1007